GENERAL KNOWLEDGE

2020

MANOHAR PANDEY

ARIHANT PUBLICATIONS (INDIA) LTD.

卐 **Administrative & Production Offices**

Regd. Office
'Ramchhaya' 4577/15, Agarwal Road, Darya Ganj, New Delhi -110002
Tele: 011- 47630600, 43518550; Fax: 011- 23280316

卐 **Head Office**
Kalindi, TP Nagar, Meerut (UP) - 250002
Tele: 0121-2401479, 2512970, 4004199; Fax: 0121-2401648

卐 **Sales & Support Offices**
Agra, Ahmedabad, Bengaluru, Bhubaneswar, Bareilly, Chennai, Delhi, Guwahati, Hyderabad, Jaipur, Jhansi, Kolkata, Lucknow, Meerut, Nagpur & Pune

卐 **ISBN** : 978-93-13191-67-4

卐 **Price** : ₹185.00

Published by : Arihant Publications (India) Ltd.

For further information about books Published by Arihant
log on to www.arihantbooks.com or email to info@arihantbooks.com

 /arihantpub /@arihantpub Arihant Publications /arihantpub

CONTENTS

CURRENT AFFAIRS

NATIONAL

General Election 2019

Narendra Modi has been sworn in as the 16th Prime Minister of India on May 30, 2019 after a landslide victory in the 2019 Lok Sabha election. By winning 303 seats, the Bharatiya Janata Party got the decisive mandate to rule the country for the next 5 years. This was the longest election in the country in terms of the number of days the polling is held for. The 2019 Lok Sabha polls conducted in seven phases spread across 39 days.

Position of Different Political Parties in Lok Sabha 2019

Party	Seats
Bharatiya Janata Party	303
Indian National Congress	52
Dravida Munnetra Kazhagam	23
All India Trinamool Congress	22
Yuvajana Sramika Rythu Congress Party	22
Shivsena	18
Janata Dal (United)	16
Biju Janata Dal	12
Bahujan Samaj Party	10
Telangana Rashtra Samithi	9
Lok Jan Shakti Party	6
Samajwadi Party	5
Nationalist Congress Party	5
Communist Party of India (Marxist)	3
Indian Union Muslim League	3
National Conference	3
Telugu Desam Party	3
Shiromani Akali Dal	2
All India Majlis-E-Ittehadul Muslimeen	2
Communist Party of India	2
Apna Dal (Sonelal)	2
Aam Aadmi Party	1

Aroma Mission Launched in Meghalaya

Meghalaya Chief Minister Conrad K. Sangma launched a new project to boost medicinal and aromatic plants cultivation named "Aroma Mission" on May 29, 2019. "Aroma Mission" a project of Rs.18 crore launched to give importance for agriculture and allied sectors so that farmers earn the benefits from it.

India's First Tree Ambulance Launched

Vice President M. Venkaiah Naidu flagged off a unique service called 'Tree Ambulance' in Chennai to revive and provide care to trees on May 27, 2019. The Tree Ambulance service has been founded by, Dr. K. Abdul Ghani, also known as Green man of India. Helpline number to avail the service-9941006786.

DRDO Conducts Successful Test of Akash-1S

The DRDO successfully conducted the second test firing of the medium range Akash-1S surface to air defence missile system in Balasore off the Odisha coast on May 27, 2019. Akash-1S is a new version of the missile fitted with an indigenously developed seeker, capable of striking down enemy fighter jets, air-to-surface missiles as well as ballistic missiles and drones very effectively.

Schedule for 2024 Moon Mission Unveiled

National Aeronautics and Space Administration (NASA) unveiled schedule for 2024 Moon mission 'Artemis' on May 26, 2019. The Mission is named 'Artemis' after the Greek mythological goddess of the Moon and twin sister to Apollo. This Mission has committed to take a female astronaut to the surface of the moon for the first time.

Air Launched Version of BrahMos Test-Fired

The Indian Air Force (IAF) successfully conducted the second test firing of the air version of BrahMos missile on May 22, 2019 from its frontline Su-30 MKI fighter aircraft. The first testing was done on November 22, 2017 making IAF the first air force in the world to successfully fire an air launched 2.8 Mach surface attack missile of this category on a sea target.

Indian Navy Successfully Test-Fires MRSAM

The Indian Navy has successfully test-fired a Medium Range Surface to Air Missile (MRSAM) on May 17, 2019.

MRSAM will enhance anti-air warfare capability of the Indian Navy. The test-firing of the missile was undertaken on the western seaboard by Indian naval ships Kochi and Chennai.

Singapore India Maritime Bilateral Exercise Held

INS Kolkata and INS Shakti of the Indian Navy participated in a three-day Asia Pacific naval and maritime event titled the International Maritime Defence Exhibition Asia (IMDEX Asia-2019) held in Changi Exhibition Centre, Singapore. SIMBEX scheduled from May 16 to 22, 2019. It is the longest uninterrupted naval exercise that India has with any other nation.

Exercise Bull Strike

The military drill 'Exercise Bull strike' was conducted on May 14, 2019 to showcase joint operations capability of the armed forces. During the exercise, the army personnel got the chance to display their prowess by undertaking company level airborne operation at Teressa island, Andaman Nicobar.

Test Flight of ABHYAS Drone

The Defence Research and Development Organisation (DRDO) successful conducted the test flight of ABHYAS drone on May 14, 2019 from Integrated Test Range (ITR) at Chandipur in Balasore, Odisha.

ABHYAS drone is a High-speed Expendable Aerial Target (HEAT) designed for autonomous flight with the help of an autopilot.

'Yuvika 2019' Organised

The first edition of the Young Scientist Programme 'Yuvika2019' (YUva VIgyani KAryakram) was inaugurated by Indian Space Research Organisation (ISRO) Chairman Dr. K. Sivan through video mode in Bengaluru on May 13, 2019.

It is a two week summer vacation residential programme that was conducted from May 13 to 26, 2019 over four ISRO centres in Bengaluru, Thiruvananthapuram, Ahmedabad and Shillong. 107 students which includes 3 students from each from each State/Union Territory have been selected for Yuvika 2019.

Cyclone Fani Hits Odisha and West Bengal

Cyclone Fani with a maximum wind speed of 240-250 kmph, is one of the most biggest and fiercest cyclonic storm over the east coast in nearly two decades.

The word Fani (pronounced as Foni) means snake was suggested by Bangladesh. According to the government, around 10000 villages and 52 towns in Odisha got affected by cyclone Fani. Fani was picked up from a pool containing 64 names suggested by eight countries in the North Indian Ocean basin. (Eight Countries are India, Sri Lanka, Bangladesh, Maldives, Myanmar, Oman, Pakistan and Thailand).

Group Sail Military Exercise

INS Kolkata and Shakti carried out Group Sail with naval ships of Japan, Philippines and the United States of America in the South China Sea from May 3 to 9, 2019. The ships undertook various exercises enroute which included formation manoeuvering, underway replenishment runs, cross-deck flying and exchange of Sea Riders.

BSNL Launched 'Bharat Fibre'

BSNL launches 'Bharat fibre' for high-speed broadband Internet service in Pulwama on May 1, 2019. BSNL became the First operator to start optical fiber-based high-speed broadband service in Pulwama. The Bharat Fibre services with reliable and high-speed internet are provided on the optical fibre by FTTH (fibre-to-the-home) service up to the customer premises.

KIIFB's Masala Bonds in London Stock Exchange

Pinarayi Vijayan, The Chief Minister of Kerala, rang the bell at London Stock Exchange for listing of Kerala Infrastructure Investment Fund Board's (KIIFB) masala bonds. KIIFB is the first state-owned entity to issue masala bonds. Kerala is also the first state in India to issue masala bonds.

RBI Released 'Vision 2021'

The Reserve Bank of India has released its vision documents on digital payment named Payment and Settlement Systems in India : Vision 2019-21. It shows the vision of RBI for growth of Digital Payment in India.

The move comes as the apex bank expects the number of digital transactions to increase more than four times to 8,707 crores in December 2021.

ISRO's New Commercial Arm Inaugurated

NewSpace India Limited (NSIL), the commercial arm of Indian Space Research Organisation (ISRO), was officially inaugurated in Bengaluru.

NSIL's main objective is to scale up industry participation in Indian space programmes.

India Banned Boeing 737 Max 8 Planes

India on March 13, 2019 banned the use of Boeing 737 Max 8 aircraft by the country's airline companies in the aftermath of Ethiopian Airlines crash. These planes will be grounded till appropriate modifications and safety measures are undertaken to ensure their safe operations.

11 More State DD Channels through DD Free Dish

Prasar Bharati has brought 11 more State DD Channels on the Satellite footprint of India through DD Free Dish on March 9, 2019. It is for the first time that the States of Chhattisgarh, Goa, Haryana, Himachal Pradesh, Jharkhand, Manipur, Meghalaya, Mizoram, Nagaland, Tripura and Uttarakhand have got their own DD channel.

Dictionary of Martyrs Released

Prime Minister Narendra Modi released the **Dictionary of Martyrs : India's Freedom Struggle (1857-1947)** in New Delhi on March 7, 2019. This five-volume dictionary contains an account of the martyrs from India's First war of Independence in 1857, to India's Independence in 1947.

Arbitration Committee for Ayodhya Dispute

The Supreme Court appointed an arbitration panel on March 8, 2019 to mediate in a decades-long dispute over a controversial plan to build a Hindu temple on the ruins of a 16th-century mosque in Ayodhya (Uttar Pradesh). The court appointed former judge FM Kalifulla to head the 3-member panel that includes spiritual guru Sri Sri Ravi Shankar and senior lawyer Sriram Panchu.

PM-SYM Yojana Launched

Prime Minister Narendra Modi launched the Pradhan Mantri Shram Yogi Maan-dhan (PM-SYM) Yojana at Vastral (Gujarat) on March 5, 2019. The scheme will assure a monthly pension of ₹ 3000 for the enrolled unorganised sector workers during their old age.

New Coin of ₹ 20 Announced

The government on March 7, 2019 has announced new ₹ 20 coin which will be shaped like a 12-edged polgyon (dodecagon). The ₹ 20 coin will weigh 8.54 gm and its outside diameter will be 27 mm.

One Nation, One Card Launched

PM Narendra Modi on March 4, 2019 launched the indigenously-developed **National Common Mobility Card** to enable people to pay multiple kinds of transport charges.

Young Scientist Programme Launched

Indian space agency ISRO on March 4, 2019 announced the launch of a special programme for schood children called Young Scientist Programme or YUva VIgyani KAryakram (YUVIKA) from this year. The programme is primarily aimed at imparting basic Knowledge on Space Technology, Space Science and Space applications to the younger ones.

Three World Records at Kumbh 2019

Kumbh 2019, the 49-day long biggest religious congregation on earth at Prayagraj (Uttar Pradesh) formally concluded on March 5, 2019. Kumbh 2019 has been placed in Guinness World Records in three sectors. These include the largest traffic and crowd management plan; the biggest painting exercise of public sites under 'Paint My City scheme and ; biggest sanitation and waste disposal mechanism.

Indo-Russia Rifles Limited Inaugurated

PM Narendra Modi on March 3, 2019 inaugurated Indo-Rusia Rifles Limited Unit at Ordnance Factory Board (OFB) in Korwa (Amethi, Uttar Pradesh). It is an Indo-Russian joint venture that will manufacture the new Kalashnikov AK-203 rifles.

National Mineral Policy 2019 Approved

The Union Cabinet has approved National Mineral Policy 2019 on February 28, 2019. The aim of National Mineral Polity 2019 is to have a more effective, meaningful & implementable policy that brings in further transparency, better regulation and enforcement, balanced social and economic growth as well as sustainable mining practices.

Pradhan Mantri JI-VAN Yojana Approved

The Union government has approved the Pradhan Mantri JI-VAN (Jaiv Indhan-Vatavaran Anukool fasal awashesh Nivaran) Yojana on February 28, 2019. The scheme is for providing financial support to Integrated Bioethanol Projects using lignocellulosic biomass and other renewable feedstock.

National Policy Software Products 2019 Approved

The Union government has approved the National Policy on Software Products 2019 on February 28, 2019. The policy will lead to the formulation of several schemes, initiatives, projects and measures for the development of software sector in the country as per the roadmap envisaged therein.

New Railway Zone Approved

The Union Cabinet on February 28, 2019 approved the setting up of a new Railway Zone at Vishakhapatnam (Andhra Pradesh). **Southern Coast Railway** will be 18th Railway zone of the Indian Railways.

PM Modi Unveiled Largest Bhagavad Gita

Prime Minister Narendra Modi unveiled world's largest Bhagavad Gita at the ISKON temple in New Delhi on February 26, 2019. Measuring over 2.8 m and over 800 kg, the giant Bhagavad Gita is one of the kind in the world. It has the original verses of Bhagavad Gita along with commentary.

National War Memorial Inaugurated

Prime Minister Narendra Modi on February 25, 2019 inaugurated the National War Memorial, at the India Gate complex in New Delhi. The memorial comprises four concentric circles, with names of 25942 soldiers inscribed in golden letters on granite tablets.

Mega Exercise Vayu Shakti 2019

The Indian Air Force on February 16, 2019 carried out a mega exercise named Vaya Shakti 2019 in Pokhran (Rajasthan). It involved alomost all variants of its fighter jets and attack helicopters.

PM Launched 'PM-KISAN'

The Prime Minister Narendra Modi launched the PM-KISAN scheme from Gorakhpur on February 24, 2019. With the launch, the first instalment of ₹ 2000 will be directly credited to the bank accounts of selected beneficiary farmers.

Vande Bharat Express Train Flagged Off

Prime Minister Modi launched India's first semi-high speed train on November 15, 2019. The express, initially called Train 18, which was rechristened to Vande Bharat Express will run between Delhi & Varanasi. It will travel from Delhi to Varanasi in 9 hours and 45 minutes.

Interim Budget 2019-20 Presented

Union Minister for Finance, Corporate Affairs, Railways and Coal, Piyush Goyal presented the Interim Budget 2019-20 in Parliament on February 1, 2019. The major highlights are :

- **Income up to ₹ 5 lakh** exempted from Income Tax; **Standard deduction** raised to ₹ 50000, a hike of ₹ 1000 for salaried class.
- **Gratuity limit** increased from ₹ 10 lakh to ₹ 30 lakh.
- Allocations to **Defence budget** crosses ₹ 3 lakh crore for the first time.

- **PM Kisan Samman Nidhi Yojana** will provide assured income support of ₹ 6000 per year to small and marginal farmers with landholding below 2 hectares.
- ₹ 3000 pension for unorganised sector workers earning up to ₹ 15000 through a mega pension scheme **Pradhan Mantri Shram-Yogi Maandhan.**
- New separate Department of Fisheries for welfare of 1.5 crore fishermen.
- A programme for genetic upgradation of cow **Rashtriya Kamdhenu Aayog.**
- Outlay for **Rashtriya Gokul** Mission increased to ₹ 750 crore.
- Total expenditure increased by over 13% to ₹ 2784200 crore.
- The announcement of setting-up of 22nd AIIMS in Haryana.

70th Republic Day Celebrated

India celebrated its 70th Republic Day on January 26, 2019.

The theme of the 70th Republic Day parade was **Life of Gandhi,** and South African President **Cyril Ramaphosa** was the Chief Guest at the event. During the parade, a desi tune **Shankhanaad** was played for the first time instead of a martial tune, which has been played since British time.

'Nari Shakti' Chosen as Hindi Word of the Year 2018

Oxford Dictionaries has chosen Nari Shakti (Women Empowerment) as the Hindi Word of the Year 2018, on January 26, 2019. 'Nari Shakti' word is used to symbolise women who are capable to take charge of their lives.

15th PBD Convention Held

The 15th edition of Pravasi Bharatiya Divas (PBD) convention was held from January 21-23, 2019 in Varanasi (Uttar Pradesh). The theme of the convention was **Role of Indian Diaspora in Building New India.** Mauritius Prime Minister Pravind Jugnauth was the Chief Guest at the 15th PBD.

Vibrant Gujarat Global Summit 2019

The ninth edition of Vibrant Gujarat Summit was held from January 18-20, 2019 in Gandhinagar. The theme of the event was **Shaping a New India.** Five Heads of States from Uzbekistan, Rwanda, Denmark, Czech Republic and Malta were took part in the event.

National Museum of Indian Cinema Inaugurated

Prime Minister Narendra Modi inaugurated National Museum of Indian Cinema (NMIC) in Mumbai on January 19, 2019. The Museum will have detailed information about the history of Indian film industry.

DD Science and Science Initiatives Launched

The Ministry of Science & Technology on January 15, 2019 launched two science communication initiatives **DD Science and India Science.**

Women's Recruitment in Military Police

The union government on January 18, 2019 has decided to induct women in Personnel Below Officer Rank (PBOR) role in Corps of Military Police for the first time ever. The women will be inducted into the military police in a graded manner, and will **comprise 20%** of its total strength.

Commemorative Coin in Honour of Guru Gobind Singh Jee

Prime Minister Narendra Modi released a commemorative coin of ₹ 350 to mark the birth anniversary celebrations of Guru Gobind Singh Jee on January 13, 2019.

Gaganyaan Mission to be Launched by December, 2021

The ISRO on January 11, 2019 said that Gangayaan mission would be launched by December, 2021.
This will be preceded by two manned missions, slated for December, 2020 and July, 2021.

Longest Suspension Bridge Opened in Arunachal Pradesh

Arunachal Pradesh CM Pema Khandu inaugurated India's longest 300-m single lane steel cable suspension bridge on January 9, 2019. The bridge across the **Siang river** at Yingkiong in Upper Siang district has been named **Byorung Bridge**.

GST Exemption Limit Doubled

The 32nd meeting of GST council was held at Vigyan Bhawan (New Delhi) on January 10, 2019. During the meeting, the GST council doubled the limit for exemption from payment of GST to ₹ 40 lakh, and ₹ 20 lakh for the north eastern Sates.

Committee to Boost Digital Payments

The Reserve Bank of India (RBI) has constituted a High-Level Committee on deepening of digital payments to encourage digitisation of payments and enhance financial inclusion on January 8, 2019. The five-member committee in headed by UIDAI's former chairman **Nandan Nilekani**.

106th India Science Congress

The 106th Indian Science Congress (ISC) was held from January 3-7, 2019 at Lovely Professional University in Jalandhar (Punjab). The theme of 106th ISC was **Future India-Science and Technology**.

Missiles Test-fired

Missile	Description
Guided PINAKA	India successfully carried out third trial of Guided PINAKA weapon system from Pokhran ranges (Rajasthan) on March 12, 2019.
QRSAM	The DRDO on February 26, 2019 successfully test-fired indigenously developed Quick Reach Surface to Air Missile (QRSAM) from Chandipur (Odisha).
HeliNa	India successfully tested indigenously developed Helicopter launched anti-tank guidied Missile 'HeliNa' on February 8, 2019.
LR-SAM	The DRDO has successfully test-fired Long Range Surface to Air Missile (LR-SAM) from naval warship INS-Chennai on January 24, 2019.
NGARM	India on January 18, 2019 tested a new indigenous air-launched missile named New Generation Anti-Radiation Missile (NGARM).

Armed Forces Exercises

Name (Duration)	Participant	Venue	Description
Al Nagah III (March 12-25)	India and Oman	Jabel Al Akhdar (Oman)	It is the third in the series of bilateral joint military exercise between India and Oman. The first two exercises were held in January, 2015 and March, 2017 in Oman and India respectively.

Name (Duration)	Participant	Venue	Description
Sampriti 2019 (March 2-15)	India and Bangladesh	Tangail (Bangladesh)	It was the eighth edition of Sampriti military exercise. The aim of the exercise is to increase mutual cooperation, bonhomie and camaraderie between the two armies.
Cobra Gold 2019 (February 12-24)	29 Nations including India, USA and China	Chonburi (Thailand)	It is the largest joint military exercise of the Asia-Pacific region. Around 4500 personnel from the Army, Navy and Air forces participated in the exercise.
Hand-in-Hand 2018 (December 10-23)	India and China	Chengdu (China)	It was the first bilateral military exercise in China post-Doklam. It focused on joint counter-terrorism operations in urban and jungle terrains.
AviaIndra 18 (Dec 10-22 and Sep 17-28)	India and Russia	Jodhpur (Rajasthan) and Lipetsk (Russia)	It is an Air Force level exercise between India and the Russian Federation. The aim of the exercise is focused towards anti-terrorist operations in a bilateral scenario.
Indra Navy 2018 (December 9-16)	India and Russia	Bay of Bengal & Vishakhapatnam Port	This year's exercise was the 10th iteration of the Indra Navy series between the two countries.
SHINYUU Maitri-2018 (December 3-7)	India and Japan	Agra (Uttar Pradesh)	Indian Air Force and Japanese Air Self Defence Force (JASDF) participated in this bilateral exercise. The theme of the exercise was joint Mobility Humanitarian Assistance & Disaster Relief (HADR) on Transport aircraft.
Konkan-18 (November 28-December 6)	India and the UK	Goa	The bilateral Konkan exercise provides a platform for the Indian Navy and Royal Navy (UK) to build interoperability and share best practices.
INDRA 2018 (November 18-28)	India and Russia	Jhansi (Uttar Pradesh)	It was the 10th annual exercise of armies of India and Russia.
Vajra Prahar 2018 (November 19-December 2)	India and the USA	Bikaner (Rajasthan) and Seattle (USA)	It was a joint special forces exercise between armies of both nations. The aim of the exercise was to enhance the interoperability of the two armed forces and further the military-to-military cooperation.

Satellites Launched by the ISRO

Satellite	Description
GSAT-31	India's 40th communication satellite GSAT-31 was successfully launched from Kourou (French Guiana) on February 6, 2019. It has the mission life of around 15 years.
Microsat-R and Kalamsat-V2	India's PSLV-C44 successfully launched world's lightest and student-made satellite Kalamsat-V2 and Microsat-R (imaging satellite) on January 25, 2019.
GSAT-7A	ISRO's GSLV-F11 successfully launched the communication satellite GSAT-7A from Sriharikota on December 19, 2018. It is the 39th communication satellite of ISRO.
GSAT-11	India's heaviest and most advanced high throughput communication satellite GSAT-11 was successfully launched from French Guiana on December 5, 2018.

Heads of Various Governments who Visited India

Name (Designation)	Descritpion
Mohammed bin Salman (Crown Prince, Saudi Arabia)	He paid his first state visit to India on February 19-20, 2019. During the visit, India and Saudi Arabia signed five important agreements.

Name (Designation)	Descritpion
Mauricio Macri (President, Argentina)	He paid an official state visit to India from February 17-19, 2019. During the visit, both the nations signed 10 agreements in various sectors including defence, agriculture and tourism.
Cyril Ramaphosa (President, South Africa)	He visited India from January 25-26, 2019 as a State Guest of Honour for Republic Day 2019. He is the second President of South Africa after Nelson Mandela to be the Chief Guest at the Republic Day.
Pravind Jagnauth (Prime Minister, Mauritius)	He was on official visit to India from January 20-28, 2019 as the Chief Guest at the 15th Pravasi Bharatiya Divas (PBD) convention, held in Varanasi (Uttar Pradesh).
Erna Solberg (Prime Minister, Norway)	She paid a State visit to India from January 7-9, 2019. During the visit, both the nations signed an MoU on India-Norway Ocean Dialogue and the establishment of the Joint Task Force on Blue Economy.
Dr. Lotay Tshering (Prime Minister, Bhutan)	He paid a State visit ot India from December 27-29, 2018 at the invitation of PM Modi. The visit took place during the Golden Jubilee year of the establishment of formal diplomatic relations between India and Bhutan.
Ibrahim Mohamed Solih (President, Maldives)	Maldivian President Solih paid an official visit to India with First Lady Fazna Ahmed from December 16-18, 2018. It was Solih's first visit abroad after assuming the office of President of Maldives.

India's Position in Various Global Indices

Name (Released On)	India's Rank	Top-3 Nations	Issuer and Objective
Inclusive Internet Index 2019 (February 27, 2019)	47th (Previously Same)	1. Sweden 2. Singapore 3. The USA	It is prepared by Economist Intelligence Unit (EIU) for Facebook. It is based on the Scores of Availability, Affordability, Relevance and Readiness categories.
International Intellectual Property Index (February 7, 2019)	36th (Previously 44th)	1. The USA 2. The UK 3. Sweden	US Chamber of Commerce's GIPC released the index under the title 'Inspiring Tomorrow'. India's score represents the largest gain of any country measured on the index.
Corruption Perception Index (January 28, 2019)	78th (Previously 81st)	1. Denmark, 2. New Zealand, 3. Finland	Germany based NGO Transparency International released the index. It highlights a connection between healthy democracies and successfully fighing corruption in the public sector.
Democracy Index (January 10, 2019)	41st (Previously 42nd)	1. Norway, 2. Iceland, 3. Sweden	The 11th edition of EIU Democracy Index reveals that political participation is on the rise in almost every region of the world.

State Visits of the Prime Minister Narendra Modi

Nation(s) (Duration)	Description
South Korea (February 21-22, 2019)	During the visit, India and South Korea signed six agreements. PM Modi also conferred upon the Seoul Peace Prize 2018 by the Seoul Peace Prize Cultural Foundation.
Argentina (November 29-December 1, 2018)	PM Modi visited Argentina for the G20 Summit 2018. During the visit, he also attended Russia-India-China Trilateral meeting, in which RIC leaders exchanged views on expanding mutual cooperation in international forums.

INTERNATIONAL

IMD World Competitiveness Rankings 2019

India has moved up one place to rank 43rd in the 2019 edition of the IMD World Competitiveness Rankings, mainly due to its robust economic growth, a large labour force and its huge market size. The index has been topped by Singapore, followed by Hong Kong and The USA at second and third position respectively.

First UN-Habitat Assembly

The first session of the UN-Habitat Assembly held from May 27-31 ,2019 at UN-Habitat in Nairobi, Kenya. The special theme for the UN-Habitat Assembly is : 'Innovation for Better Quality of Life in Cities and Communities'. India has been elected to the Executive Board of the first UN-Habitat Assembly.

Trump to Meet New Japanese Emperor

Donald Trump, President of United States, made history on May 27, 2019 by becoming the first leader in the world to meet with the new emperor of Japan. The US President is on a four-day state visit to Japan.

Russia Launched Nuclear Powered Ice Breakers

Russia's nuclear energy agency, Rosatom has come up with the nuclear-powered ice breaker name as Ural, on May 25, 2019 at the Baltic Shipyard in St. Petersburg.

Ural is the third of the new Special class of nuclear-powered ice-breakers. The first two are Arktika and Sibir.

Pakistan Successfully Test-Fired Shaheen-II

Pakistan successfully test-fired a long-range ballistic missile Shaheen-II on May 24, 2019, capable of carrying a nuclear warhead, capable of hitting targets as far as 1,500 kilometers away. The launch was aimed at ensuring operational readiness of the Army Strategic Forces Command.

Declared Algeria and Argentina Malaria-Free

WHO officially declared Algeria and Argentina as malaria-free countries after recording no new cases for more than three years. Now, the numbers of malaria free countries increased to 38 from 36. Argentina reported the last indigenous case in 2010 while in Algeria it was reported in 2013.

SCO Foreign Ministers Meeting

External Affairs Minister Sushma Swaraj attended a two-day meeting of the Shanghai Cooperation Organisation Bishkek, in Kyrgyzstan on May 21, 2019. The SCO was founded at a summit in Shanghai in 2001 by the presidents of Russia, China, Kyrgyz Republic, Kazakhstan, Tajikistan and Uzbekistan. Along with India, Pakistan was also granted SCO membership in 2017.

Saudi Arabia Approved Permanent Residency

The Saudi government has approved for the first time a scheme that gives permanent residency to certain expatriates, allowing them to own real estate in the kingdom and reside with their families without a Saudi sponsor. The 'Privileged Iqama' system will offer a permanent residence scheme and one that can be renewed annually to highly skilled expatriates and owners of capital funds.

Same-sex Marriage Allowed in Taiwan

Taiwan became the first Asian-nation to legalise same-sex marriage on May 24, 2019. The Taiwan lawmakers passed a law allowing same-sex couples to form 'exclusive permanent unions' and to apply for a 'marriage registration' with government agencies.

Ireland Declare Climate Emergency

Ireland has become the second country in the world to declare a climate and biodiversity emergency on May 11, 2019.

It happened after the Oireachtas (Irish parliament) report on Climate Action was accepted by the government and opposition parties without a vote.

Ireland followed in the footsteps of the United Kingdom, which declared a climate emergency earlier this month (May 2019).

New 'Sovereign Internet' Law in Russia

Russian President Vladimir Putin signed into law a 'sovereign internet' bill that will allow Russian authorities to isolate the country's internet to expand the Government Control of the Internet.

The new move requires Internet providers to install equipment for routing Russian web traffic through servers in Russia which will allow the Russian intelligence agencies of state authorities to control public information.

UK Becomes First Parliament to Declare Climate Emergency

The UK Parliament passed a motion a national declaration of an Environment and Climate Emergency on May 1, 2019.

Hence the Parliament of the UK has become the first parliament, or the UK has become the first country to pass a declaration on climate emergency. This move marks a serious emergency in dealing with climate change.

Space X Launched Falcon-9 Rocket

Space X launched its 17th commercial resupply mission to the International Space Station (ISS) by using Falcon 9 rocket with Dragon Spacecraft. The 213-foot-tall rocket lifted off from Cape Canaveral Air Force Station in Florida.

Global Influenza Strategy 2019-30 Released

The WHO on March 11, 2019 released a Global Influenza Strategy for 2019-30 aimed at protecting people in all countries from the threat of influenza. The goal is to prevent seasonal influenza, control the spread of influenza from animals to humans and prepare for the next influenza pandemic.

World Bank Released WBL Report 2019

The World Bank, on March 1, 2019 released annual report named **Women, Business and the Law 2019**. According to the report, currently only six nations (Belgium, Denmark, France, Latvia, Luxembourg and Sweden) gave women and men equal rights.

Second North Korea-US Summit

The second summit meeting between North Korean leader Kim Jong-un and US President Donald Trump was held in Hanoi (Vietnam) on February 27-28, 2019. The meeting was abruptly cut short as the both leaders failed to reach an agreement over how North Korea should denuclearise.

INSTEX to Support Trade with Iran

France, Germany and the United Kingdom (UK) announced the creation of **Instrument for Supporting Trade Exchanges (INSTEX)** on January 30, 2019. It is a Special Purpose Vehicle (SPV) aimed at facilitating legitimate trade between European economic operators and Iran.

National Emergency in USA

President Donald Trump on Nov. 15, 2019 declared a national emergency to fulfill his pledge to construct a wall along the US-Mexico border. Bypassing Congress, Trump announced that he would use executive action to siphon billions of dollars from federal military construction and counterdrug efforts for the wall.

Abu Dhabi Included Hindi as Third Official Court Language

In a landmark decision, Abu Dhabi on February 10, 2019 has included Hindi as the third official language used in its courts, alongside Arabic and English, as part of a move designed to improve access to justice. This is aimed at helping Hindi speakers to learn about litigation procedures, their rights and duties without a language barrier.

Macedonia to Become 30th NATO Member

NATO States have signed an agreement with Macedonia on February 6, 2019, clearing the way for the Balkan nation to become the NATO's 30th member. Last month's accord with Greece ended one of the world's longest diplomatic disputes, paving the way for Skopje to join NATO and the European Union.

WEF Annual Meeting 2019 Held

The World Economic Forum (WEF) Annual Meeting 2019 was held from January 22-25, 2019 in Davos-Klosters (Switzerland). It was focused on **Globalisation 4.0 : Shaping a Global Architecture in the Age of the Fourth Industrial Revolution.**

SPORTS AND GAMES

CRICKET

IPL 2019

Mumbai Indians defeated the Chennai Super Kings by 1 run in the finals to win their record fourth title in Indian Premier League (IPL) on May 12, 2019 at Rajiv Gandhi International Cricket Stadium, Hyderabad. The 2019 season of the IPL was the twelfth season since the professional Twenty20 cricket league was established by the BCCI in 2007.

Australia Tour of India 2019

Australian cricket team played two T? and five ODI matches during the tour India from February 24 to March 13, 2019. **Australia** won both T20 and ODI series with 2-0 and 3-2 score respective Usman Khwaja (Australia) won Player the Series award for ODI series, while Glen Maxwell (Australia) for T20 series.

Irani Cup 2018-19

Ranji champions **Vidarbha** beat Rest of India in Nagpur on February 16, 2019 to retain the Irani Cup. Vidarbha has now become the third team after Mumbai and Karnataka to clinch two Irani Cup titles in a row.

Ranji Trophy 2018-19

Vidarbha on February 7, 2019 defeated Saurashtra by 78 runs to win the final of Ranji Trophy 2018-19 edition and lift the coveted domestic trophy for the second consecutive time.

India-New Zealand ODI Series 2019

India won an emphatic series win after beating New Zealand in the fifth and final ODI at Wellington by 35 runs on February 2, 2019. Chasing 253, New Zealand team was bowled out for 217 runs in 44.1 over.

GOLF

PGA Championship 2019

American golfer Brooks Koepka returned to the top of the world rankings after his nerve-jangling second straight US PGA Championship victory at Bethpage Black.

He set a record in the lowest 36-hole score in Major golf history and seized a record seven-stroke lead after two rounds of the US PGA Championship.

FOOTBALL

UEFA Europa League

English football club Chelsea beat Arsenal 4-1 to win the UEFA Europa League final on May 29, 2019 at the Olympic Stadium in Baku, Azerbaijan.

With this win, Chelsea has earned the right to play against the winners of the 2018–19 UEFA Champions League in the 2019 UEFA Super Cup.

Indian Women's League 2019

Sethu FC has clinched their first ever Indian Women's League trophy after defeating Manipur Police 3-1 at the Guru Nanak Stadium in Ludhiana on May 22, 2019. The Sethu FC is an Indian women's football club based in Tamil Nadu. The 2018-19 season is the third season of the Indian Women's League. The league is ran by the All India Football Federation (AIFF).

Premier League

Manchester City clinched their fourth Premier League title (Football) after winning the 2018-19 season on May 13, 2019. Manchester City registered a 4-1 victory against Brighton to accumulate 98 points, while Liverpool, who were also in the title race, finished second with 97 points.

I-League 2018-19

Chennai-based team **Chennai City FC** beat Minerva Punjab in Coimbatore (Tamil Nadu) on March 9, 2019 to win I-League 2018-19 title. Chenniai City FC team have become the eighth different champion of the top Indian professional football league since its inception in 2007.

AFC Asian Cup 2019

Qatar produced the most famous moment in its sporting history on February 1, 2019 after defeating Japan 3-1 in the final of the Asian Cup in UAE. Qatar secured the victory courtesy of goals from the competition's top scorer Almoez Ali, Abdelaziz Hatim and Akram Hassan Afif.

FIFA Club World Cup 2018

The 15th edition of FIFA Club World Cup on concluded on December 22, 2018. Spanish Club **Real Madrid** won the title for the fourth time after beating Al-Ain Club (UAE).

TENNIS

Italian Open 2019

The Italian Open 2019, also known as the Rome Masters, was held from May 13 to 19, 2019.

Rafael Nadal of Spain defeated Novak Djokovic of Serbia in the final to claim his ninth Italian Open title.

The Czech Republic's Karolina Pliskova beats United Kingdom (UK's) Johanna Konta in finals and won women's singles title in this tournament.

Madrid Open 2019

Serbian tennis superstar Novak Djokovic defeated Greece's Stefanos Tsitsipas 6-3, 6-4 in the Madrid Open final, claiming his third title at the clay-court event and 33rd ATP Masters 1000 crown on May 12, 2019. Kiki Bertens of Netherlands beats Simona Halep of Romania in finals to win women's singles title. Jean-Julien Rojer (Netherlands) / Horia Tecau (Romania) won Men's Double and Hsieh Su-wei (Taiwan)/ Barbora Strýcová (Czech Republic) won Women's Double.

Dubai Championships 2019

Swiss tennis stars **Roger Federer** and **Belinda Bencic** won men's and women's singles titles respectively at the Dubai Tennis Championships 2019, on March 2, 2019. Federer defeated Stefanos Tsitsipas (Greece) in the final, while Bencic outplayed Petra Kvitova (Czech Republic).

Qatar Open 2019

Beligan woman tennis player **Elise Mertens** won the women's singles title at the Qatar Open tennis tournament 2019 on February 16, 2019. She defeated Simona Halep (Romania) in the final. It was the 17th edition of the tournament, which took place in Doha (Qatar).

Australian Open 2019

First grand slam tennis tournament of the year Australian Open 2019 was concluded on January 27, 2019. Serbian tennis star **Novak Djokovic** and Japanese player **Naomi Osaka** won men's and women's singles titles at the championship.

Sydney International 2019

Czech Republic's tennis star **Petra Kvitova** defeated Asleigh Barty (Australia) in the women's singles final of Sydney International hard court tennis tournament 2019 at Sydney (Australia) on January 12, 2019. Australian tennis player **Alex de Minaur** won men's singles title.

Brisbane International 2019

Japan's **Kei Nishikori** and Czech Republic's **Carolina Pliskova** won men's and women's singles title at the Brisbane International Hard Court tennis tournament 2019 on January 6, 2019.

Hopman Cup 2019

Tennis legend Roger Federer won the Hopman Cup for the record third time after defending champion **Switzerland** beat Germany 2-1 in the final on January 5, 2019.

BADMINTON

All England Open 2019

All England Open Badminton Championships 2019 was held in Birmingham (England) from March 6-10, 2019. Japanese player **Kento Momota** defeated Victor Axelsen (Denmark) to win the men's singles title. In women's singles final, **Chen Yufei** from China defeated Tai Tzu-ying (Chinese Taipei).

83rd Senior National Championships

Saina Nehwal defeated PV Sindhu in straight games in the marquee clash of the tournament to retain her women's singles crown at the 83rd Senior Badminton Nationals in Guwahati on February 16, 2019. **Sourabh Verma** completed a hat-trick of titles at the Senior Badminton Nationals, claiming the men's singles crown after defeating young Lakshya Sen in straight games.

Indonesia Masters 2019

Indian badminton star **Saina Nehwal** and **Anders Antonsen** (Denmark) won women's and men's singles titles respectively at the Indonesia Masters badminton tournament 2019 on January 27, 2019.

SPORTS PERSONALITY

Igor Stimac

Croatian World Cupper Igor Stimac was on May 15, 2019 appointed head coach of the Indian football team for a two-year term. The national team has been without a coach since the departure of Stephen Constantine in January, following the creditable show at the AFC Asian Cup.

Sana Mir

Pakistan off-spinner Sana Mir bagged the title of the most successful women ODI's spinner in the world after she dismissed Sune Luus from South Africa in the third ODI of ICC Women's Championship on May 12, 2019. It was Sana's 147th ODI wicket in her 118th appearance.

Kumar Sangakkara

Kumar Sangakkara, former Sri Lanka captain has been named as the first non-British president of Marylebone Cricket Club (MCC). He succeeds Anthony Wreford. He will take up his one-year post in October.

Dipa Karmakar American toymaker 'Mattel', in celebration of its 60th anniversary, introduced new Barbie dolls honouring role models from 18 countries including India's Olympian gymnast Dipa Karmakar, on March 9, 2019. Karmakar become India's first female gymnast to qualify for the final vault event.

Anil Kumble Fomer Indian leg spinner Anil Kumble has been re-appointed as Chairman of the ICC Cricket Committee for the final three-year term, on March 2, 2019. Anil Kumble has been the Chairman of the committee since 2012.

Sanath Jayasuriya Former Sri Lanka batsman Sanath Jayasuriya on February 26, 2019 banned for two years after admitting to obstruct an anti-corruption probe by tempering with evidence sought by the ICC. He has been banned from all forms of cricket for two years.

Abhijeet Gupta Grandmaster Abhijeet Gupta won the Cannes International Open Chess Trophy after taking an easy draw with Pier Luigi Basso (Italy) in the ninth and final round on February 25, 2019. Abhijeet finished with 7.5 points. He registered 6 wins and 3 draws at the tournament.

Sunil Chhetri Star Indian football player Sunil Chhetri was awarded the first ever **Football Ratna** by Football Delhi on February 18, 2019. Chhetri who stays second in the list of goal scorers among active players in world football at the moment, has begun his football career in Delhi.

Vani Kapoor Vani Kapoor on February 1, 2019 became the first Indian to earn a card for the Australian Ladies PGA Tour (LPGA). She achieved this feat after came through its first ever qualifying tournament at Ballarat Gold Club (Australia).

OTHER EVENTS

BWF Launches 2 New Formats of Game

The Badminton World Federation (BWF) has launched two new formats of the game namely AirBadminton and Triples on May 19, 2019.

The main difference between the traditional badminton and the two new formats will be the shuttlecock and the design and dimensions of the court.

Khelo India Youth Games 2019

The second edition of Khelo India Youth Games was concluded in Pune (Maharashtra) on January 20, 2019. The theme of the event was **5 Minute Aur**. **Maharashtra** became Overall Champion after topped the medals tally with 227 medals (85 gold, 61 silver and 81 bronze), while Haryana (62 gold, 56 silver and 60 bronze) and Delhi (48 gold, 37 silver and 51 bronze) finished second and third respectively.

Youth Olympic Games 2018

The third edition of the Youth Olympic Games was held in Buenos Aires, Argentina between October 6 and 18, 2018. Indian weightlifter **Jeremy Lalrinnunga** grabbed the first ever gold medal in weightlifting battling under the men's 62 kg weight category. Shooters **Manu Bhaker** and **Saurabh Chaudhary** had won the gold medal under 10 m air pistol category in their individual events.

AWARDS & HONOURS

NATIONAL

CEAT Cricket Awards 2019

Virat Kohli has bagged the International Cricketer of the year award while Smriti Mandhana was honoured with the International women cricketer of the year award during the CEAT International Cricket Awards 2019. Kohli has accumulated 10843 runs in the ODI cricket and scored 6613 runs in the longest format. Whereas, Mandhana has 1951 runs under her belt in ODI cricket and 1298 runs in the shortest format.

Swachh Survekshan Awards 2019

President Ram Nath Kovind presented the Swachh Survekshan Awards 2019 in New Delhi on March 6, 2019. **Indore** was awarded as the Cleanest City in India, **Bhopal** Cleanest Capital & **Ujjain** Cleanest City (3 lakh to 1 million category).

Bharat Ratna 2019

The President of India Ram Nath Kovind conferred the Bharat Ratna Award to Nanaji Deshmukh (posthumously), Dr. Bhupen Hazarika (posthumously) and Pranab Mukherjee, on January 25, 2019.

Pradhan Mantri Rashtriya Bal Puraskar 2019

The President Ram Nath Kovind conferred Pradhan Mantri Rashtriya Bal Puraskar 2019 to 26 children, including **Arunima Sen, Aryamaan Lakhotiya, Eiha Dixit, Ayushman Tripathy, Megha Bose** and 21 others.

Padma Awards 2019

The Ministry of Home Affairs announced the Padma Awards 2019, on January 25, 2019. The list comprises 4 Padma Vibhushan, 14 Padma Bhushan and 94 Padma Shri awards.

Padma Vibhushan Awardees

Teejan Bai	Art-Vocals-Folk
Ismail Omar Guelleh (Foreigner)	Public Affairs
AM Naik	Trade & Industry
Balwant Moreshwar Purandare	Art-Acting-Theatre

Padma Bhushan Awardees

John Chambers (Foreigner)	Trade & Industry
Sukhdev Singh Dhindsa	Public Affairs
Pravin Gordhan (Foreigner)	Public Affairs
Mahashay Dharam Pal Gulati	Trade & Industry
Darshan Lal Jain	Social Work
Ashok Laxmanrao Kukade	Medicine

Kariya Munda	Public Affairs
Budhaditya Mukherjee	Art-Music-Sitar
Mohanlal Viswanathan Nair	Art-Acting-Film
S. Nambi Narayan	Science & Technology (Space)
Kuldip Nayar (Posthumous)	Journalism
Bachendri Pal	Mountaineering
VK Shunglu	Civil Service
Hukumdev Narayan Yadav	Public Affairs

Saraswati Samman 2017

KK Foundation conferred Saraswati Samman 2017 to Gujarati poet **Sitanshu Yashashchandra** in a ceremony held at National Meseum (New Delhi) on January 22, 2019. He has been honoured for his poetry collection in Gujarati named 'Vakhar'.

Gandhi Peace Prize 2015-18

The Ministry of Culture on January 16, 2019 announced Gandhi Peace Prize for the year 2015, 2016, 2017 and 2018. **Vivekanand Kendra, Kanyakumari** (2015), **Akshaya Patra Foundation** and **Sulabh International** (2016), **Ekal Abhiyan Trust** (2017) and **Yohei Sasakawa** (2018) were declared winners respectively.

INTERNATIONAL

Nine Dots Prize 2019

Indian playwright and journalist Annie Zaidi has been named for the 2019 Nine Dots Prize on May 30, 2019 for her essay Bread, Cement, Cactus. The book will be published by Cambridge University Press in May 2020.

Global Asian of the Year 2018-19

Bengaluru-based medical doctor Hema Divakar was honoured with the 'Global Asian of the Year 2018-19' award in Dubai on May 23, 2019. Hema received the award for her yeomen services and contributions to the women's healthcare ecosystem, in India.

Joan Miro Prize

Indian artist Nalini Malani has won the Joan Miró Prize for 2019. The award is named after Spanish painter and sculptor Joan Miró. He was one of the most influential artists the 20th century.

Sasakawa Award 2019

United Nations Office for Disaster Risk Reduction (UNDRR) has conferred the Sasakawa Award 2019 for Disaster Risk Reduction to Dr. Pramod Kumar Mishra.

The award was announced at the Award Ceremony during the ongoing 6th Session of Global Platform for Disaster Risk Reduction (GPDRR) 2019 at Geneva on May 17, 2019.

Man Booker International Prize

Jokha Alharthi, an author from Oman, has won the prestigious Man Booker International Prize 2019 for her book 'Celestial Bodies' on May 22, 2019.

Her original work 'Sayyidat el-Qamar ' has been translated into English by Marilyn Booth under the title Celestial Bodies. She is the first Arabic-language writer to win the prize.

91st Academy Awards

The 91st annual Academy Awards were given on February 25, 2019. For the first time in 30 years, there was no host to usher the audience from category to category. *The List of Major Awards were as follow*

Best Actor	Rami Malek (Bohemian Rhapsody)
Best Actress	Olivia Colman (The Favourite)
Best Director	Alfonso Cuarón (Roma)
Best Picture	Green Book
Best Documentary	Free Solo
Best Costume Design	Black Panther (Ruth E Carter)
Best Film Editing	Bohemian Rhapsody (John Ottman)

Dan David Prize 2019

Indian historian **Sanjay Subrahmanyam** has won prestigious Dan David Prize of Israel for the year 2019 for his work on inter-cultural encounters between Asians, on February 10, 2019. He shares the award in the category of 'Past time dimension' with Prof. Kenneth Pomeranz (USA).

Laureus World Sports Awards 2019

Prestigious Laureus World Sports Awards 2019 were presented in Monaco on February 18, 2019. Some important winners are

Category	Winner
Sportsman of the Year	Novak Djokovic (Serbia, Tennis)
Sportswoman of the Year	Simone Biles (USA, Gymnastics)
Comeback of the Year	Tiger Woods (USA, Golf)
Breakthrough of the Year	Naomi Osaka (Japan, Tennis)
Team of the Year	French Football Team

72nd BAFTA Awards

To honour the best national and foreign films of 2018, 72nd British Academy Film Awards (BAFTA) were presented at the Royal Albert Hall (London) on Feb 10, 2019. Some of the important winners are

Category	Winner
Best Film	Roma (Mexico)
Best British Film	The Favourite
Best Actor	Rami Malek
Best Actress	Olivia Colman
Best Director	Alfonso Cuaron
Best Animation Film	Spider-Man: Into the Spider Verse

Sheikh Saud International Prize

The first Sheikh Saud International Prize for Materials Research has been awarded to eminent scientist **CNR Rao** on January 20, 2019. It is started by the Centre of Advanced Materials of United Arab Emirates (UAE).

61st Grammy Awards

The 61st Grammy Awards ceremony was held on February 10, 2019 at Staples Centre in Los Angeles (USA). Some of the important winners are

Category	Winner
Record of the Year	This is America
Album of the Year	Golden Hour
Song of the Year	This is America
Best New Artist	Dua Lipa
Best Pop Vocal Album	Sweetener
Best Dance/Electronic Album	Women Worldwide
Best Rock Album	From the Fires

ICC Awards 2018

The International Cricket Council (ICC) announced the winners of ICC Awards 2018 on January 22, 2019. Indian captain **Virat Kohli** won ICC Cricketer of the Year, ICC Test Player of the Year and ICC One Day Player of the Year awards, while **Rishabh Pant** decleared winner of ICC Emerging Player of the Year award.

Sheikh Saud International Prize

The first Sheikh Saud International Prize for Materials Research has been awarded to eminent scientist **CNR Rao** on January 20, 2019. It is started by the Centre of Advanced Materials of United Arab Emirates (UAE).

Nobel Prizes 2018

Field	Winner(s)
Physiology (Medicine)	James P. Allison (USA) and Tasaku Honjo (Japan)
Physics	Arthur Ashkin (USA), Gerard Mourou (France) and Donna Strickland (Canada)
Chemistry	Frances H. Arnold (USA), George P. Smith (USA) and Sir Gregory P. Winter (UK)
Peace	Dennis Mukwege (Congo) and Nadia Murad (Iraq)
Economic Sciences	William D. Nordhaus (USA) and Paul M. Romer (USA)

PERSONS IN NEWS

NATIONAL

Jaganmohan Reddy

YSR Congress Party Leader YS Jaganmohan Reddy took oath as the new Chief Minister of Andhra Pradesh on May 30, 2019.

Naveen Patnaik

Naveen Patnaik, took oath as the CM of Odisha in Bhubaneswar on May 29, 2019 for the consecutive 5th time.

Pema Khandu

BJP leader Pema Khandu , took oath as the Chief Minister of Arunachal Pradesh on May 29, 2019. BJP had won 41 seats in the 60-member Arunachal Pradesh Assembly.

PS Golay

Sikkim Krantikari Morcha (SKM) president Prem Singh Tamang, popularly known as PS Golay took oath as the Chief Minister of Sikkim.

Priyanka Mohite

A mountaineer from Satara, Maharashtra, Priyanka Mohite, has become the first Indian woman to successfully scale Mount Makalu on May 25, 2019. It is the fifth-highest mountain in the world with a height of 8,481 metres.

Vijaya Mulay

The renowned filmmaker and film historian Vijaya Mulay, has passed away at her south Delhi residence on May 19, 2019. Vijaya Mulay is best known for her 1974 film Ek Anek Aur Ekta.

AK Sikri

Justice AK Sikri has been appointed Chairperson of the News Broadcasting Standards Authority (NBSA) on May 15, 2018. He is a former judge of Supreme Court of India.

MB Balakrishnan

Former South Asian Games gold-medalist and Swimming Champion MB Balakrishnan passed away in road accident in Chennai on May 14, 2019.

The Tamil Nadu based player won the 100 m and 200 m backstroke events at the South Asian Games.

R. Gandhi

The RBI has appointed former deputy governor Rama Subramaniam Gandhi as an additional director on the board of Yes Bank for two years from May 14, 2019. The appointment has been made under sub-section (1) of Section 36 AB of the Banking Regulation Act, 1949.

GS Lakshmi

GS Lakshmi has been appointed to the ICC International Panel of Match Referees on May 13, 2019, becoming eligible to referee international matches with immediate effect. With this, She has become the first ever woman to be inducted to Match Referees panel of ICC.

Thoppil Mohamed Meeran

Noted Tamil author and Sahitya Akademi winner Thoppil Mohammed Meeran passed away on May 11, 2019.

Meeran authored the novels Oru Kadalora Kiramathin Kathai (1988, The Story of Sea Side Village), Turaimugam (1991, Harbour), Koonan Thoppu (1993, The Grove of a Hunchback), Saivu Narkkali (1995, The Reclining Chair) and Anju vannam theru (2011).

Kidari Sravan Kumar

Tribal welfare minister of Andhra Pradesh, Kidari Sravan Kumar resigned from his ministerial post on May 10, 2019.

He was given the charge of the ministry on November 11, 2018, after the sudden demise of his father KS Rao.

M. Jayshree Vyas

M. Jayshree Vyas has been appointed as the first independent woman director of Bombay Stock Exchange (BSE) on May 7, 2019. Jayshree Vyas was working as Managing Director (MD) of Shree Mahila Sewa Sahakari Bank, Ahmedabad, since 1986.

Virat Kohli

Virat Kohli is the first cricketer in the world ever to break into the 100 million category for followers on social media. Virat Kohli has Facebook (37.1 million), Twitter (29.4 million) and Instagram (33.5 million) to his name.

Aarohi Pandit

Captain Aarohi Pandit, has become the world's first woman on May 15, 2019 to cross the Atlantic Ocean solo in a Light Sports Aircraft (LSA) christened as 'Mahi'.

Dia Mirza

Indian actress Dia Mirza has been named as one of the 17 advocates for the ambitious Sustainable Development Goals (SDGs) by United Nations on May 12, 2019.

Mujibur Rahman

India and Bangladesh in a meeting agreed to jointly produce the film based on the life and works of Bangabandhu Sheikh Mujibur Rahman and documentary of Bangladesh Liberation War 1971.

Bhaskar Khulbe

Senior IAS officer Bhaskar Khulbe has been **re-employed as Secretary to Prime Minister** Narendra Modi for six months, on March 10, 2019. He was appointed as the Secretary (PMO) in August, 2016.

Sitanshu Ranjan Kar

Indian Information Service (IIS) officer Sitanshu Ranjan Kar was given a **six-month extension** as principal Director General of Press Information Bureau (PIB), on March 10, 2019.

Jagdish Mukhi

Jagdish Mukhi sworn-in as the **Governor of Mizoram** on March 9, 2019. He succeeded Kummanam Rajasekharan, who resigned a day before. Jagdish Mukhi is also the Governor of Assam.

Raghuram Rajan

Former RBI Governor Raghuram Rajan honoured with **Yashwantrao Chavan National Award 2018** for his contribution to economic development, on March 12, 2019. The award is given every year by the Yashwantrao Chavan foundation (Maharashtra).

G. Sateesh Reddy

India's aerospace scientist and Chief of the DRDO G.Sateesh Reddy has been conferred the **Missile Systems Award 2019** by American Institute of Aeronautics and Astronautics (AIAA), on March 3, 2019. He is the first Indian to win the award.

V. Dhananjay Kumar

Former Union Minister Venur Dhananjay Kumar died in Mangaluru (Karnataka) at the age of 67 years on March 4, 2019. He served as the Union Minister for Civil Aviation and Tourism (1996), Union Minister of State for Finance (1999-2000) and Union Minister of State for Textiles (2000-03).

Sushma Swaraj

External Affairs Minister Sushma Swaraj attended the 44th Session of Council of Foreign Ministers (CFM) of OIC as **Guest of Honour**, which held in Abu Dhabi (UAE) on March 1-2, 2019.

Hasmukh Adhia

Former Finance Secretary Hasmukh Adhia has been appointed as **Non-Executive Chairman** of **Bank of Baroda** on March 1, 2019. He has been appointed for a period of three years.

Ajay Narayan Jha

Senior IAS officer Ajay Narayan Jha joined the **15th Finance Commission** as its **Member** on March 1, 2019. He joined in place of Shaktikanta Das who had resigned as a Member of the Commission after being appointed as Governor of the RBI.

Govind Prasad Sharma

Educationist and author Govind Prasad Sharma has been appointed as the **Chairman of National Book Trust (NBT)** on February 25, 2019.

Uma Nath Singh

Former Chief Justice of Meghalaya High Court Uma Nath Singh has been appointed as the **Lokayukta of Nagaland** on February 22, 2019.

Rishi Kumar Shukla

Madhya Pradesh cadre (1983 batch) IPS officer Rishi Kumar Shukla took charge as **Director of CBI** on February 4, 2019. He replaced Alok Kumar Verma for the post.

Krishna Sobti

Renowned **Hindi fiction writer and essayist** Krishna Sobti was **passed away** at the age of 93 years on January 25, 2019.

Ravneet Gill

The RBI gave its approval to apppoint Ravneet Gill as the next **MD and CEO of Yes Bank**, on January 24, 2019. He replaced Rana Kapoor for the post.

Shivakumara Swami

Siddaganga Math (Tumakuru, Karnataka) **seer** Sri Shivakumara Swami was passed away on January 21, 2019. He was 111 years old.

Rakesh Asthana

Former CBI officer Rakesh Asthana was appointed as new **Director General** of **Bureau of Civil Aviation Security** (BCAS) on January 18, 2019.

Satyarup Siddhanta

West Bengal-based IT professional Satyarup Siddhanta on January 16, 2019, became the **youngest person** in the world to achieve a dual feat— climbing both the seven summits and seven volcanic summits.

INTERNATIONAL

James Marape

James Marape has been sworn in as the 8th Prime Minister of Papua New Guinea by the National Parliament on May 30, 2019. He is former finance minister of this country.

Peter O'Neill

The Prime Minister of Papua New Guinea, Peter O'Neill, has resigned from the post on May 26, 2019. Mr O'Neill had been the prime minister for seven years. He has handed over the leadership responsibility to Sir Julius Chan, who would now serve on the post for third term.

Theresa May

The British Prime Minister Theresa May has announced to quit her position as the prime minister of United Kingdom on May 24, 2019. She announced after failing to come up with an agreement with her ministers to lead Britain out of the European Union (Brexit). She will remain as a lame-duck prime minister until a new leader is chosen, probably by the end of July, 2019.

Joko Widodo

Joko Widodo has been re-elected as Indonesia's president on May 19, 2019. According to the elections commission, Widodo and his vice-presidential running mate Ma'ruf Amin won the election by a 55.5% to 44.5% margin over Subianto and Sandiaga Uno.

Volodymyr Zelenskiy

Ukrainian TV star Volodymyr Zelenskiy was sworn in as the country's new president on May 15, 2019. Election victory with 73.22% of the vote against incumbent Petro Poroshenko.

Cyril Ramaphosa

South African President Cyril Ramaphosa's ruling ANC won re-election with an absolute majority in parliament on May 15, 2019.
The African National Congress (ANC) held a comfortable lead with 57.73%.

Tijjani Mohammad Bande

Tijjani Mohammad Bande, a professor from Nigeria, has been appointed as the new President of the United Nations General Assembly on May 11, 2019.

Boubou Cisse

Mali's president Ibrahim Boubacar Keïta on May 5, 2019 named a new government under Prime Minister Boubou Cisse. Mali President announced the new executive comprising 37 members under Prime Minister Boubou Cisse.

Laurentino 'Nito' Cortizo

The Panama Electoral Tribunal announced Laurentino 'Nito' Cortizo as the winner of Panama's presidential election (with 95% of votes counted) on May 5, 2019. He will succeed Juan Carlos Varela Rodríguez. This was the 6th presidential election in Panama.

Tod D. Wolters

US Air Force General Tod D. Wolters has been sworn in as the top military officer of the 29 Nation NATO Military alliance. He declared as the Supreme Allied Commander Europe during the ceremony at NATO's (The North Atlantic Treaty Organization) military headquarters in Mons, southern Belgium on May 2, 2019.

Jack Farj Rafael Jacob

Lieutenant General (retired) Jack Farj Rafael (JFR) Jacob honoured with a plaque on the Wall of Honour at the Ammunition Hill by Israel.

Kane Tanaka

Guiness World Records on March, 9, 2019 officially confirmed Kane Tanaka from Fukuoka (Japan) as the **oldest person living** at **116 years.** She was born prematurely on January 2, 1903.

Jagjit Pavadia

Jagjit Pavadia has been re-elected on May 7, 2019 for a five-year term on International Narcotics Control Board (INCB) by the 54-member UN Economic and Social Council. She will begin her second five-year term from March 2, 2020.

Padma Lakshmi

Indian-American television personality and food expert Padma Lakshmi has been appointed by the **United Nations Development Programme (UNDP)** at its **Goodwill Ambassador** on March 7, 2019.

Medha Narvekar

Indian-American Medha Narvekar has been named **Vice-President and Secretary** of the **University of Pennsylvania**, on March 1, 2019. She will replace Leslie Kruhly for the post on July, 1, 2019.

Jores Alferov

Renowed **Russian Scientist** Jores Ivanovich Alferov has **died** in Saint Petersburg at the age of 89 years, on March 1, 2019. He was the inventor of the heterotransistor and the **winner of 2000 Nobel Prize in Physics** together with Herbert Kroemer (Germany).

Kelly Knight Craft

US President Donald Trump has nominated Kelly Knight Craft as the next **US Ambassador to the United Nations (UN)** on February 22, 2019.

Suman Kumari

Suman Kumari has become the **first Hindu woman** to be appointed as a **civil judge in Pakistan** on January 29, 2019. Ms. Kumari, who hails from Qambar-Shahdadkot in Sindh province, will serve in her native district.

Newly Appointed Presidents & Prime Ministers

The Personality (Designation)	Description
Mohammad Shtayyeh (PM, Palestine)	Palestinian President Mahmoud Abbas appointed Mohammad Shtayyeh as the Palestinian Prime Minister on March 11, 2019.
Kaja Kallas (PM, Estonia)	Reform Party's Kaja Kallas is elected as first female Prime Minister of Estonia on March 8, 2019.
Muhammadu Buhari (President, Nigeria)	He has been re-elected as the President of Nigeria on February 28, 2019.
Christophe Joseph Marie Dabire (PM, Burkina Faso)	President Kabire on January 21, 2019 appointed Christophe Joseph Maric Dabire as the new Prime Minister of Burkina Faso.
Andry Rajoelina (President, Madagascar)	He was sworn-in as Madagascar's President on Janaury 19, 2019.

The Personality (Designation)	Description
Nicolas Maduro (President, Venezuela)	Venezuelan President Nicolas Maduro was sworn-in for a second term on January 10, 2019.
Jair Bolsonaro (President, Brazil)	Former paratrooper Jair Bolsonaro took charge as new Brazilian President on January 1, 2019.
Sheikh Hasina (PM, Bangladesh)	She was elected Bangladesh Prime Minister for the third straight term on December 31, 2018.
Ranil Wickremesinghe (PM, Sri Lanka)	Former PM Ranil Wickremesinghe sworn back in as Sri Lanka's Prime Minister on December 15, 2018 after being deposed two months earlier.
Andres Manuel Obrador (President, Mexico)	He took oath of office as Mexico's first leftist President in over 70 years on December 1, 2018.

WHO'S WHO

President Ram Nath Kovind
Vice-President M Venkaiah Naidu
Prime Minister Narendra Modi

Cabinet Ministers

Minister	Portfolio
Narendra Modi	Prime Minister and also in-charge of : Ministry of Personnel, Public Grievances and Pensions; Department of Atomic Energy; Department of Space; and All important policy issues; and All other portfolios not allocated to any Minister.
Rajnath Singh	Defence
Amit Shah	Home Affairs
Nitin Jairam Gadkari	Road Transport and Highways; Micro, Small and Medium Enterprises
DV Sadananda Gowda	Chemicals and Fertilizers
Nirmala Sitharaman	Finance; Corporate Affairs

Minister	Portfolio
Ramvilas Paswan	Consumer Affairs, Food and Public Distribution
Narendra Singh Tomar	Agriculture and Farmers Welfare; Rural Development; Panchayati Raj
Ravi Shankar Prasad	Law and Justice; Communications; Electronics and Information Technology
Harsimrat Kaur Badal	Food Processing Industries
Thaawar Chand Gehlot	Social Justice and Empowerment
Dr. S Jaishankar	External Affairs
Ramesh Pokhriyal 'Nishank'	Human Resource Development
Arjun Munda	Tribal Affairs
Smriti Zubin Irani	Women and Child Development; Textiles
Dr. Harsh Vardhan	Health and Family Welfare; Science and Technology; Earth Sciences
Prakash Javadekar	Environment, Forest and Climate Change; Information and Broadcasting
Piyush Goyal	Railways; Commerce and Industry
Dharmendra Pradhan	Petroleum and Natural Gas; Steel
Mukhtar Abbas Naqvi	Minority Affairs
Prahlad Joshi	Parliamentary Affairs; Coal; Mines
Dr. Mahendra Nath Pandey	Skill Development and Entrepreneurship
Arvind Ganpat Sawant	Heavy Industries and Public Enterprise
Giriraj Singh	Animal Husbandry, Dairying and Fisheries
Gajendra Singh Shekhawat	Jal Shakti

Ministers of State (Independent Charge)

Minister	Portfolio
Santosh Kumar Gangwar	Labour and Employment (Independent Charge)
Rao Inderjit Singh	Statistics and Programme Implementation (Independent Charge); and Planning (Independent Charge)

Minister	Portfolio
Shripad Naik	Ayurveda, Yoga and Naturopathy, Unani, Siddha and Homoeopathy (AYUSH) (Independent Charge); Defence
Jitendra Singh	Development of North Eastern Region (Independent Charge); Prime Minister's Office; Personnel, Public Grievances and Pensions; Department of Atomic Energy; Department of Space
Kiren Rijiju	Youth Affairs and Sports (Independent Charge); Minority Affairs
Prahlad Singh Patel	Culture (Independent Charge); Tourism (Independent Charge)
Raj Kumar Singh	Power (Independent Charge); New and Renewable Energy (Independent Charge); Skill Development and Entrepreneurship
Hardeep Singh Puri	Housing and Urban Affairs (Independent Charge); Civil Aviation (Independent Charge); Commerce and Industry
Mansukh Mandaviya	Shipping (Independent Charge); Chemicals and Fertilizers

Ministers of State

Minister	Portfolio
Faggansingh Kulaste	Steel
Ashwini Kumar Choubey	Health and Family Welfare
Arjun Ram Meghwal	Parliamentary Affairs; Heavy Industries and Public Enterprise
General (Retd) VK Singh	Road Transport and Highways
Krishan Pal Gurjar	Social Justice and Empowerment
Danve Raosaheb Dadarao	Consumer Affairs, Food and Public Distribution
G. Kishan Reddy	Home Affairs
Parshottam Rupala	Agriculture and Farmers Welfare
Ramdas Athawale	Social Justice and Empowerment

Sadhvi Niranjan Jyoti	Rural Development
Babul Supriyo	Environment, Forest and Climate Change
Sanjeev Kumar Balyan	Animal Husbandry, Dairying and Fisheries
Dhotre Sanjay Shamrao	Human Resource Development; Communication; Electronics and Information Technology
Anurag Singh Thakur	Finance; Corporate Affairs
Angadi Suresh Channabasappa	Railways
Nityanand Rai	Home Affairs
Rattan Lal Kataria	Jal Shakti ; Social Justice and Empowerment
V. Muraleedharan	External Affairs; Parliamentary Affairs
Renuka Singh Saruta	Tribal Affairs
Som Parkash	Commerce and Industry
Rameswar Teli	Food Processing Industries
Pratap Chandra Sarangi	Micro, Small and Medium Enterprises; Animal Husbandry, Dairying and Fisheries
Kailash Choudhary	Agriculture and Farmers Welfare
Debasree Chaudhuri	Women and Child Development

Governors and Chief Ministers

State	Governor	Chief Minister
Andhra Pradesh	ESL Narasimhan	Jaganmohan Reddy
Arunachal Pradesh	BD Mishra	Pema Khandu
Assam	Jagdish Mukhi	Sarbananda Sonowal
Bihar	Lalji Tandon	Nitish Kumar
Chhattisgarh	Anandiben Patel (Add. Charge)	Bhupesh Baghel
Delhi	Anil Baijal (Lt. Governor)	Arvind Kejriwal
Goa	Mridula Sinha	Manohar Parrikar
Gujarat	OP Kohli	Vijay Rupani
Haryana	Satyadev Narayan Arya	Manohar Lal Khattar
Himachal Pradesh	Acharya Dev Vrat	Jai Ram Thakur
Jammu-Kashmir	Satyapal Malik	President's Rule
Jharkhand	Droupadi Murmu	Raghubar Das
Karnataka	Vajubhai R. Vala	HD Kumaraswamy
Kerala	P. Sathasivam	P. Vijayan
Madhya Pradesh	Anandiben Patel	Kamal Nath
Maharashtra	C. Vidyasagar Rao	Devendra Phadnavis
Manipur	Najma Heptulla	N. Biren Singh
Meghalaya	Tathagata Roy	Conrad Sangma
Mizoram	K. Rajasekharan	Zoramthanga
Nagaland	PB Acharya	Nephiu Rio
Odisha	Ganeshi Lal	Naveen Patnaik
Punjab	VP Singh Badnore	Amarinder Singh
Rajasthan	Kalyan Singh	Ashok Gehlot
Sikkim	Ganga Prasad	Prem Singh Tamang
Tamil Nadu	Banwarilal Purohit	EK Palanisami
Telangana	ESL Narasimhan	K. Chandrashekhar Rao
Tripura	Kaptan Singh Solanki	Biplab Deb
Uttar Pradesh	Ram Naik	Adityanath Yogi
Uttarakhand	Baby Rani Maurya	Trivendra Singh Rawat
West Bengal	Kesari Nath Tripathi	Mamata Banerjee

Chiefs of Defence Forces

Name of Force	Chief
Air Force	Air Chief Marshal BS Dhanoa
Army	General Bipin Rawat
Navy	Admiral Karambir Singh
Integrated Defence Staff	Lt. General Satish Dua

Heads of Financial Institutes/Organisations

Person	Designation
Shaktikanta Das	Governor, Reserve Bank of India
Sandeep Somani	Chairperson, FICCI
SB Mathur	Chairperson, Unit Trust of India
Harsha Kumar Bhanwala	Chairperson, NABARD
Chhatrapati Shivaji	CMD, SIDBI
S. Kalyanaraman	Chairperson, National Housing Bank
Balkrishna Goenka	Chairperson, ASSOCHAM
Rajan Bharati Mittal	Chairperson, International Chamber of Commerce
Saurabh Chandra	Chairperson, Multi Commodities Exchange
Sunil Mehta	Chairman, Indian Banks' Association
AV Girija Kumar	CMD, Oriental Insurance Company
Deepak Kumar	Director, Employees State Insurance Corporation
CS Makarand Iele	President, Institute of Company Secretary of India

Important National Officials

Designation	Name
Chief Justice of India	Ranjan Gogoi
Chairperson, National Human Rights Commission	HL Dattu
Chairperson, National Commission for Backward Classes	Bhagawan Lal Sahni
Chairperson, National Commission for Minorities	Syed Ghayorul Hasan Rizvi
Chairperson, Central Board of Direct Taxes	Sushil Chandra
Chairperson, National Commission for Scheduled Tribes	Nand Kumar Sai
Chairperson, University Grants Commission	Dhirendra Pal Singh

Designation	Name
Chairperson, National Commission for Scheduled Castes	Ram Shankar Katheria
Chairman, Indian Space Research Organisation	Sivan K.
Chairman, Atomic Energy Commission	Kamlesh Vyas
Chairperson, 15th Finance Commission	NK Singh
Governor, Reserve Bank of India	Urjit Patel
Chairman, Securities & Exchange Board of India	Ajay Tyagi
Chairperson, TRAI	Ram Sevak Sharma
Chairperson, NABARD	Harsh Kumar Bhanwala
Chairperson, National Highways Authority of India	Sanjeev Ranjan
Chairperson, Central Board of Film Certification	Prasoon Joshi
Chairperson, Central Board of Secondary Education	Anita Karwal
Chairperson, IRDAI	SC Khuntia
Chairperson, Press Council of India	CK Prasad
Director General, BSF	Rajanikant Mishra
Director General, SSB	Kumar Rajesh Chandra
Director General, CRPF	Rajiv Rai Bhatnagar
Director General, ITBP	SS Deshwal
Director General, CISF	Rajesh Ranjan
Chief Election Commissioner	Sunil Arora
Attorney General	KK Venugopal
Solicitor General	Tushar Mehta
President, NASSCOM	Debjani Ghosh
President, Press Trust of India	N. Ravi
President, Staff Selection Commission	Ashim Khurana
Director General, Delhi Metro Rail Corporation	Mangoo Singh
Chairman, Union Public Service Commission	Arvind Saxena

> **Note** In this book, we were unable to update some new facts. Given below is the page numberwise updation of such facts.

Page 201

- NH 548 and NH 118 are the shortest National Highways of India, each with the length of 5 km.

Page 226

Environment Related Important International Agreements/Conference

Agreement/Conference	Place
Katowice Climate Conference (CoP24)	Katowice Poland (2018)

Page 254

- Salary of Vice-President is ₹ 4,00,000 per month.

Page 260

Speakers of Lok Sabha
(As on 21 June, 2019)

Name	Tenure	
Sumitra Mahajan	06.06.2014	16.06.2019
Om Birla	19.06.2019	Till Date

- M. Thambidurai was the Deputy Speaker of Lok Sabha till 25 May, 2019.

Page 264

- Salary of Chief Justice of India is ₹ 2.8 lakh per month and salary of other judges of supreme court is ₹ 2.5 Lakhs per month.

Page 271

- Telangana is the 25th High Court in India. It was established in 2019 and its seat is in Hyderabad.

Page 272

- Salary of Chief Justice of High Court is ₹ 2,50,000 and Judge of High Court is ₹ 2,25,000.

Page 278

Election Commissioner of India
(As on 21 June, 2019)

Name	Tenure	
Om Prakash Rawat	23.01.2018	1.12.2018
Sunil Arora	02.12.2018	Till date

Page 284

- The Hundred and two Amendment Act 2018 provided Constitutional Status to National Commission for Backward Classes.
- The Hundred and three Amendment Act 2018 Provided 10% reservation for economically weaker section of society.

Page 306-307

Major Government Schemes Launched in 2018-19

Programme	Year of Begining	Objectives Description
Ayushman Bharat Yojana	2018	To provide ₹ 5 lakh health insurance to 10 crore poor families.
Kisan Samman Nidhi	2019	To provide ₹ 6000 per year financial assistance to those farmers having Cultivable area upto 2 hectares.

Page 467

Top Super Computers of the World

Name	Country	Operating System
IBM Summit (2018)	America	IBM

Page 491

- Statue of Unity (Gujarat) is the tallest statue in India.

Page 494

- The Victorian and Art Deco Ensemble of Mumbai was declared UNESCO World Heritage Site in 2018.

Page 505

- 2018 was observed as the UN International Year of Indigenous Languages.

Page 514-515

Books Awarded with Prize

Books	Award	Authors	Year
Less (fiction)	Pulitzer Prize	Andrew Sean Greer	2018
Flight	Man Booker Prize	Olgo Tokarczuk	2018
Post Box No. 203	Sahitya Akademi Award	Chitra Mudgal	2018
Vakhar	Saraswati Saumman	Sitanshu Yashaschandra	2018
Home Fire	Oranze Prize	Kamila Shamsie	2018

Page 523

- 2018 Commonwealth Games were held on Gold Coast, Queensland, Australia.
- The Asian Games or Asiad 2018 were held in Jakarta Palembang, Indonesia.

Page 525

- 2018 ICC Women's World Twenty 20 was hosted in the West Indies from 9 to 24 November 2018. Women team of Australia won the World T20 2018 title.
- The 2018 Hockey World Cup was held at Kalinga stadium, Bhubaneshwar, India in 2018.

Page 538

- INS Karanj is third submarine of the first batch of zix Kalvari class submarine. It is a diesel-electric attack submarine, that was launched on 31th January, 2018.

Page 548

Indians winning Ramon Magsaysay Award

Recipient	Year
Bharat Vatwani	2018
Sonam Wangchuk	2018

Page 549

- Catriona Gray of Phillipines has been crowned Miss Universe 2018.
- Vanesa Ponce of Mexico has been crowned Miss World 2018.
- Nguyen Phuong Khankh of Vietnam has been crowned 2018 Miss Earth.

Page 550

- Centre for Science and Environment India received Indira Gandhi Peace Prize 2018.
- Pranab Mukherjee, Bhupen Hazika (Posthumously) and Nanaji Deshmukh (Posthumously) won 2019 Bharat Ratna.

Page 553

- In 2018, Saikhom Mirabai Chanu (Weightlifting) and Virat Kohli (Cricket) have won Rajiv Gandhi Khel Ratna Award.

Page 555

- Vinod Khanna has received Dada Saheb Phalke Award for the year 2017.

Page 557

Amitav Ghosh has received Jnanpith Award for the year 2018.

INDIAN HISTORY

ANCIENT INDIA

THE EARLY MAN

- The fossils of the early human being have been found in Africa about 2.6 million years back, but there are no such evidence in India. So, it appears that India was inhabited later than Africa.
- The recent reported artefacts from **Bori** in Maharashtra suggest that the appearance of human beings in India was around 1.4 million years ago.
- The evolution of the Earth's crust shows four stages. The fourth stage is divided into **Pleistocene** (most recent) and **Holocene** (present).
- Man is said to have appeared on the Earth in the early Pleistocene.
- The early man in India used tools of stone roughly dressed by crude clipping. This period is therefore, known as the **Stone Age**, which has been divided into
  - The Palaeolithic or Old Stone Age
  - The Mesolithic or Middle Stone Age
  - The Neolithic or New Stone Age

The Palaeolithic Age (500000 BC-9000 BC)

- The Palaeolithic culture of India developed in the pleistocene period or the ice age.
- It seems that Palaeolithic men belonged to the Negrito race. **Homo Sapiens** first appeared towards the end of this phase.
- Palaeolithic men were hunters and food gatherers. They had no knowledge of agriculture, fire or pottery, they used tools of unpolished, rough stones and lived in cave rock shelters. They are also called **Quartzite men**.
- This age is divided into three phases according to the nature of the stone tools used by the people and change in the climate.
  - Early or Lower Palaeolithic
  - Middle Palaeolithic
  - Upper Palaeolithic

Phases of the Palaeolithic Age

Age	Tools	Climate	Sites
Early	Hand axes, cleavers and choppers	Humidity decreased	Soan valley (Punjab)
Middle	Flakes-blades, points, borers and scrapers	Further decrease in humidity	Valleys of Soan, Narmada and Tungabhadra rivers.
Upper	Scrapers and burin	Warm climate	Caves and rockshelters of this age have been discovered at Bhimbetka near Bhopal.

The Mesolithic Age
(9000 BC- 4000 BC)

- It intervened as a transitional phase between the **Palaeolithic Age** and the **Neolithic Age**.
- In this age, climate became warm and dry, which brought about changes in fauna and flora and made it possible for human beings to move to new areas.
- The Mesolithic people lived on hunting, fishing and food- gathering. At a later stage, they also domesticated animals.
- The characteristic tools of the Mesolithic Age are microliths, pointed cresconic blades, scrapers, etc made up of stones.
- **Adamgarh** in Madhya Pradesh and **Bagor** in Rajasthan provide the earliest evidence for the domestication of animals.
- The people of Palaeolithic and Mesolithic ages practiced painting. **Bhimbetka** in Madhya Pradesh is a striking site of **Pre-historic painting** of Mesolithic age.

The Neolithic Age
(4000 BC-1800 BC)

- The people of this age are characterised by the use of polished stone tools. They particularly used stone axes.
- It is interesting that in **Burzahom** dogs were buried with their masters in their graves.
- The Neolithic settlers were the earliest farming communities. They produced ragi and horse-gram (*kulathi*). Neolithic sites in Allahabad district are noted for the cultivation of rice in the sixth millenium BC. They domesticated cattle, sheeps and goats. They wove cotton and wool to make clothes.
- Hand made pottery and use of potter wheel first appeared during the Neolithic age.

- Neolithic men lived in caves and decorated their walls with hunting and dancing scenes. They knew the art of making boats. In the later phase, people lived a more settled life and lived in circular and rectangular houses made of mud and reed.
- Koldihwa in UP revealed a three fold cultural sequence: Neolithic, Chalcolithic and iron age. **Mehargarh** in **Baluchistan** is the oldest Neolithic site in India (7000 BC).
- Important sites include Chhotanagpur region, Central India and South of the Krishna river. **Belan valley** of Vindhays and middle part of the Narmada valley shows all the three phases of Stone age.

Chalcolithic Culture
(1800 BC-1000 BC)

- The end of the Neolithic period saw the use of metals. Copper was the first metal to be used.
- Chalcolithic culture refers to the stone-copper phase. People also used hand-axes and other objects made up of copper ware.
- Chalcolithic people were primarily rural communities. They domesticated animals and practised agriculture. They were not acquainted with burnt bricks and lived in thatched houses. They venerated the mother Goddess and worshipped the bull.
- The people of Chalcolithic culture were the first to use *painted pottery*. Black and red pottery painted with white line design was most popular.
- The **Malwa ware** is considered the richest among the Chalcolithic ceramics.
- Important sites of this phase are spread in Rajasthan, Maharashtra, West Bengal, Bihar, Madhya Pradesh etc.

INDUS VALLEY CIVILISATION

- Indus civilisation is one of the four earliest civilisations of the world along with the civilisations of Mesopotamia (Tigris and Euphrates), Egypt (Nile) and China (Hwang Ho).
- The civilisation forms part of the proto-history of India and belongs to the **Bronze age**.
- The most accepted period is 2500-1700 BC (by Carbon-14 dating).

It can be divided into following sub-parts
- Early Phase 2900-2500 BC
- Middle (mature) Phase 2500-2000 BC
- Later Phase 2000-1750 BC
- **Dayaram Sahni** first discovered Harappa in 1921.
- **RD Banerjee** discovered Mohenjodaro or **Mound of the Dead** in 1922.

Nomenclature of Indus Valley Civilisation

- **Indus Valley Civilisation** as it flourished along the Indus river.
- Harappan Civilisation named by John Marshall after the first discovered site, Harappa.
- **Saraswati-Sindhu Civilisation** as most of the sites have been found at the Hakra-Ghaggar river.

Geographical Spread

- The civilisation covered parts of Sind, Baluchistan, Afghanistan, West Punjab, Gujarat, Uttar Pradesh, Haryana, Rajasthan, Jammu and Kashmir, Punjab and Maharashtra.
- **Mundigak** and **Shortughai** are the two sites located in Afghanistan.
- West-Sutkagendor on Makran coast (Pak-Iran Border) East-Alamgirpur in Uttar Pradesh (River Hindon).
- North-Manda in Jammu (River Chenab). South-Daimabad in Maharashtra (River Pravara) are major sites.

Some New Discoveries

- **Ganverivala** in Pakistan by Rafeeq Mugal.
- **Rakhigarhi** in Sind (Haryana) by Rafeeq Mugal.
- **Dholavira** on bank of river Luni in Gujarat excavated by RS Bist and JP Joshi is largest and latest excavated site in India.
- **Bhirrana** oldest Harappan site has said to be the mounds at Bhirrana village on the banks of Ghaggar river.

Town Planning

- It was not uniform. A unique feature was the grid system i.e. streets cutting across one another at right angles, dividing the town into large rectangular blocks.

Indus Cities *At a Glance*

City	Province	River Bank	Year of Discovery	Archaeologist(s)
Harappa	Pakistani Punjab	Ravi	1921	Daya Ram Sahni
Mohenjodaro	Sind	Indus	1922	RD Banerjee
Sutkagendor	Baluchistan	Dasht	1931	Aurel Stein
Rangpur	Gujarat	Meedar	1931	MS Vats
Chanhudaro	Sind	Indus	1931	MG Majumdar
Ropar	Indian Punjab	Sutlej	1953	YD Sharma
Lothal	Gujarat	Bhogava Sabarmati	1957	SR Rao
Kalibangan	Rajasthan	Ghaggar	1959	BB Lal
Alamgirpur	Uttar Pradesh	Hindon	1974	YD Sharma
Banawali	Haryana	Ghaggar	1974	RS Bisht

- The towns were divided into two parts: upper part or citadel and lower part.
- The fortified **citadel** on the Western side housed public buildings and members of ruling class.
- Below the citadel on the Eastern side, lay the **lower town** inhabited by the common people.
- **Underground Drainage System** connected all houses to the street drains made of mortar, lime and gypsum. They were covered with either brick or stone slabs and equipped with its 'Manhole'. This shows developed sense of health and sanitation.
- **The Great Bath** (Mohenjodaro) It was used for religious bathing. Steps at either end leads to the surface. There were changing rooms alongside.
- **The Granaries** (Harappa) six granaries in a row were found in the citadel at Harappa.
- Houses were made up of *burnt bricks*. They were often two or more storeyed, varied in size, with a square courtyard around, which had a number of rooms. Windows did not face the main streets. They had tiled bathrooms.
- **Lamp-posts** were erected at regular intervals. It indicates the existence of street lighting.

Agriculture

- It was the backbone of the civilisation. The soil was fertile due to inundation in the river Indus and flooding.
- The Indus people sowed seeds in the flood plains in November, when the flood water receded and reaped their harvests of wheat and barley in April, before the advent of next flood.
- They used wooden plough share (ploughed field from Kalibangan) and stone sickles for harvesting.
- *Gabarbands* or *nalas* enclosed by dam for storing water were a feature in parts of Baluchistan. Grains were stored in granaries.

- **Crops Produced** wheat, barley, dates, peas, sesamum, mustard, millet, ragi, bajra and jowar. At Lothal and Rangpur, rice husks were found.
- **They were First to Produce Cotton** in the world, which Greek called as *Sindon* derived from Sind. A fragment of woven cotton cloth was found at Mohenjodaro.
- Well irrigation is evident from Alladinho, dams and irrigation canals from Dholavira. Sugarcane was not known to Indus people.

Domestication of Animals

- Animal rearing was practiced, evident from the discovery of the Humped Bull.
- They domesticated buffaloes, oxens, sheep, asses, goats, pigs, elephants, dogs, cats etc.
- Camel bones are reported at Kalibangan and remains of horse from Surkotada.

Trade

- Agriculture, industry and forest produce provided the basis for internal and external trade.
- Trade was based on **barter system**. Coins were not evident, bullock carts, pack animals and boats were used for transportation.
- Weights and measures were made of limestone, steatite etc. generally in cubical shape. They were in multiple of sixteen.
- Several sticks inscribed with measure marks have been discovered. It points that linear system of measurement was in use.
- Foreign trade flourished with Mesopotamia or Sumeria (Iraq), Central Asia, Persia, Afghanistan and Bahrain.
- Sumerian text refers to trade with Meluha (Indus). Dilmun (Bahrain) and Makan (Makran coast) were two intermediate stations.
- Lothal (artificial dockyard), Surkotada, Sutkagendor, Prabhas, Bhatrao, Kalibangan, Dholavira, Daimabad were **coastal towns** of the civilisation.

Towns Associated with Different Industries

- **Daimabad** Bronze industry.
- **Lothal** Factory for stone tools and metallic finished goods.
- **Balakot** Pearl finished goods, bangle and shell industry.
- **Chanhudaro** Beads and bangles factory. It was the only city without a citadel.

- Major Exports were agricultural products, cotton goods, terracotta figurines, pottery, steatite beads (from Chanhudaro), Conch-shell (from Lothal), ivory products, copper etc.

Major Imports

Imports	From
Gold	Kolar (Karnataka), Afghanistan, Persia (Iran)
Silver	Afghanistan, Persia (Iran), South India
Copper	Khetri (Rajasthan), Baluchistan, Arabia
Tin	Afghanistan, Biha
Lapis Lazuli and Sapphire	Badakhshan (Afghanistan)
Jade	Central Asia
Steatite	Shaher-i-Sokhta, Kirthar hills
Turquoise	Iran
Amethyst	Maharashtra

Art and Craft

- Harappans used stone tools and were well acquainted with bronze. Bronze was made by mixing copper (from Khetri) with tin.
- **Bead Making** and jewellery of gold, silver precious stone were made. Cotton fabrics were used in summers and woollen in winters.
- Both men and women were very fond of ornaments and dressing up.
- **Pottery** both plain (red) or painted (red and black) pottery was made. Pots were decorated with human figures, plants, animals and geometrical patterns and *ochre* was painted over it.

- **Seals** were made of steatite pictures of one horned bull, buffalo, tiger, rhinocerous, goat and elephant are found on the seals. They marked ownership of property.
- **Mesopotamia** seals were found from Mohenjodaro and Kalibangan; Persian seal was obtained from Lothal. Most important one is the **Pashupati seal**.
- **Metal Images** Bronze image of a nude woman dancer (identified as *devadasi*) and stone steatite image of a bearded man (both are obtained from Mohenjodaro).
- **Terracotta Figurines** Fire baked clay was used to make toys, objects of worship, animals (monkey, dogs, sheep, cattle, humped and humpless bulls), cattle toys with movable head, toy-carts, whistle shaped like birds and both male and female figurines.
- They played dice games. Gambling was their favourite time pass. No clear evidence of music.

Religious Practices

- **Chief Female Diety** A terracotta figure where a plant is shown growing out of the embryo of a woman, represents Mother Goddess (Goddess of Earth).
- **Chief Male Diety** Pashupati Mahadeva (Proto-Shiva), represented in seals as sitting in a yogic posture on a low throne and having three faces and two horns. He is surrounded by an elephant, a tiger, a rhino and a buffalo and two deers appear at his feet.
- *Lingam* and *yoni* worship was prevalent. Trees (pipal), animals (bull, birds, dove, pigeon) unicorn and stones were worshipped. No temples have been found, though idolatry was practiced.
- Indus people believed in ghosts and evil forces and used amulets for protection against them. Fire altars are found at Lothal and Kalibangan.
- Evidence of snake worship is also found.

Burial Practices

- General practice was placing the dead body in the in North-South direction.
- **Mohenjodaro** Three forms of burial were Complete, Fractional and Post Cremation.
- **Kalibangan** Two forms of burial- Circular and Rectangular Grave.
- **Surkotada** Pot-burial, Dholavira Megalithic burial.
- **Lothal** Double burial.
- **Harappa** East-West axis; R-37 and H cemetery.

Script

- It was pictographic in nature. Fish symbol is most represented.
- Overlapping of the letters show that it was written from right to left in the first line and then left to right in the second line. This style is called *Boustrophedon*.

DECLINE OF THE CIVILISATION

The Harappan culture flourished about till 1800 BC, then it began to decline. There is no unanimity among historians, regarding the exact reason for the decline of this urban civilisation. There are many different theories that show the decline of the Indus culture.

Decline of Indus Civilisation (Different Views)

Views	Thinkers
External Aggression	Wheeler, Piggot and Gordon-Childe
Inundation	MR Sahani
Epidemic	KVR Kennedy
Tectonic Disturbances (e.g. Dholavira)	Marshall and Raikes
Sudden decline	Wheeler
Climatic change	RL Stein and AN Ghosh
Deforestation, Scarcity of resources, Ecological Imbalances	Fairservis
Flood (e.g. Mohenjodaro)	Marshall, SR Rao, Maickey
The Destruction due to change in course of River Ghaggar	GF Holes

Important Harappan Sites

City	Archaeological Finds
Harappa (*Gateway city*)	Two row of six granaries with brick platform, work men's quarter, stone symbol of *lingam* and *yoni*, virgin-Goddess, clay figures of Mother Goddess, wheat and barley in wooden mortar, copper scale and mirror, vanitybox, dice. **Sculpture** Dog chasing a deer (bronze), nude male and nude dancing female (stone), red sand stone male torso.
Mohenjodaro (*Mound of the Dead*)	The great bath, The great granary (largest building), multi-pillared assembly hall, college, proto-Shiva seal, clay figures of Mother Goddess, Dice. **Sculpture** Bronze dancing girl, steatite image of bearded man.
Kalibangan (*Black Bangle*)	Decorated bricks, bangle factory, wheels of a toy cart, wells in every house.Remains of a massive brick wall around both the citadel and lower town (lower town of Lothal is also fortified), bones of camel, tiled floor. Mother Goddess figurines are absent here.
Chanhudaro (*Lancashire of India*)	Inkpot, lipstick, carts with seated driver, *ikkas* of bronze, imprint of dog's paw on a brick. Only city without citadel.
Daimabad	Bronze images of charioteer with chariot, ox, elephants and rhinoceros.

City	Archaeological Finds
Amri	Actual remains of rhinoceros.
Alamgirpur	Impression of cloth on a trough.
Lothal (*Manchester of Indus Valley Civilisation*)	Rice husk, fire altars, grinding machine, tusks of elephant, granomy, terracotta figure of horse and seal, dying vat, painted jar (bird and fox), teracotta ship, houses with entrance on main streets, impressions of cloth on some seals, modern day chess, instrument for measuring 180, 90 and 45 degree angles.
Ropar	Buildings made of stone and soil. Dog buried with humans. One inscribed steatite seal with typical Indus pictographs; oval pit burials.
Banawali	Oval shaped settlement, only city with radial streets, lack of systematic drainage pattern. Toy plough, largest number of barley grains.
Surkotada	Both citadel and lower town fortified with stone wall. First actual remains of horse bones. Cemetry with four pot burials.
Dholavira	Only site to be divided into three parts. Giant water reservoir, unique water harnessing system, dams and embankments, a stadium, rock-cut architecture.
Sutkagendor	Two fold division of township Citadel and Lower Town.

THE ARYAN AND THE VEDIC AGE

Original Home and Identity

- The word *Aryan* literally means *of high birth*. *Veda* means *mantra* and *slokas* and also knowledge and conscience.
- The location of the original homeland of the Aryans is still controversial, but the most accepted theory is that they migrated from Central Asia in several groups between 2000-1500 BC and settled in Eastern Afghanistan, modern Pakistan, Punjab and Western UP.
- This region is popularly known as the land of seven rivers or '*Sapta Sindva*' (the Indus, its five tributaries Vitasta, Askini, Vipas, Parushni, Sutudri and the Saraswati).

Note *The Central Asian theory is also proved by the Boghazkai Inscription (Turkey), which mentions four Vedic Gods : Indra, Varuna, Mitra and Nasatya.*

Rigvedic or Early Vedic Period (1500-1000 BC)

- Early Vedic people had knowledge of rivers Yamuna, Saraswati, (Nanditara) and Ganga. Ocean was mentioned as *Samudra* (referred to collection of water and not sea) snow mountains (*Himvat*) and desert land (*Dhawa*). So, they lived in *Sapta Sindva* region.

Rivers Mentioned in the Rig Veda

Rigvedic Names	Modern Names
Sindhu	Indus
Vitasta	Jhelum
Askini	Chenab
Parushni	Ravi
Vipas	Beas
Shutudri	Sutlej
Gomati	Gumal
Krumu	Kurram
Ghaggar Drishadvati	Ghaggar
Suvasthu	Swat
Kubha	Kabul
Nandi tara	Saraswati
Sadanira	Gandak
Gumal	Gomati

- Aryans came into conflict with the indigenous inhabitants called **Dasas** (early branch of Aryans) and **Dasyus** (Original inhabitants). **Dasyuhatya** or slaughter of *Dasyus* is repeatedly mentioned in the *Rig Veda*.

The Dasarajna War

- This battle was fought on the bank of the Parushni river (Ravi), **Sudas**, the son of Divodas and the Bharata king of Tritsu family won over an alliance of ten tribes (Five Aryans and Five non-Aryans) and killed their leader **Purusukta**.
- The battle broke out due to a dispute between **Vashistha** (*priest of Bharatas*) and **Visvamitra** (*priest of alliance*).

Economy

- Aryans followed a mixed economy consisting of both agriculture and pastoralism.
- They possessed better knowledge in agriculture ploughshare is mentioned in Rig Veda. It was made up of wood and was drawn by the ox. They were acquainted with sowing, harvesting, threshing and knew about different seasons.
- The reference of cow in the *Rig Veda* shows that *Rigvedic Aryans* were predominantly pastoral people. The term for war in the *Rig Veda* is *Gavishthi* or search for cows. The horse was almost as important as cow.
- **Cow** was the standard unit of exchange. Gold coins like *Nishka*, *Krishna* and *Satmana* were also in use. *Godhuli* was used as a measure of time and *Gavyuti* as measure of distance.

Polity

- The election of the king was by the tribal assembly called **Samiti**.
- Several tribal or clan based assemblies existed such as the Sabha, Samiti, Vidatha and Gana.
- The **Samiti** was the National Assembly of the people, while the **Sabha** was Council of Elders.

- King was assisted by many functionaries. Most important functionary was the **Purohita,** the religious advisor of the king, followed by the Senani, the head of the army.
- The voluntary offerings to the chief by the people was called **Bali**.
- There was no regular or standing **army**. However, there were groups of infantry and charioteers.
- Weapons made of stone, wood, bone and metal were used.

Society

- Kinship was the basis of society's structure. People gave their primary loyalty to the tribe, which was called **Jana**.
- An other term that stands for tribe in the *Rig Veda* is *Vis*.
- *Vis* was divided into *grama*. When *grama* clashed with one another, it caused the *Sangrama* or war.
- The term family (*Kula*) is rarely mentioned in the *Rig Veda*. Patriarchial family structure was prevalent.
- Varna was the term used for colour of people, which were classified into four *Varnas*.
- **Brahmins** (teachers and priests), **Kshatriyas** (rulers and administrators), **Vaishyas** (merchants and bankers), **Sudras** (artisans and labourers).

Rigvedic Gods

- Rigvedic people believed in nature worship and not in erecting temples or idol worship. They performed *Yajnas* in open areas.
- **Soma** was considered to be the God of plants and an intoxicating drink is named after him.
- The ninth *mandala* of the *Rig Veda* i.e. 'Soma Mandala' is attributed to *Soma*.
- Some female divinities such as **Aditi** and **Usha**, represented the appearance of the dawn.

Types of Deities

God	Associated Field
Indra/Purandar (Most Important)	Breaker of Forts
Agni	Fire God
Varuna	Water God and upholder of natural order
Surya	God with Seven horse driven chariot
Savitri	God of light to whom Gayatri Mantra is addressed
Mitra	Solar God
Pushan	God of marriage, also guarded roads
Vishnu	One, who covered Earth in Three steps-Upakrama
Rudra	God of Animals
Dyaus	Eldest God and Father of the World
Ashwin/Nastya	God of health, youth and immortality
Sindhu	River Goddess
Yama	God of death
Marut	Personified storm

Types of Marriages

Eight types of marriages were in practice during the Vedic period :

Brahma	Marriage of a duly dowered girl to a man of the same class.
Daiva	A daughter is given to a sacrificial priest, as a part of his fee.
Arsa	A token bride-price of a cow is given in place of the dowry.
Prajapatya	The father gives the girl without dowry and without demanding the bride-price.
Gandharva	Love marriage.
Asura	Bride was bought from her father.
Rakshasa	Marriage by capture .
Paishacha	Marriage by seduction.

Important Rituals

- **Rajasuya**—The king's influence was strengthened by rituals. The king performed this sacrifice, which was supposed to confer supreme power on him.
- **Asvamedha**—A king performed the *Asvamedha,* which meant unquestioned control over the area, in which the royal horse ran uninterrupted.
- **Vajapeya**—A king performed the *Vajapeya* or the chariot race, in which the royal chariot was made to win the race against his kinsmen.

LATER VEDIC AGE (1000-600 BC) (PAINTED GREYWARE PHASE)

- Later *Vedic* texts refer to rivers Narmada, Sadanira etc. Vindhya mountain and territorial division of India into *Aryavarta* (Nothern India), *Madhyadesa* (Central India) and *Dakshinapatha* (Southern India). Aryans expanded from Punjab over the whole Western UP covered by Ganga-Yamuna Doab (Aryavarta).
- The expansion towards East is indicated in a legend of *Satapatha Brahmana* i.e. how Videha Madhava migrated from the Saraswati region, crossed Sadanira and came to the land of Videha (modern Tirhut).

Polity

- Formation of large kingdoms; for all practical purposes, Kingship became hereditary. Assembly lost its importance and royal power increased at their cost. *Vidhata* totally disappeared. Women were no longer permitted to attend assemblies.
- The term **Rashtra** indicating territory, first appeared in this period.
- *Taittariya Brahmana* refers to the theory of divine origin of kingship.
- *Satapatha Brahmana* refers to Twelfth *Ratninas* or civil functionaries of the time.

Twelve Ratninas (*Shatapatha Brahmana*)

Purohita	The Priest
Mahishi	Chief Queen
Yuvaraja	Crown Prince
Suta/Sarathi	The Royal herald/the Charioteer
Bhagadugha	Tax collector
Akshavapa	Accountant
Palagala	Friend of king
Govikarta	Head of forest department
Senani	The General
Gramani	Head of the village
Kshatri	Gateman/Chamberlain
Sangrahitri	Treasurer

- There was development of judiciary. Kings administered the criminal court. Serious crimes were the killing of an embryo, homicide, the murder of a Brahmin, stealing of gold and drinking *sura*. Treason was a capital offence.

Society

- The fourfold division of society became more clear. Initially based on occupation, it later became hereditary.
- **Brahmin**—The growing cult of sacrifice enormously added to the power of *Brahmins*.
- **Kshatriyas**—They constituted the warrior class.
- **Vaisyas**—They were the agriculturalists, cattle rearers, traders, artisans and metal workers.
- **Shudras**—Lowest in the social hierarchy and born to serve the upper three varna.
- The **Ashram system** was formed to attain four *purusharthas* (*Dharma, Artha, Kama* and *Moksha*). *Jabala Upanishada* gives the earliest reference to four ashramas i.e. the stages of life—*Brahmacharya, Grihastha, Vanaprastha* and *Sanyasa*.

- Position of women declined. *Aitareya Brahmana* states that daughter is the source of misery while a son is the protector of family. *Maitrayani Samhita* mentions three evils—liquor, woman and dice. Polygamy became frequent.
- However, some of the women had got higher education as indicated by the Yajnavalkya-Gargi dialogue in *Vrihadarnyaka Upanishada*.
- In this period, *pratiloma vivah* was not permitted.

Economy

- Agriculture became the chief economic activity. Manure was wheat, rice, barley, beans and seasum.
- New occupational group emerged, such as fisherman, washerman, dyers, door-keepers and footmen.
- Tin, silver and iron was now known to the people.
- Merchants were organised into Guilds, as indicated by the terms-*Ganas* (corporations) and *Sresthins* (eldermen).

Religion

- Rituals became important in the cult of sacrifice.
- *Prajapati* became the supreme God. *Vishnu* was conceived as the preserver and protector of people.
- *Pushan*, responsible for well being of cattle, became the **God of Shudras**.
- Towards the end of the Vedic age, a section of society began to resent the priestly domination.

16 Sanskaras

1. Garbhadhana	9. Karnachhedana
2. Pumsavana	10. Vidyarmbha
3. Simantonnayan	11. Upanayana
4. Jatakarma	12. Vedarambha
5. Namakaran	13. Samavaratana
6. Nishkramana	14. Vivaha
7. Annaprashana	15. Vanprastha
8. Chudakarma	16. Antyesti

The Vedic Literature

- The word **Veda** comes from the word **Vid**, means to know or knowledge.
- Vedic texts are divided between **Sruti** (based on hearing) and **Smriti** (based on memory).
- *Veda* are divided into **Samhitas**.

Rig Veda

- One of the oldest religious text in the world.
- Collection of hymns, composed around 1700 BC, contains 1028 hymns and is divided into 10 *mandalas*.
- II to VII are the earliest *mandalas*, each of which is ascribed at a particular family of Rishi Gritsamad, Visvamitra Vamadeva, Atri, Bhardwaja, Vashistha. *VIII mandala* is ascribed to Kanvas and Angiras. *IX mandala* is the compilation of Soma hymns.
- The *Xth mandala* contains the famous *Purushasukta* hymn which explains that the four *varnas* were born from the mouth, arms, thighs and feet of the creator *Brahma*.
- The IIIrd *mandala* contains the **Gayatri Mantra**, which was compiled in the praise of Sun God Savitri.
- Saraswati is the deity river in the *Rig Veda*.

Sama Veda

- *Sama Veda* derives its roots from '*saman*', which means **melodies**. It is a collection of melodies. The hyms of the *Sama Veda* were recited by Udgatri at the *Soma* sacrifice.
- It contains *Dhrupad Raga*.

Yajur Veda

- Deals with the procedures for the performance of sacrifices. The beliefs and rituals of non-Aryans are written in it.
- *Two text of Yajur Veda*
  - **Shukla** (White) *Yajur Veda*
  - **Krishna** (Black) *Yajur Veda*

Atharva Veda

- It is a book of magical formulae. It contains charms and spells toward off evil and disease.

The Upanishadas

- The term *Upanishadas* is the knowledge acquired by sitting close to the teacher (*Guru*).
- Also called *Vedarita*, because they denote the last phase of Vedic period.
- They are spiritual and philosophical in nature and they reveal the aim of *Vedas*. They define the doctrine of *Karma*, *Atman* (soul), *Brahma* (God), origin of universe.
- There are 108 *Upanishadas* and the period of 800 BC to 500 BC is known as period of *Upanishadas*. 11 are predominant and they are called *mokhya Upanishadas*.

Brahmanas

- These are the prose commentaries on various vedic hymns. They explain the *Vedas* in an orthodox way. They explain the hidden meaning behind the hymns. They are ritualistic by nature.
- The most important is the 'Shatapatha Brahmana' attached to the *Yajur Veda*. It recommends one hundred sacred paths.

The Aranyakas

- The sages dwelling in the forests explained the Vedic scriptures to their pupils in the form of *Aranyakas*. These have magical power and they form the concluding part of *Brahmanas*. It provides details of the *rishis*, living in jungle.

Vedangas

- They are the *limbs of the Vedas. These are treaties of Science and Arts.*
  - *Shiksha* (deals with pronounciation) (phonetics).
  - *Kalpa* (deals with rituals)
  - *Vyakarana* (Grammar)
  - *Nirukta* (Etymology)
  - *Chhanda* (Metrics)
  - *Jyotisha* (Astronomy)
- Panini wrote **Ashtadhyayi** (4th century BC) on *Vyakarana*.

Upavedas
There are four Upavedas—
- **Dhanurveda** (*Upaveda* of *Yajur Veda*) : Deals with art of warfare.
- **Gandharvaveda** (*Upaveda* of *Sama Veda*) : Deals with art and music.
- **Shastrashastra** : Deals with military technology (associated with *Atharva Veda*)
- **Ayur Veda** (*Upaveda of Rig Veda*) : Deals with medicine.

Philosophy
Six systems of Hindu philosophies, given by six philosophers of ancient India.

Nyaya (analysis)	— Gautama	*Vaisesika*	— Kannada
Sankhya	— Kapila	*Yoga* (application)	— Patanjali
Purva Mimansa	— Jaimini	*Uttar Mimansa*	— Vyasa

Puranas
- These include mythology, cosmogony, various legends, folk beliefs, law codes and miscellaneous topics.
- It refers to the change in the mode of worship (from sacrifice to idol worship), and visual appeal of deities as against worship of ideas.

Sutras
Sutra literature is divided into three classes
- **Srauta Sutra** (dealing with large public sacrifices).
- **Griha Sutra** (dealing with rituals connected with birth, naming, marriage).
- **Dharma Sutra** (explain social and local customs).

Epic
- **Mahabharata**, written by Ved Vyas, is older than the '*Ramayana*'. Originally, the *Mahabharata* consisted of 880 verses then it was raised to 24000 verses. The final compilation brought the number of verses to 100000.
- **Ramayana** written by Valmiki originally consisted of 6000 verses, which was raised to 12000 and finally 24000 verses.

Smritis
- **Dharma Shastra** is the other name for the Smritis, which are the law books written in *sloka* form.
- The important *Smritis* are *Manav Dharma Shastra, Vishnu Dharma Shastra, Yajnavalkya Smriti* and *Narada Smriti*.
- **Manav Dharma Shastra** or **Manusmriti** is the oldest and most famous. Manu is supposed to be the first king and law maker.
- Later on, some minor *Smritis* and commentaries like the **Mitakshara** were compiled.

PRE-MAURYAN AGE

- The material advantages brought about by the use of the iron implements in Eastern UP and Bihar in 6th century BC helped in the formation of large territorial states.
- Use of iron tools in agriculture produced surplus, which could be taxed by the princes to finance their military and administrative needs.
- Thus, many *Janapadas* sprung up in the 6th century BC, the larger of which were called **Mahajanapadas**.

THE MAHAJANAPADAS

- The *Anguttara Nikaya* of *Suttapitaka*, *Mahavastu* (Buddhist literature) and *Bhagavati Sutta* (Jain literature) mentions the list of 16 *Mahajanapadas*.

They were of two types

- **Non-Monarchial/Republican** States Kamboj, Kuru, Koliyas (Ramgrama), Malla, Moriya (Pipplivana), Shakya (Kapilvastu), Vajji (Panchal), Lichchhavis (Vaishali), Bhaggas (Sumsumasa), Kalamas (Kesaputta), Videhas (Mithila), Jnatrikas (Kundalgrama).
- **Monarchical States** Anga, Avanti, Chedi, Kashi, Kosala, Gandhara, Magadh, Matsya, Sursena, Vatsa.
- People now owned stronger allegiance to the *Janapada* or territory than the *jana* or tribe they belonged to.
- **Asmaka** was the Southernmost *Mahajanapada*.
- **Vatsa** was earlier a *Kuru* clan.
- **Vajji** was confederacy of eight republican clans.

THE REPUBLICAN STATES

- The republics, unlike the monarchies were ruled by tribal oligarchies and the *Brahmanas* had no place.
- The ruling class belonged to the same class and *varna*. **Lichchhavis** are said to be the oldest republic in the world.

Administration

Raja (King), *Uparaja* (Vice-King), *Senapati* (Commander) and *Bhandagarika* (treasurer).

Mahajanapadas and their Capitals

	Mahajanapadas (Location)	Capital(s)
1.	Gandhara (Between Kabul and Rawalpindi).	Taxila
2.	Anga (Bhagalpur and Mungher in Bihar).	Champa
3.	Magadha (Patna and Gaya district of Bihar).	Girivraj, Rajagriha (Bimbisara); Patliputra (Udayin); Vaishali (Shishunaga); Patliputra (Ashoka)
4.	Kasi (Varanasi district, UP).	Varanasi
5.	Vajji (Vaishali district, Bihar).	Vaishali
6.	Malla (South of Vaishali district, UP).	Kusinagara and Pava
7.	Chedi (river Ken, Bundelkhand area).	Sothivati-nagar or Shuktimati
8.	Vatsa (river Yamuna, Allahabad and Mirzapur district in UP).	Kaushambi
9.	Kosala (Eastern UP).	Sravasti and Ayodhaya (Saket)
10.	Kuru (Ganga Yamuna doab, Delhi-Meerut region).	Hastinapur and Indraprastha
11.	Panchala (Ganga-Yamuna doab, Rohilkhand).	Ahichhatra, Kampilya
12.	Matsya (Jaipur-Bharatpur-Alwar district).	Viratnagar/Bairath
13.	Surasenas (Mathura region).	Mathura
14.	Asmaka (river Godavari) (near Paithan in Maharashtra).	Patna or Patali
15.	Avanti (Malwa).	Ujjain (Northern capital), Mahismati (Southern capital)
16.	Kamboja (Hazara district of Pakistan).	Rajapur or Hataka

MAGADHA EMPIRE

- The period from 6th century BC to 4th century BC saw the struggle for supremacy amongst the four *Mahajanapadas*- Magadha, Kosala, Vatsa and Avanti.
- Ultimately, Magadha emerged as the most powerful and prosperous kingdom in the North India.
- The founder of Magadha was **Jarasandha** and **Brihadratha**. But, the growth started under the Haryankas, expansion took place under the **Shishunagas** and **Nandas** and reached its zenith under the Mauryas.
- **Extent** Former districts of Patna, Gaya and parts of Shahabad.

Causes of the Rise of Magadha

- Advantageous geographical location of the capital cities.
- Abundance of natural resources such as iron, helped in preparing effective weapons.
- The alluvial soil of the Gangetic plains and sufficient rainfall were very conducive to agriculture produce.
- Unorthodox character of Magadhan society and ambitious rulers.

HARYANKA DYNASTY

Bimbisara (544 BC- 492 BC)

- He built the capital city **Rajgir** (Girivraja), which was surrounded by five hills, the openings in which were closed by stone walls on all sides. This made Rajgir impregnable.
- He was contemporary to Gautama Buddha and Mahavira and the first king to have standing army and *makaira*, for which he is known as *Seniya*.
- He defeated Anga King Brahmadatta and strengthened his, own position by matrimonial alliances.

- His three wives belonged to royal family of Koshala (**Mahakosaladevi,** sister of Prasenjit ruler of Kashi), Lichchhavi (**Chellana**, sister of Chetaka) and Madra clan of Punjab. (**Khema,** daughter of Madra king).
- He sent his personal physician, Jivak to his rival Avanti king **Chandapradyota Mahasena** of Ujjain, to cure him of jaundice.
- The Gandhara ruler of Taxila, Pukku Sati, sent on embassy to Bimbisara.

Ajatashatru
(492 BC- 460 BC)

- He was son of Chellana and Bimbisara. He occupied the throne by killing his father.
- He adopted an aggressive policy of expansion and gained complete control over Kasi.
- He defeated his maternal uncle Prasenjit, king of Kosala and married his daughter Vijjira.
- He destroyed Vaishali (capital of the Lichchhavis) after a protracted war of sixteen years, by sowing the seeds of discord amongst the people of Vaishali.
- **Sunidha and Vatsakar** Ajatashatru's diplomatic ministers, **Mahashilakantaka** a war engine, which catapulted big stones and **Rathamusala** a kind of chariot with a mace; helped him to defeat the Lichchhavis.
- He fortified Rajagriha to meet the threat from Avanti. He also built the fort of Rajagriha and Jaladurga (a water fort) at Patali village on the bank of river Ganges.
- He patronised the first Buddhist Council and Buddha died during his reign.

Udayin (460 BC-444 BC)

- Son and successor of Ajatashatru.
- He built the fort upon the confluence of the Ganga and the Son rivers at Pataliputra (Patna), thus, transferred the capital from Rajgriha to the new city **Pataliputra**.
- Udayin was succeeded by weak rulers Anuruddha, Munda and Naga Dasak.

SHISHUNAGA DYNASTY(412 BC-344 BC)

- Shishunaga was the minister of Nag-Dasak and was elected by the people.
- He destroyed the Pradyota dynasty of Avanti. This ended the hundred year old rivalry between the two states and Avanti became a part of Magadh. He temporarily shifted the capital to Vaishali.

Kalashoka (Kakavarin)

- He succeeded Shishunaga.
- He transferred the capital from Vaishali to Pataliputra and convened the second **Buddhist Council** in Vaishali (38ⴰ BC).
- Sabakami was the President of this council.

NANDA DYNASTY (344 BC-323 BC)

It is considered to be the first non-Kshatriya dynasty and ruled for 100 years.

Mahapadmananda

- Mahapadmananda, the great conqueror and founder of the Nanda dynasty, also known as 'Ekarat', 'Eka-chhatra' (sovereign ruler) or Sarvakshatrantaka i.e. uprooter of the Kshatriyas (by Puranas) Ugrasena i.e. owner of huge army (Pali texts). He is also described as "The first empire builder of Indian History."
- He conquered **Koshala** and **Kalinga** (and from here, he brought an image of the Jina as victory trophy).
- Succeeded by his eight sons, last one being Dhanananda.

Dhanananda (The Last Nanda Ruler)

- Alexander invaded North-Western India during his reign (326 BC), but the huge army of Dhanananda deterred Alexander from advancing towards Gangetic valley.
- He is probably referred to as Agrammes or Xan-drames in the Greek texts.
- **Chandragupta Maurya**, assisted by Kautilya overthrew Dhanananda to establish Mauryan dynasty in 321 BC.

FOREIGN INVASIONS

Iranian Invasion

- The archaemenian ruler of Iran, took advantages of the political disunity on the North-West frontier of India.
- **Cyrus** of Persia (588 BC-530 BC) was the first foreign conqueror, who penetrated well into India. He destroyed the city of Capisa (North of Kabul). He enrolled Indian soldiers in the **Persian Army**.
- **Darius**–I, grand son of Cyrus invaded North-West India in 516 BC and annexed Punjab, West of Indus and Sind.
- **Xerxes,** the successor of Darius, employed Indians in the long war against the Greeks.

Impacts of Iranian Invasion

- Iranian contact gave an impetus to Indo-Iranian trade.
- There was cultural exchange in the form of Kharoshthi script from Iran to India. Some of Ashoka's inscriptions in North-West India were written in this script.
- Iranian influence is perceptible in sculpture, e.g. the bell-shaped capitals.

Alexander's Invasion

- Alexander, the king of Macedonia destroyed the Iranian empire. From Iran, he marched towards India, attracted by its great wealth and divided polity.
- Alexander conquered Kabul in 328 BC. He moved to India through the unguarded Khyber pass and reached Orhind near Attock in 326 BC.
- **Ambhi**, the ruler of Taxila, readily submitted to Alexander. He got the first and strongest resistance from **Porus**.
- Alexander defeated Porus in the **Battle of Hydaspas** on the banks of the river Vitasta (Jhelum), but was impressed by his bravery, so he restored to Porus, his kingdom and made him his ally.
- After the **Battle of Sakala**, Alexander proceeded upto Beas with a view to conquer the East, but his fatigued army refused to cross the river.
- So, he was forced to retreat. He placed the North-Western India under the Greek Governor **Selucus Nikator**.
- He remained in India for 19-months (326-325 BC) and died in Babylon (323 BC) at the age of 33 years.

Impacts of Alexander's Invasion

- Opening up of new trade routes between North-West India and Western Asia.
- Indians learnt from the Greeks in the fields of coinage, astronomy, architecture and sculpture (Gandhara school).
- Many Greek settlements were established, like Alexandria in Kabul and Sind, Boukephala in Jhelum.
- Alexander's invasion paved the way for the expansion of the Mauryan empire in that area.
- His historians have left valuable accounts related to Indian geography, social and economic conditions, which enable us to build the Indian chronology of the times.

Pre-Mauryan Society

- Division of society into four classes necessitated the formation of *Dharmasutras*.
- Shudras were ill-treated, while all privileges were cornered by the Brahmanas and Kshatriyas.
- Restrictions were imposed on women and they were not entitled to education or the *Upanayana* ceremony.
- *Dharmasutras* condemned *Vaishyas* for lending money.

Pre-Mauryan Economy

- Agricultural production increased. *Varihi* and *Sali* were new varieties of rice; *Karisa*, *Nivartan* and *Kulyavapa* were units of land measurement; **Sita** was the state's land.
- Development of industry and crafts. **Sreni** was the guild or corporation.
- Spurt in trade. *Sartha* referrred to caravans and *Sresthi* to bankers. *Anathapindaka*, was a *Sresthi* of Sravasti, who donated *Jetuvana Vahana* to the Buddha. *Mendaka* was another rich *Sresthi* of Rajagriha.
- **Pottery** Northern black polished ware was used.

Immediate Causes of the Rise of Heterodox Sects

- Division of the society into four *varnas*.
- Reaction of the Kshatriyas to the Brahmins supremacy.
- The desire of the Vaishyas to improve their social position, with an increase in their economic position.
- To preserve cattle wealth.
- Desire to go back to simple life. The use of Sanskrit in Vedic texts was not understandable to the masses.

RELIGIOUS ENVIRONMENT

The 6th century BC was the period of great religious upheaval or intellectual revolution. Of the various sects that emerged in this period, Jainism and Buddhism were the most prominent.

This marked the beginning of second Urbanisation in India, also known as the age of the Buddha.

JAINISM

- It was founded by **Rishabhnath**. He is described as an incarnation of *Narayana* in *Vishnu Purana* and the *Bhagavata Purana*.
- There were 24 *Tirthankaras* (guru), the first one was Rishabhnath (emblem-bull).
- *Rig Veda* mentions two Tirthankaras-Rishabh Dev and **Arishtanemi**.
- The 23rd Tirthankara was **Parsavanath** (symbol-serpent). He was the prince of Banaras, who abandoned the throne and led the life of a hermit. He died at Sammet Sikhar/Parasanath hill in Hazaribagh district of Jharkhand.
- The 24th Tirthankara was Vardhaman Mahavira (Emblem-lion).

Life of Mahavira

- Vardhman Mahavira or *Jina* (conqueror) was born to Siddhartha (head of Jnatrika clan) and Trishla (Lichchhavi princess and sister of Chetak) in 540 BC at **Kundalgram** near Vaishali in Bihar.
- He was married to Yashoda and had a daughter **Priyadarsena**, whose husband Jamali became his first disciple.
- **Renunciation** at the age of 30, he became an ascetic and joined an order founded by Parsavanath, but left it later. He wandered for six years with Gosala (founder of Ajivika Sect).
- **Kaivalya** (perfect knowledge) attained at the age of 42, under a sal tree at Jimbhika grama in Eastern India on the banks of the river Rijupalika.
- **First Sermon** at Pava to his eleven disciples known as Ganddharas. He also founded a Jain *Sangha* at Pava.
- **Death** at the age of 72 in 468 BC at Pavapuri near Rajagriha.
- He became the head of a sect *Nirgranthas* (free from fetters), later called as '*Jinas*.'

- He was called the *Jaina* or *Jitendriya* (one who conquered his senses); *Kevalin* (perfect learned), *Nirgranthas* (from all bonds), *Arihant* (blessed one) and *Mahavira* (the brave).

Teachings of Mahavira

- Rejected the authority of the *Vedas* and did not believe in existence of God.
- He believed that every object possesses a soul, so he professed strict non-violence.
- Attainment of salvation by believing in penance and dying of starvation.
- Universal brotherhood (equality) and non-belief in caste system.
- He believed in *karma* and transmi-gration of soul.

Jaina Philosophy

- **Syadavada** All our judgements are necessarily relative, conditional and limited. It is the theory of 'may be' and seven modes of prediction are possible. Absolute affirmation and negation is wrong.
- **Anekantavada** Doctrine of mayness of reality.
- **Three Ratnas** (Way to *Nirvana*) :
  - Right faith (*Samyak Vishwas*)
  - Right knowledge (*Samyak Jnan*)
  - Right conduct (*Samyak Karma*)
- **Five Cardinal Principles**
  - Non-injury (*Ahimsa*).
  - Non-lying (*Satya*).
  - Non-stealing (*Asteya*).
  - Non-possession (*Aparigraha*).
  - Observing celibacy (*Brahmacharya*).
- *Mahavratas*-monks, who observed the five principles.
- *Anuvratas* lay members who observed the five principles.

The first four principles were given by Parsavanath, while the fifth was added later by Lord Mahavira.

Five Instruments of Knowledge
- *Mati jnana*—Perception through activity of sense organs including the brain.
- *Avadhi jnana*—Clairvoyant perception.
- *Shruta jnana*—Knowledge revealed by scriptures.
- *Manahparyaya jnana*—Telepathic knowledge.
- *Keval jnana*—Omniscience or Temporal knowledge.

Sects of Jainism
- After the death of Mahavira, during the reign of king **Chandragupta Maurya**, a severe famine led to a great exodus of Jaina monks from Ganga valley to the deccan. This migration led to a great schism in Jainism.
- **Bhadrabahu,** who led the emigrants, insisted on the retention of the rule of nudity, which led Mahavira establish the sect of the **Digambaras**.
- **Sthulabhadra**, the leader of the monk, who remained in the North allowed his followers to wear white garments termed as the **Svetambaras**.

Jain Church
- Arya Sudharman, one of the disciple of Mahavira, became the *Thera* (Potiff) of Jaina Church after his death. Later, he was succeeded by **Jambu**, **Sambhutavijaya** and **Bhadrabahu** (contemporary to Chandragupta Maurya).

Spread of Jainisim
- *In later times, Jainism was chiefly concentrated in two regions :*
  - Gujarat and Rajasthan-*Svetambara* sect.
  - Mysore—*Digambara* sect.

Importance of Jainism
Led to the growth of many regional languages like Suraseni, out of which grew the Marathi, Gujarati, Rajasthani and Kannada.

Causes Behind the Decline of Jainism
- Extreme observance of *ahimsa,* penance and austerity.
- No patronage from later kings.
- The Jainas did not make any efforts to spread their religion.

Jaina Councils

Council	Year	Venue	Chairman	Royal Patron	Developments
First Jaina Council	300 BC	Pataliputra	Sthulabhadra	Chandragupta Maurya	Compilation of 12 *Angas* to replace 14 *Purvas.*
Second Jaina Council	AD 512	Vallabhi	Devridhigani Kshmasramana	—	Final compilation of 12 *Angas* and 12 *Upangas.*

BUDDHISM

Founded by Gautama Buddha (also called *Sakyamuni* or *Tathagata*) known originally as Siddhartha.

Gautam Buddha

- He was born (Symbol-lotus and bull) in 563 BC at **Lumbini** (Sakya tribe of Kapilvastu) on Vaiskha Purnima day in Kshatriya clan.
- His father **Suddhodhana** was the Saka ruler, his mother **Mahamaya** died after 7 days of his birth, so he was brought up by stepmother **Gautami**.
- Married at 16 to **Yashodhara**, enjoyed the married life for 13 years and had a son named Rahul.
- Great Renunciation or *Mahabhinish-kramana* (Symbol-horse) at the age of 29 years after witnessing four scenes in a sequence (old man, sick man, dead body and an ascetic).
- **Nirvana** or enlightenment (symbol-Bodhi tree) at 35 years of age at Uruvella **(Bodh Gaya)** under a pipal tree on the banks of Niranjan (Phalgu) river on the 49th day of meditation.
- First Sermon or **Dharmachakra Pravartana** (symbol-8 spoked wheel) at **Sarnath**, where his five disciples had settled.
- Death at the age of 80 years in 483 BC at **Kusinagar** in UP in the Malla republic (Mahaparinirvana).

Major Events of Buddha's Life

Events	Symbols
Janma (*Birth*)	Lotus and Bull
Mahabhinishkramana (*Renunciation*)	Horse
Nirvana/Sambodhi (*Enlightenment*)	Bodhi tree
Dhramachakra pravartana (*First Sermon*)	Wheel
Mahaparinirvana (*Death*)	Stupa

Teachings of Buddha

(a) Four Noble Truths (Arya Satyas)

1. The world is full of sorrows (*Sabbam Dukkam*).
2. The cause of sorrow is desire (*Dwadash Nidan/Pratitya Samutpada*).
3. If desires are conquered, all sorrows can be removed (*Nirvana*).
4. This can be achieved by following the 8-fold path (*Ashtangika Marga*).

- The second truth, is based on Buddha's doctrine of *Paticheha Samutpada* or *Pratitya Samutpada* i.e. law of dependent origination or causation.

(b) Eight-Fold Path (Ashtangika marga)

- Right understanding
- Right thought
- Right speech
- Right action
- Right means of livelihood
- Right effort
- Right mindfulnes awareness
- Right concentrations meditation

(c) Three Jewels (Triratnas)

- Buddha (the enlightened)
- Dhamma (doctrine)
- Sangha (order)

(d) Code of Conduct

- Do not covet the property of others
- Do not commit violence
- Do not use intoxicants
- Do not speak a lie
- Do not indulge in corrupt practices

(e) Belief in Nirvana

- Also known as *moksha* or salvation. It refers to a belief in the concept of ultimate bliss, whereby the person gets freedom from the cycle of birth and death.

(f) Belief in Ahimsa

- Law of Karma and *Madhya Marga/Madhyama Pratipada* (the middle path).

Buddhist Sangha

It consisted of monks (*Bhikshus* or *Shramanas*) and nuns, who acted as a torch bearer of the *dhamma*. The worshippers were called *Upasakas*.

Sects of Buddhism

- **Vajrayana** Its followers believed that salvation could be attained by magical power, which they called *vajra*.
- The chief divinity of the sect is *Taras*. Bengal and Bihar (Eastern India) was the main area of its concentration.
- **Hinayana** (the Lesser Vehicle).
- **Mahayana** (the Greater Vehicle).

Buddhist Scriptures

Hinayana Literature (in Pali)

- Tripitakas
  - **Vinaya Pitaka** rules of monastic discipline for monks.
  - **Sutta Pitaka** collection of Buddha's sermon.
  - **Abhidhamma Pitaka** Philosophies of Buddha's teachings.

Causes of the Decline of Buddhism

- Incorporation of rituals and ceremonies, it originally denounced.
- Reform in *Brahamanism* and rise of *Bhagavatism*.
- Buddhists took up the use of Sanskrit (earlier Pali), started practicing idol worship, receiving offerings and huge donation.

Importance of Buddhism

- Promotion of trade and commerce.
- Stressed upon the **Doctrine of Ahimsa**.
- Improvement in condition of women and down trodden sections.
- Spread of Indian culture to other parts of Asia.
- Promotion of Pali language and education through Residential Universities (Taxila, Nalanda).

Spread of Buddhism

- Mahayanism in Central Asia, China and Japan, Hinayanism in Ceylon, Thailand and other parts of South-East Asia.
- King Ashoka sent Buddhist missions under his son Mahendra and daughter **Sanghamitra** to Sri Lanka.
- Kanishka was the patron of Mahayana sect of Buddhism.

Buddhist Councils

Buddhist Council	Year	Venue	Chairman	Royal Patron	Development (s)
First Council	483 BC	Saptaparni cave, Rajgriha	Mahakassaapa	Ajatashatru (Haryanka Dynasty)	Compilation of Sutta Pitaka and Vinaya Pitaka by Ananda and Upali respectively.
Second Council	383 BC	Vaishali	Sabakami	Kalasoka (Shisunaga Dynasty)	Monks were split into Sthavirmadins and Maha sanghikas.
Third Council	250 BC	Patliputra	Mogaliputta Tissa	Ashoka (Maurya Dynasty)	Compilation of Abhidhamma Pitaka.
Fourth Council	AD 72	Kundalvan, Kashmir	Vasumitra (Chairman) and Ashwaghosha (Vice-Chairman)	Kanishka (Kushan Dynasty)	Division of Buddhists into Hinayana and Mahayana.

Some Famous Buddhist Scholars

Ashvaghosha, Nagarjuna, Asanga, Vasubandhu, Buddraghosha, Dinnaga and Dharmakirti.

Bodhisattvas

- Vajrapani (holds thunderbolt).
- Manjushri (holds books describing 10 *paramitas*).
- Maitreya (the future Buddha).
- Avlokitesvara/Padmapani (lotus bearer).
- Kshitigrha (guardian of purgatories).
- Amitabha/Amitayusha (The Buddha of heaven).

Buddhist Architecture

Buddhism takes the credit for

- First human statues to be worshipped.
- Stone-pillars depicting the life of Buddha at Gaya, Sanchi and Bharhut.
- Gandhara art and the beautiful images of the Buddha.
- Cave architecture in the Barabar hills at Gaya and in Western India around Nashik.
- Art pieces of Amaravati and Nagarjunakonda.
- Traditional names of buddhist places.
- **Stupa** relics of Buddha or some prominent monks.
- **Chaitya** Prayer hall.
- **Vihara** residence.

Buddhist Universities

Buddhist Universities	Location	Founder
Nalanda	Badagaon, Bihar	Kumargupta-I
Vikramshila	Bhagalpur, Bihar	Dharmapala (*Pala ruler*)
Somapuri	North Bengal	Dharmapala (*Pala ruler*)
Jagadal	Bengal	Ramapala (*Pala ruler*)
Odantpuri	Bihar Sharif, Bihar	Gopala (*Pala ruler*)
Vallabhi	Gujarat	Bhattarka (*Maitrak rule*)

Similarities between Buddhism and Jainism

- Both opposed Brahmanical domination and caste system, but upheld the essence of Vedas, preached truth, non-violence, celibacy and detachment from material comforts, believed in *karma* and rebirth and were liberal towards women.

Differences *between* Buddhism and Jainism

	Buddhism	Jainism
Followers	Monks	Lay man
Salvation	Moderate one	Extreme one
Spread	Died in India, but spread to foreign lands	Confined to India and survived
Ahimsa	Liberal Policy	Over-emphasis
Soul	Did not believe in soul	Believed in soul

Other Heterodox Sects

Sect	Founder	Theory
Ajivikas	Gosala Maskariputra (Makhali)	Believed in fate called 'Niyati'
Amoralism	Purana Kassapa	Sankhya Philosophy
Lokayata or Charvaka School	Ajita Keshakambalin	Uchchedavada (annihilationism)
Hindu Vaisesika School	Pakudha Katyayana	Sorrow, happiness and life are indestructible like Earth, water etc.

THE MAURYAN EMPIRE

ORIGIN OF MAURYAS

- **Mudrarakshasa**—Mauryas were connected with the Nandas and were called them Vrishal/Kulhina (of low clan).
- **Buddhist Tradition** Chandragupta was a Kshatriya (Sakya clan). The region was full of peacocks (mors), so became famous as 'Moriyas'.
- **Puranas** They belonged to the Moriya clan (low caste).
- *Junagarh rock inscription* of Rudrada-man (AD 150) suggests that Mauryans might have been of *Vaishya* origin.

Sources
Literary Sources

- **Arthashashtra of Kautliya** (*Chanakya* or *Vishnugupta*) Written in Sanskrit by Prime Minister of Chandragupta Maurya, it is a treatise on state craft and public administration under *Mauryas*. The book is in 15 parts.

Buddhist Literature

- *Ashoka vadana and Divyavadana* Information about Bindusara and Ashoka's expeditions to Taxila.
- *Dipavamsa and Mahavamsa* (Sri Lankan chronicles) Ashoka's role in spreading of Buddhism in Sri Lanka.
- **Jatakas** Socio-economic conditions of Mauryan period.
- *Sthaviravali Charita or Parisistha-parvan of Hemachandra* (A biography of Chanakya) Chandragupta's conversion to Jainism.
- *Mudrarakshasa of Vishakhadatta* in Sanskrit, an account of prevailing socio-economic conditions and about how Chandragupta overthrew the Nandas with the help of Chanakya.
- **Indica of Megasthenese** Socio-economic and administrative structure under Mauryas; Indians free from slavery; 7-castes system and usuary in India.

Various Edicts of Mauryan Age

Edicts	Content	Location
A. Rock Edicts		
▪ 14 Major Rock Edicts	Ashoka's principle of government and policy of *Dhamma*.	Kalsi (Dehradun, Girnar (Gujarat), Yerragudi (Andhra Pradesh), Mansehra (Pakistan), Sopara (Bombay), Dhauli and Jaugada (Orissa), Shahbazgarhi (Pakistan).
▪ Two separate Kalinga Edicts	Kalinga War and new system of administration after war (All men are my children - *Dhauli*).	Dhauli or Tosali and Jaugada (Orissa).
▪ Minor Rock Edicts	Personal history of Ashoka and summary of his *Dhamma*.	South and central parts of the empire.
B. Pillar Edicts		
▪ 7 Pillar Edicts	Appendix to the Rock Edicts.	Delhi topra, Delhi-Meerut, Rampurva, Lauriya-Araraj, Lauriya-Nandangarh and Allahabad-Kosam.
C. Other Edicts		
▪ Queen's Edict	Refers to Karuvaki mother of Tivala/Tivara, the 2nd Queen.	On Allahabad Pillar
▪ Bhabru Edict	Ashoka's faith in Buddhism	Bairat (Rajasthan)
▪ Nigalisagar Pillar Edict	Stupa of Buddha at Kanakamuni was enlarged.	Nigalisagar (Nepal)
▪ Rummindei Pillar	Ashoka visited Lumbini and reduced land tribute.	Rummindei/Lumbini (Nepal).
▪ 3 Barbara cave Edicts	Donation to Ajivikas.	Barbara hills (Gaya, Bihar).

- **Puranas** Chronology and lists of Mauryan kings.
- **Others Account of Diodorous**, Pliny, Plutarch (Chandragupta as *Androcottus*), Arrian and Justin (Chandragupta as *Sandrocottus*).

Epigraphical Evidences

- **Ashoka's Edicts and Inscriptions** Ashoka's edicts were first deciphered by **James Princep** in 1837. It was written in Prakrit language and 3 scripts *viz* Kharoshthi in North-West, Greek and Aramaic in West and Brahmi in Eastern India.

Quick Digest

- Inscriptions of Skandgupta and Rudradaman are also found at Girnar. The pillar Edict VII is the last edict to be issued by Ashoka.
- Mahasthan and Sohgura copper plate inscriptions issued by Chandragupta Maurya, deals with relief measures adopted during famine.
- Latest discovery-3 Ashokan minor rock edicts from Sannati village (Karnataka).

Chandragupta Maurya (321 BC-298 BC)

- Also called as **Sandrocottus/** Androcottus by Greek scholars.
- He entered into an alliance with Parvartaka and with the help of Chanakya, he dethroned the last Nanda ruler Dhanananda and founded the Mauryan dynasty with the capital at Pataliputra.
- Chandragupta defeated Selucus Nikator, the general of Alexander in North-West India in 305 BC. Selucus surrendered a vast territory in return for 500 elephants. Hindukush became the boundary between the two states. There was a matrimonial alliance between them.
- Selucus also sent the Greek Ambassador, **Megasthenese**, to the court of Chandragupta Maurya.
- Chandragupta embraced Jainism and went to Chandragiri hill, at Sravanbelagola with Bhadrabahu, where he died of slow starvation (*Salekhna*).

- Chandragupta was the first Indian ruler to unite the whole North India. Both trade and agriculture flourished during his reign. Weights and measures were standarised, money came into use and sanitation and famine relief measures were undertaken by the states.

Bindusara (298 BC-273 BC)

- Greeks called him **Amitro Chates** (derived from Sanskrit word *Amitraghata* i.e. slayer of foes); *Vindupala* (Chinese texts;), *Sinhasena-* Jain text; *Bhadrasara* (*Yayu Purana*).
- He extended the kingdom further to the Peninsular region of India as far South as Mysore.
- Antiochus I, the Selucid king of Syria, sent his Ambassador, **Deimachus** to his court.
- Pliny mentions that Ptoleny Philladelphus of Egypt sent **Dionysius** as his Ambassador to the court of Bindusara.
- **Taranath**—the Buddhist monk, credits him for conquering the land between the two seas.
- Antiochus I sent some sweet wine and dried figs to Mauryan court on Bindusara's request, but denied to send a sophist explaining that Greek law forbid a sophist to be sold.
- He patronised Ajivika sect.

Ashoka (273 BC-232 BC)

- He was the greatest Mauryan ruler; Governor of Taxila and Ujjain previously. His rule extended to the whole of sub-continent except to the extreme South. It also included Afghanistan, Baluchistan, Kashmir and valleys of Nepal.
- A Buddhist text **Dipavasma** says that he usurped the throne after killing his 99 brothers, except the youngest one, **Tissa** in the war of succession that lasted for four years.

- He fought **Kalinga War** (261 BC) in the 9th year of his rule. The miseries of war caused deep remorse to Ashoka, and therefore he abandoned the policy of physical conquest (*Bherighosa*) in favour of cultural conquest (*Dhamma ghosha*).
- However, Ashoka retained Kalinga after conquest. This proves that he was not an extreme pacifist and changes in his policies were mainly for administrative purposes.
- He embraced Buddhism under **Upagupta**.
- He sent his son Mahendra and daughter Sanghamitra to Ceylon as Buddhist missionaries with a sapling of original pipal tree.
- He inaugurated the **Dhammayatras** from the 11th year of his reign by visiting Bodh Gaya; also appointed *Dhamma Mahamatras* (officers of righteousness) to spread the message of *Dhamma*.

Ashoka's Dhamma

- It was a code of conduct and a set of principles to be adopted and practiced by the people to build up an attitude of social responsibility and preserve the social order. It ordained to pay respect to elders, mercy to slaves and emphasised truth, non-violence and tolerance.

LATER MAURYAS

- Following the death of Ashoka, the Mauryan dynasty lasted for 137 years, the empire was divided into Western and Eastern parts.
- **Brihadratha**, the last Mauryan ruler, was assassinated in 184 BC by his Brahmin Commander in-chief, **Pushyamitra Shunga**, who established the Shunga dynasty.

Mauryan Administration

- The Mauryan state was a welfare state, with highly centralised government.
- **Central Administration** King was the Nucleus, assisted by *Mantri Parishad*, *which included* :

- **Yuvaraj** the crown Prince
- **Gopa** the *Purohit* Chief Priest
- **Senapati** Commander-in-Chief of Army and other ministers.

Provincial Administration

Provinces	Capital
Uttarapatha (North)	Taxila
Avantipatha (West)	Ujjain
Prachyapatha (West)	Kalinga
Dakshinpatha (South)	Suvarnagiri
Central Province	Pataliputra

Some Important Rock Edicts

Major Rock Edicts	Content
MRE I	Prohibition of animal sacrifice
MRE II	Refers to Cholas, Pandyas, Satya putras and Kerala putra (kingdom of South) and care for man and animals
MRE III	Liberality to Brahmins
MRE IV	Non-violence; courtesy to relations
MRE V	Appointment of Dhamma Mahamatras
MRE VII	Tolerance among all sects
MRE VIII	Dhammayatras
MRE IX	Charity, kinship, Dhamma
MRE XII	Religious tolerance
MRE XIII	Kalinga war; Bheri Ghosa to Dhamma Ghosa

Art and Architecture

- Mauryan art is classified into two groups by **Ananda Coomaraswamy**
1. **Popular/Folk Art** Sculptures of *Yaksha* and *Yakshini* e.g. *Yaksha* of Parkham (Mathura); *Yakshini* from Vidisha (MP) and Didarganj (Patna).
2. **Royal/Court Art** Royal Palace of Chandragupta Maurya at Kumharar, Patna (*Fa Hien* referred it as the *creation of God*), city of Patliputra Ashokan pillars; stupas and caves.
- Mauryans introduced stone masonry on a large scale.
- **Pillars** represent the masterpiece of Mauryan sculpture e.g.

- *Single lion capital* Rampurva and Lauriya Nandangarh.
- *Four lion capital* at Sarnath and Sanchi.
- *Carved elephant* at Dhauli and *engraved elephant* at Kalsi.

Causes of the Fall of the Mauryan Empire

Brahmanical reaction (**HP Shastri**), financial crisis, oppressive rule, weak successors; highly centralised administration (Romila Thapar); Pacific policy of Ashoka (HC Ray Chaudhary); Partition of the empire are some of the probable causes of decline of Mauryan empire.

- **Stupas** were built throughout the empire, to enshrine the relics of Buddha e.g. Sanchi and Bharhut.

Significance of Mauryan Rule

- The emblem of Indian Republic has been adopted from the lion capital of Ashokan pillar at **Sarnath**.
- Many Gurukuls and **Buddhist** *monasteries* (Taxila and Banaras) developed with royal patronage.
- *Literary developments* e.g. Arthashashtra (Kautilya); Kalpasutra (Bhadrabahu), Katha Vastu (Buddhist text), Bhagwati Sutra, Acharanga Sutra and Dasavalik (Jaina text).

POST-MAURYAN PERIOD

Mauryans were succeeded by many ruling dynasties from Central Asia in North-West India and by native rulers (Shungas, Kanvas, Satvahanas) in the Eastern, central and Deccan region of India.

FOREIGN STATES

The Indo-Greeks

- A series of invasions began in about 200 BC. The weak Mauryan king failed to restrict them. The first to invade India were the Indo Greeks, who ruled Bactria lying South of the Oxus river in the area covered by North Afghanistan. They occupied a large portion of North-Western India and moved upto Ayodhya and Pataliputra.
- The most famous Indo-Greek ruler was **Menander** (165-145 BC) or Milinda. He had his capital at *Sakala* (modern Sialkot in Punjab). He invaded the Ganga Yamuna doab. He was converted to Buddhism by Nagasena. Menander and Nagasena's conversation were recorded in the book Milindapanho or *'the questions of Milinda.'*
- They were the first rulers in India to issue coins. The Greek rule introduced features of Hellinistic art in the North-West frontier of India.

e.g. Gandhara art and Military Governorship.
- The Sanskrit term for astrology Horshastra is derived from the Greek term horoscope.

The Shakas or Scythians (AD Ist to 4th Century)

- The Greeks were followed by the Shaka.
- There were five branches of Shakas ruling from Afghanistan, Punjab, Mathura, (where it ruled for about two centuries.), Ujjain (rules over) Western India and Deccan.
- A king of Ujjain, who called himself **Vikramaditya** defeated Shakas. An era called the *Vikram Samvat* is recorded from the event of his victory over the Shakas i.e. 57 BC.
- The most famous Shaka ruler in India was **Rudradaman** (AD 130-150).
- He repaired the Sudarshan lake in the semi arid zone of Kathiawar and issued the first ever longest inscription in Chaste Sanskrit at Junagarh.
- Other important Saka ruler in India were *Nahapana*, Ushavadeva, Chastana, Ghamatika etc.

Sudarshana Lake

- It was constructed by **Pushyagupta** the Governor of Saurashtra under **Chandragupta Maurya**.
- **Tushasp** constructed dam on the lake during the reign of **Ashoka Maurya**. First reconstruction by Governor Survishakh under Saka Satrap Rudradaman and second by **Chakrapalit** under **Skandgupta**.

The Parthians
(AD 1st to 3rd Century)

- Originally, the Parthians lived in Iran, from where they moved to India and replaced Shakas.
- They occupied only a small portion of North-Western India as compared to the Greeks and Shakas.
- The most famous Parthian king was **Gondophernes**, in whose reign **St Thomas** came to India for the propagation of Christianity.

The Kushanas
(AD 1st to 3rd Century)

- The Kushanas (Yuechis or Tochanians) replaced the Greeks and Parthians. They were nomadic people from steppes of North Central Asia. Their empire included a good part of Central Asia, portion of Iran, a portion of Afghanistan, almost the whole of Pakistan and North India.
- The first Kushana dynasty was founded by *Kujala Kad-phises*. *Wima Kadphises* (the 2nd ruler) issued gold coins in India. Kanishka founded the 2nd Kushana dynasty.

Kanishka (AD 78-101)

He was also known as *Second Ashoka* and was the most famous Kushana ruler. He had two capitals–Purushpur and Mathura.

- Kanishka started an era in AD 78, which is now known as **Saka era** and is used by Government of India.
- He patronised the fourth Buddhist Council in Kashmir, where the doctrine of **Mahayana** form of the Buddhism was finalised.

- Kanishka patronised the following persons :
  Ashwaghosha *Buddhacharita*
  Nagarjuna *Madhyamik sutra*
  Vasumitra *Chairman of the fourth Buddhist Council*
  Charaka *Charakasamhita*.
- The last Kushana ruler was **Vasudeva I.** This shows that successors of Kanishka bore typical Indian names as Vasudeva.

Impacts of Central Asian Contact

- The Shaka-Kushana phase registered a distinct advance in building activities. The use of burnt brick for flooring and that of tiles for both flooring and roofing, construction of brick well and red ware pottery became prevalent.
- They introduced better cavalry and tunic, trousers and long heavy coat and also. They also brought cap, helmets, and boots, which were used by warriors. The Kushanas were the first rulers in India to issue gold coins. Kanishka controlled the famous silk route in Central Asia.
- The Kushana empire gave rise to Gandhara and Mathura Schools of Art. The famous headless erect statue of Kanishka shows artistic creations of Mathura School. Vatsyayana wrote *Kamasutra* in this period.

Gandhara School of Art

- It exhibits the influence of Greek and Roman art; patronised by Shakas and Kushanas. The school specialised in Buddha and Bodhi-sattva images, stupas and monasteries. They used blue schist stone.
- Buddhas of this school of art are gentle, graceful and compassionate.

Mathura School of Art

- The Buddha of the Gandhara School of Art were copied here, but in a refined way.
- The majority of creations consisted of nude, seminude figures of female, *Yakshinis* or *Apsara* in an erotic pose.
- The image exhibited not only masculinity and energetic body, but also grace and religious feeling.

Amaravati School of Art

- Lord Buddha depicted in the form of a *Swastika* mark. Also depicted Buddha in the human form for the first time.
- The ornate bull or 'Nandiswara', situated in the Amareswara temple, is also an Amaravati piece of art.

NATIVE STATES

The successors of Ashoka were weak kings, so Mauryan empire gradually declined. The last ruler of Mauryan dynasty was killed by his own commader-in-Chief Pushyamitra Shunga who founded the **Shunga dynasty**.

Shunga Dynasty
(185 BC-73 BC)

- **Pushyamitra Shunga** ruled from Vidisha (MP). He defeated Bactrian king, Dematrius and conducted two *Ashvamedha Yajnas* (Chief priest- Patanjali). He is considered to be the prosecutor of Buddhism.
- However, the Buddhist Stupa at Bharhut was built during his reign.
- The Greek Ambassador **Heliodorus** visited the court of fifth Shunga king **Bhagabhadra** and set-up a pillar in honour of Lord Vasudeva near Vidisha (Madhya Pradesh).
- Shunga king **Agnimitra** was hero of *Kalidasa's Malvikagnimitram.*
- The Shungas marked as the revival of Hindu culture, Sanskrit language and Bhagavatism.
- The great Sanskrit Grammarian, Patanjali was patronised by them.
- The famous book on Hindu Law *Manusmriti* was compiled during this period.
- **Later Kings** Vasumitra, Vajramitra, Bhagabhadra, Devabhuti. All of them were Brahmanas.
- **Shunga Art** Bharhut Stupa, gateway railing surrounding the Sanchi Stupa built by Ashoka, Vihara, Chaitya and Stupa of Bhaja (Poona), Nasika Chaitya, Amaravati Stupa etc.

Kanva Dynasty
(73 BC-28 BC)

- Kanva was a minor dynasty founded by **Vasudeva**, who killed the last Shunga king **Devabhuti**. Its capital was at Patliputra.
- **Bhumimitra** and Narayana succeeded Vasudeva. All the rulers were Brahmins.
- The last ruler, Susarman, was killed by Andhra king Simuka.

The Cheti Dynasty
of Kalinga

- The Hathigumpha inscription of Kharavela—the third ruler of the dynasty, gives information about the Chetis. Kharavela pushed his kingdom upto Godavari in the South, and recovered the Jaina image from Magadha.
- He was a follower of Jainism. He constructed residential caves for Jain monks on the Udaygiri hill near Bhubaneshwar, Orissa.

The Satavahana Dynasty

- The Satavahanas are considered to be identical with the Andhra, who are mentioned in the *Puranas*.
- The earliest inscriptions of the Satavahanas belong to the first century BC, when they defeated the Kanvas and established their power in parts of Central India.
- They were successors of Mauryas in the Deccan and Central India.
- The founder of this empire was **Simuka,** after the assassination of last Kanava King Susarman.
- **Gautamiputra Satakarni** (AD 106-130) was the greatest ruler of this dynasty.
- Assumed the title of **raja-raja** and **maharaja**.
- His capital was at Paithan or Pratisthan on the banks of the river Godavari in Aurangabad district.

- **Vasishthiputra Sri Satkarni**, the 24th ruler, married the daughter of Saka Satrap Rudradaman, but was twice defeated by him.
- **Yajna Sri Satkarni** (AD 165-194), the later king of Satavahanas, 'recovered North Konkan and Malwa from Shaka rulers. His coins figured 'ship with double mast'.
- **Pulamayi III** was the last Satavahana ruler, succeeded by Ikshavakus in the 3rd century BC.

Important Aspects of the Satavahanas

- They issued mostly lead coins (apart from copper and bronze). Satavahanas were the first rulers to make land grants to Brahmins. There is an instance of grants being made to Buddhist monk, which shows they also promoted Buddhism.
- Satavahana rulers called themselves Brahmins. Gautamiputra Satkarni boasted that he was a true Brahmin.
- They performed Vedic rituals and worshipped Gods like Krishna, Vasudeva and others.
- Stupas at Nagarjuna konda and Amaravati in Andhra Pradesh became important seats of Buddhist culture under the Satavahanas.
- In the Satavahana phase, many *chaityas* e.g. Karle caves in Western deccan, Nashik and Kanheri and Viharas were cut out of solid rocks in the North-Western Deccan. The official language of Satavahanas was Prakrit and the script was Brahmi.
- Provinces were called **Ahara,** and the officials were known as Amatyas and **Mahamatyas**.

THE AGE OF THE GUPTAS

- The fall of Kushana empire towards the middle of AD 3rd century led to the establishment of the empire of the Guptas.
- Although the Gupta empire was not as large as the Mauryas, it kept North India politically united for more than a century.
- Their period is generally regarded as the **Golden Age of Hinduism.**
- Guptas belonged to the *Vaishya* caste.
- **Sri Gupta** was the founder of Gupta dynasty. Sri Gupta was followed by his son *Ghatotkacha* and was followed by his son Chandragupta. Both assumed the title of **Maharaja**.

Chandragupta I (AD 319-335)

- He greatly raised the power and prestige of his dynasty by his matrimonial alliances and conquests.
- He married the Lichchhavi princess **Kumara Devi** and issued Chandragupta I Kumaradevi type gold coins (Dinaras).
- Chandragupta-I is also said to have started a new era Gupta Era, which starts from 26th February AD 320, the coronation date of Chandragupta I.
- He established his authority over Magadha, Saketa and Prayaga.
- He was the first Gupta king to adopt the title of **Maharajadhiraja**. He issued gold coins.

Samudragupta (AD 335-380)

- Son and successor of Chandragupta I. He was a great conqueror.
- The long inscription in the pillar of Allahabad (*Prayag Prasasti*) enumerated by his court poet Harisena informs about the people and the countries that were conquered by *Samudragupta*. Because of his bravery and generalship, he came to be called the **Napoleon of India** by VA Smith.

- **Virasen** was his Commander- in-Chief during Southern campaign. Vasubandhu, a famous Buddhist scholar, was his minister. Samudragupta's arms reached as far as Kanchi, Tamil Nadu, where the Pallavas were compelled to recognise his suzerainty.
- Samudragupta annexed the territories after defeating the monarchs in North India, but did not annex territories in South India. His authority over Java, Sumatra and Malaya island proves that he maintained a strong navy.
- Samudragupta is said to have composed numerous poems of high merit. Some of his coins represent him playing the *Veena*. He also performed *Ashvamedha* sacrifices.
- The Allahabad pillar inscriptions mention the title **Dharma Prachar Bandhu** i.e. he was the upholder of Brahmanical religion.
- According to Chinese sources, **Meghavarman**, the ruler of Sri Lanka, sent a missionary to Samudragupta for a permission to build a **Buddhist temple at Gaya**.
- He was a Vaishnavite.

Chandragupta II (AD 380-415)

- According to Devi Chandraguptam of Vishakhadutta, Samudragupta was succeeded by Ramagupta.
- Ramagupta was a coward. He surrendered his queen **Dhruvadevi** to the Saka invader. He was also the only Gupta ruler to issue copper coins.
- Chandragupta II, the younger brother of **Ramagupta**, invaded the enemy's camp, killed the Saka ruler and Ramagupta; occupied the throne and married Dhruvadevi.
- He proved to be a great ruler and extended his empire by conquests and matrimonial alliances. He married **Kubernaga** of Naga dynasty and married his daughter Prabha-Vatigupta, with the Vakataka prince Rudrasena II.
- **Mehrauli Iron Pillar Inscription** (Delhi) claims his authority over North-Western India and a good portion of Bengal. It says that the king defeated the confederacy of Vangas and Vahilkas (Bulkh). **Virasena's Udaygiri** cave inscription refers to his conquest of the whole world.
- Chandragupta II conquered **Western Malwa** and Gujarat, from the Shaka Kshatrapas Rudra Simha III. The conquest gave Chandragupta the Western sea coast, famous for trade and commerce. This contributed to the prosperity of Malwa and its Chief city Ujjain. Ujjain was made the second capital by Chandragupta II.
- He issued silver coins (first Gupta ruler to issue silver coins) and adopted the title *Vikramaditya* and *Sakari* in memory of his victory.
- The court of Chandragrugupta II at Ujjain was adorned by nine scholars known as **Navaratna,** including Kalidasa and Amarsimha.
- **Harisena** was the court poet and the minister.
- **Fa Hien**—The Chinese piligrim visited India at his time.

Kumaragupta (AD 415-455)

- He founded the **Nalanda University**.
- Worshipper of Lord Kartikeya.
- In the last year of his reign, the empire was invaded by the Turko-Mongol tribe, the Hunas. During the war with the Hunas, Kumaragupta died.

Skandagupta (AD 455-467)

- He repulsed the ferocious Hunas attacks twice. The heroic feat entitled him the title Vikramaditya (also mentioned in the Bhitari Pillar Inscription).
- During his period Sudarshana lake was repaired and its embankments were rebuilt.
- The continuous attack of the Hunas weakened the Guptas economy and the decline of empire began soon after the death of Skandagupta.

Reasons of the fall of Gupta Empire

- The weak successors of Skandagupta could not check the growing Huna power.
- Rise of feudatories in Bihar, Bengal and Madhya Pradesh.

Gupta Kings, their Titles and Coins

Gupta Kings	Titles	Gold Coins (Dinaras)
Chandragupta I	Maharajadhiraja or king of the kings	Kumaradevi type
Samudragupta	Kaviraj (Prayag Prasati), Ashvamedha, Vikram, Param Bhagvat, Sarva-rajoch Chetta (uprooter of all kings).	Dhanurdhari-Archer, Garud, Axe, Ashvamedha, Vyagnra hanam (Tiger killing), Veena Vadan, Playing flute type.
Chandragupta II	Vikramaditya, Sakari Devagutpa/Devashri/Devaraja, Narendra Chandra Sinh Vikram, Param Bhagvata etc.	Ashvarohi, Chhatradhari, Chakra-Vikram type etc.
Kumaragupta	Mahendraitya, Ashvamedha Mahendra and Mahendra Sinh	Gajarohi, Khadgadhari, Gajarohi Sinh-nihanta, Khang-nihanata, (i.e. rhinocerous slayer) Kartikeya and Apratighmudra type.
Skandagupta	Vikramaditya, Kramaditya, Param Bhagvat, (on coins); Shakropama (Kahaum Pillar inscription); Devaraja (Arya Manjushri Mula Kalpa).	Archer king and queen, Chhatra and horseman type.

Gupta Administration

- Gupta administration was highly decentralised and quasi-feudal in character.
- Gupta Kings adopted pompous titles such as *Parameshvara*, *Maharajadhiraj*, *Parambhattarka*, which signify that they ruled over the lesser kings in their empire. The practice of appointing Kumara (crown prince) came in vogue.
- Kings were assisted by *Mantriparishad/ Mantrimandal* (Council of Ministers) as referred in the *Prayag Prasasti*.

Administrative Units *and their* Heads

Unit	Headed by
▪ Bhukti (province)	Uparika
▪ Vishayas (district)	Vishyapati
▪ Nagar/Peth	Purapala/Nagar Pati
Village (sub-district)	Gramika

- **City Administration** Paura was the council responsible for city administration. It included the President of the city corporation, Chief representative of the guild of merchants, a representative of the artisans and the Chief Accountant. It comprised of local representatives.
- **Army Military** Chariots receded into the background and cavalry came to the forefront. The Gupta empire maintained a large standing army, but essentially the military organisation was feudal in character.
- **Senabhakta** It was a form of tax i.e. the army was to be fed by the people whenever, it passed through the countryside. Forced labour or *Vishti* was also practised in royal army.
- **Revenue** Land revenue was the chief source of state's income. It varied from $\frac{1}{4}$th to $\frac{1}{6}$th of the produce. The number of taxes increased.

* During the Gupta's rule, land grants (Agarhara and Devagrahara grants) also included transfer of royal rights over salt and mines, which were earlier states monopoly during Mauryas. **Judiciary** For the first time, civil and criminal law were clearly defined and demarcated.
* **Coinage** Guptas issued the largest number of gold coins, which were called **dinaras** in their inscriptions. Silver coins were called the Rupayakas.

Important Officials

Official	Field of Work
Maha Pratihari	Chief usher of Royal Palace
Dandapashika	Chief officer of the Police department
Mahaprajapati	Chief officer of elephant corps
Vinayasthitisthapak	Chief officer of religious affairs
Mahashvapati	Chief of Cavalry
Mahadandanayaka	Minister of Justice

Society

* **The Supremacy of the Brahmins continued** They accumulated wealth on accounts of numerous land grant and claimed many privilege.
* The position of the **Shudras** improved, and they were permitted to listen epic, *puranas* and to worship a new God, Lord Krishna.
* *Varna system* got strengthened due to the large scale proliferation of castes, chiefly because of assimilation of foreigners into the Indian society, absorption of tribal people into Brahminical society through land grants and transformation of guilds into class due to the decline of trade and urban centres.
* The Position of women declined; The first example of immolation of widow after death of her husband (*Sati*) appeared in Gupta times. (Also referred in the Eran inscription, which mentions that the wife of Goparaja, Commander of Bhangupta, performed

Sati). Polygamy and pre-puberty marriages were common. Women were not given the right to property except for *stridhana*, in the form of garments and jewellery.

Religion

* **Bhagavatism** centred around the worship of *Vishnu* or Bhagavad.
* *Bhagvad Gita* was written in this period. It preached the doctrine of incarnation or *Avatar*.
* Idol worship in the temple became a common feature. The Gods were unified with their respective consorts. Thus, *Parvati* got associated with *Shiva* and *Laxmi* with *Vishnu*.
* Gupta kings followed a policy of tolerance towards the different religious sects.
* There was an evolution of Vajrayanism as well and Buddhist tantric cult.
* **Buddhism** no longer received royal patronage in the Gupta period.

Economy

Land was classified into five groups :
* *Khila* — Waste land
* *Kshetra Bhoomi* — Cultivable land
* *Vastu Bhoomi* — Habitable land
* *Charagah Bhoomi* — Pasture land
* *Aprahata Bhoomi* — Forest land

* According to Pahadpur copper plate inscription of Buddhagupta, state was the exclusive owner of land.
* Poona plates of Prabhavati Gupta refers to the land survey conducted during the period.
* *Pushtapala* was the officer incharge for maintaining records of all land transactions.
* **Trade** There was a decline in trade with the Roman empire after AD 3rd century, while the South-East Asian trade increased.

- Ports on West coast to trade with Mediterranean and West Asia—Bharoach, Chaul, Kalyan and Cambay.
- Ports on East coast to trade with South-East Asia—Tamralipti, Ghantashala and Kandura.

Taxes

Bhaga King's share in the produce, to be paid by cultivators.

Bali (Earlier a voluntary offering) an additional and oppressive tax during Gupta period.

Bhoga Periodic supplies of fruits, firewoods etc., which the villagers had to furnish to the king.

Uparika An extra tax levied on all subjects.

Gupta Art

Gupta period is also called The **Golden Age of Ancient India**.

- **Samudragupta** is represented on his coins playing the Veena and **Chandragupta II** is credited with maintaining in his court, nine luminaries or great scholars viz, Kalidasa, Amarsimha, Dhanavantri, Varahmihira, Vararuchi (Vartika-a comment on Ashtadhyayi), Ghatakarna, Kshapranak, Velabhatt and Shanku.
- Over two metre high bronze images of the **Buddha of Gupta period has been recovered from Bhagalpur**.
- For the first time, we get in the Gupta period images of **Vishnu, Shiva** and some other Hindu Gods.
- Buddha sitting in *Dharmachakra mudra* (Sarnath) and Buddha images of Bamiyan belong to this period.
- **Brahminical Image** The Great Boar (Varah) carved in relief at the entrance of a cave at Udayagiri.
- **Paintings** Ajanta paintings and paintings at Bagh (Madhya Pradesh) are of this time. They belong to the Buddhist Art.
- In this period the Gandhara School of Sculpture was replaced by regional centres at Banaras, Pataliputra and Mathura.
- **Stupas**—Mirpur Khas (Sindh), Ratnagiri (Orissa) and Dhammekh (Sarnath).

Gupta Architecture

- The Gupta age marks the beginning of main style of temple architecture in India namely the Nagara and Dravida style (shikhar style) with **Garbhagriha** (shrine room in which the image of God is kept).
- Square sanctum sanctorum and a pillared porch.

Religious Literature

- **Hindu Texts** Many old religious books were re-written e.g. Vayu Purana, Vishnu Purana, Manu Smriti (translated into English under the title of "Institutes of Hindu law" William Jones), **Ramayana** and **Mahabharata**.
- **New Text** Narad Smriti, Parashar Smriti, Katyana Smriti and Brihat Smriti.
- **Jain Texts** Nyayavartam written by Sidhsena.
- **Buddhist Texts** Abhidharma Kosha written by Dignaga, Vishudhimagga written by Buddhghosa.
- Mrichchakatikam (i.e. the clay cart) is the love story of a poor Brahmin Charudatta and virtuous courtsean Vasantasena. The work is notable for its realistic depiction of city life.

Quick Digest

- *Brahmasidhanta*, was translated into Arabic under the title "Sind Hind".
- **Ritusamhara, Meghdootam** and **Raghuvamsham** are epics and not plays.
- **Bhasa** wrote 13 plays in this period.
- There was a development of Sanskrit grammar based on **Panini** and **Patanjali**. Amarkosha was compiled by Amarasimha.

Other Literary Works

Author	Book
Sudraka	Mrichchakatikam
Bharavi	Kiratarjuniya
Dandin	Dasa Kumar Charita and Kavyadarshan
Bhasa	Svapnavasavadattam, Charudatta
Vishakhadatta	Mudrarakshasa Devi Chandraguptam
Vishnu Sharma	Panchtantra and Hitopodesha
Amarismha	Amarkosh
Iswara Krishna	Sankhya Kanika
Vatsyayana	Kamasutra (earliest book on sex)
Bhattin	Ravan Vadha
Varahamihira	Panchasiddhantika, Brihad Samhita

Astronomy (Science)

- Aryabhatta, the great mathematician wrote **Aryabhatiyam** and Surya Siddhanta. He placed the value of first line number and the **use of zero** ('0').
- **Varahamihira** wrote *Panchsiddhantika* and *Brihadsamhita*. He said the Moon moves round the Earth and Earth together with the Moon, move round the Sun.
- **Brahmagupta** was a great mathematician. He hinted the law of gravitation in *Brahma Siddhanta*. *Vagabhatta* was a distinguished physician.
- Dhanvantri was famous for the *knowledge of Ayurveda*.
- *Romaka Siddhanta*, a book on astronomy was compiled.
- Palakapya wrote *Hastyagarveda*, a treatise on the disease of elephants.
- Bhaskara wrote *Mahabhaskarya* and *Laghu Bhaskarya*.

THE HARSHA PERIOD

PUSHYABHUTI/ VARDHANA DYNASTY

- Harsha belonged to Pushyabhuti dynasty, which ruled from Thaneswar. Pushyabhutis were the feudatories of Guptas, but had assumed independence after Hunas' invasion.
- **Prabhakar Vardhana** (AD 580-605) was its first important ruler succeeded by **Rajyavardhan** (AD 605-606).
- Grahavarman (Maukhari ruler of Kannauj), husband of Rajyashri (sister of Rajyavardhana) was murdered by Devagupta (ruler of Malwa) in alliance with Shashanka (ruler of Bengal).
- Rajyavardhana killed Devagupta but was himself killed by Shashanka in AD 606.

Harshavardhan (AD 606-647)

- Harsha, also known as **Siladitya,** ascended the throne in AD 606 and from this year, *Harsha Era* began.
- Harsha made **Kannauj** his capital.
- The early history of Harsha's reign is constructed from a study of the book *Harshacharita*.
- Harsha is called the last great Hindu emperor of India, but he was neither a staunch Hindu nor the ruler of the whole country.
- In Eastern India, he faced opposition from Shaivite king Shashanka of Gauda, who cut off the Bodhi tree of Bodhgaya.
- Harsha defeated Dhruvasena II, the Maitraka ruler of Vallabhi.

- Harsha was defeated in Deccan by Pulakesin-II, the Chalukyan king of Vatapi. Harsha's administration became more feudal and decentralised.
- The Chinese pilgrim **Hiuen Tsang** visited India during Harsha period. He informs us that the revenue of Harsha was divided into four parts, one for the king, second for the scholar, third for the officer and fourth for religious purposes.
- Harsha used to celebrate a solemn festival at Prayag after every five years.
- After the death of Harsha in AD 657, the empire once again broke up into petty states and the throne was usurped by his minister Arunashva.
- Harsha was a **Shaivite**. He also granted revenue of 200 villages for the maintenance of Nalanda University. It is said that   Harsha brought '5 indies' under his control (Punjab, Kannauj, Bengal, Bihar and Orissa).

Tripartite Struggle

The struggle for supremacy between the Palas, the Gurjara - Pratihara and the Rashtrakutas for the possession of Kannauj (Farrukhabad District, UP) at the end of AD 8th century is known as the Tripartite struggle in history.

Art and Architecture

Vesara/Deccan Style

- It was started by the **Chalukyas**.
- Examples include Vesara style temples at Aihole (town of temples), Jinendra temple (Meguti temples), Vishnu temple, Lad Khan temple (God Surya), Durga temple, Nagara style temple at Pattadakal, Papanatha temple, Dravida style temple at Pattadakal, Virupaksha temple and Sangamesvara temple.

Pallava Art/Dravida Style

- The *Shikhara* had influence of Java, Cambodia and Annam.
  Examples of Pallava Arts :
  - *Bhairawkona temple*
  - *Ananteshwar temple at Undavalli*
  - *Mandapa temple*
  - *Ratha temple* of Mamallapuram
  - Kailashnath and Vaikunth
  - Perumal Temple at Kanchi
  - Shore Temple at Mamallapuram
  - **Pallava Sculpture** Based on Buddhist tradition e.g. descent of the Ganges and Arjuna's penance at Mamallapuram.

Rashtrakuta Style

The rock-cut temple of Kailash (Shiva) at Ellora, was built by Krishna I.

Hoyasalas Style

Temple of Hoyasaleshwar at Dwarsamudra.

Other Dynasties and Rulers

Dynasty	Capital	Founder	Famous Rulers	Other Features
Palas (Eastern India)	Pataliputra, Gaur	Gopala	**Dharma Pala** Revived Nalanda University and founded Vikramshila University defeated Bhoja (Pratihara) amogvarsha (Rashtrakuta) and won kannauj. **Devapala** won Orissa and Assam. **Mahikala** defeated by Rajendra Chola.	They traded with South-East Asia and were replaced by Senas in Bengal.
Gurjara Pratiharas (SW Rajasthan) (AD 733-1019)	1. Jodhpur 2. Malwa	Harichandra	**Mihir Bhoja** He worshipped Lord Vishnu and adopted the title *Adi Varaha*.	They originated in Geyanta region of Rajasthan.
Vakatakas (Deccan and Central India)	Vatsagumla, Paunar	Vindhyashakti	**Pravarsena I** performed four *Ashvamedha Yagyas*.	Chandragupta II married his daughter Prabhavati to the Vakataka king Rudrasena.
Eastern Gangas of Orissa	Kalingnagar, Cuttack	Anantavarman Chodagong Deva	**Narshima Deva I** built the Sun temple at Konark.	Anantavarman built the Jagannath temple at Puri.
Western Gangas (AD 350-999)	Kolar, Talakal	Konganivarman Madhava	**Dunvirta**	Constructed Jain monuments at Sravanbelagola.
Senas of Bengal	Vikrampura, Vijaypura	Vijaysena	**Ballasena** **Lakshmansena**	They were overthrown by Deva dynasty.
Hoysalas	Dwarasamudra	Vishnu Vardhan	**Vira Ballal** defeated the Chalukyan ruler Somesvara IV.	Hoysala art and architecture was of a high standard. The minute carving of Hoysala temple is their most attractive feature.
Rashtrakutas (AD 750-1142)	Manyaket or Malkhed	Dantidurga (earlier served the Chalukyas of Badami)	**Amogvarsha** He is compared to Vikramaditya in giving patronage to men of letters. He wrote the Ist Kannad Poetry, Kavi Rajamarg and also wrote Prashnottar Mallika.	Rashtrakutas are credited with the building of cave shrine of Elephanta. It was dedicated to Mahesh and (*Trimurti*) counts among the most magnificient art creations of India.

Dynasty	Capital	Founder	Famous Rulers	Other Features
Pallavas (AD 560-903) of **Tondainadu** (land of creepers)	Kanchi	Simhavishnu	**Krishna II** constructed Kailash temple at Ellora in Dravidian sytle. **Krishan III** set-up Pillar of victory and a temple at Rameshwaram. **Narasimhavarman-I** (AD 630-668) occupied Chalukayan capital at Vatapi and assumed the title Vatapikonda.	They were orthodox Brahmanical Hindus. Both the Chalukyas and Pallavas tried to establish their supremacy over land between Krishna and Tungabhadra.
Chalukyas of Badami	Vatapi (Badami)	Pulakesin I	**Pulakesin-II** He was contemporary of Harsha and was able to check Harsha in conquering Deccan, but was defeated and killed by Pallava ruler Narasimhavarman-I. The Chinese pilgrim **Hiuen Tsang** visited his kingdom.	Many of the painting and sculptures of the Ajanta and Ellora caves were completed during Chalukyan Art developed the Deccan or Vesara style. They perfected the art of stone building, that is stones finally joined without mortar.
Chalukyas of Kalyani	Kalyani	Tailap II (defeated the Parmar king Munj)	**Somevara I** (AD 1043-1068) He shifted the capital from Manyakhet to Kalyani. **Vikramaditya IV** (AD 1070-1126) He started the Chalukya- Vikram era.	Bilhana, the writer of *Vikramdevacharita* and *Mitakshara* in Yagyavalkya Smriti, adorned the court of Vikramaditya IV.
Yadavas	Devagiri	Bhillana	**Ramchandra**	Ramachandra was defeated by Malik Kafur.

Sangam Age
(AD First-Third Century)

- The land South of Krishna river was divided into three kingdoms

Kingdom	Location	Capital	Emblem	Famous Port	Famous Rulers	Other Features
Chola (Cholamandalam)	North- East of Pandyas between Penner and Vellar rivers.	Uraiyur (famous for cotton trade and Puhar)	Tiger	Puhar	**Elara** was the earliest known Chola king. He conquered Sri Lanka and ruled over it for 50 years. **Karikala** founded the capital city Puhar/Kaveripatnam and constructed embankment along **Cauveri** river. (kallanai)	The Cholas maintained an efficient Navy. Their economy was based on trade of cotton cloth. The Chola kingdom was destroyed by the attack of Pallavas from the North.
Chera	Part of Kerala and Tamil Nadu	Vanji or Karur	Bow	Muzris Todi, Bandar	**Udiyangera** is one of the earliest known Chera rulers. This title of **Udiyangera**, was given to him because it is said that he served both the armies of Kurukshetra War. **Senguttuvan/Red Chera**, was the greatest Chera king. He invaded the North and crossed Ganga. He is remembered for building a temple of 'Kannagi'-**the Goddess of chastity and founded the famous Pattini cult.**	It has well-established trade with Romans and also set-up two regiments at *Muzris* to protect their interests. They built the temple of Augustus at Muzris.
Pandya	Southernmost part of India	Madurai	Carp (fist)	Korkai, Saliyur	**Mudukudumi** was the earliest known Pandyan ruler. **Nedunjelian** was the most important king of Pandya. He accused Kovalan of theft. As a result, the city of Madurai was laid under a curse by Kannagi (Kovalan's wife).	This kingdom was first mentioned by Megasthenes, who says that their kingdom was famous for pearl and was ruled by a woman. Also finds mention in the *Ramayana* and *Mahabharata*.

- The Pandyan kings profited from trade with Roman empire and sent embassies to Roman emperor-**Augustus** and **Trojan.**

Sangam Regions

Panchtinai (five Tamilregions)	Inhabitants	Occupation
Kurinji (hilly backwoods or montane)	Kurvar, Vetar	Hunting, Gathering
Palai (Pastoral tract)	Eyinar, Maravar	Cattle lifting, Highway Robbery
Mullai (Pastoral tract)	Ayar, Idaiyar	Shifting Agriculture, Animal husbandry
Marutam (Wetland)	Ulavar, Vellalar	Plough Agriculture
Neital (littoral/coastal)	Paratavar, Valayar	Fishing, Salt extraction

Sangam Literature

- The word *Sangam* is associated with a college or assembly of Tamil scholars and poets, flourished under the royal patronage of the Pandyan kings.
- The whole Sangam age is called Golden or Augustan age. According to Tamil sources, the father of Tamil literature is 'Agastya.'

Tamil Sangams

Sangams	Venue	Chairman	Surviving Text
1st	Ten-Madurai	Agastaya	—
2nd	Kapatapuram Alvai	Agastaya (founder) Tolakappiyan (later chairman)	Tolakappiyam (Tamil Grammar)
3rd	North Madurai	Nakkirar	Ettutogai Patinenki lakanakku, Pattu-Pattu

Important Sangam Works

- *Tolkappiyam* by Tolkappiyar (Tamil Grammar).
- *Tirukkural or Kural* by Tiruvalluvar is sometimes called the *Fifth Veda* or *Bible of the Tamil land*. It explains the doctrine of *Dharma, Artha, Kama* and *Moksha*.
- *Aggatiyam* comprises grammar of letters and life, in three parts, written by saint Aggatiyar.

Epics

- **Silappadikaram** meaning, the jewelled anklet by Ilango Adigal is an epic, dealing with love story of Kovalan and Madhavi, also called *Illiyad* of Tamil Poetry.
- **Manimekalai** is one of the two greatest epics and a sequel to *Silappadikaram*, written by Seetalai Sattannar.
- **Sevaga Chintamani** (Sivaga Sindamani), a third epic by a Jaina Tiruttakadeva. It has elements of Jainism.
- **Bharatman** was written by Perudevanar.

Sangam Economy

The land was very fertile with proper irrigation facilities. The chief local God was **Murugan**, also called as Subramaniya.

Revenue Terminologies

- Karai — Land tax
- Irai — Tribute paid by feudatories and booty collected in war
- Iravu — Extra demand or forced gift
- Ulgu — Custom duties
- Variyar — Tax collector
- Variyam — A well-known unit of territory yielding tax

THE CHOLAS

- The ancient capital of Cholas was **Palayarai.**
- **Vijayalaya** revived the Chola empire in the AD 9th century. He took the title of *Narkesari*.
- **Aditya Chola** defeated the Pallava king Aparajit, captured Tondamandalam and took the title of 'Maduraikonda.' He built a Siva temple at Tanjore.
- **Parantaka I** established his authority over the North-Eastern part of Sri Lanka. His copper-plate inscription informs us about the administration of the Cholas.
- **Rajaraja I** (AD 985-1014) attacked Sri Lanka. He permitted the Shailendra king to build the *Churamani Buddhist Vihara* at Nagapattanam. He himself built the Rajarajeshwara temple (Saiva temple) at Tanjore. He is known as **Rajaraja-The Great** in history.
- **Rajendra I** (AD 1014-1044) conquered the complete Sri Lanka and made Anuradhapur as his capital.

- He defeated the Pala king Mahipala and took the title of *Gangaikondacholam* and he also built the Cholamandalam lake and the city of Gangaikonda Cholapuram. He won the Java, Sumatra and Malaya areas from the Shailendra king.
- **Rajendra III** was the last king of the dynasty.

Other Aspects of the Cholas

- **Administration** The Chola empire was divided into *mandalams* and then into *valadus*. The most important feats of Chola administration was local-self **Government**. Each village was divided into 30 wards. Several committees were constituted under the *Gram Sabha* for various purposes.
- Cholas maintained a strong navy. *Kasu* or *Kalanju* was their gold coin.
- **Literature** Bentak Madhav wrote commentary on *Rig Veda* in this period.
- Jayanodar wrote *Phalingtuparni* and Shekilar wrote *Periyapuranam* in the court of Kullotunga I.
- **Kamban, Kuttana** and **Pugalendi** were considered as *three gems of Tamil Poetry*. Kamban wrote *Ramavataram* and *Kamba Ramayana*.
- **Architecture** The dancing figure of *Shiva* called *Nataraja* was made during Chola period.
- The Chola style of architecture is called **Dravida Style** in the temples, the *vimana* or the tall pyramid tower dominated the whole structure of the shrine. *Gopurams* and *Garbhagriha* are the two other important structures.
- The best specimens of the temple are Vijayala-Choleshwar and the Nageshwar Koranganatha temple.

Chola Temples

Temple	Location	Builder
Kailashnath temple	Kanchipuram	King Rajasimha
Vrihadeshwar temple	Tanjore	Rajaraja I
Koranganatha temple	Srini wasanIlur	Parantak I
Airawteshwar temple	Darasuram	Rajaraya II
Kampahre-shwar temple	Tribhuvan	Kullotung III
Gangaikonda Cholapuram	Gangaikonda Cholapuram	Rajendra I

RELIGIOUS DEVELOPMENTS VAISHNAVISM

- Lord Vasudeva was first worshipped in Western India. Besnagar inscription (2nd century BC) states that the cults received royal patronage. Soon, Vasudeva was identified with Narayana and Krishna.
- **Chandogya Upanishada** gives first reference to Lord Krishna as the son of Devaki and student of *Rishi* Ghor Angiras. *Matsya Purana* refers to the ten incarnations of *Vishnu*.
- This cult emphasised on *Bhakti* and *Ahimsa*.

SAIVISM

- Shiva is identified with the *Rig Vedic* God *Rudra*. He was worshipped in form of *linga* (phallus).
- **Matsya Puranas** and Anusashan festival of *Mahabharata* refers to *lingam* worship. *Gundimallam linga* is the oldest idol of *Shiva*, excavated from Renugunta in Andhra Pradesh.
- **Mahabhashya** of **Patanjali** mentions Saiva cult as *Shiva Bhagvat*. *Vamana Purana* refers to four schools of *Saivism*—Pasupati, Saiva, Kapalika and Kalmukha.
- *Pasupatal* is the oldest cult founded by **Lakulisa**.

- **Kapalika** is the tantric cult who worship Mahakal, Kapala bhrit and Bhairav.
- *Kalmukha* another tantric cult, flourished in Karnataka.
- *Aghoris* worshipped Goddesses Sitala and Kali
- *Kanphata or Gora khnati* cult was propounded by Gorakhnath in Eastern Bengal.
- *Suddhasaiva* cult was expounded by Srikanat Sevacharya.
- *Virasiva or* Lingayat cult was founded by Basava.
- Rashtrakutas built the Kailasa temple of Ellora and the Kushana kings inscribed *Shiva* and *Nandi* on their coins.

SHAKTI DHARMA

- It refers to the worship of the female deity. It is first mentioned in the *Mahabharata*.
- The *Tantric Devi hymn* in the 10th *mandala* of the *Rig Veda* is devoted to the worship of Goddesses.

CHRISTIANITY

- This religion was founded by Jesus Christ. He was born to Mother Mary and Joseph in **Bethlehem** near Jerusalem. His birth day (25th December) is celebrated as the holy festival, **Christmas**.
- His first two disciple, Andrews and Peter, were hanged in AD 33 by the Roman Governor Portius.
- **Bible** is the holy book of Christians and the sign of 'Cross' is their holy symbol.

ISLAM

- **Hazrat Muhammad Saheb** founded the Islamic religion. He was born to Amina (mother) and Abdullah (father) at Mecca in AD 570.
- He was married to *Khajida* (a widow) at the age of 25 yrs. His daugher, Fatima, was married to Ali Hussain.
- Hazrat Muhammad attained supreme knowledge or enlightment in AD 610 in the **Hira Cave** near Mecca. His teachings are compiled in the *Holy Kuran*.
- 24th September (AD 622), the day Hazrat Muhammad started his journey from Mecca to Medina marks the beginning of the **Hijri Era**.
- He died on 8th June, AD 623 and was buried at Medina.
- After his death, Islam divided into the *Shia* and the *Sunni* cults. His successors were known as *Khalifa*.
- The Turkish ruler, **Mushtafa Kamal Pasha**, ended the designation of *Khalifa*.
- The birthday of *Muhammad Saheb* is celebrated as Eid-mild-un-Nabi.

ZOROASTRIANISM (PARSI)

Parsi religion was founded by *Prophet Zoroaster* (Zarathustra).

His teachings are compiled in the holybook-Zend Avesta. His followers believed in one God-Ahur.

Some Important Temples of Ancient India

Temple	Builder	Dynasty
Jagannath temple, Puri	Narsinghdev	Ganga
Sun temple of Konark	Yasho Varman	Ganga
Kandariya and Mahadev temple, Khajurao	Krishna-I	Chandela
Kailash temple of Ellora	Krishna-I	Rashtrakuta
Elephanta	Narsingh Varman-I	Rashtrakuta
Mamallapuram temple	Narsingh Varman-II	Pallava
Kailashnath temple of Kanchi	Narsingh Varman-II	Pallava
Baikuntha Perumal Temple of Kanchi	Narsingh Varman-II	Pallava
Jain temple of Dilwara	Vimala	Minister of Solanki ruler

MEDIEVAL INDIA

THE RAJPUTS

- They emerged as a powerful force in Northern India in AD 9th and 10th centuries.
- **Origin :** Four of the Rajput clans claim to have descendant from a mythical figure that arose out of a sacrificial fire pit near Mount Abu, i.e. of Agnikula origin. They are
  — Chauhans of East Rajasthan.
  — Pratihara Pariharas of South Rajasthan.
  — Chalukyas/Solankis of Kathiawar.
  — Parmars/Pawars of Malwa
- However, the most accepted theory is that Rajputs were of a foreign origin, who came as conquerors and settled in West India.
- *The two main clans of Rajputs are*
- *Surya Vansha* (Sun family)
- Chandra Vansha (Moon family)

Some Important Rajput Kingdoms

Rajput Kingdoms	Capital(s)	Founder
Chauhan/Chahaman of Delhi-Ajmer	Delhi	Vasudeva
Pawar of Malwa	Ujjain, Dhar	Sri Harsha
Pratihara of Kannauj	Avanti, Kannauj	Nagabhatta I
Rashtrakuta of Malkhand	Manyakheta	Dantidurga (Dantivarman II)
Chalukya/Solanki of Kathiawar	Aniha/vada	Mularaja I
Kalchuri/Haihaya of Chedi	Tripuri	Kokkala I
Chandela of Jejakabhukti	Khajuraho, Mahoba, Kalinjar	Nannuk Chandela
Gadhawal/Rathor of Kannauj	Kannauj	Chandradeva
Tomars of Delhi and Haryana	Dhillika	—
Guhilota/Sisodiya of Mewar	Chittor	Bappa Rawal, Hammir I

SOME IMPORTANT RAJPUT RULERS

- **Jai Chand Gadhawal/Rathor** (1169-94 AD) assisted Muhammad Ghori against Prithviraj Chauhan in the Second battle of Tarrain (1192), but was himself killed by Ghori in the battle of Chandawar (1194).
- **Prithviraj Chauhan** (1178-92) He was the Chahamana ruler of Delhi and Agra who fought two battles with Muslim invader Muhammad Ghori. **First Battle of Tarrain** (1191) Prithviraj defeated Muhammad Ghori. **Second Battle of Terrain** (1192) Prithviraj was defeated and killed by Muhammad Ghori.
- **Bhoja Parmar** (1010-55) **of Malwa** He was a great conqueror and a patron of literature and was also known as **Kaviraj**.

Architectural Works

- **Kandariya Mahadeva** temple at Khajuraho, built by Chandellas of Bundelkhand (AD 1000).
- **Dilwara temple** at Mount Abu (West Indian style of architecture) built by Siddharaja Solanki of Gujarat.
- **Angkorvat Temple** at Cambodia built by Suryavarman II. It is dedicated to Lord Vishnu and built on Dravidian model.
- **Sun Temple** at Konark (Orissa).
- **Lingaraja Temple** at Bhubaneshwar (Orissa).

Literary Works

- *Kathasaritasagar* by Somadeva.
- *Vikramdeva Charita by* Bilhana (biography of Chalukya King Vikramdeva VI).
- *Rajtarangini* of Kalhana (history of Kashmir).
- *Gita Govinda* of Jayadeva (in Sanskrit).
- *Chachanama* The history of Sind.

ARAB CONQUEST OF SIND

Md Bin Qasim Invasion (AD 712) Md Qasim of Iraq was the first Muslim to invade India. He defeated the ruler of Sind, Dahir and the province was given to Omayyad Khilafat.

TURKISH INVASIONS
Mahmud of Ghazni

- Towards the close of the AD ninth century, the vast empire of Arab broke up and the Turks who got the upperhand over the *Khalifas* of Baghdad, established many independant principalities. One of such Turk state was founded by **Alapigin** with **Ghazni** as his capital in about AD 933.

- In those days, Punjab and the North-West of India were ruled by **Jaipal** of the Shahiya dynasty (Hindustani). **Subuktigin,** the ruler of Ghazni of that period, fought with Jaipal and defeated him.

- Mahmud Ghaznavi was the eldest son of Subuktigin, born in AD 971 and ascended the throne in AD 998.

- For India, the only memory of Mahmud is that of a plunderer and destroyer of temples. Mahmud is said to have made **17 raids** into India. The initial raids were directed against the Hindustani rulers. In AD 1001, the Hindustani ruler **Jaipal** again was defeated by Mahmud.

- His son **Anandapala** succeeded the throne. A decisive battle between Mahmud and Anandapala was fought in AD 1008-09 at **Waihind** during his sixth expedition.

- In other expeditions Mahmud plundered Nagarkot, Thaneshwar, Kannauj, Mathura and Somnath.

- He plundered **Somnath temple** in AD 1025 (his sixteenth raid).

- In AD 1026, Mahmud defeated the *Jats*. He died in AD 1030. The objective of Mahmud's expeditions was to plunder and loot. He was not interested in expanding his empire to India.

Quick Digest

- Mahmud is considered as a hero of Islam by medieval Muslim historians because of his stout defence against the Central Asian Turkish tribal invaders.

- Secondly, because he was closely associated with the renaissance of the Iranian spirit.

- A high water mark in the Iranian renaissance was reached with **Firdausi's Shah Namah.**

- He patronised three persons, contemporary to him: **Firdausi** (court poet), **Alberuni** (scholar) and **Utbi** (court historian).

- Alberuni wrote '*Kitab-ul-Hind*'.

MUHAMMAD GHORI

- The Ghaznavi state was no longer a powerful state after Mahmud Ghazni. His successors were weak which resulted into the emergence of a powerful empire called Seljuk empire. But towards the middle of the 12th century, another group of Turkish tribe man shattered the power of the Seljuk Turks.

- The power of the Ghurids increased under Sultan Alauddin, who earned the title the **World burner**, because he ravaged Ghazni and burnt it into the ground.

- The rising power of the Khawarizm empire severely limited the Central Asian ambition of the Ghurids.

- In 1173, Muizzudin Muhammad (Muhammad Ghori) ascended the throne at Ghazni, while his elder brother was ruling at **Ghur**. Muizzudin Muhammad conquered **Multan** and Kutch.

- In 1178, he attempted to penetrate into **Gujarat** by marching across the Rajputana desert, but was completely rooted out by the Gujarat ruler.

- He realised the necessity of creating a suitable base in Punjab before venturing upon the conquest of India. He conquered **Peshawar, Lahore** and **Sialkot**.

- At that period, the Chauhan power had been steadily growing. Chauhans had captured Delhi from the *Tomars* around the middle of the century.

- At the age of 11, Prithviraj ascended the throne at Ajmer and began a career of conquest. He invaded the Chandellas of Bundelkhand in a battle near Mahoba.
- Both Prithviraj and Muhammad Ghori's attention towards the Punjab and Ganga valley brought the two ambitious rulers into conflict. In the First Battle of **Terrain** (1191) the Ghori forces were completely rooted out by Prithviraj.
- It a said that **Jaichand**, the ruler of Kannauj (Gahadavala kingdom) did not help Prithviraj during the Second battle of Terrain because Prithviraj had abducted, Jaichand's daughter Sanyogita, who was in love with him.
- **Prithviraj Raso**, written by court poet of Prithviraj, Chand Bardai, the depicts the life story of Prithviraj and his love story.
- The defeat laid the foundation of Muslim rule in India.
- Later on in 1194, Jaichand of Kannauj was also defeated at the Battle of Chandawar.

- Muhammad Ghori died in AD 1206, leaving the charge with Qutub-ud-din Aibak.
- The Sultanate of Delhi had five ruling dynasties with 34 kings.

> ### Battle of Terrain
> - The Second Battle of Terrain (1192) is regarded as one of the turning point in Indian history. The better organised and well prepared Turkish force defeated the Indian forces.
> - Prithviraj was defeated by Muhammad Ghori. Prithviraj was allowed to rule over Ajmer for sometime. But was executed on a charge of conspiracy after some time.

Causes of the Turkish Success

- Political disunity among Rajput and internal rivalries.
- No Central Government.
- Unguarded frontiers, even after repeated attacks.
- Organised military and ambitious Turkish invaders.

THE DELHI SULTANATE

THE ILBARI OR SLAVE DYNASTY (1206-1290)

- After Muhammad Ghori's death, all the Muslim rulers who ruled over India from AD 1206-1290 were either slaves or were descendants of the slave ruler. So, the Dynasty is generally known as the **Slave Dynasty**.
- The dynasty is also called Ilbari Dynasty, as all the rulers of this dynasty except Aibak belonged to the Ilbari tribe of Turks.

Qutubuddin Aibak (1206-1210)

- Originally a slave, Qutubuddin, because of his merit and loyal service was rose to the post of Viceroy by Muhammad Ghori.

After Ghori's death, Aibak ruled over **Delhi** and founded his dynasty.
- Lahore and later, Delhi was his capital.
- For his generosity, he was given the title of **Lakh Baksh**.
- He constructed two mosques **Quwwat-ul-Islam** at **Delhi** and *Adhai Din ka Jhopra* at **Ajmer**.
- He also began the construction of **Qutub Minar** in the honour of famous Sufi Saint Khwaja Qutub-ud-Din Bakhtiyar Kaki.
- Aibak was great patron of learning, and patronised writers like *Hasan-ul-Nizami*, author of *Taj-ul-Massin* and Fakhruddin, author of *Tarikh-i-Mubarak-Shahi*. He fell from the horse while playing *chaugan* (Polo) and died.

Aram Shah (AD 1210)

After Qutubuddin's death, his son Aram Shah succeeded him. Aram Shah proved quite incompetent. Some of the nobles rose to the occassion and invited Aibak's son-in-law and Governor of Badaun, Iltutmish to ascend the throne. He deposed Aram Shah and secured the throne for himself.

Iltutmish (AD 1210-1236)

- He is considered to be the greatest slave king and the real consolidator of the Turkish conquest in India.
- He made Delhi the capital in place of Lahore and was the son-in-law of Aibak.
- Iltutmish, during the early years of his reign, first consolidated his position by suppressing the revolts of the ambitious nobels.
- In AD 1215, he defeated **Yaldoz**, who established himself as the independent ruler of Ghazni. He sent expeditions against the Rajputs in Ranthambor, Jalor, Gwalior, Ajmer and Malwa.
- During his period, the **Mongols** under their leader **Changez Khan** made their appearance for the first time in India. He saved Delhi Sultanate from the wrath of **Changez Khan** by refusing shelter to Khwarizm Shah, Jalaluddin Mangobanni, to whom Changez Khan was chasing.
- He got his authority (Sultanate of Delhi) recognised by the **Caliph of Baghdad** (*khalifa*), as a member of world fraternity of Islamic states.
- He completed the construction of **Qutub-Minar**.
- He constituted a corp of 40 loyal slave *Amins*, known as **Turkan-i-Chahalgani** or *Chalisa*.
- He started Iqta system in Delhi Sultanate. This is an assignment of land in lieu of salary, which he distributed to his officers. Every *Iqtadar* had to maintain law and order, and collect revenue. After deducting his salary and the expenses of the government, he sent the surplus amount to the Central Government.
- He introduced the Silver Tanka and Copper Jital.
- He patronised Minhaj-us-Siraj, author of Tabaqat-i-Nasiri.
- He is called the *father of Tomb Building* (built Sultan Garhi in Delhi).

Rukunuddin Firoz (AD 1236)

- Iltutmish appointed his daughter Raziya as his successor.
- But most of the nobles could not reconcile themselves to the idea of a woman ruling over them and so they placed one of his son Rukunuddin Firoz on the throne. He was a worthless person who left the work of the government in the hand of his mother, **Shah Turkan**.
- Finally throne was given to Raziya when he was out of the capital to curb a rebellion in Awadh against him.

Raziya Sultan (AD 1236-1240)

- She was the first and the last Muslim woman ruler of Medieval India.
- Raziya successfully crushed the rebellions that occurred in Multan Lahore and Jhansi. The *wazir* **Nizam-ul-Mulk Junaidi**, who had opposed her elevation to the throne, was defeated by Raziya.
- She also sent an expedition against **Ranthambhor** to control the Rajput.
- She discarded the female apparel and started holding the court with her face unveiled.
- Her attempt to create a party of nobles loyal to her and the appointment of a non-Turk, **Yakut** to the high office led to opposition.
- She herself led an expedition against the rebellious Governor of **Lahore** and forced him to acknowledge her suzerainty.
- There was again a serious rebellion in Bhatinda. **Altunia**, Governor of Bhatinda refused to accept the suzerainty of Razia. Razia, accompanied by Yakut, marched against Altunia.
- However, Altunia murdered Yakut and imprisoned Razia. Subsequently, Razia married Altunia and both of them marched towards Delhi. In AD 1240, Razia, became the victim of a the conspiracy and was assassinated near Kaithal (Haryana) by the *jats*.
- After Raziya, the battle of succession continued in which the following rulers ruled insignificantly.

Ghiyasuddin Balban (1265-1286)

- Balban ascended the throne in 1265, after killing all members of Iltutmish's family. He himself was a member of the *chalisa* or *chahalgani*, but he broke the power of *chahalgani* and restored the prestige of the crown.
- He created a strong centralised army and established the military department *Diwan-i-Arz*. He ordered the separation of military affairs from finance department (*diwan-i-wazarat*). He also appointed spies.
- He declared the Sultan as, the 'representative *of God on the Earth*'. The Persian court model influenced Balban's conception of kingship. He took up the title of **Zil-i-Ilahi** (Shadow of God) and impressed upon the people that king was the deputy of God (*Niyabat-i-Khudai*).
- He refused to laugh and joke in the court, and even gave up drinking wine. To emphasise that the nobles were not his equals. He introduced Persian etiquettes like **Sijda** and **Paibos**. (prostration before and kissing the monarch's feet).
- Balban started the festival of *Nauroz*. He adopted the policy of Blood and Iron
- He was a patron of Persian literature, and showed special favour to **Amir Khusro**.

Kaiqubad (AD 1287-90)

Grandson of Balban, he was put on the throne by Fakruddin, the *kotwal* of Delhi. But, Kaiqubad was killed by the Khalji rulers. This led to the end of Ilbari dynasty and establishment of the Khalji dynasty.

THE KHALJI DYNASTY (AD 1290-1320)

A group of Khalji nobles led by Jalaluddin Khalji, overthrew the incompetent successors of Balban in AD 1290. The Khalji rebellion was welcomed by the non-Turkish nobility. The Khaljis did not exclude the Turks from high offices, but ended the Turkish monopoly.

Jalaluddin Khalji (AD1290-1296)

- He was the first ruler of the Delhi Sultanate to clearly put forward the view that the state should be based on the willing support of the governed and that since the large majority of the people in India were Hindus, the state in India could not be a truly Islamic state.
- He adopted the policy of tolerance and avoiding harsh punishment.
- The most important aspect of his reign was the invasion of Devagiri in 1294, by his nephew and son-in-law Alauddin Khalji.
- He married his daughter to **Ulugh Khan**, a descendant of Changez Khan to win his goodwill.

Alauddin Khalji (1296-1316)

- He came to the throne by treacherously murdering his uncle and father-in-law Jalaluddin Khalji.
- He proclaimed himself as Sultan winning over the nobles and soldiers to his side by the lavish use of gold.
- He massacred the rebellious nobles, relatives, family members and the Mongols who had settled in Delhi. Alauddin gave harsh punishment even to the wives and children of all nobles.
- Alauddin framed a series of regulations to prevent the nobles from conspiring against him. They were forbidden to hold banquets of festivals or to form marriage alliances without the permission of the Sultan.
- To discourage the festival parties, he banned the use of wines and intoxicants. He also instituted a spy service to keep himself informed of all that the nobles said and did.
- He firstly conquered Gujarat and married Raja's wife Kamla Devi. He acquired Malik Kafur from there.
- Then he captured Ranthambhor, Chittor and Malwa.
- Malik Kafur was sent towards South to expand the territory.

- He defeated Yadava king of Devagiri, Ramchandra Deva, Kakatiya king Pratap Rudra Deva I, Hoyasala king of Dwar, Samudra king Vira Ballala III and Pandyas of Madurai (King Mahavarman Kulshekhara).
- He is said to have reached as far as Rameshwaram, where he built a mosque.
- Alauddin strengthened the North-West frontier, under his trusted commander Ghazi Malik.

Administrative Reforms of Alauddin Khalji

- First Sultan to have a permanent army. He paid soldiers in cash.
- In order to avoid the problems created by the nobles, Alauddin issued four important ordinances.
- Confiscation of religious endowments and free grants of lands.
- Reorganised the spy system.
- Prohibited the use of wine and intoxicants.
- Laid down that the nobles should not have social gatherings and they should not inter-marry without his permission.
- He introduced the system of *Dagh* or branding the horses and *Chehra* or detailed description of each soldier.

Revenue Reforms of Alauddin Khalji

- Measured the cultivable land and fixed the land revenue. *Bishwa* was declared to be the standard of measurement.
- The state demanded half of the produce.
- The post of special official called **Mustakharaj** was created for the purpose of collection of revenue.
- Alauddin is credited to have built many forts, and the most important of them is **Alai Fort**.
- He also constructed the **Alai Darwaja**, the entrance gate of the Qutub Minar.
- He also built the palace of thousand pillars called 'Hazar Situn,' Hauz Khas and Jamait Khana Mosque and built his capital at Siri. He adopted the title **Sikandar-i-Sahni**.

- He was the first Turkish sultan who separated religion from politics. He proclaimed kingship knows no kinship.
- He patronised many great poets in his court like Amir Khusro and Mir Hasan Dehlvi.

Market/Economic Reforms

- *Alauddin controlled the market by many regulations*
- Fixed the cost of all commodities.
- He set-up three markets at Delhi.
- All goods for sale were brought to the open market called 'Sarai-Adl'.
- He established the market control department under a minister called **diwan-i-riyasat**.

Successors of Alauddin Khalji

- After the death of Alauddin in 1316, Malik Kafur *Hazar Dinari* seized the throne, but he could not rule for long and nominated Shihabuddin (Alauddin's sixteenth son) as king.
- Shihabuddin was deposed by Qutbuddin Mubarak Shah (1316-20).
- **Nasiruddin Shah** (AD 1320) killed Mubarak Shah and himself was killed by Ghazi Malik the Governor of Dipalpur.
- This ended the 30 years rule of Khalji dynasty and established the Tughlaq dynasty on throne.

THE TUGHLAQ DYNASTY (AD 1320-1414)

Ghiyasuddin Tughlaq (AD 1320-1325)

- Ghazi Malik or Ghiyasuddin Tughlaq was the founder of Tughlaq dynasty or the dynasty of the Qaraunah Turks. He was the first Sultan of Delhi who took up the title of *Ghazi or* slayer of the infidels.
- He liberalised Alauddin's administrative policies and took a keen interest in construction of canals and formulated the famine policy. The judicial and police arrangements were made efficient.
- He gave up the land measurement system and started the *Batai System* or sharing of crops. Efficient *Postal service* was restored.

- He sent his son, Jauna Khan to re-establish the authority in Warangal (Kakatiya) and Madurai (Pandyas).
- He built the city of *Tughlagabad* near Delhi and made it his capital.
- Sufi saint, Shaikh Nizam-ud-din Aulia said Delhi is far away, in regard to him.
- He died in 1325, after a fall from a high raised pavillion. *Ibn Battuta*, the Moroccan traveller, who was in Delhi at that time, opined that his death was due to sabotage arranged by his son, Jauna Khan (Muhammad-bin- Tughlaq).

MUHAMMAD-BIN-TUGHLAQ (AD 1325-1351)

- **Jauna Khan** ascended the throne under the name Muhammad-bin- Tughlaq. He was one of the most extra-ordinary king who ever sat on the throne of Delhi. He was an expert in Arabic, Persian Astronomy, Philosophy, Maths and Medicine.
- He applied his rational and innovative mind in every aspect of administration but achieved little success as he was very hasty in nature.

Five Ambitious Projects of Muhammad-Bin-Tughlaq

His five ambitious projects were

Taxation in the Doab (1326)

The Sultan made an ill-advised financial experiment in the Doab between the Gangas and the Yamuna. He not only increased the rate of taxation, but also revived and created, some additional *Abwabs* or Cessess.

Transfer of the Capital (1327)

The most controversial step was the transfer of capital from Delhi to Deogiri. He renamed Deogiri as Daulatabad.

Introduction of Token Currency (1329)

Muhammad Tughlaq decided to introduce Bronze coin, instead of the silver coin which would have the same value.

The Khurasan Expedition (1329)

Under the vision of Universal Conquest, he decided to conquest Khurasan and Iraq and mobilised a huge army for this purpose.

Qarachil Expedition (1330)

This expedition was launched, in Kumaon hills in the Himalayas, allegedly to counter Chinese incursions. The attack was successful, but when the rainy season set in, the invaders suffered terribly. He died in **Thatta** (Sind), while campaigning against a Turkish slave *Taghi*.

Diwan-i-Kohi

A new department of agriculture *Diwan-i-Kohi* was set-up. He built the fortress of Adilabad and the city of "*Jahanpanah*".

Ibn-Battuta

The famous Moroccan traveller Ibn-Battuta came to Delhi in 1334 and acted as the *Qazi* of the capital for 8 years. He recorded the contemporary Indian scene in his *Safranamah (Rahela)*.

Firoz Shah Tughlaq (1351-1388)

- Firoz Tughlaq faced the problem of preventing the imminent break up of Delhi Sultanate. So he tried to appease the nobility, the army and the Battuta theologians.
- He made the *Iqta system* hereditary.
- He extended the principle of heredity to the army. The soldiers were not paid by cash but by assignments on land revenue of villages (*Vajeha*). This technique led to many abuses.
- In order to encourage agriculture, the Sultan paid a lot of attention to irrigation. He repaired a number of canals. The first canal was from Sutlej to Ghaggar. The second canal carried water from Yamuna to Hissar. He imposed *Haq-i-Sharb* or *Hasil-i- Sharb* i.e. water tax.
- He encouraged the practice of slavery and selected young boys from the conquered territory for the purpose. *Diwan-i-Bandagon* was created as the department for slaves.

- Built new towns of Fatehabad, Hissar, Jaunapur (in memory of Muhammad Tughlaq) and Firozabad. During his Bengal campaign, he renamed Ikdala as **Azadpur and Pandua** as **Firozabad.**
- He brought two pillars of Ashoka from Topara and Meerut, to Delhi and repaired Qutub-Minar when it was struck by lightning.
- He established a hospital at Delhi, known as *Darul-Shifa.*
- A new department of *Diwan-i- Khairat* was set-up to make provision for the marriage of poor girls.
- Introduced two new coins – *Adha* (50% *Jital*) and *Bikh* (25% *Jital*).
- Mathura was destroyed during his period.
- He made **Jaziya** a separate tax and he imposed this tax upon the Brahmans for the first time in the history of Sultanate.
- **Barani**, the historian, was in his court. He wrote *Tarikh-i-Firozshahi and Fatwa-i-Jahangiri.*
- He died in AD 1388.

THE LATER TUGHLAQS (1388-1414)

- After Firozshah Tughlaq, Ghiyasuddin Tughlaq Shah-I succeeded. He was repalced by **Abu Bakr Shah** in AD 1389.
- The states of Malwa, Sharqi (Jaunpur) and Gujarat broke away from the Sultanate.
- Abu Bakr was replaced by Nasiruddin Muhammad in AD 1390. Nasiruddin Muhammad was replaced by **Ala-ud-din Sikandar Shah** for a brief period in 1394, but regained the throne after Sikandar's death.
  He ruled till AD 1412. During his period, Timur invaded India.

Timur's Invasion

- Timur, the head of the Chaghtai Turks and the ruler of Mongols in (Central Asia) invaded India in 1398, during the reign of Nasiruddin Muhammad Tughlaq.

- He robbed people. He is said to have inflicted on India more misery, than had ever before been done by a conquerer in a single invasion.
- Timur nominated **Khizr Khan** to rule over Punjab and himself returned to Central Asia. He died on his way to conquer China in AD 1404.

Taxation System

Firoz Shah Tughlaq introduced new system of taxation according to the *Quran.*

- **Kharaj**   A land tax of 1/10th of the procedure of land.
- **Zakat**   2.5% tax on property (by Muslim only).
- **Jaziya**   A tax by non-Muslims (even by Brahmins).
- **Khams** 1/6th of the booty captured during war.

THE SAYYID DYNASTY (AD 1414-50)

- **Khizr-Khan** (1414-21) founded the Sayyid dynasty and claimed to have descended from the prophet of Islam.
- He helped Timur in his invasion, so was given the governship of Lahore.
- Khizr Khan took the title of **Rayat-i-Ala** and not of a king. The coins were struck and *Khutba* was read in the name of Timur and his successor Shahrukh.
- Khizr Khan's three successors were incapable rulers. Mubarak Shah (1412-33) led successful expeditions against Mewatis, Katehars and the Gangeti Doab area. He was killed and deposed by the nobles.
- **Muhammad Shah** (1434-43) ruled on a very small area, rest being governed by nobles. **Alauddin Shah Alam** (1443-1451) was the last Sayyid king who retired as a coward, descending in favour of Bahlol Lodhi. Thus, the Sayyid Dynasty was replaced by the Lodhi Dynasty.
- Yahya-bin-Ahmed-bin-Abdullah Sirhindi wrote *Tarikh-i-Mubarak* Shahi (History of Muhammad Shah of Sayyid Dynasty).

THE LODHI DYNASTY
(AD 1451-1526)

Considered as the first Afghan dynasty of India. They were ruling over **Sirhind**, while Sayyids ruled over India.

Bahlol Lodhi (AD 1451-1489)

- Founder of Lodhi dynasty in India.
- Revived Sultanate to quite an extent.
- Annexed entire Sharqi kingdom and issued Bahlol coins.
- Never sat on the throne, used to sit on carpets alongwith *Amins*.

Sikandar Lodhi
(AD 1489-1517)

- Noblest of the three Lodhi rulers, real name was **Nizam Khan** (Son of Bahlol Lodhi). Conquered Bihar and Bengal in AD 1504, he built a new city Agra and made it his capital. He was the son of Bahlol Lodhi.
- He was a Muslim fanatic and broke the sacred images of Jwalamukhi temple at Nagarkot and ordered the temple of Mathura to be destroyed.
- He set-up an efficient espionage and judiciary system and introduced the system of auditing of accounts.
- He encouraged agriculture. For measurement of land, he introduced *Gaj-i-Sikandari*.
- He was a poet and wrote verses in Persian under the pen-name of **Gulrukhi**.
- He repaired the Qutub Minar.

Ibrahim Lodhi (1517-1526)

- Ibrahim Lodhi arrested the absolute power of the Sultan. As a result, some of the nobles turned against him. At last, Daulat Khan Lodhi the Governor of Punjab, invited Babur to overthrow Ibrahim.
- He captured Gwalior and was defeated by Rana Sanga of Mewar.
- He was defeated and killed at the hands of Babur in the **First Battle of Panipat in AD 1526**. This marked the end of the Delhi Sultanate.

Causes of the Decline of the Delhi Sultanate

- Despotic, autocratic and military forms of government.
- Wars of succession.
- Financial instability.
- Vastness of the empire and improper administrative control.
- Unsuccessful experiments of Muhammad -bin-Tughlaq. Timur's invasion.
- Incompetent nobility and increase in number of slaves during Firoz Tughlaq.

THE SULTANATE ADMINISTRATION

- The Turkish Sultans in India declared themselves *Lieutenants of Painful*, which meant that they included the name of Caliphate of Baghdad in Khutba, but he had only moral position.
- Political, legal and military authority was vested in the Sultan. He was responsible for administration.
- He was the Commander-in-Chief of the military forces.
- The country was divided into *Iqtas*, which were distributed among the nobles, officers and soldiers for the purpose of administration and revenue collection. *Iqtadars* could be transferred.
- The key figure in the administration was *Wazir*. In the earlier period, the *Wazir* was primarily a military leader, but now he began to be considered more as an expert in the revenue affairs and supervised the collection of income and expenditure.
- The head of military department was called *Ariz-i-Mamalik*. The responsibility of *Ariz* was recruitment, payment and inspection of army.
- *Diwan-i-Risalat* dealt with religious matters. It was presided over by a *Chief Sadr* or *Chief Qazi*. The *Qazi* dispensed civil law based on Muslim law (*Sharia*).
- *Diwan-i-Insha,* headed by *Dahir-i-Muma lik, managed the royal correspondence.*
- The rulers posted intelligence agents called *Barids* in different parts of the empire to keep themselves informed.

- *Wakil-i-Dar* was responsible for the maintenance of proper decorum at the court. The province were divided into *Shiqs* and headed by *Shiqdars*. The next unit was *Parganas*, groups of hundred villages, headed by the *Chaudhary*. *Pargana* was also headed by *Amil*. *Khuts* were the landowners.

CULTURAL DEVELOPMENTS

Art and Architecture

- Archs and domes are a special feature of Muslim architecture. This required stronger cement, thus, finer quality of mortar became widespread in North India.
- For decoration, the Turks used, geometrical and floral designs with verses from the *Quran*. Hindu motifs like bell, lotus and swastik etc were also used e.g. *Adhai Din ka Jhompra* at Ajmer, tomb of Ghiyasuddin Balban in Mehrauli (Delhi).

Other Developments

- **Quwwat-ul-Islam** mosque, Delhi Built by Qutubuddin Aibak.
- **Adhai din ka Jhopra** Ajmer : Qutubuddin Aibak.
- **Alai Darwaja**, Qutub Minar : Alauddin Khalji
- **Jamat Khan Masjid** at *dargah* of Nizamuddin Auliya : Alauddin Khalji
- **Siri** (city), Hauzkhas tank, *Hazar Situn* : Alauddin Khalji.
- **City of Tughlaqabad** founded by Ghiyasuddin Tughlaq. City of Jahanpanah and Adilabad fort : Muhammad-bin-Tughlaq.
- **City of Jaunpur** Hissar, Firozabad : Firoz-shah Tughlaq.

Literary Sources

Book	Author
Khazyan-ul-Futuh	Amir Khusro
Tughlaq Namah	Amir Khusro
Tarik-i-Alai	Amir Khusro
Tabaqat-i-Nasiri	Minhaj-us-Siraj
Tarikh-i-Firozshahi	Ziauddin Barni
Gita Govind	Jayadeva
Mitakshara	Vigyaneshwara
Dayabhaga	Jimuta Vahana
Ashiqa and Khizr khan	Amir Khusro
Amuktamalyada	Krishnadeva Raya
Futuhat-i-Firozshahi	Firoz Shah
Parasana Kaghava	Jayadeva
Khamsah	Amir Khusro
Miftahul Futuh	Amir Khusro

Music

- New musical modes and instruments like *Rabab* and *Sarangi*, were introduced.
- Amir Khusro introduced many Persian Arabic *ragas*. He also invented the *Sitar*.

Paintings

Arabs introduced paper in the 15th century which encouraged painting.

Literature

- Many Sanskrit works like *Rajatarangani* and *Mahabharata* were translated into Persian. Udayraja wrote *Raja Vinoda* on Mahmud Begarha.
- Zai Nakshabi translated Sanskrit stories into Persian under the title *Tuti Namah*.
- Merutanga wrote *Prabandha Chintamani*.

Amir Khusro

- He was a Persian poet (AD 1253-1325) associated with royal courts of more than seven rulers of the Delhi Sultanate.
- He was also a musician and invented the *Sitar*. He innovated *Khayal* (a style of singing).
- In his book Tarikh-i-Alai, he gave an account of the conquests of Alauddin Khalji.
- His book *Ashiqa*, contains the love story of Deval Rani and Khizr Khan.
- In his book *Nur-Siphir* or nine skies, he gave the story of Sultan Mubarak Shah. He also lived in the court of Ghiyasuddin Tughlaq and wrote *Tughlaqnamah*.
- Khusro is also known as *Tuti-i-Hind* or '*Parrot of India*'.

PROVINCIAL KINGDOMS

Gujarat

- Disintegrated from Delhi in AD 1397, under Zaffar Khan, who assumed the title of *Sultan Muzaffar Shah*.
- Ahmed Shah I (his grandson), built a new city Ahmedabad and also built Jama Masjid and Tin Darwaza at Ahmedabad.
- Mahmud Beghra was another prominent ruler, in whose reign, the Portuguese set-up a factory at Diu.
- Sanskrit scholar, Udayraja, was his court poet. Akbar annexed Gujarat in AD 1573.

Malwa

- The state was annexed by Alauddin Khalji in AD 1305 and remained a part of the Sultanate until its Governor, Dilawar Khan Ghuri, declared his independence in AD 1435.
- **Hasan Shah** was a powerful ruler of Malwa. He built Jama Masjid, Hindol Mahal and Jahaz Mahal at Mandu. Next ruler, Mahmud Khalji, was defeated by Rana Kumbha.
- Malwa became a part of Gujarat in AD 1531 and was annexed to the Mughal state in AD 1562.

Kashmir

- Shamsuddin Shah became the first Muslim ruler of Kashmir in AD 1339.
- **Zainulabdin** (AD 1420-70) was the greatest ruler of Kashmir, also known as *'Badshah'* and *the Akbar of Kashmir*.
- He accepted the policy of tolerance, introduced the art of shawl making in Kashmir, built Zaina Lanka and an artificial island in the Wular lake.
- Later ruled by Chak Dynasty, whose ruler submitted to Akbar in AD 1586.
- It is believed that women played an important role in the history of the Kashmir.

Mewar

- The capital city Chittor was captured by Alauddin Khalji in AD 1303, but Rajput rule was soon restored by Rana Hamir (AD1326-64).
- Rana Kumbha Karan (AD 1433-68) was the greatest ruler of Mewar. He built the famous victory tower **Vijay Stambh** at Chittor, to commemorate his victory over Mahmud Khilji of Malwa. His court was adorned by Mandan, who wrote many books on architecture namely, *Parsad Mandan* and *Rupa Mandan*.
- **Rana Sangram Singh** or **Rana Sanga** (1509-28) defeated Mahmud II of Malwa and Ibrahim Lodhi. But, he was defeated by Babur in the **Battle of Khanwa** (AD 1527).

Bengal

- Disintegrated from Delhi during the reign of Muhammad-bin- Tughlaq.
- In AD 1342, Iliyas Khan founded the new Iliyas Shahi Dynasty.
- Ghiyasuddin Azam established friendly relations with China and established trade and commerce.
- The famous poet, Maladhar Basu, compiler of *Sri-Krishna Vijay*, was patronised by the Sultans and was given the title of *Gunaraja Khan.*
- Chaitanya and Shankaradeva belonged to this period. Sher Shah Suri occupied Bengal in AD 1538.

VIJAYANAGARA KINGDOM (AD 1336-1580)

The Sangamas (AD 1336-1485)

- The kingdom was founded in AD 1336 in response to the Tughlaq authority in South India.
- Vijayanagara Kingdom and the city was founded by Harihara I and Bukka. (Two of the five sons of Sangama).
- Harihara and Bukka were originally the feudatories of the of Kakatiyas. They were brought to the centre by Muhammad-bin-Tughlaq, converted to Islam and were sent to South to control the rebellion, but motivated by a Bhakti Saint Vidyaranya they reconverted into Hindu. They established the Vijayanagara kingdom in AD 1336.

Harihara I (AD 1336-56)

Conflict with the Bahmani kingdom for supremacy over three areas : Raichur doab (between Krishna and Tungabhadra), Krishna-Godavari Delta and Marathwada.

Bukka I (AD 1356-79)

- Renamed the city of Vidyanagar as Vijayanagara.
- The royal Ambassadors from Malabar and Ceylon, adorned his court.
- Restored peace between the warring Vaishnavas and the Jains.

Devraya-I (AD 1406-22)

- He constructed a dam across the Tungabhadra to bring the canal into the city. Italian traveller Nicolo Conti visited the kingdom during his reign.
- **Srinatha** was his court poet, who wrote *Haravilasam*.
- There was a **Pearl Hall** in his palace, where he honoured the men of eminence.

Devraya-II (AD 1423-46)

- He was the greatest Sangama ruler. The Commanders believed that he was an incarnation of *Indra*. He wrote *Mahanataka Suddhanidhi*. He took the title 'Ganga Betekara' i.e the elephant hunter. Persian Ambassador Abdul Razzaq, the envoy of Shahrukh, visited his court.
- The Sangama dynasty was replaced by Saluva dynasty, which lasted for two decades.
- The king was a scholar in Kannada and Sanskrit.

The Saluvas (AD 1486-1505)

- Saluva Narsimha was the (AD 1486-91), founder of the dynasty, native of the Kalyam region.

Tirumal (1491) and Immadi Narasimha (1491-1505)

- Ruled under the regency of Narsa Nayak.
- **Vasco Da Gama** came to India (Calicut) during the reign of Immadi in AD 1498.
- Ultimately, a new dynasty called the Tuluva dynasty was founded by Vir Narasimha.

The Tuluvas (AD 1505-1570)

- **Vira Narsimha** (AD 1505-09) Killed Immadi of Saluva dynasty and established the Tuluva dynasty. He was the son of Narsa Nayaka.
- **Krishnadevaraya** (AD 1509-29) was the greatest ruler of the dynasty. Portuguese traveller, **Domingo Paes**, wrote high about him. Berbosa also came as a traveller. Also Friar Louis, the Ambassador of the Portuguese Governor, Albuquerque, resided in his court.
- His period was known as "Golden age of Telugu literature."
- He was a warrior, an administrator and a patron of art and literature. He defeated the Gajapati ruler of Orissa and took the title **Yavanaraja Sthapnachaya** (restorer of the Yadava of Bidar).
- His political ideas are contained in the Telugu book *Amuktamalayada*. He also wrote Sanskrit drama *Jambavati Kalyanam*.
- As a great patron of literature, he was known as *Abhinava Bhoja*, *Andhra Pitamaha* and *Andhra Bhoja*. Sri Vyasatirtha was his guru.
- Eight great poets of Telugu, known as *Ashta Diggaja* adorned his court.
- He was a contemporary to Babur.
- **Achyuta Raya** (AD 1529-42) Succeeded Krishnadevaraya. A Portuguese traveller Fernao Nuniz came during his reign.
- **Sadasiva** (1543-76) was the last ruler of the dynasty.
- **Battle of Talikota** (AD 1565) Between the alliance of Ahmednagar, Bijapur, Golkonda and Bidar at one side and Sadasiva on the other side. Sadasiva was defeated.
- Caesar Frederick, the Portuguese traveller, visited his court (AD 1567-68).

The Aravidus (AD 1570-1650)

• The dynasty was founded by **Thirumala**, brother of Rama Raya. He shifted the capital to Penugonda and divided the empire into three linguistic sections.

Vijayanagara Architecture

• Important temples are Vithalswami and Hazara temples at Hampi, Varadraja and Ekambarnatha temples at Kanchipuram, and Parvati temples at Chidambaram.

• The stories of *Ramayana* and *Mahabharata* were inscribed on the walls of the temples; e.g. Vithalswami and Hazara Ram temple.

• Vibrant combination of Chalukyan, Hoysalan, Pandyan and Cholan styles.

Vijayanagara Society

• Only empire in Medieval India, which employed women in the services. Women even went to battles.

Vijayanagara Trade

• Accounts of Nuniz and Paes indicate a dependence on foreign trade for maintenance of the two most important bases of the Vijayanagara empire the cavalry and its fire arms.

Vijayanagara Coins

• They issued gold coins called **Varahas** or **Pagodas**. (*Varahas*, because the most common symbol was Varaha the boar an incarnation of *Vishnu*). These help us know that they were the worshippers of Vishnu.

The Nayankara System

• Under this system, military chiefs were assigned certain pieces of land called *Amaram*. These chiefs, known as **nayaks**, had revenue and administrative rights on their lands.

• They were required to maintain elephants, horses and soldiers in certain numbers, which were included in the royal army during wars.

• They also had to pay a sum of money to the central exchequer. In course of time, the *nayaks* began to assert their military, administrative and economic powers, which later became a major cause of the decline of the Vijayanagara empire.

The Ayagar System

• It involved the Constitution of a Twelve-member official group by the centre to maintain administration at the village level. These officials, called the *Ayagars*, were village functionaries and constituted of groups of families.

• They were given, for their service, a portion of or a plot in the village, which were tax-free. The *Ayagars* were hereditary officials and there was to be no sale or purchase of land without their permission.

BAHMANI KINGDOM

• The Bahmani kingdom of Deccan was founded by **Hasan Gangu**, whose original name was Ismail Mukh. The capital was Gulbarga. Hasan Gangu took the title of **Alauddin Hasan, Bahaman Shah** (AD 1347-58) became the first king of Bahmani in AD 1347.

• At the time of his death, his dominion had four provinces- Gulbarga, Daulatabad, Berar and Bidar.

• **Mahmud Shah I** (1358-75) son of Bahaman Shah, established a council consisting of eight ministers and decentralised his provincial administration. He fought with Vijayanagara. He was succeeded by his son Ala-ud-din Mujahid Shah.

• **Firoz Shah** (1397-1422) was the most remarkable figure in the Bahmani kingdom. He was determined to make Deccan the cultural centre of India. He inducted Hindus in his administration to large extent. He built an observatory at **Daulatabad**. He founded the city of **Firozabad** on the bank of the river Bhima. Firoz defeated Devaraya I.

• Firoz Shah was succeeded by his brother **Ahmed Shah I** (AD 1422-36). He shifted his capital from Gulbarga to Bidar.

• Ahmed Shah is known as *Wali* or saint, due to his association with Gisudiraz.

• Inlaying of zinc with silver and gold, and **Bidri ware** was introduced in his period.

- Ahmed Shah was succeeded by his son **Alauddin-II** (AD 1436-58) and Humayun. **Humayun** (AD 1458-61) was so cruel, that he got the title of *Zalim*.
- Humayun was succeeded by his son **Nizam Shah** (1461-63) and then by **Muhammad Shah-III** (AD 1463-82). Mahmud Gawan was the Prime Minister of Muhammad. **Nikitin**, a Russian merchant, visited Bidar during his reign.
- After Gawan's execution by the discontented noble, the Bahmani kingdom started declining.
- The last ruler of Bahmani kingdom was **Kalim Ullah Shah** (AD 1524-27).
- After the break-up of Bahmani kingdom, *five Muslim separate states were formed as follow* :
  1. **Nizam Shahis of Ahmednagar** founder-Ahmed Nizam Shah, later annexed by Shahjahan.
  2. **Adshahis of Bijapur** (1490-1686) founded by Yusuf Adil Shah. It was annexed by Aurangazeb.
     Greatest ruler of the kingdom was Ibrahim Adil Shah. He introduced *Dakhini* in place of Persian language. Another ruler Muhammad Adil Shah built the **Gol Gumbaz**.
  3. **Imad Shahis of Berar** (1490-1574) founded by Fateullah Khan II Mad-ul-Mulk with Daulatabad as capital. Later, it was conquered and annexed by one of the Nizam Shahi rulers of Ahmednagar.
  4. **Qutub Shahis of Golconda** (1518-1687)   founded by Quli Qutub Shah. He built the famous Golconda fort and made it his capital.
- Muhammad Quli Qutab Shah was the greatest of all. He founded the city of Hyderabad.
- He built the famous **Charminar**. Most important port of Qutub Shahi kingdom was Masulipatnam. The kingdom was annexed by Aurangzeb (1687).
  5. **Barid Shahis of Bidar** (1528-1619) founded by Ali Barid. Annexed by *Adil Shahis of Bijapur*.

RELIGIOUS MOVEMENTS

The Sufi Movement

Mystics who are called *Sufis*, rose in Islam at a very early stage.

- These saints had nothing to do with the state. They laid great emphasis on love as a bond between God and the individual soul.
- *Sufi* came out of the word **sooph** meaning **wool**. They advocated life of purity and renunciation. Sufism sprang from the doctrine of *Wahadat-ul-Wujud* or unity of being. This doctrine was propounded by Ibn-ul-Arabi.
- One and the earliest Sufis was Rabia, a woman.
- Sufis organised 12 orders or *silsilas*. A silsila was generally led by a prominent mystic, who lived in a *khanqah* or hospice alongwith his disciple. The link between the teacher or *pir* and his disciples or *murids* was a vital part of Sufism. Every *pir* nominated a successor or *wali* to carry out his work.
- Sufi orders are broadly divided into *Ba-shara* that is those which followed the Islamic law (shariat) and *Be-shara*, that is those which were not bound by it.

Sufi Order	Founder	Popular Saints	Other Features
Chisti (*Delhi and Doab region*)	Khwaja Abdul Chisti (in Heart)	Khwaja Muinuddin Chisti (India) Bakhtiyar Kaki, Nizamuddin Auliya, Nasiruddin Chirag-i-Delhi Nizamuddin Aullia also known as Tahbul-i-Illahi (beloved of God).	They adopted musical recitation, called *sama*, to create mood of nearness to God.
Suhrawardi (*Punjab and Sind*)	Shaikh Shihabuddin Suhrawardi	Shaikh Bahuddin Zakariya	Saints had big *jagirs* and a close contact with the state.
Firdausi	Shaikh Badruddin of Samark	Shaikh Shamsuddin Yahiiya (Bihar)	Yahiya believed in pantheistic monotheism and was the disciple of Khwaja Nizamuddin Firdausi.
Qadiri	Shaikh Abdul Qadiri	Shah Niamatullah Syid Muhammad Jilani	**Dara Shikoh**, the eldest son of Shahjahan was the follower of this order.
Naqshbandi	Khwaja Pir Muhammad	Khwaja Bagi Billah Shailkh Ahmed Sirhindi	—

Sufi Terminology

Sufi Words	Meanings
Shaikh/Murid/Pir	Spiritual teacher
Tasawwuf	Sufism
Murid	Disciple
Khanqah	The hospice
Sama	Musical recital
Raksa	Dance
Fana	Self annihilation
Khalifah	Successor

The Bhakti Movement

- The Bhakti Movement, which stressed mystical union of the individual with God, was initiated in South India by popular saint poets called **Alvars**, who represented the emotional side of Vaishnavism, through collective songs called *Prabandhas*.

- It declined in the AD 10th century, but was again revived as a philosophical and ideological movement by *Acharyas* like

Ramanuja, whose disciple Ramananda took it to North India.

- **South India** : Shiva and Vishnu
  North India : Rama and Krishna

- The real development of *Bhakti* took place in South India between the 7th and the 12th centuries. The *Bhakti* saints came usually from the lower caste. They disregarded caste, encouraged women to join and taught in the local vernacular language.

- They considered that God has either a form (*Saguna*) or was formless (*Nirguna*).

Ramanuja (AD 1017-1137)

In the 11th century, Ramanuja tried to assimilate *Bhakti* to the tradition of the *Vedas*. According to him, **Moksha** (salvation) can be obtained through **Karma**, **Gyan** and **Bhakti**. He gave the concept of Vishishtadvaita.

Jnandeva (AD 1275-96)

Progenitor of *Bhakti Movement* in Maharashtra.

Namdeva (1270-1350)

He was a *Nirguna Upasaka*. Some of his *abhangas* are included in the *Guru Granth Sahib*.

Ekanath (AD 1533-99)

- Born in Patan in Aurangabad published the first receivable edition of **Janesvari** (**Marathi Gita**).

- He condemend caste system and accepted disciple from the lower caste.

Tukaram (AD 1598-1650)

He was a contemporary of Shivaji, the greatest Marathi Bhakti poet and his views are similar to that of Kabir. Great devotee of Vithal, a form of God Vishnu.

Ramadas (1608-81)

He was the spiritual guru of Shivaji. Established *ashrams* all over India. He wrote Dasabodha, a didactic work, which gave advice on all aspects of life.

Guru Nanak (1469-1538)

- Founder of Sikh faith in India.
- He has born in **Talwandi**, now **Nankana** Sahib to a Khatri family. He composed hymns and sang them with the help of a *rabab*.
- He laid emphasis on one God. By repeating his name with love and devotion, one could get salvation without distinctions of caste, creed and sect. He was against idolatory, undertaking pilgrimage and other ritualistic conducts.
- In course of time, his teachings gave rise to Sikhism.
- Nanak began the practice of community kitchen or Guru-ka-Langar.
- He named the formless God as Akal Purush.
- His teachings are compiled in the Adi Granth.

Vallabhacharya (1479-1531)

- He emphasised on the worship of Krishna as an incarnation of the almighty God.
- Lived in the court of Krishnadeva of Vijayanagara.
- He taught that there was no difference in *Atma* and *Paramatma*. By means of *Bhakti*, one can get salvation and merge in him. He founded the **Pushti sect**.

Ramananda (15th century)

- The founder of *Bhakti Movement* in North India.
- He discarded caste rules and included among his disciples, men of all castes.
- He was greatly influenced by the teachings of Ramanuja.
- Among his disciples were Raidas, the cobbler, Kabir the weaver, Dhanna the farmer, Sena the barber and Pipa the Rajput.

Kabir (1440-1510)

- He was a weaver.
- Represented *Nirguna Bhakti* tradition. His followers organised themselves as Kabir Panthis.
- His teachings contained Dohas, which are sung till today.
- He was not merely a *Bhakti* poet, but also a social reformer. He spoke in language of common man. He emphasised on simplicity of the religious practice be it Brahminism or Islam.
- He advocated the Bhakti marga and dedication to a formless supreme being.

Chaitanya (1486-1533)

- Born in Nadia district of West Bengal.
- Regarded as the founder of modern *Vaishnav Sect* of Bengal.
- He preached during the reign of Sultan Alauddin Shah of Bengal and Gajpati ruler of Orissa. He died in Puri. His biography is the Chaitanya Charitmala.
- Philosophy of Chaitanya was called Achityabhedaveda.
- His disciples considered him as the incarnation of *Krishna*.

Surdas (1483-1563)

Disciple of Vallabhacharya and devotee of lord Krishna and Radha. He wrote Sur *Suravali*, *Sahitya Ratna* and Sursagar (belonged to *Saguna school*).

Dadu Dayal

Nirguna Bhakti tradition, founded Brahma Sampradaya and Parabrahma Sampradaya; preached service to humanity.

Nimbarakacharya

Worshipper of Krishna and Radha and contemporary of Ramanuja.

Madhavacharya (1238-1317)

According to him, the release from transmigration could be secured only by means of knowledge and devotion. Jayatirtha was his successor.

Mirabai (1498-1546)

Married to **Bhojraj**, she was the Rathore princesss of Mevata and daughter in-law of Rana Sanga of Mewar. She belonged to the Krishna cult of Vaishnavism.

Tulsidas (1532-1623)

Born in Brahmin family in Varanasi and belonged to Ram Bhakti cult of Vaishnavism. He wrote *Ramcharitmanas*, *Gitawali*, *Kavitawali*, *Vinay Patrika* etc.

Vidyapati

* *Maithilili* saint poet.
* Wrote Padavali i.e. thousands of love ballads on Radha and Krishna. He also wrote *Kirtilata Kirtipataka*.

Narsingh Mehta

Saint from Gujarat, who wrote songs in Gujarati, depicting the love of Radha and Krishna. He authored Mahatma Gandhi's favourite bhajan *'Vaishnava jan ko'*.

Purandar Das (1480-1564)

Vaishnava saint, composer of Karnataka, who laid the foundation of Carnatic music.

Shankara Deva (1449-1568)

Vaishnava saint from Assam.

Thyagaraja (1767-1847)

Telugu saint and greatest composer of Carnatic music.

THE MUGHAL EMPIRE

Babur (AD 1526-1530)

* He was the descendant of Timur on his father's side and Changez Khan on his mother's side. His family belonged to the Chagtai section of the Turkish race and were commonly known as Mughals.
* Originally ruled over Ferghana (Afghanistan).
* He was invited to attack India by Daulat Khan Lodhi, Subedar of Punjab, Alam Khan Lodhi, uncle of Ibrahim Lodhi and **Rana Sanga.**
* He was successful in his fifth expedition. In the First **Battle of Panipat** in AD 1526, he finally defeated Ibrahim Lodhi.
* Defeated Rana Sanga of Mewar in **Battle of Khanwa** in 1527. Babur took the title of 'Ghazi' after this.
* Defeated another Rajput ruler Medini Rai in **the Battle of Chanderi** in AD 1528.
* In AD 1529, he defeated Muhammad Lodhi (uncle of Ibrahim Lodhi) in the **Battle of Ghaghra**.

* The battle of Ghaghra was the Ist battle which was fought on land and water simultaneously in medieval India.
* Babur was the first ruler to entitle himself 'Badshah'.
* He wrote **Tuzuk-i-Babari** or *Babarnama* in Turkish. It was translated into Persian by *Abdul Rahim Khan-i-Khanan* and in English by Madam Bebridge.
* His victory led to rapid popularisation of gunpowder and artillery in India.
* After the Kushanas, he was the first to have brought Kabul and Kandhar into the Indian empire.
* He died in AD 1530 and was buried at Aram Bagh in Agra. Later his body was taken to Aram Bagh at Kabul.

Humayun (AD 1530 - 40 and 1555 -56)

* He was the son of Babur and Maham Anaga begum.
* Babur had divided his empire among the three brothers of Humayun (Kamran, Hindal and Asakari). So, Humayun had to face real problems ascending to the throne.

- His first campaign was against Kalinjar.
- In AD 1533, the first siege of Chunar and the March of Gaur was stopped by Jalal Khan Sher Khan (Sher Shah) offered nominal submission by sending his son **Qutb Khan** to Humayun's court.
- The second siege of Chunar was stopped by Jalal Khan, Sher Shah's son in 1538. Humayun occupied Gaur where Sher Shah had left wine, women and opium to delay Humayun who renamed it as Jannatabad (Paradise).
- The **Battle of Chausa** (1539) was fought between **Sher Shah** and **Humayun's** army. Humayun was badly defeated and escaped. He was saved by **Nizam**.
- The **Battle of Kannauj** (Bilgrama) (1540) : Humayun was again defeated by Sher Shah and had to flee.
- He passed nearly 15 years in exile. He wandered in Sindh during the reign of Shah Hussain Arghuna, and then reached the Iranian Court.
- He got a chance to return in AD 1555. By that time, Sher Shah and his son Islam Shah, who ruled upto 1553, had died. Muhammad Adil Shah was fond of pleasure and the entire affairs of his state were governed by Hemu, his minister.
- **Bairam Khan**, his most faithful officer helped him. The Mughals occupied Lahore without any march towards Delhi. After the Battle of Machhiwara against the Afghans, and Battle of Sirhind against Sikandar Shah, Humayun's second coronation was organised. In AD 1556, he fell from the stairs of the library (Sher Mandal, Delhi) and died. Dinpanah was his second capital.

Akbar (AD 1556 -1605)

- Akbar was born to Hamida Banu begum at Amarkot in Rana Veersal's palace in AD 1542.
- Akbar was 14 years old when he was crowned at **Kalanaur** in 1556. Akbar already had shown his calibre at the battle field, when he captured Sirhind from Sikandar Shah, AD 1555.
- Bairam Khan represented him in the Second Battle of Panipat in AD 1556 against Muhammad Adil Shah Sur's *Wazir*, Hemu. Akbar defeated Hemu and reoccupied Delhi and Agra.
- Between 1556-1560, Akbar ruled under Bairam Khan's regency. The fort of Gwalior, Jaunpur, Ajmer and Ranthambore were successfully occupied. Later, Akbar asked Bairam Khan to proceed to Mecca. On the way near Patna, Bairam Khan was murdered.
- He also ended the interference from the **Petticoat Government**, (1560-62) represented by Maham Anaga and Adham Khan's Junta.
- Akbar conquered **Malwa** in AD 1561, defeating Baz Bahadur. He was later made the *Mansabdar*, to honour his skill as a musician.
- Akbar's earliest campaigns was against Rani Durgawati of Garh-Katanga (Gond and Rajput principalities).
- The two powerful forts of Rajasthan-Ranthambor and Chittor (Rana Udai Singh guarded by Jaimal) were captured by the Mughals.
- Akbar's deccan campaign began with the siege of **Ahmednagar** (defended by Chand Bibi).
- Akbar's East campaign was against Asirgarh, resulting into the annexation of Khandesh (1601).
- Akbar followed the policy of reconciliation with the Rajputs. In AD 1562, he married the eldest daughter of Raja Bharmal of Jaipur, Harakha Bai.
- In 1570, he married princesses of Bikaner and Jaisalmer, 1584. Prince Salim was married to the daughter of Raja Bhagwan Das.
- He won Gujarat in 1572. In order to commemorate his victory of Gujarat, Akbar build **Buland Darwaja** at Fatehpur Sikri.

- Raja Maan Singh conquered Bihar, Bengal and Orissa for him.
- In 1586, Akbar conquered Kashmir and in 1593, he conquered Sindh.
- At the time of Akbar's death in AD 1605, his empire included Kashmir, Sindh, Kandahar and extended as far as the Godavari in the Deccan.
- He was buried at Sikandara near Agra.

Navratnas in Akbar's Court

Abul Fazal	He was the *Wazir* of Akbar. He wrote the **Akbarnamah** and also led the Mughal imperial army in its war in Deccan.
Faizi Abul	Fazal's brother and historian in Akbar's court. His famous work *Lilavati* is on Mathematics. Akbar appointed him as a teacher for his son.
Tansen	Believed to be one of the greatest musicians of all time. He was born to a Hindu family.
	He served as the court musician to **king Ramchandra** of Mewar and was sent to Akbar's court.
	He accepted Islam at the hands of great Sufi saint **Shaikh Muhammad Ghaus** of Gwalior.
	It was believed that **Tansen** made miracles, such as bringing rain and fire through his singing of *the ragas*, such as **Megh Malhar** and **Deepak**.
Birbal	Courtier in the administration of Akbar. His actual name was **Mahesh Das**.
	He was conferred the title of Raja by Akbar. He frequently had witty and humorous exchanges with Akbar.
Raja Todarmal	He was Akbar's Finance Minister.
	He introduced standard weights for measurement and undertook revenue districts. His revenue collection arrangement came to be called the **Todarmal's Bandobast**.
	His systematic approach to revenue collection became a model for the future Mughals as well as the British.
Raja Man Singh	He was the Raja of Amber, a *Mansabdar* and a trusted General of Akbar.
	He was the grand son of Akbar's father-in-law Bharmal and the adopted son of Raja Bhagwan Das.
	He assisted Akbar in many battles including the well known **Battle of Haldighati**.
Abdul Rahim Khan-e-Khana	He was a poet and the son of Bairam Khan, known for his Hindi couplets.
Faqir Azio Din	He was the chief advisor of Akbar, sufi mystic.
Mullah Do Piaza	He was among the Mughal emperor's chief advisor.

Important Aspects of Akbar's Rule

- Akbar reorganised the central machinery of administration, on the basis of division of power between various departments.
- He abolished the *Jaziya* and pilgrimage tax, and the forcible conversion of prisoners of war. The use of beef was also forbidden.
- He believed in Sulh-i-Kul, that is peace for all.
- He built an **Ibadat Khana** at Fatehpur Sikri to discuss religious matters. He invited many distinguished persons, such as Purshottam Das (Hindu) Maharaji Rana (Parsi), Harivijaya Suri (Jain), Monserate and Aquaviva (Christian).
- To curb the dominance of the *Ulema*, Akbar introduced a new *Khutba* written by Faizi and proclaimed *Mahzarnamah* in 1579, which made him the final interpreter of Islamic law (*Mujtahid Iman-i-Adil*), in case of any controversies.

- It made him *Amir-ul-Momin* (leader of the faithful) and *Amir-i-Adil* (a just ruler).
- His liberation is reflected again in the pronouncement of *Tauhid-i-Ilahi* or Din-i-Ilahi, which propounded Sufi divine monotheism. Birbal, Abul Fazl and Faizi joined the order.
- Akbar established the painting *karkhana*, headed by Abdus Samad.
- Ralph Fitch (1585) was the first Englishman to visit Akbar's court.
- Abul Fazal wrote '*Akbarnamah*', the appendix of which was called *Ain-i-Akbari*.
- His land revenue system was known as Todarmal Bandobast or *Zabti system*.
- *Mansabdari System* was another feature of administration during Akbar's reign to organise the nobility as well as the army. He was the first Mughal ruler to separate religion from politics.
- Sufi saint Shaikh Salim Chisti blessed Akbar with a son who was named Salim (Jahangir). Akbar shifted his court to Fatehpur Sikri from Agra, in honour of the saint.
- Birbal was killed in the battle with the Yusufzai tribe (1586).
- Abul Fazal was murdered by Bir Singh Bundela (1601). In 1579, Akbar issued '*Decree of Infallibility*'.
- Persian was made the official language of Mughal empire.
- He culminated '*Din-i-illathi*', which recognised no prophets.

Maharana Pratap

A Rajput ruler of Mewar, he belonged to the Sisodia clan of Suryavanshi Rajputs. He was a son of Udai Singh II. In 1568, during the reign of Udai Singh II, Mewar was conquered by Akbar.

Battle of Haldighati was fought on 18th June, 1576, in which Maharana Pratap was defeated by Akbar's army, led by Raja Maan Singh. Maharana had to flee the field on his trusted horse-**Chetak**. Thereafter, Pratap had to retreat into the **Aravallis**, from where he continued his struggle through the tactics of guerilla warfare. Rana Pratap died of injuries sustained in a hunting accident.

Jahangir (AD 1605-1627)

- Akbar's eldest son, prince Salim, assumed the title of *Nuruddin Muhammad Jahangir* and ascended the throne.
- He was born at Fatehpur Sikri near Agra in 1569. He was given a proper education by his tutor Rahim Khankhana.
- In AD 1585, he married **Manbai**, the daughter of his maternal uncle-Raja Bhagwan Das.
- In AD 1587 he married **Jodhabai** or Jagat Gosain, the daughter of Udai Singh, who gave birth to prince Khusro (Shahjahan). He mostly lived in Lahore, which he adorned with gardens and buildings.
- The eldest son of Jahangir, Khusro revolted against him, but was suppressed. Khusro received patronage of Guru Arjun Dev (5th Sikh Guru). Guru Arjun Dev was executed for his blessings to the rebel prince.
- **Rana Amar Singh** (son of Maharana Pratap) of Mewar, submitted before Jahangir in AD 1615. Rana Amar Singh was made a *Mansabdar* in the Mughal court.
- His greatest failure was loss of Kandahar to Persia in 1622.
- Jahangir's wife Nurjahan (daughter of Itamad-daulah) exercised tremendous influence over the state affairs. She was made the official Badshah Begum.
- Coins were stuck in her name and all royal *farmans* beared her name.
- She got high positions for her father (Itamaduddaulah) and her brother (**Asaf Khan**).
- He restored Muhammad faith and prohibited the sale of Tobacco.
- Nurjahan married her daughter by Sher Afghani to Jahangir's youngest son, Shahryar and she supported him for the heir apparent.

- Jahangir's military general, Mahabat Khan revolted and abducted him but Nurjahan saved him due to her diplomatic efforts.
- He was justice loving, a huge bell with a chain of 30 yards was placed at the gate of royal palace in Agra and anybody who sought justice from the emperor had to strike the bell. This bell was called *Zanzir-i-Adil*.
- Jahangir faced a formidable opponent in Malik Amber of Ahmednagar.
- Captain Hawkins (1608-11) and Sir Thomas Roe (1615-1616) visited Jahangir's court.
- **Pietxa Valle**, the famous traveller, came during his reign.
- Production of Tobacco (brought by the Portuguese) started in his reign.
- He was buried at Lahore.
- He wrote his autobiography, Tuzuk-i-Jahangiri in Persian.

Mehrunnisa

Nurjahan's actual name was **Mehrunnisa**. She was the widow of Sher Afgani. Jahangir married to her and confered the title 'Nurjahan to her.'

Shahjahan (AD 1628-58)

- Born to Jodhabai or Jagat Gosain in Lahore in 1592. His real name was Khurram. He was the youngest prince to be appointed as the Governor of Deccan, at the age of 15.
- In AD 1612, he got married to Arjamand Bano Begum (known as Mumtaz Mahal), daughter of Asaf Khan.
- He marched against Khan Jahan Lodhi, the Governor of Deccan and Jujhar Singh Bundela, the independent ruler of Bundelkhand.
- Shahjahan's policy of annexing Deccan was successful. Ahmednagar was annexed while Bijapur and Golconda accepted his suzerainity.
- The Portuguese established their control over Satgaon, through a Shahi firman. They started misusing their authority. Shahjahan ordered Qasim Khan in 1532 to drive the Portuguese out of Hughli.

- In 1639, Shahjahan secured Kandahar and immediately fortified it. But Persia wrested Kandahar from Mughals in 1649. Shahjahan failed to recover Kandahar.
- Shahjahan was the second Indian ruler to invade Central Asia.
- Two French travellers : **Bernier** and **Tavernier** and the Italian traveller **Nicolo Manucci** visited during his reign. **Peter Mundi** described the famine that occurred during Shahjahan's reign. His reign is considered as the Golden age of the Mughal empire.
- The last 8 years of Shahjahan were very painful, because of the brutal war of succession between his four sons.
- He was imprisoned by his son Aurangzeb in Agra fort and died in captivity in AD 1658. He was buried at Taj Mahal (Agra) besides his loving wife.

War of Succession

- Among Shahjahan's four sons, the eldest son Dara Shikoh was the Governor of Punjab, Shuja was Governor of Bengal, Aurangzeb was Governor of Bengal and Murad was Governor of Gujarat.
- **Battle of Bahadurgarh** February 1658, was fought between Shuja and Dara, Shuja was defeated.
- **Battle of Dharmat** April 1658, where combined forces of Aurangzeb and Murad, defeated Dara.
- **Battle of Samugarh** May 1658, Dara led Mughal forces on behalf of Shahjahan against Aurangzeb. In this decisive battle, Shahjahan was put into prison by Aurangzeb in the Agra fort.
- **Battle of Khanjawa** December 1658, between Aurangzeb and Shuja. Shuja was defeated and fled to Arakan.
- **Battle of Devtrai March 1659**, Dara was defeated and executed by Aurangzeb. His dead body was paraded on the streets of Delhi.

Aurangzeb (AD 1658-1707)

- He was the third son of Shahjahan born in Ujjain.
- Aurangzeb, made the victory of Deccan in 1636. Aurangzeb's first tenure was upto 1644.

- Aurangzeb's second term as Viceroy in Deccan began in 1653 and continued uptil 1658.
- He took the title of '**Alamgir**' in 1659. He was called a **Zinda pir** or the 'living saint.'
- Under him, the Mughal empire reached its greatest extent and the largest single state ever known in India.
- He forbaded the inscription of *Kalma* on the coins, also forbaded *Sati* and Jharokha-darshan. He ended the celebration of *Nauroz* (singing in the court) and in 1679, reimposed *Jaziya*.
- Mutasib (regulation of moral conduct) were appointed. He ended the use of almanacs and weighing of the emperor. Aurangzeb compiled the Fatwa-i- Alamgiri.
- The Hindu *Mansabdar*, however, maintained their high proportions during his rule.
- Thus, the Mughal empire stretched from Kashmir in the North to Jinji in the South and from Hindu Kush in the West to Chittagong in the East.
- Aurangzeb died in AD 1707 and was buried at Khuldabad (Daulatabad) near Aurangabad.
- He built '**Bibi ka Maqbara**', similar to Taj Mahal in Aurangabad.

Revolts under Aurangzeb

- Aurangzeb's rule can be broadly divided into two periods, in the first 23 years, he concentrated in the North, when Maratha power under Shivaji emerged and the second period (1682-1707) is marked by his pre-occupations with the affairs of Deccan.
- **Sikhs** In 1675, he ordered the arrest and execution of the ninth Sikh Guru, **Guru Tegh Bhadur**. Against this, Guru Gobind Singh organised his followers into a military force called *Khalsa*, but he was also murdered in AD 1708 by an Afghan at Nanded in Deccan. Later, Banda Bairagi continued the war against Mughals.
- **Marathas under Shivaji** Shivaji was a powerful king. Aurangzeb conspired with Jai Singh of Amber against Shivaji in 1665. Shivaji visited Mughal court on the request of Jai Singh, but was imprisoned. He managed to escape in 1674 and declared himself an independent monarch.
- After his death in 1680, his son and successor, Sambhaji was executed by Aurangzeb in 1689. Later, the Marathas, Rajaram and Tarabai, continued the movement against the Mughals.
- The **Jats** revolted under **Gokla**, **Rajaram** and **Churaman**.
- The **first Afghan Rebellion** was by Yusuf Shahi tribes of Afghanistan of Roshni Sect.
- The **Second Afghan Rebellion** was led by Ajmal Khan.
- **Marwar** He annexed Marwar in AD 1678. The campaigning was led by Akbar II (Son of Aurangzeb) against Durgadas, General of Ajit Singh (Son of Raja Jaswant Singh). Akbar II died in the battle. This gave a serious blow to Rajput Mughal alliance.
- Bijapur and Golconda were annexed in AD 1686 and AD 1687, respectively.
- **Ahoms** In 1662, Mir Jumla Aurangzeb's ablest general led the expedition against Ahoms.

Religious Policy of Aurangzeb

Aurangzeb was a Sunni orthodox Muslim, who wanted to convert India from **Dar-ul-Harb** to **Dar-ul-Islam**. His religious policy was a departure from the policy of tolerance and universal peace followed by Akbar. He replaced the solar calender by the lunar *Hira,* dismissed court musicians and royal painters, appointed Muhtasibts (court sensors) from amongst the *Ulema*, to enforce *sharia*'t.

Causes of the Fall of the Mughal Empire

- Weak and incompetent successors.
- Wars of succession.
- Aurangzeb's Deccan, religious and Rajput policies.
- Jagirdari crisis.
- Growth of Marathas and other regional powers.
- Foreign invasions of Nadir Shah (1739) and Abdali.

LATER MUGHALS

Bahadur Shah-I (AD 1707-1712)

- Real name is **Muazzam**, ascended the Mughal throne with the title **Bahadur Shah**. He also assumed the title Shah Alam-I.
- Pursued pacifist policy and was therefore, known as **Shah Bekhabar**.
- He made peace with Guru Gobind Singh and Chatrasal. He granted Sar Deshmukhi to Maratha and released Shahu.
- He forced Ajit Singh of Marwar to submit but later recognised him as the Rana of Marwar. He defeated Banda Bahadur at Lohgarh.
- He was not able to eliminate *Jaziya*, but he supported music.

Jahandar Shah (AD 1712-1713)

- Jahandar Shah won the war of succession due to the support of Zulfiqar Khan, the most powerful Iranian noble of the time.
- He was the first puppet Mughal emperor.
- Jai Singh of Amber was given the title of Mirza Raja Sawai and Ajit Singh was awarded the title of **Maharaja**. He abolished Jaziya.

Farrukhsiyar (AD 1713-1719)

- Ascended the throne with the help of Sayyid brothers (Abdullah Khan and Husasain Khan) who were the *Wazir* and the *Mir Bakshi* respectively.
- Zulfiqar Khan was murdered.
- Banda Bahadur was executed at Gurudaspur. Farrukhsiyar was murdered by the Sayyid brothers with the help of Marathas, in AD 1719.
- Surman Commission visited his court.

Muhammad Shah (AD 1719-1748)

- Ascended the throne with the help of Sayyid brothers (king makers.). Sayyid brothers were killed under a conspiracy hatched by the nobles in 1720.
- Nizam-ul-mulk was appointed as the *Wazir*, but he relinquished the post in 1722 and marched towards Deccan and found an autonomous state Hyderabad.

- During his reign, Bengal acquired virtual independence during the governership of **Murshid Quli Khan**.
- **Saadat Khan** (Burhan-ul-Mulk), who was appointed as the Governor of Awadh, laid down the foundation of the autonomous state.
- **Nadir Shah** invaded India in AD 1739 and defeated Muhammad in the battle of Karnal (1739) and he took away *Takht-i-Taus* (Peacock throne) and the Kohinoor diamond.
- **Ahmed Shah Abdali** raided the kingdom for the first time during his reign.
- He was a pleasure loving king and was nicknamed **Rangeela**.

> ### Kohinoor Diamond
>
> Most sources agree that the Kohinoor was mined at *Rayalseema* in Andhra Pradesh. It was first owned by the Kakatiya dynasty. From then onwards, the stone passed through the hands of successive rulers of the Delhi Sultanate, finally passing to Babur in 1526. ShahJahan had the stone placed into his ornate Peacock Throne. It was taken away by Nadir Shah in 1739 along with the Peacock Throne.

Ahmed Shah (AD 1748-54)

Ahmed Shah Abdali invaded Delhi many times and Punjab and Multan were ceded to him.

Alamgir II (AD 1754-1759)

Ahmed Shah Abdali occupied Delhi during his reign. He defeated the Marathas in the **Third Battle of Panipat in 1761**. In this battle, Marathas were led by Sadashiv Rao Bhau, while the *Peshwa* at that time was Balaji Bajirao.

Shah Alam-II (1759-1806)

- He crowned himself under **Shujauddaula's** protection in Bihar and remained in exile for 12 years.
- He fought the **Battle of Buxar** in AD 1764 and was defeated by the British. He lived for several years at Allahabad as a pensioner of the East India Company.

By the **Treaty of Allahabad**, the emperor received the territories of Allahabad and Kara and an annual tribute of 26 lakhs from Bengal.

- By a *farman*, the emperor confirmed the English gains and granted them the *Diwani* of Bengal, Bihar and Orissa.

Akbar-II (AD 1806-37)

- The king gave Raja Rammohan Roy, the title of **Raja**.
- Lord Hastings ceased to accept the sovereignty of Mughals and claimed the status of pensioner of the East India Company.

Bahadur Shah-II (1837-1862)

- He was the Last Mughal Emperor. He was confined by the British in the Red Fort.
- During the 1857 sepoy revolt, he was proclaimed the emperor of India by the rebels. He was deported to Rangoon and died there.
- He used to write *Shairis* in the pen-name of Zafar.

Socio Economic Conditions

- **Society** Society was stratified into several classes. Both *Sati* and child marriage were readily practiced. *Purdah system* was in vogue, both among the Hindus and the Muslims.
- **Economy** Both trade and commerce flourished with the European nations. Cotton, Indigo, Opium and tobacco was produced. Mughal rulers encouraged agriculture, industries and crafts.
- **Ports** Surat, Cambay, Cochin and Masulipattnam.

Central Administration

- Akbar organised the central machinery of administration on the basis of the division of power between various departments and through checks and balance. The king was the head of all powers.
- The *wakil* (deputy of the king) was stripped off of all his powers after Bairam Khan's death.

Wazir : The Prime Minister.

Diwan : His responsibility were in three fields : Executive, revenue and finance.

- **Mir Bakshi** He was the head of the military department, similar to that of Ariz-i-mamalik, under Delhi Sultanate.
- **Mir Saman or Khan Saman** Incharge of the royal households, like building, roads, gardens etc.
- **Sadr-us-Sudur** Incharge of religious matters, religious endowments and charities.
- **Chief Qazi** Head of the Judiciary department after the king.
- **Barids** Intelligence officers.
- **Mustaufi** Auditor-General.

Provincial Administration

- Mughal empire was divided into 12 Subas (provinces). After expansion of the empire, it became 15 during Akbar, 11 during Jahangir, 22 during Shahjahan and 21 during Aurangzeb.
- **Subedar** Head of the province (governor).
- **Provincial Diwan** Dealt with finance, directly responsible to *central diwan*.

District or Sarkar

- **Fauzdar** Administrative head of the *Sarkar*.
- **Amil/Amalguzar** Collecting revenues and patrolling the roads.
- **Kotwal** Duty was to maintain law and order in *sarkar* besides, trial of criminal cases and regulations of prices.

Pargana

- **Siqdar** Administrative head of the *Pargana*.
- **Amin/Qanungo** They were revenue officials.

Village

- **Lambardar**   Village Headmen
- **Patwari**   Village Accountant

Mansabdari System

- Mansabdari system (1595-96) showed a noble's civil and military capacity. In its broad aspect, the mansab or rank awarded to an individual fixed both his status in the official hierarchy as well as his salary.
- Twin ranks   Zat and Sawar were alloted. The Zat indicated the noble's personal status and the Sawar rank, the actual number of horsemen he was expected to maintain.

Revenue Administration

- The empire was divided into Khalisa (crown land), Jagirs (land granted to nobles) and Inam Madad-i-Maash Suyurghal (land granted to religious and learned men).
- **Dashala System of Raja Todarmal** : Under this system the average produce of different crops at the average price prevailing over the last 10 years were calculated. 1/3rd of the average produce was the state's share. For the measurement of land, 'Bigha' was adopted as the standard unit.
- **Zabti System** was based on the measurement and asessment of land.

- Methods of revenue collection
  - **Rai** Yield per unit area.
  - **Kankut** Based on estimate.
  - **Zabti** Based on the yields of crops.
- **Jagirdari System** In this system, every Jagirdar was assigned land in proportion to his salary.
- **Ijara System** The Government began contracting the land with the middle man, also known as revenue farmers, who were supposed to pay fixed amount to the government, however, were left free to collect whatever they could, from the farmers leading to their exploitation.

Mughal Paintings

- The Mughals introduced new themes depicting the court, battle scenes and added new colours (peacock blue and Indian red).
- Jaswant and Dasawant were two famous painters of Akbar's court.
- Mughal painting reached to its zenith during Jahangir's rule. Jahangir was a great patron of painting.

Mughal Architecture

Ruler	Architecture Built
Babur	Mosques at Kabuligarh (Panipat) and at Sambhal (Rohilkhand).
Humayun	City of Dinpannah, Jamali mosque and mosque of Isa Khan at Delhi .
Haji Begum (wife of Humayun)	Humayun Tomb.
Akbar	Agra fort; Jahangiri Mahal in Agra fort based on design of Manmandir; Lahore Palace, Allahabad fort, temple of Govind-deva at Vrindavana and several buildings at Fatehpur Sikri that included Panch Mahal (planned on Buddhist Vihara), Diwan-i-khas, Jodhabais' Palace, Diwan-i-Aam, Buland Darwaja (Iranian style). He began to build his own tomb at Sikandara which was completed by Jahangir.
Jahangir (Indo-Persian style)	Moti Mosjid at Lahore, own Mausoleum at Shahdara.
Nurjahan	Itamaduddaulas marble tomb at Agra in **pietra dura** technique.
Shahjahan	**At Agra** Taj Mahal, Moti ki Masjid, Khanas Mahal, Sheesh Mahal, Musamman Burz (Jasmine Palace where he spent his last years). **At Delhi** Jama Masjid, Red Fort (Diwan-i-Khas and Rang Mahal). **Others** : Shalimar Bagh (Lahore), City of Shahjahandabad (Red Fort and Taqht-i-Taus i.e. Peace throne), Nahor-i-Faiz.
Aurangzeb	Moti Masjid at Delhi, Bibi-ka-Makbara (tomb of his wife Rabbia-ud-Douna) at Aurangabad, Badshahi mosque at Lahore.

Mughal Era Painting

Ruler	Famous Painters		Other Features
Humayun	▪ Mir Sayyid Ali ▪ Abdus Samad		
Akbar	▪ Adbus Samad ▪ Khusro kuli ▪ Basawan ▪ Daswan	▪ Farrukh Beg ▪ Jamshed	Introduction of Persian style Daswan illustrated 'Razma Namah' (Persian Mahabharat) and Akbarnama.
Jahangir	▪ Bishan Das ▪ Ustad Mansur (animal paintings)	▪ Abdul Hassan	Painting reached at its zenith, use of halo (divine light) started.

Mughal Period Literature

Scholars	Works
▪ Khan Abdur Rahman	Translated **Tuzuki-i-Baburi** from Turki to Persian during Akbar's reign.
▪ Abul Fazal	Ain-i-Akbari, Akbarnama.
▪ Abdul Qadir Badauni	Kitab-ul-Ahadish, Tarikh-i-Alffi, Muntakhab-ul-Tawarikh.
▪ Khwaja Nizamuddin	Tabaqat-i-Akbari
▪ Jahangir	Tuzuk-i-Jahangiri (in Persion).
▪ Hamid	Padshah Namaah
▪ Khafi Khan	Muntakhab-i-Lubab
▪ Dara Shikoh	Translated Upanishadas and Bhagavada Gita, Safinat-ul-Auliya, Hasrat-Ul-Arifim.
▪ Mirza Muhammad Quzim	Alamgirnamah
▪ Ishwar Das	Fatuhat-i-Alamgiri
▪ Muhammad Salih	Shahjahanama

SHERSHAH SURI AND AFGHAN EMPIRE (1540-55)

- His real name was **Farid**.
- He was born to **Hasan**, a Jagirdar of Sasharam and Hajipur. Ibrahim Lodhi transferred his *jagir* to him.
- He joined Babar Khan Lohanis service and then appointed as the Deputy Governor of Bihar.
- He usurped the throne as 'Hazarat-i-Ala'.
- He gained Chunar by marrying a widow Lad Malika.
- **Battle of Chausa** In 1539, he captured Chausa from Humayun. He assumed the title of Shershah as emperor.
- He also issued coins and Khutba was read in his name. The whole area from Bengal to Banaras was under his empire.

- **Battle of Kannauj** He also annexed Kannauj after defeating Humayun.
- **Battle of Samel** (1544) Defeated Rajput forces of Marwar.
- The campaign of Bundelkhand was the last campaign of his life. While besieging its fort at Kalinjar, Sher Shah got burned due to fire in the bundle of rockets in 1545.

Administration

- For administrative convenience, Shershah divided his whole empire ⸱o 47 divisions called Sarkars and ⸱urther into smaller Parganas.
- *Pargana*, composed of number of villages and was under the charge of *Shiqdar*, who looked after the law, the order and general administration of the *Pargana*. The *Amil* or *Munsif* looked after the collection of land revenue in the *Pargana*.

Central Departments	
• *Diwan-i-Wazarat*	revenue and finance
• *Diwan-i-Ariz*	military
• *Diwan-i-Insha*	dispatches.
• *Diwan-i-Rasalat*	correspondence.

- Civil cases of the pargana was headed by Amin and criminal cases by a Qazi or *Mini-i-Adal*.
- He introduced the principle of local responsibility for local crimes.

Revenue System

- Land was measured using the **Sikandari-gaz** ; one-third of the average produce was fixed as tax.
- The peasant was given a Patta and Qabuliyat, which fixed the peasants rights and taxes.
- *Zamindars*, were removed and taxes were directly collected.

Others

- Shershah introduced a regular postal service.
- He introduced silver *rupiya*.
- He promoted trade and commerce by reducing the number of customs duty at collection points.
- Shershah improved the transportation by building roads. The roads built by Sher Shah were termed as 'the arteries of the empire'. **Sarais** were built on the road. He restored the old imperial road Grand Trunk from Sonargaon in Bengal to Peshawar.
- He built **Purana Qila**, alongwith Grand-Trunk. He also built his tomb at Sasaram in Bihar.
- Malik-Muhammad Jayasi wrote Padmavat (Hindi) during his reign.
- Tarikh-i-Shershahi was written by Abbas Khan Sarwani, his court historian.

THE MARATHA AGE

Shivaji

- Shivaji belonged to the Bhonsle Clan of Marathas. Shivaji's father Shahji Bhonsle was a military commander under Nizam Shahi ruler of Ahmednagar.
- Shivaji was born to Jijabai in the hill fortress of Shivner. Shivaji's early career and life was influenced by Jijabai, his mother, Dadaji Kondev, the manager of his father's Jagir and Guru Ramdas, his spiritual teacher.
- Dadaji Kondev gave him training in civil and military administration.
- Before that, in 1646, he conquered the fort of Torna and built forts at Raigarh and Pratapgarh. In 1647, he assumed full charge of his *Jagir*.
- In 1659, Shivaji killed Afzal Khan, Ambassador of Ali Adil Shah (Sultan of Bijapur), in a meeting with his tiger paws. The Sultan then acknowledged the independent status of Shivaji.

- Later, Shaista Khan, a Governor of Deccan, was deputed by Aurangzeb to put down the rising power of Shivaji in 1660. Shivaji lost Poona and suffered several defeats, till he made a bold attack on Shaista's military camp at night and plundered Surat and later Ahmednagar.
- Raja Jai Singh of Amber was then appointed by Aurangzeb to put down Shivaji (1665) and Jai Singh succeeded in besieging Shivaji in the fort of Purandhar. Consequently, the Treaty of Purandhar (1665) was signed according to which, Shivaji ceded some forts to the Mughals and paid a visit to the Mughal court at Agra. Shivaji also agreed to help Mughals in their attack on Bijapur.
- Shivaji visited Agra with his son Shambhaji in 1666. He was put on house arrest but escaped from there.
- He, very soon, conquered the forts which he had surrendered to the Mughals. He defeated the Mughal forces in the **Battle of Salher** in 1672.

- He was crowned in 1674 at Raigarh and assumed the title of **Haindava Dharmodharak** (protection of Hinduism) and Chhatrapati. He became the sovereign ruler of Maharashtra. He died in 1680.

Shivaji's Administration

- Shivaji divided the territories under his rule into three provinces (prants), each under a Viceroy. Provinces were divided into *Prants*, which were subdivided into *Parganas or Tarafs*. The lowest unit was village, headed by a headman or *patel*.
- Shivaji was helped by **Ashtapradhan** (eight ministers), which was unlike a Council of Ministers, for there was no collective responsibility. Each minister was directly responsible to Shivaji.
- His administrative reforms were guided by Malik Amber of Ahmednagar.

Shivaji's Revenue Administration

- Assessment of land revenue was based on measurement. The Kathi of Amber was adopted as the unit of measurement.
- **Chauth** was one-fourth of the land revenue paid to the Marathas so as not to be subjected to Maratha's raid.
- **Sardeshmukhi** was an additional levy of 10 per cent (1/10th) on those lands of Maharashtra, over which the Marathas claimed hereditary right, but which formed part of the Mughal empire.

MARATHAS AFTER SHIVAJI

- There was a dispute of succession between Sambhaji and Rajaram.
- Son of Shivaji, Sambhaji (1680-89) succeeded the throne. He was an incapable ruler and poor diplomat.
- **Prince Akbar**, the rebellious son of Aurangzeb took shelter with him. Sambhaji was executed by Aurangzeb and his infant son, Shahu, was taken captive by Aurangzeb. Sambhaji was succeeded by Rajaram in 1689.
- **Rajaram** (1689-1700) was killed in 1700 by Aurangzeb. His widow **Tarabai** put her infant son, Shivaji II, on the throne.
- After Aurangzeb's death in 1707, Shahu, the grandson of Shivaji and son of Sambhaji was released by Bahadur Shah. He claimed the throne and this led to a civil war between Shahu and Tarabai. Shahu emerged victorious in the **Battle of Khed**, with the help of Balaji Vishwanath. After this, Shahu ruled from Satara and Tarabai from Kolhapur. From now onwards, the rule of *Peshwa* started. They became virtual rulers of the state.

Shivaji's Ashtapradhan

Ashtapradhan	Department
Peshwa (*Mukhya Pradhan*)	Prime Minister, Finance
Sar-i-Naubat/Senapati	Military Commander
Majumdar or Amatya	Accountant General (*revenue and finance minister during the Peshwas*)
Waqenavis/Mantri	Intelligence, posts and household affairs
Surunavis or Sachiv	Minister for Correspondence
Dabir or Sumanta	Foreign Minister and Minister of royal ceremonies
Nyayadhish	Administration of Justice
Pandit Rao	Charity and religious affairs

THE PESHWAS
(AD 1713–1818)

Balaji Viswanath (1713–1720)

- He excelled in diplomacy and won over many Maratha chiefs to the side of Shahu. Shahu honoured him with title of '**Sena Karta**' in 1708, and made him his *Peshwa* in 1713. The *Peshwa* concentrated all the powers in his office. He became the functional head of the Maratha empire.
- He concluded an agreement with the Sayyid brothers, by which the Mughal emperor (Farrukhsiyar) recognised Shahu as the king of *Swarajya*.
- He also helped Sayyid brothers in over throwing Farrukhsiyar.

Baji Rao (1720-1740)

- He was a bold and brilliant commander and was considered the greatest exponent in guerilla tactics after Shivaji. Maratha power reached its zenith under him.
- Under his leadership, the Marathas compelled the Mughals first to give them the right to collect *chauth* of the vast areas and then to cede those areas to the Maratha kingdom.
- He conquered Salsettle and Bassin from Portuguese in 1733. He also defeated the Nizam-ul-Mulk near Bhopal and concluded the treaty of **Durai Sarai**, *via* which he got Malwa and Bundelkhand (1737).

Balaji Baji Rao
(Nana Sahib) (1740-1761)

- In an agreement with the Mughal emperor (Ahmed Shah), the *Peshwa* agreed to protect the Mughal empire from internal and external enemies in return for the *chauth*.
- In the Third Battle of Panipat in 1761, between Maratha and Ahmed Shah Abdali, Viswas Rao, the son of Nana Sahib died.

Peshwa Madhav Rao I (1761-1762)

- Balaji Baji Rao was succeded by his younger son Madhav Rao I. Raghunath Rao, the eldest surviving member of Peshwa family, became regent to the young *Peshwa* and de-facto ruler of the state.
- After the death of Madhav Rao, Peshwaship had lost its all power.

LATER PESHWAS

- Narayan Rao (1772-73)
- Sawai Madhav Rao (1773-95)
- Baji Rao II (1795-1818)

MODERN INDIA

ADVENT OF THE EUROPEANS

Portuguese

- The Cape Route from Europe to India was discovered by **Vasco da Gama**. He reached Port of Calicut via Cape of Good Hope (Africa) on 17th May, 1498 and was received by the Hindu ruler of Calicut, **Zamorin**. This led to the establishment of trading stations at **Calicut**, **Cochin** and **Cannanore**.
- Cochin (1502) was the initial capital of the Portuguese in India, later on replaced by **Goa**.
- The first Governor of Portuguese in India was **Francisco Almeida** (1505-09). He introduced '**The Policy of Blue Water**'.
- **Alfonso d' Albuquerque** arrived in India in 1503 and became Governor of the Portuguese in India in 1509. He captured Goa from the ruler of Bijapur in 1310 and introduced the policy of Imperialism.
- **Nino-da-Cunha** (1529-1538) transferred the capital from Cochin to Goa in 1530. He acquired Diu and Bassein from Bahadur Shah of Gujarat (1534).
- Portuguese acquired Daman in 1559. They lost Hugly in 1631, during the reign of Shah Jahan.
- In 1661, the Portuguese king gave Bombay to Charles II of England as dowry, for marrying his sister.
- First Portuguese factory was established at **Calicut**.
- The famous Jesuit Saint, **Francisco Xavier** arrived in India with Martin Alfonso de Souza (1542-45).
- Gradually, almost all of their territories were lost to Marathas (Salsette and Bassein in 1739), Dutch and English. Only Goa, Diu and Daman remained with them until 1961.

Dutch

- The Dutch East India Company established factories in India at Masulipatnam in 1605, Pulicat (1610), Surat (1616), Bimlipatam (1641), Karaikal (1645), Chinsura, Kasimbazar, Patna, Balasore, Nagapatam and Cochin.
- They replaced the Portuguese as the most dominant power in European trade with East.
- Pulicat was their main centre in India till Nagapatam replaced it in 1690.
- The Dutch conceded to British after their defeat in the **Battle of Bedera** in 1759.

English

- Before the establishment of the East India Company, **John Mildenhall**, an English merchant came to India over land route to trade with Indian merchants in 1599.
- The English East India Company was formed by a group of merchants in 1599 known as **Merchant Adventures**.
- Jahangir issued a *farman* to **Captain Hawkins** (1609) permitting him to establish a factory at Surat.
- **Sir Thomas Roe** visited Jahangir's court (1615) as an ambassador of king James I to seek permission to trade in India.
- First factory was built at Surat (1608). Surat was replaced by Bombay acquired from Charles-II on lease as the headquarters on the West coast in 1687.
- In 1639, obtained Madras from Raja of Chandragiri with permission to build a fortified factory, which was named **Fort St George**.
- In 1690, Job Charnock, established a factory at Sutanati and the *Zamindari* of three villages Sutanati, Kalikata and Govindpur were acquired by the British (1698). These three villages grew as city of Calcutta.
- The factory at Sutanati was fortified and named **Fort William** in 1700.
- In 1717, John Surman obtained royal *farman* from Mughal emperor Farrukhsiyar. This *farman* is also called the *Magna Carta of the British rule* in India as it gave large concessions to the company.

Danes

- The Danes arrived in India in 1616. They established settlement at **Tranqueber** (Tamil Nadu) in 1620 and **Serampore** (Bengal) in 1676. Serampore was their headquarters.
- They were forced to sell their settlements to the British in 1854.

French

- The French East India Company was formed in 1664 by **Colbert** under state patronage during the reign of **Louis XIV**.

- The first French factory was established at Surat by **Francois Caron** in 1668 and second at **Masulipatnam** in 1669.
- They occupied **Mahe, Yanam** and **Karaikal**.
- The foundation of Pondicherry was laid in 1673, which afterwards became their capital. They also developed a factory at Chandernagar.
- The Governors, **Lenoir** and **Dumas** revived the French power in India between 1720-42 and the Anglo-French conflict started with the arrival of Governor Dupleix in 1742.

INDEPENDENT STATES

HYDERABAD

- Founded by Nizam-ul-Mulk Asaf Jahan in AD 1724. His original name was **Chin Qilich Khan** but emperor Farrukhsiyar conferred on him the titles of *'Khan-i-Duran'* and later *'Nizam-ul-Mulk'*.
- Puran Chand was his *diwan*.
- Carnatic was one of the *Subah* of Deccan hence, it was under Nizam of Hyderabad.
- Nizam of Hyderabad became independent of Delhi and deputy Governor of Carnatic made himself independent of Hyderabad, hence assumed the title *'Nawab of Carnatic'*.
- Saadautullah Khan of Carnatic made his nephew Dost Ali as his successor at Carnatic without the approval of Nizam. This caused rivalry between Carnatic and Hyderabad.
- Hyderabad remained independent until it became a part of Independent India. The Nizam provided assistance to the British during the 1857 Revolt.

AWADH

- Founded by **Saadat Khan Burhan-ul-Mulk**. Emperor Muhammad Shah appointed him as Governor of Awadh in AD 1722.
- Committed suicide in 1739 and was succeeded by his nephew Safdar Jung.

- The highest post of his government was held by Maharaja Nawab Rai. This shows his religious tolerance towards the Hindus.

MYSORE

- **Haider Ali** started his career as a soldier in Mysore state, promoted to Commander-in-Chief and later to *Faujadar* at Dindigul.
- In 1761, he overthrew Nanjaraja and established his authority over Mysore. He established a Modern Arsenal in Dindigul.
- In 1769, he repeatedly defeated the British in **First Anglo-Mysore War** and reached the walls of Madras. He died in 1782 during **Second Anglo-Mysore War**.
- **Tipu Sultan** (1782-99) succeeded Haider Ali. He planted the **Tree of Liberty** at Srirangapatnam and became a member of the *Jacobian Club*.
- He died in 1799, fighting at the gates of Srirangapatnam during the 4th **Anglo-Mysore War**.
- He was tolerant and enlightened in his approach towards other religions. He gave money for the construction of image of Goddess Sarda on the Shrinageri temple. The famous temple of Sri Rangnath was situated barely a hundred yards from his palace. He assumed the title of *Padshah* in 1797.

BENGAL

- **Murshid Quli Khan** (1717-27) He was made Governor of Bengal (1717) and Orissa (1719). He transferred capital of Bengal from Dacca to Murshidabad. He died in 1727.
- **Shuja-ud-din** (1727-39) He was granted Governorship of Bihar by Mughal emperor Muhammad Shah Rangeela.
- **Sarfaraz Khan** (1739-40) Alivardi Khan deposed and killed Shuja-ud- din's son, Sarfaraz Khan and made himself Nawab.
- **Alivardi Khan** (1746) Bribed Muhammad Shah Rangeela and legalised his position by receiving a *farman* from him. He prevented the English and French fortifications at Calcutta and Chandranagar respectively.

Shiraj-ud-Daula (1756-57)

- Under the *farman* of 1717, the Company had rights to import or export their goods in Bengal without paying tax and right to issue passes or *dastaks*. *Dastaks* were misused for private trade by Company's servants.
- In 1756, Siraj-ud-Daula seized the English factory at Kasimbazar and marched to Calcutta and occupied Fort William. **Black hole tragedy** took place. Robert Clive recovered Calcutta and **Treaty of Alinagar** was signed on 2nd January, 1757.
- **Battle of Plassey** On 23rd June, 1757, English won the battle against Siraj-ud-daula, and compelled the Nawab to concede all the demands.
- Mir Jafar, (*Mir Bakhsh*), Manik Chand (Officer incharge of Calcutta), Aminchand (rich Sikh merchant), Jagat Seth (banker), Khadim Khan (Commander of Nawab's army) all were on the English side.
- Mir Madan and Mohan Lal, Nawab's soldiers, fought bravely.
- Nawab was killed by Mir Jafar's son Miran.

Mir Jafar (1757-60)

- Mir Jafar was the first Nawab of Bengal, Bihar and Orissa under the British rule in India.
- He granted free trade right to the Company in Bengal, Bihar and Orissa.
- In 1760, Mir Jafar was replaced by his son-in-law, Mir Qasim.

Mir Qasim (1760-64)

- Mir Qasim ceded Burdwan, Midnapur and Chittagong. He shifted his capital from Murshidabad to Monghyr.
- Mir Qasim soon revolted as he was angry with the British for misusing *dastaks* (free duty passes).
- **Battle of Buxar** He formed an alliance with Nawab of Awadh, Shuja-ud-daula and Mughal Emperor Shah Alam-II and fought with the British army at Buxar on 22nd October, 1764. Mir Jafar was again put on the throne by the Britishers.
- On Mir Jafar's death, his son Nizam-ud-daula was placed on the throne and he signed a treaty on 20th February, 1765, by which the Nawab had to disband most of his army and to administer Bengal through a deputy *subedar* nominated by the company.
- Robert Clive became the first Governor of Bengal in 1765.
- After the Battle of Buxar, the Company gave Shah Alam-II a subsidary of ₹ 26 lakh and secured *Diwani* of Arrah and Allahabad.
- The important outcome is the **Treaty of Allahabad**.

Treaty of Allahabad (August, 1765)

- English got the *Diwani* rights (right to collect revenue) of Bengal, Bihar and Orissa) and gave 26 lakhs.
- The Dual Government of Bengal was established in 1765, wherein the company got the right to collect revenue but the *Nizamat right* (duty of administration) was with the Nawab.
- **Warren Hastings** ended the **Dual System** of Government in 1772.

ASCENDANCY OF THE BRITISH

Carnatic Wars

First War (AD 1746-48)

- A war between France and England.
- Nawab of Carnatic's army was defeated by French under Dupleix, in the **Battle at St Thome**. Afterwards, the French besieged Madras.
- The war ended with Treaty of **Aix-la-Chapelle** (1748), which also ended the Austrian war of succession.

Second War (AD 1749-54)

- Dupleix alligned with Muzaffar Jung (Hyderabad) and Chanda Sahib (Carnatic).
- After initial victory of the French, ultimately Robert Clive emerged victorious.
- War ended with **Treaty of Pondicherry/ Treaty of Godehu**.
- The **Siege of Arcot** (1751) made Clive a national hero in England.

Third War (AD 1758-63)

- French Governor **Count de Lally** captured Fort St David.
- French were defeated by British in the decisive **Battle at Wandiwash** in AD 1760. Pondicherry was returned to France by **Treaty of Paris**.
- Local version of "seven years war" in Europe.

Anglo-Mysore Wars

First War (1766-69)

Haider Ali defeated the British, **Treaty of Madras signed**.

Second War (1780-84)

- Warren Hastings attacked French port Mahe, which was in Haider Ali's territory. Haider Ali led a joint front with Nizam and Maratha and captured Arcot. In 1781, Haider Ali was defeated at Porto Novo by Eyre Coote.
- **Treaty of Mangalore** (1784) was signed by Tipu Sultan on the basis of all mutual restitution of conquests.

Third War (1789-92)

- Marathas and Nizam aided the British, Lord Cornwallis captured Bangalore.
- **Treaty of Seringapatnam signed;** Tipu ceded half of his territories.

Fourth War (1799)

- Lord Wellesley attacked, Tipu died while fighting.
- Tipu used the iron (–) cased rockets in the 3rd and 4th **Anglo- Mysore Wars**.
- It placed England on the military supremacy in India.

Anglo-Maratha Wars

First War (1775-82)

- English favoured Raghunath Rao to become the *Peshwa* but were defeated and signed the **Convention of Wadgaon**.
- British later signed **Treaty of Salbai** renouncing the cause of Raghunath Rao.

Second War (1803-06)

The Peshwas signed the **Treaty of Bassein** (1802), which was a treaty for subsidiary alliances.

Third War (1817-19)

Lord Hastings moved against Marathas and Marathas were decisively defeated.

Anglo-Sikh Wars

Began after the death of Ranjit Singh in 1839.

The Sikhs (Punjab)

- **Guru Nanak** (1469-1539) Born in Talwandi, he was the first Sikh guru and established **Nanak Panth**.
- **Guru Angad** (1539-52) Invented **Gurumukhi** script for Punjabi language.
- **Guru Amardas** (1552-74) Divided his spiritual empire into 22 parts called *Manjis*, which was put under the charge of a Sikh. Mughal Emperor Akbar visited him.
- **Guru Ramdas** (1575-81) Founded the city of Amritsar. He dug a tank (sarovar) and constructed **Harmandir Sahib** in the midst of the tank.
- **Guru Arjun Dev** (1581-1606) He compiled the **Adi Granth**. Completed the construction of Amritsar and founded the cities of Taran and Kartarpur. He was executed by Jahangir.
- **Guru Har Govind Rai** (1606-45) Transformed Sikhs into warrior class and defeated Mughal army at Sangrama. Fortified Amritsar and built **Akal Takhqt** at Golden Temple. Took the title of *'Padshah'* and founded the city of Kiratpur in Kashmir.
- **Guru Har Rai** (AD 1645-61)He met Dara Shikoh, son of Aurangzeb.
- **Guru Har Kishan** (1661-64) Ramraya established separate seat of Guru at Dehradun.
- **Guru Teg Bahadur** (1664-75) Executed by Aurangzeb at Delhi. Sis Ganj Gurudwara marks the site of his martyrdom.
- **Guru Gobind Singh** (1675-1708) (born in Patna) He organised a community of warriors called Khalsa (Baisakhi Day, 1699), summoned the assembly of Sikhs at Anantpur and 5 persons were selected (*Panj Piaras*), who took the water of immortality.
- The Sikhs were required to keep *5 k's viz Kesh, Kripan, Kachcha, Kangha* and *Kara*. He compiled **Dasween Padshah ka Granth**. He was stabbed to death by a Pathan in 1708.
- **Maharaja Ranjeet Singh** (1792-1839) Born in 1780 at Gujranwala, he founded the Sikh rule in Punjab. He occupied Lahore in 1799 and made it his capital. He annexed Amritsar (1802), Ludhiana, Kangra, Multan, attacked Kashmir and Peshawar. He died in 1839.
- **Successors of Ranjit Singh** Kharak Singh (1839-40), Naunihal Singh (1840), Sher Singh (1841-43), Dalip Singh (1843-49).

First War (1845-46)

Sikh were defeated, **'Treaty of Lahore' ended the war.**

Second War (1948-49)

Dalhousie annexed Punjab. Sir John Lawrence became the first Commissioner of Punjab.

Anglo-Burmese Wars

Burma was united by king **Aloung Paya** between 1752-60. His successor Bodopaya repelled many Chinese invasions and conquered the states of Arakan and Manipur (1813).

First War (1824)

In 1824, British Indian authority declared war on Burma and occupied Rangoon and reached the capital Ava, peace came in 1826 by **Treaty of Yandabo.**

Second War (1852)

Annexation of Pegu, the capital province only remained free.

Third War (1885)

British attacked over Burma and Thibaw surrendered. In 1935, Burma was separated from India. Movement of Burma reached a new height under leadership of U Aung San and Burma got independence.

Anglo-Afghan Wars

First War (1839-42) or Auckland's Folly

- In 1839, British replaced Dost Muhammad by placing Shah Shuja. British faced a popular revolt but were able to re-occupy Kabul. However, they had to restore the throne to Dost Muhammad. British occupied Kabul in 1842.

Second War (1878-80)

- British India attacked Afghanistan during period of Sher Ali. Sher Ali was defeated by Lord Lytton and his sons signed the **Treaty of Gandamak** (Yakub Khan).
- British adopted the principle of non-interference.

Third War

- Durand line was reaffirmed between British India and Afghanistan.
- **Treaty of Rawalpindi** was signed.
- Afghan independence with full sovereignty in Foreign Affairs.

ECONOMIC AND COMMERCIAL POLICY

The 'gradual development of Economic and Commerical Policy has been traced through three stages of British colonialism by **RP Dutta**.

Phases of Economic Policy

Early Phase (1600-1757)

The East India Company was purely a trading company, dealing with import of goods and precious metals into India and export of spices and textiles.

Mercantile Phase (1757-1813)

They imposed their own prices and had no relation with the cost of production. The Company used its political power and monopolised trade and dictated terms to the weavers of Bengal. The Company used revenue of Bengal to finance exports of Indian goods.

Industrial Phase (1813-1858)

The British mercantile industrial capitalist class exploited India. Charter Act of 1813, allowed 'one way free trade' for British citizens resulting in Indian markets flooded with cheap and machine made imported goods from Britain. Indians not only lost their foreign markets but their Indian markets also.

Finance Imperialism

(1858 Onwards)

This phase saw export of capital from India and also chains of British controlled banks, export import firms and managing agency houses. Exploitation through railways is the best example of finance Imperialism.

Drain of Wealth Theory

- "Drain of Wealth" refers to a portion of National Product of India, which was not available for consumption of its own people.
- **Dadabhai Naoroji** first cited the drain of wealth theory in his book titled **Poverty and Un-British Rule in India**.
- RC Dutt blamed the British policy for Indian economic ills in his book **Economic History of India**.
- Drain of wealth began in 1757 after Battle of Plassey. In 1765, the company acquired the *diwani* of Bengal and began the purchase of Indian goods out of the revenue of Bengal and exported them. These purchases were known as Company's investments.

LAND REVENUE SYSTEMS

Permanent Settlement

- Introduced in **Bengal**, **Bihar** and **Orissa**, districts of **Banaras** and Northern districts of **Madras** by Lord Cornwallis in 1793.
- John Shore planned this settlement.
- Assured of their ownership, many *zamindars* stayed in towns and exploited their tenants.
- It declared *zamindars* as the owners of the land. Hence, they could keep 1/11th of the revenue collected to themselves while the British got a fixed share of 10/11th of the revenue collected. The *zamindars* were free to fix the rate.

Ryotwari Settlement

- Introduced in Bombay, Madras and Assam. Munro and Charles Reed recommended it.
- In this, the direct settlement was made between the Government and the *Ryots*.
- The revenue was based on the basis of the quality of the soil and the nature of the crop. The revenue was fixed for a period not exceeding 30 years. It was based on the 'Scientific Rent Theory of Ricardo.'
- The position of the cultivator became more secure.

Mahalwari System

- Introduced in the area of **Ganga valley**, North-West Frontier Provinces parts of **Central India** and **Punjab**.
- **Revenue Settlement** was to be made by village or estates with landlords. A settlement was made with the village, which maintained a form of common ownership known as **Bhaichara** or with **Mahals**, which were group of villages. Revenue was periodically revised.

REVOLT OF 1857

CAUSES OF THE REVOLT

- **Political** Nana Sahib was refused pension as he was the adopted son of Peshwa Baji Rao-II to lead the revolt at Kanpur.
- **Awadh** (Lucknow) was annexed in 1856, on charge of maladministration and Jhansi was annexed owing to the **Doctrine of Lapse**.

Military Discrimination

Indian soldiers were paid low salaries, they could not rise above the rank of *Subedar* and were racially insulted.

Religious Discrimination

The social reforms by British was against the people's will (widow remarriage, abolition of sati, school for girls, Christian missionaries etc). Soldiers were asked to use the *Enfield Rifles* with greased (by pork or beef) cartridges.

Economic Grievances

Heavy taxations, discriminatory tariff policy; destruction of traditional handicrafts that hit peasants, artisans and small zamindars.

Outbreak of the Revolt

- **Bengal Resentment** in which 19 native infantries of Behrampur, refused to use the newly introduced Enfield Rifle.
- **Mangal Pandey** 34th native infantry fired at the sergeant major of his regiment. Known as a part of Mutiny of Barrackpur.

- Mangal Pandey was hanged.
- On 10th May, 1857, the sepoys at Meerut refused to use Enfiled Rifles and revolted. The mutiny spread throughout Uttar Pradesh and sepoys moved to Delhi crying **March to Delhi**.
- At Delhi, Bahadur Shah II was declared '*Shahenshah-i-Hindustan.*'
- Where the rulers were loyal to the British, the soldiers revolted as in Gwalior and Indore. In some places, people revolted before the sepoys.
- In the beginning, the rebels were successful. Europeans were killed, police stations and law courts were attacked and revenue records were destroyed. But, the revolt was soon suppressed.

Centres of Revolt and their Leaders

- **Delhi** Bahadur Shah II, General Bakht Khan
- **Kanpur** Nana Sahib/Dhondhu Pant (adopted son of Baji Rao-II) Tantia Tope, Azimullah khan
- **Jhansi** Rani Lakshmi Bai
- **Lucknow** Begum Hazrat Mahal, her son Birjis Qadir.
- **Faizabad** Maulavi Ahamdullah
- **Bareilley** Khan Bahadur Khan
- **Bihar** (Arrah) Kunwar Singh, Zamindar of Jagdishpur.

Suppression of the Revolt

- **John Lawrence** remarked, "Had a single leader of ability arisen among them we must have been lost beyond redemption." Delhi was captured on 20th September, 1857 by **John Nicholson** and Bahadur Shah II was deported to Rangoon, where he died in 1862. His sons were shot dead at Delhi.

- Jhansi was captured by Hugh Rose on 17th June, 1858. Rani Lakshmi Bai died in the battle field.
- Lucknow was recaptured on 21st March, 1858 by Colin Campbell, **Havelock** and **Outram**.
- Nana Sahib and Hazrat Mahal both escaped to Nepal.
- **William Taylor** and **Edgre** suppressed the revolt at Arrah. Tantia Tope was betrayed by a friend. He was captured and executed on 15th April, 1859.

Rani Lakshmi Bai

Rani Lakshmi Bai, nicknamed Manu, was married to Raja Gangadhar Rao in 1842. The couple adopted a child in 1853 but Lord Dalhousie wished to annex Jhansi under the Doctrine of Lapse. Rani did not surrender and died fighting at Kalpi near Jhansi during the Revolt of 1857.

Causes Behind the Failure of the Revolt

- Lack of unity and poor organisation of the revolt. All the classes of the society were not effected or participated in the revolt.
- Lack of common motive for participating in the revolt. Some of the rulers like **Scindhias**, **Nizam** and **Holkars** helped Britishers in reppressing the revolt.
- The military equipments of rebels were inferior.

- The most significant feature of the revolt was the exhibition of Hindu–Muslim Unity.
- Concentrated on the Northern part of India.

The following historians had different views on the revolt.

Historian	Views on the revolt
VD Savarkar	'First war of Independence.'
RC Majumdar	'Neither 'first' nor 'national' nor a war of independence.'
Disraeli	'A national revolt rooted indeep mistrust.'
Malleson	'Sepoy mutiny'.

Impacts of the Revolt

- In August 1858, the British Parliament passed an Act, which put an end to the rule of the Company. The responsibility of the administration of British India passed into the hands of the **British Queen** and the Parliament.
- An office of the Secretary of State for India with a 15 members' council was constituted for the administration of India.
- The designation of the **Governor- General** was changed to **Viceroy**, who was to act as a representative.
- 'Doctrine of Lapse' was withdrawn. Princely states were assured against annexation.
- The British pursued the **divide and rule** policy.
- Increase in the number of **white soldiers** in the army.
- Total expense of the suppression was borne by the Indians.

Opinions on the Nature of the 1857 Revolt

Opinion-Maker	Nature of Revolt
Sir John Seeley	Wholly unpatriotic and selfish sepoy mutiny with no native leadership
T R Holmes	A conflict between civilsation and barbarism
Outram and Taylor	A Hindu-Muslim conspiracy
VD Savarkar	Indian War of Independence
Bipin Chandra	The entire movement lacked a unified and forward looking programme to be implemented after the capture of power
SN Sen	What began as a fight for religion ended as a war of independence
Benjamin Disraeli	Is it a military mutiny or is it a national revolt?
Dr RC Majumdar	The so called First National War of Independence 1857, is neither First, nor National, nor War of Independence

GOVERNOR-GENERALS OF BENGAL

Warren Hastings (1772-85)

- He became Governor of Bengal in 1772 and first Governor-General of Bengal in 1773, through the **Regulating Act** of 1773.
- He abolished the **dual system of administration**.
- Divided Bengal into districts and appointed collectors and other revenue officials.
- Established India's first Supreme Court in Calcutta.
- He founded **Asiatic Society of Bengal** with William Jones in 1784 and wrote introduction to the first English translation of the **Gita** by **Charles Wilkins**.
- Started *Diwani* and *Faujdari adalats* and the district level *Sadar diwani* and *Nizmat adalats* (appellate courts).
- He redefined Hindu and Muslim laws. A translation of code in Sanskrit appeared under the title 'Code of Gentoo laws'.
- First Anglo-Maratha War occurred during his period, which ended with **Treaty** of **Salbai** (1776-82).
- Second Anglo-Mysore War (1780-84), ended with **Treaty of Mangalore**.
- Rohilla War in 1774.
- Pitts India Act, 1784 and Edmund Burke Bill, 1783 was passed.
- Deprived *zamindar* of their judicial powers. Maintenance of records was made compulsory.
- Impeachment proceedings started against him in Britain on the charges of taking bribes. After a trial of 7 years, he was finally acquitted.

Lord Cornwallis (1786-1793)

- First person to codify laws (1793). The code separated the revenue administration from the administration of justice.
- He introduced *Izaredari System* in 1773.
- He started the **Permanent Settlement of Bengal**.
- He created the post of **District Judge**. He is known as **Father of Civil Services in India**.

- Third Anglo-Mysore War and the **Treaty of Seringapatnam**.
- He undertook police reforms.
- Reform of the Judiciary (1793) setting up courts at different levels and separation of revenue administration from Judicial administration.

Sir John Shore (1793-1798)

- He played an important role in planning the **Permanent Settlement**.
- He introduced **First Charter Act** (1793).
- He was famous for his policy of non-interference.
- **Battle of Kharla** between Nizam and Marathas (1759).

Lord Wellesley (1798-1803)

- Introduced the system of **Subsidiary Alliance**. Madras presidency was formed during his tenure.
- **In Fourth Anglo-Mysore** War 1799, Tipu Sultan died.
- First subsidiary treaty with Nizam of Hyderabad.
- Second Anglo-Maratha War.
- In 1800, he set-up **Fort William College** in Calcutta. He was famous as *Bengal Tiger*. He brought the Censorship of Press Act, 1799.

Subsidiary Alliance

- The subsidiary alliance system was used by Wellesley to bring Indian states within the orbit of British political power.
- Under this system, the ruler of the allying Indian state was compelled to accept the Permanent Stationing of a British force within his territory and to pay a subsidy for its maintenance. British promised that they will not interfere in the internal affairs but this was a promise they seldom kept.
- It disarmed the Indian states and threw British protectorate over them.
- First to accept subsidiary alliance was **Nizam of Hyderabad** 1798, the second was the Nawab of Awadh, 1801.
- The Peshwa, the Bhonsle, the Scindhia and Rajputs of Jodhpur, Jaipur accepted the subsidiary alliance.

Sir George Barlow (1805-07)
- Vellore mutiny (1806, by soldiers).
- Second Anglo-Maratha War ended.

Lord Minto I (1807-1813)
- Treaty of Amritsar (1809) with Ranjit Singh.
- The Charter Act of 1813 ended the monopoly of East India Company in India.

Lord Hastings (1813-23)
- Adopted the policy of intervention and war.
- Anglo-Nepal War (1813-23).
- Third Anglo-Maratha War (1817-18).

- Introduced the Ryotwari settlement in Madras by Thomas Munro, the Governor.
- **Treaty of Sangli** with Gorkhas (1816).
- **Treaty of Poona** (1817) with the the Peshwa.
- Suppression of Pindaris (1817-1818).

Lord Amherst (1823-28)
- First Anglo Burmese War (1824-26), signed **Treaty of** Gandaboo in 1826 with lower Burma of Pegu, by which British merchants were allowed to settle on Southern coast of Burma.
- Acquisition of Malaya Peninsula and Bharatpur (1826).

GOVERNOR-GENERALS OF INDIA

Lord William Bentinck (1828-1834)
- Most liberal and enlightened amongst all the Governor-Generals of India,
- Regarded as the '**Father of Modern Western Education in India**'.
- Abolition of Sati in 1829.
- Suppression of *Thugi* (1830).
- Passed the Charter Act, of 1833.
- Deposition of Raja of Mysore and annexation of his territories (1831).
- Abolition of Provincial court of Appeal and appointment of commissioners instead. **He was the First Governor-General of India**.
- **First Medical College** was opened in Calcutta in 1835.
- **Treaty of Friendship** with Ranjit Singh (1831).
- Annexed Coorg (1834) and Central Cachar (1831).

Sir Charles Metcalfe (1834-36)
Passed the famous Press Law, which liberated the press in India. He is known as the **liberator of press**.

Lord Auckland (1836-42)
- First Afghan War (1836-42).
- Death of Ranjit Singh (1839).

Lord Ellenborough (1842-44)
- Brought an end to the Afghan War (1842).
- Abolished Slavery
- Sind was annexed by Charles Napier. He was appointed as **First Governor of Sind**.

Lord Hardinge (1844-48)
- First Anglo-Sikh War and the Treaty of Lahore.

Lord Dalhousie (1848-56)
- Second Anglo-Sikh War (1848-49) and annexation of Punjab.
- Abolished titles and pensions.
- Widow Remarriage Act (1856).
- Introduced Doctrine of Lapse.
- **Woods Educational Despatch** of 1854.
- Introduction of the **Railway, Telegraph** and the **Postal System** in 1853.
- Establishment of a separate **Public Works Department** in every province.
- An **Engineering College** was established at Roorkee.
- Planned to open universities in Calcutta, Bombay and Madras on the model of Universities of London.
- Second Anglo-Burmese War (1852).
- Santhal uprisings (1855-56).
- Charter Act of 1853.

VICEROYS OF INDIA

Lord Canning (1856-1862)

- Revolt of 1857.
- Universities of Calcutta, Bombay and Madras were opened in 1857.
- He was last Governor-General appointed by the East India Company and the **first Viceroy**.
- Passed the **Government of India Act of 1858**, which ended the rule of the East India Company.
- The Doctrine of Lapse was withdrawn. The **Indian Penal Code** (1859) was passed. Income tax was introduced for the first time in 1858.
- The Indigo riots in Bengal.
- The **Indian Councils Act of 1861** was passed, which proved to be a landmark in the constitutional history of India.
- Indian High Court Act, (1861). Under this act, High Courts were opened in 1865.
- Bombay and Madras founded in 1857.

Lord Elgin-I (1862-63)

- Wahabi Movement suppressed.

Sir John Lawrence (1864-69)

- High Courts were established at Calcutta, Bombay and Madras in 1865. War with Bhutan in 1865.
- The **Punjab Tenancy** Act, was passed.

Lord Mayo (1869-72)

- Introduction of financial decentralisation in India and made the first Provincial Settlement in 1870.
- He established the **Department of Agriculture and Commerce**.
- He organised the Statistical Survey of India. In 1872, the first **Census** was done in India. He established the **Rajkot College** in Kathiawar and **Mayo College** at Ajmer.

- He was the only **Viceroy to be murdered** in office by a convict in the Andaman in 1872.
- He introduced state railways.

Lord Northbrook (1872-76)

- In 1872, Kuka Rebellion in Punjab led by Ram Singh. Famine in Bihar (1876).
- He resigned over Afghanistan question.
- Trial of Gaekwads of Baroda.

Lord Lytton (1876-80)

- Most unpopular Viceroy of India.
- Arranged the Grand Darbar in **Delhi** (in 1877), when the country was suffering from severe famine.
- Passed the Royal Title Act, (1876) and Queen Victoria was declared as **Kaiser-i-Hind**.
- He passed Arms Act, (1878) the infamous **Vernacular Press Act,** (1878) and lowered the maximum age of ICS from 21 to 19 years.
- **Seco**nd **Anglo-Afgan War** 1878-80.
- Famine Commission under Starchy was appointed by him in 1878.
- In 1876, **Deccan Agrarian Relief** Act was passed.

Lord Ripon (1880-1884)

- He was appointed by the Liberal Party under Gladstone. Repealed the Vernacular Press Act in 1882.
- The first Factory Act, came in 1881 (Improve the labour condition).In rural areas, Local Boards were set-up in 1889, Madras Local Board Act, was passed. He was famously known as "**Father of Local Self Government**".
- First Official Census in India (1881).
- Famine code was adopted (1883).
- Appointed **Hunter Commission** for Educational reforms in 1882.
- **Ilbeqrt Bill Controversy** (1883-84), which empowered Indian Judges to inquire into European cases.
- Foundation of **Punjab University**.

Lord Dufferin (1884-88)

- Third Anglo-Burmese War and annexation of Burma (1885).
- Formation of **Indian National Congress** (INC) in 1885.
- Bengal Tenacy Act, in 1885.
- Dufferin called the Indian National Congress as 'microscopic minority'.

Lord Lansdowne (1888-94)

- Factory Act, of 1891.
- Indian Council Act, of 1892.
- Civil Services were classified- Imperial, Provincial and Subordinate services.
- In 1891, Age of Consent Act, under which marriage of girl below 12 years was prohibited.
- Appointment of **Durand Commission in 1893** to define the line between British India and Afghanistan.

Lord Elgin II (1894-1899)

- The Santhal uprising of 1899.
- Munda uprising of 1899.
- Lyall Commission appointed after famine.
- Assassination of two British officials by the Chapekar brothers in 1897.
- Plague spread in Bombay.

Lord Curzon (1899-1905)

- Appointed a Police Commission in 1902 under Andrew Frazer.
- Universities Commission appointed in 1902, under Thomas Railey.
- **Indian Universities Act**, passed in 1904.
- Famine Commission under Macdonell.
- A new Department of Commerce and Industry established.
- Partition of Bengal (16th October, 1905).
- The risings of the frontier tribes in 1897-98 led him to create the North-Western Frontier Province.
- He passed the **Ancient Monuments Protection Act**, (1904) to restore India's cultural heritage. Thus, the **Archaeological Survey of India was established**.
- Passed the **Indian Coinage and Paper Currency Act**, (1899) and put India on a gold standard.
- **PUSA Agricultural Institute** in 1903.

Lord Minto-II (1910-1916)

- Swadeshi Movement.
- **Surat split** (split in Congress between the moderates and the extremists, 1907).
- **Indian Councils Act**, 1909 and Morley-Minto Reforms.
- Foundation of Muslim League, 1906.
- Newspapers Act, 1908.

Lord Hardinge-II (1910-1916)

- Annulment of the Partition of Bengal in 1911.
- Bomb was thrown at Hardinge near Chandni Chowk, but escaped unhurt.
- Transfer of capital from **Calcutta to Delhi** in 1911.
- Darbar in Delhi and Coronation of George V in 1911.
- In 1912, Bihar and Orissa separated from Bengal and, became a new state.
- Establishment of **Hindu Mahasabha** by Madan Mohan Malviya (1915).
- Gandhiji came back to India from South Africa (1915).

Lord Chelmsford (1916-21)

- Government of India Act, 1919 also known as Montague-Chelmsford Reforms.
- Repressive Rowlatt Act, (1919).
- **Jallianwala Bagh Massacre** (13th April, 1919).
- **Home Rule Movement** both by Tilak and Annie Beasant.
- **Saddler Commission** on Education in 1917.
- Appointment of **Hunter Commission** to look into Jallianwala Bagh Tragedy.
- Chambers of Prince, 1921, established.
- Non Co-operation Movement Started, Khilafat movement initiated.
- An Indian Sir SP Sinha was appointed as the Governor of Bengal.
- Death of Tilak (1920).

Lord Reading (1921-1926)

- Rowlatt Act was repealed along with Press Act of 1910.
- Holding of simultaneous examination for the ICS in England and India from 1923. Prince of Wales visited India in November, 1921.
- Moplah Rebellion (1921) took place in Kerala.
- Chauri-Chaura incident and withdrawal of Non-Coperation Movement.
- Formation of Swaraj Party by CR Das and Motilal Nehru (1923).
- Communist Party of India founded by MN Roy (1925).
- Kakori Train Conspiracy (1925).
- Vishwabharati University (1922).
- Lee Commission (1924) for public services. **Young Hilton Committee** for currency notes (1926).
- Royal Commission on agriculture.
- **RSS** founded in 1925.
- Murder of Swami Shraddhanand.

Lord Irwin (1926-1931)

- Simon Commission visited India in 1928. Buttler Commission in 1927.
- Deepawali declaration by Lord Irwin (1929).
- All India Youth Congress, 1928.
- Nehru Report, 1928.
- Lahore Session of the Congress, (1929) and Poorna Swaraj declaration.
- First Round Table Conference 1930, Congress boycotted it.
- Civil Disobedience Movement, 1930 started with.
- **Dandi March** (12th March, 1930).
- Gandhi-Irwin Pact, 5th March, 1931.
- Sharda Act, 1929, under which marriageable age of girls (14 years) and boys (18 years) was raised.
- Jawaharlal Nehru and Subhash Chandra Bose founded **Independence of India League**.

Lord Wellington (1931-1936)

- Second and Third Round Table Conferences.
- Communal Award by Mcdonald (British PM). **Government of India Act, 1935.**

- **Poona Pact** was signed.
- During his period Orissa was separated from Bihar (1936) and a new province **Sind** was created (1936), Burma separated from India as well in 1935.
- All India Kisan Sabha, 1936.
- Foundation of Congress Socialist Party, 1934.

Lord Linlithgow (1934-44)

- First General Election (1936-37) Congress Ministries.
- SC Bose president of 51st INC (1938).
- Forward Bloc founded in 1939.
- **Deliverance day** by Muslim League 1939.
- Lahore Resolution of Muslim League (1940) demand of Pakistan.
- **August Offer**, 1940.
- "Divide & Quit" at the Karachi Session (1940). Passing of Quit India resolution (1942).
- In Haripura Session (1939) of Congress, declared *Complete Independence*.
- **Cripps Mission**, 1942.
- **Quit India Movement**, 1942.
- In 1943, Muslim League celebrated 'Pakistan day'.

Lord Wavell (1943-47)

- **CR Formula** (Rajaji Formula), 1944.
- **Wavell Plan and Shimla Conference**, 1945.
- Cabinet Mission came to India in May, 1946. The Congress and the Muslim league both rejected its proposals.
- Muslim League celebrated 16th August, 1946 as '**Direct Action Day**'.
- INA trials and the Naval Mutiny, 1946.

Lord Mountbatten

- **June third plan**.
- Last British Viceroy of British India.
- First Governor-General of free India.
- Boundary commissions under **Radcliffe**.
- Introduction of Indian **Independence Bill** in the House of Commons.

C Rajagopalachari

- **Last Governor-General of Free India**.
- The only Indian Governor-General to remain in office from 21st June, 1948 to 25th January, 1950.

GROWTH OF MODERN EDUCATION IN INDIA

First Phase (1758-1812)

- Initially, the East India Company was not interested in the development of education. Some minor exceptions were efforts by individuals.
- The **Calcutta Madrasa** established by Warren Hastings in 1781, for the study of Muslim law.
- The **Sanskrit College** established by Jonathan Duncan at Banaras in 1791, for the study of Hindu law and philosophy.
- **Fort William College** established by Wellesley in AD 1800, for training of Civil Servants of the Company in Indian languages and customs (closed in AD 1802).

Second Phase (1813-1853)

- For the first time, the British Parliament included in 1813 Charter, a clause under which the Governor-General-in-Council was bound to keep a sum not less than one lakh rupees, for education. However, the company used this fund for promoting Indian language and literature.
- The charter allowed the Christian missionaries to spread their religious ideas in India.
- The greatest importance of the 1813 Act was that the Company, for the first time, acknowledged state responsibility for promotion of education in India.
- Establishment of **Calcutta College** in 1817 with the efforts of Raja Ram Mohan Roy for imparting Western education. Three Sanskrit colleges were set-up at Calcutta.
- In 1823, a **General Committee of Public Instruction** was appointed to look after the development of education in India, but failed due to Orientalist-Anglicist controversy over the nature of education i.e. traditional or Western and the medium of instruction.

- The controversy was settled by **Macaulay's Education Policy** 1835, which was approved by Lord William Bentinck. The policy favoured English education to a traditional one.
- In 1844, Lord Hardinge decided to give government employment to Indians educated in English schools. This further boosted the Western education in India.
- **Bethune school** was founded by JED Bethune at Calcutta (1849), **Agricultural Institute at Pusa** (Bihar) and **Engineering Institute at Roorkee**.

Third Phase (1854-1900)

- In 1854, Charles Wood prepared a despatch on an Educational System for India, which came to be called the *Magna Carta of Education* in the country. According to Wood's scheme
  (i) The government needed to spread Western education through English medium for higher education. But Vernacular primary schools should be set-up in rural areas.
  (ii) A **grants-in-aid system** to encourage private enterprises involvement in education.
  (iii) A department of public instruction to be set-up in each of the five provinces.
  (iv) Universities in Calcutta (1857), Bombay (1857) and Madras (1857) were established.
  (v) Teacher's training institutions.
  (vi) Promotion of Education for Women.
- Most of Wood's proposals were implemented, which led to Westernisation of the Indian Educational System.

Sergeant Plan, 1944

- The Sergeant Plan, worked out by the Central Advisory Board of Education in 1944, called for elementary and higher secondary schools, universal, free and compulsory education for children in the 6-11 age group and a six-year school course for the 11-17 age group.
- Though, the plan aimed to reconstruct education in 40 years, it was later restricted to 16 years.
- Sir John Sergeant was the Educational Advisor to the Government of India.

- In 1882, Lord Ripon appointed the Hunter Commission under Sir WW Hunter. The commission's views were restricted to primary and secondary education. It emphasised over the state's role in extending education, female education and to involve private enterprise in education.
- As a result, Punjab (1882) and Allahabad (1887) Universities were established.

Fourth Phase (1901-1920)

- Lord Curzon appointed University Commission under Sir Thomas Rayleigh Based on his report, the **Indian Universities Act** was passed in 1904.

SOCIAL AND CULTURAL UPRISINGS

Brahmo Samaj

- Founded by Raja Rammohan Roy (1771-1833).
- He is regarded as the first great leader and reformer of modern India. He was one of the earliest propagators of modern education.
- He started **Atmiya Sabha** in 1814. **Brahmo Sabha** in 1828 and **Brahmo Samaj** in 1830.
- He was deeply influenced by monotheism, anti-idolatry of Islam, Sufism, ethical teachings of Christianity, liberal and rationalist doctrine of the West.
- He laid emphasis on human dignity and criticised social evils.
- He launched a movement for the abolition of *Sati* through his journals **Sambad Kaumudi** (1819), **Precepts of Jesus** in 1820.
- He was a gifted linguist. He knew more than a dozen languages including Sanskrit, Persian, Arabic, English, French, Latin, Greek and Hebrew. He was opposed to Sanskrit system of education.
- He gave enthusiastic assistance to David Hare, who founded the famous **Hindu College in Calcutta** in 1817.

- Established a **Vedanta College** (1825), in which courses both in Indian and Western, Social and Physical sciences were offered.
- He wrote **A Gift to monotheists** or *'Tuhafat-ul-Muwaihidin'* in Persian in 1809.
- Other important leaders of Brahmo Samaj were **Devendranath Tagore**, who joined in 1848 and **Keshab Chandra Sen** in 1858.
- Later, there was a split and in 1866-Devendranath Tagore founded **Adi Brahmo Samaj** and **Tattva Bodhini Sabha** and **Brahmo Samaj of India** was founded under the leadership of Keshab Chandra Sen.
- Anand Mohan Bose started Sadharan Brahmo Samaj.
- Justice MG Ranade founded the **Prarthana Samaj**.

Arya Samaj

- The first Arya Samaj unit was founded by Swami Dayanand Saraswati in 1875 in Bombay.
- Swami Dayanand Saraswati was born in 1824 in Gujarat. His original name was Mula Shankar.
- He was known as the earliest Neo-nationalist. He looked on the Vedas as 'India's Rock and Ages'. His motto was **go back to the Vedas** and **India for the Indians**.

- Arya Samaj stood for four-fold Varna System determined by merit and not by birth; for equal rights for men and women.
- Opposed untouchability, caste discrimination, child marriage and supported widow remarriage and intercaste marriages.

Brahmo Ideas

The purpose of Brahmo Samaj was to purify Hinduism and to preach monotheism. It was opposed to idol worship, priesthood and ritualistic worship; Emphasised on worship through prayer, meditation and reading from the *upanishada*.

- He wrote three books-**Satyartha Prakash, Veda-Bhashya Bhumika** and **Veda Bhashya**.
- In 1886, Lala Hansraj instituted Dayanand Anglo Vedic (DAV) school in Lahore. In 1902, **Gurukul Pathshala** was established at Haridwar.
- After the death of Dayanand in 1883, difference occured in Gurukul section and DAV section. While Gurukul section laid emphasis on the traditional pattern of education, the DAV stood for the spread of English education.
- The Arya Samaj started the **Shuddhi Movement** to convert non-Hindus to Hinduism. Other prominent Arya Samajists were Lala Hansraj, Pt Guru Dutt, Lala Lajpat Rai and Swami Shraddhanand.

Ramakrishna Mission

- It was established by Swami Vivekanand to carry on humanitarian relief and social work after death of his **Guru Ram krishna Paramhansa** in 1897.
- His original name was **Narendranath Dutt**. He was born in Calcutta in 1863.
- He stressed on social action and proclaimed the essential oneness of all religions and condemned any narrowness in religious matters.
- He attended the Parliament of religions held at Chicago in 1893 and published two papers **Prabhudha Bharata** in English and **Udbodhana** in Bengali.

- He urged people to inculcate the spirit of liberty, equality and free thinking.
- He worked for emancipation of women.
- He emerged as a preacher of **Neo Hinduism**. He advocated the **Doctrine of Service**-the service of all human beings. He was considered as the Spiritual Father of the Modern Nationalist Movement.
- Irish woman **Margaret Noble** (Sister Nivedita) popularised Ramakrishna Mission after Vivekananda's death.

Dharma Sabha

- The orthodox Hindus organised the Dharma Sabha under leadership of Raja **Radhakant Dev** in 1830 to counter Brahmo Samaj.
- It was opposed to reforms and protected orthodoxy, but played an active role in promoting Western Education even to girls.

Paramhansa Mandali

- Founded by Dadoba Pandurang and Bal Shastri Jambhekar in 1849. The Mandalis believed in **One God**.
- Members took food cooked by low caste people. Believed in permitting widow remarriage and in education of women.

Veda Samaj

- Called Brahmo Samaj of the South. Started by **Sridharalu Naidu**.
- He translated books of *Brahmo Dharma* into Telugu and Tamil.

The Prarthana Sabha

- Founded in 1867 by **MG Ranade**.
- Prominent leaders were **Dr Atmaram Pandurang** and **RG Bhandarkar** and **NG Chandavarkar**.
- It rejected idolatry, denied the *vedas*, and adopted the method of *Congregational Worship*.

Young Bengal Movement

- During the late 1820 and early 1830, there emerged a radical intellectual trend among the youth in Bengal, which came to be known as the 'Young Bengal Movement'.
- It was founded by **Henry Louis Vivian Derozio**. He was a teacher in Hindu College in Calcutta.

- They believed in truth, freedom and religion. Supported women's education.
- Derozio edited the papers-**Calcutta Gazzette** and India **Gazette**.

Swami Narayan Sampradaya

Founded by **Swami Sahajananda** in Gujarat to protest against luxurious practices of Vaishnavism.

Namdhari/Kuka Movement

- Founded by Bhai Balak Singh and Baba Ram Singh, in North-West frontier province, Ludhiana, in 1841.
- Spread the true spirit of Sikhism, opposed to all caste distinctions.

Indian Reform Association

- Founded by **Keshab Chandra Sen** in Calcutta in 1870.
- Objective was to create public opinion against child marriages and for legalising the Brahma form of marriage. Promoted intellectual and social status of women.

Theosophical Society

- Founded by **Madam HP Blavatsky** and **Col HS Olcott** in New York in 1875.
- In 1882, its headquarters were shifted to Adyar (Tamil Nadu).
- The Theosophical Society of India was founded by **Annie Beasant**. She founded Central Hindu College in 1898, which later became Banaras Hindu University in 1916.
- They drew inspiration from Indian thought and culture. It advocated the revival and strengthening of ancient religion of Hinduism, Zoroastrianism and Buddhism. It accepted the law of *Karma* and was inspired by *Upanishada*, *Sankhya*, *Yoga* and *Vedanta*.

Deccan Education Society

- Founded by **MG Ranade**, VG **Chibdonkar**, **GG Agarkar** in Pune 1884.
- Objective was to contribute to the cause of education and culture in Western India. The society founded the **Ferguson College**.

Seva Sadan

- Founded by **Behramji M Malabari** in Bombay in 1885.
- Campaign against child marriage, enforced widowhood and care for socially exploited women.

Indian National Social Conference

- Founded by **MG Ranade** and **Raghunath Rao in Bombay** in 1887.
- Focus was to abolish polygamy and *Kulinism* and promote intercaste marriages. The conference is also referred as **Social Reform Cell** of the INC.

Madras Hindu Association

Founded by **Viresalingam Pantalu** in Madras in 1892. Movement concerned with plight of women and to combat **devadasi system**.

Bharat Dharma Mahamandala

- Founded by **Pandit Madan Mohan Malaviya** and **Pandit Din Dayal Sharma** in Varanasi (1929).
- It was an organisation of orthodox Hindus.

The Servants of India Society

- Founded by Gopal Krishna Gokhale in Bombay (1905).
- Worked for famine relief, tribal welfare.

Poona Seva Sadan (1909)

Founded by **GK Devadhar** and **Ramabai Pande** in Pune for economic upliftment and employment of women.

Niskam Karma Math (1910)

Founded by **Dhondo Keshav Karve** of Pune. Worked for social reform, selfless service to mankind, educational progress in women.

The Bharata Stri Mandal (1910)

Founded by **Saralabala Devi Chaudharani** in Calcutta. It was the First All India Women Organisation.

Seva Samiti (1914)

Founded at Allahabad by Pandit Hridayanath Kunzru to promote education and reform criminal and fallen elements in the society.

The Indian Women's Association

Founded by Annie Beasant in Madras (1917), for upliftment of women.

Rahanumai Mazdayasan Sabha

Founded in Bombay by SS Bengali, Naoroji Furdonji and JB Nacha (1831). It was the Socio-religious organisation of the Parsis, founded for the restoration of Zoroastrian religion to its pristine glory and social regeneration of the Parsi Community through modern education.

Khudai Khidmatgar Movement

Started by **Khan Abdul Gaffar Khan** in NWFP (1929).

Lokahitawadi

Started by **Gopal Hari Deshmukh**. He advocated Western education and free education for upliftment of women. As a votary of national self-reliance, he attended Delhi durbar in 1876, wearing hand spun **khadi cloth**.

Radha Swami Movement

- Started by **Tulsi Ram** (Shiv Dayal Saheb or Swami Maharaj) in 1861.
- He was a banker of Agra.
- He preached belief in guru's supreme position, one supreme being and on simple social life.

Deva Samaj

- Started by **Shiv Narain Agnihotri** in 1887.
- It preached high moral and social conduct.
- Deva Shastra tells us about the ideals of Deva Samaj.

Caste Movements and Organisations

Movements	Location	Leaders	Courses
Satya Shodhak Samaj (1873)	Maharashtra	Jyotiba Phule	• To fight against Brahaminical domination and to liberate low caste people by educating them. • Started a school for untouchables. • His books *Ghulamgiri* and *Sarvajanik Satyadharma Pustak* questioned the traditional customs and beliefs of the society.
Shri Narayan Dharma Paripalan Yogam or SNDP Movement (1902-03)	Kerala	Shri Narayan Guru He also launched the **Aravipuram movement**	• This movement was opposed to religious disabilities against lower castes. Demanded free entry of people of lower castes to the temples.
Temple Entry Movement	Kerala	TK Madhavan Sri Narayana Guru N Kumaran Asan	• To allow lower castes to enter into the temples.
Bahujan Samaj (1910)	Satara Maharashtra	Mukundrao Patil	• Opposed to exploitation of the lower castes by the upper caste Brahmin landlords and merchants.
Self-respect Movement	Madras	EV Ramswami	• Anti-Brahmin; advocated wedding without priest, forcible temple entry.
Harijan Sevak Sangh (1932)	Pune	Mahatma Gandhi	• For removal of untouchability and social discrimination against untouchables.
Dravid Monnetra Kazhagam (1949)	Madras	CN Annadurai	—

Tribal Movements

Revolts	Year	Area
Chaur Uprising	1966-70	Bengal and Bihar
Kol Uprising	1824-28, 1839, 1899	Gujarat
Bhil Uprising	1818-31	Western Ghat
Rampa Rebellion	1879	Coastal Andhra
Khasi Rising	1846-48, 1855, 1914	Orissa
Kuki Rising under Rani Gaidilieu	1917-19	Manipur
Ho Rising	1820,1822, 1832	Singhbhum and Chhotanagpur
Singpo Rising	1830-39	Assam
Kol Rising under Buddha Bhagat	1831-32	Ranchi, Singhbhum, and Hazaribagh
Khond Rising under Chakrabisai	1846-48, 1855, 1941	Khandmal area in Orissa
Naikad Revolt under Roop Singh and Joria Bhagat	1858-59, 1868	Gujarat
Kachhag Revolt under Sambhudaan	1882	Chhachar area of Assam
Bhil Rising under Govind Guru	1913	Baswana and Durgapur area of South Rajasthan
Oraon Revolt under Jatra Bhagat	1914-15	Chhotanagpur area
Tharo Kuti Rising under Jadonand and Rani Gaidilieu	1917-19	Manipur
Munda Revolt under Birsa Munda	1899-1900	Chhotanagpur area
Rampa Rebellion under Allari Sita Ram Raju	1923-24	Andhra Pradesh

Muslim Socio-Religious Movements

Movement	Location	Leaders	Courses
Fairazi Movement (1804)	Faridpur, Bengal	Haji Shariatullah, Dudhi Miyan	Emphasis on strict monotheism and to rid the Muslim society of non-Islamic social customs.
Deoband Movement (1867)	Deoband	Mohammad Qasim Nanutavi, Rashid Ahmed Ganghoi	Against Western education and promoted classical studies in Islam. Supported Indian National Congress and opposed the Aligarh Movement.
Aligarh (1875)	South	Sir Syed Ahmed Khan	Liberalisation of Indian Islam and modernisation of Indian Muslim through religious reinterpretation and modern education. Urdu Journal-*Tahzib-al-aklaq*. Founded Aligarh school in 1875, that grew into Aligarh Muslim University.
Ahmadiyya Movement (1889-90)	Faridkot	Mirza Ghulam Ahmed of Qadiyan	Believed in universal religion for all humanity, opposed to Islamic orthodoxy and spread of Eastern liberal education among the youth.
Ahrar Movement	—	Riza Khan and Ali Brothers	Against Aligarh Movement.

THE INDIAN NATIONAL MOVEMENT

THE INDIAN NATIONAL CONGRESS

- The **National Conference** in 1883, decided to invite prominent public men and associations to discuss questions on general concern.
- **Indian National Union**–1884 was formed by AO Hume. The National Conference and the Indian National Union merged to form the Indian National Congress in 1885.
- The first meeting of INC was organised by **AO Hume** at Gokuldas Tejpal Sanskrit College on 28th December, 1885 in Bombay. AO Hume was a retired British Civil Servant. Meeting was presided over by Womesh Chandra Bonnerjee and attended by 72 delegates.
- It was the first organised expression of the Indian National Movement on an all India scale. In 1886, the delegates to Congress became 436.
- The venue of first meeting was changed from Pune to Bombay due to out break of Cholera in Pune. Kadambini Ganguly was the first woman graduate of Calcutta University to address the Congress Session in 1889.
- **Safety Valve Theory** British historians argue that Hume's main purpose was to provide a *safety valve* to the growing discontent among the educated Indians.
- **Opposition to Congress** By Syed Ahmed Khan, Raja Shiva Prasad of Banaras and Lord Dufferin (then Viceroy).

Quick Digest

- Ist President of INC   *WC Bonnerjee*
- Ist Woman President   *Annie Besant*
- Ist Muslim President   *Badruddin Tayabji*
- Ist English President   *George Yule*
- Gandhi became President   *1924, Belgaum*
- Jawaharlal Nehru became   1929, Lahore
  President
- Subhash Bose became   1938,Haripura
  President

Objectives and Methods of Work

Moderate Phase, (1885-1905)

- Development and consolidation of feeling of national unity irrespective of race, caste, religion or province.
- Peaceful constitutional agitations, prayer and petitions were the instruments of work.
- They succeeded in passing the Indian Councils Act of 1892, which allowed some members to be indirectly elected by Indians, but keeping the official majority intact.

Moderate Leaders

- AO Hume, DB Naoroji, Badruddin Tayabji, MG Ranade, WC Banerjee, SN Banerjee, Pherozeshah Mehta, C Shankaran Naiyar, MM Malviya, VS Shrinivas Shastri, Tej Bahadur Sapru, GK Gokhale, Anand Mohan Bose, E Dinesh Wacha, Ras Bihari Ghosh, Mohanlal Ghosh, P Anand Charlu, CY Chintamani, RC Dutt, S Subrahmanyam Aiyer, KT Tailang, Madhusudan Das, Rahimtulla M Sayani.
- They worked to create a strong public opinion to arouse consciousness and national spirit. They persuaded the British Government and British public opinion to introduce reforms in India.

Extremist Phase (1905-17)

Cause for the Rise of Extremists

- Dissatisfaction with the methods and achievements of moderates.
- Growing consciousness about the exploitative character of the British rule. Loss of Britain in the Boer wars (1899-1902) demolished the myth of whiteman supremacy.
- Reactionary policies of Curzon-University Act (1904), Indian Official Secrets Act (1904) to restrict freedom of press and partition of Bengal.
- Extremists gave the idea of India's independence the central place in India's politics.

Methods of the Extremists

- Promotion of Swadeshi and Boycott of foreign goods. Non-Co-operation with Britishers (Passive Resistance).

  Extremist leaders- Lala Lajpat Rai, Bal Gangadhar Tilak, Bipin Chandra Pal, Sir Aurobindo Ghosh, Chakravarti Bose, T Prakasham and Chidambaram Pillai.

- They want to take the movement outside Bengal.

Partition of Bengal

- Through a royal proclamation, **Lord Curzon** ordered Partition of Bengal creating East Bengal and Assam out of rest of Bengal on **16th October, 1905**.
- The objective was to set up a communal gulf between the Hindus and Muslims.
- The Indian National Movement entered its second phase after the Partition of Bengal.
- The British said that the existing province of Bengal was too big to be efficiently administered by a single Provincial Government.
- The Indian National Congress and the nationalists of Bengal firmly opposed the Partition. Within Bengal, different sections of population— zamindars, merchants, lawyers, students and even women rose up in spontaneous opposition to the partition of their province.
- **Divide and Rule** The nationalists could see that it was a deliberate attempt to divide the Bengal's territory on religious grounds as for Eastern part Muslims will be in majority and for the Western part, the Hindus.
- **Rabindranath Tagore** composed the National Song Amar Sonar Bangla for the occasion. This song was adopted as National Anthem by Bangladesh in 1971, after its liberation from Pakistan.

The Anti-Partition Movement

- The Anti-Partition movement was initiated on 7th August, 1905. On that day, a massive demonstration against the partition, was organised in the Town Hall in Calcutta.
- The partition took effect on 16th October, 1905.

> - **Banaras Session of INC,** 1905- Presided by GK Gokhale—first call for Swadeshi.
> - **Meeting of INC at Calcutta** 7th August, 1905—Resolution to boycott British goods was adopted.

The Swadeshi and Boycott

- It had its origin in the Anti-Partition movement of Bengal. Mass meetings were held all over Bengal, where *Swadeshi or* the use of **Indian goods** and the boycott of **British goods** were proclaimed and pledged. Public burning of foreign cloth were organised and shops selling foreign cloths were picketed.
- An important aspect of the Swadeshi Movement was the emphasis placed on self reliance or Atmashakti.
- Acharya PC Roy organised his famous Bengal Chemical Swadeshi stores.
- The **Swadeshi Movement** had several consequences like flowering of nationalist poetry, prose, journalism, self-reliant and constructive activity, coupled with opening up of many national educational institutions.
- Nationalist Educational Institutions were founded *e.g.,* Bengal Technical Institute, Bengal National College.
- BC Pal and Chidambram Pillai led **Vandemataram** Movement in Madras.
- Lala Lajpat Rai and Ajit Singh led the movement in Punjab.

Why Swadeshi Movement Failed?

- Severe government repression.
- Split in nationalists at Surat.
- Lack of effective organisation.
- The movement was rendered leaderless.

Formation of Muslim League

- Set-up in 1906, under the leadership of Aga Khan, Nawab Salimullah of Dhaka and Nawab Mohsin-ul-Mulk.
- League supported Partition of Bengal, opposed the Swadeshi Movement, demanded special safeguards for its community and separate electorate for Muslims.

- **Calcutta Session of INC** (1906) Dadabhai Naoroji, the President of the session, declared that Self Government or *Swaraj,* like that of United Kingdom was the goal of Indian people.

SURAT SPLIT (1907)

- The INC splited into two groups during the session at Surat in 1907. Extremists were led by **Lal, Bal, Pal,** while Moderates were led by GK Gokhale.

Moderates

- They demanded mild constitutional reforms, economic relief, administrative reorganisation and protection of civil rights.

Extremists

- They were dissatisfied with the achievement of the moderates. They realised that the true nature of British was exploitative.
- There were 3 groups of extremists The **Maharashtrian** group (headed by Bal Gangadhar Tilak), **the Bengal group** (represented by BC Pal and Aurobindo) and **the Punjab group** (led by Lala Lajpat Rai).
- Aurobindo published **New lamps for old** in the **Indu Prakash** in 1954–94. It was the first systematic critique of the moderates.

Indian Councils Act of 1909 or the-Morley Minto Reforms

- Number of elected members in the imperial and provincial legislative councils increased.Separate electorates introduced for Muslims.
- Non-official members to be elected indirectly. Thus, election introduced for the first time.
- Legislatures could pass resolutions, ask questions and supplementaries and vote for separate items on the budget.
- One Indian to be taken in Viceroy's executive council. Satyendra Sinha was first Indian member to the executive council.

- **Annulment of Partition** In 1911, the government announced annulment of the Partition of Bengal. Western and Eastern Bengal were to be reunited.

Ghadar Party (1913)

- Formed by Lala Hardayal, Taraknath Das and Sohan Singh Bakhna.
- The war period witnessed the growth of revolutionary movement not only in India, but outside India as well, by the Indians.
- Indian revolutionary in the United States of America and Canada had established the Ghadar (Rebellion) Party in 1913. Most of the members of the party were Punjabi Sikh peasants and ex-soldiers, who migrated.
- The party was built around the weekly paper *'The Ghadar'*, which carried the caption *Angrezi raj ka Dushman.*
- Headquarters were at **San Francisco**.
- The outbreak of the first World War provided the Ghadarites with an opportunity to free India from a government, which was indifferent to their cause.
- They began to return India in thousands for a cooridinated revolt, but unfortunately the authorities came to know about their plans and took immediate action. The rebellious regiments were disbanded and their leader were either imprisoned or hanged.
- Some of the prominent Ghadar leaders were—Baba Gurumukh Singh, Kartar Singh Saraba, Sohan Singh Bakhna, Rahmat Ali Shah, Bhai Paramanand and Mohammad Barkatullah.
- To carry out other revolutionary activities, *"Swadesh Sevak Home"* at Vancouver and United India House at Seattle was set-up.

Komagata Maru Incident (1914)

- Komagata Maru was a Japanese steam ship that carried Sikh and Muslim immigrants from Punjab to Vancouver, Canada. But the ship was forced to return back to India by the Canadian authorities. The ship docked at Budge in Calcutta. The Britishers considered the passengers as dangerous political agitators and tried to arrest Baba Gurdit Singh from among them. Police opened fire on them and 19 passengers died in the incident.

Home Rule Movement (1916)

- After **Tilak's** return having served sentence of six years in **Mandlay**, he tried securing the readmission of himself and other extremists into the Indian National Congress. With the need being felt for popular pressure to attain concessions, disillusionment with Morley-Minto reforms and wartime miseries. Tilak and **Annie Besant** readied to assume leadership.
- The Home Rule League was pioneered on lines of a similar movement in Ireland. Muslim League supported the movement. Its objective was to work for social and political reforms.

Tilak's Home Rule Movement

- It started in April, 1916 at Poona. Tilak's league was to work in Maharashtra, Karnataka, Central Province and Berar excluding Bombay. Tilak linked up the question of *Swaraj* with the demand for the formation of linguistic states and education in Vernacular language.
- He gave the slogan *"Swaraj is my birth right and I shall have it."* Tilak's newspapers **Maratha** and **Kesari** were organs for home rule.

Annie Besant's Home Rule Movement

- Started with Subramaniyam Iyer at Adyar in September, 1916. Annie Besant's league worked in rest of India.
- Annie Besant's newspapers New India, **Commonwealth** and Young India became important for this movement. She coined the term Commonwealth.
- George Arundale was the organising secretary of the movement.
- Many moderate nationalists, who were dissatisfied with the Congress inactivity, joined home rule agitation. In June 1917, Annie Beasant was arrested, popular pressure forced the government to release her in September, 1917.

Lucknow Session of the Congress (1916)

- Presided by a moderate Ambika Charan Majumdar. The growing nationalist feeling in the country produced two historic developments at the Lucknow Session of the Indian National Congress in 1916. Firstly-the two wings of the Congress were reunited. The Lucknow Congress was 1st united Congress. *i.e.,* brought about an union of moderates and extremists.
- Secondly at Lucknow, the Congress and the All India Muslim League sank their old differences and put up a common political demand for representative government and dominion status, before the government. Congress accepted the separate electorates. This led to **Congress-League Pact.**

Montague Declaration (1917)

- A British policy was announced after the Lucknow pact, which came to be known as the August Declaration. It aimed at "increasing association of Indians in every branch of the administration for progressive realisation of responsible government in India. The declaration formed the basis of **Montague-Chelmsford Reforms,** of 1919.

Rowlatt Act (1919)

- In 1919, a **Sedition Committee** headed by **Justice Rowlatt** led to the Rowlatt Act. This act authorised the government to imprison any person without trial and conviction by the Court of Law for 2 years. The law also enabled the government to suspend the right of Habeas Corpus, which had been the foundation of Civil Liberties in Britain. It led to a countrywide agitation and marked the foundation of Non-Cooperation Movement.
- During March and April 1919, the country witnessed a remarkable political awakening in India. There were hartals, strikes, processions and demonstrations.

Gandhi's Return to India

- Gandhi returned to India in January, 1915. He did not join any political organisation that did not accept the creed of non-violent *Satyagraha*.

During 1917 and 1918, he was involved in three struggles.

Champaran Satyagraha (1917)

- Ist Civil Disobedience Movement.
- To look into the problems of indigo planters *(tinkathia system)*

Ahmedabad Mill Strike (1918)

First hunger strike. To settle disputes between the mill owners of Ahmedabad and the workers.

Kheda Satyagraha (1918)

First Non-Cooperation Movement. Due to failure of crops, the farmers, with Gandhi, withheld the revenue to get remission based on revenue code.

Jallianwala Bagh Massacre (13th April, 1919)

- The dissatisfaction against Rowlatt Act led to mass agitations. The government was determined to suppress the mass agitation. A large but unarmed crowd had gathered on **13th April, 1919** at **Amritsar** (Punjab) in the **Jallianwala Bagh**, to protest against the arrest of their popular leaders Dr Saif-ud-din Kitchlew and Dr Satyapal. **General Dyer**, the Military Commander of Amritsar, decided to terrorise the people of Amritsar into complete submission. Jallianwala Bagh was a large open space, which was enclosed on three sides and had only one exit. General Dyer surrounded the Bagh, closed the exit with his troops and then ordered his men to shoot into the crowd. Thousands were killed and wounded.
- On 13th March, 1940, Sardar Udham Singh killed O'Dyer, when the latter was addressing a meeting in Coxton Hall, London.

- **Rabindranath Tagore** returned his knighthood in protest.
- **Hunter Commission** was appointed to inquire into it.

The Khilafat Movement

- During the first World War, **Turkey** allied with Germany and Austria against British. The Indian Muslim regarded the Sultan of Turkey as their spiritual leader, *Khalifa*.
- After the war, the British removed the *Khalifa* from his power and fragmented Turkey. Hence, the Muslim started the **Khilafat Movement** in India, for the restoration of *Khalifa's* position.
- The leaders were Ali brothers (Shaukat Ali and Mohammed Ali), Maulana Azad, Hakim Ajmal Khan and Hasrat Mohani. Gandhi saw this as an opportunity to bring about Hindu-Muslim unity against the British, although CR Das opposed it initially.
- The Central Khilafat Committee met at Allahabad. The meeting was attended by number of Congress and Khilafat leaders. In this meeting, a programme of non-cooperation towards the government was declared. This included **boycott** of titles conferred by the government, boycott of civil services, army and police, *i.e.*, of all **government jobs**.

Non-Cooperation Movement (1920)

- It was the first mass based political movement under Gandhi.
- The decision to not cooperate in the most peaceful manner with the government and its laws, was endorsed at the annual session of the Congress held at **Nagpur**, in 1920. The Nagpur Session also made changes in the Constitution of the Congress.
- Anti-Rowlatt agitation, Jallianwala Bagh tragedy, Khilafat Movement, general economic distress during and after the war were the reasons for Non-Cooperation Movement.
- The **Tilak Swarajya Fund** started financing the Non-Cooperation Movement. The movement envisaged boycott of school, colleges, law courts, foreign cloth and advocated the use of Charkha.

Revolutionary Organisations in India

Organisation	Year	Founder	Place
Mitra Mela	1899	Savarkar Brothers	Poona
Anushilan Samiti (I)	1902	Gyanendranath Bose	Midnapur
Abhinav Bharat	1906	VD Savarkar	Poona
Swadesh Bandhav Samiti	1905	Ashwini Kumar Dutt	Barisal
Anushilan Samiti (II)	1907	Barindra Ghosh and Bhupendra Dutt	Dhaka
Bharat Mata Society	1907	Ajit Singh and Amba Prasad	Punjab
Hindustan Republican Association	1924	Jogesh Chandra Chatterji Sachindranath Sanyal	Kanpur
Naujawan Sabha	1926	Bhagat Singh	Lahore
Hindustan Socialist Republican Association	1928	Chandrashekhar Azad	Delhi

Revolutionary Organisations Formed Outside India

Organisation	Year	Founder	Place
India House	1905	Shyamaji Krishna Verma	London
Abhinav Bharat	1906	VD Savarkar	London
Indian Independence League	1907	Tarak Nath Das	USA
Ghadar Party	1913	Lala Hardayal, Tarak Nath-Das and Sohan Singh Bhakna	San Francisco
Indian Independence League	1914	Lala Hardayal and Birendra	Berlin
Government Indian Independence League	1942	Ras Bihari Bose	Tokyo
Indian National Army	1942		

- Boycott of the forthcoming visit of Prince of Wales in November, 1921.
- Popularisation of **Charkha** and **Khadi** and **Jail Bharo** by Congress volunteers.
- The movement demanded-*Swaraj* or self rule and Redressal of the Punjab wrongs and Khilafat issue.
- Lala Lajpat Rai organised educational Boycott in Punjab.
- CR Das, C Rajagopalachari, Saif-ud-din Kitchlew, VB Patel, Aruna Asaf Ali and Motilal Nehru gave up their legal practice.
- The Congress Session at Allahabad in December, 1921 decided to launch a **Civil Disobedience Movement**. But before it could be launched, the angry peasants (mob) attacked on a police station at **Chauri Chaura** in Gorakhpur district of Uttar Pradesh on 5th February, 1922. This changed the whole situation and Gandhiji was compelled to withdraw the Non-Cooperation Movement.

Spread of Non-Cooperation Movement

- United Province became a strong base for the Non-Cooperation Movement.
- Agrarian-riots under the leadership of **Baba Ramchandra**, **Eka Movement** under **Madari Pasi**.
- In Punjab–**Akali Movement** for reform and control of *Gurudwaras*.
- In Andhra Pradesh, the Non-Cooperation Movement was a great success. **Alluri** Sitaram Raju organised the tribals in Andhra and combined their demands with those of the Non-Cooperation Movement.

The Swarajists

- Major developments in Indian politics occurred during 1922–28. Differences arose among leaders after the withdrawal of the Non-Cooperation Movement. One school of thought headed by **CR Das** and **Motilal Nehru** advocated that nationalists should end the boycott of legislative council, enter them, obstruct their working according to official plans, expose their weaknesses, transform them into arenas of political struggle and thus use them to arouse public enthusiasm. They were *'pro-changers'*.

- Sardar Vallabhbhai Patel, Dr Ansari, Babu Rajendra Prasad and others opposed council entry. They were known as 'no changers'.

- In December, 1922, CR Das and Motilal Nehru formed Congress- Khilafat Swarajya Party, with CR Das as President and Motilal Nehru as Secretary. It worked within the Congress.

- In the 1923 elections, the Swarajists won 42 seats out of the 101 elected seats in the Central Legislative Assembly. With the cooperation of other Indian group, they repeatedly out-voted the government in the Central Assembly and in several of the provincial councils.

- Swarajists were split by Communalism. The responsivists offered cooperation to the government to safeguard the Hindu interests. Madan Mohan Malaviya and Lala Lajpat Rai founded the **Independent Congress Party**, later in 1933. It was recognised as Congress Nationalist Party.

Simon Commission (1927)

- In 1927, the British Government appointed the **Indian Statutory Commission,** known popularly by its chairman Simon to go into the question of further Constitutional Reform.

- The committee had to review the working of the dyarchy system, introduced by Montague Chelmsford Reform of 1919 and to report to what extent a representative government can be introduced in India.

- All the members of the commission were white.

- The Indians protested, against the Simon Commission, because of the exclusion of Indians from the Commission and in the fear that the foreigners would discuss and decide upon India's fitness for self government.

- The National Congress decided to boycott the commission in its **Madras Session** in 1927, presided over by Dr Ansari.

- The Muslim League and **Hindu Mahasabha** decided to support the Congress.

- The Commission's arrival in India led to a powerful protest. On 3rd February, 1928, the Commission was greeted with Hartals and black flag demonstrations, under the slogan Simon Go Back.

- The government used brutal suppression and police attacks to break the popular opposition.

- At Lahore, Lala Lajpat Rai was severely beaten in a Lathi charge and he succumbed to his injuries on 17th November, 1929.

Nehru Report (1928)

- All important Indian leaders and parties tried to meet the challenge of the Simon Commission by getting together and trying to evolve an alternative scheme of Constitutional Reforms. Nehru report was tabled in 1928 by **Motilal Nehru**.

- It remains memorable as the first major Indian effort to draft a constitutional framework for whole India with lists of central and provincial subjects and Fundamental Rights.

- However, the recommendations evoked a debate concerning the goal of India-Dominion status or Complete independence.

- Other members of committee—Tej Bahadur Sapru, Ali Imam, MS Aney, Mangal Singh, Sohaib Qureshi, GR Pradhan and SC Bose.

Outcome of the Nehru Report

- It demanded responsible government both at the centre and in the provinces. But, it advocated dominion status, not complete independence.

- It demanded Universal Suffrage. It rejected separate communal electorate. It proposed Muslim reservation in the centre and provinces, where they were in minority.

The report recommended equal rights for women, freedom to form unions and disassociation of the state from religion in any form.

It demanded for reorganisation of the North-West provinces on lingustic basis.

Jinnah's 14 points (9th March, 1929)

- Jinnah, the leader of Muslim League did not accept the Nehru Report and drew up a list of fourteen demands, which became famous as *14 points of Jinnah*.

Lahore Session (1929)

- This session was presided by Jawaharlal Nehru. Gandhi came back to active politics by that time.
- Draw in talks broke down on the issue of dominion status, which the British were reluctant to give.
- This session passed a resolution of Poorna Swaraj (Complete independence) as its ultimate goal.
- On 31st December, 1929 the newly adopted tricolour, was hoisted and 26th January, 1930 was fixed as the **First independence day**.
- The Congress Session also announced a Civil Disobedience Movement under the leadership of Mahatma Gandhi.
- Congress decided to boycott the first Round Table Conference.

Civil Disobedience Movement (1930)

- Before starting the Civil Disobedience Movement, Gandhiji placed an **Eleven point ultimatum** before Irwin for administrative reforms and stated that if Lord Irwin accepted them, then there will be no agitation.
- The Civil Disobedience Movement was started by Gandhi on 12th March, 1930 with his famous Dandi March. Together with 78 chosen followers, Gandhi walked nearly 375 km from Sabarmati Ashram to Dandi, a village on the Gujarat sea-coast.

- Salt production had geographical limitations. So, in other parts of the country, the movement included– picketing of liquor shops and auctions, no revenue campaign in Bardoli, defiance of forest laws in Maharashtra, Karnataka and the central provinces, refusal of *chaukidari* tax in Eastern India, *prabhat pheris*-singing of National Songs.
- The notable feature of the movement was a wide participation of women.

Spread of Civil Disobedience Movement

- **Peshawar** Under the leadership of Khan Abdul Gaffar Khan popularly known as the frontier Gandhi, The Pathans organised the society of **Khudai Khidmatgars** (servants of God) known popularly as Red Shirts. They were pledged to non-violence and freedom struggle. Two platoons of Garhwali soldiers refused to open fire on non-violent mass demonstrations.
- North-East India Manipur took a brave part in it and Nagaland produced a brave heroine, **Rani Gaidilieu**, who at the age of 13 responded to the call of Gandhi. The young Rani was captured in 1932 and sentenced to life imprisonment. She was released only after the independence of India. **Chittagong** Armoury raided by Surya Sen in 1930.
- **Darshana** It was led by Sarojini Naidu, Imam Saheb and Maniklal Gandhi.
- In Madras, **Rajagopalachari** led a march from Trichionopoly to Vedaranyam along the Coromandal coast. In Kerala, **K Kelappan** marched from Calicut to Payannur.
- The government, adopted ruthless repression, lathi charges and firing on unarmed crowd of men and women. Over 90000 Satyagrahis including Gandhiji and other Congress leaders were imprisoned. **Congress was declared illegal**. Meanwhile, the British Government summoned the **First Round Table Conference** in London, in 1930, to discuss the Simon Commission report. But, the National Congress boycotted the conference and its proceedings proved abortive.
- Dandi March was led by Gandhi from Sabarmati Ashram.

First Round Table Conference (12th November, 1930)

- Congress boycotted the conference.
- Muslim League was represented by Mohammad Ali, Agha Khan, Fazlul Haq, MA Jinnah and Hindu Mahasabha by Moonje and Jayakar.
- Tej Bahadur Sapru, Chintamani and Srinivas Shastri (Liberals) appeared.
- Princes of Hyderabad, Mysore attended it. No result came out of the conference.
- The government now made attempts to negotiate an agreement with the Congress, so that it could attend the Round Table Conference.
- Moderate statesman Jaikar, Sapru and Srinivas Shastri initiated efforts to break the ice between Gandhiji and the government. The negotiation between Irwin and Gandhi in 5th March, 1931 came to be known **Gandhi-Irwin Pact** or known **Delhi Pact**.

Gandhi-Irwin Pact

- Under this pact, the government agreed to release all those political prisoners, who had remained non-violent. The Right to make salt for consumption was agreed to.
- The Congress was to suspend Civil Disobedience Movement and take part in Second Round Table Conference.

Karachi Session (1931)

- It endorsed the Gandhi–Irwin Pact. This Session is also memorable for its resolution on Fundamental Right and National Economic Programme, with the efforts of Jawaharlal Nehru and Subhash Chandra Bose.
- Six days before this session, Bhagat Singh, Sukhdev, Rajguru were executed.

Second Round Table Conference

- Gandhiji went to England in September, 1931, to attend the Second Round Table Conference. But the British Government refused to concede the basic nationalist demand for freedom on the basis of the immediate grant of dominion status with complete control over defence, external affairs and finance.
- The Congress officially suspended the movement in 1933 and withdrew it in 1934. Gandhiji resigned from active politics.

Poona Pact (Communal Award)

- McDonald announced the proposal on minority representation, known as the **Communal Award** in **1932**. Under this the depressed classes (Muslims, Sikhs, Indian Christians, Anglo Indians, Women and Backward Classes) were to be considered as a minority, would be entitled to the right of separate electorate. Gandhi reacted strongly to the proposal. He considered the depressed class as the integral part of Hindu society.
- He thought that there was no need to protect the depressed classes through representation, rather the need was to eradicate untouchability.
- Gandhi restored to fast unto death in Yervada Jail against this separate electorate for depressed class, which Ambedkar was insisting on. This resulted into the Poona-Pact between Gandhi and Ambedkar on 25th September, 1932.
- 147 seats were to be alloted to the depressed classes in the provincial legislature as against 71 provided by the Communal Award. The pact also called for adequate representation of depressed classes in civil services.
- Gandhiji coined the word *Harijan* for depressed classes and their upliftment became his prime concern. All India Anti Untouchability League was started in September, 1932. On 8th May, 1933 Gandhiji decided to begin a 21 day fast for self purification for the *Harijan* cause.
- He started the Individual Civil Disobedience on 1st August, 1933.

Impacts of Civil Disobedience Movement

- The Congress swept polls in most provinces in 1937. The left parties emerged as an alternative in politics.
- Some Congress activists formed Socialist group.
- Nehru and Subhash Bose emerged as leaders.

Third Round Table Conference

- Held in London in 1932.
- The Congress did not participate.
- The discussion led to Government of India Act, 1935.

Government of India Act, 1935

- The discussions of the Third Round Table Conference and Simon Commission report eventually led to the passing of the Goverment of India Act of 1935. The act provided for the establishment of an **All India Federation** and a new system of government for the Provinces on the basis of provincial autonomy.
- It abolished the Council of India, established by the Government of India Act, 1858.
- The act provided for a Federal Court and a Federal Bank.
- The Congress rejected the 1935 Act and demanded the convening of a constitutional assembly elected on the basis of adult franchise to frame a Constitution for independent India.

Second World War

- Lord Linlithgow declared India to be at war without the prior assent of the **Central Legislature**. The Congress Ministry resigned in the wake of the war.
- Congress agreed to support Britain only in return of independence being granted. The viceroy could promise this only after the war. In October-November 1939, the Congress Ministries resigned in protest. The Muslim League observed this as the **Deliverence Day** (22nd December, 1939). The Satyagraha was kept limited so as not to embarass Britain's war effort by a mass upheaval in India.
- The viceroy refused to accept preconditions set by the Congress. (Constituent Assembly for establishment of Responsible Government at the Centre). But, the British Government desperately wanted the active cooperation of Indians in the war effort. To secure this cooperation, it sent to India in March, 1942, a mission headed by a Cabinet Minister Sir Stafford Cripps and before that the August Offer.

August Offer (1940)

The **Viceroy Linlithgow** put forward a proposal that included-

- Dominion status in the unspecified future.
- A post war body to enact Constitution.
- Expansion of Governor-General's council with representation of the minorities.
- Establishment of a War Advisory Council.
- Congress rejected this offer as there was no suggestion for a National Government. Muslim League accepted it.

Individual Satyagraha

- Congress rejected the August offer because Congress was convinced that the British would not modify their policy in India. Gandhi decided to start the Individual Satyagraha.
- **Vinoba Bhave** was the first to offer individual Satyagraha, by 15th May, 1941 and more than 250000 Satyagrahis had been jailed.
- *Delhi Chalo Movement* began.

Cripps Mission, 1942

- Sir Stafford Cripps declared that the aim of British Policy in India was "the earliest possible realisation of self-government in India". The British Government's refusal of accepting immediately the Congress demand was the cause of failure of the mission.

Constitutional Proposal of the Cabinet Mission

(a) Dominion status to be granted after the war.

(b) Constitution making body to be elected from provincial assemblies and nominated by the rulers in case of princely states.

(c) Individual princes could sign a separate agreement with the British.

(d) British would however, control the defence for war period.

The British Government undertook to accept and implement the Constitution in two conditions:

- Any province(s) unwilling to accept the Constitution could form a separate union with separate Constitution.

- The new Constitution making body and the British Government would negotiate a treaty to sort out matters arising out of transfer of power to Indian hands.
- Gandhi termed this proposal as a post dated cheque in a crashing bank.
- Though, Cripps proposal failed but it provided legitimacy to the demand for Pakistan by accomodating it in the provision for provincial autonomy.

Quit India Movement, 1942

- The All India Congress Committee met at **Bombay** on 8th August, 1942. It passed the famous **Quit India** resolution and proposed to start off a non-violent mass struggle under **Gandhi's leadership.**
- It is also called Vardha proposal and leaderless revolt.
- Gandhi told the British to quit and leave India in God's hand. His message was **Do or Die**.
- Repressive policy of the government and indiscriminate arrest of the leaders provoked people to violence.
- Nehru was lodged in **Almora jail**, Maulana Azad in **Bankura** and Gandhi was kept in **Agha Khan's palace**, Poona. In many areas, government lost control and the people established *Swaraj*. Parallel governments were established.
- In Satara, Pratisarkar was set up under Nana Patil and in Baliya under Chittu Pande. Others were in Talcher and Bihar. In Bengal, Tamluk Jatiya Sarkar functioned in Midnapore.
- Underground revolutionary activity also started by **Jaiprakash Narain** and **Ramanandan Mishra** escaped from Hazaribagh Jail and organised an underground movement.
- In Bombay, the socialist leaders continued their underground activities under leaders like **Aruna Asaf Ali**. Congress radio was established with **Usha Mehta** as its announcer and Rammanohar Lohia in Bihar.
- School and college students and women actively participated, workers went on strikes. There were no communal clashes during the movement.

- The merchant community and capilatist did not participate. Muslim League kept aloof and the Hindu Mahasabha condemned the movement. Communist party did not support the movement. Rajagopalachari also did not participate.

Demand for Pakistan

- In 1930, Md Iqbal for the first time suggested that the Frontier Province, Sind, Baluchistan and Kashmir be made the Muslim state within the federation.
- Chaudhary Rehmat Ali coined the term '**Pakistan**' (later Pakistan).
- The fear of Muslims to be subjugated by Hindus in free India was realised by Jinnah and he demanded for the creation of Pakistan.
- **Pakistan Resolution** Muslim League first passed the proposal of Separate Pakistan in its Lahore Session in 1940 (called Jinnah's Two-Nation theory). It was drafted by Sikandar Hayat Khan, moved by Fazlul Haq and seconded by Khaliquzzaman. It rejected the federal scheme envisaged in the Government of India Act, 1935. In December 1943, the Karachi Session of the Muslim League adopted the slogan–'*Divide and Quit*'.

> ### Gandhiji's Fast
> (10th February– 7th March, 1943)
> Gandhiji undertook a 21 day fast for condemning the violence of the people during the Quit India Movement.

Rajagopalachari Formula (1944)

- Also known as Rajaji formula (1944), Rajagopalachari proposed that a commission could be appointed for demarcating district in the North-West and East, where Muslims were in absolute majority. Plebiscite would be held on the basis of adult suffrage, that would ultimately decide the issue of separation from Hindustan.
- If majority decides in favour of forming a separate sovereign state then such could be accepted.

- Jinnah objected this as he wanted Congress to accept two-nation theory and wanted only Muslims of the North-West and East to vote in the plebiscite.
- Desai-Liaqat Pact reached no settlement between the league and Congress.

Shimla Conference or Wavell Plan (1945)

- Proposed by **Lord Wavell.**
- Suggested to set up a new executive council with only Indian members. The viceroy and commander in chief would be the only non-Indian members of the council.
- It would work under the existing Constitution. But the door was open for discussion of new Constitution.
- Hindus and Muslims would have equal representation. Jinnah demanded the Muslim League to have absolute choice in choosing the Muslim members, so he rejected the plan.

The Indian National Army

- The idea of Indian National Army (INA) was first conceived in Malaya by **Mohan Singh**, an Indian officer of the British Indian Army.
- The Japanese handed over the Indian prisoners of war to Mohan Singh, who tried to recruit them into an Indian National Army. By the end of 1942, 40000 men were ready to join the INA. The outbreak of the Quit India Movement gave a fillip to the INA.
- In March, 1942, a conference of India was held in Tokyo and **Indian Independence League** was formed. At **Bangkok Conference**, Ras Bihari Bose was elected as President of the league.
- Subhash Bose escaped to Berlin in 1941 and set-up **Indian League** there.
- In 1943, he arrived at Singapore. Earlier, he had left the Congress after having differences with Gandhi and formed the **Forward Bloc** in 1939.
- In Singapore, he was assisted by Ras Bihari Bose. In October, 1943, he set up a provisional Indian Government with headquarters at **Rangoon** and **Singapore**.

INA Trials

- The INA commanders **PK Sehgal**, **Shah Nawaz** and Gurbaksh Dhillon were put on trial at the Red Fort.
- Defence of INA prisoners in the court was organised by Bhulabhai Desai, Tej Bahadur Sapru, Kailash Nath Katju, Nehru and Asaf Ali.
- Muslim League also joined the country wide protest. 12th November, 1945 was celebrated as INA Day.

The Cabinet Mission

- The Attlee Government announced in February 1946, the decision to send a high powered mission of three British Cabinet members (**Patrick Lawrence**, secretary of state for India, **Stafford Cripps**, President of the Board of Trade and **AV Alexander,** first Lord of Admirality) to India to find out ways and means for a negotiated and peaceful transfer of power to India.
- The British bid for a united and friendly India and they rejected the demand for a full-fledged Pakistan.
- The Congress demanded that power should be transferred to one centre and that minorities demands be worked out in a framework ranging from autonomy to Muslim-majority province to self determination or recession. The plan failed on the issue of the nature of grouping. Congress wanted the grouping to be optional till the formation of Constituent Assembly, but Jinnah was in the favour of compulsory grouping.

Jinnah's Direct Action Resolution

- He was alarmed by the election results of the Constituent Assembly (Congress won 209 of the total 273 seats) and was afraid of being totally eclipsed in the Constituent Assembly.
- On 29th July, 1946, Jinnah withdrew his earlier acceptance to the plan and fixed 16th August, 1946 as **Direct Action Day**. Calcutta, Noakhali and Garmukteshwar were the storm centres. Jinnah celebrated Pakistan Day on 27th March, 1947.

Interim Government (1946)

- Interim Government headed by **Jawaharlal Nehru** was sworn on in 2nd September, 1946. Muslim League refused to join initially. Wavell persuaded the league to join in October, 1946. The **Constituent Assembly** begins its session in **9th December, 1946** and Dr Rajendra Prasad was elected its President, but, the league did not attend. Liaqat Ali Khan of Muslim League was made the Finance Minister.

Attlee's Statement (20th February, 1947)

- A deadline of 30th June, 1948 was fixed for transfer of power, even if the Indian politicians had not agreed by that time on the Constitution.
- British power and obligations *vis-a-vis* the princely states would lapse with transfer of power but these would not be given to any successor government.
- **Mountbatten** was to replace Wavell as the Viceroy.
- Partition of the country was implicit in the provision that if the Constituent Assembly was not fully representative, than power would be transferred to more than one Central Governments.

Mountbatten Plan (3rd June, 1947)

- As Viceroy, Mountbatten proved more decisive and quick in taking decisions than his predecessors.
- His task was to explore the option of unity or division till October, 1947 and then advise the British Government on the form of transfer of power.
- **3rd June Plan** In case of partition, two dominions and two Constituent Assemblies would be created. The plan declared that power would be handed over by 15th August, 1947.
- The plan was put in effect without the slightest delay.
- The Legislative Assemblies of Punjab and Bengal decided in favour of partition of these two provinces. Thus, East Bengal and West Punjab joined Pakistan. West Bengal and East Punjab remained with India. Referendum in

Sylhet resulted in the incorporation of that district in East Bengal.

- The referendum in NWFP decided in favour of Pakistan.
- Princely states were given the option to join either of the two dominions or remain independent.
- Boundary Commission was to be set up if partition was effected.
- Mountbatten's formula was to divide India, but retain maximum unity.
- Punjab and Bengal Assemblies would meet in two groups, Hindus and Muslims, to vote for partition.

Indian Independence Act, 1947

- On 18th July, 1947, British Parliament ratified the Mountbatten Plan as the **Independence of India Act, 1947**.
- The act provided for the creation of two independent dominions of India and Pakistan. Each dominion was to have a Governor– General to be responsible for effective operation of the act.
- Sovereignity of British power was to be abolished.

INDEPENDENCE OF INDIA

- On 15th August, 1947, India got independence. Jinnah became the first Governor-General of Pakistan. India requested Mountbatten to continue as the Governor-General of India.
- Assembly and Councils of the states were to be automatically dissolved.
- For the transitional period that is till a new Constituion was adopted by each dominion, the government of the two dominion were to be carried on in accordance with the Government of India Act, 1935.

Integration of States

- **Vallabhbhai Patel**, played the most important role in the integration of states. Except Kashmir, Hyderabad and Junagarh, all states signed an instrument of accession with Indian Government. On October 1947, the Pakistani troops invaded Kashmir and in the crisis, the Maharaj of Kashmir acceded to the Indian Union.

- Through a referendum in the state of Junagarh in February 1948, Junagarh was merged in the Indian Union. The Nawab left for Pakistan.
- Due to the pressure of internal anarchy and military action in the state, the Nizam of Hyderabad was forced to join the Indian Union.

- **Integration of French Colonies** Pondicherry, Chandranagar, Mahe, Karaikal and Yaman were integrated (by the end of 1954).
- **Integration of Portuguese Colonies** Dadra and Nagar Haveli (1954); Goa and Daman and Diu (1961).

IMPORTANT NATIONAL LEADERS

Dadabhai Naoroji (1825-1917)

- He was the first Indian to demand *Swaraj* in the Calcutta Session of INC, 1906.
- He was also known as the *Indian Gladstone, Grand Old Man of India*.
- He was first Indian to be elected to the *House of Commons* on Liberal Party ticket.
- He highlighted the draining of wealth from India by the British and its effect in his book *Poverty and Un-British Rule in India* (1901).

Annie Besant (1847-1933)

- She founded the Theosophical Society in India and started the Home Rule League.
- She established Central Hindu School and College at Banaras (later BHU).
- She was elected the President of the Calcutta Session of INC, 1917.
- She did not attend the 1920 Session at Nagpur due to growing differences with Gandhiji, as she felt that Government of India Act, 1919 were a means to free India.
- She edited famous Newspapers — *New India and Commonweal*.
- She prepared — The Lotus Song, a translation of *Gita* into English.

Bal Gangadhar Tilak (1857-1920)

- He was awarded with the title *Lokmanya*.
- He established new English school at Poona. He was the editor of *Maratha* in English and *Kesari* in Marathi.

- He joined INC in 1891 and moved an Arms Act Resolution.
- He celebrated the Ganapati pooja and the Shivaji festival.
- He collaborated with Agarkar and set up institutions to give economically feasible education to people.
- He was called Bal, Lala lajpat Rai was called Lal and Bipin Chandra Pal was called Pal.
- They were called as the trio of *Lal, Bal, Pal*, an extremist group.
- He founded the Home Rule League in 1916 and helped in ushering the Lucknow Pact and the Reforms Act at the Amritsar Congress in 1919.
- He demanded *swaraj* and gave the slogan *Swaraj is my birth right and I shall have it.*
- Valentine Chirol described him as the *Father of Indian unrest*.
- He wrote the books *The Artic Home of Vedas* and *Gita Rahasya*.

Bankim Chandra Chattopadhyay (1833-1894)

- He was a great scholar best known for the composition of the hymn **Bande Mataram**.
- His first novel was **Durgesnandini**, published in 1864 and he started the journal *Bangadarsan*.

Bipin Chandra Pal (1858-1932)

- He was awarded with the title Mightiest Prophet of Nationalism by Aurobindo Ghosh.
- He supported the 'Age of Consent Bill, (1891), Swadeshi Movement and fought for the cause of the Assam tea-gardeners.

- He started Newspapers- *Paridaashak* (weekly); *Public Opinion and Tribune* (editor); *Swaraj* (English weekly in London); *Hindu Review* (English monthly); *Independent* (daily); and *Democrate* (weekly).

Rabindranath Tagore (1861-1941)

- He was a poet, philosopher, educationist, internationalist and a patriot.
- His elder brother, Satyendranath Tagore was the first Indian to become an ICS.
- His first poem was published in the *'Amrita Bazar Patrika'* and then he wrote *'Banaphul'* (story) and *'Bhanusinher Padavali'* (series of lyrics).
- He founded Shantiniketan near Bolpore on 22nd December, 1901.
- He wrote *Gitanjali*, which fetched him the Nobel Prize in 1913.
- He inaugurated Raksha Bandhan festival to oppose the Partition of Bengal (1905).
- He founded the Vishva Bharati University.
- In 1915, British Crown granted him a *knighthood*, which he renounced after the Jallianwala Bagh Massacre.
- His compositions were chosen as National Anthem by two nations
  1. India—*Jana Gana Mana*
  2. Bangladesh—*Amar Sonar Bangla*

Lala Lajpat Rai (1865-1928)

- He was a courageous man so, he was called *The Lion of Punjab* (*Sher-a-Punjab*).
- He was inspired by Mahatma Hans Raj. Being an Arya Samajist, he helped in establishment of the DAV College at Lahore.
- He withdrew his name from the presidency list of the INC at its Surat session. He was the President of the special session of the Congress at Calcutta, 1920.
- He opposed the withdrawal of Non-Cooperation Movement in 1922. He founded Swaraj Party with Motilal Nehru and CR Das.
- He was injured during a demonstration against Simon Commission in 1928.
- He was the editor of the Bande Matram, The Punjab and The People.

Gopal Krishna Gokhale (1866-1915)

- Gandhiji regarded him as his political guru.
- He was the President of the Banaras Session of INC, 1905, supported the Swadeshi Movement.
- He was the founder of the Servants of Indian Society in 1905, to train people, who would work as national missionaries.

Mahatma Gandhi (1869-1948)

- Gandhi came to India in 1915. He already had *Satyagrahas* in South Africa. In 1907, *Satyagraha* was done against compulsory registration and passes for Indians. In 1910, against immigration restrictions, and de-recognition of Non-Christian Indian marriages.
- He followed the doctrine of Ahimsa.
- The **Champaran Satyagraha** in 1917, against the *Tinkathia* System led by him was his first success in India.
- The **Ahmedabad Satyagraha,** where there was a dispute between the mill owner and workers over the 'plague bonus' was also a success. Gandhi then advised the worker to go on strike and he undertook a **hunger strike,** after which the mill owners were pressurised to accept the tribunal award of 35 per cent increase in wages.
- **Kheda Satyagraha** The peasants of Kheda district were in extreme distress due to the failure of crops and the government ignored their appeals for the remission of land revenue. Gandhiji advised them to withhold the revenue and fight until death.

Facts about Gandhi

- **Name** Mohan Das Karam Chand Gandhi.
  Titles:
- Mahatma (by Rabindranath Tagore, 1917).
- Malang Baba/Nanga Fakir (by Kabailas of North-West Frontier, 1930).
- Indian/Traitor Faqir (by Winston Churchill, 1931).

- Half Naked Saint (by Franq Mores, 1931).
- Rashtrapita (by Subhash Chandra Bose, 1944).
- **Birth** 2nd October, 1869 at Porbandar in Gujarat.
- **Mother** Putali Bai.
- **Father** Karam Chand Gandhi.
- **Political Guru** Gopal Krishna Gokhale.
- **Private Secretary** Mahadev Desai.
- **Influenced by** John Ruskin (Unto the last); Leo Tolstoy; Thoreau; Emerson; the Bible; the Gita.
- **As an Editor**
- *Indian Opinion* (1903-15) in English, Gujarati, Hindi and Tamil.
- *Harijan* (1919-31) in English, Gujarati and Hindi.
- *Young India* (1933-42) in English and Gujarati.
- **Literary works**
Hind Swaraj (1909)
My Experiments with Truth (Auto Biography, 1927).

Sarojini Naidu (1879-1949)

- Popularly known as the *Nightingale* of India, she was a nationalist and poetess from Uttar Pradesh.
- She was married to Dr Govindarajulu Naidu in 1893.
- Under the guidance of Gopal Krishna Gokhale, she became the first woman to participate in the India's struggle for independence.
- She participated in the Dandi March with Gandhiji and presided over the Kanpur Session of Congress in 1925.
- She was the first woman to become the Governor of Uttar Pradesh State.
- Her famous books include — **The Golden Threshold** (1905), **The Feather of the Dawn; The Bird of Time** (1912) and **The Broken Wing** (1917).

Chakravarthi Rajagopalachari (1879-1972)

- He was a politician and lawyer from Tamil Nadu.
- He gave up his practice during Non-Cooperation Movement.

- He held the post of the General-Secretary of the INC in 1921-1922 and was a member of Congress Working Committee from 1922 to 1924.
- He started the Civil Disobedience Movement in Tamil Nadu and was arrested for leading a Salt March from Trichinapoly to Vedaranniyam on the Tanjore coast.
- He was elected as the Chief Minister of Madras in 1937 elections.
- He resigned from Indian National Congress in 1942 for not accepting the Cripps' Proposal.
- He prepared the CR Formula for Congress-League Cooperation.
- He served as the Governor of Bengal (August-November, 1947) and was the first and last Indian Governor-General of India (1948-50).
- He became the Minister of Home Affairs in the country's first cabinet.
- He founded the Swatantra Party in 1959. His rational ideas are reflected in the collection **Satyameva Jayate.**
- He was awarded with the *Bharat Ratna* in 1954.

Dr Rajendra Prasad (1884-1963)

- He participated in Swadeshi Movement (established Bihari Students, Conference), Champaran Satyagraha, Non-Cooperation Movement, Civil Disobedience Movement and Quit India Movement.
- He founded the National College at Patna.
- He was elected as the Minister Incharge of Food and Agriculture in the Interim Government (1946).
- He was the President of the Constituent Assembly.
- He became the first President of the Indian Republic. He was honoured with *Bharat Ratna* in 1962.
- He edited the newspaper—*Desh* (Hindi weekly).

Jawaharlal Nehru (1889-1964)

- He became the General Secretary of the Indian National Congress in 1928 and its President in 1929.

- The Independence resolution was passed under his Presidentship at the Lahore Session.
- He was the first Prime Minister of Republic India (from 1947 to 1964), also known as *Architect* of *Modern India*. He authored the Doctrine of Panchseel and believed in the policy of non-alignment.
- **Books**—*The Discovery of India, Glimpses of World History, A Bunch of Old Letters, The Unity of India, Independence and After, India and the World,* etc.
- His autobiography was entitled as *Auto-biography*.

Dr Bhimrao Ambedkar
(1891-1956)

- Dr Ambedkar was the great leader of the depressed class and an eminent jurist.
- He set up a network of colleges in the name of People's Education Society.
- He founded the Depressed Classes Institute (1924) and Samaj Samata Sangh (1927).
- He participated in all the Three Round Table Conferences of London and signed the Poona Pact with Gandhiji in 1932.
- He was in the Governor-General's Executive Council from 1942 to 1946 and organised the Indian Labour Party and Scheduled Caste Federation.
- He became the Chairman of the Drafting Committee of Indian Constitution.
- As the first Law Minister of the Independent India, he introduced the **Hindu Code Bill**.
- He started *The Republican Party* in 1956.
- He embraced Buddhism towards the end of his life.

Subhash Chandra Bose
(1897-1945)

- He passed the Indian Civil Services Examination in 1920 in England, but left it on Gandhiji's call of Non-Cooperation Movement.
- He founded the independence for India League with Jawaharlal Nehru.
- He was elected as the President of INC at its Haripura Session (1938) and Tripuri Session (1939), but resigned from Tripuri due to differences with Gandhiji.
- He founded the Forward Bloc (1939) and Kisan Sabha.
- He escaped to Berlin in 1941 and met Hitler. He took the charge of Indian Army (*Azad Hind Fauz*) in 1943 in Singapore and set up Indian Provisional Government there.
- He addressed Mahatma Gandhi as the *Father of the Nation*.
- He supposedly died in a plane crash in 1945.
- He gave the famous slogans — *Dilli Chalo* and *Jai Hind*.
- *The India Struggle* was his autobiography.

Bhagat Singh (1907-1931)

- He was a member of Hindustan Socialist Republican Association.
- He started the 'Militant Naujawan Bharat Sabha' in Punjab.
- He killed British official Saunders in 1928 and was involved in Lahore Conspiracy and bombed the Central Legislative Assembly.
- He was executed on 23rd March, 1931.

Books/Journals and Newspapers

Author/Editor	Work
Aurobindo Ghosh	▪ Karmayogi
	▪ New lamp for old
	▪ Bhawani Mandir
Bankim Chandra Chatterjee	▪ Anand Math
	▪ Durgesh Nandini
BR Ambedkar	▪ Mook Nayak
	▪ Bahishkrit Bharat
Dadabhai Naoroji	▪ Rast Goftar
	▪ Voice of India
	▪ Poverty and Un-British Rule in India
Dayanand Saraswati	▪ Veda Bhasya Bhumika
	▪ Satyartha Prakash
Gopal Krishna Gokhale	▪ Nation
	▪ Sudharak
Jawaharlal Nehru	▪ Discovery of India
	▪ National Herald
	▪ Wither India
	▪ Soviet Asia
MK Gandhi	▪ Navjeevan
	▪ Young India and Harijan
	▪ Indian opinion
Madan Mohan Malviya	▪ Hindustan
	▪ Leader
RN Tagore	▪ Letters from Russia
	▪ Gora
Raja Ram Mohan Roy	▪ Sambad Kaumudi
	▪ *Mirat-ul-Akhbar*
	▪ Barga-Dutta
Vivekanand	▪ Prabhudha Bharat Udbodhana
	▪ Prachya aur Pashchaya
Annie Beasant	▪ New India, Commonwealth
BG Tilak	▪ Kesari and Maratha
BK Nanda	▪ Biography of Gokhale
B Upadhyay	▪ Sandhya
Bal Shastri Jambekar	▪ Darpan
Barindra Kumar Ghosh and Bhupendra Dutta	▪ Yugantar
Bhartendu Harish Chandra	▪ Kavivachan Sudha
Bipin Chandrapal	▪ Paridarshak
Curzon	▪ Philosophy of the East
Dayal Singh Majeetia	▪ Tribune

Author/Editor	Work
Deenbandhu Mitra	▪ Neel Darpan
Derozio	▪ East Indian
Devendranath Tagore	▪ Indian Mirror
EV Ramaswamy Naiker	▪ Kudi Anasu
G Subramaniya Aiyar	▪ Swadesh Mitram
G Subramaniya Aiyar, Viraraghavachari and Subba Rao Pandit	▪ The Hindu
Ghulam Hussain	▪ Inquilab
Harish Chandra Mukherjee	▪ Hindu Patriot
Henry Vivian Derozio	▪ India Gazette
Hunters	▪ Indian Musalmans
Ishwar Chandra Vidyasagar	▪ Som Prakash
James Augustus Hicky (1780)	▪ Bengal Gazette
Jyotiba Rao Phule	▪ Ghulam Giri
KK Mitra	▪ Sanjivani
KM Panikkar	▪ The Hindustan Times
MA Azad	▪ India wins freedom
MG Ranade	▪ Essays in India economics
MN Roy	▪ India in Transition
Madam Bhikaji Cama	▪ Bande Mataram
Maulana Abul Kalam Azad	▪ Al-Hilal
Maulana Mohammad Ali	▪ Comrade
Mukundrao Patil	▪ Din Mitra
Muzaffar Ahmed	▪ Navyug
PC Rai	▪ History of Hindu Chemistry
Pherozshah Mehta	▪ Bombay Chronicle
RC Dutt	▪ Economic History of British India
RP Dutt	▪ India Today
Robert Knight	▪ Indian Statesman
Robert Knight and Thomas Bennett	▪ Bombay Times
SA Dange	▪ The Socialist
Subhash Chandra Bose	▪ Indian struggle

Important Dates/Years of India's Freedom Struggle

Date/Year	Importance
1905	Partition of Bengal announced; to come in force from 16th October 1906.
1906, December 31	Muslim League founded at Dacca
1908, April 30	Khudiram Bose executed.
1908, July 22	Tilak sentenced to six years on charges of sedition.
1909, May 21	Morley-Minto Reforms of Indian Councils Act, 1909.
1911	The coronation or *Delhi durbar* held at Delhi, in which the Partition of Bengal is cancelled.
1911	Delhi becomes the new capital of India.
1912, December 23	Bomb thrown on Lord Hardinge, on his entry into state Delhi.
1914, November 1	Ghadar Party formed at San Francisco.
1914, June 16	BG Tilak released from jail.
1914, August 4	Outbreak of the First World War.
1914, September 29	Komagatamaru ship reaches Budge Budge (Calcutta port).
1915, January 9	Gandhiji arrives in India.
1915, February 19	Death of Gopal Krishna Gokhale.
1916, April 28	BG Tilak finds Indian Home Rule League with its headquarters at Poona.
1916, September 25	Another Home Rule League started by Annie Besant.
1917, April	Mahatma Gandhi launches the Champaran campaign in Bihar to focus attention on the grievances of indigo planters.
1917, August 20	The Secretary of State for India, Montague, declares that the goal of the British Government in India is the introduction of Responsible Government.
1918	Beginning of Trade Union Movement in India.
1918, April	**Rowlatt (Sedition) Committee** submits its report. **Rowlatt Bill** introduced on February 16, 1919.
1919, April 13	Jallianwala Bagh tragedy
1919, December 5	**The House of Commons** passes the **Montague-Chelmsford Reforms** or the **Government of India Act, 1919.** The new reforms under this act came into operation in 1921.
1920	First meeting of the **All India Trade Union Congress.** (under Narain Malhar Joshi).
1920, December	The Indian National Congress (INC) adopts the Non-Cooperation Resolution.
1920-22	Non-Cooperation Movement, suspended on February 12, 1922 after the violent incidents at Chauri Chaura on February 5, 1922.
1922, August	Moplah rebellion on the Malabar coast.
1923, January 1	Swarajist Party formed by Motilal Nehru and others.
1924	The Communist Party of India starts its activities at Kanpur.
1925, August	Kakori Train Conspiracy case.
1927, November 8	The British Prime Minister announces the appointment of the Simon Commission to suggest future constitutional reforms in India. Simon Commission arrives in Bombay on February 3, 1928 and all-India hartal. Lala Lajpat Rai assaulted by police at Lahore.

Date/Year	Importance
1928	Nehru Report recommends principles for the New Constitution of India. All-parties conference considers the Nehru Report, August 28-31, 1928.
1928, November 17	Death of Lala Lajpat Rai.
1929	Sharda Act passed prohibiting marriage of girls below 14 and boys below 18 years of age with effect from 1930.
1929, March 9	All-Parties Muslim Conference formulates the 'Fourteen Points' under the leadership of Jinnah.
1929, April 8	Bhagat Singh and Batukeshwar Dutt throw a bomb in the Central Legislative Assembly.
1929, October 31	Lord Irwin's announcement that the goal of British policy in India was the grant of the Dominion status.
1929, December 31	The Lahore Session of the INC adopts the goal of complete independence—*Poorna Swarajya* for India; Jawaharlal Nehru hoists the tricolour of Indian Independence on the banks of the river Ravi at Lahore.
1930, January 26	First Independence Day observed.
1930, February 14	The Working Committee of the INC meets at Sabarmati and passes the Civil Disobedience resolution.
1930, March 12	Mahatma Gandhi launches the Civil Disobedience Movement with his epic Dandi March (March 12 to April 6). First phase of the Civil Disobedience movement : March 12, 1930 to March 5, 1931.
1930, November 30	First Round Table Conference begins in London to consider the report of the Simon Commission.
1931, March 5	Gandhi-Irwin pact signed. Civil Disobedience Movement suspended.
1931, March 23	Bhagat Singh, Sukh Dev and Rajguru executed.
1931, September 7	Second Round Table Conference.
1931, December 28	Gandhiji returns from London after the deadlock in Second Round Table Conference. Launches Civil Disobedience Movement. The Indian National Congress declared illegal.
1932, January 4	Gandhiji arrested and imprisoned without trial.
1932, August 16	British Prime Minister Ramsay Macdonald announces the infamous "Communal Award".
1932, September 20	Gandhiji in jail, begins his epic "fast unto death" against the Communal Award and ends the fast on 26th September, after the Poona Pact.
1932, November 17	The Third Round Table Conference begins in London (17th November to 24th December).
1933, May 9	Gandhiji released from prison as he begins his fast for self-purification. Indian National Congress suspends Civil Disobedience Movement but authorises *Satyagraha* by individuals.
1934	Gandhiji withdraws from active politics and devotes himself to constructive programmes.
1935, August 4	The Government of India Act (1935) passed.
1937	Elections held in India under the Act of 1935 (February 1937). The Indian National Congress contests elections, and forms ministries in several provinces (July, 1937).
1938, February 19-20	Haripura session of Indian National Congress. Subhash Chandra Bose elected Congress President.
1939, March 10-12	Tripuri session of the Indian National Congress.
1939, April	Subhash Chandra Bose resigns as the president of the Indian National Congress.
1939, September 3	Second World War (1st September). Great Britain declares war on Germany; the Viceroy declares that India too is at war.

Date/Year	Importance
1939, October 27-November 5	The Congress ministries in the provinces resign in protest against the war policy of the British Government.
1939, December 22	The Muslim League observes the resignation of the Congress ministries as Deliverance Day.
1940, March	Lahore Session of the Muslim League, passes the Pakistan Resolution.
1940, August 10	Viceroy Linlithgow announces August Offer.
1940, August 18-22	Congress Working Committee rejects the August Offer.
1940, October 17	Congress launches Individual Satyagraha Movement.
1941, January 17	Subhash Chandra Bose escapes from India; arrives in Berlin (March 28).
1942, March 11	Churchill announces the Cripps Mission.
1942, August 7-8	The Indian National Congress meets in Bombay; adopts 'Quit India' resolution.
1942, August 9	Gandhiji and other Congress leaders arrested.
1942, August 11	Quit India Movement begins; the Great August Uprising.
1942, September 1	Subhash Chandra Bose establish the Indian National Army 'Azad Hind Fauj'.
1943, October 21	Subhash Chandra Bose proclaims the formation of the Provisional Government of Free India.
1943, December	Karachi Session of the Muslim League adopts the slogan 'Divide and Quit'.
1944, January 25	Wavell calls Shimla Conference in a bid to form the Executive Council of Indian political leaders.
1946, February 18	Mutiny of the Indian naval ratings in Bombay.
1946, March 15	British Prime Minister Attlee announces Cabinet Mission to propose a new solution to the Indian deadlock; Cabinet Mission arrives in New Delhi (14th March); issues proposal (16th May).
1946, July 6	Jawaharlal Nehru takes over as Congress President.
1946, August 6	Wavell invites Nehru to form an Interim Government; Interim Government takes office (2nd September).
1946, December 9	First session of the Constituent Assembly of India starts. Muslim League boycotts it.
1947, February 20	British Prime Minister Attlee declares that the British Government would leave India not later than June, 1948.
1947, March 24	Lord Mountbatten, the last British Viceroy and Governor-General of India, sworn in (March 24, 1947 to June 21, 1948).
1947, June 3	Mountbatten Plan for the partition of India and the announcement (4th June) that transfer to power will take place on 15th August.
1947, August 15	India wins freedom.

ART AND CULTURE OF INDIA

RELIGION

Religion is a collection of belief systems, cultural systems and world views that relate humanity to spirituality and sometimes to moral values. Religion is different from private belief in its social character.

Hinduism

- It consists of a collection of intellectual and philosophical points of views, rather than a rigid system of beliefs.
- There is no specific founder of the religion.
- Its roots can be traced to the historical Vedic religion of the Iron age India.
- Hinduism is the third largest religion in the world after Christianity and Islam.
- Prominent texts are *Vedas, the Ramayana* and *Mahabharata.*

Islam

- Prophet Mohammed is the founder of Islam.
- Quran is the Holy book of Islam.
- Islam is the second largest religion in the world.
- Most Muslims belong to two denominations-Shia and Sunni.
- Islam arrived in India in the AD 8th century.

Christianity

- Jesus is the founder of Christianity.
- Bible is the Holy book of Christianity.
- Christian religion is mainly divided into 2 streams-Catholic and Protestant.
- Christianity is the world's largest religion.
- Holy texts of the Christianity are the Old Testament and the New Testament.

Sikhism

- Guru Nanak is the founder of Sikhism.
- Guru Granth Sahib is the Holy book of Sikhism. Sikhism is the third largest religion of India.
- Sikhism developed in India during 16th and 17th centuries.

Buddhism

- Mahatma Buddha is the founder of Buddhism. Buddhism is the indigenous religion of India.
- Holy book of Buddhism are the *Tripitak as.*
- The three Jewels of Buddhism are *Buddha, Dhamma* and *Sangha.*
- Buddhists generally classify themselves as either *Theravada* or *Mahayana.*

Jainism

- Mahavira Swami is the founder of Jainism.
- Jainism is a religion indigenous to the Indian subcontinent.
- Holy book of Jainism is the *Kalpa Sutras.*
- The main doctrines of Jainism are *Anekantavada, Syadvada* and *Nayavada.* The two sects of Jainism are Svetambara and Digambara. Jaina holy texts consist of Purvas, Agamas, Angas and Upangas.

LANGUAGES

Sanskrit

- Sanskrit is the mother of many Indian languages.
- Sanskrit is the most ancient language of our country.
- The Vedas, Upanishads, Puranas and Dharmasutras are all written in Sanskrit.
- It is one of the twenty-two languages listed in the Indian Constitution.
- The Dharmasutras, the Manusmriti, Arthashastra and Gita Govinda are the famous books in Sanskrit.
- Panini, Kautilya, Kalhana and Jayadeva are the famous writers of Sanskrit.

Pali

Pali is an Indo-Aryan language, which was used for the earliest Buddhist scriptures. Pali literature is mainly concerned with Theravada Buddhism.

Telugu

- The Vijyanagara period was the golden age of Telugu literature.
- Eight Telugu literary luminaries are popularly known as *Ashtadiggajas*.
- Ramakrishna was the author of *Panduranga Mahatmayam*, which was considered as one of the greatest poetical works of Telugu literature.

Kannada

- Kannada language developed fully after the AD 10th century. The earliest known literary work in Kannada is *Kavirajamarg,* written by the Rashtrakuta King Nripatunga Amoghavargha I.
- Pampa, known as the father of Kannada, wrote his great poetic works Adi Purana and Vikramarjiva Vijaya in the AD 10th century.

Malayalam

- The language of Malayalam emerged around the AD 11th century. By 15th century, Malayalam was recognised as an independent language.
- *Bhasa Kautilya*, a commentary on *Arthashastra* and *Kokashndisam* are two great works.
- Rama Panikkar and Ramanujan Ezhuthachan are well known authors of Malayalam literature.

Tamil

- Tamil is the mother language of the Dravidian language family.
- The Sangam literature is a collection of long and short poems composed by various poets in praise of numerous heroes and heroines.
- There are about 30000 lines of poetry, which are arranged in eight anthologies called *Ettuttokai.*

Persian and Urdu

- Urdu emerged as an independent language towards the end of the AD 4th century.
- Urdu as a language was born out of the interaction between Hindi and Persian.
- Urdu became more popular in the early 18th century.
- The earliest Urdu poet is supposed to be Khusrau.
- Urdu has given us a new form of poem, that is called a *nazm*.

Hindi

- Hindi is a direct descendant of the Sanskrit language, through Prakrit and *Apabhramsha*.
- It is spoken largely in North India.
- Evolution of Hindi literature can be better understood through four stages of Adi Kal, Bhakti Kal, Riti-kavya Kal and Adhunik kal.

LITERATURE

Bengali Literature

- Raja Ram Mohan Roy wrote in Bengali besides English, which gave an impetus to Bengali literature.
- Ishwar Chandra Vidhyasagar (1820-91) and Akshay Kumar Dutta (1820-86) were the two other writers of this early period.
- Sharat Chandra Chatterji (1876-1938) and RC Dutta, a noted historian and a prose writer, too contributed to the making of Bengali literature.
- But the most important name that influenced the whole of India was that of Rabindra Nath Tagore (1861-1941). Novels, dramas, short stories, criticism, music and essays, all flowed from his pen. He won the Nobel Prize for literature in 1913 for his *Geetanjali.*

Assamese Literature

- Like Bengali, Assamese also developed in response to the Bhakti movement.
- Shankaradeva, who introduced Vaishnavism in Assam helped in the growth of Assamese poetry. Even the *Puranas* were translated in Assamese.

- The earliest Assamese literature consisted of *buranjis* (court chronicles). Shankaradeva has left several devotional poems, which people sang with rapturous pleasure, but it was only after 1827 that more interest was shown in producing Assamese literature.

Oriya Literature

- Oriya language shows the maximum influence of Sanskrit. It originated in the AD 9th century and its literary development took place in the 13th century.
- Worth mentioning in Oriya literature are Fakirmohan Senapati and Radha Nath Ray, whose writings deserve considerable attention in the history of Oriya literature.
- The works of Upendra Bhanja (1670-1720) were important as they ushered a new period of Oriya literature. In Odisha, the works of Saraladasa are regarded as the first works of Oriya literature.

Punjabi Literature

- Punjabi is a language with several shades. It is being written in two scripts, Gurumukhi and Persian.
- Guru Nanak was the first poet in Punjabi. Some other contemporary poets, mostly Sufi saints, used to sing in this language.
- Guru Gobind Singh, the 10th guru, was educated in Patna (Bihar), where he learnt Persian and Sanskrit.
- He has composed two *savaiyyas* in Punjabi, but these are not a part of the Adi Granth. Similar is the popularity of *Bulley Shah*, who was a Sufi saint. He has composed a large number of songs.

Indian Literature in English Language

- English came into India with the British and soon became a language of formal education. Some of the early Indian works in English were written by Raja Rammohan Roy, Henry Vivian Derozio and Madhusudan Dutt. Aurobindo Ghosh wrote his epic poem *'Savitri: A Legend and a Symbol'* in English.

- India's only Nobel laureate in literature Rabindranath Tagore wrote some of his work originally in English and did some of his own English translation from Bengali. Sarojini Naidu and Jawaharlal Nehru also wrote in English. Nehru's 'The Discovery of India' and 'Glimpses of World History' are quite popular.
- Some notable Indian poets, who write in English are Nissim Ezekiel, Dom Moraes, Arun Kolakar and Dilip Chitre. Other notable Indian writers are Khushwant Singh, Salman Rushdie, Vikram Seth, Arundhati Roy, Kamala Markandaya, Kiran Desai, Jhumpa Lahiri etc.

MUSIC

The music of India is said to be one of the oldest unbroken musical traditions in the World.

Many different legends have grown up concerning the origin and development of Indian classical music.

Hindustani Music

Classical Music

- Hindustani classical music originated in North India around the 13th and 14th centuries. In contrast to Carnatic music, the Hindustani classical music was not only influenced by ancient Hindu musical traditions and Vedic philosophy, but also by the Persian elements.
- Hindustani music is based on the *Raga* system. The *Raga* is a melodic scale, comprising of notes from the basic seven - *Sa, Re, Ga, Ma, Pa, Dha* and *Ni*.
- On the basis of notes included in it, each *raga* attains a different character. The form of the *raga* is also determined by the particular pattern of ascent and descent of the notes, which may not be strictly linear.
- Hindustani classical music is primarily vocal-centric. The major vocal forms associated with Hindustani classical music are the *khayal, ghazal, dhrupad, dhammar, tarana* and *thumri*.

Thumri

It is an informal vocal form of Hindustani classical music and is said to have begun with the court of Nawab Wajid Ali Shah, the Nawab of Oudh.

Dadra

It refers to two separate, but originally linked concepts in Hindustani classical music. The *Dadra tala* consists of six beats in two equal divisions of three. It is mostly performed in Agra and in the Bundelkhand region.

Qawwali

It is a form of Sufi devotional music. Originally, it was performed at mainly Sufi shrines or *dargahs*. Its roots can be traced back to 8th century Persia. Songs in *qawwali* are mostly in Urdu and Punjabi languages.

Ghazal

It is a poetic form consisting of rhyming couplets and a refrain, with each line sharing the same meter.

It is an ancient form originating in 6th century Arabic verse. It spread into South Asia in the 12th century, due to the influence of Sufi mystics.

Hori

It is a genre of semi-classical singing, which is popular in Uttar Pradesh and Bihar. It comes under the category of season songs.

Kirtan

It is a call and response chanting or responsory performed in Indian devotional traditions. It is closely associated with the Bhakti movement.

Gharana

There is a rich tradition of *Gharanas* in classical Hindustani music. These schools or *Gharanas* have their basis in the traditional mode of musical training and education. Every *Gharana* has its own distinct features.

Gwalior Gharana

This is the oldest among all the *Khayal Gayaki* (vocal) styles. The distinctive feature of this style of singing has been noted to be its lucidity and simplicity.

Agra Gharana

The Agra Gharana places great importance on developing forcefulness and deepness in the voice, so that the notes are powerful and resonant.

Kirana Gharana

It derives its name from the birth-place of Abdul Kharim Khan of Kirana near Kurukshetra. In the Kirana style of singing, the *swara* is used to create an emotional mood by means of elongation and use of *Kana-s*.

Rampur Sahaswan Gharana

In Rampur Sahaswan Gharana, there is a stress on the clarity of *swara* and the development and elaboration of the *raga* is done through a stepwise progression.

Patiala Gharana

Patiala Gharana is regarded as an off-shoot of the Delhi Gharana. The *Patiala Gharana* is characterised by the use of greater rhythm play and by *Layakari* with the abundant use of *Bols,* particularly Bol tans.

Delhi Gharana

The *Delhi Gharana* was represented by Tanras Khan and Shabbu Khan. The highlights of *Delhi Gharana* are pleasing *vistaar* and exquisite compositions.

Bhendi Bazaar Gharana

The most distinctive feature of the Bhendi Bazaar Gharana is the presentation of *Khayal*, which is open voice, using Akar. There is a stress on breath-control and singing of long passages in one breath is highly regarded in the *Gharana*.

Banaras Gharana

The *Banaras Gharana* evolved as a result of great tilting style of *khayal* singing known by *Thumri* singers of Banaras and Gaya.

Mewati Gharana

The *Mewati Gharana* gives importance to developing the mood of the *raga* through the notes forming it and its style is *Bhava Pradhan*. It also gives equal importance to the meaning of the text.

Musical Instruments and Instrumentalists

Instruments	Instrumentalists

Stringed Instruments

	Instruments	Instrumentalists
1.	Rudra Veena	Asad Ali Khan, Zia Moin-ud-din Dagar
2.	Santoor	Shiv Kumar Sharma,
3.	Sarod	Buddhadev Dasgupta, Ali Akbar Khan, Amjad Ali khan, Bahadur Khan, Sharan Rani, Zarin S Sharma
4.	Sarangi	Ustad Binda Khan
5.	Sitar	Ravi Shankar, Hara Shankar Bhattacharya, Nikhil, Banerjee, Vilayat Khan, Mustaq Ali Khan
6.	Surb Ahar	Sajjad Hussain, Annapurna
7.	Veena	Doraiswamy Iyengar, Chittibabu, Emani Sankara Shastri, Dhanammal, S Bala Chandran, KR Kumaraswamy
8.	Violin	Gajanan Rao Joshi, MS Gopal Krishnan, TN Krishnan, Baluswamy, Dikshitar, Dwaran Venkataswamy Naidu Lalyuli G Jayaraman, Mysore T Chowdiah, VG Jog

Wind Instruments

	Instruments	Instrumentalists
9.	Flute	TR Mahalingam, N Ramani, Hari Prasad Chaurasia, Pannalal Ghosh
10.	Nadaswaran	Sheikh Chinna Moula, Neeruswamy Pillai, Rajaratanam Pillai
11.	Shehnai	Bismillah Khan

Percussion (Strikting Thumping) **Instruments**

	Instruments	Instrumentalists
12.	Mridangam	Palghat Mani Iyer, Karaikudi R Mani, Palghat Raghu
13.	Pakhawag	Pt Ayodhya Prasad, Gopal Das, Babu Ram Shanker Pagaldas
14.	Tabla	Zakir Hussain, Nikhil Ghosh, Kishan Maharaj, Alla Rakha Khan, Pandit Samta Prasad, Kumar Bose, Latif Khan
15.	Kanjira	Pudukkotai Dakshinamurthi Pillai

Instruments Vocalists

Carnatic	MS Subbulakshmi, Balamuralikrishna, Bombay Jaishree, HK Raghavendra, Aryakudi Ramanujan Iyenegar Venkataram, Sitarajam, Mani Krishnaswamy, Akhil Krishnan, ML Vasanthakumari, MD Ramanathan, GN Balasubramaniam
Dhrupad	Ustad Rahim Fahim-ud-din Dagar, Zahir-ud-din Dagar, Wasif-ud-din Dagar, Bundecha Bandhu, Pt Abhay Narayan Mallick, Pt Ritwik Sanyal, Uday Bhawalkar
Hindustani	Shubha Mudgal, Madhup Mudgal, Mukul Shivputra, Pandit Jasraj, Parveen Sultana, Naina Devi, Girija Devi, Ustad Ghulam Mustafa Khan, Gangubai Hangal, Krishna Hangal, V Rajput, Kumar Gandharva, Faiyyaz Khan, Mallikariun Mansur.
Thumri	Ustad Bade Ghulam Ali Khan, Ustad Mazhar Ali Khan, Ustad Zawad Ali Khan, Poornima Chaudhary, Shanti Heerananda, Naina Devi, Rita Ganguly
Qawwali	Ghulam Hasan Niyazi, Sultan Niyazi, Ghulam Farid Nizami, Hussain Khan Bandanawaji, Aslam Sabaari, Chand Nizami

DANCE

Indian Classical Dances

India has an old tradition of thousands of years in regard to fine arts and classical and folk music and dances. Some of the world-famous dance forms that originated and evolved in India are Bharatnatyam, Kathak, Kathakali, Kuchipudi, Manipuri, Mohiniattam and Odissi.

Bharatnatyam

- Bharatnatyam is one of the most popular classical Indian dances. Bharatnatyam is more popular in South Indian states of Tamil Nadu and Karnataka.
- The music accompanying this dance is Carnatic music. It evolved out of the *Devadasi system* of South Indian temples. Two famous styles are Pandanallur and Tanjore.
- Famous dancers associated with Bharatnatyam are E Krishna Iyer, Rukmini Devi Arundale and Anna Pavlova.

Kathak

- Kathak is one of the most important classical dances of India. Kathak is said to be derived from the word *katha,* meaning the art of storytelling.
- Famous centres are Lucknow and Jaipur. Lucknow school depicts Mughal Court etiquette, while the Jaipur school depicts stories of Rajput kings and Gods. Famous exponents are Sitara Devi, Sambhu Maharaj, Uma Sharma Shovana Narayan etc.

Kathakali

- Kathakali is the classical dance form of Kerala. The word *Kathakali* literally means **story play.**
- Kathakali is considered as one of the most magnificent theatres of imagination and creativity.
- Famous exponents of Kathakali are Vallathol Narayan Menon, Kunju Kurup, Guru Gopinath etc.

Kuchipudi

Kuchipudi is one of the classical dance forms of South India. Kuchipudi exhibits scenes from the Hindu epics, legends and mythological tales. Famous exponents of Kuchipudi are Lakshmi Narayan Shastri, Raja and Radha Reddy, Swapana Sundari and Yamini Krishnamurti.

Manipuri

- Manipuri is one of the six major classical dances of India. The most striking part of Manipuri dance is its colourful decoration, lightness of dancing foot, delicacy of *abhinaya* (drama), lilting music and poetic charm. Manipuri dance is not only a medium of worship and delight but also essential for all socio-cultural ceremonies of Manipuri people. Popular exponents are Javeri sisters, Rita Devi, Nirmala Mehta, Guru Bipin Singh etc.

Mohiniattam

- Mohiniattam from Kerala is a solo female dance and is known for its rhythmic and unbroken flow of the body movements. Mohiniattam has the grace and elegance of Bharatanatyam and vigour of Kathakali.
- Famous exponents of this dance form are Kalyani Amma, Vaijayanthimala, Bharati Shivaji and Hema Malini.

Odissi

- Odissi is one of the famous classical Indian dances from Odisha state.
- It is a graceful and sensous dance style and involves the *tribhanga* (three bends) posture.
- The (three bends) symbolise the means to escape the limitations of the body.
- Famous **dancers** of Odissi are Indrani Rehman, Sonal Mansingh, Kiran Sengal, Rani Karna, Sharon Lowen and Myrta Barvie.

Folk Dances and Tribal Dances in India

States	Dances
Maharashtra	Kathakeertan, Lezim, Dandaniya, Tamasha, Gafa, Dahikala, Lavani, Mauni, Dasavtar
Karnataka	Huttari, Suggi Kunitha, Yakashagana
Kerala	Kaikottikali, Kaliyattam, Tappatikkali
Tamil Nadu	Kolattam, Pinnal Kolattam, Kummi, Kavadi, Karagam
Andhra Pradesh	Ghanta Mardala, Veedhi Natakam, Burrakatha
Odisha	Ghumara Sanchar, Chadya Dandanata, Chhau
Paschim Banga	Kathi, Chhau, Baul, Kirtan, Jatra, Lama
Asom	Bihu, Khel, Gopal, Rash Lila, Tabal Chongli, Canoe
Punjab	Giddha (women), Bhangra (men)
Jammu and Kashmir	Rauf, Hikat
Himachal Pradesh	Jhora, Jhali, Dangli, Mahasu, Jadda, Jhainta, Chharhi
Haryana	Jhumar, Ras Leela, Phag dance, Daph, Dhamal, Loor, Gugga, Khoria, Gagor
Gujarat	Garba, Dandiya Rass, Tippani, Gomph
Rajasthan	Ginad, Chakri, Gangore, Teratali, Khayal, Jhulan Leela, Jhuma, Suisini
Bihar	Jata Jatin, Jadur, Chhau, Kathaputli, Bakho, Jhijhiya, Samochakwa, Karma, Jatra, Natna
Uttar Pradesh	Nautanki, Thora, Chappeli, Raslila, Kajri
Madhya Pradesh	Karma
Meghalaya	Laho
Goa	Mando
Mizoram	Khantumm
Uttarakhand	Choliya, Pandav Nritya, Jagars, Jhora

Classical Dancers of India

Dance	Dancer
Bharatnatyam	Bala Saraswati, CV Chandrasekhar, Leela Samson, Mrinalini Sarabhai, Padma Subramanyam, Rukmini Devi, Sanyukta Panigrahi, Sonal Mansingh, Yamini Krishnamurti
Kathak	Bharti Gupta, Birju Maharaj, Damayanti Joshi, Durga Das, Gopi Krishna, Kumudini Lakhia, Sambhu Maharaj, Sitara Devi
Kuchipudi	Josyula Seetharamaiah, Vempathi Chinna Sathyam
Manipuri	Guru Bipin Sinha, Jhaveri Sisters, Nayana Jhaveri, Nirmala Mehta, Savita Mehta
Odissi	Debaprasad Das, Dhirendra Nath Patnaik, Indrani Rahman, Kelucharan Mahapatra, Priyambada Mohanty
Kathakali	Mrinalini Sarabhai, Guru Shankaran, Namboodripad, Thottam Shankaran, Kutti Nayyar, Shankar Kurup, KC Pannikar, TT Ram Kulti Nayyar, etc
Mohiniyattam	Protima Devi, Sanyukta Panigrahi, Sonal Mansingh, Pankaj Charan Das, Kelucharan Mahapatra, Madhvi Mudgal, etc

ARCHITECTURE

Indian architecture, which has evolved through centuries, is the result of socio-economic and geographical conditions of the region. Indian architecture evolved in various stages in different parts and regions of the country. Apart from the natural evolution Indian architecture was generally affected by many great and important historic developments.

Rajput Architecture

- The Rajputs were great patrons of art and architecture, the finest examples being their forts and palaces. The Rajput palaces are complex compositions built as inner citadels surrounded by the city and enclosed by a fortified wall as at Chittorgarh and Jaisalmer. Some forts, such as those at Bharatpur and Deeg, were protected by wide moats.
- The palaces of Jaisalmer, Bikaner, Jodhpur, Udaipur and Kota represent the maturity of the Rajput style.

Deccan Style

- The architecture of the Deccan is marked by its distinct originality and independence of style, unlike the architectural styles of the other provinces, which combined both the temple architecture and the Islamic building ideals. It derived its elements from the architectural styles of the Sultan of Delhi and that of the distant Persia.
- Some key features of this style are the presence of bulbous domes with lotus neck, military style of architecture, presence of thick walls and combination of gateway and mosque-like *Charminar.*

Mughal Style

- The medieval period saw great developments in the field of architecture. With the coming of Muslims to India, many new features came to be introduced in buildings. The development of Muslim style of architecture of this period can be called the Indo-Islamic architecture or the Indian architecture influenced by Islamic Art.

- The Indo-Islamic style was neither strictly Islamic nor strictly Hindu.
- The earliest building of this period is Quwwat-ul-Islam Mosque and the Qutub Minar at Delhi.

PUPPETRY

- The early puppet shows in India dealt mostly with histories of great kings. Princes and heroes and also political satire in rural areas.
- Slowly, this art form emerged from the precincts of the temple and villages to reach out to the outside world performing on various social and contemporary themes in Indian towns and cities.

PAINTING

The history of Indian paintings is just about as old as the history of the people of India. The most primitive instances of paintings in India can be traced back to cave paintings.

Mughal School

- This school has a specific style of South Asian painting. Usually, it was confined to miniatures either as book depictions or as individual works to be kept in albums.
- This practice materialised from Persian miniature painting, with Indian influences of Hindu, Buddhist and Jain.
- It wonderfully blossomed during the Mughal Empire. Later, this school of painting reached other Indian courts of Muslims and Hindus and afterwards Sikhs.
- Akbar and Jahangir were exceptionally great patrons of this painting. Mughal School of painting revolved around court scenes, portraits, hunting scenes, lovers, battle fronts etc.

Rajput School

- This school progressed and thrived during the 18th century in the majestic Rajputana courts.
- This school of painting flooded from the approach of Mughal painting.

- A typical style of painting with particular common characteristics came up in every Rajput realm.
- This school illustrated an assortment of themes like landscapes, events from the *Mahabharata, Ramayana,* Krishna's life and about human beings.

Cultural Heritage

Site	State
Mahabodhi Temple	Bihar
Red Fort	Delhi
Qutub Minar	Delhi
Humayun's Tomb	Delhi
Champaner Achaelogical Park	Gujarat
Churches of Old Goa	Goa
Jantar Mantar	Jaipur
Hampi	Karnataka
Pattadakal	Karnataka
Chhatrapati Shivaji Terminus	Mumbai, Maharashtra
Ajanta Caves	Maharashtra
Ellora Caves	Maharashtra
Sanchi Stupa	Madhya Pradesh
Khajuraho	Madhya Pradesh
Rock Shelters of Bhimbetka	Madhya Pradesh
Elephanta Caves	Maharashtra
Konark Sun Temple	Odisha
Mahabalipuram	Tamil Nadu
Great Living Chola Temples	Tamil Nadu
Agra Fort	Uttar Pradesh
Taj Mahal	Uttar Pradesh
Fatehpur Sikri	Uttar Pradesh
Mountain Railway of India	Paschim Banga

Bengal School

- This school was a fashion of art, which progressed during the British Raj of India in early 20th century.
- Indian Nationalism was greatly linked to this painting. British art administrators also supported and promoted it.
- Raja Ravi Verma and Abanindranath Tagore were amongst the pioneer artists of this school. Today's renowned artists, who belong to this School include Nilima Dutta, Sudip Roy, Paresh Maiti and Bikash Bhattacharjee.

WORLD HISTORY

Mesopotamian Civilisation

- It is the oldest civilisation of the world. Mesopotamia is the land between the rivers Tigris and Euphrates.
- Mesopotamians were the first to use **potter's wheel**, to make glass ware, to evolve a proper system of writing called **Cuneiform**. Cuneiform script was deciphered by **Henry Rawlinson**.
- Mesopotamians discovered **sexagesimal system** of counting (based on sixties), Pythogoras theorem and the length of day and night.

Chinese Civilisation

- The earliest civilisation was by the **Shang** (Chou) **Dynasty**, followed by the Chin and Han dynasties.
- In 3rd century BC, the ruler of China dynasty built the **Great Wall.**
- Chinese script was pictographic and their calendar was a combination of solar-lunar calendar.
- Silk became the chief item of export during the Hangs.
- The two major religions were Taoism and Confucianism. They invented water clock, abacus and umbrella.

Iranian Civilisation

- This civilisation developed in around 6th century BC by the Achaemenid Empire under its first ruler, Cyrus. His capital was at Pasaragadae.
- His successors were Darius I and Darius III. The Achaemenids introduced the use of gold and silver coins.
- Their main religion was **Zoroast- rianism**, founded by Zarathustra or Zoroaster. Their official language was **Aramaic**.

Greek Civilisation

- The civilisation developed around 800 BC, when the small villages clustered to form city-states.
- They worshipped Zeus (Sky God), Poseidon (Sea God), Apollo (Sun God), Athena (Goddess of victory) etc.
- In the Battle of Marathon (490 BC), Greeks defeated King Darius I. Alexander was the greatest Greek ruler.
- The Olympic Games originated in Greece. *Iliad* and *Odyssey* are among the best epics of the world written by Homer.

Roman Civilisation

- Italy was the centre of the civilisation. The city of Rome was founded by Romulus in 1000 BC on the bank of river Tiber.
- The war between Carthage and Rome is known as **Punic War** (264 BC to 146 BC).
- Julius Caesar, one of the generals, murdered Pompey, another general and occupied the throne. He was attached to the Egyptian queen Cleopatra. Caesar was succeeded by Octavian and Diocletion.
- Romans worshipped the planets. They developed the Latin language.
- Lucretius, Seneca, Cicero and Marus were the famous Roman philosophers and Horace and Virgil were the poets. Tacitus and Pliny were the historians.
- They invented 'concrete', useful for constructing buildings.

Renaissance

- The Renaissance or "Revival of learning" started in the AD 14th century in Italy.
- The fall of constantinople by the Turks in 1453 led to the dispersal of scholars throughout Italy. Renaissance led to the revival of classical learning, art and architecture humanism. Renaissance writers-Dante, Petrorch, Boccacciro and Machiavelli, came to the fore.
- Renaissance painters—Leonardo da Vinci (The last Supper and Monalisa), Michelangelo (The last Judgement and the fall of man) and Raphael (Madonna) emerged during Renaissance.
- The movement also helped in the development of printing press.

Reformation (16th Century)

- This movement was started in Germany by **Martin Luther**, by publicly protesting the sale of Letters of Indulgence.
- It was a revolt against **Roman Catholic Church**. As a result, Western Europe was split between Roman Catholic and protestant countries.

Glorious Revolution of England (1688)

- This revolution started against the policies of **King James II**. He tried to secure freedom of worship for Catholics.
- This united the **Whigs** and **Tories** of Anglican Church against him, and they invited William of Orange to occupy English throne.
- James II threw the great seal into the river Thames and fled to France. The event is known as **Glorious or Bloodless Revolution**.
- It ended the despotic rule of the Stuarts, established the modern budgetary system and the **Bill of Rights** (1689) was passed that settled down the problem of succession.

Industrial Revolution

- It began in Britain in AD 1750 with the invention of **Spinning Jenny** by Hargreaves, **Water frame** by Richard Arkwright (1769), **Mule** by Samuel Crompton (1779), **Power loom** by Emmund Cartwright (1785) and **Steam engine** by James Watt (1769).
- This fastened the production of cloth and better quality yarn were produced. The economic progress also affected the culture and society of the people.

American Revolution

- **George Washington**, the first President of America was the pioneer of this revolution.
- **Boston Tea Party** (1773) A group of citizens of Boston dumped the crates of tea, loaded on a ship of East India Company into the sea. This was because of the problem on tea tax.

- On 4th July, 1776, the **Declaration of Independence** was issued by Thomas Jafferson.
- The war ended with the Treaty of Paris in AD 1783.
- **Benjamin Franklin** established the American Philosophical Society. Americans were the first to have a written Constitution.

French Revolution

- The Revolution initiated on 5th May, 1789 during the kingship of Louis XVI.
- The immediate cause of the revolution was the extravagant expenditure and inefficiency by Louis XV and Louis XVI. Other causes were social inequality, heavy taxation etc.
- Montesquieu, Voltaire and Rousseau were the French writers and thinkers of the period.
- **Liberty, Equality and Fraternity** were the watch of the revolution.

Unification of Germany

- This was the result of the **Blood and Iron Policy** of Bismarck, the Prime Minister of King William I.
- After the Napoleonic war (1792-1855), the 38 independent states were unified under the king of Prussia. From 1815 to 1850, Austria ruled over the German confederation.
- Bismarck defeated Austria and dissolved the German confederation.
- He founded a new confederation of 22 states in 1866. The unification was completed with the Prussia-France War (1870), in which the French Emperor Louis Bonaparte was defeated.
- **William I**, the king of Prussia was declared as the Emperor of Germany at Versailles in France.

IMPORTANT WARS OF THE 20th CENTURY

Russo-Japanese War (1904-05)

The conflict arising from the rivalry of Russia and Japan for control of Manchuria and Korea resulted in the war. Russia was forced to surrender Korea, the Liaotung Peninsula and Sakhalin to Japan.

First World War (1914-18)

International conflict began between Austria and Serbia. The chief contestants were the Central Powers (Germany and Austria) and the Triple Entente (Britain, France and Russia). Many other countries joined as the war began. The naval blockade of Germany caused severe food shortages and helped to end the war.

Sino-Japanese Wars (1931-33)

Two wars between China and Japan, marking the beginning and the end of Japanese imperial expansion on the Asian mainland. The first war in 1894-95 arose from rivalry for control of Korea. The second war in 1937-45 developed from Japan's seizure of Manchuria.

Second World War (1939-45)

International conflict arising from disputes provoked by the expansionist policies of Germany in Europe and Japan in the far East. The axis powers- Germany, Italy and (after September 1940) Japan-controlled most of Europe and much of Northern Africa, China and Asia. The United States stayed out of the war until 7th December, 1941.

Arab-Israeli War (1948-1949, 1956, 1967, 1973-1974)

Conflict between Israel and the Arab states. After the creation of the state of Israel (14th May, 1948), troops from Egypt, Iraq, Lebanon, Syria and Trans Jordan (Modern Jordan) invaded the new nation. Simmering Arab-Israeli hostilities exploded into war in 1967, when Israel, assailed by Palestinian guerillas, launched a massive primitive strike against Egypt, the Arab world's leading state.

Korean War (1950-1953)

Conflict between North Korea, supported by China and South Korea supported by UN forces dominated by the USA. Negotiations continued for two years before a truce was agreed on in July 1953.

Vietnam War (1954-1975)

Conflict between US backed South Vietnam and the Viet Cong, who had the support of communist North Vietnam. It followed the partition of Vietnam. In 1975, South Vietnam was overrun by North Vietnamese forces, and the country was united under Communist rule.

Iran-Iraq War (1980-1990)

War began shortly after the Iranian Revolution of 1979. Iraq wanted control over oil-rich Iranian border territory.

Falkland War (1982)

Military conflict between Great Britain and Argentina on the question of sovereignty over the Falkland Islands led to the war. Britain won the war.

Gulf War (1991)

Military action by a US led coalition to expel Iraqi forces from Kuwait. Kuwait was liberated (26th February, 1991) and a ceasefire was declared on 28th February.

Bosnian War (1992-98)

Ethnically rooted war in Bosnia and Herzegovina, a republic of Yugoslavia with a multiethnic population-Muslims, Serbs and Croats.

US-Afghan War (2001)

Military action by US against Afghanistan in protest against the 11th September's, attack on WTC Towers.

Gulf War II (2003)

Military action by a US led coalition to oust Saddam Hussain from power in Iraq. It was conducted on the pretext of Iraq possessing Weapons of Mass Destruction (WMD).

FAQs (Indian History)

1. Who was the first Governor-General of Bengal?

2. The Battle of Wandiwash (1760) was fought between whom?

3. Who granted the permission to establish the French factory at Masulipatnam?

4. The trade monopoly of East India company was ended by which Act?

5. Sir Thomas Roe visited the court, of which Mughal emperor?

6. In which year was Harappan Civilisation discovered?

7. Water Management System of Harappan times has been unearthed at?

8. Which animal was not represented on the seals and terracotta art of the Indus Valley Civilisation?

9. Which Governor General is associated with Doctrine of Lapse?

10. Which place was the capital city of Tipu Sultan?

11. Patanjali is known for the compilation of which book?

12. Which Veda contains an account of magical charms and spells?

13. In ancient India, the earliest capital of Magadh kingdom was at

14. A Buddhist council during the reign of Ashoka was held at

15. Where did Lord Buddha breathed his last?

16. Who founded the independent Sultanate of Bengal?

17. Who is also known as Nigantha Natoputra?

18. Chinese traveller Hiuen-Tsang studied, at which university?

19. Under which system of assessment, the Britishers collected revenue directly from the farmers?

20. Who started the Public works Department in India (1848)?

21. Who gave the theory of economic drain in his book, "Poverty and the Un British Rule in India"?

22. Megasthenes was an ambassador, of which Greek king?

23. The division of Mauryan society in 7 classes is particularly mentioned, in which book?

24. Who was the first Mauryan ruler to conquer Deccan?

25. Who was first to decipher the Brahmi script of Ashoka?

26. Charaka was the famous court physician of which king?

27. The first President of All India Trade Union Congress was

28. The first Governor General and Viceroy of British India was

29. Which Chinese general defeated Kanishka?

30. Who was the founder of pattini cult related to worship of Kannagi?

31. The silver coins of Gupta period were Known as

32. The second session of INC was presided over by

33. Who was the first Muslim President of INC?

34. Who was the first Indian to become member of the British Parliament?

35. Which period marks the beginning of Indian temple architecture?

36. Which extremist leader dominated the Lucknow Pact in December, 1916?

37. The Prayag Prasasti/Allahabad Pillar Inscription is associated, with which ruler?

38. The rock-cut temples of Mahabalipuram were built under the patronage of king?

39. Two great religious conferences were held by Harshavardhan at

40. The subject matter of Ajanta painting pertains to to religion

41. In which movement did Gandhiji made the first use of Hunger Strike?

42. From where did Acharya Vinoba Bhave start the individual Satyagraha in 1940?

43. Use of white marble, long legs and slender frames-were the characteristic features of which ancient art forms of India.

44. First major inscription in classical sanskrit is that of

45. Who attended the Congress of Oppressed Nationalist at Brussels in 1927, on behalf of the Indian National Congress?

46. Who was the last British Viceroy of India?

47. Who was the President of Indian National Congress, when the Mountabatten Plan was accepted?

48. The final arrangements for Indian independence was worked out by which plan?

49. Who constructed the Jagannath temple at Puri?

50. Who advocated on behalf of Indian National Army in 1946 in the Red Fort trials?
51. Alberuni visited India, with which muslim invader?
52. For which movement did Gandhiji give the slogan, 'Do or Die'?
53. The khilji Sultans of Delhi were, of which tribe?
54. Who was the Governor General of India during the launch of Civil Disobedience Movement?
55. Qutub Minar was completed, by which Sultan?
56. Who Presided over the All India Khilafat Conference at Delhi(1919)?
57. In the sultanate period, the highest rural authority for land revenue was
58. Which Committee was appointed by the British Government to investigate in Jallianwala Bagh massacre?
59. The city of Jaunpur was founded in the memory of
60. The congress in Travancore launched a Civil Disobedience Movement against, which Dewan of Travancore state?
61. Who was the Chairman of Joint Parliamentary Committee (1935), that led to the framing of the Act of 1935?
62. Which Congress President negotiated with both Cripps Mission and Lord Wavell?
63. Who constructed the monumental Rayagopurams in front of temples at Hampi and Tirupati?
64. 'A Forgotten Empire,' written by the historian Robert Sewell refers to which empire?
65. Tulsidas composed his 'Ramcharitamanasa' in the reign of
66. Which Maratha Peshwa followed the ideal of 'Hindu pada-Pashahi'?
67. The Laxman Era was started in AD 1119, by which dynasty?
68. Mahaballipuram was established by the
69. The Balkan Plan for fragmentation of India was framed by
70. Who organised the Chittagong Armoury raid?
71. The leader of Bardoli Satyagrah(1928) was
72. Yahya bin Ahmed Sirhindi, the author of 'Tarikh -i-Mubaraqshahi', lived in the period of which dynasty?
73. In the Delhi Sultanate, an administrative unit called *Pargana* was headed by
74. Which muslim ruler was hailed as the Jagadguru by his subjects because of his belief in secularism?
75. Where is the Vijaya Vithala temple, having its 56 carved pillars emitting musical notes located?
76. Who was the founder of Sufi order in India?

Answers

1. Warren Hastings, 2. English and French, 3. Abdulla Qutub Shah, 4. Charter Act of 1833, 5. Jahangir, 6. 1921, 7. Dholavira, 8. Cow, 9. Lord Dalhousie, 10. Srirangapattanam, 11. Yoga Sutra, 12. Atharava Veda, 13. Rajgir (Girivaraja), 14. Pataliputra, 15. Kushinagar, 16. Murshid Quli khan, 17. Vardhman Mahavira, 18. Nalanda, 19. Ryotwari, 20. Lord Dalhousie, 21. Dada Bhai Naoroji, 22. Seleucus Nikator 23. Indica of Megasthenes, 24. Bindusara, 25. James Princep, 26. Kanishka, 27. Lala Lajpat Rai, 28. Lord Canning, 29. Pen chao, 30. Sengattivan, 31. Rupyaka, 32. Surendranath Banerjee, 33. Badar-ud- din Tayabji, 34. Dadabhai Naoroji, 35. Gupta period, 36. Bal Gangadhar Tilak, 37. Samudragupta, 38. Pandya Kings, 39. Kannauj and Prayag, 40. Buddhism, 41. Ahmedabad Strike, 1918, 42. Pavnar in Maharashtra, 43. Amravati School of Art, 44. Rudradaman, 45. Jawaharlal Nehru, 46. Lord Mountbatten, 47. JB Kripalani, 48. Cabinet Mission Plan, 49. Anant Varman, 50. Bhulabhai Desai, 51. Mahmud Ghaznavi, 52. Quit India Movement, 53. Turks, 54. Lord Irwin, 55. Iltutmish, 56. MK Gandhi, 57. Choudhary, 58. Hunter Commission, 59. Mohammad-bin Tughlaq, 60. CP Rama Swami Aiyer, 61. Lord Linlithgow, 62. Abul Kalam Azad, 63. Krishna Deva Raya, 64. Vijayanagara Empire, 65. Akbar, 66. Baji Rao I, 67. Senas, 68. Pallavas, 69. Lord Mountbatten, 70. Surya Sen, 71. Sardar Vallabhbhai Patel, 72. Sayyid, 73. Amil, 74. Ibrahim Adil Shah-II, 75. Hampi, 76. Khwaja Muin-ud-din Chisti

GEOGRAPHY

WORLD GEOGRAPHY

- Geography is the science that studies the lands, the features, the inhabitants and the phenomena of the Earth.
- The word geography adopted in the 2nd century BC by the Greek Scholar **Eratosthenes**.

Branches of Geography

Geography is divided into two main branches i.e. physical geography and human geography.

Some Contributors to Geography

- **Eratosthenes** was the first person to calculate the circumference of the Earth and also calculate the tilt of the Earth's axis.
- **Anaximander** created the first map of world.
- **Ainville** made the first map of India.
- **Ptolemy** first presented India on the world map.
- **Anthropogeography** was written by **Friedrich Ratzel**.

Human Geography

Human geography is a branch of the geography that studies the world, its people, communities and cultures with an emphasis on relations of land across space and place.

The fields of human geography are as follow:
- Cultural geography
- Development geography
- Economic geography
- Health geography
- Historical geography
- Political geography
- Population geography
- Settlement geography

Physical Geography

Physical geography deals with the physical environment and the various process that bring about changes in the physical environment on the Earth surface.

The fields of physical geography are as follow:
- **Geomorphology** It is the scientific study of landforms and processes that shape them.
- **Hydrology** It is the study of the movement, distribution and quality of water on Earth, including the hydrological cycle, water resources and environmental watershed sustainability.
- **Climatology** It is the study of climate, scientifically defined as weather conditions averaged over a period of time.
- **Pedology** It is the study of soils in their natural environment.
- **Glaciology** It is the study of glaciers and ice sheets.
- **Biogeography** It is the study of relationships of organisms with their environment.

Universe

- The study of universe is known as Cosmology.
- The universe is commonly defined as the totality of everything that exists including all physical matter and energy, the planets, stars, galaxies and the contents of intergalactic space.
- The universe comprises of billions of galaxies. The galaxies are made up of millions of stars held together by the force of gravity and these stars account for most of the masses of the galaxy. **Andromeda** is our nearest galaxy.
- Our own galaxy is called the **Milky Way** (or the Akash Ganga) and it contains about 300 billion stars and one of these is our Sun. Planets and other objects revolve around the Sun and make up the solar system with the Sun at the centre.
- In AD 140, **Ptolemy** propounded the theory that the Earth was the centre of the universe and the Sun and the other heavenly bodies revolved around it.
- In 1543, **Copernicus** said that the Sun is the centre of universe and not the Earth.
- **Kepler** supported Copernicus but said that the Sun is the centre of solar system and not the universe.
- In 1924, **Edwin Hubble** first demonstrated existence of galaxies beyond Milky Way.
- *Structurally, the galaxies are found in three forms*
  (i) **Spiral** have a central nucleus with great spiral arms. Milky Way and Andromeda are the examples.
  (ii) **Elliptical** without spiral arms.
  (iii) **Irregular** with no shape.

Evolution of Universe

The three main theories put forward to explain the origin and evolution of the universe are

(i) **Big Bang Theory** (Proposed by Georges Lemaitre) Big Bang was an explosion that occurred 13.8 billion years ago, leading to the formation of galaxies of stars and other heavenly bodies.

(ii) **Steady State Theory** Bondi, Gold and Fred Hoyle developed this theory and states that although the universe is expanding, it nevertheless does not change its appearance over time, it has no beginning and no end.

(iii) **The Pulsating Theory** According to this theory, the universe is supposed to be expanding and contracting alternately i.e. pulsating. At present, the universe is expanding.

NASA has launched the Cosmic Background Explorer (COBE) and the Wilkinson Microwave Anistropy Probe (WMAP) missions to study the radiation present in the universe.

Stars

- Stars are heavenly bodies made up of hot burning gases, thus shining by their own light.
- If the star is bigger than the Sun but not more than twice as big, it will turn into a **Neutron star** or **Pulsar**. They are formed due to novae or super novae explosion.
- A star's colour indicates the temperature of its surface. Blue colour denotes maximum temperature, then comes yellow, then red etc.

Evolutionary Stages of a Star

1. **Proto Star** It is the stage, where the helium core become increasingly heavy, accompanied with expanding outer layers.
2. **Red Giant** This stage results into the swelling and reddening of the outer regions of the star. Such stars of gigantic dimension is called **Red Star**.
3. **White Dwarf** If the mass of the star is relatively small like that of our Sun, the gases that reach the outer layer are expelled. As these expelled gases cool and contract, the star becomes a White Dwarf.

Stars: Quick Digest

- Brightest star outside solar system is Sirius, also called as **Dog Star**.
- Closest star to our solar system is Proxima Centauri (4.2 light years away). Followed by Alpha Centauri (4.3 light years away) and Barnard's Star (5.9 light years away).

Concept of Black Hole and Chandrashekhar Limit

- There is an upper limit to the mass of stars, above which two things are possible
  1. Explosion of the star to form neutron stars called **Pulsar**.
  2. Collapse and compaction of the star to form Black Holes.
- Therefore, the black holes are formed due to collapse and compaction under gravity, at the end of the life cycle.
- A renowned Indian Physicist Chandrashekhar had predicted an upper limit to the mass of stars, which is called as Chandrashekhar limit. It is 1.44 times the mass of the Sun.
- *Some of the units used for the calculation of these distances are as follows:*

Units of Distance

Unit	Description of the Unit
Light year	It is the distance that light can travel in 1 year. Our solar system is less than 1 light day across.
Astronomical unit	It is the average distance between the Sun and the Earth. 1 light year = (almost) 60000 Aus
Parsec	It is the distance from the Earth to a star that has parallax of 1 arc second. The actual length is about 3.262 light years.

SOLAR SYSTEM

- The solar system comprises the Sun, 8 planets, their Moon and other non-stellar objects, which are believed to have been developed from the condensation of gases and other lesser bodies.

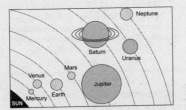

- The Sun is at the centre of the solar system and all the planets revolve around it in elliptical orbit. It is the nearest star to the Earth.

- The size of solar system has been estimated to be about 10^5 AU.

Components of the Solar System

Our Solar System consists of

- the Sun, Eight planets (excluding Pluto) and their respective satellites.
- interstellar debris such as asteroids, meteoroids, comets. The electrically charged gases, called **Plasma**.
- interplanetary dust particles.
- the components of solar system other than planets dwarf planets and satellites are called as **Small Solar System Bodies** (SSSB).

Origin of the Solar System

Various theories were given to explain the Origin of the Solar System.

Hypothesis	Propounder
Gaseous Hypothesis	Kant
Nebular Hypothesis	Laplace
Planetesimal Hypothesis	Chamberline and Moulton
Tidal Hypothesis	Sir James Jeans and Harold Jeffreys
Binary Star Hypothesis	HN Russell
Supernova Hypothesis	F Hoyle
Interstellar Dust Hypothesis	Otto Schmidt
Electromagnetic Hypothesis	H Alfven
Protoplanet Hypothesis	G Kuiper
Nebular Cloud Hypothesis	Dr Von Weizsacker

THE SUN

- The Sun accounts for more than 99 per cent of the mass of the Solar System and due to this, the Sun exerts immense gravitational pull to keep the planets rotating around it in definite elliptical orbit.
- The Sun is the major source of energy of the solar system. The energy is provided by the nuclear fusion reaction, that converts hydrogen into helium in the core of the Sun.

- The glowing surface of the Sun that we see is called as **Photosphere**. Above the photosphere is the red coloured **Chromospheres** and beyond it is the magnificent corona, which is visible during eclipses.
  - Hydrogen and helium are the main gases present in the Sun.
  - It has a surface temperature of about 6000°C.
  - It takes 224 million years to complete one circle (revolution) around the galactic circle called **cosmic year**.
  - The Sun is 1300000 times bigger than the Earth in terms of volume.
- Superimposed on Sun's white light are hundred of dark lines called **Fraunhofer lines**. Each line indicates some elements present in the Solar System.

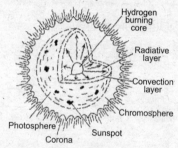

Layers of the Sun

Specifics of the Sun

Average distance from the Earth	149598900 km
Diametre	1391980 km
Temperature of the core	15000000°C
Rotation speed	25.38 days (with respect to equator); 33 days (with respect to poles)
Time taken by sunlight to reach the Earth	8 min and 16.6 sec

Concepts Associated with the Sun

- **Solar Winds** The Sun is continuously emitting streams of photon in all directions either as spiral streams called **Solar Wind** or **bouts of incandescent material** called **Solar Flares**. Solar flares being hot ionised gases pose danger to satellite communication.

- **Aurora** The constituent particles of the solar wind are trapped by the Earth's magnetic field and enter the Earth's upper atmosphere as Aurora. It is described as Aurora Borealis in the Northern hemisphere and Aurora Australis in Southern hemisphere.
- **Plages and Sunspots** The surface of the Sun is continuously changing. Bright spots are called **Plages** and dark spots are called **Sunspots**. The Sunspots are cold and dark regions on the Sun's surface with a periodicity of 11 years. These spots greatly influence the global climate.

PLANETS

- Planets are opaque bodies, which continuously revolve around and are lighted by the Sun. There are **eight planets** in the solar system.
- The sequence of planets according to their size (in descending order) is Jupiter, Saturn, Uranus, Neptune, Earth, Venus, Mars and Mercury.
- The sequence of planets according to their distance from the Sun is Mercury, Venus, Earth, Mars, Jupiter, Saturn, Uranus and Neptune.

Classification of Planets

1. **Inner Planets** Include Mercury, Venus, Earth and Mars.
2. **Outer Planets** Include Jupiter, Saturn, Uranus and Neptune.

Inner Planet	Outer Planet
They are called as **Terrestrial** or **Rock** planets. They are nearer to the Sun.	They are called as **Jovian** or **Gaseous** planets. They are far away from the Sun.
They have very few natural satellites (or moons) or no satellites.	They have a large number of natural satellites (or moons).
They have a core of molten metals.	They have ring system around the Sun.
They move faster and have a shorter period of revolution.	They move rather slowly and have a longer period of revolution.

Specifics of the Planets

Biggest Planet	Jupiter
Biggest Satellite	Ganymede
Blue Planet	Earth
Green Planet	Uranus
Brightest Planet	Venus
Brightest Star Outside Solar System	Sirius (Dog Star)
Closest Star of Solar System	Proxima Centauri
Coldest Planet	Neptune
Evening Star	Venus
Farthest Planet from Sun	Neptune
Planet with Maximum Number of Satellites	Jupiter
Fastest Revolution in Solar System	Mercury
Hottest Planet	Venus
Densest Planet	Earth
Fastest Rotation in Solar System	Jupiter
Morning Star	Venus
Nearest Planet to Earth	Venus
Nearest Planet to Sun	Mercury
Red Planet	Mars
Slowest Revolution in Solar System	Neptune
Slowest Rotation in Solar System	Venus
Smallest Planet	Mercury
Smallest Satellite	Phobos
Earth's Twin	Venus
Only Satellite with an Atmosphere Like Earth	Titan

A Comparative Study of the Planets of the Solar System

Planets	Special Characteristics	Rotation and Revolution Time	Important Physical Properties	Satellite Systems
Mercury	Smallest and the innermost planet. It has no atmosphere. It has a cratered surface, much like the Moon.	Rotation : 58.65 days Revolution: 88 days (Fastest Revolution in the Solar System).	It has the maximum diurnal range of temperature.	No satellite
Venus	Also called as the veiled planet, known as (**Evening and Morning star**) as it is seen in the East in morning and in the West in the evening. It is the brightest object in solar system because of almost 70% albedo. It contains 90 to 95% CO_2. The night and day temperature almost the same.	It has the slowest rotational speed. It has almost equal rotation and revolution. Rotation (Clockwise) 257 days and Revolution: 224.7 days.	Rotates from East to West unlike the other planets. It is the hottest planet.	No satellite
Earth	The Earth is neither too hot nor too cold. It is called as the **Blue Planet** due to the presence of water.	Rotation :24 hours; Revolution : 365 days and 6 hours.	It is the densest of all and is unique for the presence of higher forms of life.	Moon is the only natural satellite.
Mars	Called as **Red Planet**. It has a thin atmosphere comprising of nitrogen and argon.	Rotation 24.6 hour. (almost equal to Earth) Revolution: 687 days.	It is marked by dormant volcanoes. Nix Olympia is the highest mountain, which is three times higher than the Mount Everest.	Two satellites : Phobos and Deimos .

Planets	Special Characteristics	Rotation and Revolution Time	Important Physical Properties	Satellite Systems
Jupiter	It is the largest planet in the solar system with a mass 2.5 times greater than the combined mass of all the remaining planets, satellites and asteroids put together. In contains hydrogen, helium, methane and ammonia. A great red spot is detected on it.	Fastest rotational velocity (9.8 hrs)	It is too massive to solidify as a planet but not massive enough to develop nuclear fusion and become a star. It gives off more energy than it receives from the Sun, because of the heat inside.	It has 67 satellites. Some of the prominent satellites are: Europa, Callisto and Ganymede. These are called as **Galileon Moons**.
Saturn	It is the 2nd largest planet and is surrounded by a set of eight rings, which are made up of primordial dust and ice particles.	Rotation in 10.3 hours. Revolution in $29\frac{1}{2}$ years.	It has the least density of all the satellites. 30 times less dense than the Earth.	It has 62 satellites, the largest being Titan.
Uranus	It is unique as its axis of rotation is inclined at 98° to its orbital plane.	Unlike the others, which spin on their axis, Uranus actually rolls, apparently from North to South.	Surrounded by a system of 9 faint rings.	It has 27 satellites. The prominent are Miranda Ariel etc.
Neptune	It is a penultimate planet, has a dynamic atmosphere, which contains an the Earth sized blemish called the **Great Dark Spot** that is reminiscent of Jupiter's Great Red Spot .	Rotation 15.7 days and Revolution 165 years.	It has 5 faint rings .It appears as **Greenish Star.**	It has 14 satellites. The prominent are Triton and Nereid.

Pluto is not a Planet Now

- Pluto was discovered by Clyde Tombaugh in 1930.
- The redefinition of planet by the International Astronomical Union (IAU) on 24th August, 2006 states that, in the solar system, a planet is a celestial body that
  - it is in orbit around the Sun.
  - it has sufficient mass so that it assumes a hydrostatic equilibrium (nearly round) shape.
  - it has cleared the neighbourhood around its orbit.
- A non-satellite body fulfilling the first two rule is classified as a Dwarf planet. So, Pluto is considered as Dwarf planet.

THE MOON

The study of Moon is called Selenology.

Specifics of the Moon

Distance from Earth	382200 km
Diameter	3475 km
Mass (with respect to Earth)	1 : 8.1
Ratio of Gravitational Pull of Moon and Earth	1 : 6
Highest Mountain	35387 ft (Leibnitz Mountain)
Time Taken by Moonlight to Reach Earth	1.3 s
Rotation speed	3680 kmph
Speed of Revolution around Earth	3680 kmph
Revolution Period around Earth	27 days, 7 h, 43 min and 11.47s

Rotation Period	27 day, 7 h, 43 min and 11.47s
Atmosphere	Absent
Part of Moon not visible from Earth	41%
Maximum distance from Earth (Apogee)	406000 km
Minimum distance from Earth (Perigee)	356400 km
Circumference	11000 km

- Moon is also known as the **fossil planet**.
- The Moon is the only natural satellite of the Earth.
- The Moon has no atmosphere, no twilight and no sound.
- The size of the Moon is one-fourth (1/4th) the size of the Earth.
- Gravitational pull of the Moon is one-sixth (1/6th) that of the Earth.
- Silicon, iron, magnesium etc elements are found mainly on the Moon's surface.

Interstellar Debirs :

Asteroids, Meteoroids, Comets

Various Aspects	Asteroids or Planetoids	Comets	Meteoroids/Meteors
Constitutents and Genesis	Composed of rocks, dust and metal. They cannot retain their atmosphere due to small size.	Comets may originate in a huge cloud called the **Oort cloud** that is thought to surround the solar system. It is composed of frozen gases and dust.	Meteoroids are small fragments of rocks and metal. Under the Earth's gravitational field, they become white hot through friction as they fall through the atmosphere and are seen as the **Meteors** or **Shooting stars.**
Shape and Size	No definite shape, rather same as of Planetoids or small planet.	Comets have a head and tail, where the tail always points away from the Sun because of the solar wind and the radiation pressure.	No definite shape.
Orbit	They orbit the Sun in the asteroid belt, which lies between the orbits of Mars and Jupiter.	They have an extremely eccentric orbit but with definite periodicity.	Meteoroids travel through space. Meteors are scattered in the interplanetary space of the solar system.

The Earth

- Earth is the third planet from the Sun and the densest and the fifth-largest of the eight planets in the solar system. It is also the largest of the solar system's four terrestrial planets. Earth is also called as **Blue Planet**.
- The age of the Earth is estimated at about 4.6 billion years. The history of the Earth is studied in terms of geological eras, periods and epochs. The whole history is divided into three Eras-**Palaeozoic**, **Mesozoic** and **Cenozoic**.

Geological History of the Earth

Period	Beginning (years ago)	Remarks
Cenozoic Era Quaternary Period		
Holocene Epoch	10000	Modern man
Pleistocene Epoch	2 million	Homo Sapiens
Tertiary Period		
Pliocene Epoch	5 million	Early human ancestor
Miocene Epoch	24 million	Flowering plants and trees
Oligocene Epoch	38 million	Early horses, cats, dogs, camel
Eocene Epoch	55 million	Rabbits, hare
Palaeocene Epoch	63 million	Small mammals : Rats, mice
Mesozoic Era		
Cretaceous Period	138 million	Extinction of dinosaurs
Jurassic Period	205 million	Age of dinosaurs
Triassic Period	240 million	Frogs and turtles
Palaeozoic Era		
Permian Period	290 million	Reptile dominate, Replace amphibians
Lower Carboniferous Period	330 million	1st Reptiles
Upper Carboniferous Period	360 million	Fish
Devonian Period	410 million	Amphibians
Silurian Period	435 million	Corals
Ordovician Period	500 million	Graptolites
Cambrian Period	570 million	Trilobites
Pre-Cambrian Time	4.5 billion	Bacteria

Composition of Whole Earth

1. Iron—35%
2. Oxygen—30%
3. Silicon—15%
4. Magnesium—13%
5. Nickel—2.4%
6. Sulphur—1.9%
7. Calcium—1.1%
8. Aluminium—1.4%
9. Others—0.5%

Specifics of the Earth

Age	4.6 billion years
Mass	5.9×10^{24} kg
Volume	1083×10^{12} Km^3
Mean Density	5.513 g/cm^3
Shape	An oblate spheroid or a geoid
Radius of Earth	6400 km
Total surface area	509700000 sq km
Land area (29%)	148400000 sq km
Water area (71%)	361300000 sq km
Rotation time	23 hours 56 minute and 4.09 seconds
Revolution time	365 days, 5 hours, 48 minutes and 45.51 seconds
Orbit speed about the Sun	29.8 km/second
Mean surface temperature	14°C
Highest temperature recorded	58°C Al-Aziziyah
Mean Distance from the Sun	149598500 km
Inclination of polar axis from orbital plane	23° 26 min and 59 s
Deepest ocean point	11034 m, Mariana Trench (Pacific Oceans)
Time coordinate of Earth	Longitude
Temperature coordinate of Earth	Latitudes

THE EARTH'S MOVEMENT

- *The Earth moves in space in two distinct ways:Rotation and Revolution.*
  (i) It rotates on its own axis from West to East once in every 24 hours. It causes day and night.
  (ii) It revolves around the Sun in an orbit once in every 365¼ days. It causes the seasons and the year.

Rotation of Earth

- Spins on its imaginary axis from West to East in 23 hours, 56 minutes and 40.91 seconds.
- The rotational speed at equator is maximum (1667 km/hr) and then decreases towards the poles, where it is zero.
- The days and the nights are equal at the equator.
  The rotation of the Earth has the following implications such as:
  - Causation of day and night.
  - Change in the direction of winds and ocean currents.
  - Rise and fall of tides everyday.
  - A difference of one hour between the two meridians which are 15° apart.

REVOLUTION OF EARTH

- It is the Earth's motion in elliptical orbit around the Sun. It takes 365 days, 5 hours, 48 minutes and 45.51 seconds. It leads to one extra day in every fourth year.
  The revolution of the Earth results in
  - changes of season.
  - variation of the length of the days and nights at different times of the year.

Shifting of the wind belts.

Below figure shows the revolution of the Earth and its effects on seasons and the variations of lengths of day and night.

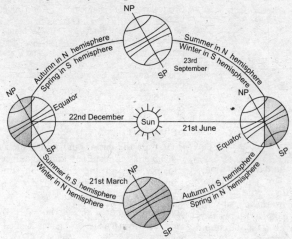

Revolution of the Earth

Major Difference Between Rotation and Revolution of Earth

Rotation	Revolution
Turning around the Earth on its own axis.	Movement of the Earth around the Sun.
Earth takes 24 hours to complete one rotation.	The Earth takes 365.25 days to complete revolution.
Rotation causes day and night.	Revolution along with inclination of the Earth on its axis causes change in seasons.

Earth's Position *wrt* Moon

Apogee	Perigee
The period of the farthest distance between the Moon and the Earth is called Apogee. It is about 407000 km.	The period of the nearest distance between the Moon and the Earth is called **Perigee**. It is about 364000 km.

Earth's Position *wrt* Sun

Perihelion	Aphelion
The period of the nearest distance between the Earth and the Sun is Perihelion. It happens on 3rd January and the distance is 147 million km.	The period of the farthest distance between the Earth and the Sun is Aphelion. It happens on 4th July and the distance is 152 million km.

Tilt of the Earth's Axis

- The axis of the Earth is inclined to the plane of ecliptic (the plane, in which the Earth orbits round the Sun) at an angle of 66½° giving rise to different seasons and varying lengths of day and night.
- If the axis were perpendicular to this plane, all parts of the globe would have equal days and nights at all times of the year.

- The Earth is tilted about 23.5° from a line perpendicular to ecliptic plane.

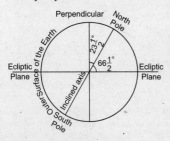

Equinoxes

- These are the days, when days and nights are equal. Under this situation, the Sun is vertically overhead at the equator. It happens on two days of the year i.e. 21st March and 23rd September.
- 21st March: Vernal Equinox.
- 23rd September: Autumnal Equinox.

Solstice Summer Solstice

- After the March equinox, the Sun appears to move Northward and is vertically overhead at the Tropic of Cancer on 21st June. This is known as Summer Solstice.
- On 21st June, the Northern hemisphere will have its longest day and shortest night. The Southern hemisphere will have shortest day and longest night.

Winter Solstice

- On 22nd December, the Sun is overhead at the Tropic of Capricorn. This is the winter solstice, when the Southern hemisphere will have its longest day and shortest night.
  A summary of daylight hours in the Northern and Southern hemisphere is as follows:

Winter Solstice

Longest day in the Northern hemisphere	21st June
Shortest day in the Northern hemisphere	22nd December
Equal day and night in the Northern hemisphere	21st March and 23rd September
Longest day in the Southern hemisphere	22nd December
Shortest day in the Southern hemisphere	21st June
Equal day and night in the Southern hemisphere	21st March and 23rd September

Seasons

- They are the periods into which the year can be divided as a result of the climatic conditions, mainly due to the changes in duration and intensity of solar radiation.
- *There are four seasons such as*:

Spring	Summer	Autumn	Winter
When the Sun is directly overhead the equator. (21st March)	When the Sun is directly overhead Tropic of Cancer -the North temperate zone experiences summer. (21st June)	When the Sun returns to the equator and the North temperate zone experiences the season of autumn. (23rd September)	The Sun is at the Tropic of Capricorn and the North temperate zone experiences winter. (22nd December)

Latitude

- Latitude is the angular distance of a point on the Earth surface from the centre of the Earth, measured in degree. These lines are called **parallels** of **latitude** and on the **globe** they are circles. The circumference of the circles decreases from equator to pole and at the pole it converses to a point.
- The distance between any two parallels of latitude is always equal. One degree latitude = Approx 111 km. The most important lines of latitudes are Equator (0°), the Tropic of Cancer (23½°N), the Tropic of Capricorn (23½°S), the Arctic Circle (66½°N) and the Antarctic Circle (66½°S).

Longitude

- Longitude is the angular distance of a point on the Earth surface along the equator, East or West from the **Prime meridian**. On the globe, they form semi-circles from pole to pole passing through the equator.

- Prime meridian is the semi-circle from pole to pole, from which all the other meridians radiate Eastwards and Westwards up to 180°. In 1884, it has been decided that the zero meridian is one that passes through the Royal Astronomical Observatory at Greenwich near London. 180° meridian (International Date Line) is exactly opposite to the prime meridian. Such points are called antipodal points.

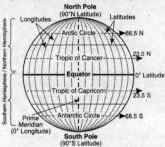

Latitude and Longitude on the Earth

Universal Time (Standard time) and Time Zones

- To avoid confusion about having many local times within one country, a particular meridian is chosen for the whole country, whose time is known as **standard time**.
- The Indian Government has accepted the meridian of 82.5 degree East for standard time, which is 5 hrs 30 mins ahead of the Greenwich Mean Time.

- The Earth is divided in 24 longitudinal zones, each being 15 degree or 1 hour apart in time (360 degree = 24 hours, 360/24 =15 degree in 1 hour) or 1 degree in 4 minute are called Standard Time Zones.
- Larger countries such as USA, Russia and Canada, which have greater East-West stretch have to adopt several time zones for practical purposes.
- Russia has as many as 11 time zones.
- Both USA and Canada have five time zones, *viz,* the Atlantic, Eastern, Central, Mountain and Pacific time zones.
- A simple memory aid for time is East-Gain-Add (EGA) and West-Lose-Subtract (WLS).

International Date Line

- It is the 180 degree meridian running over the Pacific Ocean, deviating at Aleutian Island, Fiji, Samoa and Gilbert Island.
- This is the International Date Line, where the date changes by exactly one day, when it is crossed.
- Samoa and Tokelau shifted his position back to West of the date line on 30th December, 2011.

ECLIPSES

- An eclipse occurs when the Sun, the Moon and the Earth are in a straight line. There are two types of eclipses-Solar and Lunar eclipse.
- Generally, a total of seven eclipse including solar and lunar eclipses, take place in a year.

Lunar Eclipse	Solar Eclipse
■ It is the situation, when the Earth comes between Sun and Moon.	■ It is the situation, when the Moon comes between Sun and Earth.
■ It occurs only on a full Moon day. But, it does not occur on every full Moon day because the Moon is so small and the plane of its orbit is tilted about 5 degree with respect to the Earth's orbital plan.	■ It occurs only on a new Moon day. But, it does not occur on every new Moon day because of the inclination of the Moon's orbital plan.
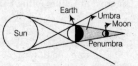 Diagram of Lunar Eclipse	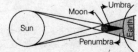 Diagram of Solar Eclipse

Diagram of Lunar and Solar Eclipse

EARTH'S INTERIOR

The interior of Earth is divided into three parts

  (i) Crust   (ii) Mantle   (iii) Core

The Crust

- The crust is the outermost and the thinnest layer of the Earth. This layer has the least density and its thickness varies about 8 to 40 km. **Mohorovicic Discontinuity** or Moho, marks the lower limit of the crust and this discontinuity is identified on the basis of rock density.
- Thickness of the crust is more in the continents and lesser in the oceans while density of continental crust is lower than oceans.
- The rocks forming the crust of the Earth are rich in lighter minerals like silica and aluminium. Hence, this layer is also called as **Sial** (silica and aluminium). The average density of this layer is 2.7 gm/cm^3.
- Due to presence of minerals like silica and magnesium in the rocks forming this layer of the Earth known as **Sima** (silica and magnesium).
- Sial and Sima together form Earth crust.

The Mantle

- This layer is the intermediate layer of the Earth in terms of both its location and density.
- It is about 2900 km in thickness, composed of minerals in a semi-solid state.
- It is divided into further two layer upper mantle and lower mantle. The upper part of the mantle is called the **Asthenosphere**, which is about 250 km thick.

- The average density of this layer is about 5.68 gm/cm^3.
- The transitional zone separating the mantle from the core is called the **Gutenberg Discontinuity**.

The Core

- The core is the innermost layer of the Earth and occupies its centre. It is about 3500 km in radius.
- The core is further divided into two layers : outer core and inner core.
- The outer part of the core is believed to have the properties of a liquid and the innermost part of the core (about 1255 km in radius) may be called **solid** or **crystalline**.
- This layer is also known **as Nife** (nickel and iron), because this layer contain large concentration of iron and nickel.
- Temperature of the core is between 2200°C and 2750° C.
- Density of this part of the Earth is 13.6 gm/cm^3 and is many times greater than the average density of the Earth (5.53 gm/cm c^3).

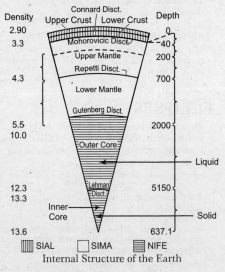

Internal Structure of the Earth

Discontinuities

The various layers are separated by discontinuities, which are evident in seismic data.

- **Conroad** discontinuity lies between upper crust and lower crust.
- **Mohorovicic** discontinuity between crust and mantle.
- **Repetti** discontinuity lies between upper mantle and lower mantle.
- **Gutenberg** discontinuity between core and mantle. Here, the Earth's density as well as velocity of 'P' waves increases.
- **Lehmann** discontinuity divides upper core and lower core.

Composition of the Earth's Crust

Elements	Percentage (%)	Elements	Percentage (%)
Oxygen	46	Calcium	3.6
Silicon	28	Sodium	2.8
Aluminium	8	Potassium	2.6
Iron	6	Magnesium	1.5

Continental Drift Theory

- This theory is given by **Alfred Wegener**, in 1915, to explain the origin and evolution of the continents and the oceans. According to this theory, about 250 million years ago, there was only one continent named Pangea means All Earth and it was surrounded by one mass of water body, named **Panthalassa**.
- The present shape of the continents and oceans is due to the break up of Pangaea.
- This breaking process started about 200 million years ago.
- The Northern rift cuts Pangea from East to West creating **Laurasia** in the North and **Gondwanaland** in South. A shallow sea called **Tethys** was situated between the Laurasia and the Gondwanaland.

Sea Floor Spreading Theory

- The concept of sea floor spreading was first formulated by **Harry Hess** in the year of 1960.
- According to this theory, the mid oceanic ridges were situated on the rising thermal convective current coming from mantle.
- The oceanic crust moves in opposite directions from mid oceanic ridges and thus there is continuous upwelling of new molten materials along the mid oceanic ridges. These molten masses cool down and solidify to form new crust.

Plate Tectonics Theory

- Plate tectonic is a scientific theory that describe the large-scale motions of Earth's lithosphere.
- The word tectonics comes from the Greek word meaning builder.
- The theory of Plate tectonics states that the lithosphere is divided into several rigid segments, which include both oceanic and continental crusts. These segments are called **plates** and they are moving on the **asthenosphere**, which is not a liquid, but a solid which flows under stress.
- About 20 such plates have been identified. There are seven major plates such as Eurasia, Antarctica, North America, South America, Pacific, African and Indian Plate.
- There are various intermediate sized plates such as China, Philippine, Arabian, Iran, Nazca, Cocos, Caribbean and Scotia Plates.

Plate Margins

Depending upon the type of movement, plate margins are of three types :

(i) **Divergent Plate Margin** (Constructive margins)

(ii) **Convergent Plate Margin** (Destructive margins)

(iii) **Parallel Plate Margin** (Conservative margin or Transform Boundary)

- Collision can occur between two oceanic plates, one oceanic and one continental plate or two continental plates.

Types of Plate Boundary

Divergent Plate Boundary	Convergent Plate Boundary	Transform Fault Boundary
When the plates move apart with the upwelling of material from the mantle, divergent plate boundary results.	A convergent plate boundary is one, where two plates collide, one plate bending downward and subducting below the other.	They are located, where plates slide past one another without the creation or destruction of crust.
Formation of the mid-oceanic ridges are the example of divergent plate margin.	Deep oceanic trench is formed adjacent to the zone of subduction. Fold mountains are the result of convergent plate boundary.	San Andreas fault along the West coast of Mexico is a famous transform fault.

FORCES AND PROCESSES AFFECTING THE EARTH'S CRUST

- Appearance of the surface of the Earth keeps changing.
- These changes are produced under the influence of two type of forces.

These are given below :

Exogenetic or External Forces

- The forces affecting the surface of the Earth from outside are called the **external** or **exogenetic** forces.
- **Weathering** and **Erosion** are the examples of external forces.

Endogenetic or Internal Forces

- The forces originating in the interior of the Earth are called the **internal** or the **endogenetic forces**.
- **Volcanoes**, **Earthquakes** and **Landslide** are the examples of internal forces.
- *These forces are of two types*:

Sudden Endogenetic Forces

- Sudden endogenetic forces are the result of long period preparation deep within the Earth.
- But their cumulative effects on the Earth's surface are quick and sudden.

Diastrophic Forces

- Diastrophic forces include both vertical and horizontal movements which are caused due to forces deep within the Earth. These diastrophic forces operate very slowly and there effects become visible after thousands and millions of years.

- These forces termed as **constructive forces** effect larger areas of the globe and produce meso-level reliefs e.g. **mountains, plateaus, plains, lakes, big faults** etc.
- These diastrophic forces are further subdivided into two groups namely epirogenetic force and orogenetic force.

Epirogenetic Force

- It causes upliftment and subsidence of continental masses through upward movements and are infact, vertical movements. These forces and resultant movements affect larger parts of the continents. These are further divided into two type: upward movement and downward movement.

Orogenetic Force

- Orogenetic movement is caused due to endogenetic forces working in horizontal movement. Horizontal forces and movements are also called as **tangential forces**.
Orogenetic or horizontal forces work in two ways, namely
  (i) in opposite direction and
  (ii) towards each other.
- When it operates in opposite direction, called tensional force. Tensional force create faulting **cracking** and **fracture**. **Tensional forces** are also called as **divergent forces**.
- The force, when operates face to face, is called **compression force** or convergent force. Compression force create **folding** and **warping**.

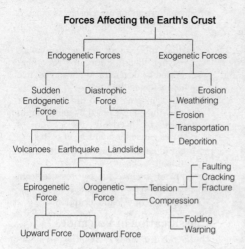

Forces Affecting the Earth's Crust

EARTHQUAKES

- It refers to the vibration of the Earth's surface caused by the endogenetic forces of Earth.
- The magnitude or intensity of energy released by an earthquake is measured by the **Richter Scale**, whereas the damage caused is measured by modified **Mercalli Intensity Scale**.
- The place of origin of earthquake is called **focus**. The place on the ground surface, which is perpendicular to the focus or hypocentre is called **Epicentre**.
- **Seismology** is the special branch of geology that deals with the study of earthquake.

Earthquake Waves

Earthquake waves are seismic waves that are created when energy builds up in rocks and they fracture.

Earthquake waves are basically of two types : body wave and surface wave.

Body Waves

They are generated due to the release of energy at the focus and move in all directions travelling through the body of the Earth. The body wave interact with the surface rocks and generate new set of waves called **Surface Wave**. There are two types of body waves Primary and Secondary wave.

1. Primary Wave

Primary Wave (P Waves) These are the waves of short wavelength and high frequency. They are longitudinal waves and can travel through solid, liquid and gases.

2. Secondary Wave

Secondary Wave (S Waves) These are the waves of short wave length and high frequency. They are transverse waves, which travel through all solid particles.

Surface Waves or Long Waves (L Waves)

They are the waves of long wavelength, confined to the skin of the Earth's crust. It causes most of the earthquake's structural damage.

THE EARTHQUAKE ZONES IN INDIA

The Indian plate is moving from South to North at the speed of **5 cm/year** and the Eurasian Plate is static on its own position, so there is a collision between Indian Plate and Eurasian Plates. Due to this collision, the earthquakes occurs in the Himalayan regions of India. The collision also results in the increase of the height of Himalayas at the speed of **1 cm/year**.

- The second most important earthquake zone is Parallel to Punjab and Rann of Kachchh. It occurs due to the movement between the transform boundaries of Eurasian and Indian Plates.
- Earthquakes occur in Assam, Arunachal Pradesh, Nagaland, Tripura, Manipur, Mizoram, Andaman and Nicobar Islands, Jammu and Kashmir, the North-Western region of Uttar Pradesh and the Northern region of Bihar etc.

Distribution of Earthquakes

Most of the world earthquake occur in

- the zones of young fold mountain
- the zones of folding and faulting
- the zone of junction of continental and oceanic margin
- the zone of active volcanoes
- along different plate boundaries
  The traditional zones of earthquakes
  - Circum Pacific belt
  - Mid Continental belt
  - Mid Atlantic belt

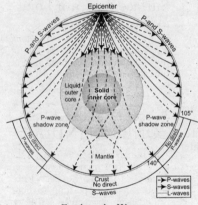

Earthquake Waves

SHADOW ZONE

- There are some specific area where earthquake waves do not occur or occur rarely such areas are termed as Shadow zone.
- It is located between 105° and 140° from epicentre.

VOLCANISM

- Volcanism includes all phenomena connected with the movement of heated material from the interior towards the surface of the Earth.
- A volcano is a vent or opening, through which heated materials consisting of gases, water, liquid lava, fragments of rocks are ejected from the highly heated interior to the surface of the Earth.

- Volcanic eruptions are closely associated with several integrated processes such as:
- Gradual increase in temperature with increasing depth, due to the heat generated by degeneration of radioactive elements inside the Earth.
- Origin of magma due to the lowering of the melting point caused by reduction in pressure of overlying rocks due to fractures caused by splitting of plates.
- Origin of gases and water vapour due to heating of water.
- Ascent of magma due to pressure from gases and vapour.
- Occurrence of volcanic eruption.

Classification of Volcanoes

On the Basis of Mode of Eruption

Central Eruption or Explosive Type	Fissure Eruption or Quiet Eruption
Here the magma comes with great force through the small vent and spread to a distant position. e.g. Hawaiian type, Strombolian type, Pelean type, Vesuvious type, Volcanian type.	Large quantities of lava quietly flow up from fissures and spread out over the surrounding areas. Successive flow of lava results in the growth of lava plateau. e.g. Deccan Plateau.

On the Basis of Periodicity of Eruptions

Active Volcano	Dormant Volcano	Extinct Volcano
Volcano which errupt periodically e.g. Etna, Stromboli, Mayon	Volcano which become quiet after their eruption for some time e.g. Fujiyama, Krakatoa, Barren Island	They have no indication of future eruption

Various Volcanic Belts

- **Circum-Pacific Belt** (*Fire girdle of the Pacific or the fire ring of the Pacific*). It extends across the Kamchatka Peninsula, Kurile Islands, the Islands of Japan, Philippines, New Guinea, New Zealand and the Soloman Islands.
- **Highest Volacanic Peaks** Cotopaxi (South America), Fujiyama (Japan), Valley of ten thousand smokes (Alaska).

- **Mid-Continental Belt** (Volcanic zones of convergent continental plate Margins). It includes volcanoes of Alpine mountain chain, the Mediterranean sea and the fault zone of Eastern Africa of Stromboli, Vesuvius, Etna, Kilimanjaro etc.
- **Mid-Atlantic Belt**, in which the volcanoes are fissure eruption type, e.g. Iceland, Canary Islands, Cape Verde, Azores etc.

Important Volcanic Mountains

Names	Height (m)	Country	Location	Last Notified Eruption
Ojos del Salado	7084	Argentina-Chile	Andes	1981
Guallatire	6060	Chile	Andes	1960
Cotopaxi	5897	Ecuador	Andes	1975
Lascar	5592	Chile	Andes	1968
Tupungatito	5640	Chile	Andes	1964
Popocate-petl	5451	Mexico	Altiplano de Mexico	1920
Nevado del Ruiz	5400	Colombia	Andes	1985

Weathering

It is the process of disintegration or decomposition of rocks in situ by natural agents. It is a static process. *There are three types of weathering*

1. **Physical Weathering** (or mechanical weathering)
   - It involves rock disintegration without any change in the chemical constituents of the rocks.
   - The factors responsible for physical weathering are temperature change, crystallisation of water into ice, the pressure release mechanism.
2. **Chemical Weathering** It involves the decomposition due to chemical changes. There are various chemical processes, which cause chemical weathering such as Solution, Oxidation, Carbonation, Hydration, Hydrolysis and Chelation.

The Process of Chemical Weathering

Process	Mechanism of Chemical Weathering
Solution	It involves the dissolution of soluble particles and minerals from the rocks with the help of water.
Oxidation	It represents addition of oxygen to form oxides.
Carbonation	It is the reaction of carbonate or bicarbonate ions with minerals.
Hydration	It is the process of addition of water to the minerals.
Hydrolysis	It is the process wherein both minerals of rocks and water moleclues decompose and react in such a way that new mineral compounds are formed.

3. **Biological Weathering** Plants and animals including man largely control it.
   It is divided into three types such as
   (i) Faunal weathering   (ii) Floral weathering   (iii) Anthropogenic weathering

Erosion

It involves removal of rock material and then transpor- tation of it. Therefore, erosion is performed by mobile agents such as streams, winds, waves and underground water.

ROCKS

- The solid part of the Earth's crust are called **rocks**.
- The rocks are made up of two or more minerals.
- Minerals are obtained from rocks. A rock can be defined as an aggregate of minerals.
  Rocks are classified in three main types depending on the process of their formation
  (i) Igneous   (ii) Sedimentary   (iii) Metamorphic

Igneous Rocks

- Formed due to the cooling, solidification and crystallisation of hot and molten magma.
- They are called as the **primary rocks** as all the other rocks are formed directly or indirectly from the igneous rocks.
- It is believed that the igneous rocks are formed during each period of geological history of Earth.
- They are hard, granular and crystalline rocks, less affected by chemical weathering.
- Moreover, it does not have any fossil or does not form any strata or layers of lava.

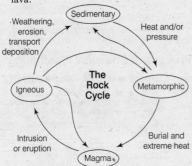

The Formation of Rocks

CLASSIFICATION OF IGNEOUS ROCKS

On the basis of Mode of Occurrence :

- Intrusive Rocks They are formed due to the solidification of rising magma below the surface of the Earth, e.g. Granite, Lapolith, Batholiths, Sills etc
- **Extrusive Rocks** They are formed due to cooling and solidification of hot and molten magma at the Earth surface, e.g. Basalt, Gabbro etc.

On the basis of Silica Content

- Acidic : It has more silica content e.g. Granite.
- Basic : It has less amount of silica content e.g. Gabbro.

Sedimentary Rocks

- The word 'Sedimentary' is derived from the Latin word *sedimentum*, which means settling.
- It is formed due to the aggregation and compaction of sediments derived from the older rocks, plants, animals and contains fossils of plants.
- The sedimentary rocks can be classified on the basis of the nature of sediments : mechanically, chemically and organically formed rocks.

Mode of Formation

Mechanically Formed	Chemically Formed	Organically Formed
Sandstone Conglomerate	Gypsum, Salt rock	Limestone, Coal, Peat, Dolomite

Metamorphic Rocks

- These are the changed form of Igneous and Sedimentary rocks.
- These are the rocks, which change either in form or composition without disintegration.
- Already formed metamorphic rocks are metamorphosed and this process is called **metamorphosis**.
- The agents of metamorphism are heat, compression and solution.

Rock Transformation

Sedimentary Rocks	Metamorphic Rocks
Limestone	Marble
Sandstone	Quartzite
Shale/Clay	Slate, Phyllite, Schist
Coal	Diamond

Original Rocks	Metamorphic Rocks
Sandstone	Quartzite
Limestone	Marble
Shale and Mudstone	Slate
Granite	Gneisse
Coal	Graphite Coal
Clay	Slate

Landforms

Classification of Landforms

- *There are four major landforms such as mountains, hills, plateau and plains.*

Landform	% of the total Global Surface Area
Plains	41
Plateau	33
Hills	14
Mountains	12

Mountains

Based on their mode of formation four main types of mountain can be distinguished.

Fold Mountains

- It is formed due to the compressive forces generated by endogenetic forces (earthquake, landslide etc.)
- Example of fold moutains : Himalayas, Alps, Andes, Rockies, Atlas etc.
  On the basis of age, fold mountains are grouped into
  - (a) **Young/New Fold Mountains** It came into existence after the continental drift. e.g. Himalayas, Andes, Rockies, Alps. Himalayas are regarded as the youngest mountains in the world.
  - (b) **Old Fold Mountains** They belong to pre-drift era, then subject to denudation and uplift. e.g. Pennines (Europe), Appalachians (US), Aravallis (India) etc.

Fold Mountains

Block Mountains

- It is formed when great block of Earth's crust may be raised or lowered due to tectonic activities.
- The land between the two paralled faults either rises forming Block mountains or horsts or subsides into a depression termed as Rift valley or Graben.

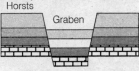

Block Mountains

- Example of Block mountain : Vindhyan and Satpura in India, the Vosges in France and Black forest in Germany (through which Rhine river flows).

Volcanic Mountains

- They are formed due to the accumulation of volcanic material.
- It is also called as **Mountains of Accumulation.**
- Examples : Mt Fuji (Japan), Cotopaxi in Andes, Vesuvius and Etna in Italy, Mt Mayon (Philippines) etc.

Residual or Dissected Mountains

- They are formed as a result of erosion of plateaus and high planes by various agents of erosion.
- Examples : Catskill mountains of New York, Sierras of Spain, Highlands of Scotland and Nilgiri, Parasnath, Girnar, Deccan Plateau and Rajmahal of India.

Major Mountain Ranges

Ranges	Locations	Length (km)
Andes	South America	7200
Himalayan, Karakoram and Hindu kush	South Central Asia	5000
Rockies	North America	4800
Great Dividing Range	East Australia	3600
Atlas	North-West Africa	1930
Caucasus	Europe	1200
Alaska	USA	1130
Alps	Europe	1050

Plateaus

- Tabular upland having relief of more than 500 feet may be defined as plateau.
- Tibetan plateau (5000 m) is the highest plateau in the world.

Major Plateaus

Plateau	Locations
Tibetan Plateau	Between Himalayas and Kunlun mountains
Deccan Plateau	Southern India
Arabian Plateau	South-West Asia
Plateau of Brazil	Central-Eastern South America
Plateau of Mexico	Mexico
Plateau of Colombia	USA
Plateau of Madagascar	Madagascar
Plateau of Alaska	North-West North America
Plateau of Bolivia	Andes Mountains
Great Basin Plateau	South of Colombia Plateau, USA
Colorado Plateau	South of Great Basin Plateau, USA

According to their mode of formation and their physical appearance, plateaus may be grouped into the following types:

Tectonic Plateau These are formed by Earth movements, which cause uplift and are normally of a conside rable size and fairly uniform altitude.

- When plateau are enclosed by Fold moutains, they are known as **Intermont Plateau.**
- Examples of Tectonic Plateau are: Tibetan Plateau between the Himalayas and the Kunlun and the Bolivian Plateau between two ranges of the Andes.

Volcanic Plateau These are formed by accumulation of lava. e.g. North-Western part of Deccan Plateau (India).

Dissected Plateau Through the continual process of weathering and erosion by running water, ice and winds, high extensive plateau are gradually worn down, and their surface made irregular as example is the Scottish Highlands.

Plains

- A relatively low-lying and flat land surface with least difference between its highest and lowest points is called a Plain.
- The plains are divided into structural, erosional and depositional plains.

Classification of Plains

Structural Plain	Erosional Plain	Depositional Plain
Formed due to the uplift of a part of the sea floor e.g. the Great Plain of USA.	Formed when the elevated tract of land is worn down to a plain by the process of erosion. e.g. Plain of North Canada.	Formed by filling up of sediments into depressions along the foothills, lakes and seas e.g. Indo Ganga Plain.

ATMOSPHERE

Atmosphere is a thick gaseous envelope surrounding the Earth from all sides and attached to Earth through the force of gravitation.

Significance of Atmosphere

- Acts as a filter because it absorbs the various unwanted radiation.
- Source to various gases.
- Supports life forms in biosphere.

Extent of Atmosphere

Almost 97% of effective atmosphere confines within the height 29 km of the Earth's surface.

So, the vertical distribution of the atmosphere is not uniform and even not homogeneous.

It extends about 600 miles from the sea level.

Composition of Gases

The percentage composition of the various gases in atmosphere upto 50 km is given below:

Gases	Percentage Composition	Significance
Nitrogen	78.08%	Acts as dilutent and is generally chemically inactive.
Oxygen	21%	Inhaled by biotic components for survival. Oxygen is also essential for combustion of burning matter.
Argon	0.93%	Inert gas.
Carbon dioxide	0.03%	Being a greenhouse gas, it increases the temperature of the lower atmosphere.
Neon	0.0018%	Inert gas.

Composition of Atmosphere

- The atmosphere is composed of gases, vapours and particulates.
- Gases such as Helium, Ozone and Hydrogen etc are present in traces.
- Ozone gas absorbs the ultraviolet radiations and save the biosphere from its adverse impact.

Layers of Atmosphere

Troposphere

- It extends up to 18 km from the Earth's surface. Thickness varies from 8 km at the poles to 18 km at the equator.
- At every **165 m**, there is a drop of 1° C (or 6.4° C per km). This is called **Normal Lapse Rate of Temperature.**
- **Tropopause** separates troposphere from stratosphere.
- This, layer accounts for practically the entire water vapour, all dust particles and most of the Carbon dioxide contained in the atmosphere. Due to this all weather phenomena such as condensation, precipitation and storms etc occur in the troposphere only.

Stratosphere

- The stratosphere extends up to about 50 km, where **stratopause** separates it from the mesosphere.
- In this layer, the temperature increases with increase in height. This phenomenon is known as **temperature inversion.**
- The temperature rises in this layer from about –60°C at the tropopause to 0°C at stratopause.

- The part of the stratosphere, in which there is a concentration of ozone is often called **ozonosphere**. It absorbs ultraviolet radiation, which is harmful for us.
- Stratosphere is free from dust particles and also from atmospheric turbulences. Hence, this layer is considered ideal for flying of jet aircrafts.

Mesosphere

- Mesosphere extends above the stratopause up to a height of about 80 km.
- In this layer, the temperature decreases with height like in the troposphere and it falls from about 0° C at its base to about – 100° C at 80 km height. It is considered the coldest layer of the atmosphere.
- The upper limit of the mesosphere is marked by the **Mesopause**, a transitional layer separating it from the ionosphere.

Ionosphere

- Ionosphere is located above the mesosphere and extends up to about 600 km. This layer is also called as **ionosphere** because it contains electrically charged ions that reflect the radio waves back to the Earth thus making radio communication possible. Absorption of solar radiation by ionised particles cause an increase in temperature with increasing height in the ionosphere.
- Due to large concentration of ionised particles in this layer the ionosphere acts as a protective layer against meteorites, that are burnt in this layer.

Thermosphere

- The zone between the 85 km and 600 km above the surface is often called **Thermosphere**. In this layer, the temperature increases with increasing altitude. The upper limit of the thermosphere, the **thermopause** is generally taken at an altitude of about 600 km.
- The day temperature at 600 km altitude exceed $1400°C$ while night temperature remain about $225°C$.
- The upper part of the thermosphere contains only the lighter gases like helium and hydrogen.

Exosphere and Magnetosphere

- The outermost part of the atmosphere of the Earth is called **Exosphere**.
- This zone of the atmosphere is about 10,000 km thick.
- The upper limit of the exosphere is uncertain as this layer acts as a transitional layer between the Earth's atmosphere and the space. The outer part of the exosphere is called **Magnetosphere**.

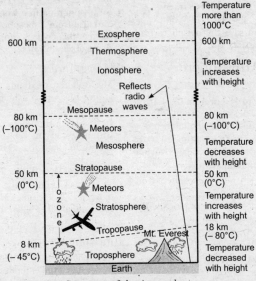

Structure of the Atmosphere

Chemical Composition of the Atmosphere

- **Homosphere up to 90 km** In this region, the proportion of various constituents is same throughout. But these days concentration of CO_2 is increasing due to global warming whereas concentration of O_3 is decreasing due to growing industrialisation. Thus, disturbing the homogeneity.
- **Heterosphere** The recent data from the satellites studies suggested that beyond about 100 km the lightest gases separates out, forming several concentric layers around the Earth. Four distinct layers of gases are mostly registered.

Insolations

- Solar radiation that is intercepted by the Earth is known as **Insolation**.
  - Insolation is measured with the help of **Pyranometers**.

The amount of insolation depends on following factors:
  (i) The area and nature of the surface.
  (ii) The inclination of the rays of the Sun.
  (iii) Distance between the Earth and the Sun.
  (iv) Length of the day.
  (v) The transparency of the atmosphere.

- As the angle of the Sun's rays decreases poleward, the amount of insolation received also decreases in that direction.
- The Earth's surface does not absorb all the energy that it receives. The proportion of the solar radiation reflected from the surface is called **Albedo**.
- On an average, insolation is highest near the equator, marginally lower at the tropics and lowest at the poles.

Heat Budget of the Earth

- The Earth receives energy continuously from the Sun, its temperature is almost constant except the long-term climate changes. This is because the atmosphere loses an amount of heat equal to the gain through insolation. This mechanism of maintaining the same temperature by the atmosphere is called the **Heat Budget** or **Heat Balance**.
- Let us assume that **100 units** of energy reach the top of the atmosphere of the Earth, **14 units** are absorbed directly by the atmosphere and **35 units** are lost to space through reflection.
- The remaining **51 units** reach the Earth's surface and are absorbed by the Earth due to which the surface gets heated.
- The heated surface of the Earth starts radiating energy in the form of long waves and this process is called **Terrestrial Radiation**.

- Out of the total 51 units given up by the surface in the form of terrestrial radiation, the atmosphere (mainly CO_2 and water vapour) absorbs about 34 units and the remaining 17 units escape to space.
- In this way, the atmosphere receives a total of $14 + 34 = 48$ units and this amount is radiated back to space by the atmosphere.
- The total loss of energy to space thus amounts to 100 units. 35 units reflected by the atmosphere. 17 units lost as terrestrial radiation 48 units from the atmosphere. 100 units back to space.
- In this way, no net gain or loss of energy occurs in the Earth's surface.
  The transfer of heat is done by two ways
  (i) Earth's surface to atmosphere
  (ii) From equator to poles

Atmospheric Pressure

- Air is an extremely compressible gas having its own weight. The pressure exerted by air due to its weight is called **atmospheric pressure** on the Earth's surface.
- Atmospheric pressure is neither the same for all the regions nor the same for one region all the time.
- Atmospheric pressure is affected by various factors such as altitude, temperature and Earth's rotation.

Influence on the Atmospheric Pressure

Altitude Air pressure increases, when air descends due to the decrease in volume. When air raises its volume increases and the outward pressure of its molecule is spread over a larger area and its pressure decreases.

Temperature The pressure of air rises, when its temperature falls. Low temperature at the poles cause the air to contract–high pressure develops; whereas the high temperature along the equator cause the air to expand–low pressure develops.

These layers in the order of height are

Layers	Height (km)
Molecular Nitrogen	100-200
Atomic Oxygen	200-1100
Helium Layer	1100-3500
Hydrogen	No upper limit

The order is in decreasing order of the atomic mass.

THE GLOBAL PRESSURE BELTS

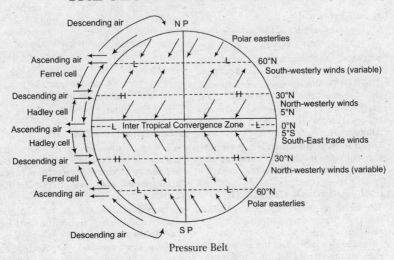

Pressure Belt

Equatorial Low Pressure Belt

• It is located on either side of the geographical equator in a zone extending between 5°N and 5°S. Its location is not stationary and there is a seasonal drift of this belt with the Northward (summer solstice) and Southward (winter solstice) migration of the Sun.

• It is thermally induced because of the intense heating of the ground surface by the almost vertical Sun rays.

• It represents the zone of convergence of North-East and South-East trade winds. This convergence zone is characterised by light and feeble winds. And because of the frequent calm conditions this belt is called as a **belt of calm** or **doldrums**.

Subtropical High Pressure Belt

• It extends between 30° to 35° in both the hemisphere.

• It is not thermally induced, but dynamically induced as it owes its origin to the rotation of the Earth and sinking and settling down of winds.

• Here the convergence of winds at higher altitude above this zone results in the subsidence of air from higher altitudes. Thus, descent of wind results in concentration of their volume and ultimately causes high pressure.

• This zone of high pressure is also called as **Horse Latitude**.

Sub-Polar Low Pressure Belt

- It extends between 60° to 65° in both the hemisphere.
- The low pressure belt does not appear to be thermally induced because there is low temperature throughout the year and as such there should have been high pressure belt instead of low pressure belt. Thus, it is dynamically induced.
- It is more developed and regular in Southern hemisphere than in Northern hemisphere because of the over dominance of water (ocean) in the Southern hemisphere.

Polar High Pressure Belt

- High pressure persists at the poles throughout the year because of the prevalence of very low temperature all the year round.

Shifting of Wind Belts

- The entire system of pressure and wind belts follows the movement of midday Sun. In June, when the Sun is over the Tropic of Cancer, all the belts move about 5°–10° North of their average position.
- In the same manner, when the Sun is overhead at the Tropic of Capricorn in December, all the belts swings 5°–10° South of their average position.

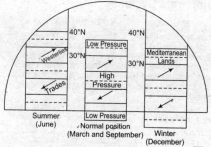

Shifting Wind Belts

Wind System

- The pressure difference is the major cause of the genesis of the wind system. The air moves from high pressure to low pressure.
- The slope of pressure from high to low is called as **pressure gradient**, which is also called as **barometric slope**.

- The imaginary line joining the points having same pressure is called **isobars**. The direction of air movement should be perpendicular to the isobars because the direction of pressure gradient is perpendicular to the isobars, but the direction is deviated from the expected one due to **Coriolis force** caused by the rotation of the Earth.
- Thus, the factors that control the air motion are as follows:
  - Pressure gradient
  - Rotation of Earth and Coriolis force
  - Frictional force
  - Centrifugal action of wind
- The winds blowing parallel to the isobars generally at the height of 600 m is called **geostropic wind**.

Wind Direction and Related Laws

- The Coriolis force generated due to the rotation of Earth acts as a deflective force to the wind direction. Because of the Coriolis force, all the winds are deflected to the **right in the Northern hemisphere** while they are deflected to the **left in the Southern hemisphere** with respect to the rotating Earth.
- This is referred to as **Farrel's Law**. The Coriolis force is absent along the equator, but increases progressively towards the pole.

Primary Movement (Permanent Winds)

- Trade winds
- Polar winds
- Westerllies

Secondary Movement

- Cyclone : Tropical and Temperate, Thunderstorms and Tornado
- Anti cyclone
- Seasonal wind i.e. Monsoon
- Tertiary Movement

Primary Wind Movement (Permanent Winds)

These winds include trade wind, westerlies and polar winds.

Trade Wind

- These are steady currents of air blowing from the sub-tropical high pressure belt towards the equatorial low pressure belt.
- Under the influence of the Coriolis forces they flow from the North-East in the Northern hemisphere and from South-East in the Southern hemisphere.

Westerlies

- The permanent winds blowing from the sub-tropical high pressure belt to the sub-polar low pressure belt in both the hemisphere is called **Westerlies**.
- The general direction of the westerlies is South-West to North-East in the Northern hemisphere and North-West to South-East in the Southern hemisphere.
- Because of the dominance of the land masses in the Northern hemisphere the Westerlies become more complex and complicated and become less effective during summer seasons and more vigorous during winter seasons. The Westerlies become more rigorous in the Southern hemisphere because of the lack of land and dominance of oceans.
- Their velocity increases Southward and they become stormy so they are called **roaring forties** between latitudes 40°-50°. South latitudes, **furious fifties** at 50° South latitude and **screaming sixties** at 60° South latitudes.

Polar Winds

Polar winds blows from polar high pressure belt to sub-polar low pressure belt. They are **North-Easterly in Northern hemisphere and South-Easterly in the Southern hemisphere.**

Secondary Wind Movement

Seasonal winds are the winds, which reverse its direction completely every 6 months is called Seasonal winds. The best example is Monsoon winds.

CYCLONES

Cyclones are the centres of low pressure surrounded by closed isobars having increasing pressure outward and closed air circulation from outside towards the central low pressure in such a way that

- Air blows inward in anti-clockwise direction in the Northern hemisphere.
- Air blows inward in clockwise direction in the Southern hemisphere.

Cyclones are mainly of two types
(i) Tropical Cyclone   (ii) Temperate Cyclone

Cyclone Distribution

Cyclone	Region
Typhoons	China Sea
Tropical Cyclones	Indian Ocean
Hurricanes	Caribbean Sea
Tornadoes	USA
Willy Willies	Northern Australia

Differences Between Tropical and Temperate Cyclones

Tropical Cyclone	Temperate Cyclone
They are found in the trade wind belt, between 8-20 degree North and South. But not found between 0 to 8 degree as there is no coriolis force.	Normally found between 30 to 65 degree North and South in the sub-polar frontal zone, where cold polar air mass meets the warm tropical air mass.
It travels from East to West in the Easterly wind belt.	It moves from West to East embedded in the Westerly wind belt.
Tropical cyclones are much smaller with a diameter of about 200 to 500 km.	They forms over a much large area with the diameter 300 to 1500 km.
Tropical cyclones are non frontal in nature.	Temperate cyclones are frontal in nature.
It is formed only over the oceans.	It is formed either over continents or over the oceans.
Tropical cyclone can form only in the summer.	They can form both in summer as well as in winter.
It does not have definite lifecycle and weather forecasting is very difficult.	It takes more time to dissipate as it has a more definite lifecycle.

Anticyclone

- They are the wind system, which has the highest air pressure at the centre and lowest at the outer margins surrounded by circular isobars where wind blows
  - from centre to outward in clockwise direction in Northern hemisphere.
  - from centre to outward in anti-clockwise direction in Southern hemisphere.
- They are high pressure system and common in sub-tropical belts and practically absent in the equator region.
- They are generally associated with rainless fair weather and that's why they are called as **weatherless phenomena**.

Thunderstorms

- Thunderstorms are local storm characterised by swift upward movement of air and heavy rainfall with cloud thunder and lightening.
- Structurally, thunderstorms consist of several convective cells, which are characterised by strong updraft of air.

Tornado

- Tornadoes are very strong tropical cyclones of smaller size. In the Mississippi valley (US), they are called **Twisters**.
- They are more destructive than cyclones as the speed of winds is very high, exceeding 220 km per hour.

Jet Stream

- The strong and rapidly moving circumpolar Westerly air circulation in a narrow belt of a few hundred kilometres width in the upper limit of troposphere is called **Jet Stream**.
- Their circulation path is wavy and meandering.
- The extent of the Jet Streams narrows down during the summer season because of their Northward shifting while these extend up to 20° North latitude during winter season.

HUMIDITY

- Humidity of air refers to the content of the water vapour present in the air at a particular time and place. Humidity is measured by an instrument called **hygrometer**. Another instrument used for the same purpose is **sling psychrometer**.

The atmospheric humidity is expressed in a number of ways such as:

Way of Measurement of Humidity	Definition
Humidity Capacity	The capacity of air of certain volume at certain temperature to retain maximum amount of moisture content.
Absolute Humidity	The total weight of moisture content per volume of air at definite temperature is called absolute humidity.
Specific Humidity	The mass of the water vapour in grams contained in a kilogram of air and it represents the actual quantity of moisture present in a definite air.
Relative Humidity	It is the ratio of the amount of water vapour actually present in the air having definite volume and temperature (i.e. absolute humidity) to the maximum amount the air can hold (i.e. humidity capacity).

Relative Humidity

$$= \frac{\text{Absolute humidity}}{\text{Humidity capacity}} \times 100$$

- **Condensation** is the change of physical state of matter from gaseous phase into liquid phase and is the reverse of **vaporisation**.
- When the relative humidity reaches 100%, the air is completely saturated. The air temperature is said to be as **dew-point**.
- **Smog** (Smoke + Fog) is a form of fog that occurs in areas, where the air contains a large amount of smoke.
- **Fog** is made from the droplets of water suspended in the lower layer of the atmosphere. Fog is not considered as a form of precipitaion. Visibility of less than 1 km is the internationally recognised definition of fog.

- **Haze** is formed by water particles that have condensed in the atmosphere and visibility lie between 1 km to 2 km.
- **Frost** is the moisture on the ground surface that condenses directly into ice, i.e. when condensation occurs below freezing point.

Tertiary Movement (Local Winds)

Wind	Nature	Region
Land Breeze	Warm	Land breeze blows from land to sea.
Sea Breeze	Cold	Sea breeze blows from sea to land.
Chinook (*snow eater*)	Warm	Rockies (*USA and Canada*)
Sirocco	Hot	North Africa
Fohn	Warm	Alps/Europe
Khamsin	Hot	Egypt
Blizzard	Cold	Siberian, Canada, USA
Bora	Cold	Yugoslavia
Southerly Buster	Cold	Australia
Purga	Cold	Russian, Tundra
Bire	Cold	France
Cape Doctor	Cold	South African coast
Harmattan (*The Doctor*)	Hot	Sahara to Guinea Coast (*Ghana, Nigeria etc*)
Zonda	Warm	Argentina, Chile/Andes
Brick Fielder	Hot	Australia
Samun	Hot	Iran
Levanter	Cold Wind	Spain
Norwester	Hot Wind	New Zealand
Leveche	Hot	Algeria, Morocco
Santa Ana	Warm	USA (*California*)
Berg	Warm	South Africa
Yoma	Warm	Japan
Karaburan	Hot	Tarim Basin
Black Roller	Hot/Dusty	North America
Kalbaisakhi	Hot	North India
Mistral	Cold	France to Mediterranean (*Rhine valley*)

PRECIPITATION

On the basis of its origin, precipitation may be classified into four main types

- **Convectional Rainfall** It occurs due to thermal convection currents caused due to insolational heating of ground surface.

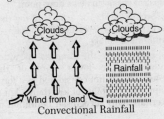

Convectional Rainfall

- **Orographic Rainfall** occurs due to ascent of air forced by mountain barrier.

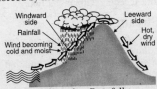

Orographic Rainfall

- **Frontal Rainfall** It occurs due to upward movement of air caused by convergence of cold air masses against warm air masses.
- **Cyclonic Rainfall** When the air is caused to rise upward due to cyclonic circulation, the resulting precipitation is called cyclonic rainfall. The average weather conditions over a large area are called the **climate of a place**.

- The factors, which control the weather and the climatic conditions are latitude, altitude, unequal distribution of land and water, ocean current, air pressure and wind, mountain barrier, nature of ground surface, different types of atmospheric storms etc.

Types of Precipitation

Convectional Precipitation	Orographic Precipitation	Cyclonic Precipitation
■ It occurs daily in the afternoon in the equatorial regions. ■ It is of very short duration but occurs in the form of heavy rainfall. ■ It occurs through thick, dark and extensive cumulo-nimbus clouds. ■ It is accompanied by cloud, thunder and lightening.	■ The wind ward slope receives the maximum amount of rainfall, whereas the leeward side receives less rainfall. ■ The windward slopes of the mountains at the time of rainfall are characterised by cumulus clouds while leeward slope has stratus clouds. It can occur in any season.	■ Rainfall associated with the temperate cyclone occurs, when two extensive air masses of different physical properties converge. ■ In tropical regions two extensive air masses of similar physical properties converge to form tropical cyclones, wherein lifting of air is almost vertical and very often associated with convection.

Clouds

- Clouds are the masses of small water droplets or tiny ice crystals.
- Clouds are classified according to their appearance, form and height.
  There are four groups
    (i) High Clouds 6000 m to 12000 m
    (ii) Middle Clouds 2100 m to 6000 m
    (iii) Low Clouds below 2100 m
    (iv) Clouds of great vertical extent 1500 m to 9000 m

The different types of clouds are given Latin names, which are the combination of the following words:

- **Cirrus** means looking like a feather and used to describe the very high clouds.
- **Cumulus** means looking like a heap. It is used to describe the clouds having flat bases and rounded tops.
- **Stratus** means lying in level sheets. It is used for layer type of clouds.
- **Alto** means high.
- **Nimbus** means rain cloud.

Types of Clouds

High Clouds	Middle Clouds	Low Clouds	Clouds with Great Vertical Extent
Cirrus Composed of small ice crystal, white, wispy and fibrous in appearance.	**Alto-cumulus** Composed of water droplets in layers and patches.	**Strato-cumulus** Large globular masses, bumpy looking, soft and grey in appearance forming a pronounced regular and sometimes wavy pattern.	**Cumulus** Round topped and flat based forming a whitish grey globular mass, consists of individual cloud units.
Cirro-cumulus Composed of ice crystals, but globular or rippled in appearance.	**Alto-stratus** Composed of water droplets, forming sheets of grey or watery looking clouds.	**Nimbo-stratus** Dark grey and rainy looking, dense and shapeless, often gives continuous rains.	**Cumulo-nimbus** They have a great vertical extent, white or black globular masses, whose rounded tops often spread out in the form of anvil. It is characterised by convectional rain, lightning and thunder.

Types of Clouds

High Clouds	Middle Clouds	Low Clouds	Clouds with Great Vertical Extent
Cirro-stratus Looks like a thin white almost transparent sheet, which causes the Sun and Moon to shines through it with a characteristic 'halo'.		**Stratus** These are low, grey and layered, almost fog like in appearance, bringing dull weather and often accompanied by drizzle.	Noctilucent clouds, they are made of ice crystals. They are normally too faint to be seen.

Climate

Weather refers to the sum total of the atmospheric conditions in terms of temperature, pressure, wind, moisture, cloudiness, precipitation and visibility of a particular place at any given time.

Great Deserts

Name	Country/ Region
Sahara (*Libyan, Nubian*)	North Africa
Australian (*Gibson, Simpson, Victorian Great Sandy*)	Australia
Arabian (*Rub-al-Khali, An-Nafud*)	Arabia
Dast-e-Lut (*Barren Desert*)	Iran
Dast-e-Kavir (*Salt-e-Kavir*) (*Salt Desert*)	Iran
Desier to de Sechura	Peru
Atacama	North Chile
Patagonia	Argentina
Kalahari	Botswana
Namib	Namibia

World Climatic Types

Climatic Zone	Climatic Types	Rainfall	Natural Vegetation
Equatorial Zone (0°-10°N and S)	1. Hot, wet equatorial	Rainfall all the year (80 inches)	Equatorial rain forests
Hot Zone	2. (a) Tropical Monsoon	Heavy summer rain (60 inches)	Monsoon forests
(10°-30°N and S)	(b) Tropical Marine		
	3. Sudan type	Rain mainly in summer (70 inches)	Savana (Tropical grassland)
	4. Desert	Little rain (5 inches)	Desert vegetation and scrub
	(a) Saharan type		
	(b) Mid latitude type		
Warm Temperate Zone (30°N-45°S)	5. Western margin (Mediterranean type)	Winter rain (35 inches)	Mediterranean forests
	6. Central Continental type (Steppe type)	Light summer rain (20 inches)	Steppe, temperate grassland
	7. Eastern Margin	Heavier summer rain (45 inches)	Warm, wet forests and bamboo
	(a) China type		
	(b) Gulf type		
	(c) Natal type		

Cool Temperate Zones (45°N-65°S)	8. Western Margin (British Type)	Rain in autumn and winter (30 inches)	Deciduous forests
	9. Central Continental (Siberian Type)	Light summer rain (25 inches)	Coniferous forests
	10. Eastern Margin (Lauritian Type)	Moderate summer rain (40 inches)	Mixed forests (coniferous and deciduous)
Cold Zone (65°N-90°S)	11. Arctic or Polar	Very light summer rain (10 inches)	Tundra, mosses, lichens
	12. Mountain Climate	Heavy rainfall (variable)	Alpine, fern, coniferous, pastures, snow

Hot Wet Equatorial Climate

Distribution	Climate	Natural Vegetation	Economy
Found between 5°N -10°S of the equator. It is found mainly in the lowlands of Amazon, Congo, Malaysia and the East Indies.	Mean monthly temperature around 24-27 degree C. Diurnal and annual range of temperature is small. Convectional rainfall with annual rainfall of 250 cm.	Tropical rain forest with multitude of evergreen trees such as mahogany, ebony. Lianos, epiphytic and parasitic plants are also found.	Sparsely populated primitive people live as hunter and gatherer in the forests. Practice of shifting cultivation is prevalent.

Tropical Monsoon and Tropical Marine Climate

Distribution	Climate	Natural Vegetation	Economy
▪ Found between 5°-30° latitudes on either side of the equator. It is found mainly in India, Burma, Thailand, Laos, Cambodia, Northern Australia .	▪ Summer and winter seasons are sharply differentiated due to the North and Southward movement of the Sun. ▪ Average temperature of warm dry summer months ranges between 27-32° C. ▪ Orographic and Cyclonic Rainfall ▪ Monsoon rain through South-West monsoon winds.	▪ Normally deciduous. ▪ Most of the forest yield valuable timber like teak, sal, acacia etc.	▪ Agriculture based economy. ▪ Agriculture crops includes rice, sugarcane, jute etc.

The Sudan or Savanna Climate

Distribution	Climate	Natural Vegetation	Economy
▪ Located between 5°-20° latitude on either side of the equator. ▪ Mostly found in Llanos of Orinoco valley, the Campos of Brazil, hilly areas of Central America, Southern Zaire etc.	▪ Alternate hot, rainy and cool dry season. Mean high temperature throughout the year is between 24 and 27 degree C. ▪ The extreme diurnal range of temperature is a characteristic of Sudan type of climate. ▪ The average annual rainfall ranges between 100 cm and 150 cm.	▪ Characterised by tall grass and short trees (flat top). ▪ Trees are deciduous and hard. ▪ Scrubland is well represented by a number of species in Australia like mallee, mulga, spinifex grass etc.	▪ Tribes live in the Savanna lands. ▪ Some tribes live as Pastoralists like the **Maasai**. ▪ **Hausa** are settled as cultivators in Northern Nigeria.

Hot Desert and Mid - Latitudinal Desert Climate

Distribution	Climate	Natural Vegetation	Economy
■ Major hot deserts are located on the Western coasts of continents between latitudes 15°N-30°S.	■ Lie on the sub-tropical high pressure belt, where air is descending. ■ Relative humidity is extremely low. ■ Rainfall is convectional type with violent thunder storm. ■ The diurnal temperature is very high.	■ Vegetation is mostly Xerophytic or drought resistant scrub. Plants that exist in deserts have highly specialised means of adapting themselves to the arid environment such as few or no leaves, needle shaped leaves etc.	■ Inhospitable conditions of the deserts are barrier to economic development. ■ The **Bushmen** of the Kalahari and the **Bindibu** of Australia are primitive tribes.

Warm Temperate Western Margin : Mediterranean

Distribution	Climate	Natural Vegetation	Economy
■ This is found in California, in parts of Western and South Australia, in South-Western South Africa in parts of Central Chile and around the Mediterranean region.	■ The climate is characterised by hot, dry summers and cool, **wet winters**. ■ During summer, regions of Mediterranean climate are dominated by sub-tropical high pressure cells causing no or little rainfall.	■ Evergreen trees such as oak and eucalyptus, jarrah and kari are found. ■ Evergreen coniferous trees are pines, firs, cedars and cypresses.	■ Economy is based on cultivation of fruits, wine making and cereal growing and a wide range of citrus foods.

Temperate Continental Steppe Climate

Distribution	Climate	Natural Vegetation	Economy
■ Pustaz of Hungary, Prairies of North America, Pampas of Argentina and Uruguay, Bush Veld of South Africa.	■ Continental climate with extremes of temperature. ■ Winters are very cool.	■ It has the scanty vegetation of the sub-arid lands of continental Eurasia.	■ Grazing of animals, extensive and mechanised wheat cultivation.

Warm Temperate Eastern Margin : *China Type* (Gulf Type Climate)

Distribution	Climate	Natural Vegetation	Economy
■ Found on the Eastern margin of the continents in warm temperate latitudes.	■ Characterised by warm moist summer and a cool dry winter. ■ Uniform distribution of rainfall throughout the year is an important feature.	■ Evergreen broad leaved forests and deciduous forests.	■ Rice, tea and mulberries are extensively grown in monsoon China. ■ Other important crops are corn, tobacco and cotton.

Cool Temperate Western Margin : British Type

Distribution	Climate	Natural Vegetation	Economy
▪ From Britain, this belt stretches far inland into the lowlands of North-West Europe including regions such as Northern and Western France, Belgium, the Netherland, Denmark, Western Norway.	▪ It is under the permanent influence of the Westerlies. ▪ Summers are in fact never very warm. Winters are mild. ▪ As the rain bearing winds come from the West, the Western margins have the heaviest rainfall.	▪ Deciduous forest some of the common species are oak, elm, birch, beech, poplar etc.	▪ Fishing is important in Norway and British Columbia. ▪ Market gardening is widely practised in North-Western Europe.

Cool Temperate Continental : Siberian (Boroeal Type)

Distribution	Climate	Natural Vegetation	Economy
▪ Experienced only in Northern hemisphere. ▪ On its polar side, it merges into the Arctic Tundra and in Southern side, it fades into the temperate steppe climate.	▪ Characterised by a bitterly cold winter of long duration and a cool brief summer. ▪ The winter precipitation is in the form of snow.	▪ Here the Coniferous forest belt of Eurasia and North America are the richest source of the softwood. ▪ The major species are pine, fir spruce and larch.	▪ Saw mills for the softwood are prevalent. ▪ Many of the **Samoyeds** and **Yakuts** of Siberia and some of the Canadians are engaged in hunting, trapping and fishing.

Cool Temperate Eastern Margin : Laurentian

Distribution	Climate	Natural Vegetation	Economy
▪ It is found in North-Eastern North America and the Eastern Coast of Asia. ▪ It is absent in Southern hemisphere because only a small portion of Southern continents extend South of the latitude of 40° South.	▪ It has cold dry winter and warm, wet summers. ▪ Winters temperature may be well below freezing point and snow falls to quite a depth.	▪ Generally forest is Coniferous. Some of the important species are oak, maple and birch.	▪ Lumbering and its associated timber, paper and pulp industries are the most important economic under-taking.

Arctic and Polar

Distribution	Climate	Natural Vegetation	Economy
▪ It is found mainly in North of the Arctic circle.	▪ Characterised by a very low mean annual temperature. Winter are long and very severe, summers are cool and brief. ▪ Precipitation is mainly in the form of snow falling in winter.	▪ The greatest inhibitating factor is the region's deficient in heat. ▪ There are no trees in the Tundra. ▪ Such an environment can support only the lowest form of vegetation, mosses, lichens and sedges.	▪ The few people, who live in the Tundra live a semi-nomadic life. **Eskimos** live in Greenland, Northern Canada and Alaska. ▪ In the Eurasian Tundra, there are other nomadic tribes such as the **Lapps** of Northern Finland and Scandinavian, the Samoyeds of Siberia, **Yakuts**, **Koryaks** and **Chuckshi** of North-Eastern Asia.

Famous Grasslands of the World

Grasslands	Countries
Steppe	Eurasia
Pustaz	Hungary
Prairie	USA
Pampas	Argentina
Veld	South Africa
Downs	Australia
Cantebury	New Zealand

Some Important Isopleth

Isopleth	Reaction
Isohels	Sunshine
Isohyets	Rainfall
Isonif	Snow
Isocline	Slope
Isotherms	Temperature
Isobars	Equal Pressure
Isabath	Equal depth in sea
Isohaline	Salinity
Isohypse	Elevation above sea-level
Isodapane	Equal transportation cost
Isobrants	Thunder storm at the same time

HYDROSPHERE

The water component of the Earth is called hydrosphere which covers about 70% of the surface of Earth. It includes the oceans, seas, lakes, ponds, rivers and streams.

Composition of Hydrosphere

Storage Component	% of Water
Oceans	97.6
Ice capes and glaciers	2.05
Ground water	0.68
Soil moisture	0.01
Saline lakes and inland seas	0.008
Lakes	0.009
Freshwater rivers	0.0001
Atmosphere	0.0009

OCEANS

There are four oceans. In the order of their size they are: Pacific ocean, Atlantic ocean, Indian ocean and Arctic ocean. The average depth of oceans is about 4 km.

Major Oceans

Ocean	Important Information
Pacific	It is the largest and deepest ocean. Most of the islands of the ocean are volcanic or of coral origin. Mariana Trench, the world's deepest trench with depth 11033 km is in Pacific ocean.
Atlantic	It has the longest coast line. It is the busiest ocean for trade and commerce since its sea routes connect the two most industrialised regions, namely Western Europe and North-Eastern United States of America. Atlantic ocean is still widening. Puerto Rico Trench is the deepest point of this ocean.
Indian	Only ocean named after a country. It is deeper than the Atlantic ocean. Here the number of continental islands is more than that of volcanic islands. Sunda (farlier known as java) Trench is the deepest point of this ocean.
Arctic	It is the smallest ocean and lies within the Arctic circle. The North pole lies in the middle of the Arctic ocean. Most of the part of the ocean is frozen and hence least saline and the shallowest among all the oceans. Nansei Trench is the deepest point of this ocean.

Relief of the Ocean Basin Continental Shelf

- The shallow sub-merged extension of the continent is called the **continental shelf**.
- Extends to a depth of 100 fathoms (1 fathoms = 1.8 m).
- Average width 70 km; average slope 17 feet/mile or about 1°.
- Continental shelf covers 7.5% area of the oceans. It extends over 13.3% of the Atlantic ocean 5.7% of Pacific ocean and 4.2% of Indian ocean.
- If mountains extend along the coast, the shelf will be narrower.
- About 20% petrol and gas are found here. They also provide the richest fishing ground in the world.

Continental Slope

- Extends seawards from the continental shelf.
- Depth-200-2000 fathoms (3660 m).
- Average slope 2 to 5 degrees.

- The boundary between shelf and slope is known as **Andesite Line**, names after the **Andesite Rock**.
- They cover about 8.5% of the total ocean area.

Continental Rise

- Continental rise is an area at the foot of the slope, slightly rising due to the accumulation of debris transported over the slope.
- Average slope-0.5° to 1°.
- Oil deposits occur here.

Abyssal or the Deep Sea Plains

- It is the deepest and most extensive part of the oceanic floor.
- Average depth 3000 m to 6000 m.
- It covers about 75.9% of total oceanic area.
- Parts of the Abyssal plains are occupied by raised ridges or submarine mountains and by very deep trenches or canyons.

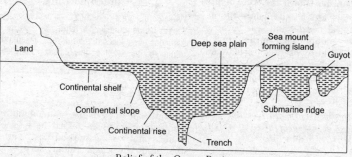

Relief of the Ocean Basin

Deeps/Trenches

- Trenches are narrow and steep sides depressions. Trenches are formed, when two plates of the Earth's crust are moving together and one is being pushed down below the other.
- Mariana trench (Challenger deep) is the deepest trench in the world situated in the NW Pacific oceans, near Philippines. It is more than 11 km deep.

Oceanic Ridges

- Oceanic Ridges are formed by the volcanic activity along the spreading boundary of plates.
- It is thousands of km long and hundreds of km wide mountain range on the oceanic floor.
- Their summits may rise above the sea level in the form of Islands i.e. Azores Island of Iceland.

Sea Mounts and Guyouts

A ridge rising more than 1000 m above the ocean floor is called **seamount**. Flat topped sea mounts are called **Guyouts**.

- Both of them are formed by the volcanic activity.
- Largest number of sea mounts and Guyouts are found in the Pacific.

Submarine Canyons

- Submarine canyons are the deep gorges on the ocean floor and are restricted to the continental shelves, slopes and rises.
- Many submarine canyons are found along the mouths of major rivers e.g. Hudson canyon.

CORAL REEFS

- Coral reefs are formed due to accumulation and the compaction of skeletons of lime secreting organisms known as **Coral Polyps**.
- Corals are found mainly in the tropical oceans and seas because they require high mean annual temperature of ranging between 20°C to 25°C.
- Corals do not live in deeper waters due to lack of sufficient sunlight and oxygen.

On the basis of nature, shape and mode of occurrence, the coral reefs is classified into four types:

Fringing Reefs

- It develop along the continental margins or along the islands.
- The seaward slope is steep and vertical while the landward slope is gentle.
- They are usually attached to the coastal land, but occasionally they are separated from the shore by a shallow and narrow lagoon called **Boat Channel**.
- This type of reefs are found near Rameshwaram in the Gulf of Mannar and Andamans.

Barrier Reefs

- Largest coral reefs off the coastal platform, but parallel to them. The reef lies at a distance away from the coast. Hence, a broad lagoon develops between the reef and the shore.
- The Great Barries Reef of Australia is the largest barrier reef in the world. In India found in Nicobar and Lakshadweep.

Patch Reefs

- Patch reefs are isolated and discontinious patches lying shoreward of offshore reef structures. These are found in the Palk bay, Gulf of Mannar and Gulf of Kutch.

Atoll

- A reef of narrow growing corals of horse shoe shape and crowned with palm trees is called an **atoll**.
- It is formed around an islands or in an elliptical form on a submarine platform.
- Funafuti atoll of Ellice Islands is a famous atoll also found in Lakshadweep and Nicobar.

Coral Bleaching

When corals are stressed by changes in conditions such as temperature, light or nutrients, they expel the symbiotic algae living in their tissues, causing them to turn completely white, this phenomenon is known as coral bleaching.

SALINITY

- Salinity is defined as the total amount of salt content in grams contained in 1 kg of sea water and is expressed as part per thousand. The oceanic salinity not only affects the marine organism and plant community, but also affects the physical properties of the ocean such as temperature, pressure, density, waves and currents.
- Average salinity in Southern hemisphere is more than that of Northern hemisphere.
- Iso-halines represent the salinity distribution in the surface of the sea. These are the lines joining places having an equal degree of salinity. The main source of salinity is dissolution of the rocks of oceanic crust, which contain salts.
- Poles have minimum salinity because of addition of fresh water in the form of icebergs and excessive snowfall.

- Variation in salinity causes vertical circulation of water. More saline water freezes slowly while the boiling point of saline water is higher than the fresh water.
- Salinity also increases the density of water.

Composition of Sea Water

Salt	Percentage Composition (%)
Sodium Chloride	77.8
Magnesium Chloride	10.9
Magnesium Sulphate	4.7
Calcium Sulphate	3.6
Potassium Sulphate	2.5
Others	0.5

Most Saline Water Bodies

Water Bodies	Percentage Composition (%)
Lake Assel (Djibuti)	34.8
Lake Van (Turkey)	33
Dead Sea (West Asia)	33.7
Great Salt Lake (USA)	32.0

Salinity on an average decreases from equator to poles. The highest salinity is recorded near the tropics rather than the equator because of the heavy precipitation in the equatorial region.

Controlling Factors of the Oceanic Salinity

The salinity of oceans and different seas depends on a number of factors such as evaporation, precipitation, influx of the river water, prevailing wind, ocean currents and sea waves etc.

Controlling Factor	Relation with Salinity
Evaporation	Greater the evaporation, higher the salinity.
Precipitation	Higher the precipitation, lower the salinity.
Influx of river water	Big voluminous rivers pour down immense volume of fresh water into the oceans and salinity is reduced at the mouth.
Atmospheric pressure	Anticyclonic conditions with stable air and high temperature increases the salinity of the surface water of the ocean.
Circulation of oceanic water	Ocean currents affect the spatial distribution of salinity by mixing sea waters.

MOVEMENTS OF OCEANIC WATER

Waves

- Waves are the oscillatory movements in water mainly produced by winds, manifested by an alternate rise and fall of the sea surface.
- The waves are the important agents of erosion in the coastal regions, where they carve out various landforms like caves, bays, gulfs, capes and cliffs.
- Seismic waves or Tsunamis are the waves caused by earthquakes in volcanic eruptions in the sea bottom.
- The Tsunamis, which hit the coast in South-East Asia on 26th December, 2004, caused havoc in that region.

Ocean Currents

- An ocean current is a continuous, directed movement of ocean water generated by the forces acting upon it, such as breaking waves, wind, coriolis effect, temperature and salinity differences and tides caused by the gravitation pull of the Moon and the Sun.
- Ocean currents circulate in clockwise direction in Northern hemisphere and in anti-clockwise direction in Southern hemisphere.

Ocean currents are of two types:

(i) **Warm Currents** The ocean currents flowing from lower latitude to higher latitude are called as warm currents.

(ii) **Cold Currents** The ocean currents flowing from higher latitude to lower latitude are called as cold currents.

CURRENTS OF NORTH PACIFIC OCEAN

Warm Currents

- **North Equatorial Current** It flows Westwards from the Western Coast of Mexico to the Philippines.
- **Kuroshio Current** It is an extension of North Equatorial Current near Japan Coast. It flows towards North.
- **Alaska Current** It flows along the Coast of British Columbia and the Alaska Peninsula.

Cold Currents

- **Oyashio Current** It flows down from Bering Sea towards Japan from North pole and it joins Kuroshio currents.
- **Kuril Current** It flows down from sea of Okhotsk and joins Kuroshio current to the North of Japan.
- **West Wind Drift** It flows towards Alaska.
- **Californian Current** It is an extension of Alaskan currents. It joins finally North Equatorial current and completes clockwise circulation of water.

Currents of South Pacific Ocean

Warm Currents

- **East Australian Current or Great Barrier Current** It flows towards East coast of Australia from equator towards Pole.
- **South Equatorial Current** It originates due to South-East trade winds and flows Westwards and bifurcates near New Guinea.
- **Counter Equatorial Current** It extends upto Panama Bay. It flows exactly on equator from West to East.

Cold Currents

- **Peruvian Current** (Humboldt current). It flows from South pole towards equator on the Coast of Chile and Peru.

- **West Wind Drift** It flows from Tasmania to Chile Coast of South America.

Currents of North Atlantic Ocean Warm Currents

- **North Equatorial Current** It is present between Equator and 10°N.
- **Cayenne Current** It flows adjacent to French Guinea and enters into Carribean Sea and Gulf of Mexico.
- **Florida Current** Cayenne current near Florida (US Coast) is called Florida current.
- **Antilles Current** It flows to the East of West Indies and Other Islands.
- **Gulf Stream** It flows from US coast towards North-West Europe under the influence of westerly winds.
- **North Atlantic Drift** Gulf Stream bifurcates into
    (i) North Atlantic Drift (warm)
    (ii) West Wind Drift (cold) and Canaries current (cold)

Cold Currents

- **Labrador Current** It orginates in Baffin Bay and Davis Strait and merges with Gulf Stream near Newfoundland. Newfoundland is a famous zone of fishing, commonly known as **Grand Bank**.
- **Irminger Current or East Greenland Current** It flows between Greenland and Iceland and merges with North Atlantic drift.
- **Canaries Current** It flows along the Western Coast of North Africa between Madeira cape verde and it joins North equatorial current.
- **West Wind Drift** It flows towards UK.

Currents of South Atlantic Ocean Warm Currents

- **South Equatorial Current** It flows between equator and 10°.
- **Brazilian Current** It flows to the East Coast of Brazil from equator towards pole.

Cold Currents

- **Falkland Current** It flows along the South-East Coast of South America from South to North.
- **Benguela Current** It flows from South to North near the 'Cape of Good Hope'.
- **West Wind Drift** It is continuence of Brazilian and Falkland current.
- **Guinea Current** It flows near Coast of Guinea (Africa).

Currents of the Indian Ocean

- The Asiatic Monsoon influences the currents of the North Indian Ocean, while the currents of South Indian ocean are influenced by the atmosphere's anti-cyclonic circulation.
- **North Equatorial Current** The current flows from East to West and upon reaching the East Coast of Africa, a good portion turns Southward, crosses the equator, and becomes the Mozambique current.
- **Mozambique Current** The Mozambique current flows South along the East Coast of Africa from the vicinity of the equator to about 35°S, where it becomes Agulhas Stream.
- **Agulhas Stream** The Agulhas stream flows Westward along the Southern West of Madagascar and joins the Mozambique current along the East African coast.
- **West Wind Drift Current** It flows across the Indian ocean to the waters South-West of Australia.
- **North-East Monsoon Drift** It flows along the coast of India during winter.
- **South-West Monsoon Drift** It flows along the coast of India during Summer.
- **South Equatorial Current** It is a significant Pacific, Atlantic and Indian ocean current that flows East-West between the equator and about 20 degrees South.
- **Somalia Current** It is an ocean boundary current that runs along the coast of Somalia and Aman in the Western Indian ocean and is analogous to the Gulf Stream in the Atlantic Ocean.
- There is no counter equatorial current in the Indian ocean rather only monsoonal currents which change their direction with respect to seasons.

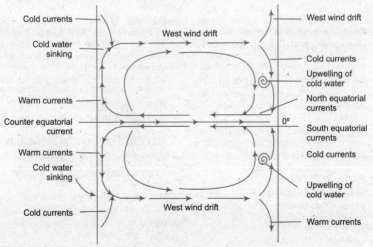

Pattern of Oceanic Current Movement

TIDES

• The rise and fall of the sea level as a result of the forces between the Earth, the Moon and the Sun is called a **tide**. The interval between two tides is 12 hours and 26 minutes.

Spring Tides

• When the Earth, the Moon and the Sun are in a straight line also called **SYZYGY** the Sun assists the gravitational pull of the Moon, creating a condition of higher high tides and lower low tides known as **spring tides**.

Neap Tides

• When the Sun and Moon are at right angles to the Earth, the Sun partially contracts the pull of the Moon, producing lower high tides typical of a Neap tide.

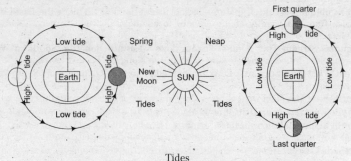

Tides

Continents of the World

Asia, Africa, North America, South America, Europe, Australia and Antarctica are the seven continents.

Continent's Earth Area

Continents	% of Earth Area
Asia	29.5
Africa	20.4
North America	16.3
South America	11.8
Antarctica	9.6
Europe	7.1
Australia	5.3

ASIA

It has 49 and 5 disputed countries.

Latitude 10° S and 80° N

Longitude 25° E and 170° W

Area 44579000 sq km
(approx 30% of the World)

Population 4.427 billion

Oceans and Seas Arctic Ocean, Pacific Ocean, Indian Ocean, Red Sea, Gulf of Aden, Persian Gulf, Gulf of Oman, Arabian Sea, Bay of Bengal, China Sea, Yellow Sea, Okhotsk and Bering Sea.

Highest Point Mt Everest (8848 m)

Lowest Point Dead Sea (– 396 m)

Straits Strait of Malacca, Bering Strait

Islands Kurile, Sakhalin, Honshu, Hokkaido, Taiwan, Borneo, Sumatra and Java, Celebes, New Guinea, Philippines, Sri Lanka, Bahrain and Cyprus.

Peninsulas Kamchatka Peninsula, Peninsula of Korea, Peninsula of Indo-China, Malay Peninsula, Indian Peninsula and Arabian Peninsula.

- It is the largest continent in the world both in term of the population and area.
- It is situated entirely in the Northern hemisphere except some of the islands of Indonesia.
- To the North of it lies the Arctic ocean, to the East the Pacific ocean, to the South, the Indian ocean and to the West lies Mediterranean sea. It is separated from Europe by the Ural mountains, the Caspian sea, the Black sea, the Caucasus mountain and the strait of Dardanelles in the West.

Important Information of Asia

- **Caspian Sea** is the world's largest lake and five times larger than the Lake Superior. It separates Europe from Asia.
- **Dast-e-Kavir** is the largest salt desert of the world situated in the Northern Iran.
- **Lop Nor Lake** in China is a site for numerous nuclear tests.
- **Hwang Ho** is called as China's Sorrow. It flows through loess land, hence it is also called as **Yellow river**.

- Quinling mountains divide China into North and South China.
- Amur river forms the boundary between Russia and China.
- **Yangtze Kiang** is the longest river of Asia.
- Mekong river flows through China, Thailand-Laos border, Cambodia and Vietnam to South China sea.
- Laos is the only landlocked country in South-East Asian Peninsula.
- Group of islands is called an **Archipelago**. Indonesia is the largest archipelago in the world.
- Irawaddy river is known as the **lifeline** of **Myanmar**. It falls into Gulf of Martaban. In Gulf of Martaban pearls are found.
- Lake Van of Turkey is the most saline water body in Asia.
- Fujiyama, a volcanic mountain is the highest peak of Japan.
- Japan is the most industralised nation of Asia.
- Myanmar is called land of **mountains** and **rivers**.
- Pakistan is called **country of canals**.
- Japan is called land of **Rising Sun**.
- **Dead Sea**, the third saltiest water body in the world, is a landlocked sea. It lies between Israel and Jordan.

Physical Aspects of Asia

Mountains	Himalayas, Karakoram, Kailash, Kunlung Shan, Tienshan, Altai, Sayan, Yablonovy, Stanvoy, Kolyma, Verkhoyansk, Pegu Yoma, Arakan Yoma, Hindukush, Elburz, Sulaiman, Kirthar, Makran, Zagros, Pontic, Taurus.
Rivers	Ob, Yenisey, Amur, Yalu, Hwang Ho, Sikiang, Mekong, Tigris, Eupharates, Amu Darya and Syr Darya.
Lakes	Baikal, Balkash, Van Golu, Turnool, Asad, Dead Sea, Tonle Sap Toba, Lop Nor, Caspian Sea and Sea of Gallilee.
Plains	Manchurian, Great Plain of China, West Siberian Plain, Mesopotamian.
Deserts	Rub-al-Khali, Al Nafud, Dasht-I-Kavir, Dasht -I-Lut, Gobi.
Plateaus	Ladakh, Tibet, Yunan, Takla Makan, Pamir, Armenian, Iranian, Mongolia, Alban, Indo-China, Shan, Deccan, Baluchistan, Arabian, Anatolia, Loess.
Mountains from Pamir Knot	South-West: Sulaiman
	South-East: Himalaya, Karakoram and Kunlun
	North-East: Tien Shan
	North-West: Hindukush
Mountains from Armenian Knot	South-West : Taurus
	South-East: Zagros
	North-East: Elburz
	North-West: Pontic

Japan Cities

Cities	Famous For
Tokyo	Electrical Instruments
Yokohama	Precision Instruments
Nagoya	Automobiles
Osaka	Cotton Textiles
Nagasaki	Ship Building

*Osaka is called the **Manchester of Japan**.*

AFRICA

It has 54 countries.

Latitude 35° S and 37° N
Longitude 50° E and 17° W
Population 1022234000 (2nd)
Area 30065000 sq km (approx) (20.4 % of the world)

Oceans and Seas Indian Ocean, Red Sea, Atlantic Ocean, Gulf of Guinea, Mediterranean Sea.
Highest Point Kilimanjaro (5895 m)
Lowest Point Lake Assal (-156.1 m)
Straits Strait of Bab-el-Mandeb and Straits of Gibraltar.
Islands Madagascar, Cape Verde Islands, the Comoros, Mauritius and Seychelles.
Plateaus The entire continent is a plateau.
Three types of palm trees are found in Africa *viz* Coconut palm, Oil palm and Date palm.

- It is the second largest continent after Asia and about nine times the size of India.
- It is situated South of Europe and South-East of Asia. It is bound by Mediterranean sea in the North, the Atlantic ocean in the West and South-West, the Indian ocean in the East and Red sea in the North-East.

- Africa belongs to all four hemispheres and bulk of the continent lies in tropics. It is joined to Asia by the narrow isthmus of Suez and separated from Eurasia at three different points (Strait of Gibraltar, Suez canal and the strait of Bab-el-Mandeb).
- It is the only continent, which is crossed by Tropic of Cancer, Equator and Tropic of Capricorn.
- It is also called as **Dark Continent** because the greater part of its vast interior remained little known to the outside world until the last century.

Physical Aspects of Africa

Mountains	Atlas, Ethiopian Highlands, Mt Kenya, Mt Elgon, Mt Kilimanjaro, Drakensberg, Mt Cameroon, Mt Rouwenzori, Katanga Plateau and Jos Plateau
Rivers	Nile, Zaire or Congo, Niger, Orange, Limpopo, Zambezi
Lakes	Kariba, Nyasa, Mweru, Tanganyika, Edward, Tana, Nasser, Chad, Volta and Assal, Victoria
Deserts	Sahara, Sahel, Libyan, Arabian, Nubian, Namib and Kalahari

Important Information of Africa

- **Lake Victoria** is the largest lake of Africa, which is located between Uganda, Kenya and Tanzania. It is source to White Nile river. The equator passes through it.
- **Nasser lake** is a man-made lake, which lies on Nile river and located between Egypt and Sudan.
- **Nile river** is the longest river of the world and life blood of Egypt.
- The White Nile and the Blue Nile meet at Khartoum (Sudan) to form Nile.
- **Congo river** cuts equator twice.
- Port Harcourt of Niger is located on Niger Delta.
- The Zambezi river includes the **Victoria fall**, one of the largest falls in the world. It makes the natural political boundary between Zambia and Zimbabwe.
- The **Orange river** forms the natural boundary between South Africa and Namibia.

- The **Limpopo river** cuts the Tropic of Capricorn twice and it separates South Africa from Botswana and Zimbabwe.
- The highest peak of Africa is **Mt Kilimanjaro** and is located in Tanzania.
- The three points, where Africa almost touches Eurasia are Gibraltar, Suez and Bab-el-Mandeb.
- The highest temperature in the world has been recorded at **Al-Aziziyah** (Libya) as 58°C making it the hottest place in the world.
- **Swahili** is a famous language of Africa.
- **Sahara desert** is the largest single stretch of desert, which is 5500 km from East to West and 1900 km from North to South.
- **Kalahari desert** is the home of the Africa's one of the oldest races, the Kalahari Bushmen.
- Food crops such as wheat, rice, maize and cash crops such as cotton, coffee, cocoa, oil palm, sugarcane, rubber, tobacco are prominent in Africa.
- Africa is rich in mineral deposits and these minerals are mostly found on the plateau, South of the Equator. The minerals found in Africa are diamond, gold, copper, bauxite, platinum, iron ore, petroleum, manganese etc.

NORTH AMERICA

It has 23 countries.

Latitude 7° N and 84° N

Longitude 20° W and 180° W

Area 24235280 sq km (approx) (16.3 %)

Population 528720588 (4th)

Major Deserts Chihuahuan, Colorado, Mujave, Sonoran

Oceans and Seas Atlantic Ocean, Caribbean Sea, Gulf of California, Gulf of Alaska, Bering Sea and Hudson Bay.

Islands Greenland, Baffin, Victoria, New Foundland, Cuba, Jamaica and Haiti.

Highest Point Meckinley (6194 m)

Lowest Point Death Valley (-85.9 m)

- It is the 3rd largest continent after Asia and Africa. It is surrounded by the Atlantic ocean in the East, Gulf of Mexico in the South, the Pacific ocean in the West and the Arctic in the North. To the North it is separated from the Easternmost tip of Siberia by the **Bering Strait**.
- 49° latitude parallel forms the boundary between Canada and USA and 100° W longitude divides the North America into more or less two equal parts.

Physical Aspects of North America

Mountains	Brook's range, Alaska, Aleutian ranges, Cascade range, Rocky mountains, Coast range, Sierra Nevada etc.
Rivers	Mississippi-Missouri, St Lawrence, Colorado, Columbia, Sacramento, Rio Grande, Yukon, Mackenzie, Nelson, Saskatchewan Peace etc.
Lakes	Great Bear, Great Salve, Athabasca, Winnipeg, Superior, Michigan, Huron, Erie, Ontario, Great Salt and Mead.
Plateaus	Columbia-Snake, Colorado and Mexican.
Peninsula	Ungava, Yucatan and Kenai.

Important Information of North America

- Canada has the longest coast line in the world.
- Canada is the second largest country (in area) in the world.
- USA is the fourth largest country in area and third largest country (in population) in the world.
- 49th parallel forms the boundary between Canada and USA. It is the longest boundary between two countries.

- Erie Canal, **Great Lakes waterways**, St Lawrence Seaway are some of the most important Canals of North America. North America is rich in mineral resources such as iron ore, petroleum and natural gas, copper, gold, silver, nickel, sulphur, coal etc. The Prairie region of North America is ideally suited for the cultivation of wheat.

- The coniferous forests of the North America provides large quantities of soft wood. The prominent trees are fir, pine, larch and spruce etc.

- **Lake Superior** is the largest sweet water lake in the world.

- Maize, wheat and barley are the important cereals grown in North America.

- Canada is the largest producer of newsprint in the world.

- The **Panama Canal** connects Atlantic and Pacific ocean. By using Panama canal, the distance from New York to San Francisco can be shortened to nearly 23200 km.

SOUTH AMERICA

It has 13 countries.
Latitude 12° N and 55° N
Longitude 35° W and 81° W
Area 17820770 sq km (approx 12 %)
Population 385742554 (5th)

Highest Point Aconcagua (6960 m)
Lowest Point Valdes Peninsula (-39.9 m)
Straits Strait of Magellan
Deserts Atacama and Patagonia

- South America has been divided into three physical divisions namely two Eastern highlands, the central plains, the Western mountains and the Western coastal strips.

- **Cotopaxi** in Ecuador is one of the highest active volcanoes in the world.

- Paraguay and Bolivia are the only landlocked countries.

- **Pampas** is the most fertile region of South America and **Alfa-Alfa grasses** are found here.

- It is the fourth largest continent and roughly triangular in shape.

- It is situated to the South of North America, mostly in Southern hemisphere. It is surrounded by Caribbean sea in the North, Atlantic ocean in the East, Antarctica ocean in the South and Pacific ocean in the West.

- South America as well as Mexico, Central America and West Indies are collectively known as **Latin America**.

Physical Aspects of South America

Mountains	Western Mountains, Andes, Brazilian highlands and Guiana Highlands
Rivers	Amazon, Magdalena, Orinico, Parana and La Plata
Lakes	Maracaibo, Titicaca, Popo
Plateaus	Bolivian and Patagonia

Important Information of South America

- It contains the world's highest waterfall i.e. **Angel falls** in Venezuela on Orinoco river.

- It contains the world's 2nd longest river after Nile and the largest river by volume i.e. Amazon river.

- The longest mountain range of the world i.e. the Andes lies in South America.

- Moreover, the driest place on Earth i.e. **Atacama desert**, the largest rain forest i.e. the Amazon rain forest, the highest capital city i.e. Lapaz (Bolivia), the highest commercially navigable lake i.e. Lake Titicaca are situated in South America.

- **Llanos and Campos** are the Savanna grassland in South America. Selvas are the equatorial rainforests of Amazon basin. Some of the countries of South America are specialised in coffee plantation (Brazil, Ecuador, Columbia and Venezuela etc), maize cultivation and wheat cultivation.

- South America is rich in minerals such as petroleum, aluminium, bauxite, copper, gold, lead, nickel, nitrates, diamond coal etc.
- Brazil has the world's largest reserves of iron in Serra dos carajas hills.
- Brazil is also known as the **coffee bowl of the world**, because it is the largest producer of coffee.
- Brazil is the only country through which both equator and one of the tropics (Tropic of Capricorn) passes.

EUROPE

Latitude 35° N and 73° N
Longitude 25° W and 65° E
Area 10530750 sq km (approx) (7.1 %)
Population 731000000

Ocean and Seas Atlantic Ocean, Arctic Ocean, Mediterranean Sea, Caspian Sea, Black Sea, White Sea, North Sea, Norwegian Sea, Baltic Sea, Gulf of Bothnia, Gulf of Finland, Bay of Biscay, Aegean Sea and Adriatic Sea.

Highest Point Mt Elbrus (5642 m)

Lowest Point Caspian Sea (-28.0 m)

Straits Strait of Gibraltar

Lakes Lake Ladoga, Onega, Peipus, Vanern, Vattern

Islands British Isles, Iceland, Sardinia, Sicily, Crete

- Greenland, the world's largest island belongs to Denmark.

Important Gulf and Bays

Gulf of Bothnia	Sweden and Finland
English Channel	Britain and France
Gulf of Lions	South of France
Bay of Biscay	France and Spain

- Wheat is the most important crop of Europe. The **Ruhr** in Germany is the biggest and richest coal field of Europe. Other coal fields in Germany are Saar and Saxony.

- It is the second smallest continent in the world, by area, after Australia.
- Europe is situated between Ural mountains in the East and Atlantic ocean in the West, in the West of Asia and North of Africa.
- To the North of Europe lies Arctic ocean, to the South lies the Mediterranean sea, the Black sea and the Caucasus mountain and to the East Ural mountains and the Caspian sea.
- **Balkan States** It is a group of 9 countries namely Serbia and Montenegro, Slovenia, Croatia, Bosnia Herzegovina, Macedonia, Bulgaria, Greece, Romania Albania and Kosovo. However, Montenegro became an independent state in 2006 and Kosovo in 2008.
- **Baltic States** It is a group of three countries namely Estonia, Lithuania and Latvia. Iceland, Norway, Sweden and Denmark are collectively called as **Scandinavian** countries. The world's most Northerly capital is **Reykjavik**.

Physical Aspects of Europe

Mountains	Vesuvius, Appennines, Vosges, Alps, Mt Etna, Dinaric Alps, Carpathian, Pindus, Ural, Caucasus, Black Forest, Mt Stromboli, Kjolen, Pennine, Cantabarian Pyrenees, Sierra Morena and Sierra Nevada
Rivers	Po, Tiber, Rhine, Ebro, Garrone, Loire, Seine, Weser, Elbe, Wista, Onega, Dvina, Mezen, Volga, Don, Dnieper, Dneister and Danube, Rhine
Peninsula	Iberian, Balkan and Kola

Important Information of Europe

- Copenhagen, capital of Denmark is known as the key to the Baltic.
- Finland is known as the land of forests and lakes.
- Both intensive and extensive cultivation are done in Europe with a great variety of crops due to the occurrence of different kinds of soil and climate. On the steppes, wheat, sugar beet and sun flowers are the major crops, whereas in the Mediterranean region, fruit cultivation is prominent. Moreover, cattle, sheep and pigs are reared for meat, milk and its products.

- The continental shelf areas around Europe including **Dogger Bank** are rich in fish.
- Europe is rich in minerals such as iron ore, petroleum, coal, copper etc.
- United Kingdom is the name given to the combination of Great Britain and Northern Ireland. Great Britain consists of England, Scotland and Waves.
- UK is one of the most industrialized nations of the world, though it lacks the raw material. It is self sufficient in petrol.
- France is the third largest country in Europe. Russia is the largest country of the world and the highest populated country of Europe.
- Vatican city is in Rome, Italy. It is the smallest country of the world both in terms of area and population.

AUSTRALIA

Australia is an inland continent.

Latitude 10°41'S and 39°S

Longitude 114°E and 154°E

Area 7830682 sq km (5.3%)

Population 24 million

Highest Point Mt. Kosciusko (2228 m) in island of New Guinea

Lowest Point Lake Eyre (– 15.8 m)

- **Islands** Tasmania.
- It is the smallest continent of the world. It lies entirely in the Southern hemisphere. The Tropic of Capricorn runs almost through the middle of the continent and divides the continent in two equal parts.
- It is the only continent that is also a country and it lies between Pacific and Indian ocean. It is surrounded by Timor sea in the North-West, Arafura sea and Gulf of Carpentaria in the North, Great Barrier Reef in the North-East and Great Australian Bight in the South. To the South-East of the mainland lies the mountainous island of Tasmania.

Physical Aspects of Australia

Mountains	Great Dividing range, Darling range, Musgrave, Flinders and Australian Alps
Deserts	Gibson, Great Sandy, Great Victoria, Simpson, Little Sandy, Western desert, Rangipo and Tanami etc
Rivers	Murray, Darling and Swan

Important Information of Australia

- Australia is known as **Forgotten land**. It was discovered by Captain Cook in 1770. Australia is the largest producer of bauxite.
- It is divided into six states. The six states are Western Australia, Northern Territory, Queensland, New South Wales, South Australia and Victoria.
- Largest city of Australia is **Sydney**.
- The highest peak of Australia is **Mt Kosciusko** (2228 m).
- **Great Barrier reef** is the world's longest coral Reef and is located in the North-East of Australia. The largest lake of Australia is Eyre.
- The first European to dicover New Zealand was Abel Tasman.
- The highest peak of New Zealand is **Mt Cook** (3724 m).
- Agriculture is carried out in the Murray Darling Basin, around the river Swan in Perth and along the rainy East coast. Wheat and sugarcane are important crops. Moreover, commercial farming is a big business in Australia.
- Coal, iron ore, bauxite, uranium, gold and petroleum are the major mineral resources of Australia.
- Being a dry country, forest do not occur in continuous belt, however tropical forests are found in the North coastal region, which gets monsoon rain.
- The Australian trade is based on agriculture, animal rearing and minerals.

ANTARCTICA

• It was discovered in 1820.
• Ronald Amundsen was the first man to reach geographical South pole in Antarctica.
• It is called as the continent for science because it provides unique opportunity to scientists to learn about the world.

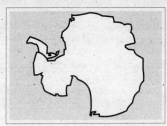

• **Mt Erebus** is the only active volcano on Antarctica.
• Mt Vinson (4897 m) is the highest peak of Antarctica.
• It is the only continent, which is completely frozen. It is, therefore, known as **White Continent**.

Highest/Lowest Points of Various Continents

Continent	Highest (m)	Lowest (m)
Asia	Mt Everest (8848)	Dead Sea (–396)
Africa	Mt Kilimanjaro (5951)	Lake Assal (–151)
North America	Mt McKinley (6194)	Death Valley (–87)
South America	Mt Aconcagua (6962)	Valdes Peninsula (–40)
Antarctica	Vinson Massif (4897)	Bentley Sub-glacial Trench (–2538)
Europe	Mt El' Brus (5642)	Caspian Sea (–28)
Australia	Kosciusko (2228)	Lake Eyre (–16)

Important Straits of the World

Strait	Water Bodies Joined	Area
Bab-al- Mandeb	Red Sea and Arabian Sea	Arabia and Africa
Bering	Arctic Ocean and Bering Sea	Alaska and Asia
Bosphorus	Black Sea and Marmara Sea	Turkey
Dover	North Sea and Atlantic Ocean	England and Europe
Florida	Gulf of Mexico and Atlantic Ocean	Florida and Bahamas Islands
Gibralter	Mediterranean Sea and Atlantic Ocean	Spain and Africa
Malacca	Java Sea and Bay of Bengal	India and Indonesia
Palk	Bay of Bengal and Indian Ocean	India and Sri Lanka
Megellan	South Pacific and South Atlantic Ocean	Chile
Sunda	Java Sea and Indian Ocean	Indonesia

Important Canals of the World

Canal	Connects
Panama	Pacific Ocean with Caribbean Sea
Suez	Mediterranean Sea to Red Sea
Erie	Atlantic Ocean to Great Lakes
Kiel	North Sea to Baltic Sea

Oceans of the World (Area wise)

Ocean	Deepest Point
Pacific	Mariana Trench
Atlantic	Puerto Rico Trench
Indian	Java Trench
Arctic	Eurasian Basin

River Side Cities

City	River
Sittwe (Myanmar)	Irawady
Baghdad (Iraq)	Tigris
Basara (Iraq)	Tigris and Euphrates
Belgrade	Danube
Berlin (Germany)	Spree
Bristol (UK)	Avon
Budapest (Hungary)	Danube
Cairo (Egypt)	Nile
Canton	Si-Kiang
Glasgow (Scotland)	Clyde
Hamburg (Germany)	Elbe
Jamshedpur	Subarnarekha
Kabul	Kabul
Karachi	Indus
Khartoum (Sudan)	Nile
Lahore	Ravi
Lisbon (Portugal)	Tangus
London (UK)	Thames
Lucknow	Gomti
Montreal (Canada)	Ottawa
Nanking	Yang-tse-Kiang
New Castle (UK)	Tyre
New Orleans (USA)	Mississippi
New York (USA)	Hudson
Paris (France)	Seine
Philadelphia (USA)	Delaware
Rome (Italy)	Tiber
Shanghai	Yang-tse-Kiang
Srinagar	Jhelum
Warsaw (Poland)	Vistula
Yangon (Myanmar)	Irawady

Major Rivers of the World

River	Origin
Nile	Victoria Lake
Amazon	Andes (Peru)
Yangtze	Tibetan Kiang Plateau
Mississippi Missouri	Itaska Lake (USA)
Yenisei	Tannu-Ola Mountains
Huang Ho	Kunlun Mountains
Ob	Altai Mountains, Russia
Congo	Lualaba and Luapula rivers
Amur	North-East China
Lena	Baikal Mountains
Mekong	Tibetan Highlands
Niger	Guinea

Important Lakes of the World

Lake	Location
Caspian	Asia
Superior	Canada and USA
Victoria	Africa
Huron	Canada and USA
Michigan	USA
Tanganyika	Africa
Baikal	Russia
Great Bear	Canada
Aral	Kazakhstan
Great Slave	Canada

List of Waterfalls

Rank	Waterfall	Location
1	Angel Falls	Venezuela
2	Tugela Falls	South Africa
3	Cataratas las Tres Hermanas	Peru
4	Olo'upena Falls	United Sates
5	Catarata Yumbilla	Peru

Major Islands of the World

Rank	Island's Name	Area (km)^2	Country
1	Greenland	2130800	Denmark
2	New Guinea	785753	Indonesia
3	Borneo	748168	Indonesia and Malaysia
4	Madagascar	587713	Madagascar
5	Baffin Island	507451	Canada
6	Sumatra	443066	Indonesia

Minerals of the World

Mineral	Leading Producer
Gold	China
Bauxite	Australia
Copper	Chile
Platinum	South Africa
Chromium	South Africa
Vanadium	China
Antimony	China
Tungsten	China
Phosphate	Morocco
Manganese	China
Diamond	Russia
Iron ore	China
Petroleum	Russia

Mines of the World

Mine	Mineral
Kimberley (South Africa)	Diamond
Lumbabashi (Zaire)	Copper
Wankee (Zimbabwe)	Coal
Witwatersrand (South Africa)	Gold
Katanga (Zaire-Zambia)	Copper and Cobalt
Kasai Province (Zaire)	Bort Diamond

Agriculture

Agricultural Produce	Leading Producer
Coffee	Brazil
Rubber	Liberia
Tea	Kenya
Oil Palm	Nigeria
Cocoa	Ghana
Coconut	Philippines
Date Palm	Egypt
Cotton	China
Wheat	China
Maize	USA
Wool	South Africa
Sisal	Brazil
Cloves	Indonesia

Industrial Cities

Country	Industry
Anshan (China)	Iron and Steel
Baku (Azerbaijan)	Petroleum
Belfast (Ireland)	Ship building
Birmingham (UK)	Iron and Steel
Chicago (USA)	Meat packing
Detroit (USA)	Automobile
Havana (Cuba)	Cigars
Hollywood (USA)	Films
Johannesburg (South Africa)	Gold Mining
Kansas City (USA)	Meat packing
Kawasaki (Japan)	Iron and Steel
Kimberley (South Africa)	Diamond mining
Krivoi Rog (Ukraine)	Iron and Steel
Leeds (UK)	Woollen textiles
Leningrad (Russia)	Ship building
Los Angeles (USA)	Petroleum
Lyon (France)	Silk textiles
Magnitogorsk (Russia)	Iron and Steel
Manchester (UK)	Cotton textile
Milan (Italy)	Silk textile
Multan (Pakistan)	Pottery
Munich (Germany)	Lenses
Nagoya (Japan)	Automobiles
Philadelphia (USA)	Locomotives
Pittsburg (USA)	Iron and Steel
Plymouth (USA)	Ship building
Rourkela (India)	Iron and Steel
Sheffield (UK)	Cutlery
Vladivostok (Russia)	Ship building
Wellington (New Zealand)	Dairying
Arizona (USA)	Optics
Bhiwandi (India)	Power looms
Vijayawada (India)	Auto parts
Bhagalpur (India)	Silk

Changed Names of Cities, States and Countries

Old Name	New Name
Abyssinia	Ethiopia
Angora	Ankara
Basutoland	Botswana
Batavia	Jakarta
British Guiana	Guyana
Burma	Myanmar
Cape Canaveral	Cape Kennedy
Cawnpore	Kanpur
Central Provinces	Madhya Pradesh
Ceylon	Sri Lanka
Christina	Oslo
Cochin	Kochi
Constantinople	Istanbul
Dacca	Dhaka
Dutch East Indies	Indonesia
Dutch Guiana	Surinam
Gold Coast	Ghana
Holland	The Netherlands
Ivory Coast	Cote D'Ivoire
Madagascar	Malagasy
Malaya	Malaysia
Mesopotamia	Iraq
Nippon	Japan
Northern Rhodesia	Zambia
Nyasaland	Malawi
Peking	Beijing
Persia	Iran
Petrograd	Leningrad
Quilon	Kollam
Rangoon	Yangon
Rhodesia	Zimbabwe
Saigon	Ho Chi Minh City
Sandwich Islands	Hawaiian Islands
Siam	Thailand
South-West Africa	Namibia
Spanish Guinea	Equatorial Guinea
Zaire	Republic of Congo

Important International Boundary Lines

Name of Boundary Line	In Between Countries
Radcliffe Line (1947)	India and Pakistan
Macmohan Line (1914)	India and China
Durand Line (1896)	Pakistan and Afghanistan
Hindenburg Line	Germany and Poland
Maginot Line	France and Germany
Order Neisse Line	Germany and Poland
Siegfried Line	Fortification between Germany and France
38th Parallel Line	North and South Korea
49th Parallel Line	USA and Canada
24th Parallel Line	Pakistan claims that it is the boundary between India and Pakistan in Rann of Kutch
17th Parallel Line	North Vietnam and South Vietnam (presently not in use)

Famous Tribes of the World

Abhors	People of Mongolian blood living between Assam and Eastern tribes
Afridis	Tribes residing in the North-West Frontier (Pakistan)
Bantus	Negroes living in the Central and South Africa
Boers	The Dutch settlers of South Africa
Cossacks	People living in the Southern and Eastern Frontiers of Russia
Eskimos	Inhabitants of Greenland and of Arctic regions
Flemings	A term used for the People of Belgium
Hamites	Inhabitants of North-West Africa
Khirgiz	People living in Central Asia
Kurds	Tribes living in Kurdistan (Iraq)
Magyars	Inhabitants of Hungary
Maoris	Inhabitants of New Zealand
Negroesz	Mostly found in Africa
Pygmies	Short sized people found in Congo basin in Africa
Red Indians	Original inhabitants of North America
Semites	Caucasian people of ancient times
Zulus	People of South Africa living in certain part of Natal

INDIAN GEOGRAPHY

- India is the 7th largest country in the world with an area of 3287263 sq km, which is 2.42% of world's area.
- India is the second most populous country in the world with a population of 1.21 billion (2011), which is 17.44% of the world.
- Indian sub-continent is located in the Northern and Eastern hemisphere.
- India shares longest boundary with Bangladesh (4096 km), followed by China (3488 km), Pakistan (3323 km), Nepal (1751 km), Myanmar (1643 km), Bhutan (699 km) and Afghanistan (106 km).
- In India, the Tropic of Cancer (23.5°N latitude) passes through 8 States (Gujarat, Rajasthan, Madhya Pradesh, Chhattisgarh, Jharkhand, West Bengal, Tripura and Mizoram).
- **Islands** Andaman and Nicobar Islands in the Bay of Bengal; Lakshadweep, Amindive and Minicoy in the Arabian Sea.
- **Indian Standard Time** (IST) The 82°30' E longitude is taken as the Standard Time Meridian of India, as it passes through middle of India (from Naini, near Allahabad).
- The 82° 30' E Meridian also dictates time in Sri Lanka and Nepal.
- In the South, on the Eastern side, the Gulf of Mannar and the Palk Strait separates India from Sri Lanka.

INDIA : BASIC INFORMATION

- Latitudinal extent — 8°4' North to 37° 6' North
- Longitudinal extent — 68°7' East to 97° 25' East
- North-South extent — 3214 km
- East-West extent — 2933 km
- Land Frontiers — 15200 km
- Total Coastline — 7516.6 km
- Number of States — 29
- Number of Union Territories — 7
- Land Neighbours (7) — Pakistan, Afghanistan, China, Nepal, Bhutan, Bangladesh and Myanmar
- States with Longest Coastline — Gujarat
- Active Volcano — Barren Island in Andaman and Nicobar Islands
- Southern most point — Indira Point or Pygmalion point in Great Nicobar
- Southern most tip of mainland — Kanyakumari
- Northern most point — Indira Col
- Western most point — West of Ghaur Mota in Gujarat
- Eastern most point — Kibithu in Arunachal Pradesh

Indian States Situated on the Border

Country	Indian States Situated on the Border
Pakistan (4)	Gujarat, Rajasthan, Punjab and Jammu and Kashmir
Afghanistan (1)	Jammu and Kashmir
China (5)	Jammu and Kashmir, Uttarakhand, Himachal Pradesh, Sikkim and Arunachal Pradesh
Nepal (5)	Uttar Pradesh, Uttarakhand, Bihar, West Bengal, Sikkim
Bhutan (4)	Sikkim, West Bengal, Assam and Arunachal Pradesh
Bangladesh (5)	West Bengal, Assam, Meghalaya, Tripura and Mizoram

PHYSICAL FEATURES

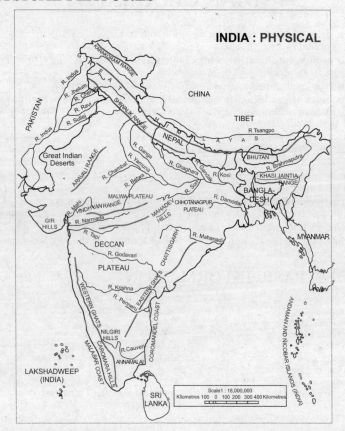

INDIA : PHYSICAL

Physiographic divisions of India are as follows:

- The Himalayan Range of Mountains
- The Peninsular Plateau
- The Great Plains of India
- The Coastal Plains
- The Islands of India

The Himalayas

- Himalayas means 'Abode of snow' and they are young fold mountains of tertiary period, which were folded over Tethys sea due to inter-continental collision.
- They are one of the youngest fold mountain ranges in the world and comprises mainly sedimentary rocks.

- They stretch from the Indus river in the West to the Brahmaputra river in the East.
- The Pamirs, popularly known as the **Roof of the World** is the connecting link between the Himalayas and the high ranges of Central Asia.
- The total length is about 2500 km with varying width of 240 to 320 km and a total area of 500000 km².

They consists of three parallel ranges such as:

(i) Himadri (Greater Himalayas)

(ii) Himachal (Lesser Himalayas)

(iii) Shiwaliks (Outer Himalayas)

Inner Himalaya or Greater Himalaya (Himadri)

- Northern most part of the Himalayan range, it is the world's highest part with an average altitude of 6100 m above sea level.
- It includes world's highest peak, Mt Everest (8848 m) located in Nepal. It is known as **Sagarmatha in Nepal** and **Chomolangma in China**.
- Zaskar range is situated on the Western part of Greater Himalayas. It includes Nanga Parbat (8126 m Kashmir-Himachal region) and Nepal Dhaulagiri (8172 m).

Other Important Peaks

- Kanchenjunga (8598 m, Sikkim) Makalu (8481 m in Nepal) Mansalu (8156 m Nepal) Nanga Parbat (8108 m Jammu and Kashmir) Kamet and Nandadevi.

Important Passes in Inner Himalaya

Pass	Location	Connectivity
Karakoram Pass	Jammu and Kashmir	India to China
Burzil Pass	Jammu and Kashmir	Kashmir valley to Central Asia
Zojila Pass	Jammu and Kashmir	Sriñagar to Leh
Shipki la Pass	Himachal Pradesh	Shimla to Gartok (Tibet)
Jelep la Pass	Sikkim	Kalimpong West Bengal to Lhasa (Tibet)
Yang yap Pass	Arunachal Pradesh	Entry of Brahmaputra river

Middle Himalaya or Lesser Himalaya (Himachal)

- *From West to East middle Himalaya is divided into following ranges:*
  - Pirpanjal range (Jammu and Kashmir). It is longest range of the middle Himalaya
  - Dhauladhar range (Himachal Pradesh)
  - Mussoorie range (Uttarakhand)
  - Nagtibba range (Uttarakhand)
  - Mahabharat range (Nepal)

Important Passes in Middle Himalaya

Pass	Location	Connectivity
Pirpanjal Pass	Jammu and Kashmir	Jammu-Srinagar road passes from this pass
Banihal Pass	Jammu and Kashmir	Jammu-Srinagar NH-IA passes from this pass. Jawahar tunnel (India's longest road tunnel)
Rohtang Pass	Himachal Pradesh	Kullu-keylang road passes from this pass

- Average height of the Middle Himalaya is 3700-4500 km.
- Mountains and valleys are disposed in all direction.
- Important hill resorts are Shimla, Ranikhet, Almora, Nainital and Darjeeling.

Outer Himalayas (Shiwalik)

- Shiwaliks are characterised by fault scraps anticlinals crest and synclinical hills.
- Average elevation is 900-1200 m.
- It is the youngest part of the mountain.
- It forms the foothills of Himalayas.

Trans Himalayan Zones

- This zone lies to the North of the Great Himalayas.
- Some important ranges of this zone are Karakoram and Ladakh etc. The highest peak in region is K2 or Godwin Austin or Qagir (8611m in Pak occupied Kashmir). Mount K2 is also the 2nd highest peak of the world and the highest peak of India, located in Karakoram range.
- Mt Rakaposhi is the highest peak in Ladakh range and the steepest peak in the world.
- Siachin glacier is second largest glacier of the world outside the polar region (more than 72 km) and is located in Nubra valley. Ladakh, Baltaro, Biafo, Batura, Hispar are the other important glaciers in this region.

Mountain Peaks : Quick Digest

Highest peak of India	Godwin Austin (K2)
Highest peak of Satpura	Dhupgarh
Highest peak of Aravalli	Gurushikhar in Mount Abu
Highest peak of Western Ghat	Anaimudi
Highest peak of Eastern Ghat	Mahendragiri
Highest peak of Nilgiri	Doda Beta
Highest peak of Naga hills	Saramati
Highest peak of Andaman and Nicobar	Saddle peak

Himalayan Mountain Peaks

Peak	Height (m)	Country
Mt Everest	8848	Nepal-China
Mt K2	8611	PoK (India)
Kanchenjunga	8586	Nepal-India
Lhotse	8511	Nepal-China
Makalu	8481	Nepal-China
Cho oyu	8201	Nepal-China
Dhaulagiri	8172	Nepal
Manaslu	8163	Nepal
Nanga Parbat	8125	Pakistan
Annapurna	8078	Nepal
Gasherbrum I	8068	Pakistan-China
Broad peak	8047	Pakistan-China

Mountain Peaks in India

Highest Peak	Height (m)	State
Mt K2	8611	PoK (India)
Kanchenjunga	8586	Sikkim
Nanda Devi	7817	Uttarakhand
Saltoro	7742	Jammu and Kashmir
Kangto	7090	Arunachal Pradesh
Reo Purgil	6816	Himachal Pradesh
Saramati	3841	Nagaland
Sandakphu	3636	West Bengal
Khayang	3114	Manipur
Anaimudi	2695	Kerala
Doda Beta	2636	Tamil Nadu

The Great Plain

- To the South of the Himalayas and to the North of the peninsula lies the great plains of North India.
- It extends from West to East for 2400 km having an average width in between 150-300 km.
- The plains are formed by depositional works of three major river systems Indus, Ganga and Brahmaputra.
- The vast plains of North India are alluvial in nature and the Western most portion is occupied by the desert.
- It is composed of Bhangar (old alluvium), Khadar (new alluvium) in the river bed, Bhabar (porous gravel ridden plains at the foothills of Shiwalik and Streams disappear here) and Terai (damp, thick forest area, where Bhabar streams reappear).

Difference Between Bhangar and Khadar

Bhangar	Khadar
These are low plains. composed of older alluvium.	The deposit of fresh alluvium every year brought by the Himalayas rivers makes this belt of Northern plains.
It contains calcareous deposits locally known as **Kankar**.	It does not contain calcareous deposits of calcium.

Difference Between Terai and Bhabar

Terai	Bhabar
Terai is a broad long zone South of Bhabar plain.	Bhabar is a long narrow plain along the foothills.
It is a marshy damp area covered with dense forest.	It is a pebble studded zone of porous beds.
It is 20-30 km wide.	It is 9-16 km wide.
It is suitable for agriculture.	It is unsuitable for agriculture.

Sub-Divisions of the Great Plain

The Rajasthan Plain	Thar or Great Indian desert is the Western most region of the Great Indian plain. A semi-arid plain, lying to the East of Thar desert is known as **Rajasthan Bagar**. The Luni is the only South-West flowing river of the region.
The Punjab-Haryana Plain	It extends from Punjab in the West to Yamuna (Haryana) in East. They are composed of Dhaya (Heavily gullied bluffs) and Bets (Khadar Plains).
The Ganga Plain	It extends from Delhi to Kolkata across the states of Uttar Pradesh, Bihar and West Bengal. The Ganga and its tributaries deposit large amount of alluvium and make this extensive plain more fertile.
The Brahma-putra Plain	Low level plain formed by Brahmaputra river system is situated between Eastern Himalaya in North and lower Ganga plain and Indo-Bangladesh border in the West.

- The Punjab - Haryana plain is drained by five rivers and the intervening area between the river is known as doab. *From South to North doabs are as follows:*

Doab	Region
Bist Doab	Between Beas and Sutlej
Bari Doab	Between Beas and Ravi
Rachna Doab	Between Ravi and Chenab
Chaj Doab	Between Chenab and Jhelum
Sind Sagar Doab	Between Jhelum and Indus

- The Sambhar (largest), Didwana and Kuchaman lakes are situated to the North of Luni basin.

The Peninsular Plateau

- Rising from the height of 150m above the river plains up to an elevation of 600-1000 m is the irregular triangle known as the peninsular plateau.
- It is composed of the old cystalline, igneous and metamorphic rocks.
- It covers a total of 160000 km² (about half of total land area of the country).

- Narmada, which flows through a rift valley divides the region into two parts: the Central Highlands in the North and the Deccan plateau in the South.
- The Deccan plateau is the largest plateau in India.

Plateaus of Peninsular India

The Central Highland

- The Central Highlands lie to the North of the Narmada river covering a major area of the Malwa plateau.
- The Aravalis range is bounded by the Central Highlands on the North-West and Vindhyan range on the South.
- It is also called as **Madhya Bharat Pathar**.

The Deccan Plateau

- The Deccan plateau is a triangular land lying to the South of the river Narmada. It is made up of lava flows in the cretaceous era through the fissure eruptions.
- It comprises Maharashtra plateau, Karnataka plateau and the Telangana and Rayalseema plateau (Andhra Pradesh).
- The general slope is from West to East.
- The Eastern and Western Ghats demarcate the Eastern and Western edges of the Deccan plateau.

Meghalaya Plateau

- This plateau is separated from main block of the peninsular plateau by a gap called **Garo-Raj Mahal gap**.
- From East to West, the plateau comprises Garo, Khasi, Jaintia and Mikir hills.

The Bundelkhand Upland

- It is located to the South of Yumana river between Madhya Bharat Pathar and the Vindhyan scrap lands and is composed of granites and gneiss.

The Marwar Upland

- It lies East of Aravali range, made up of sandstone, shale and limestone of Vindhyan period.

Chhotanagpur Plateau

- It covers mostly Jharkhand, Chhattisgarh and Purulia of West Bengal.
- It is composed mainly of Gondwana rocks with patches of granites and gneisses and Deccan lavas.

Hill Ranges of the Peninsula

Aravali Range

- Aravalis are one of the world's oldest fold mountain running in North-East to South-East direction from Delhi to Palanpur in Gujarat. It is an example of relict mountain.
- It separates the fertile regions of Udaipur and Jaipur regions from the semi-arid regions of Rajasthan.
- Piplighat, Barr, Dewair and Desuri passes allow movements by roads and railways.

Vindhyan Range

- This range acts as a water divide between Ganga system with the river system of South India. The Maikal range forms a connecting link between Vindhya and Satpura.

Satpura Range

- It is a series of seven mountains running in East-West direction South of Vindhya and in between the Narmada and Tapi.
- It comprises Rajpipla hills, Mahadeo hills and Maikal Range.

Eastern Ghats

- It comprises the discontinuous and low hills that are highly eroded by the rivers such as the Mahanadi, the Godavari, the Krishna, the Cauveri etc.
- Some of the important ranges include the Javadi hills, the Velikonda range, the Nallamalai hills, the Mahendragiri hills etc.

Western Ghats

- Western ghats are locally known by different names such as **Sahyadri** in **Maharashtra**, Nilgiri hills in Karnataka and Tamil Nadu and Anaimalai hills, Cardamom hills in Kerala.

- It runs from the South of the valley of river Tapi to Kanyakumari.
- The Sahyadris upto 16° North latitude are mainly composed of basalt.

There are three important passes in the Sahyadris

(i) Thalghat (between Mumbai and Pune)

(ii) Palghat (between Palakkad and Coimbatore)

(iii) Bhorghat (between Mumbai and Nashik)

- The Eastern and the Western Ghats meet each other at the Nilgiri hill.

Difference Between Eastern Ghat and Western Ghat

Eastern Ghat	Western Ghat
Located East to Deccan Plateau.	Located West to Deccan Plateau.
They are parallel to Eastern Coast i.e. Coromandel and Northern Circar etc.	They are parallel to Western Coast, i.e. Konkan, Malabar etc.
Mahanadi, Cauveri, Godavari, Krishna etc rivers are drawn in this land.	Narmada, Tapi, Sabarmati and Mahi etc rivers are drawn in this land.
Mahendragiri with an altitude of 1501 m is the highest peak here.	Anaimudi with an altitude of 2695 m is the highest peak here.

The Coastal Plains

On the basis of location and active geomorphological processes, *it can be broadly divided into*

- Eastern coastal plain
- Western coastal plain

The Eastern Coastal Plain

- The East coastal plain extends from the deltaic plains of the Ganga in the North to Kanyakumari in the South for 1100 km with an average width of 120 km.
- Utkal plain extends from deltaic plains of Ganga to the Mahanadi delta for about 400 km.
- Andhra coastal plain extends from the Southern limit of Utkal plains to Pulicat lake (Andhra Pradesh). It has large deltas of Krishna and the Godavari rivers.

- Tamil Nadu plains extends from the North of Chennai to Kanyakumari in the South. Coromandel coast is a part of this plain. It has the deltaic plains of Cauveri and is popularly called as **the Granary of South India.**

The Western Coastal Plain

It is about 1500 km long from Surat to Cape Comorin.

These plains are sub-divided into six Western Coastal Plain :

1. **Kachchh Plains** An island surrounded by sea and lagoons.
2. **Kathiawar Plains** It extends from Rann of Kuchchh to Daman in the South.
3. **Gujarat Plains** East to Kachchh and Kathiawar formed by the rivers Narmada, Tapi, Mahi and Sabarmati.
4. **Konkan Coast** It extends from Daman to Goa for a distance of about 500 km.
5. **Karnataka or Kanara Coast** It extends from Goa to Mangalore in narrow belt.
6. **Malabar Coast/ Kerala Coast** It extends between Mangalore and Kanyakumari. The back waters locally called **kayals** are the shallow lagoons. The largest among these is Vembanad lake followed by Ashtamudi.

Difference Between Eastern and Western Coast

Eastern Coast	Western Coast
Smooth outline	Dissected outline
Occurrence of deltas	Occurrence of estuaries
Less rainfall	More rainfall
Broader	Narrower
Long rivers	Small rivers

Islands

- India has large number islands, most of which are located in two groups
  - Andaman and Nicobar group
  - Lakshadweep group
- Group of islands is called **archipelago**.

Andaman and Nicobar Group

- It is located in Bay of Bengal.
- There are nearly 203 islands in Andaman group, whereas the Nicobar group of islands consist of 7 big and 12 small islands.
- **Ten degree channel** separates Andaman group from Nicobar Duncan passage lies between South Andaman and Little Andaman group.

Lakshadweep Group

- It is located in Arabian sea.
- Minicoy is the second largest and Southern most island and the Nott island is the largest island of this group.
- Minicoy is separated from rest of the Lakshadweep by Nine Degree Channel.
- **Eight degree channel** separates Lakshadweep group from Maldives.

DRAINAGE SYSTEM OF INDIA

- Water drains in two directions of the main water divide line of India. 90% of land water drains into Bay of Bengal and the rest drains into Arabian sea.
- Those Himalayan rivers, which originated before the formation of Himalaya are known as **Antecedent rivers**, such as-Indus, Brahmaputra and Sutlej.
- India is blessed with hundreds of large and small rivers, which drains the length and breadth of the country.

In India, the rivers can be divided into two main groups:

(i) Himalayan rivers   (ii) Peninsular rivers

The river basins have been divided into three parts such as:

River Basins

Major	Medium	Minor
River basin with catchment area of 20000 sq km and above.	River basin with catchment area between 2000- 20000 sq km.	River basin with catchment area below 2000 sq km.
It accounts for 85% of the total run off all the rivers.	It accounts for 7% of the total run off.	It accounts for 8% of the total run off.

Himalayan Rivers

Himalayan river system is divided into three major river systems:

The Indus System

- The Indus, also known as **Sindhu**, is the Western most of Himalayan rivers in India.
- It is one of the largest river basins of the world covering an area of 1165000 sq km (in India it is 321289 sq km) and a total length of 2880 km (in India 1114 km).
- It originates from a glacier near Bokhar Chu in the Tibetan region near **Mansarovar lake**.
- In Tibet, it is known as **Singi Khamban** or **Lion's mouth**.
- In Jammu and Kashmir, its Himalayan tributaries are Zanskar, Dras, Gartang, Shyok, Shigar, Nubra, Gilgit etc.
- Its most important tributaries, which join Indus at various places, are Jhelum, Chenab, Ravi, Beas and Sutlej.
- According to Indus Water Treaty signed between India and Pakistan in 1960, India can utilise only 20% of the total discharge of Indus, Jhelum and Chenab.

Indus River System

River	Source	Length (km)	Falls into
Indus	Near Manasarovar Lake	2880	Arabian Sea
Jhelum	Verinag	724	Chenab
Chenab	Bara Lacha Pass	1180	Indus
Ravi	Near Rohtang Pass	725	Chenab
Beas	Near Rohtang Pass	460	Sutlej
Sutlej	Manasarovar-Rakas Lake	1450	Chenab

The Ganga System

- The Ganga system is the second major drainage system of India.
- It rises in the Gangotri glacier near **Gaumukh** (3900 m) in the Uttarakhand. Here, it is known as the **Bhagirathi**. At Dev Prayag, the Bhagirathi, meets the **Alaknanda**, hereafter, it is known as the **Ganga**. The Alaknanda has its source in the Satopanth glacier above Badrinath.
- The Alaknanda consists of the Dhauli and the Vishnu Ganga, which meet at Joshimath or Vishnu Prayag.
- The other tributaries of Alaknanda such as the Pindar joins it at Karna Prayag, while Mandakini or Kali Ganga meets it at Rudra Prayag.
- It is 2525 km long of which 1450 km is in Uttarakhand and UP, 445 km in Bihar and 520 km in West Bengal.
- The left bank tributaries of Ganga are Ramganga, Gomti, Kali or Sharda, Gandhak, Kosi, Mahanadi.
- The right bank tributaries of Ganga are Yamuna and Son. Yamuna joins the Ganga at Allahabad. Kosi is called as **Sorrow of Bihar** while Damodar is called as **Sorrow of Bengal** as these cause floods in these regions. Hooghly is a distributory of Ganga flowing through Kolkata.

Ganga River System

River	Source	Length (km)
Ganga	Gangotri Glacier	2525
Yamuna	Yamunotri Glacier	1376
Chambal	Near Mhow	960
Ramganga	Garhwal district	596
Ghaghra	Near Gurla Mandhata peak South of Manasarovar	1080
Son	Amarkantak Plateau	780
Damodar	Chhotanagpur Plateau	541
Gandak	Tibet-Nepal border	425*
Kosi	Sikkim-Nepal-Tibet Himalaya	730*

* length in India

The Brahmaputra System

- It is one of the largest river of the world.
- It is known as **Tsangpo in Tibet**, **Dihang** or **Siang** in **Arunachal Pradesh**, **Brahmaputra** in **Assam** and **Jamuna** in **Bangladesh**.
- **Brahmaputra** forms largest number of riverine islands. Majuli is the largest riverine island in the world.
- The combined stream of Ganga and Brahmaputra forms the biggest delta in the world, the Sundarbans, covering an area of 58752 sq km. Its major part is in Bangladesh.
- Brahmaputra is volume wise largest river of India, whereas lengthwise Ganga is the longest in India.

Brahmaputra River System

Name	Source	Total Length	Information
Brahmaputra or Tsangpo	Rises in Chemayungdung glacier in the Kailash range.	2900 km	Mariam La pass separates it from Mansarovar lake. Important tributaries are Subansiri, Kameng, Dhansiri, Dihang, Lohit, Tista, Manas, Dihing etc

The Peninsular River System

Peninsular river system can be divided in two groups:

East Flowing Rivers (or Delta forming rivers)

- East flowing rivers form Delta.
- East flowing rivers fall in Bay of Bengal.

West Flowing Rivers (or Estuaries forming rivers)

- West flowing rivers do not form delta.
- West flowing rivers fall in Arabian Sea.

East Flowing Rivers

Rivers	Source	Length	Tributaries
Mahanadi	North foothills of Dandakarnaya	857 km	Seonath, Hasdeo, Ib, Mand, Tel, Ong and Jonk.
Godavari	Triambak plateau of North Sahyadri near Nashik	1465 (longest river of Peninsular India.	Penganga, Wardha, Wainganga Indravati, Sabari, Manjira.
Krishna	North of Mahabaleshwar in the Western ghat	1400 km	Bhima, Tungabhadra, Ghat Prabha, Malaprabha, Musi and Koyna.
Cauveri	Rise in Brahmgiri range in Western ghat	800 km	Herongi, Hemavati, Shimsa, Arkavati, Kabani, Bhavani and Amravati etc.

West Flowing Rivers

River	Source	Length	Tributaries
Sabarmati	Mewar in Aravalli range	371 km	It falls into Gulf of Khambat and its tributaries are Hathmati, Sedhi, Wakul.
Mahi	Rises from Vindhyan range	583 km	Flows in Madhya Pradesh, Rajasthan and Gujarat.
Narmada (*largest West flowing peninsular river system*)	Amarkantak plateau	1312 km	Tributaries : Hiran, Tawa, Banjar, Shar, Shakkar and Burhner. It flows into Gulf of Khambat. It flowes through, Madhya Pradesh, Maharashtra and Gujarat. Famous waterfalls Dhuandhar and Kapildhara are located on this river.
Tapi	Rises near Multai on the Satpura range	724 km	Also known as **Twin** or **handmaid** of **Narmada** Tributaries **Purna, Betul, Arunavati, Ganjal** etc.
Luni	Rises from Aravalis	495 km	Also called **salt river**. It is finally lost in the marshy grounds at the head of the Rann of **Kachchh**.

Difference Between Delta and Estuary

Delta	Estuary
It is the triangular deposition of alluvium at the mouth of river at its fall into the sea.	It is the funnel shaped mouth of river. High tidal actions form an estuary.
Excess deposition of silt and soil forms a delta.	Tidal waves drudge the slit out and an estuary is formed.
It is more fertile land.	It is useful for navigation.

Differences Between Himalayan River System and Peninsular System

Himalayan Rivers	Peninsular Rivers
They have large basins and catchment areas.	They have small basins and catchment areas.
They are the example of antecedent drainage.	They are the example of consequent drainage.
They are perennial in nature, i.e. the water flows throughout the year.	They are seasonal in nature and receive water only from rainfall.
These rivers are still in their youthful stage.	These rivers have already reached their maturity stage.
These rivers form meanders.	Little scope for meander formation.

Important Waterfalls of India

Waterfall	Height (km)	River	State
Kunchikal	455	Varani	Karnataka
Jog/Gersoppa	260	Sharavati	Karnataka
Rakim Kund	168	Gaighat	Bihar
Chachai	127	Bihad	Madhya Pradesh
Keoti	98	Mahanadi	Madhya Pradesh
Sivasamudram	90	Cauveri	Karnataka

Important Indian Towns on Rivers

Town	River
Jamshedpur	Subarnarekha
Delhi	Yamuna
Kanpur	Ganga
Surat	Tapi
Ferozpur	Sutlej
Allahabad	At the confluence of the Ganga and Yamuna
Varanasi	Ganga
Haridwar	Ganga
Badrinath	Alaknanda
Ludhiana	Sutlej
Srinagar	Jhelum
Ayodhya	Saryu

Town	River
Ahmedabad	Sabarmati
Patna	Ganga
Kota	Chambal
Jabalpur	Narmada
Panji	Mandavi
Ujjain	Kshipra
Guwahati	Brahmaputra
Kolkata	Hooghly
Cuttack	Mahanadi
Hyderabad	Musi
Nashik	Godavari
Lucknow	Gomti

Important River Projects and their Beneficiary States

Project	River	Purpose	Beneficiary States
Bhakra Nangal Project	Sutlej	Power and irrigation	Punjab, Himachal Pradesh, Haryana and Rajasthan
Damodar Valley	Damodar	Power, irrigation and flood control	Jharkhand and West Bengal
Hirakud	Mahanadi	Power and irrigation	Odisha
Tungabhadra Project	Tungabhadra	Power and irrigation	Andhra Pradesh and Karnataka
Nagarjunasagar Project	Krishna	Power and irrigation	Andhra Pradesh, Telangana
Gandak River Project	Gandak	Power and irrigation	Bihar, Uttar Pradesh, Nepal (joint venture of India and Nepal)
Kosi Project	Kosi	Flood control, Power and irrigation	Bihar and Nepal
Farakka Project	Ganga, Bhagirathi	Power, irrigation, avoid accumulation of slit to improve navigation	West Bengal
Beas Project	Beas	Irrigation and power	Rajasthan, Haryana, Punjab and Himachal Pradesh
Indira Gandhi Canal Project (*Rajasthan Canal Project*)	Sutlej, Beas and Ravi	Irrigation	Rajasthan, Punjab and Haryana
Chambal Project	Chambal	Power and irrigation	Madhya Pradesh and Rajasthan
Kakrapara Project	Tapi	Irrigation	Gujarat
Ukai Project	Tapi	Power and irrigation	Gujarat
Tawa Project	Tawa (Narmada)	Irrigation	Madhya Pradesh
Poochampad Project	Godavari	Irrigation	Telangana
Malaprabha Project	Malaprabha	Irrigation	Karnataka
Durgapur Barrage	Damodar	Irrigation and navigation	Karnataka, West Bengal and Jharkhand

Project	River	Purpose	Beneficiary States
Mahanadi Delta Project	Mahanadi	Irrigation	Odisha
Iddukki Project	Periyar	Hydroelectricity	Kerala
Ramganga Multipurpose Project	Chuisot stream near Kalagarh	Power and irrigation	Uttarakhand
Matatilla Project	Betwa	Multipurpose power and irrigation	Uttar Pradesh and Madhya Pradesh
Tehri Dam Project	Bhilangana, Bhagirathi	Hydroelectricity	Uttarakhand
Rihand Scheme	Rihand	Hydroelectricity	Uttar Pradesh
Kundah Project	Kundah	Hydroelectricity and irrigation	Tamil Nadu
Mandi Project	Beas	Irrigation	Himachal Pradesh
Shivasamudram Project	Cauveri	Irrigation	Karnataka
Tata Hydel scheme	Bhima	Hydroelectricity	Maharashtra
Mahi Project	Mahi	Irrigation	Gujarat
Thein Project	Ravi	Irrigation	Punjab

THE CLIMATE OF INDIA

- India has tropical monsoon type of climate. It is greatly influenced by the presence of Himalayas in the North as they block the cold masses from Central Asia. It is because of Himalayas that the monsoon shed their water in India.
- The Tropic of Cancer (23.5°N) divide India into two almost equal climatic zones, namely, the Northern zone (sub-tropic) and the Southern zone. (tropic).
- The sub-tropical climate of the Northern zone gives it cold winter seasons and hot summer seasons.
- The Southern tropical climate zone is warmer than the North and does not have a clear cut winter season.

The Southern zone has the midday Sun almost vertically overhead at least twice every year and the Northern zone does not have the midday Sun vertically overhead during any part of the year.

Factors Influencing the Climate of India

The factors influencing the climate of India are as follows:

- **Location and Latitudinal extent** The Tropic of Cancer passes through the middle of the country. The region to the South of Tropic of Cancer experiences tropical climate, whereas the region to the North of the Tropic of Cancer experiences warm temperate climate.
- **Distance from Sea** The areas near to the sea experience maritime climate, whereas the areas away from the sea experience continental climate.
- **The Northern Mountain Range** The Northern Himalayan range protects India from the bitterly cold and dry winds of Central Asia during winter. Moreover, it acts as a physical barrier for the rain bearing South-West monsoon.
- **Physiography** The physiography has great impact on the major elements of climate such as temperature, atmospheric pressure, direction of wind and amount of rainfall.
- **Monsoon Wind** It is the most dominating factor of Indian climate. The South-West summer monsoon from the Arabian sea and the Bay of Bengal bring rainfall to the entire country. Besides the North-East winter monsoon travelling from land to sea causes rainfall along the Coromandel coast after acquiring moisture from the Bay of Bengal.

Western Disturbances

These are the depressions generated over the Mediterranean sea and enter India after crossing over Iraq, Iran, Afghanistan and Pakistan under the influence of Westerly jet stream. After reaching India, they move Eastwards, causing light rain in the Indo-Gangetic plains and snowfall in Himalayan belt.

- **Upper Air Circulation** The upper air circulation of India is dominated by a westerly flow. An important component of this flow is the Jet stream. The Western cyclonic disturbances experienced in North and North Western parts of the country are brought in by this Westerly flow.

- **Tropical Cyclones** The tropical cyclones generated in Arabian sea and Bay of Bengal during the South-West monsoon and the retreating monsoon seasons influence the weather conditions of the Peninsular India.

- **El Nino and La Nina** El Nino is a narrow warm current, which occasionally appears off the coast of Peru in December by temporarily replacing the cold Peru current.

- The warming of tropical Pacific waters affect the global pattern of pressure and wind systems including the monsoon winds in the Indian ocean. La Nina is the reverse of El-Nino. It is a harbinger of heavy monsoon showers in India.

- **Southern Oscillation** Whenever the surface level pressure is high over the Indian ocean, there is low pressure over the Pacific ocean and *vice versa*. This inter-relation of high and low pressure over the Pacific and the Indian ocean is called **Southern Oscillation**.

Seasons in India

- Indian climate is characterised by distinct seasonality. Indian Meteorological Department (IMD) has recognised *the following four distinct seasons:*

  (i) The cold seasons or winter season.

  (ii) The hot weather season or summer season.

  (iii) The South-West monsoon season or rainy season.

  (iv) The season of the retreating monsoon or cool season.

Seasons and their Climatic Features

Season	Temporal Aspect	Precipitation	Other Climatic Features
Winter Season	November to March	Cause rainfall in sub-Himalayan belt by Western disturbances	Clear sky, low temperature and humidity high range of temperature
Summer Season (Pre-monsoon)	March to June	Only 1% rainfall of total Indian rainfall mostly by storms by convective current	Dry season, high temperature and low humidity
Rainy Season	June to September	Rainfall through South-West monsoon	High heat, high humidity, extensive cloud and several spells of moderate to heavy rainfall are the characteristics
Cool Season	Mid September to November	Retreating monsoon causes rainfall in Tamil Nadu and adjoining areas of Andhra Pradesh and Kerala	No cloud, severe and devastating tropical cyclone, clear sky

Local Storms in India

Name	Significance
Norwester Kalbaisakhi	It is a spring storm showers and causes rainfall in Assam and West Bengal.
Mango Shower	Thunderstorm causing rainfall in Southern plateau helps in mango ripening.
Cherry Blossoms	Thunderstorm causing rainfall in Karnataka helps in flowering of coffee.
Kalbaisakhis	Storms in West Bengal during summer due to the strong convective movement.

Climatic Regions of India

Trewartha's Classification

- Dr Trewartha's scheme has been most satifactory of all classifications of the Indian climatic regions. He presented a modified form of Koppen's classification.
- Dr Trewartha's classification divides India into four major regions of the A, B, C and H types. The A type refers to tropical rainy climate, where high temperatures are consistent. The B type stands for a dry climate with high temperatures, but little rainfall. The C type indicates a region with dry winters, where low temperatures range between 0°C and 18°C. The H type indicates a mountain climate. The A, B, and C types are further sub-divided.

Climatic Regions of India

Climate Type	Areas	Characteristics
▪ Tropical Rain Forests Climate (Am)	Western Ghats, West Coastal Plains, Parts of Assam and Tripura.	High temperature throughout the year, heavy seasonal rainfall, annual rainfall 200 cm (May to November).
▪ Tropical Savanna Climate (Aw)	Most of Peninsular region (except leeward side of Western Ghats).	Dry winters, annual rainfall varies from 76 cm to 150 cm.
▪ Tropical Semi-Arid Steppe Climate (Bs)	Rainshadow belt running Southward from Central Maharashtra to Tamil Nadu	Low rainfall varies from 38 cm to 80 cm and temperature from 20° to 30°C.
▪ Tropical and Sub-tropical Steppes Climate (Bsh)	Punjab, Haryana, and Kachchh region.	Temperature varies from 12°-35°C
▪ Tropical Desert Climate (Bwh)	Western parts of Barmer, Jaisalmer and Bikaner districts of Rajasthan and parts of Kachchh.	Scanty rainfall (mostly in form of cloud burst), high temperature
▪ Humid Sub- tropical Climate with dry Winters (Caw)	South of Himalayas.	Mild winters and extremely hot summers
▪ Mountain Climate (H)	Mountainous region (above 6000 m or more).	Rainfall varies from 63.5 cm to 254 cm. (Mostly during South-West Monsoon).

Annual Rainfall

India can be divided into the following regions depending upon the annual average rainfall received by these regions

Distribution of Rainfall

Areas of Very High Rainfall (above 200 cm)	Areas of High Rainfall (100-200 cm)	Areas of Low Rainfall (50-100 cm)	Areas of Very Low Rainfall (below 50 cm)
It includes almost whole of Assam, Nagaland, Meghalaya, Mizoram, Arunachal Pradesh, Sikkim, parts of Manipur, West Bengal and the Western Coast from Thiruvananthapuram to Mumbai.	It includes Eastern slopes of Western Ghats, major parts of Northern Plain, Odisha, Madhya Pradesh, Andhra Pradesh and Tamil Nadu.	It includes large parts of Gujarat, Maharashtra, Western Madhya Pradesh, Andhra Pradesh and Eastern Rajasthan etc.	It Include arid and semi-arid area and include large areas of Western Rajasthan, Kachchh and most of the region of Ladakh (Jammu and Kashmir).

FOREST AND NATURAL VEGETATION

According to state records, the forest area covers 23.28% of the total land area of the country.

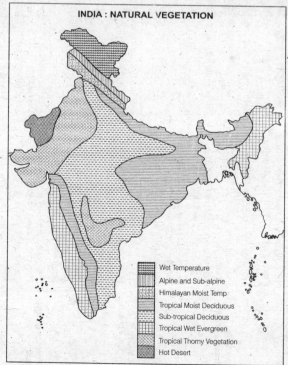

INDIA : NATURAL VEGETATION

Wet Temperature
Alpine and Sub-alpine
Himalayan Moist Temp
Tropical Moist Deciduous
Sub-tropical Deciduous
Tropical Wet Evergreen
Tropical Thorny Vegetation
Hot Desert

Forest in India

Forest Type	Distribution	Climatic Conditions	Characteristics	Species
Tropical Evergreen Forests	▪ Rainy slopes of Western Ghats. ▪ NE India except Arunachal Pradesh. ▪ Eastern part of West Bengal and Odisha. ▪ Andaman and Nicobar Islands.	▪ Rainfall > 200 cm. ▪ Relative Humidity > 70% ▪ Average temperature is about 24°C. ▪ Hot and Humid climate.	▪ Height of trees is 40 to 60 m. ▪ Leaves are dark green and broad.	Mahogany, Mahua, Bamboo, Cones, Ironwood, Kadam, Irul, Jamun, Hopea, Rubber tree, Toon, Telsur etc.
Tropical Moist Deciduous Forests	▪ Eastern parts of Sahyadris (Western Ghats). ▪ North-Eastern part of Peninsula. ▪ Middle and lower Ganga valley. ▪ Foothills of Himalayas in Bhabar and Tarai regions. ▪ These cover about 20% India's forest area.	▪ 100 to 200 cm rainfall per annum. ▪ Moderate temperature.	▪ 30 to 40 m high trees. ▪ Due to deficiency of water, they shed their leaves in dry season (onset of summer).	Sal, Teak, Arjun, Mulberry, Kusum, Sandalwood, Siris, Haldi, Khair, Mango, Banyan tree etc.
Tropical Dry Deciduous Forests	▪ Large parts of Maharashtra, Telangana and Andhra Pradesh. ▪ Parts of Punjab, Haryana and Eastern parts of Rajasthan. ▪ Northern and Western parts of Madhya Pradesh. ▪ Tamil Nadu. ▪ Southern parts of Uttar Pradesh.	▪ 50 to 100 cm rainfall. ▪ Moderate humidity.	▪ 6 to 15 m high. ▪ Roots are thick and long.	Teak, Sal, Bamboo, Mango, Acacia, Neem, Shisham etc.
Dry Forests or Arid Forests	▪ Rajasthan and adjoining areas of Haryana, Gujarat and Punjab. ▪ Rainshadow areas of Peninsular India.	▪ Low rainfall (less than 50 cm per annum). ▪ Relative humidity is less.	▪ Thorny vegetation. ▪ Roots are very long. ▪ Leaves are small.	Cactus, Thorny Bushes, Kikar, Babool, Date Palm, Acacia, Khair, Euphorbias etc.
Mountainous Forests or Himalayan Forest	▪ In Himalayan region	▪ Due to increase of altitude the temperature decreases hence Himalayan forests contain all the varieties of world except equatorial forest.	▪ Each vegetation belt occurs at relatively 300 m more height in Eastern Himalayas.	Sal, Teak, Chir, Deodar, Oak, Olive, Chestnut, Conifers, Spruce and Lirch etc..

Soils in India

Indian Council of Agricultural Research (ICAR) has divided Indian soils into eight major groups.

Type of Soils	States where Found/Occurrence	Compositions	Crops Grow
▪ Alluvial	Punjab, Haryana, Uttar Pradesh Bihar, Jharkhand	Rich in potash and lime, but deficient in nitrogen and phosphoric acid.	Large variety of Rabi and Kharif crops such as wheat, rice, sugarcane, cotton and jute.
▪ Black (or Regur soil)	Deccan Plateau, Valleys of Krishna and Godavari, Andhra Pradesh, Madhya Pradesh and Tamil Nadu	Rich in iron, lime, aluminium, magnesium, calcium, but lacks in nitrogen, phosphorus and humus.	Cotton, sugarcane, jowar, tobacco, wheat, rice.
▪ Red	Eastern parts of Deccan Plateau, Tamil Nadu, Goa, Odisha and Meghalaya	Rich in iron and potash, but deficient in lime, nitrogen phosphorus and humus.	Wheat, rice, cotton, sugarcane and pulses.
▪ Laterite	Summits of Eastern and Western Ghats, Assam hills, Andhra Pradesh, Karnataka, West Bengal and Odisha	Rich in iron but poor in silica, lime, phosphorus, potash and humus.	Tea, coffee, rubber, cashew and millets.
▪ Desert	West and North-West India, Rajasthan, North Gujarat and Southern Punjab.	Rich in soluble salts, but deficient in organic matter.	Generally, unsuitable for cultivation, but with irrigation useful for cultivation of drought-resistant lime, millets, barley, cotton, maize and pulses.
▪ Mountain	Hills of Jammu and Kashmir Uttarakhand and Assam Hills	Rich in iron and humus, but deficient in lime.	with fertilizers, tea, fruits and medicinal plants can be grown.
▪ Saline and Alkaline	Drier parts of Bihar, Jharkhand, Uttar Pradesh, Haryana, Punjab, Rajasthan and Maharashtra	Many salts such as sodium, magnesium and calcium.	Unfit for agriculture.
▪ Peaty and Marshy	Kerala, coastal regions of Odisha, Tamil Nadu and Sundarbans of West Bengal	Contain large amount of soluble salts and organic matter, but lack in potash and phosphates.	Useful for rice and jute cultivation.

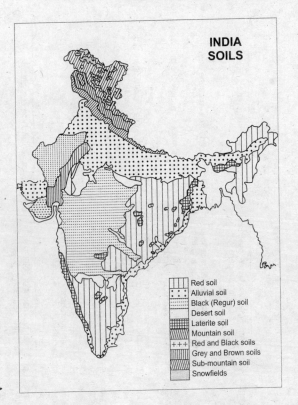

INDIA SOILS

▥	Red soil
⠐	Alluvial soil
⋯	Black (Regur) soil
	Desert soil
▦	Laterite soil
▨	Mountain soil
+++	Red and Black soils
▥	Grey and Brown soils
▧	Sub-mountain soil
	Snowfields

AGRICULTURE IN INDIA

India is essentially an agricultural land. Two-thirds of its population still lives on agriculture. Agriculture is a primary activity which includes farming, animal rearing and fishing. *There are three crop seasons in India*

(i) **Kharif** Sown in June/July, harvested in September/October. e.g. rice, jowar, bajra, ragi, maize, cotton and jute.

(ii) **Rabi** Sown in October/December, harvested in April/May e.g. wheat, barley, peas, rapeseed, mustard, grains.

(iii) **Zaid** They are raised between April/June e.g. melon, watermelon, cuccumber, toris, leafy and other vegetables.

Types of Farming

Shifting Agriculture

- It is practised by the tribal groups in the forest areas of Assam, Meghalaya, Nagaland, Manipur, Tripura, Mizoram, Arunachal Pradesh, Odisha, Madhya Pradesh, Jharkhand and Andhra Pradesh.

Various Names of Shifting Agriculture

States	Names of Shifting Cultivation
Assam	Jhum
Kerala	Ponam
Andhra Pradesh and Odisha	Podu
Madhya Pradesh	Beewar, Mashan, Penda and Beera

- In this type of agriculture, a piece of forest land is cleared mainly by tribal people by felling and burning of trees and crops are grown.
- Dry paddy, buck wheat, maize, small millets, tobacco and sugarcane are the main crops grown under this type of agriculture.

Intensive Farming

- This is a system of farming, in which the cultivator uses large amount of labour and capital on a relatively small area.
- In regions, where the size of population is big, but land is less, this type of farming is done.
- Agriculture is done with the help of manual labour.

Extensive Farming

- This is a system of farming, in which the cultivator uses a limited amount of labour and capital on a relatively large area.
- This type of agriculture is practised in regions, where population size is small and land is enough.
- Agricultural is done with the help of machines.

Green Revolution

It is the phrase generally used to describe the spectacular increase that took place during 1968 and is continuing in the production of foodgrains in India.

The components of Green Revolution are as follows:

- High Yield Variety Seeds
- Irrigation
- Use of Fertilizers
- Use of Insecticide and Pesticide
- Command Area Development
- Consolidation of Holdings
- Land Reforms
- Supply of Agricultural Credit
- Rural Electrification
- Rural Roads and Marketing
- Farm Mechanisation
- Agricultural Universities

Impact of Green Revolution

Positive Impact

- Increase in agricultural production
- Reduction of the import of foodgrains
- Capitalistic farming
- Industrial growth
- Rural employment

Negative Impact

- Inter-crop imbalance
- Environmental impacts
- Increase in regional imbalance
- Unemployment due to mechanisation
- Negligence of other crops

Major Crops and Producing States

Crop Type	Crop Name	Major Producers
Cereals	Wheat	Uttar Pradesh, Punjab and Madhya Pradesh
	Rice	West Bengal and Uttar Pradesh
	Gram	Madhya Pradesh and Tamil Nadu
	Barley	Maharashtra, Uttar Pradesh and Rajasthan
	Bajra	Maharashtra, Gujarat and Rajasthan
Cash Crops	Sugarcane	Uttar Pradesh and Maharashtra
	Poppy	Uttar Pradesh and Himachal Pradesh
Oil Seeds	Coconut	Kerala and Tamil Nadu
	Linseed	Rajasthan Madhya Pradesh and Haryana
	Groundnut	Gujarat, Andhra Pradesh and Tamil Nadu
	Rape seed and Mustard	Rajasthan, Madhya Pradesh and Haryana
	Sesame	Uttar Pradesh and Rajasthan
	Sunflower	Andhra Pradesh and Maharashtra Karnataka

Crop Type	Crop Name	Major Producers
Fibre Crops	Cotton	Maharashtra and Gujarat
	Jute	West Bengal and Bihar
	Silk	Karnataka and Kerala
	Hemp.	Madhya Pradesh and Uttar Pradesh
Plantations	Coffee	Karnataka and Kerala
	Rubber	Kerala and Karnataka
	Tea	Assam and Kerala
	Tobacco	Gujarat, Maharashtra and Madhya Pradesh
Spices	Pepper	Kerala, Karnataka and Tamil Nadu
	Cashewnuts	Kerala, Tamil Nadu and Andhra Pradesh
	Ginger	Kerala and Uttar Pradesh
	Turmeric	Andhra Pradesh and Odisha

Growing Conditions of Some Important Crops

Crop	Temperature	Rainfall	Soil
Rice	Not above 25°C	150-300 cm	Clay or Loamy, Alluvial
Wheat	10°–15°C (Winter), 21°–26°C (Summer)	80 cm	Well-drained loams and clay loam
Cotton	21°–30°C, but not below 20°C, 200 frost free days	50-75 cm	Black soil (Regur) alluvial or laterite soils
Sugarcane	32°–38°C	100-150 cm	Any type of soil that can retain moisture
Jowar	Not below 16°C	<100 cm	Variety of soils including clayey and sandy
Jute	24°–35°C	Rainfall of 150 cm, with 90% humidity	Light sandy or clayey loams
Tea	13°–32°C	125-375 cm, grown on hill slopes	Well drained, deep friable loams or forest soils rich in organic matter
Coffee	23°–28°C	150-200 cm	Rich well-drained friable loams containing good amount of vegetable mould
Bajra	25°–30°C	40-50 cm	Sandy loams, red and black soils
Ragi	20°–30°C	50-100 cm	Red, sandy loams and light black
Pulses	20°–35°C	50-75 cm	Dry, light soil
Rubber	25°–35°C	150-200 cm	Rich well-drained soils
Tabacco	15°C – 35°C	50-100 cm	Well-drained loamy soil, alluvial or black soils

MINERAL RESOURCES

Three types of minerals are as follows:

   (i) **Metallic**   Iron-ore, copper, aluminium, tin, lead, gold and silver.
  (ii) **Non-Metallic** Coal, mica, manganese, petroleum and sulphur.
 (iii) **Radioactive**   Uranium and thorium.

Metallic Mineral Mines

Metallic Mineral	Mines
Iron	Kemmangundi, Sandur and Hospet(Karnataka) Barbil-Koira (Odisha), Bailadila and Dalli-Rajhara (Chhattisgarh), North Goa
Manganese	Found in Karnataka, Odisha, Madhya Pradesh, Maharashtra
Chromite	Found in Odisha, Bihar, Karnataka, Maharashtra and Andhra Pradesh
Copper	Malanjkhand Belt (Balaghat ,Madhya Pradesh), Khetri-Singhana Belt (Jhunjhun), Singhbhum (Jharkhand)
Bauxite	Found in Odisha, Gujarat , Jharkhand, Maharashtra, Chhattisgarh
Gold	Kolar and Hutti (Karnataka), Ramgiri in Anantapur (Andhra Pradesh)

Non-Metallic Mineral Mines

Non-Metallic Mineral	Mines
Limestone	Found in Andhra Pradesh, Rajasthan, Madhya Pradesh, Gujarat, Chhattisgarh
Dolomite	About 90% of the dolomite is found in Madhya Pradesh, Chhattisgarh, Odisha, Gujarat, Karnataka , West Bengal
Asbestos	Rajasthan , Andhra Pradesh and Karnataka
Gypsum	Found in Rajasthan and Jammu and Kashmir
Graphite	Occurs in Kalahandi, Bolangir (Odisha) and Bhagalpur (Bihar)

Atomic Mineral Mines

Atomic Mineral	Mines
Uranium	Jadugoda (Jharkhand) , Gaya (Bihar), Saharanpur (Uttar Pradesh), Monazite sands of Kerala coast. Found as by-product in copper mines of Udaipur
Thorium	Derived from Monazite sand. Found in Kerala, Jharkhand , Bihar, Tamil Nadu and Rajasthan
Lithium	Found in Lepidolite and Spodumene. Lepidolite is found in Jharkhand, Madhya Pradesh and Rajasthan, Baster region
Zirconium	Found along Kerala coast and alluvial rocks of Ranchi and Hazaribagh
Beryllium	Occurs in Nellore district, Andhra Pradesh, Sikkim, Jammu and Kashmir
Antimony	Occurs is Lahaul and Kangra district of Himachal Pradesh and district of Madhya Pradesh

Industries in India

Industries	Details

Cotton Textile Industry

- The first modern Cotton textile mill was established in Bombay in 1854 by local Parsi entrepreneurs with the name of Bombay spinning and weaving comapny.
- Mumbai is called Cottonopolis of India.
- Ahmedabad is called Manchester of India.
- Coimbatore is called Manchester of South India.
- Kanpur is called Manchester of Uttar Pradesh.
- **Distribution** Maharashtra (Mumbai, Solapur, Pune, Kolhapur, Satara, Wardha, Aurangabad and Amravati), Gujarat (Ahmedabad, Vadodra, Rajkot, Surat, Bhavnagar, Porbandar, Maurvi and Viramgam), Tamil Nadu (Chennai, Tirunelveli, Madurai, Tuticorin, Salem, Virudhnagar and Pollachi), Karnataka (Bengaluru, Belgaum, Mangalore, Chitradurga, Gulbaraga and Mysore), Uttar Pradesh (Kanpur, Etawah, Modinagar, Moradabad, Bareilly, Agra, Meerut and Varanasi), Madhya Pradesh (Indore, Gwalior, Ujjain, Bhopal), Rajasthan (Kota, Jaipur, Sriganganagar, Bhilwara and Udaipur).

Woollen Textile Industry

- The first Woollen textiles mill was set-up in 1876 at Kanpur. Jammu and Kashmir is a large producer of handloom woollen products.
- **Distribution** Punjab (Dhariwal, Amritsar, Ludhiana, Ferozpur), Maharashtra (Mumbai), Uttar Pradesh (Kanpur, Mirzapur, Agra, Tanakpur).

Jute Textile Industry

- First modern Jute mill was set-up in 1855 at Rishra near Kolkata. India is the largest producer of raw jute and jute good production, whereas it is second largest exporter of jute goods after Bangladesh.
- **Distribution** West Bengal, Bihar, Uttar Pradesh, Andhra Pradesh, Assam, Odisha, Tripura and Chhattisgarh.

Silk Textile Industry

- India is the second largest prouducer of natural silk, after China and is the only country producing all four varieties or natural silk viz Mulberry, Tasar, Eri and Muga of which Golden yellow Muga silk is unique in India.
- **Distribution** Karnataka is the leading producer followed by West Bengal, Bihar etc.

Rubber Industry

- The first factory of synthetic rubber was set-up at Bareilly.
- **Distribution** Bareilly (Uttar Pradesh), Baroda (Gujarat) Synthetic Rubber Units-Mumbai, Ahmedabad, Amritsar-Reclained Rubber Units.

Tea Industry

- Tea cultivation in India was first started in the mid-19th century in Darjeeling, Assam and Nilgiris.
- Nearly 98% of the tea production comes from Assam, West Bengal, Tamil Nadu and Kerala, while the rest of it comes from Karnataka, Terai regions of Uttarakhand, Himachal Pradesh, Arunachal Pradesh, Manipur and Tripura.

Sugar Industry

- Uttar Pradesh is the leading producer of sugar.
  Distribution Uttar Pradesh (Gorakhpur, Deoria, Basti, Gonda, Meerut, Saharanpur, Muzaffarnagar, Bijnor and Moradabad), Bihar (Darbhanga, Saran, Champaran and Muzaffarpur), Punjab (Phagwara and Dhuri) Haryana (Ambala, Rohtak and Panipat), Maharashtra (Nashik, Pune, Satara, Sangli, Kolhapur and Sholapur) and Karnataka (Munirabad, Shimoga and Mandya).

Industries	Details
Paper Industry	■ The first Paper mill in the country was set-up at Serampore (Bengal) in 1832, which failed. In 1870, a fresh venture was started at Ballygunj near Calcutta. ■ Raw material : Bamboo (70%), Salai wood (12%), Sabai (9%), Bagasses (4%) and Waste paper and Rags (5%). ■ **Distribution** Madhya Pradesh (Nepanagar), Hindustan Paper Corporation, Vellore, Mysore Paper mill, Bhadravati, Maharashtra, (Mumbai, Pune, Ballarpur and Kamptee produce Paper and Vikhroli), Andhra Pradesh (Rajahmundry and Sirpur), Madhya Pradesh (Indore, Bhopal and Shahdol), Karnataka.
Iron and Steel	■ **Distribution** Bhadrawati (Karnataka), Jamshedpur (Jharkhand), Durgapur, Burnpur (West Bengal), Bokaro (Jharkhand), Rourkela (Odisha), Bhilai (Chhattisgarh), Salem (Tamil Nadu) and Visakhapatnam (Andhra Pradesh).
Ship	■ **Distribution** Cochin Shipyard , Mumbai (Mazgaon Dock), Hindustan Shipyard at Visakhapatnam and Kolkata (Garden Reach workshop). Mazgaon dock at Mumbai builts Vessels for Indian Navy.
Aircraft Industry	■ **Distribution** Hindustan Aeronautics India Limited was formed by merging two aricraft factories at Bengaluru and Kanpur. Four other factories are at Nashik, Lucknow, Koraput (Odisha) and Hyderabad.
Fertilizer Industry	■ The Fertilizer Corporation of India (FCI) was set-up in 1961. ■ National Fertilizer Limited (NFL) was set-up in 1974. ■ **Distribution** Sindri (Bihar), Nangal, Gorakhpur (Uttar Pradesh), Durgapur, Namrup, Cochin, Rourkela, Neyveli, Varanasi, Vadodra, Kanpur, Visakhapatnam and Kota.
Heavy Machinery	■ **Distribution** Durgapur, Mumbai, Ranchi, Visakhapatnam, Tiruchirapalli and Naini.
Machine Tool Industry	■ It forms the basis for the manufacturing of industrial, defence equipments, automobiles, railway engines and electrical machinery. ■ **Distribution** Hyderabad, Bengaluru, Pinjore (Haryana), Kalamassery (Kerala), Secunderabad, Ajmer and Srinagar.
Heavy Electrical Equipments	■ **Distribution** Bengaluru, Bhopal, Jammu, Tiruchirapalli, Ramchandrapuram (Hyderabad) and Jagdishpur (Uttar Pradesh).
Photo Films Industry	■ The Hindustan Photo Films Manufacturing Company at Udagamandalam (Tamil Nadu) is the only factory in the public sector, producing photo paper and films.
Glass Industry	■ **Distribution** Uttar Pradesh (Firozabad, Balijoi, Hathras, Naini, Secunderabad, Maharashtra (Mumbai, Telogaon, Pune Sitarampur), Tamil Nadu (Tiruvottiyur) and Karnataka (Belgaum, Bengaluru).

ENERGY

- India is a fast growing country and therefore the demand for energy is also continuously growing. India is exploiting almost all the sources of energy such as hydroelectricity, thermal energy, nuclear energy, solar energy and wind energy etc.
- Power development commenced in India with the commissioning of electricity supply in Darjeeling during 1897, followed by a hydropower station at Sivasamudram in Karnataka during 1902.
- Himachal Pradesh, Meghalaya, Nagaland, Sikkim and Uttarakhand are largely dependent upon hydroelectricity.
- National Hydro Power Corporation (NHPC) was set-up in 1975, under public sector for the generation of hydropower in India.
- National Thermal Power Corporation (NTPC) was set-up in 1975, for generation of thermal energy. NTPC has 18 coal based super thermal power projects and 7 gas/liquid based combined cycle projects.
- Atomic Energy Institute at Trombay was set-up in 1954 and renamed as Bhabha Atomic Research Centre (BARC) in 1967.
- Heavy Water Plants are at Vadodra, Tuticorin, Kota, Thal, Hazira and Manuguru. The first heavy water plant was set-up in Nangal in 1962.
- The Renewable Energy Programme started with the establishment of the Department of Non-Conventional Energy Sources in 1982. Indian Renewable Energy Development Agency was set-up in 1987. In 1992, DNES was converted into Ministry of Non-conventional Energy Sources.

Renewable Energy Plants

Types of Energy	Plants	States
Wind Energy	Muppandal	Tamil Nadu
	Perungudi	Tamil Nadu
	Kayattar	Tamil Nadu
	Satara	Maharashtra
	Jogimati	Karnataka
	Lamba, Mandvi	Gujarat
Geothermal Energy	Manikaran	Himachal Pradesh
	Puga Valley	Jammu and Kashmir
	Tattapani	Chhattisgarh
Tidal Energy	Gulf of Khambat	Gujarat
	Gulf of Kachchh	Gujarat
	Sundarban	West Bengal
Wave Energy	Vizhinjam	Kerala
Solar Energy	Tirupati	Andhra Pradesh

The Major Atomic Power Stations

Power Station	Location
Tarapur	Maharashtra
Rawatbhata	Rajasthan
Kalpakkam	Tamil Nadu
Narora	Uttar Pradesh
Kakrapara	Gujarat
Kaiga	Karnataka
Kudankulam	Tamil Nadu
Banswara	Rajasthan

Ultra Mega Power Plants (UMPP)

Plants	States	Capacity (MW)	Awarded to
Sasan	Madhya Pradesh	4000	Reliance
Mundra	Gujarat	4000	Tata
Krishna-patnam	Andhra Pradesh	4000	Reliance
Girye	Maharashtra	4000	NA
Tadri	Karnataka	4000	NA

Major Thermal Plants

States	Names of the Plant	States	Names of the Plant
Haryana	Faridabad, Panipat	Andhra Pradesh Telangana	Nellore, Vijayawada Ramagundam, Kothagudam
Punjab	Bhatinda, Ropar		
Delhi	Badarpur, Indraprastha		
Rajasthan	Kota	Tamil Nadu	Ennore, Tuticorin, Neyveli
Uttar Pradesh	Obra, Panki,Singrauli	Bihar	Barauni
Gujarat	Ukai, Sikka, Ahmedabad, Sabarmati	Jharkhand	Bokaro
		Odisha	Talcher, Rourkela
Madhya Pradesh	Satpura, Amarkantak, Pench	West Bengal	Kolkata, Titagarh, Durgapur
		Assam	Kamrup, Bongaigaon
Chhattisgarh	Korba, Bhilai	Jammu and Kashmir	Pampore
Maharashtra	Nashik, Uran , Chandrapur, Trombay, Dabhol		
		Tripura	Rokhia

Transport

RAILWAYS

- India has the second largest railway network in Asia and the fourth largest in the World after the USA, Russia and China. The Indian railway operate in three different gauges

Gauge	Routes (km)
Broad Gauges (l. 676 m)	46807
Meter Gauges (l. 000 m)	13290
Narrow Gauges (0.761 and 0.610 m)	3124

- It is the largest public sector undertaking of the country and it is the world's second largest railway network under single management.
- The first Indian railway line in India was operated for public traffic in 1853 between Bombay and Thane over a distance of 34 km.
- The second train ran between Howrah and Hooghly in 1854.
- The first electric train in India was 'Deccan Queen', it was introduced in 1929 between Bombay and Poona.
- The headquarters of Indian railway is in New Delhi.
- The fastest train in India is Gatiman Express whose maximum speed is 160 km/hr. it runs between Hazrat Nizamuddin to Agra Cantt.

Railway Zones

Zone	Headquarter
Central Railway	Mumbai
Eastern Railway	Kolkata
Northern Railway	New Delhi
North-Eastern Railway	Gorakhpur
North-East Frontier Railway	Malegaon
Southern Railway	Chennai
South Central Railway	Secundrabad
South-Eastern Railway	Kolkata
Western Railway	Mumbai (Church Gate)
East Central Railway	Hajipur
East Coast Railway	Bhubaneshwar
North Central Railway	Allahabad
North-Western Railway	Jaipur
South-East Central Railway	Bilaspur
South-West Railway	Hubli
West Central Railway	Jabalpur
Kolkata Metro	Kolkata

- Indian railways has the second biggest electrified system in the world after Russia.
- The total route covered is approximately 63000 km.
- The second longest train route is of 'Himsagar Express' from Jammu Tawi to Kanyakumari. It covers a distance of 3726 km and passes through ten states.
- The first metro rail was introduced in Calcutta on 24th October, 1984. The two stations connected were Dumdum and Belgachhla.

- The oldest steam engine 'Fairy Queen' still runs on rail.
- Uttar Pradesh has largest railway network in India.
- Mumbai CST is busiest railway junction of India.
- Railway track electrification was introduced in early 1920s. The first two sections from Victoria Terminus to Kurla and from Victoria Terminus to Bandra were electrified. About 26% of the rail lines have been electrified.

Indian Railways Recognised by UNESCO

Railways	Specialities
Darjeeling Himalayan Railways (1999)	Narrow gauge railway from Siliguri to Darjeeling in the State of West Bengal.
Chhatrapati Shivaji Terminus (2004)	It was opened in 1887, in the time to celebrate Queen Victoria's Golden Jubilee.
Nilgiri Mountain Railways (2005)	It connects the town of Mettupalayam with the hill station of Udagamandalam in the Nilgiri hills.
Kalka-Shimla Railways (2008)	Narrow Gauge railway in North-West India travelling along a most mountainous route from Kalka to Shimla.

The year in Bracket represents the year in which UNESCO has added the railway line to the World Heritage Site list.

Committees Constituted for Rail Security

Committees	Years
Shahnawaz Committee	1954
Kunzrou Committee	1962
Wahchoo Committee	1968
Sikri Committee	1978
Khanna Committee	1998

Vivek Express

- It has the longest train route in India connecting Dibrugarh and Kanyakumari.
- It is 8th longest in the world.
- It was started to commemorate the 150th birth anniversary of Swami Vivekananda.
- It is a weekly train with a total distance of 4227 km.
- Previously Himsagar Express was the longest express.

Konkan Railways

- It runs from Mangalore to Roha (40 km South of Mumbai).
- The network involves 3 states such as Maharashtra, Goa and Karnataka.
- It has the fastest track in India and has a total length of 738 km.
- Almost 10% of the line passes through tunnels.

Railway Manufacturing Units

- Chittaranjan Locomotive Works (CLW), Chittaranjan : steam locomotives and electric locomotives.
- Diesel Locomotive Works (DLW), Varanasi : Diesel locomotives.
- Wheel Axle Plant (WAP), Bengaluru: Wheel Axle plant
- Diesel Component Works (DCW), Patiala : Diesel components and parts.
- Rail Coach Factory (RCF), Kapurthala, Punjab : rail coaches.
- Integral Coach Factory (ICF), Chennai : Coaching stock.
- Bharat Earth Movers Ltd. Bengaluru : Rail coaches for Delhi Metro Rail Corporation.
- Durgapur and Yelahanka : Wheel Axle plant.
- Tatanagar; Metre gauge steam locomotives.
- Bhilai : Rail and Sleeper cars.
- Perambur : Rail coaches.

Diamond Quadrilateral Project

The new government at centre has promised to build the Diamond Quadrilateral Project which would connect *via* high-speed rail the cities of Chennai, Mumbai, Kolkata and Delhi.

Bullet Train in India

Railway Ministry in his white paper 'Vision 2020' envisages the implementation of regional high speed rail projects to provide services at 250-350 km/h. Six corridors have been identified for technical studies

- Delhi-Chandigarh-Amritsar
- Pune-Mumbai-Ahmedabad
- Hyderabad-Vijayawada-Chennai
- Howrah-Haldia
- Chennai-Bengaluru-Thiruvananthapuram
- Delhi-Agra-Lucknow-Varanasi-Patna

Metro Rail

City	Start	Length (km)	In operational (leu)
Calcutta	1984	28.4	
Delhi	2002	213	20.4
Bengaluru (Namma)	2011	114	16.6
Gurgaon	2013	5.1	
Jaipur	2015	35.1	
Chennai	2015	45.1	
Hyderabad	2015	71.6	
Navi Mumbai	2016	106.4	
Kochi	2016	25.6	
Lucknow	2016	35	

Mono Rail

The Mumbai Mono Rail which started its services in 2014 is the first operational Mono Rail in India. Apart from Mumbai, Chennai and Bengaluru are also has plan for mono rail.

ROADWAYS

In 1943, Nagpur Plan classified the roads into four categories:
  (i) National Highways
 (ii) State Highways
(iii) District Roads
 (iv) Village Roads

* Indian road network is the third largest in the world.
* India has a road network of over 4.42 million km.
* National highways are constructed and maintained by Central Public Works Department (CPWD).

The five Express Highways of India are as follow:
  (i) Western Express Way
 (ii) Eastern Express Way
(iii) Highway between Kolkata and Dum Dum Airport
 (iv) Highway between Sukinda mines and Paradip Port
  (v) Express Highway between Durgapur and Kolkata

National Highways

NH1	New Delhi-Ambala-Jalandhar-Amritsar-Indo-Pak Border
NH2	Delhi-Mathura-Agra-Kanpur Allahabad-Varanasi-Kolkata
NH3	Agra-Gwalior-Nashik -Mumbai
NH4	Thane -Chennai (via Pune -Belgam)
NH5	Kolkata-Chennai
NH6	Kolkata -Dhule
NH7	Varanasi -Kanyakumari
NH8	Delhi-Mumbai (*via* Jaipur-Baroda-Ahmedabad)
NH9	Pune- Machilipatnam
NH10	Delhi- Fazilka
NH11	Jaipur - Bikaner
NH12	Jabalpur-Jaipur
NH24	Delhi-Lucknow
NH27	Allahabad-Mangawan
NH28	Barauni-Lucknow
NH29	Varanasi-Pharenda and terminating of Sunali
NH47A	Kundanoor-Willington Island in Kochi

Some of the important information regarding the National Highways:
* NH44 is the longest National Highway in India.
* NH5 and NH17 run along the Eastern and the Western coast respectively.
* NH15 represents the border road in Rajasthan desert.
* NH47A is the shortest highway in the India highway network.

National Highway Development Programme (NHDP)

National Highway Development Programme consists of following projects:
* The Golden Quadrilateral connects:
* Delhi to Kolkata 1453 km (NH2)
* Delhi to Mumbai 1419 km (NH8, NH76 and NH79)
* Mumbai to Chennai 1290 km (NH4, NH7 and NH46)
* Chennai to Kolkata 1684 km (NH5, NH6 and NH60)

Total length **5846 km**, out of which maximum length is in Andhra Pradesh (1016 km) followed by Uttar Pradesh (753 km).

2. North-South and East-West Corridors
   (i) NS corridor connects Srinagar to Kanyakumari.
   (ii) EW corridor connects Porbandar (Gujarat) to Silchar (Assam).
3. To upgrade 12109 km of National Highway with 4 lanes on BOT basis. It will cover NHs after that phase 1 and 2.
   (i) NS and EW corridors cross each other at Jhansi (Uttar Pradesh).
   (ii) Total length of this project is 7300 km.
   (iii) Maximum length of corridors is in Tamil Nadu (856 km) followed by Uttar Pradesh (851 km).

AIRWAYS

- JRD Tata was the first person to take a solo flight from Mumbai to Karachi in 1931.
- In 1935, the 'Tata Air Lines' started its operation between Mumbai and Thiruvananthapuram and in 1937 between Mumbai and Delhi.
- In 1953, all the private airline companies were nationalised and Indian Airlines and Air India came into existence.
- Vayudoot Limited started in 1981 as a private air carrier and later on it merged with Indian Airlines.
- International Airports Authority of India and National Airports Authority were merged on 1995 to form Airports Authority of India. The Authority manages the Civil Aviation Training College at Allahabad and National Institute of Aviation Management and Research at Delhi.

International Airports in India

	International Airport	City
1.	Rajiv Gandhi International Airport	Hyderabad
2.	Calicut International Airport	Calicut
3.	Chhatrapati Shivaji International Airport	Mumbai
4.	Kempegowda Airport	Bengaluru
5.	Goa (Dabolim) Airport in Dabolim City	Goa
6.	Netaji Subhash Chandra Bose International Airport	Kolkata
7.	Thiruvananthapuram International Airport	Thiruvananthapuram
8.	Lokpriya Gopinath Bordoloi International Airport	Guwahati
9.	Sardar Vallabhbhai Patel International Airport	Ahmedabad
10.	Indira Gandhi International Airport	Delhi
11.	Chennai International Airport	Chennai
12.	Shri Guru Ram Das Jee International Airport	Amritsar
13.	Cochin International Airport	Kochi (Kerala)
14.	Coimbatore International Airport	Coimbatore (Tamil Nadu)
15.	Lal Bahadur Shastri Airport	Varanasi (Uttar Pradesh)
16.	Chaudhary Charan Singh Airport	Lucknow (Uttar Pradesh)
17.	Ambedkar Airport	Nagpur (Maharashtra)
18.	Tiruchirapalli Airport	Tiruchirapalli
19.	Jaipur Airport	Jaipur
20.	Veer Savarkar International Airport	Port Blair
21.	Srinagar International Airport	Srinagar (Jammu and Kashmir)

Waterways
Major Waterways of India

Numbers	Stretches of the Water Way	Specifications
NW1	Allahabad-Haldia (1620 km)	Along Ganga River
NW2	Sadiya- Dhubri (891 km)	Along Brahmaputra River
NW3	Kottapuram-Kollam (205 km)	Along Champakara and Udyogamandal Canal.
NW4	Bhadrachalam to Rajahmundry and Wazirabad to Vijaywada (1095 km)	Along Godavari and Krishna River
NW5	Mangalgarhi to Paradeep and Talcher to Dhamara (623 km)	Along Mahanadi and Brahmini River System
NW6	Lakhipur to Bhanga (121 km)	Along Barak River

Ports in India

- The Waterways Authority in India divides Indian ports into three categories, major, minor and intermediate ports.
- India has about 190 ports, with 13 major and the rest intermediate and minor.

Eastern Coast Ports

Ports of Eastern Coast	Important Fact
Kolkata	Oldest port, India's riverine port having two dock system.
Paradip	It handles iron-ore and some amounts of coal and dry cargo.
Chennai	All weather port having deep drafted berth, oil jetties, iron- ore terminals etc.
Visakhapatnam	Seaport and well known for its outstanding performance. It serves the Bhilai and Rourkela Steel Plant
Tuticorin	Artificial deep sea harbour, all weather port offer direct weekly container service to USA.
Ennore	First corporatised major port in India.

Western Coast Ports

Ports of Western Coast	Important Fact
Mumbai	It handles maximum traffic, natural harbour, it handles mostly petroleum and dry cargo.
Kandla	Tidal port and important traffic handled are crude oil, petroleum, edible oil, foodgrains.
Marmagao	It handles iron ore. It has a naval base.
New Mangalore	It is an all weather port.
Cochin	Major natural port in Willingdon Island.
Jawaharlal Nehru	It is called as Nhava Sheva.

- Largest container port of India is Jawaharlal Nehru (Nhava Sheva) port in Mumbai. The largest natural port is in Visakhapatnam.
- Kandla in Gujarat is a tidal port. It has been made into a free trade zone.
- New Mangalore port is also called the **Gateway of Karnataka**.
- Mumbai port is the busiest port of India.

Miscellaneous
Important Lakes of India

Name of Lake	State	Important Fact
Chilika Lake	Odisha	It is a saline and lagoon lake (largest saline water lake of India).
Kolleru Lake	Andhra Pradesh	It is a freshwater lake.
Loktak Lake	Manipur	It is a freshwater lake having inland drainage in Manipur.
Lonar Lake	Maharashtra	It is a meteorite crater lake in Buldhana area of Maharashtra. The water is highly charged with Sodium carbonates and Sodium chloride.
Pangong Lake	Jammu and Kashmir	It is a salty lake.
Pulicat Lake	Tamil Nadu and Andhra Pradesh border	It is a saline and lagoon lake.
Sambhar Lake	Rajasthan	It is a shallow lake, which is saline, located near Jaipur.
Tsomarari Lake	Jammu and Kashmir	It is a salty lake.
Vembanad Lake	Kerala	It is a lagoon lake.
Wular and Dal Lakes	Jammu and Kashmir	Wular lake was created due to tectonic activities.

Major Tribes of India

Tribal Groups	Found in	Tribal Groups	Found in
Abors	North-East	Kol	Madhya Pradesh and Uttar Pradesh
Angami	Nagaland	Kolam	Andhra Pradesh
Apatanis	Arunachal Pradesh	Kotas	Tamil Nadu
Badagas	Tamil Nadu	Kuki	Manipur
Baigas	Madhya Pradesh	Lahaulas	Himachal Pradesh
Bakarwals	Jammu and Kashmir	Lepchas	Sikkim
Bhils	Madhya Pradesh and Rajasthan	Lushai	Tripura
Bhotias	Uttarakhand	Murias	Madhya Pradesh
Bharia	Madhya Pradesh	Meenas	Rajasthan
Birhors	Madhya Pradesh and Jharkhand	Moplahs	Kerala
Chang	North-East	Mundas	Jharkhand
Chenchus	Andhra Pradesh, Telangana and Odisha	Mishimi	North-East
Gaddis	Himachal Pradesh	Nagas	Nagaland
Galaong	North-East	Oraons	Jharkhand and Odisha
Garos	Assam and Meghalaya	Onges	Andaman and Nicobar
Gonds	Madhya Pradesh and Jharkhand	Singpho	North-East
Gujjars	Jammu and Kashmir and Himachal Pradesh	Santhals	West Bengal, Odisha Jharkhand and Bihar
Irula	Tamil Nadu	Sangtam	North-East
Jaintias	Meghalaya	Sema	Nagaland
Jarawa	Little Andaman	Sentinelese	Andaman and Nicobar
Kanikar	Tamil Nadu	Shompens	Andaman and Nicobar
Katkari	Maharashtra and Madhya Pradesh	Todas	Tamil Nadu
Kharia	Jharkhand, Odisha and Madhya Pradesh	Uralis	Kerala
Khond	Andhra Pradesh, Bihar, Chhattisgarh, Maharashtra, Odisha, West Bengal and Madhya Pradesh	Wancho	North-East
Khas	Himachal Pradesh, Uttarakhand, Sikkim	Warlis	Maharashtra
Khasis	Assam and Meghalaya		

Nicknames of Important Indian Places

Nickname	Place
Abode of the God	Prayag (Allahabad)
Blue Mountains	Nilgiri
Boston of India	Ahmedabad
City of Buildings	Kolkata
City of Castles	Kolkata
City of Festivals	Madurai
City of Lakes	Srinagar
City of Nawabs	Lucknow
City of Rallies	New Delhi
City of Seven Islands	Mumbai
City of Temples	Varanasi
City of Weavers	Panipat
Dakshin Ganga	Godavari
Deccan Queen	Pune
Egg Bowl of Asia	Andhra Pradesh
Electronic City of India	Bengaluru
Garden City of India	Bengaluru
Garden of Spices of India	Kerala
Gateway of India	Mumbai
Golden City	Amritsar
Heaven of India	Jammu and Kashmir
Hollywood of India	Mumbai
Manchester of India	Ahmedabad
Manchester of the North	Kanpur
Manchester of the South	Coimbatore
Old Ganga	Godavari
Pink City	Jaipur
Pittsburg of India	Jamshedpur
Queen of Arabian Sea	Cochin
Queen of the Mountains	Mussoorie (Uttarakhand)
Sacred River	Ganga
Silicon Valley of India	Bengaluru
Soya Region	Madhya Pradesh
Space City	Bengaluru
State of Five Rivers	Punjab
Steel City of India	Jamshedpur (called Tatanagar)
Switzerland of India	Kashmir
Venice of the East	Kochi

Famous Hill Stations

Hill Stations	Height from Sea Level (m)	States
Coonoor	1860	Tamil Nadu
Dalhousie	2035	Himachal Pradesh
Darjeeling	2135	West Bengal
Gangtok	1850	Sikkim
Gulmarg	2730	Jammu and Kashmir
Kalimpong	1250	West Bengal
Kasauli	1895	Himachal Pradesh
Khandala	620	Maharashtra
Kodaikanal	2120	Tamil Nadu
Kullu Valley	1200	Himachal Pradesh
Lansdowne	2120	Uttarakhand
Lonawala	620	Maharashtra
Mahabaleshwar	1370	Maharashtra
Manali	2050	Himachal Pradesh
Mandi	709	Himachal Pradesh
Mannar	1160	Kerala
Mount Abu	1220	Rajasthan
Mukteshwar	1975	Uttarakhand

Hill Stations	Height from Sea Level (m)	States
Mussoorie	2500	Uttarakhand
Nainital	1940	Uttarakhand
Ooty (Udagamandalam)	2290	Tamil Nadu
Pahalgam	2200	Jammu and Kashmir
Panchgani	1200	Maharashtra
Pachmarhi	1065	Madhya Pradesh
Periyar	915	Kerala
Ranikhet	1830	Uttarakhand
Shimla	2159	Himachal Pradesh

Indian Town Associated with Industries

Town	State	Industries
Ahmedabad	Gujarat	Cotton Textiles
Agra	Uttar Pradesh	Leather, Marble, Carpets
Aligarh	Uttar Pradesh	Locks, Cutlery
Ankleshwar	Gujarat	Oil fields
Ambernath	Maharashtra	Machine Tools
Amritsar	Punjab	Woollen Clothes
Anand	Gujarat	Milk and its Products
Alwaye	Kerala	Fertilizer, Monazite Factory
Ambala	Haryana	Scientific Instruments
Bokaro	Jharkhand	Steel Plant
Bengaluru	Karnataka	Telephones, Aircrafts, Motors, Cotton Textiles, Toys
Batanagar	West Bengal	Shoes
Bareilly	Uttar Pradesh	Resin Industries, Match Factory
Bhilai	Chhattisgarh	Steel Plant
Barauni	Bihar	Chemical Fertilizer
Burnpur	West Bengal	Steel Plant
Bhurkunda	Jharkhand	Glass Industries
Bhagalpur	Bihar	Silk Industries
Bhandara	Maharashtra	Explosives
Bhadroves	Karnataka	Iron and Steel
Bongaigaon	Assam	Petroleum
Bhadoi	Uttar Pradesh	Carpets
Churk	Uttar Pradesh	Cement
Cyberabad	Telangana	Electronics, Computers, Information Technology
Chitaranjan	West Bengal	Locomotive
Cochin	Kerala	Ship Building, Coconut Oil, Rubber
Calicut	Kerala	Coffee, Coconut
Coimbatore	Tamil Nadu	Cotton Industries
Dhariwal	Punjab	Woollen Clothes
Durgapur	West Bengal	Steel
Digboi	Assam	Petroleum

Town	State	Industries
Delhi	Delhi	Textiles, Electronic
Dalmianagar	Bihar	Cement
Darjeeling	West Bengal	Tea
Dindigul	Tamil Nadu	Cigar, Tobacco
Firozabad	Uttar Pradesh	Bangle works
Guntur	Andhra Pradesh	Cotton Industries
Gwalior	Madhya Pradesh	Pottery, Tobacco
Gomia	Jharkhand	Explosives
Haridwar	Uttarakhand	Heavy Electricials
Hatia	Jharkhand	Heavy Engineering Corporation
Haldia	West Bengal	Chemical Fertilizer
Hazira	Gujarat	Artificial Rayon
Jamshedpur	Jharkhand	Iron and Steel, Locomotives, Railway Coaches
Jalandhar	Punjab	Surgical Goods and Sports Articles
Jaipur	Rajasthan	Cloth, Printing, Brass
Jharia	Jharkhand	Coal Mines
Jabalpur	Madhya Pradesh	Bidi Industry
Jainakot	Jammu and Kashmir	HMT Watch
Japla	Jharkhand	Cement
Kanpur	Uttar Pradesh	Cotton and Woollen Mills, Leather, Sugar
Katni	Madhya Pradesh	Cement
Korba	Chhattisgarh	Aluminium Factory, Thermal Plant
Koyna	Maharashtra	Aluminium Factory
Koyali	Gujarat	Petro-Chemical Industries
Kolar	Karnataka	Gold Mining Center
Kolkata	West Bengal	Jute, Leather, Electric goods
Kota	Rajasthan	Atomic Power Plant
Kanchipuram	Tamil Nadu	Silk Clothes
Karnal	Haryana	Dairy Product
Kandla	Gujarat	Chemical Fertilizers, Famous Port
Khetri	Rajasthan	Copper Industries
Ludhiana	Punjab	Hosiery
Lucknow	Uttar Pradesh	Embroidery Work, Chicken Work
Chennai	Tamil Nadu	Leather, Cigarette, Integral Coach Factory
Madurai	Tamil Nadu	Cotton and Silk Weaving
Mirzapur	Uttar Pradesh	Carpet, Pottery, Brass Industries
Muradabad	Uttar Pradesh	Brassware, Cutlery
Mathura	Uttar Pradesh	Oil Refinery
Mysore	Karnataka	Sandalwood Oil, Silk Goods
Meerut	Uttar Pradesh	Publication Work, Sports Goods, Scissors Making
Mumbai	Maharashtra	Cinema Industries, Cotton Textiles
Modinagar	Uttar Pradesh	Nylon thread
Moorie	Jharkhand	Aluminium

States/UTs of India

Andhra Pradesh

Capital Hyderabad
(Joint with Telangana)

Data of Formation 1st October, 1953
(Reorganised in June 2014 by creating Telangana as a separate state)

State Symbols

Animal   Blackbuck
Bird   Indian Roller
Tree   Neem

Neighbouring States/UTs

Maharashtra, Odisha, Karnataka, Telangana, Tamil Nadu, Sea: Bay of Bengal.

- Visakhapatnam is the major port in the state.
- Andhra Pradesh is India's eighth largest state by area and 10th largest by population.
- The Hyderabad Information Technology Engineering Consultancy City (HITEC City) is the largest information technology park in India.
- It is called the Rice Bowl of India and egg bowl of Asia.
- Andhra Pradesh has the second- longest coastline of 972 km among the state of India.

Arunachal Pradesh

Capital   Itanagar
Date of Formation 20th February, 1987
State Symbols

Animal   Mithun
Bird   Great Hornbill
Tree   Hollong
Flower   Fox tail Orchid

Neighbouring States
Assam, Nagaland.
Neighbouring Countries
Bhutan, Myanmar, China

- It is the Easternmost State of India.
- Rajiv Gandhi University is the only university in the state.
- Agriculture is the main occupation of the People of Arunachal Pradesh and Jhum (shifting cultivation) is practised.
- Arunachal Pradesh is also known as land of the rising Sun in reference to its position as the Easternmost State of India.

Assam

Capital   Dispur
Date of Formation 26th January, 1950
State Symbols

Animal   Indian one-horned Rhino
Bird   White-wing Wood Duck
Tree   Hollong
Flower   Fox-tail Orchid

Neighbouring States
Meghalaya, Arunachal Pradesh and Nagaland, Manipur, Tripura, Mizoram, West Bengal.

Neighbouring Countries   Bhutan and Bangladesh.

- Assam contributes about 15% of the world's entire tea production.
- Assam is surrounded by six of the other seven sister states : Arunachal Pradesh, Nagaland, Manipur, Mizoram, Tripura and Meghalaya. These states are connected to the rest of India *via* a narrow strip in West Bengal called the **Siliguri Corridor** or **Chicken's Neck**.

Bihar

Capital   Patna
Date of Formation 26th January, 1950
State Symbols

Animal   Gaur
Bird   Sparrow
Tree   Peepal
Flower   Marigold

Neighbouring States
Jharkhand, Uttar Pradesh, West Bengal

Neighbouring Country Nepal

- After the separation of Jharkhand from Bihar, Bihar has become a mineral less state, as the mineral-rich belt has gone to Jharkhand.
- Bihar is the 12th largest state in terms of geographical size and 3rd largest by population.
- According to Census 2011, Bihar has lowest literacy rate (63.82%).
- Gautam Buddha attained Enlightenment at Bodh Gaya, a town located in the modern day district of Gaya in Bihar.
- Vardhamana Mahavira, the 24th and the last Tirthankara of Jainism, was born in Vaishali around 6th century BC.

Chhattisgarh

Capital   Raipur
Data of Formation 1st November, 2000
State Symbols

Animal   Wild Buffalo
Bird   Hill Myna
Tree   Sal

Neighbouring States
Madhya Pradesh, Odisha, Telangana, Andhra Pradesh, Maharashtra, Uttar Pradesh and Jharkhand.

- 10th state in terms of area and 16th in terms of population.
- More than 80% of the population depends on agriculture. But, it is equally rich in mineral deposits.
- It is an important electrical power and steel producing state of India.
- Chhattisgarh is known for *Kosa* Silk and Lost Wax Art.

Goa

Capital	Panaji
Date of Formation	30th May, 1987

State Symbols

Animal	Gaur
Bird	Ruby Throated Yellow Bulbul
Tree	Matti

Neighbouring States

Karnataka, Maharashtra

Sea   Arabian Sea

- Goa is one of the favourite destination of tourists, with its famous beaches. Marmagao is the major port.
- It is the India's smallest state by area and the fourth smallest by population.
- It also has rich flora and fauna owing to its location on the Western Ghats range, which is classified as a biodiversity hotspot.

Gujarat

Capital	Gandhinagar
Date of Formation	1st May, 1960
Area	196024 sq km.

State Symbols

Animal	Asiatic Lion
Bird	Great Flamingo

Neighbouring States/UTs

Rajasthan, Maharashtra, Madhya Pradesh, Daman and Diu, Dadra and Nagar Haveli

Sea   Pakistan Sea, Arabian Sea

- Gujarat is the main producer of groundnut and cotton.
- Kandla port, on the coast of Gulf of Kachchh lies in Gujarat only.
- It has longest coastline of 1600 km.
- Gujarat has the fastest growing economy in India. It is also one of the most industrialised states of India and has per capita GDP above the national average.

Haryana

Capital	Chandigarh
Date of Formation	1st November, 1966

State Symbols

Animal	Black Buck Antelope
Bird	Black Francolin
Tree	Peepal
Flower	Lotus

Neighbouring States UTS

Punjab, Himachal Pradesh, Uttarakhand, Uttar Pradesh, Delhi, Rajasthan, Chandigarh (UT).

- Panipat is called the **Weaver City** for its handloom products. Haryana is a landlocked State in Northern India.
- Haryana is self-sufficient in food production and the second largest contributor to India's central pool of foodgrains.
- Yamuna Nagar district is the largest industrial town wholly within Haryana. It has Asia's largest paper mill belt and Asia's largest sugar mill.
- Yamuna Nagar has Asia's largest timber industry, an HPGCL thermal power plant, a hydro power plant and India's largest railway workshop. Haryana has lowest sex ratio (877).

Himachal Pradesh

Capital	Shimla
Date of Formation	25th January, 1971

State Symbols

Animal	Snow Leopard
Bird	Western Tragopan
Tree	Deodar
Flower	Pink Rhododendron

Neighbouring States

Jammu and Kashmir, Punjab, Haryana, Uttarakhand.

Neighbouring Country   China

- Population is divided into five major groups the Gaddis, Kinners, Gujjars, Pangawals and Lahaulis.
- Himachal Pradesh is known to be abundant in natural beauty.
- The economy of the Himachal Pradesh is currently the third fastest growing economy in India.
- Apples are the important fruits produced.
- Excellent opportunities are available for horticulture and cash crops.

Jammu and Kashmir

Capital	Srinagar (summer) Jammu (winter)
Date of Formation	26th October, 1947

State Symbols

Animal	Hangul
Bird	Black-necked crane
Tree	Chinar
Flower	Lotus

Neighbouring States Himachal Pradesh and Punjab

Neighbouring Countries Pakistan, Afghanistan, China.

- Jammu and Kashmir is called as the Paradise on Earth.
- Apart from agriculture, people are involved in handicrafts, like carpet making, shawl making, wood carving etc.
- Ladakh, also known as *Little Tibet*, is renowned for its remote mountain beauty and Buddhist culture.

Jharkhand

Capital	Ranchi
Date of Formation	15th November, 2000

State Symbols

Animal	Elephant
Bird	Koel
Tree	Sal
Flower	Palash

Neighbouring States

Bihar, Uttar Pradesh, Chhattisgarh, Odisha and West Bengal.

- Jharkhand is also known as the storehouse of minerals. This is because it accounts for 37.5% of country's coal reserves, 22% of the iron ore, 40% of its copper, 90% of its mica and huge deposits of bauxite, quartz and ceramics.
- The name 'Jharkhand' means *The Land of Forests*.
- Jharkhand has a concentration of some of the country's highly industrialised cities such as Jamshedpur, Ranchi, Bokaro Steel City and Dhanbad.

Karnataka

Capital	Bengaluru
Date of Formation	1st November, 1956

State Symbols

Animal	Elephant
Bird	Indian Roller
Tree	Sandal wood
Flower	Lotus

Neighbouring States Kerala, Goa, Maharashtra, Telangana, Andhra Pradesh and Tamil Nadu

Sea Arabian Sea

- Bengaluru is the most famous IT destination.
- Karnataka is famous for its sandal soap and sandal wood oil.
- It stands first in the production of electronic equipments and raw silk.
- New Mangalore is the major port.
- Many of India's premier science and technology research centres, such as ISRO, Central Power Research Institute, BEL and the Central Food Technological Research Institute are headquartered in Karnataka.

Kerala

Capital	Thiruvananthapuram
Date of Formation	1st November, 1956

State Symbols

Animal	Elephant
Bird	Great Hornbill
Tree	Coconut
Flower	Kanikonna

Neighbouring States/UTs

Tamil Nadu, Karnataka and Lakshadweep

- Kerala has highest literacy rate (93.9%) and highest sex ratio (1084) in India.
- Kerala has the highest Human Development Index in India, higher than that of most developed countries.
- Kerala is very rich in cash crops especially spices.
- Calicut, Cochin are the major ports.

Madhya Pradesh

Capital Bhopal

Date of Formation 1st November, 1956

State Symbols

Animal Swamp Deer
Bird Paradise Fly Catcher

Neighbouring States

Maharashtra, Gujarat, Rajasthan, Uttar Pradesh and Chhattisgarh.

- Madhya Pradesh, often called the heart of India, is a state in Central India.
- It is the second largest state by area and sixth largest state by population. It is primarily an agricultural state.
- Pachmarhi Biosphere Reserve in Satpura range and Amarkantak Biosphere Reserves are two of the 18 biosphere reserves in India.

Maharashtra

Capital Mumbai

Date of Formation 1st May, 1960

State Symbols

Animal Giant Squirrel
Bird Green Imperial Pigeon
Tree Mango
Flower Jarul

Neighbouring States

Gujarat, Madhya Pradesh, Telangana Andhra Pradesh, Karnataka, Goa, Dadra and Nagar Haveli and Chhattisgarh.

Sea Arabian Sea

- It is the second most populous after Uttar Pradesh and third largest state by area.
- It is the industrial powerhouse of India.
- The world famous film industry Bollywood is in Maharashtra, located in the economic capital of India, Mumbai.
- Mumbai and Jawaharlal Nehru port are the major ports.

Manipur

Capital Imphal

Date of Formation 21st January, 1972

State Symbols

Animal Sangai
Bird Mrs. Hume's Pheasant
Tree Uningthou
Flower Siroy Lilly

Neighbouring States

Mizoram, Assam and Nagaland

Neighbouring Country Myanmar

- It is known for its rich biodiversity having a number of rare plants, trees and wildlife.
- Agriculture is the major source of livelihood for the people.
- *There are four type of forests found :*
  1. Tropical Semi-Evergreen
  2. Dry Temperate Forest
  3. Sub-Tropical Pine
  4. Tropical Moist Deciduous

Meghalaya

Capital Shillong

Date of Formation 2nd April, 1970

State Symbols

Animal Clouded Leopard
Bird Hill Myna
Tree Gamari
Flower Lady Slipper Orchid

Neighbouring State Assam

Neighbouring Country Bangladesh

- Meghalaya is one of the seven sister states of India.
- The State of Meghalaya is also known as the Meghalaya plateau. It mainly consist of Archean rock formations. These rock formations contain rich deposits of valuable minerals like coal, limestone, uranium and sillimanite.
- More than 70% of the area is under forest.
- The wettest place in the world, Mawsynram (in Cherrapunji district) is in Meghalaya only.

Mizoram

Capital Aizwal

Date of Formation 20th February, 1987

State Symbols

Animal Serow (Saza)
Bird Hume's Bar tailed Pheasant
Tree Mesual Ferrea
Flower Dancing girl (Aiting)

Neighbouring States
Tripura, Assam and Manipur

Neighbouring Country Myanmar

- It is one of the seven sister states in North-Eastern India.
- Agriculture is the major occupation.
- Jhum or shifting cultivation is still prevalent.
- The biggest river in Mizoram is Chhimtuipi, also known as **Kaladan**.
- Phawngui Tlang also known as the **Blue Mountain**, situated in the South-Eastern part of the state, is the highest peak in Mizoram at 2210 m.

Nagaland

Capital   Kohima
Date of Formation 1st December, 1963
State Symbols
Animal   Mithun
Bird   Blyth's Tragopan
Tree   Alder
Flower   Rhododendron

Neighbouring States Manipur, Arunachal Pradesh and Assam.

Neighbouring Country Myanmar

- Agriculture is the most important economic activity in Nagaland, with more than 90% of the population employed in agriculture.
- Nagaland is rich in flora and fauna. About one-sixth of Nagaland is under the cover of tropical and sub-tropical evergreen forests-including palms, bamboo and rattan as well as timber and mahagony forest.

Odisha

Capital   Bhubaneshwar
Date of Formation 1st November, 1956
State Symbols
Animals   Sambar
Bird   Blue Jay
Tree   Aswattha
Flower   Asoka

Neighbouring States
Andhra Pradesh, Chhattisgarh, Jharkhand and West Bengal

- World's longest dam, Hirakud (on Mahanadi) is in Odisha only.
- Paradip is the major port in Odisha.

- Agriculture based economy, rice is the main crop. The Chilika lake is brackish water lagoon located in the Southern part of the Odisha coastal plains.

Punjab

Capital   Chandigarh
Date of Formation 26th January, 1950
State Symbols
Animal   Blackbuck
Bird   Eastern Goshawk
Tree   Sheesham

Neighbouring States Jammu and Kashmir, Himachal Pradesh, Haryana and Rajasthan

Neighbouring Country Pakistan

- Agriculture is the largest occupation in Punjab; it is the largest single provider of Wheat to India.
- Per hectare yield is maximum in Punjab.
- Bhakra dam (on Sutlej) is the highest dam of India.
- Punjab is the only state in India with a majority Sikh population.
- Various small-scale industries are operational in Punjab such as bicycle parts, sewing machine, hand tools and machine tools etc.

Rajasthan

Capital   Jaipur
Date of Formation 1st November, 1956
State Symbols
Animal   Chinkara
Bird   Great Indian Bustard
Tree   Khejari
Flower   Rohida

Neighbouring States Gujarat, Madhya Pradesh, Uttar Pradesh, Delhi, Haryana and Punjab.

Neighbouring Country Pakistan

- It is the largest state of India in terms of area. Western Rajasthan is a desert region (Thar) deserts.
- Zinc, silver, lead, salt are found in abundance.

Sikkim

Capital	Gangtok
Date Formation	16th May, 1975

State Symbols

Animal	Red Panda
Bird	Blood Pheasant
Tree	Rhododendron Niveum
Flower	Dendrobium Nobile Orchid

Neighbouring State West Bengal

Neighbouring Countries China, Nepal and Bhutan

- It is the least populous state in India and the second smallest in area after Goa.
- It is a landlocked Indian state located in the Himalayan mountains.
- Sikkim is the only state in India with an ethnic Nepali majority.

Tamil Nadu

Capital	Chennai
Date of Formations	26th January, 1950

State Symbols

Animals	Nilgiri Tahr
Bird	Emerald Dove
Tree	Palmera Palm
Flower	Kandhal

Neighbouring States

Kerala, Karnataka, Andhra Pradesh and Puducherry (UT)

Sea Bay of Bengal and Indian Ocean

Neighbouring Country Sri Lanka

- Tamil Nadu is home to many natural resources, Hindu temples of Dravidian architecture, hill stations, beach resorts, multi-religious pilgrim sites and UNESCO world heritage site. Its economy depends largely on agriculture.
- Chennai, Tuticorin and Ennore are the major ports in the State of Tamil Nadu.
- Major industries in Tamil Nadu are cotton textiles, chemical fertilizers, paper and its products, diesel engine, iron and steel, railway wagons and coaches etc.

Telangana

Capital	Hyderabad
Date of Formation	2nd June, 2014

State Symbols

Animal	Deer
Bird	Indian Roller
Tree	Jammi
Flower	Thangedu

Neighbouring States Maharashtra, Chhattisgarh, Karnataka and Andhra Pradesh.

- Two major Peninsular rivers; the Godavari and the Krishna drains the states. About two-third catchment area of both rivers lies in Telangana.
- Important hub of art and culture as many historical places, forts, temples are situated.
- Most of the population is involved in agriculture as fertile land for agriculture is available.

Tripura

Capital	Agartala
Date of Formation	21st January, 1972
Area	10491.69 sq km

State Symbols

Animal	Phayre's Langur
Bird	Green Imperial Pigeon
Tree	Agar
Flower	Nageshwar

Neighbouring States Assam and Mizoram

Neighbouring Country Bangladesh

- It is the third smallest state of India (area-wise).
- It is an agriculture based state.
- Tripura is a landlocked state in North-Eastern India.

Uttarakhand

Capital	Dehradun
Date of Formation	9th November, 2000

State Symbols

Animals	Musk Deer,
Bird	Himalayan Monal
Tree	Burans
Flower	Brahm Kamal

Neighbouring States Uttar Pradesh and Himachal Pradesh

Neighbouring Countries China and Nepal

- It has tremendous potential for hydel power. The biggest project is the Tehri Dam Project on Bhagirathi river.
- Uttarakhand is home to several important educational institutions, including the oldest engineering colleges in Asia, the Indian Institute of Technology at Roorkee and Govind Ballabh Pant University of Agriculture and Technology in Pantnagar.
- Rishikesh is widely considered as the yoga capital of the world.

Uttar Pradesh

Capital	Lucknow
Date of Formation	26th January, 1950
State Symbols	
Animal	Swamp Deer
Bird	Sarus Crane
Tree	Ashok
Flower	Palash

Neighbouring States Uttarakhand, Himachal Pradesh, Haryana, Delhi, Rajasthan, Madhya Pradesh, Chhattisgarh, Jharkhand and Bihar.

Neighbouring Country Nepal : Uttar Pradesh is the India's most populous state as well as the World's most populous sub-national entity (only 5 nations have more population than Uttar Pradesh) About 78% of the population depends on agriculture.

- Uttar Pradesh is the largest producer of foodgrains, sugarcane and oilseed.
- Small Scale Cottage Industries are spread through-out in Uttar Pradesh.
- Kanpur is the largest economic hub of Uttar Pradesh. Kanpur is also the economic capital of Uttar Pradesh.

West Bengal

Capital	Kolkata
Date of Formation	1st November, 1956
State Symbols	
Animal	Fishing Cat
Bird	White-throated King Fisher
Tree	Chatian
Flower	Shephali

Neighbouring States Odisha, Jharkhand, Bihar, Sikkim and Assam

Neighbouring Countries Nepal, Bhutan and Bangladesh.

Sea Bay of Bengal.

- Kolkata - Haldia is the major port in West Bengal. Agriculture is the mainstay of economy. It is the largest producer of rice in the country.
- West Bengal is noted for its cultural activities, with the state capital Kolkata earning the Sobriquet cultural capital of India.

Delhi

Animal	Nilgai
Bird	House sparrow
Capital	Delhi
Date of Formation	1st February, 1992

Neighbouring States Haryana and Uttar Pradesh

- Delhi is the largest metropolis by area and the second largest metropolis by population in India.
- It is the eight largest metropolis in the world by population.
- Delhi is the largest commercial centre of Northern India and is the largest centre of small industries.
- Delhi has greater number of vehicles than the total vehicles of Kolkata, Mumbai and Chennai put together.

Andaman and Nicobar Islands

Capital	Port Blair
Date of Formation	1st November, 1956
State Symbols	
Animal	Dugong or Sea cow
Bird	Andaman wood Pigeon
Tree	Andaman Padauk

- Tourism and agriculture are the mainstay of economy.
- Andaman is a group of 204 islands, while Nicobar is a group of 19 islands. Out of these, only 36 islands in Andamans and 12 islands in Nicobars are inhabited.
- Mangrove forests are found in abundance in these islands.
- India's Southern-most point, Indira Point, is located, in Nicobar only.

Chandigarh

Capital   Chandigarh

Date of Formation UT since 1966.

State Symbols

Animal   Indian Grey
               Mongoose
Bird   Indian Grey Hornbill
Flower   Dhak Flower
Tree   Mango Tree

Neighbouring States Punjab and Haryana

- Chandigarh is one of the most beautiful and well-planned places in India. It was designed by a French Architect, Le Corbusier. Chandigarh serves as a joint capital of Haryana and Punjab.

Dadra and Nagar Haveli

Capital   Silvassa
Date of Formation   11th August, 1961
Area   491 sq km
Neighbouring States Gujarat,
                         Maharashtra

- Forest cover about 40% of the total area. The rich bio-diversity makes it an ideal habitat for variety of birds and animals. This makes it a perfect spot for eco-tourism.

Daman and Diu

Capital   Daman
Date of Formation   30th May, 1987
Neighbouring State   Gujarat

- Agriculture and fishing dominate the economies of Daman and Diu.Rice, Ragi (calsa called finger millet), pulses and beans are among the main crops of Daman.

Lakshadweep

Capital   Kavaratti
Date of Formation   1st November,
                         1956

State Symbols

Animal   Butterfly Fish
Bird   Noddy Tern
Tree   Bread Fruit
Neighbouring States Kerala,
                         Karnataka
Sea   Arabian Sea

- It is the smallest Union Territory of India.
- It is a group of 25 coral islands.
- Lakshadweep is India's largest producer of coconut.

Puducherry

Capital   Puducherry
**Date of
Formation**   7th January, 1963
State Symbols

Animal   Squirrel
Bird   Koel
Flower   Cannon Ball
Tree   Vilva Tree

- In September, 2006, the territory changed its official name from Pondicherry to Puducherry, which means 'New Village' in the Tamil language. It is a former French colony, consisting of four district Puducherry, Karaikul, Yanam and Mahe.

RANK OF INDIAN STATES AND UTs (CATEGORY WISE) CENSUS, 2011

Literacy Rate

Ranks	Overall Literacy		Male Literacy		Female Literacy	
	States	Percentage	States	Percentage	States	Percentage
1.	Kerala	93.91	Lakshadweep	96.11	Kerala	91.98
2.	Lakshadweep	92.28	Kerala	96.02	Mizoram	89.40
3.	Mizoram	91.58	Mizoram	93.72	Lakshadweep	88.25
4.	Tripura	87.75	Goa	92.81	Tripura	83.15
5.	Goa	87.40	Tripura	92.18	Goa	81.84
6.	Daman and Diu	87.07	Puducherry	92.12	Andaman and Nicobar Islands	81.84

Ranks	Overall Literacy — States	Percentage	Male Literacy — States	Percentage	Female Literacy — States	Percentage
7.	Puducherry	86.55	Daman and Diu	91.48	Chandigarh	81.38
8.	Chandigarh	86.43	NCT of Delhi	91.03	Puducherry	81.22
9.	Delhi	86.34	Himachal Pradesh	90.83	NCT of Delhi	80.93
10.	Andaman and Nicobar Islands	86.27	Chandigarh	90.54	Daman and Diu	79.59
11.	Himachal Pradesh	83.78	Andaman and Nicobar Islands	90.11	Nagaland	76.69
12.	Maharashtra	82.91	Maharashtra	89.82	Himachal Pradesh	76.60
13.	Sikkim	82.20	Uttarakhand	88.33	Sikkim	76.43
14.	Tamil Nadu	80.33	Sikkim	87.29	Maharashtra	75.48
15.	Nagaland	80.11	Gujarat	87.23	Tamil Nadu	73.86
16.	Manipur	79.85	Tamil Nadu	86.81	Meghalaya	73.78
17.	Uttarakhand	79.63	Manipur	86.49	Manipur	73.17
18.	Gujarat	79.31	Dadra and Nagar Haveli	86.46	Punjab	71.34
19.	Dadra and Nagar Haveli	77.65	Haryana	85.38	West Bengal	71.34
20.	West Bengal	77.08	Nagaland	83.29	Gujarat	70.73
21.	Punjab	76.68	Karnataka	82.85	Uttarakhand	70.70
22.	Haryana	76.64	West Bengal	82.67	Karnataka	68.13
23.	Karnataka	75.60	Odisha	82.40	Assam	67.27
24.	Meghalaya	75.48	Punjab	81.48	Haryana	66.77
25.	Odisha	73.45	Chhattisgarh	81.45	Dadra and Nagar Haveli	65.93
26.	Assam	73.18	Madhya Pradesh	80.53	Odisha	64.36
27.	Chhattisgarh	71.04	Rajasthan	80.51	Chhattisgarh	60.59
28.	Madhya Pradesh	70.63	Uttar Pradesh	79.24	Madhya Pradesh	60.02
29.	Uttar Pradesh	69.72	Assam	78.81	Andhra Pradesh	59.74
30.	Jammu and Kashmir	68.74	Jharkhand	78.45	Arunachal Pradesh	59.57
31.	Andhra Pradesh	67.66	Jammu and Kashmir	78.26	Uttar Pradesh	59.26
32.	Jharkhand	67.63	Meghalaya	77.17	Jammu and Kashmir	58.01
33.	Rajasthan	67.06	Andhra Pradesh	75.56	Jharkhand	56.21
34.	Arunachal Pradesh	66.95	Arunachal Pradesh	78.69	Bihar	53.33
35.	Bihar	63.82	Bihar	73.39	Rajasthan	52.66
	National Average	74.04%		82.14%		65.46%

(According to 2011 Census) Andhra Pradesh includes state of Telangana and Andhra Pradesh.

Sex Ratio

Ranks	Sex Ratio		Child Sex Ratio	
	State	Ratio	State	Ratio
1.	Kerala	1084	Mizoram	971
2.	Puducherry	1038	Meghalaya	970
3.	Tamil Nadu	996	Andaman and Nicobar Island	966
4.	Andhra Pradesh	992	Puducherry	965
5.	Chhattisgarh	991	Chhattisgarh	964
6.	Manipur	987	Arunachal Pradesh	960
7.	Meghalaya	986	Kerala	959
8.	Odisha	978	Assam	957
9.	Mizoram	975	Tripura	953
10.	Himachal Pradesh	974	West Bengal	950
11.	Goa	968	Tamil Nadu	946
12.	Karnataka	968	Nagaland	944
13.	Uttarakhand	963	Jharkhand	943
14.	Tripura	961	Sikkim	944
15.	Assam	954	Andhra Pradesh	943
16.	West Bengal	947	Karnataka	943
17.	Jharkhand	947	Odisha	934
18.	Maharashtra	946	Manipur	934
19.	Lakshadweep	946	Bihar	933
20.	Nagaland	931	Dadra and Nagar Haveli	924
21.	Madhya Pradesh	931	Goa	920
22.	Rajasthan	928	Madhya Pradesh	912
23.	Arunachal Pradesh	938	Daman and Diu	909
24.	Gujarat	918	Lakshadweep	908
25.	Bihar	916	Himachal Pradesh	906
26.	Uttar Pradesh	908	Uttar Pradesh	899
27.	Punjab	893	Uttarakhand	886
28.	Sikkim	889	Gujarat	886
29.	Jammu and Kashmir	883	Rajasthan	883
30.	Andaman and Nicobar Islands	878	Maharashtra	883
31.	Haryana	877	Chandigarh	867
32.	Delhi	866	Delhi	886
33.	Chandigarh	818	Jammu and Kashmir	859
34.	Dadra and Nagar Haveli	775	Punjab	846
35.	Daman and Diu	618	Haryana	830
	National Average	940		914

ECOLOGY AND ENVIRONMENT

- Ecology is a science, in which study of organism is undertaken in relation to their environment. This science developed in response to the increasing awareness of inter- relationships between plants, animals and their physical habitats.
- The term ecosystem was first used by AG Tansley in 1935, who defined ecosystem as a particular category of physical system, consisting of organisms and inorganic components in a relatively stable equilibrium open and of various sizes and kinds.

Components of Ecosystem

- **Abiotic Part** is the non-living component, e.g. air, water, soil, suspended particulate matter etc.
- **Biotic Part** includes plants, animals and micro-organism.
- *The living organism in an ecosystem can be divided into three categories*

Producers

- Producers are organisms that can make organic energy resources from abiotic components of the environment. They produce their food themselves.

Consumers

- Consumers are those organisms that gather energy by consuming organic material from other organisms. Primary consumers are those organisms, who consume mainly producers, primary consumers are also known as Herbivores.
- Secondary consumers are those organisms, who consume mainly primary consumers. Tertiary consumers are organisms that consume secondary consumers. Tertiary consumers are carnivores. Omnivores feed on both producers and other consumers.
- Detritovores consume detritus (dead).

Decomposers

- Decomposers are organisms that break down dead or decaying organisms. Decomposers are heterotrophic meaning that they use organic substrates to get their energy, carbon and nutrients for growth and development e.g. bacteria and fungi.

Functions of Ecosystem

The main functions of an ecosystem are as follows:
   (i) Materials or nutrient cycle
   (ii) Biological or ecological regulation

- **Foodchain** The flow of energy from of one organism to another in a sequence of food transfer is known as a foodchain. A simple foodchain is like the following
Grass → Insect → Frogs → Snake → Hawk
- **Food Web** A network of foodchains or feeding relationships, by which energy and nutrients are passed on from one specie of living organism to another is called food web.
- **Trophic Levels** Trophic levels are the feeding position in a foodchain such as primary producers, herbivore, primary carnivore etc. Generally green plants form the first trophic level, the producers, herbivores from the second trophic level, while carnivores and omnivores form the third and even the fourth trophic levels.
- **Ecological Pyramid** An ecological pyramid is a graphical representation designed to show the number of organisms, energy relationships and biomass of an ecosystem. They are also called **Eltonian Pyramids** after Charles Elton, who developed the concept of ecological pyramids, producer organisms (usually green plants) from the base of the pyramid, with succeeding levels above representing the different tropic levels.
- Succeeding levels in the pyramid represent the dependence of the organisms at a given level on the organisms at lower level.
- **Pyramid of Biomass** Biomass is renewable organic (living) material. A pyramid of biomass is a representation of the amount of energy contained in biomass at different trophic levels for a particular time.
- It is measured in grams per meter or calories per meter. This demonstrates the amount of matter lost between trophic levels.
- **Pyramid of Energy** The pyramid of energy represents the total amount of energy consumed by each trophic level.

- An energy pyramid is always upright as the total amount of energy available for utilisation in the layers above is less than the energy available in the lower levels.
- **Biome** Biome is a large natural ecosystem, wherein we study the total assemblage of plant and animal communities. Biosphere is the largest ecosystem on the Earth, divided into biomes.

Important Biomes	Physical Characteristics	Plants	Animals
Tundra	Two seasons, dry and frozen deserts **Winter** extreme cold and snowy **Summer** flooding caused by snow melt permafrost layer (permanently frozen about 3 m below ground. **Location** far North and far South towards the polar ice caps **Average Temperature** 10°C **Rainfall now** 25 cm/yr **Snow** 10-20 cm/yr	No trees, dominated by mosses and lichens and grasses some small shrubs.	Insect blooms, large hooved mammals (caribou, musk, ox), bears wolves, small rodents (lemmings) migrate during the breeding season
Boreal Forest	Long winter, short fall and spring, 2-3 months of summer, wetter seasons, heavy rain and snow. **Location** coniferous forest, far Northern and far Southern latitudes	Trees 5-10 m high, boreal forest conifers pine, spruce, bog plants (ferns and mosses)	Diverse array of migrants from the tropics with few resident species (moose, bear, lynx, fox, voles) large insect blooms
Temperate Deciduous Forest	Four seasons **Rainfall** 80-140 cm/yr	Complex levels of vegetation deciduous trees, loose leaves in fall	Diverse array of migrants from the tropics and resident species.
Savannah	Dry three seasons **Rainfall** 90-150 cm/yr **Location** tropical to sub-tropical	Grasses, shrubs, trees short and (2m tall) clumped together (10 m tall)	Large ungulates, large predators
Temperate Grassland	Temperate and some subartic grassland (extreme Northern Prairies-steppes and some extreme Southern grasslands-Pampas of Argentina) **Rainfall** 25-70 cm/yr	Grasses	Large ungulates
Mediterranean	Mild wet winter followed by hot, dry, summer, many plants dependent on regular fires associated with Chaparral. **Location** near coastlines (California, Chile, Mediterranean)	Short trees and shrubs	Diversity of mammals, birds, insects etc that like dry habitats
Desert	Very dry **Rainfall** less than 25 cm/year **Location** primarily equatorial but some reach into temperate regions	Cactus, sagebrush, creosote and shrubs	Small rodents, reptiles
Tropical Rainforest	Very wet-heavy rainfall. **Soil** poor in nutrients **Temperature** constant throughout the year (wet and dry seasons)	Large trees-broad-leaved evergreens, epiphytes, not much forest floor vegetation (little sunlight) canopy 30-40 m above ground	Highest diversity of animals

Aquatic Biome Freshwater and Marine biomes

• **Ecological Niche** Organisms in ecosystem get evolved for particular task. This task or role, which an organism plays in ecosystem is called as ecological niche.

POLLUTION

Environmental pollution is the effect of undesirable changes in our surroundings that have harmful effects on plants, animals and human beings.

Pollutants Pollutants are substances, which cause pollution and they could be in any from solid, liquid or gaseous.

• A primary pollutant is an air pollution emitted directly from a source.
• A secondary pollution is not directly emitted as such, but forms, when other pollutants (primary pollutants) react in the atmosphere.

Primary pollutants

• Sulphur dioxide (SO_2), nitrogen oxides (NO_2), carbon monoxide (CO), chloro-fluoro carbons (CFCs), carbon dioxide (CO_2), Suspended Particulate Matter (SPM) and Ammonia (NH_3) etc.

Secondary pollutants

1. Particulate matter formed from gaseous primary pollutants and compounds in photochemical smog, such as nitrogen dioxide.
2. Ground level ozone (O_3) formed from N_2 and Volatile Organic Compounds (VOCs).
3. Peroxyacety l Nitrate (PAN) similarly formed from NO_2 and VOCs.

Air Pollution

It is the contamination of air by a variety of substances causing health problems and damaging our environment.

Air Pollutants

Some of the most common air pollutants are as follows.

• **Carbon Monoxide** (CO) is produced from incomplete combustion of fuel such as natural gas, coal and wood.
• It is also produced in tabacco smoke. It slows our reflexes and makes us feel sleepy.

• **Carbon Dioxide** (CO_2) is the principal greenhouse gas and is primarily responsible for the greenhouse effect. It can be formed from all types of common human activities, such as burning fuels and even breathing.
• **Chlorofluorocarbons** (CFCs) were generally used in great quantities in industry, for refrigeration and air-conditioning and in consumer products.
• **Ozone** (O_3) gas occurs naturally in the upper atmosphere where it shields the Earth from the Sun's dangerous ultraviolet rays. When found at ground level, however, it's a pollutant.
• **Nitrogen Oxide and Sulphur Dioxide** are major contributors to smog and acid rain. These gases both react with volatile organic compounds to form smog, which can cause respiratory problems in humans. Acid rain can harm vegetation, change the chemistry of river and lake water by lowering the pH which is harmful to animal life and react with the marble statues and buildings to decompose them.

Controls/Measures of Air Pollution

• Suitable fuel selection
• Modification in industrial processes
• Correct selection of manufacturing sites
• More efficient engines
• Awareness for using public transport so that air pollution is minimised

Water Pollution

• It is the contamination of water bodies (*e.g.* lakes, rivers, oceans, aquifers and groundwater). Water pollution occurs when pollutants are discharged directly or indirectly into water bodies without adequate treatment to remove harmful compounds.
• **Biological Oxygen Demond** (BOD) It is a measurement of amount of dissolved that is used by aerobic micro-organisms when decomposing organic matter in water. It is an important water quality parameter and is an indicator of organic pollution.

Control/Measures of Water Pollution

- Mass social awareness should be generated.
- Ground water pollution can be eliminated by maintaining strict restrictions regarding waste disposal.
- Industrial effluents should be effectively recycled, before releasing in water.
- **Government Initiatives** National Water Policy, 2002, Water (Prevention and Control of Pollution) Act, 1974, establishment of pollution control boards, oil spill response centre etc are some government initiatives to control water pollution.

Noise Pollution

- Noise can be taken as a group of loud, non-harmonious sounds or vibrations that are unpleasant and irritating to ear. Decibel is the standard for the measurement of noise. The zero on a decibel scale is at the threshold of hearing, the lowest sound pressure that can be heard, on the scale 20 db is whisper 40 db the noise in quiet office, 60 db is normal conversation; 80 db is the level at which sound becomes physically painful.

Land Pollution

- It refers to degradation or destruction of Earth's surface and soil, directly or indirectly as a result of human activities. It explains any activity that lessens the quality or productivity of the land as an ideal place for agriculture, forestation, construction, etc.

Causes of Land Pollution

- Deforestation and soil erosion.
- **Agricultural Activities** Use of highly toxic fertilisers and pesticides mining activities.
- **Overcrowded Landfills** Garbage which cannot be recycled become a part of the landfills.
- **Industrialisation** Creation of more waste by industries that needs to be disposed off.
- **Nuclear Waste** The left over radioactive material contains harmful and toxic chemicals that can affect human health. They are dumped beneath the Earth to avoid any casuality.

- **Sewage Treatment** Large amount of solid waste is leftover once the sewage has been treated. The leftover material is sent to landfill site which end up in polluting the environment.

Solutions for Land Pollution

- Make people aware about the concept of reduce, recycle and reuse.
- Practicing organic farming which uses no chemical pesticides and fertilisers in agricultural activities.
- Avoid buying packages items as they will lead to garbage.
- No littering on ground and proper disposal of garbage.
- Buy bio-degradable products.
- Organic gardening and organic food.

e-Waste

It is a term used to cover almost all types of Electrical and Electronic Equipment (EEE) that could enter into the waste stream. Although, e-waste is a general term, it can be considered to cover TVs, computers, mobile phones, white goods (*e.g.* fridges, washing machines, dryers etc) home entertainment and stereo systems, toys, toasters, kettles almost any households or business item with circuitry or electrical components with power or battery supply which are discarded.

Radioactive Pollution

- It is the release of any radioactive material into the environment. Radioactive pollution can be a very dangerous because radiation mutates DNA, causing abnormal growth and possibly cancer and this radiation remains in the environment for years, slowly diminishing over time. Radioactive pollution is mainly caused by nuclear accidents, nuclear explosion, accident during production or use of radioactive materials. There are techniques used to manage this pollution, however, we are far from keeping our planet clean of radioactive pollution.

Biodiversity

- Biodiversity refers to the variety within the living world. The term is commonly used to describe the number, variety and variability of living organisms.

- Often used as a synonym of **Life on the Earth**. It means genetic variation, species variation or ecosystem variation within an area, biome or planet.
- Biodiversity is often seen in the terms of three fundamental and hierarchically related levels of biological organisation.
- **Genetic diversity** represents the heritable variation within and between population of organisms.
- **Species diversity** refers to number of species in a site or habitat.
- **Ecosystem diversity** refers to diversity of different organisms at the ecosystem, habitat or community level.

Biodiversity Hotspots

- A biodiversity hotspot is a bio-geographic region with a significant reservoir of biodiversity that is under threat from humans. The concept of biodiversity hotspots was originated by **Norman Myers**.
- To qualify as a biodiversity hotspot on Myers 2000 edition of the Hotspot Map, a region must meet two strict criterias. It must contain at least 0.5% or 1500 species of vascular plants as endemics and it has to have lost at least 70% of its primary vegetation. India has two biodiversity hotspots—Western Ghats and Eastern Himalayas.

Biodiversity Conservation

Conservation is planned management of natural resources to retain the balance in nature and retain the diversity. It emphasises on the wise use of natural resources by accepting the idea of sustainable development. Conservation biodiversity is important in following ways.

Method of Conservation

The method of conservation of biodiversity can be classified into two groups.

In-Situ (On Site)

Conservation includ protection of plants and animals within their natural habitats or in protected areas. Protected areas are land or sea dedicated to protect and maintain biodiversity. Examples are Biosphere Reserves, National Parks, Wildlife Sanctuaries, etc.

Ex-Situ (Off Site)

Conservation of plants and animals outside their natural habitats. These include botanical gardens, zoos, gene banks of seed, tissue culture and cryopreservation.

Threatened Species

Threatened species are any species (including animals, plants, fungi, etc.) which are vulnerable to endangerment in the near future. Species that are threatened are sometimes characterised by the population dynamics measure of critical depensation, a mathematical measure of biomass related to population growth rate. This quantitative metric is one method of evaluating the degree of endangerment.

IUCN

The International Union for Conservation of Nature (IUCN) is the foremost authority on threatened species, and treats threatened species not as a single category, but as a group of three categories, depending on the degree to which they are threatened :

- Vulnerable species : A vulnerable species is one which has been categorised by the International Union for Conservation of Nature as likely to become endangered unless the circumstances threating its survival and reproduction improve.
- Endangered species : An endangered species is a species which has been categorized as likely to become extinct.
- Critically endangered species : A critically endangered (CR) species is one which has been categorised by the International Union for Conservation of Nature (IUCN) as facing a very high risk of extinction in the wild. It is the highest risk category assigned by the IUCN Red List for wild species.

IUCN Red List

The IUCN Red List of Threatened Species (also known as the IUCN Red List or Red Data List), founded in 1964, is the world's most comprehensive inventory of the global conservation status of biological species.

Climate Change

Climate change refers to long-term change in the earth's climate, especially a change due to an increase in average atmospheric temperature. Earth's climate is also changing. In the past, Earth's climate has gone through warmer and cooler periods, each lasting thousands of years.

Difference Between National Park, Sanctuary and Biosphere Reserve

National Park	Sanctuary	Biosphere Reserve
A reserved area for preservation of its natural vegetation, wildlife and natural beauty.	A reserved area for preservation of endangered species.	Multipurpose protected area to preserve genetic diversity in representative ecosystem.
Boundaries are fixed by legislation.	Boundaries are not sacrosanct.	Boundaries are fixed by legislation.

Endangered Species of India

Birds	Great Indian Bustard, Forest Owlet, Vulture, Bengal Florican, Himalayan Quail, Siberian Crane
Mammals	Flying Squirrel, Red Panda, Pygmy Hog, Kondana Rat, Snow Leopard, Asiatic Lion, One-Horned Rhinoceros
Reptiles	Gharial, Hawksbill Turtle, River Terrapin, Sispara Day Gecko
Amphibians	Flying Frog, Tiger Toad

Wildlife Conservation in India

Project	Year
Project Hangul	1970
Project Gir	1972
Project Tiger	1973
Project Olive Riddey Turtles	1975
Crocodile Breeding Scheme	1975
Project Manipur Thamin	1977
Project Rhino	1987
Project Elephant	1992
Project Red Panda	1996
Project Vulture	2006

Important Sanctuaries and National Parks

Name of Sanctuary/Park	Location
Achanakmar Sanctuary	Chhattisgarh
Bandhavgarh National Park	Madhya Pradesh
Bandipur Sanctuary	Karnataka
Banerghatta National Park	Karnataka
Bhadra Sanctuary	Karnataka
Chandraprabha Sanctuary	Uttar Pradesh
Corbett National Park	Uttarakhand

Name of Sanctuary/Park	Location
Dachigam Sanctuary	Jammu and Kashmir
Dandeli Sanctuary	Karnataka
Dudhwa National Park	Uttar Pradesh
Gandhi Sagar Sanctuary	Madhya Pradesh
Ghana Bird Sanctuary	Rajasthan
Gir Forest	Gujarat
Gautam Buddha Sanctuary	Bihar
Jaldapara Sanctuary	West Bengal
Kaziranga National Park	Assam
Kanchenjunga National Park	Sikkim
Nagarhole National Park	Karnataka
Namdapha Sanctuary	Arunachal Pradesh
Pachmarhi Sanctuary	Madhya Pradesh
Ranganthittoo Bird Sanctuary	Karnataka
Simlipal Sanctuary	Odisha
Sundraban Tiger Reserve	West Bengal
Sonai Rupa Sanctuary	Assam
Tungabhadra Sanctuary	Karnataka

Biosphere Reserves of India

Name	State	Type
Great Rann of Kachchh	Gujarat	Desert
Gulf of Mannar(UNESCO)	Tamil Nadu	Coasts
Sundarbans (UNESCO)	West Bengal	Gangetic Delta
Cold Desert	Himachal Pradesh	Western Himalayas
Nanda Devi (UNESCO)	Uttarakhand	West Himalays
Nilgiri (UNESCO)	Tamil Nadu, Kerala and Karnataka	Western Ghats
Dehang-Dibang	Arunachal Pradesh	East Himalayas
Pachmarhi (UNESCO)	Madhya Pradesh	Semi-Arid
Seshachalam Hills	Andhra Pradesh	Eastern Ghats
Simlipal (UNESCO)	Odisha	Deccan Peninsula
Achanakamar Amarkantak (UNESCO)	Madhya Pradesh, Chhattisgarh	Maikala Range
Manas	Assam	East Himalayas
Khangchendzonga (UNESCO)	Sikkim	East Himalayas
Agasthyamalai	Kerala, Tamil Nadu	Western Ghats
Great Nicobar (UNESCO)	Andaman and Nicobar Islands	Islands
Nokrek (UNESCO)	Meghalaya	East Himalayas
Dibru-Saikhowa	Assam	East Himalayas
Panna	Madhya Pradesh	Ken River

Greenhouse Effect and Global Warming

- The greenhouse gases (sometimes abbreviated as GHG) in the atmosphere absorbs and emits radiation within the thermal infrared range. The process is the fundamental cause of the greenhouse effect.
- The primary greenhouse gases in the Earth's atmosphere are water vapour, carbon dioxide, methane, nitrous oxide and ozone.
- In the Solar System, the atmosphere of Venus, Mars and Titan also contain gases that cause greenhouse effects.
- **Global Warming** is the increase of Earth's average surface temperatue due to effect of greenhouse gases, such as carbon dioxide emissions from burning fossil fuels or from deforestation.

Kyoto Protocol

- The Kyoto Protocol is a protocol to the United Nations Framework Convention on Climate Change (UNFCCC), aimed at fighting global warming.
- The UNFCCC is an international environmental treaty with the goal of achieving the "stabilisation of greehouse gas concentration in the atmosphere at a level that would prevent dangerous anthropogenic interference with the climate system".
- The protocol was initially adopted on 11th December, 1997 in Kyoto, Japan and entered to force on 16th February, 2005. Second commitment period of this protocol started in 2013 and will end in 2020.
- The **Intergovernmental Panel on Climate Change** (IPCC) has predicted an average global rise in temperature of 1.4°C to 5.8°C between 1990 and 2100. If successfully and completely implemented, the Kyoto Protocol will reduce that increase by somewhere between 0.02°C and 0.28°C by the year 2050.

Mission Included in Prime Minister's National Action Plan for Climate Change (NAPCC)

- National solar mission
- National mission for enhanced energy efficiency
- National mission on sustainable habitat
- National water mission

- National mission for sustaining the Himalayan ecosystem
- National mission for Green India
- National mission for sustainable agriculture
- National mission on strategic knowledge for climate change

REDD ++

- Reducing Emissions from Deforestation and Forest Degradation (REDD) is an effort to create a financial value for the carbon stored in forests, offering incentives for developing countries to reduce emissions from forested lands and invest in low carbon paths to sustainable development.
- 'REDD+' goes beyond deforestation and forest degradation and includes the role of conservation, sustainable management of forests and enhancement of forest carbon stocks.
- The proper implementation of REDD+ will contribute to protection of biodiversity resilience of forest ecosystems and poverty reduction.

Ozone Layer Depletion

- The ozone layer is located within the Stratosphere, about 24 km above the Earth's surface. The layer consist of ozone gas molecules that are formed as the sunlight reacts with oxygen.
- The ozone layer is very important as it protecs life on Earth by filtering the Sun's dangerous ultraviolet radiation.
- Due to increased pollution on Earth, chemicals such as Chloro Fluro Carbons (CFCs) are destroying this protective ozone layer, which could lead to increased health risks and damage agricultural and acquatic ecosystem.

Montreal Protocol on Substances that Deplete the Ozone Layer

- It is an international treaty designed to protect the ozone layer from Chloro Fluoro Carbons (CFCs).
- The treaty was opened for signature on 16th September, 1987 and entered into force on 1st January, 1989, followed by a first meeting in Helsinki, May 1989.

Bonn Climate Conference 2017

The UN Climate Change Conference, 2017 was held in November 2017 at Bonn, Germany. It was presided by Government of Fiji.

Important Environmental Organisations

Organisation	Head Office	Year
IUCN	Gland	1948
World wide Fund for nature (WWF)	Swizerland	1961
Green Peace	Amsterdam	1971
World conservation Monitoring centre	Combridge	1983
Global Environmental Facility	Washington	1991

Environment Related Important International Agreements/Conference

UN Conference on the Human Environment	Stockholm (1972)
Convention on Migratory Species	Bonn (1979)
Convention for the Protection of the Ozone Layer	Vienna (1985)
Protocol on Substances that Deplete the Ozone Layer	Montreal (1987)
Convention on the Transboundary Movement of Hazardous Wastes	Basel (1989)
Earth Summit (UN Conference on Environment and Development)	Riode-Janeiro (1992)
Convention on Prior Informed Consent	Rotterdam (1998)
UN Conference on Sustainable Development	Riode-Janeiro (2012)
Nagoya Protocol on Genetic Resources	Nagoya (2010)
Convention on Biological Diversity (CBD-CoP-11)	Hyderabad (2012)
UN Climate Change Conference (CoP-20)	Lima (2014)
Paris Climate Conference (CoP-21)	Paris (2015)
Bonn Climate Conference (CoP-23)	Bonn (2017)

Glossary

Bio Fuels produced from dry organic matter or combustible oils from plants such as alcohol from fermented sugar, black liquor from the paper manufacturing process, wood and soyabean oil.

Biogas Gas rich in methane, which is produced by the fermentation of animal dung, human sewage or crop residues in an airtight container.

Biomass Organic material, both above ground and below ground and living and dead, such as trees, crops, grasses and roots.

Carbon credit The concept of Carbon Credit came into existence as a result of increasing awareness of the need for pollution control. Carbon credits are certificates awarded to countries that successfully reduce the emissions that cause global warming.

Carbon Credits are measured in units of Certified Emission Reductions (CERs). Each CER is equivalent to one tonne of CO_2 reduction.

Carbon Footprint The Carbon Footprint is a measurement of all greenhouse gases in terms of tonnes or kg of CO_2 equivalent.

Carbon Market The Kyoto Protocol allows countries that have emissions units to spare, emissions, permitted but not 'used' to sell this excess capacity to countries that are over their targets. This is called the **carbon market**, because carbon dioxide is the most widely produced greenhouse gas and because of this other greenhouse gases will be recorded and counted in terms of their 'carbon dioxide equivalents'.

Green Tax It is a tax with a potentially positive environmental impact. It includes energy tax, transport taxes and taxes on pollution and resources. They are also called **environmental taxes**.

Biomes Biomes are regions of the world with similar climate (weather, temperature), animals and plants.
Examples of Aquatic biomes are : Fresh water, marine, Coral reef and Estuaries.
Examples of Terrestrial biomes are : Tundra, Rainforest, Savanna, Taiga, Alpine and Desert etc.

Environment The environment is the biotic and abiotic surrounding of an organisms or population and includes particulary the factor that have an influence in their survival, development and evolution.

Ecology It is the scientific study of the relations that living organisms have with respect to each other and their natural environment.

Ecosystem An ecosystem is a biological system consiting of all the living organisms or biotic components in a particular area and the non-living or abiotic components with which the organisms interact such as air, mineral soil, water and sunlight.

Biosphere The biosphere is the portion of Earth, in which all known life forms exist. If includes a thin layer of air (atmosphere), water (hydrosphere) and Earth (lithosphere).

Geosphere The atmosphere, hydrosphere, lithosphere and biosphere are together referred to as the Geosphere.

Mitigation The structural and non-structural measures undertaken to limit the adverse impact of natural hazards, environmental degradation and technological hazards.

Sustainable Development Development that meet the needs of the present generation without compromising the ability of future generations to meet their own needs.

Ecological Pyramid An Ecological Pyramid is a graphical representation designed to show the biomass or biomass productivity at each Trophic level in a given ecosystem.

Trophic Level Successive stages of nourishment as represented by the links of the foodchain.

FAQs (Geography)

1. A landmass surrounded by sea on three sides is referred to as......

2. The highest peak in the Eastern Ghat is...

3. How many states are there in India through which the Tropic of Cancer passes?

4. Which group of island is located in the Bay of Bengal?

5. Name the place in Uttar Pradesh through which the Standard Meridian of India passes.

6. Which latitude divides India into two parts?

7. How many plates are found in crust (upper part of the Earth)?

8. Which State is known as the name of Black water?

9. In which state of India does the Sun rise first?

10. Which place does India have in the geographical area of the world?

11. When was the route of Suez canal constructed?

12. The mountain ranges between the Indus and the Sutlej rivers are known as.....

13. Where is the Chilika lake situated?

14. Which is the biggest salt lake of India?

15. Which is the longest river flowing in the Thar desert?

16. In which ocean do the Tapi and Narmada rivers fall?

17. Which is the largest delta in the world?

18. Which landmass is known as the roof of the world?

19. An area drained by a single river is called...

20. Which is the biggest drainage basin of the world?

21. Which river has the largest drainage basin of India?

22. Where the rivers Sutlej, Ravi, Chenab, Beas, Jhelum join the Indus rivers?

23. According to Indus Water Treaty (1960), how much per cent of the total water can be used by the India carried by Indus River System?

24. Where does the Bhagirathi and Alakananda join?

25. The main tributary of the Ganga, Bhagirathi originates from....

26. Where does the Yamuna meet the Ganga?

27. What type of climate is there in India?

28. Which place has the maximum difference in the temperature of day and night in India?

29. El-Nino is....

30. Where does the Arabian sea branch of monsoon and the Bay of Bengal branch monsoon join to each other?

31. The rainfall of winter season in the Northen regions is locally known as....

32. Which type of vegetation is found in the Andaman and Nicobar Islands and Lakshadweep Island?

33. In which state is the Gir National Park situated?

34. When did first census take place in India?

35. When did first complete census take place in India?

36. The red colour of the red soil is due to....

37. Most of the iron in India is found in....

38. Which ocean currents is associated with the El Nino phenomenon?

39. In which periods, the Appalachian mountains were formed?

40. The lapse rate of the atmosphere is....

41. What is the most common salt in the sea water?

42. The cattle kept by the Masai are called

43. The timber of which tree is used for making cricket bats?

44. Ozone layer is found in....

45. 'Ring of Fire' refers to....

46. Willy-Willy is the tropical cyclone occurring in....

47. The atmospheric layer, which reflects radio-waves is known as....

48. Which planet is nearest to the Earth?

49. In which layer of the atmosphere do most weather phenomenon occur?

50. Clear night are colder than cloudy nights because of....

51. Where is the Hindustan Anti-biotics plant located?

52. Where is the Indian railways factory Diesel Component Works (DCW) located?

53. Duncan Pass is located between....

54. Where is Thattekad Bird Sanctuary located?

55. In which state is the Hydel-Power Project Nathpa Jhakri located?

56. Indian's most modern and well planned city Chandigarh was designed by

57. Sahyadri is the traditional name of the....

58. India's permanent research station Dakshin Gangotri is situated in....

59. On which river, the Baglihar Hydro-power Project is located?

60. Which state of India touches the boundaries of the largest number of other states?

61. The term Regur refers to....

62. Which is the junction point of the Eastern and Western Ghats?

63. The biosphere reserve Dehang Debang is located in....

64. The two volcanic islands in the Indian territory are....

65. The Eastern slopes of the Western Ghats have low rainfall because of

66. In which of the following state is the Simplipal bio-reserve located?

67. The wind blowing in the Northern plains in summers is known as....

68. In which of the following states is the Wular lake located?

69. Which is the longest river of the Peninsular India?

70. Name the state of India, where the Brahmaputra river enters first?

71. Uttarakhand, Uttar Pradesh, Bihar, West Bengal and Sikkim have common frontiers with....

72. Which two Peninsular rivers flow through troughs?

73. When was Wild Life Protection Act implemented?

74. In which state is the Corbett National Park located?

75. The latitudinal extent of India is....

76. How much area does India cover of the total geographical area of the world?

77. The length of the Indian coastline is....

78. Which state of India has the longest coastal line?

79. In which state is the Ooty or Udagamandalam located?

80. Which is the highest peak of the Western Ghat?

81. Which plateau lies between the Aravali and Vindyachal hills?

82. The Easternmost longitude of India is....

83. In which country does the Mt Everest lie?

84. In which country the peak of Kanchenjunga located?

85. The part lying between Tista and Dihang rivers is known as....

Answers

1. Peninsula, 2. Mahendragiri,
3. Eight, 4. Andaman and Nicobar Islands,
5. Allahabad, 6. 23½° N,
7. Major Seven and Small Nine, 8. Andaman and Nicobar,
9. Arunachal Pradesh, 10. Seventh, 11. AD 1869,
12. Punjab Himalaya, 13. Odisha, 14. Sambhar Lake,
15. Luni, 16. The Arabian Sea,
17. The delta of Ganga- Brahmaputra (Sundraban),
18. Pamir Granthi, 19. Drainage basin, 20. The Nile river of Egypt, 21. The Ganga river,
22. Mithankot, 23. 20%, 24. Deva Prayag,
25. Gangotri, 26. Allahabad,
27. Monsoon 28. Thar desert,
29. A warm ocean current, 30. Over the Ganga plains, 31. Mahawat,
32. Rain forest, 33. Gujarat,
34. 1872, 35. 1881, 36. Iron,
37. Dharwar Rocks, 38. Humboldt or Peruvian, 39. Paleozoic, 40. 6.5°C for every 1000 m, 41. Sodium Chloride, 42. Zebu, 43. Willow, 44. Stratosphere,
45. Circum- Pacific volcanic belt,
46. Coast of North-West Australia, 47. Ionosphere,
48. Venus, 49. Troposphere, 50. Radiation,
51. Rishikesh, 52. Patiala, 53. South and Little Andaman, 54. Kerala,
55. Himachal Pradesh,
56. Le Corbusier, 57. Western Ghats, 58. Antarctica, 59. Chenab, 60. Uttar Pradesh, 61. Black cotton soil, 62. Nilgiri Hills, 63. Arunachal Pradesh, 64. Narcondam and Barren, 65. their leeward location, 66. Odisha, 67. Loo, 68. Jammu and Kashmir, 69. Godavari, 70. Arunachal Pradesh, 71. Nepal, 72. Narmada and Tapi, 73. 1972, 74. Uttarakhand, 75. 8°4' N to 37°6'N, 76. 2.42%, 77. 7516.6 km, 78. Gujarat, 79. Tamil Nadu, 80. Anaimudi, 81. The Plateau of Malwa, 82. 97°25'E, 83. Nepal, 84. India, 85. Assam Himalayas

INDIAN POLITY

CONSTITUTION OF INDIA

- The Constitution is a set of fundamental principles according to which state organisation is governed. The idea to have a Constitution was given by **MN Roy**.
- The objective of the Constitution is to evolve a certain type of political culture that is based on the values enshrined in the Constitution and guided by the institutions established under the Constitution.
- Certain features of Indian Polity or Constitution can be understood better with a brief review of the Constitutional set-up in the preceding periods. As modern political institutions originated and developed in India mainly during the British rule, the origin and growth of the Indian Constitution has its roots in the British period of Indian history.

The Company Rule (1773-1857)

There are certain events in the British rule that laid down the legal framework for the organisation and administration in British India. These events have greatly influenced our Constitution and polity.

They are explained below in the chronological order

The Regulating Act, 1773

- To regulate and control the affairs of East India Company by British Government.
- It designated the Governor of Bengal as the Governor-General of British territories of India, who has the authority over the Presidencies of Madras, Bombay and Calcutta. The first such Governor-General was lord **Warren Hastings**.

- A Supreme Court was established in Calcutta. It prohibited the servants of the company to engage in any private trade and accept presents or bribes from natives. Sir Elijah Impey was the first Chief Justice.

Pitt's India Act, 1784

- It provided for Board of Control having 6 members (2 from British Cabinet and remaining from Privy Council).
- Set-up to guide and supervise the affairs of the company in India.

Charter Act, 1793

- Salaries for the staff and members of the Board of Control to be paid from Indian revenue.

Charter Act, 1813

- Ended East India Company monopoly of trade and provided ₹ 1 lakh grant for education in India. The Company's monopoly in trade with China and trade in tea was remained inacted.

Charter Act, 1833

- The centralisation of the powers began: the Governor-General of Bengal was to be the **Governor-General of India**. First such Governor was Lord **William Bentick**.

- All legislative, administrative and financial powers were handed over to Governor-General in council. Legislative powers were also given to Governor-General in council and Governments of residencies i.e. Bombay and Madras were deprived of their legislative powers.
- A fourth member in the Governor-General's Council was added as a law member.
- A **Law Commission** under Lord Macaulay was constituted for codification of laws.
- The company was now no more a trading body but had become political and territorial one, acting on behalf of the British Government.

Charter Act, 1853

- A separate Governor for Bengal was to be appointed.
- Legislation was treated for the first time as a separate form of executive functions.
- Recruitment of the Company's employees was to be done through competitive exams (excluding Indians).
- The number of members of the Court of Directors were reduced from 24 to 18 of which 6 were to be nominated by the crown.
- It extended the Company's rule and allowed it to retain the possession of Indian territories for the British Crown without specifying any particular period.
- It introduced for the first time, local representation in the Indian (Central) Legislative Council.

THE CROWN RULE
(1857-1947)

Government of India Act, 1858

- The power was transferred from the company to the British Crown.
- Court of Directors and Board of Control was abolished. The post of Secretary of State was established. A 15 members council was established to assist. Secretary of State was Member of British Cabinet and answerable to British Parliament.

- The Governor-General was made the **Viceroy of India.** Lord Canning became the first Viceroy of India.
- Ended dual system of government.
- Unitary, rigid and centralised administrative structure was created.

Indian Councils Act, 1861

- A fifth member from legal background, was added to the Viceroy's Executive Council. The Viceroy could now also nominate some Indians as non-official members in his council. In 1862, three Indians were nominated to the council.
- It made a beginning of representative institutions by associating Indians with the law making process.
- The Executive Council was now to be called the **Central Legislative Council**.
- **Portfolio System,** which was introduced by Lord Canning in 1859, was given recognition, so that work could be distributed among the members. The Viceroy was given the powers to issue ordinances.

Indian Councils Act, 1892

- Though it was insignificant, but it brought an element of representation for the first time by allowing discussion of budget. This act also introduced the element of election in India.
- Although, the majority of the official members were retained, the non-official members were to be nominated by the Bengal Chamber of Commerce and Provincial Legislative Councils.

Indian Councils Act, 1909
(Morley Minto Reforms)

- Lord Morley, the then Secretary of State of India and Lord Minto, the then Viceroy of India, announced some reforms in the British Parliament.
- The members of the Legislative Council could ask supplementary questions, discuss bills, move resolutions on financial statements and so on.
- The Legislative Councils, both at the centre and in the provinces was expanded.

- It retained official majority in the Central Legislative Council, but allowed the Provincial Legislative Council to have non-official majority.
- **Communal representation** was introduced because Muslims were given a separate electorates and there were reservation of seats on religious grounds.
- **Satyendra Prasad Sinha** became the first Indian to join the Viceroy's Executive Council.

The Government of India Act, 1919 (Montagu-Chelmsford Reforms)

- Samuel Montagu, the Secretary of State for India and Lord Chelmsford, Viceroy of India prepared report to introduce self-governing institutions in India.
- It relaxed the central control over the provinces by separating the central and provincial subjects.
- The powers of the Secretary of State were drastically reduced.
- The number of members of the Indian Council was reduced. Some Executive Council's members were to be Indians.
- Direct elections were introduced for the first time in the country.
- The Central Legislature was to have a **Bicameral** Legislature for the first time.
- **Dyarchy system** was introduced in the provinces. The provincial subjects of administration were to be divided into two categories: reserved and transferred. Transferred subjects were administered by the Governor with the help of ministers responsible to the Legislative Council. Reserved subjects were administered by the Governor with his Executive Council without any responsiblity towards the Legislative Council.

Simon Commission

It was constituted in 1927 to inquire the working of the Act of 1919, under the chairmanship of John Simon. It placed its report in 1930, which was examined by the British Parliament.

Government of India Act, 1935

- **Dyarchy** was abolished in the provinces, but it was introduced at the federal level.
- The division of subjects was made into three lists : Federal, Provincial and Concurrent.
- It provided for the establishment of an **All India Federation** consisting of British provinces and Princely States as unit, but the federation did not come into effect because the Indian Princely States had not joined the federation.
- It introduced **bicameralism** in 6 out of 11 provinces.
- The Federal Legislature had two chambers: The Council of State and Federal Assembly. The Council of State was to be a permanent body with one-third of its members, retiring every 2 years.
- The Governor was given powers to use their discretion in certain matters. The act provided for a federal court.
- It further extended the principle of communal representation by providing separate electorates for depressed classes, women and labour.
- It provided for the establishment of a Reserve Bank of India to control the currency and credit of the country.
- It provided for the establishment of a Federal Public Service Commission and Joint Public Service Commission for two or more provinces.

Cripps Mission, 1942

- **Dominion status** was proposed.
- Constitution of India to be made by an assembly, whose members were to be elected by provincial assemblies and nominated by princely states.
- Any provincial state not prepared to accept the Constitution could negotiate separately with Britain.

Cabinet Mission Plan, 1946

- According to this plan, there was to be a Union of India, consisting of both British India and the Indian states, with control over foreign affairs, defence and communication.

- Provinces were given the powers to legislate all subjects except foreign affairs, defence and communication.
- India was to be divided into three groups of provinces: Group A, Group B and Group C.
- The plan provided that the Union Constitution was to be framed by a **Constituent Assembly**, the members of which were to be elected on a communal basis by the Provincial Legislative Assemblies and the representatives of the states joining the union.

Mountbatten Plan

Lord Mountbatten, the Viceroy of India, put forth the partition plan, known as the Mountbatten Plan. The plan was accepted by the Congress and the Muslim League. Immediate effect was given to the plan by enacting the Indian Independence Act, 1947.

The Indian Independence Act, 1947

- It ended the British Rule in India and declared India as an independent and sovereign state from 15th August, 1947.
- The office of the Secretary of State was abolished. The crown no longer remained the source of authority.
- The act provided for the creation of two Constituent Assemblies for India and Pakistan.
- From 15th August, 1947, India ceased to be a dependency of the British Crown over the Indian states. The Governor-General and Provincial Governors acted as constitutional heads.

- The Central Legislature of India comprising of the Legislative Assembly and the Council of States, ceased to exist on 14th August, 1947 and the Constituent Assembly was to function also as the Central Legislature with complete sovereignty.

Interim Government 1946

- The Interim Government of India, formed on 2nd September, 1946, from the newly elected Constituent Assembly of India, had the task of assisting the transfer of power from British rule to Independent India.

Interim Cabinet

Name of Members	Portfolios Held
Jawaharlal Nehru	External Affairs and Common Wealth Relations
Sardar Vallabhbhai Patel	Home, Information and Broadcasting
Dr Rajendra Prasad	Food and Agriculture
Dr John Mathai	Industries and Supplies
Jagjivan Ram	Labour
Sardar Baldev Singh	Defence
CH Bhabha	Works, Mines and Power
Liaquat Ali Khan	Finance
Abdur Rab Nishtar	Posts and Air
Asaf Ali	Railways and Transport
C Rajagopalachari	Education and Arts
I I Chundrigar	Commerce
Ghaznafar Ali Khan	Health
Joginder Nath Mandal	Law

MAKING OF THE CONSTITUTION OF INDIA

- The Constituent Assembly was formed in November 1946, under the scheme formulated by Cabinet Mission Plan.
- The total strength of the assembly was 389, out of these, 296 were elected to represent the British India and 93 seats to the princely states. Out of

296 members, 292 members were to be elected by the provincial Legislatures while 4 members were to represent the four Chief Commissioner's provinces of Delhi, Ajmer-Merwara, Coorg and British Baluchistan. 93 seats reserved for 1princely states remained unfilled as

they stayed away from the Constituent Assembly.

- The Constituent Assembly, held its first meeting on **9th December, 1946** and reassembled on 14th August, 1947, as the sovereign Constituent Assembly for the dominion of India.
- It took **2 years, 11 months** and **18 days** to finalise the Constitution.
- Objective resolution was moved in the first session of the Constituent Assembly (on 13th December, 1946) by **Pandit Jawaharlal Nehru** which was adopted after considerable deliberation and debate in the assembly on 22nd January, 1947.
- **Dr Sachidanand Sinha** was the first President of the Constituent Assembly, when it met on 9th December, 1946, while later **Dr Rajendra Prasad** and HC Mukherjee were elected as the President and Vice-President of the assembly respectively.
- **Sir BN Rau** was appointed as the constitutional advisor of the Assembly.
- Seats were allotted to each province and each Indian state proportional to their respective population roughly in the ratio of **one to a million.**
- The seats in each province was distributed between Muslims, Sikhs and General in proportion to their respective population.
- Members of each community in the Constituent Assembly were elected by members of that community in the Provincial Assemblies by voting by the method of proportional representation with **single transferable vote**.
- On **26th November, 1949**, the Constitution was declared as passed. The provisions relating to citizenship, elections and provisional Parliament etc were implemented with immediate effect, i.e., from the 26th November, 1949. The rest of the provisions came into force on 26th January, 1950.

Committees of the Constituent Assembly

Constituent Assembly appointed number of committees to deal with different tasks of Constitution making.

Some of them are

Committee Name	Headed by
Union Powers Committee	Pandit Jawaharlal Nehru
Union Constitution Committee	Pandit Jawaharlal Nehru
Provincial Constitution Committee	Sardar Patel
Drafting Committee	Dr BR Ambedkar
Advisory Committee on Fundamental Rights minorities and Tribal and Excluded Areas	Sardar Patel
Rules of Procedure Committee	Dr Rajendra Prasad
State Committees (committee for negotiating with states)	Pandit Jawaharlal Nehru
Steering Committee	Dr Rajendra Prasad

Drafting Committee

The Constituent Assembly appointed a Drafting Committee on 29th August, 1947.

Dr BR Ambedkar, who was the Chairman of the Drafting Committee, submitted first Draft of Constitution of India to the President of the Assembly on 21st February, 1948 and second draft in October 1948.

Enactment of the Constitution

On 26th November, 1949, Constitution was adopted, containing a Preamble and 395 Articles, 22 Parts and 8 Schedules. The Constitution has undergone 100 Amendments in the 66 years since its enactment. The Constitutions, in its current form, consists of a Preamble, 25 Parts, 465 Articles and 12 Schedules.

Enforcement of the Constitution

The Constitution came into force on 26th January, 1950, was specifically chosen as the "date of commencement" of the Constitution because on this day in 1930, the **Poorna Swaraj** day was celebrated [Resolution was passed in Lahore Session (1929) of INC].

Sources of the Constitution of India

- The **Government of India Act, 1935** formed the basis or 'blue print' of the Constitution of India with the features of Federal systems, Office of Governor etc. Besides, the Constitution of India has borrowed certain features from foreign Constitutions as well.
- **British Constitution** First past the Post System, Parliamentary form of Government, the idea of the rule of law, law making procedure, office of the CAG, single citizenship, Bicameralism.
- **United States Constitution** Charter of Fundamental Rights, Power of Judicial Review and Independence of Judiciary, Written Constitution, Preamble, post of Vice-President.
- **Irish Constitution** Directive Principles of State Policy (Ireland borrowed it from Spain), Methods of Election of the President, Nomination of Members in the Rajya Sabha by the President.
- **Canadian Constitution** A Quasi-Federal form of Government (a federal system with a strong Central Government). The idea of residual powers, appointment of State Governors by centre and Advisory Jurisdiction of the Supreme Court.
- **Former USSR** Fundamental Duties and Five Year Planning.
- **Australian Constitution** Concurrent List, Provision regarding Trade, Commerce and Intercourse, Languages of the Preamble, Joint sitting in the Parliament.
- **Weimar Constitutions of Germany** Suspension of Fundamental Rights during the emergency.
- **South African Constitution** Procedure of Constitutional Amendment.
- **Constitution of France** Republican of liberty, equality and fraternity.
- **Japanese Constitution** Procedure estasblished by law.

SALIENT FEATURES OF THE CONSTITUTION

The salient features of the Constitution, as it stands today, are following

Lengthiest Written Constitution

- The Indian Constitution is the lengthiest in the world. Originally the Constitution had **395 Articles**, **8 Schedules** and **22 Parts**.

Blend of Rigidity and Flexibility

- The procedure of amendment of the Indian Constitution is **partly flexible** and **partly rigid**. Some provisions can be amended easily and some provisions can only be amended by passage in both Union Parliament and half of the State Legislatures.

Parliamentary Government

- India has a **parliamentary system** of government both, at the centre and in the states. The President is the head of the Union of India and the Governors are head of the states. But they act on the advice of the Council of Ministers. They have nominal powers.

Independent Judiciary

- There is a single, integrated and independent judiciary in India.
- The Supreme Court is the highest court of the land. Both Supreme Court and High Courts have been given extensive powers to interpret the Constitution and law under various provisions of the Constitution of India.

Federal System with Unitary Features

- Our Constitution contains federal features of government like division of powers, written Constitution, independent judiciary and bicameralism but a large number of unitary features like a strong centre, single citizenship, flexibility of Constitution, integrated judiciary emergency provisions etc.

Secular State

- The Indian Constitution stands for a secular state i.e. all religions in our country have the same right and support from the state, it does not uphold any particular religion as the official religion of the Indian state.

Universal Adult Franchise

- Every Indian citizen (above 18 years) has a right to vote in the elections without any discrimination of caste, sex, religion etc.

Emergency Provisions

- Indian Constitution has special provisions to meet any extraordinary situation or emergency. During emergency the Central Government becomes powerful and state comes under the total control of it.
- During emergency our federal system becomes unitary without any amendment of the Constitution.

PARTS OF THE CONSTITUTION

There are 25 parts in our Constitution, which can be described as below

■ Part-I (Articles 1-4)	Deals with territory of India, formation of new states, alterations of names and areas of existing states.
■ Part-II (Articles 5-11)	Deals with various provisions related to citizenship.
■ Part-III (Articles 12-35)	Deals with Fundamental Rights of Indian citizens.
■ Part-IV (Articles 36-51)	Deals with Directive Principles of State Policy.
■ Part-IV A (Article 51A)	Added by 42nd Amendment in 1976. Contains the Fundamental Duties of the citizens.
■ Part-V (Articles 52-151)	Deals with Government at the Union Level (Duties and Functions of Prime Minister, Minister, President, Vice-President, Attorney General, Parliament-Lok Sabha and Rajya Sabha, Comptroller and Auditor-General).
■ Part-VI (Articles 152-237)	Deals with Government at State Level (Article-152 exempts Jammu and Kashmir from the category of ordinary states.) (Duties and Functions of Chief Minister and his Ministers, Governor, State Legislature, High Court, Advocate General of the State).
■ Part-VII (Article 238)	Deals with states in part B, was repealed in 1956 by the 7th Amendment.
■ Part-VIII (Articles 239-241)	Deals with Union Territories.
■ Part-IX (Articles 243-2430) and Part-IX A (Articles 243P-243 ZG)	Part IX was added by 73rd Amendment in 1992. Contains a new schedule 'Schedule Eleven'. It contains 29 subjects related to Panchayati Raj. Part IX A was added by 74th Amendment in 1992. Contains a new schedule 'Schedule Twelve'. It contains 18 subjects related to muncipalities.
■ Part- IX B (243-ZH to 243-ZT)	Deals with the Cooperative Societies.
■ Part-X (Articles 244, 244A)	Deals with Scheduled and Tribal Areas.
■ Part-XI (Articles 245-263)	Deals with relation between Union and States.
■ Part-XII (Articles 264-300A)	Deals with distribution of Revenue between Union and States, Appointment of Finance Commission (Article 280), Contracts liabilities etc.
■ Part-XIII (Articles 301-307)	Relates to Trade, Commerce and Intercourse within the Territory of India.
■ Part-XIV (Articles 308-323)	Deals with Civil Services and Public Service Commission.
■ Part-XIV A (Articles 323A, 323B)	Deals with tribunals.
■ Part-XV (Articles 324-329A)	Deals with Elections (including Election Commission).
■ Part-XVI (Articles 330-342)	Deals with special provisions for Scheduled Castes and Scheduled Tribes and Anglo-Indian Representation.
■ Part-XVII (Articles 343-351)	Relates to Official Language.

▪ Part-XVIII(Articles 352-360)	Deals with Emergency Provisions.
▪ Part-XIX (Articles 361-367)	Miscellaneous Provisions.
▪ Part-XX (Article 368)	Deals with Amendment of Constitution.
▪ Part-XXI (Articles 369-392)	Contains Temporary, Transitional and Special Provisions.
▪ Part-XXII (Articles 393-395)	Concerns the short title, commencement, authorative text in Hindi and repeals of the Constitution.

Schedules

The Constitution of India at the time of adoption had only 8 schedules to which 4 more were added during the succeeding 66 years.

▪ First Schedule	State and UTs.
▪ Second Schedule	Salaries and Emoluments of President, Governor, Chief Judges and Auditor General.
▪ Third Schedule	Forms of Oath and Affirmations of Members of Legislatures, Ministers and Judges.
▪ Fourth Schedule	Allocation of Seats in the Rajya Sabha.
▪ Fifth Schedule	Administration and control of Scheduled Areas and Scheduled Tribes.
▪ Sixth Schedule	Administration of Tribal Areas in the state of Assam, Meghalaya, Tripura and Mizoram.
▪ Seventh Schedule	Distribution of Power between the Union and the State Government (Union List, State List and Concurrent List).
▪ Eighth Schedule	Languages.
▪ Ninth Schedule	Validation of certain Acts and Regulations.
▪ Tenth Schedule	Anti-Defection Law.
▪ Eleventh Schedule	Panchayats. (Rural Local Government)
▪ Twelfth Schedule	Municipalities (Urban Local Government)

EVOLUTION OF STATES AND UNION TERRITORIES

Dhar Commission

The Constituent Assembly appointed the SK Dhar Commission in June 1948, to study the feasibility of the reorganisation of the states on linguistic basis. It was felt that such reorganisation would fuel regional sentiments and might threaten national integration which was precarious in the background of Partition. Thus, the Dhar Commission categorically rejected the basis of linguistic formation of states.

JVP Committee

- The Congress in its Jaipur Session in 1948, appointed a three member committee to consider the recommendation of the Dhar Commission. Its members were Jawaharlal Nehru, Vallabhbhai Patel and Pattabhi Sitaramayya.
- The Committee rejected language as the basis for the reorganisation despite popular support for it.

First Linguistic State

- In October 1953, the Government of India was forced to create the First Linguistic State, known as Andhra Pradesh, by separating the Telugu speaking area from Madras Presidency (after the death of Sriramulu, a Congress person).
- Kurnool was the first capital of the Andhra State with High Court at Guntur (Presently, Hyderabad is the capital and also the High Court seat).

Fazl Ali Commission

After the creation of Andhra State, demand for creation of states on linguistic basis intensified and Fazl Ali Commission was constituted in December, 1953, which was also known as States Reorganisation Commission accepted language as the basis of reorganisations of state but rejected the theory of 'one-language-one state'. By the States Reorganisation Act (1956) and the 7th Constitutional Amendment Act, the distinction between states was abolished.

Some of them were merged with adjacent state and some other were designated as Union Territories. As a result 14 States and 6 Union Territories were created on 1st November, 1956.

Reorganisation of States

- In **1956**, there were 14 states and 6 union territories. Andhra Pradesh was created in **1953** and Kerala in **1956**.
- In **1956**, Karnataka was created.
- In **1960**, Bombay was bifurcated into Gujarat and Maharashtra.
- In **1963**, Nagaland was created as separate state.
- In **1966**, Haryana was carved out of Punjab and Chandigarh became a Union Territory.
- In **1970**, the Union Territory of Himachal Pradesh was elevated to the status of a state.
- In **1971**, Manipur, Tripura and Meghalaya were granted statehood. In **1974**, Sikkim became an associate state

of the Indian Union. By the 36th Constitutional Amendment Act (1975), Sikkim became a full fledged State of the Indian Union.

- In **1986**, Mizoram and Arunachal Pradesh came into being.
- In **1987**, Goa came into existence. In **2000**, three more new states : Chhattisgarh, Uttarakhand and Jharkhand were created.
- On **2nd June, 2014**, Telengana state came into existence, after reorganisation of Andhra Pradesh.

Union Territories

- National Capital Territory of Delhi and Puducherry are headed by the Lieutenant Governor.
- Daman and Diu, Dadra and Nagar Haveli have a common administrator. Lakshadweep is also governed by an administrator.
- Chandigarh and Andaman and Nicobar Islands are governed by a Chief Commissioner. Delhi and Puducherry have Legislative Assemblies. There are total seven Union Territories-Delhi, Puducherry, Daman and Diu, Dadra and Nagra Haveli, Chandigarh, Lakshadweep, Andaman and Nicobar Islands.
- By the **69th Constitutional Amendment Act 1991**, Delhi was given the status of National Capital Territory of India. It could legislate in certain matters except land, Police and law and order.

THE PREAMBLE

- The **Preamble** means Introduction or Preface of the Constitution or essence of the Constitution. NA Palkivala, an eminent jurist and Constitutional expert, called the Preamble as the **identity** card of the Constitution. India followed the USA to include Preamble in the Constitution. The Preamble of the Indian Constitution is based on the **Objectives**

Resolution drafted and moved by Pandit Nehru and adopted by the Constituent Assembly.
- The idea of Justice, Social, Economic and Political have been taken from the Russian Revolution (1917).
- The idea of Liberty, Equality, and Fraternity have been taken from the French Revolution (1789-1799).

Preamble of India

We, the People of India, having solemnly resolved to constitute India into a *Sovereign, Socialist, Secular, Democratic, Republic* and secure to all its citizens.

- **Justice,** Social, Economic and Political;
- **Liberty** of thought, expression, belief, faith and worship;
- **Equality** of status and of opportunity; and to promote among them all;
- **Fraternity** assuring the dignity of the individual and the **unity and integrity** of the Nation;
- **In our Constituent Assembly** on this twenty-sixth day of November, 1949, do hereby **Adopt, Enact and Give to Ourselves this Constitution.**

Significance of the Preamble

- The Preamble embodies the basic philosophy and fundamental values like political, moral and religious on which the Constitution is based.

- It contains the grand and noble vision of the Constituent Assembly.
- It reflects the dreams and aspirations of the founding fathers of the Constitution. It provides a key to the understanding and interpretation of the Constitution.

Amendability of the Preamble

- Whether, the Preamble can be amended under Article 368 or not, this question arose for the first time in **Keshavananda Bharati Case** (1973). In this case Supreme Court held that Preamble is the part of the Constitution and can be amended, subject to the condition that no amendment is done to the basic features of the Constitution.
- The Preamble has been amended only once so far, in 1976, by 42nd Constitutional Amendment Act, which added three new words **Socialist, Secular** and **Integrity.** This amendment was held to be valid.

UNION AND ITS TERRITORY

- **Articles 1-4** under Part-I of the Constitution deals with the Union and its Territories.
- Article 1 describes India, that is Bharat as a Union of States.
- According to **Article 1**, the Territory of India can be classified into three categories
  1. Territories of the States.
  2. Union Territories.
  3. Territories that may be acquired by the Government of India at any time.
- The names of the States and UTs and their territorial extent are mentioned in the First Schedule of the Constitution.
- At present, there are **29 States** and **7 Union Territories**.
- The 'Territory of India' is a wider expression than the 'Union of India' because the latter includes only states while the former includes not only states, but also UTs and territories that may be acquired by the Government of India at any future time.
- **Article 2** empowers the Parliament to admit into the Union of India, or establish, new states on such terms and conditions as it thinks fit.

- **Article 3** authorises the Parliament to
  (a) form a new state by separation from any state or by uniting two or more states or parts of states or by uniting any territory to a part of any state;
  (b) increase the area of any state;
  (c) diminish the area of any state;
  (d) alter the boundaries of any state;
  (e) alter the name of any state.
- A Bill seeking to create a new state or alter boundaries of existing states can be introduced in either House of the Parliament, only on the recommendation of the President.
- President refers the State Reorganisation Bill to the State Legislature concerned for expressing its opinion, within a specified period.
- The State Reorganisation Bill requires simple majority in both Houses of the Parliament.
- Parliament is not bound to accept or act upon the views of the State Legislature on a State Reorganisation Bill.
- **Article 4** provides that Bills under Articles 2 and 3 are not to be considered as Constitutional Amendment Bills.

CITIZENSHIP

- The Indian Constitution deals with the citizenship from **Articles 5-11** under Part II.
- Articles 5 to 8 deal that how a person became citizen of India, after Comencement of Constitution.

Acquisition of Citizenship

A citizen is a person, who enjoys full membership of the country in which he lives. Indian Constitution provides a single and uniform citizenship for the entire country. The Citizenship Act of 1955 provides for 5 ways of acquiring citizenship as described below

By Birth

Every person born in India on or after 26th January, 1950, shall be a citizen of India by birth, irrespective of the nationality of his parents.

- The children of foreign diplomats posted in India and enemy aliens cannot acquire Indian Citizenship.

By Descent

Persons born outside India on or after 26th January, 1950, but before 10th December, 1992 are citizens of India by descent if their father was a citizen of India at the time of their birth.

By Registration

The Central Government may, on an application, register as a citizen of India any person, if he belongs to any of the following categories

- A person of Indian origin, residing in India for 7 years.
- A person of Indian origin, who is ordinarily resident in any country or place outside undivided India.
- A person, who is married to citizens of India and resident of India for 7 years.
- Minor children of persons, who are citizen of India.
- A person of full age and capacity, whose parents are registered as citizen of India.

By Naturalisation

It can be acquired by a foreigner, who has resided in India for 12 years.

By Incorporation of Territory (Foreign Territory)

If any new territory becomes a part of India, the Government of India specifies the people of that territory to be citizens of India.

Loss of Citizenship

The Citizenship Act, 1955, also provides three modes of losing citizenship

1. By Renunciation

If a person gives up his Indian citizenship after acquiring the citizenship of another country.

2. By Termination

When an Indian citizen voluntarily acquires the citizenship of another country, his Indian citizenship automatically terminates.

3. By Deprivation

Deprivation of citizenship by the Government of India on the basis of fraud, false representation and concealment of material, fact or being disloyal to the Constitution.

Overseas Citizens of India (OCI)

- Citizenship Act has been amended in 2003, by which people of Indian origin, except in Pakistan and Bangladesh, will become eligible to be registered as the **Overseas Citizens of India** (OCI).
- OCIs are **entitled** to some benefits like multiple entry, multipurpose life long visas, they can live and work in India or their country of naturalisation.
- They are **not entitled** to hold constitutional posts and employment in the government is offices and they **can't vote**.
- All Persons of Indian Origin (PIO) cardholders are deemed to be Overseas Citizens of India(OCI) cardholders with effect from 9th January, 2015.

FUNDAMENTAL RIGHTS

- Rights are claims of social life and they help individuals to develop their personality. Some of the Fundamental Rights provide protection only against the state action and do not safeguard against the action of private individuals.
- The Fundamental Rights are guaranteed and protected by the Constitution to all persons without any discrimination.
- The Fundamental Rights have been described in **Articles 12-35**, Part III of Indian Constitution.
- Originally, Fundamental Rights were seven in number *viz*
  - Right to Equality.
  - Right to Freedom.
  - Right against Exploitation.
  - Right to Freedom of Religion.
  - Cultural and Educational Rights.
  - Right to Property.
  - Right to Constitutional Remedies.

Right to Property

The Right to Property (Article 31) was deleted from the list of Fundamental Rights by the 44th Amendment Act, 1978. It is made a legal right under Article-300A in Part XII of the Constitution.

- **Article 13** Laws inconsistent with or in derogation of the Fundamental Rights that are
  - All laws in force in the territory of India immediately before the commencement of the Constitution, and they are inconsistent with the provisions of this part, up to an extent such inconsistency, be void.
  - The state shall not make any law, which takes away or abridges the rights conferred by this part.
  - It provides for the doctrine of judicial review.
  - Constitutional Ammendment is not a law and hence cannot be challenged.

Right to Equality (Article 14-18)

Article 14 *Equality before law and equal protection of laws.* It says that the state shall not deny to any person equality before the law or equal protection of the laws within the territory of India. This provision confers rights to all persons whether citizens or foreigners. The concept of equality before law is an element of the concept of 'Rule of law'- propounded by AV Dicey, the British Jurist.

The rule of equality before law is not absolute. *Some of the exceptions are*

- The President or the Governor is not answerable to any court for the exercise and performance of the powers and duties of his office.
- No criminal proceedings shall be instituted or continued against the President or the Governor in any court during his term of office.
- No process for the arrest or imprisonment of the President or the Governor shall be issued from any court during his term of office.
- No civil proceedings against the President or the Governor shall be instituted during his term of office in any court in respect of any act done by him in his personal capacity, whether before or after he entered upon his office, until the expiration of 2 months next after notice delivered to him.

Article 15 *Prohibition of discrimination on certain grounds.* It says that the state shall not discriminate against any citizen on grounds of religion, race, caste, sex or place of birth. This provision prohibits discrimination both by state and private individuals.

There are three exceptions to this general rule of non-discriminations

- Any special provision for women and children.
- Advancement of any socially and educationally backward classes of citizens.
- Special provisions for any socially and educationally backward classes or Scheduled Castes and the Scheduled Tribes. Regarding their admission to educational institutions, including private educational institutions.

Article 16 *Equality of opportunity in public employment.* It provides equality of opportunity for all citizens in matters of employment or appointment to any office under the state.

- It does not bound state for prescribing the necessary qualification and recruitment tests for government services, certain posts may be reserved for the resident of a particular state.

- It also provides for the reservation of seats in promotion for the Scheduled Castes and Scheduled Tribes.

Article 17 *Abolition of untouchability.* It abolishes untouchability and forbids its practice in any form.

- The term 'untouchability' has not been defined either in the Constitution or in the Act (Protection of Civil Rights Act, 1955)

Article 18 *Abolition of titles.* It abolishes titles and makes four provisions in that regard.

1. It prohibits the state from conferring any title (except a military or academic distinction) on any body, whether a citizen or a foreigner.

2. It prohibits a citizen of India from accepting any title from any foreign state.

3. A foreigner holding any office of profit or trust under the state, cannot accept any title from any foreign state without the consent of the President.

4. No citizen or foreigner holding any office of profit or trust under the state is to accept any present, emolument or office from or under any foreign state without the consent of the President.

Right to Freedom
(Articles 19-22)

Article 19 It guarantees to all citizens the six rights. *These are*

1. Right to freedom of speech and expression.

2. Right to assemble peacefully and without arms.

3. Right to form associations or unions or co-operatives.

4. Right to move freely throughout the territory of India.

5. Right to reside and settle in any part of the territory of India.

6. Right to practice any profession or to carry on any occupation, trade or business.

- Originally, Article 19 contained seven rights. But, the right to acquire, hold and dispose of property was deleted by the 44th Amendment Act of 1978.

- These 6 rights are protected against only state action and not private individuals.

Article 20 *Protection in respect of conviction for offences.* It grants protection against arbitrary and excessive punishment to an accused person, whether citizen or foreigner or legal person like a company or a corporation. *It contains three provisions in that direction.*

1. **No Ex-Post-Facto Law** No person shall be (i) convicted of any offence except for violation of a law in force at the time of the commission of the act, (ii) nor be subjected to a penalty greater than that prescribed by the law in force at the time of the commission of the Act.

2. **No Double Jeopardy** No person shall be prosecuted and punished for the same offence more than once.

3. **No Self-Incrimination** No person accused of any offence shall be compelled to be a witness against himself.

Article 21 *Protection of life and personal liberty.* It declares that no person shall be deprived of his life or personal liberty except according to procedure established by law. This right is available to both citizens and non-citizens.

The Supreme Court has expanded the scope of Right to Life in its various judgments and *declared the following rights as part of Article 21.*

(a) Right to live with human dignity.

(b) Right to decent environment including pollution free water and air and protection against hazardous industries.

(c) Right to livelihood.

(d) Right to privacy.

(e) Right to shelter.

(f) Right to health.

(g) Right to free education upto 14 years of age.

(h) Right to free legal aid.

(i) Right against solitary confinement.

(j) Right to speedy trial.

(k) Right against handcuffing.

(l) Right against inhuman treatment.

(m) Right against delayed execution.

(n) Right to travel abroad.

(o) Right against bonded labour

(p) Right against custodial harassment.

(q) Right to emergency medical aid

(r) Right to timely medical treatment in government hospital.

(s) Right not to be driven out of a state.

(t) Right to fair trial.

(u) Right of prisoner to have necessities of life.

(v) Right of women to be treated with decency and dignity.

(w) Right against public hanging.

(x) Right to hearing.

(y) Right to information.

(z) Right to reputation.

Right to Education

Article 21A declares that the state shall provide free and compulsory education to all children of the age of **6 to 14 years** in such a manner as the state may determine. Thus, this provision makes only elementary education a Fundamental Right and not higher or professional education.

Article 22 *Protection against arrest and detention*

- No person, who is arrested shall be detained in custody without being informed of the grounds for such arrest nor shall he be denied the right to consult, and to be defended by a legal practioner of his choice.

- Every person, who is arrested and detained in custody is to be produced before the nearest Magistrate within a period of 24 hours of arrest excluding the time necessary for the journey from the place of arrest to the court of the Magistrate and such person cannot be detained in custody beyond that period without the authority of a Magistrate.

- There are some exception against these safeguards.

- It is not available to an enemy alien and a person arrested or detained under a law providing for preventive detention (detention of a person without trial).

- The detention of a perosn cannot exceed three months under Preventive Detention Law.

Right Against Exploitation (Articles 23-24)

Article 23 *Prohibition of traffic in human beings and forced labour.* It prohibits traffic in human beings, 'Begar' (forced labour) and other similar forms of forced labour.

Article 24 It prohibits the employment of children below the age of 14 years in any factory, mine or other hazardous activities like construction work or railway. But, it does not prohibit their employment in any harmless or innocent work.

- The Child Labours (Prohibition and Regulation) Act, 1986, is the most important law in this direction.

Mandal Commission

- In 1979, the Morarji Desai Government appointed the Backward Classes Commission under the Chairmanship of BP Mandal, a Member of Parliament, to investigate the conditions of the socially and educationally backward classes and suggest measures for their advancement. The commission submitted its report in 1980 and recommended 27%, jobs reservation for Other Backward Classes (OBCs).

- The advanced sections among the OBCs (the Creamy Layer) should be excluded from the list of beneficiaries of reservation.

Right to Freedom of Religion (Articles 25-28)

Article 25 *Freedom of conscience and right to freely profess, practice and propagate religion.* It says that all persons are equally entitled to freedom of conscience and the right to freely profess, practice and propagate religion.

The state is empowered by law to regulate or restrict any economic, financial, political or other secular activity which may be associated with religious practice.

Article 26 *Freedom to Manage Religious Affairs* Every religious denomination or any of its section shall have the following rights

(a) Right to establish and maintain institutions for religious and charitable purposes;

(b) Right to manage its own affairs in matters of religion;

(c) Right to acquire and own movable and immovable property; and

(d) Right to administer such property in accordance with law.

Article 27 *Freedom from taxation for promotion of a religion*. It lays down that no person shall be compelled to pay any taxes for the promotion or maintenance of any particular religion or religious denomination.

Article 28, *Freedom from attending religious instruction*. No religious instruction shall be provided in any educational institution wholly maintained out of state funds. However, this provision shall not apply to an educational institution administered by the state, but established under any endowment or trust, requiring imparting of religious instruction in such institution.

Fundamental Rights to Citizens and Foreigners

Fundamental Rights available only to citizens and not to foreigners	Fundamental Rights available to both citizens and foreigners (except enemy aliens)
1. Prohibition of discrimination on grounds of religion, race, sex or place of birth (Article 15).	Equality before law and equal protection of laws (Article 14).
2. Equality of opportunity in matters of public employment (Article 16).	Protection in respect of conviction for offences (Article 20).
3. Protection of six rights regarding freedom of (i) speech and expression, (ii) assembly, (iii) association, (iv) movement, (v) residence, and (vi) profession (Article 19).	Protection of life and personal liberty (Article 21).
4. Protection of language, script and culture of minorities (Article 29).	Right to elementary education (Article 21 A).
5. Right of minorities to establish and administer educational institutions (Article 30).	Protection against arrest and detention in certain cases (Article 22).
	Prohibition of traffic of human beings and forced labour (Article 23)
	Prohibition of employment of children in factories etc. (Article 24)
	Freedom of conscience and free profession, practice and propagation of religion (Article 25)
	Freedom to manage religious affairs (Article 26)
	Freedom from payment of taxes for promotion of any religion (Article 27)
	Freedom from attending religious instruction or worship in certain educational institutions (Article 28)

Cultural and Educational Rights (Articles 29-30)

Article 29 *Protection of interests of minorities.* It provides that any section of the citizens residing in any part of India having a distinct language, script or culture of its own, shall have the right to conserve the same.

Further, no citizen shall be denied admission into any educational institution maintained by the state or receiving aid out of state funds on grounds only of religion, race, caste or language.

Article 30 *Right of Minorities to Establish and Administer Educational Institutions :* Grants the following rights to minorities, whether religious or linguistic

(a) All minorities shall have the right to establish and administer educational institutions of their choice.

(b) In granting aid, the state shall not discriminate against any educational institution managed by a minority. The compensation amount fixed by the state for the compulsory acqusition of a minority educational institution shall not restrict or abrogate the right guaranteed to them. This provision was added by 44th Amendment Act of 1978 to protect the right of minorities in this regard. The act deleted the Right to Property as a Fundamental Right (Article 31).

- The right under Article 30 also includes the right of a minority to impart education to its children in its own language.

Right to Constitutional Remedies (Article 32)

- **Dr BR Ambedkar** said, Article 32 is the heart and soul of the Constitution.
- Supreme Court ruled that **Article 32** is a **basic feature** of the Constitution. Hence, it cannot be abridged or taken away even by way of an amendment to the Constitution. Under Article 32, Supreme Court and Article 226, High Court can issue writs of various forms;

- **Habeas Corpus** It is a Latin term which literally means, 'to have the body of,'. It is an order issued by the court to a person who has detained another person, to produce the body of the latter before it. The court then examines the cause and legality of detention. It would set the detained person free, if the detention is found to be illegal.

- **Mandamus** It literally means 'we command'. It is a command issued by the court to a public official asking him to perform his official duties that he has failed or refused to perform. It can also be issued against any public body, a corporation, an inferior court, a tribunal or government for the same purpose.

- **Quo-warranto** In the literal sense, it means "by what authority or warrant". It is issued to enquire into the legality of claim of a person to a public office. Hence, it prevents illegal usurpation of public office by a person.

- **Prohibition** Literally means 'to forbid'. It is issued by a higher court to a lower court or tribunal to prevent the latter from exceeding its jurisdiction or usurping a jurisdiction that, it does not possess. The writ can be issued only in case of a substantive public office of a permanent character created by a statute or by the Constitution. It cannot be issued in cases of ministerial office or private office.

Thus, unlike *mandamus* that directs activity, the prohibition directs inactivity. The writ of prohibition can be issued only against judicial and Quasi-Judicial authorities. It is not available against Administrative Authorities, Legislative Bodies and private individuals or bodies.

- **Certiorari** In the literal sense, it means, 'to be certified' or 'to be informed'. It is issued by a higher court to a lower court or tribunal either to transfer a case pending with the latter to itself or to squash the order of the latter in a case. It is issued on the grounds of excess of jurisdiction or lack of jurisdiction or error of law. Thus, unlike prohibition, which is only preventive, *certiorari* is both preventive as well as curative.

Limitations on the Enforcement of Fundamental Rights

- Parliament has the power to modify the application of the Fundamental Rights to the members of the **Armed Forces, Police Forces or Intelligence Organisations** so as to ensure proper discharge of their duties and maintenance of discipline among them (Article 33).
- Certain Fundamental Rights guaranteed by the Constitution may remain suspended, while a Proclamation of Emergency is made by the President under Article 352.
- **Article 34** Restriction on Rights conferred by this Part while martial law is in force in any area.
- **Article 35** Legislation, to give effect to the provisions of this part.

DIRECTIVE PRINCIPLES OF STATE POLICY

- The Directive Principles of State Policy are enumerated in Part IV of the Constitution from **Articles 36 to 51**.
- Dr BR Ambedkar, described these principles as **novel feature** of the Constitution.
- The DPSP alongwith Fundamental Rights contain the **philosophy** of the Constitution and is the **soul** of the Constitution.

Features

- These are constitutional instructions to the state in legislative, executive and administrative matters.
- It resembles the 'Instrument of Instructions' enumerated in the Government of India Act of 1935.
- They constitutes the comprehensive economic, social and political programme for a modern state.
- They promote social and economic democracy. They embody the concept of **a welfare state**'.
- These are fundamental in the governance of the country.
- They are non-justiciable.
- They apply to both Union and State Governments and all other authorities coming under the definition of 'State'.

Classification

- The Constitution does not contain any classification of directive principles. However, on the basis of their content and direction, they can be classified into three broad categories, *viz socialistic, Gandhian and liberal-intellectual*.

Socialistic Principles

These principles reflect the ideology of socialism. They lay down the framework of a democratic socialist state, aim at providing social and economic justice and set the path towards welfare state.

- **Article 38** To promote the welfare of the people by securing a social order permeated by justice-social, economic and political and to minimise inequalities in income, status, facilities and opportunities.
- **Article 39** To secure (a) the right to adequate means of livelihood for all citizens; (b) the equitable distribution of material resources of the community for the common good; (c) prevention of concentration of wealth and means of production; (d) equal pay for equal work for men and women; (e) preservation of the health and strength of workers and children against forcible abuse; and (f) opportunities for healthy development of children.
- **Article 39 (A)** To promote equal justice and to provide free legal aid to the poor.
- **Article 41** To secure the right to work, education and to public assistance in cases of unemployment, old age, sickness and disablement.
- **Article 42** To make provision for just and humane conditions for work and maternity relief.

- **Article 43** To secure a living wage, a decent standard of life and social and cultural opportunities for all workers.
- **Article 43 (A)** To take steps to secure the participation of workers in the management of industries.
- **Article 47** To raise the level of nutrition and the standard of living of people and to improve public health.

Gandhian Principles

These principles are based on Gandhian ideology. They represent the programme of reconstruction enunciated by Gandhi during the National Movement. In order to fulfil the dreams of Gandhi, some of his ideas were included as Directive Principles.

- **Article 40** To organise Village Panchayat to function as units of self government.
- **Article 43** To promote cottage industries on an individual or co-operation basis in rural areas.
- **Article 46** To promote the educational and economic interests of SCs, STs and other weaker sections of the society and to protect them from social injustice and exploitation.
- **Article 47** To prohibit the consumption of intoxicating drinks and drugs which are injurious to health.
- **Article 48** To prohibit the slaughter of cows, calves and other milch and draught cattle and to improve their breeds.

Liberal-Intellectual Principles

The principles included in this category represent the ideology of liberalism.

- **Article 44** To secure for all citizens a **uniform civil code** throughout the country.
- **Article 45** To provide early childhood care and education for all children until they complete the age of 6 years.
- **Article 48** To organise agriculture and animal husbandry on modern and scientific lines.
- **Article 48 (A)** To protect and improve the environment and to safeguard forests and wildlife.
- **Article 49** To protect objects, places and monuments of historic interest and national importance.
- **Article 50** To separate the judiciary from the executive in the public services of the state.
- **Article 51** To promote international peace and security and to maintain just and honourable relations between nations; to foster respect for international law and treaty obligations and to encourage settlement of international disputes by arbitration.

Distinction between Fundamental Rights and Directive Principles

Fundamental Rights	Directive Principles
These are negative as they prohibit the state from doing certain things.	These are positive as they require the state to do certain things.
These are **justiciable**, i.e. they are legally enforceable by the courts in case of their violation.	These are **non-justiciable**, i.e. they are not legally enforceable by the courts for their violation.
They aim at establishing political democracy in the country.	They aim at establishing social and economic democracy in the country.
These have legal sanctions.	These have moral and political sanctions.
They promote the **welfare of the individual**. Hence, they are personal and individualistic.	They promote the **welfare of the community**. Hence, they are societarian and socialistic.
The courts are bound to declare a law **violative** of any of the Fundamental Rights as unconstitutional and invalid.	The courts cannot declare a law **violative** of any of the Directive Principles as unconstitutional and invalid. However, they can uphold the validity of a law on the ground that it was enacted to give effect to a directive.

New Directive Principles

Article 39A To provide free legal aid to the poor (42nd Amendment Act, 1976).

Article 39(f) To secure opportunities for healthy development of children (42nd Amendment Act, 1976).

Article 43A To take steps to secure the participation of workers in the management of industries. (42nd Amendment Act, 1976).

Article 43 B To promote professionally run co-operative societies added by the 97th Constitutional Amendment Act, 2011.

Article 48 A To protect and improve the environment and to safeguard forests and wild life. (42nd Amendment Act, 1976).

Article 38(2) It added one more Directive Principle, which requires the state to minimise inequalities in income status, facilities and opportunities under Article 38. (44th Amendment Act, 1978)

Directives Outside Part IV

- Apart from the directives included in part IV, there are some other Directives contained in other parts of the Constitution.

- Claims of members of Scheduled Castes and Scheuled Tribes will be taken into consideration, consistent with the maintenance of efficiency in administration, in the appointment to Public Services. (Article 335).

- It is the duty of every state and local authority to provide adequate facilities for instruction in the mother tongue at the primary stage of education to children belonging to minority classes (Article 350 A).

- It shall be the duty of the Union to promote Hindi language amongst the people of India, so that it may serve as a medium of expression for all the elements of the composite culture of India (Article 351).

FUNDAMENTAL DUTIES

- The Fundamental Duties in the Constitution serve as a reminder to the citizens that while enjoying their rights, they should also be conscious of their duties towards the country. We have borrowed Fundamental Duties from the Constitution of former Soviet Union.

- Originally, Constitution did not contain Fundamental Duties. In 1976, the FDs of citizens were added by **42nd Constitutional Amendment Act** (1976) on the recommendations of Swaran Singh Committee. Originally, ten FDs were added. In 2002, one more duty was added. Thus, today there are 11 Fundamental Duties.

List of Fundamental Duties

According to **Article 51 A**, it shall be the duty of every citizen of India

(a) to abide by the Constitution and respect its ideals and institutions, the National Flag and the National Anthem;

(b) to cherish and follow the noble ideals that inspired the national struggle for freedom;

(c) to uphold and protect the sovereignty, unity and integrity of India;

(d) to promote harmony and the spirit of common brotherhood amongst all the people of India transcending religious, linguistic and regional or sectional diversities and to renounce practices derogatory to the dignity of women;

(e) to defend the country and render national service, when called upon to do so;

(f) to value and preserve the rich heritage of the country's composite culture;

(g) to protect and improve the natural environment including forests, lakes, rivers and wildlife and to have compassion for living creatures;

(h) to develop scientific temper, humanism and the spirit of inquiry and reform;

(i) to safeguard public property and to objure violence.

(j) to strive towards excellence in all spheres of individual and collective activity so that the nation constantly rises to higher levels of endeavour and achievement.

(k) to provide opportunities for education to his child or ward between the age of six and 14 years./ This duty was added by the 86th Constitutional Amendment Act, 2002.

Justice Verma Committee and Fundamental Duties

- Justice Verma Committee report on teaching Fundamental Duties to citizens was set-up in 1999 and the report was presented in 2000. It recommended reorienting approaches to school curriculum and teacher's education programmes and incorporating Fundamental Duties in higher and professional education. **National Commission to Review the Working of the Constitution** (NCRWC) report in 2002 recommended to implement the Justice Verma Committee recommendations.

- In 2003, Supreme Court directed the Central Government to enact a Law for the enforcement of Fundamental Duties by citizens as suggested by Justice Verma Committee.

UNION EXECUTIVE

PRESIDENT

Article 52 provides the office of the President of India. The President is the head of the Indian State. He is the first citizen of India and acts as the symbol of unity, integrity and solidarity of the nation.

Qualification of the President

Under **Article 58**, a person to be eligible for election as President *should fulfil the following qualifications*

- He should be a citizen of India. He should have completed 35 years of age.
- He should be qualified for election as a member of the Lok Sabha.
- He should **not hold any office of profit** under the Union Government or any State Government or any local authority or any other public authority.

Election of the President
(Article 54)

The President is elected **not directly** by the people but by members of electoral college consisting of the elected members of both the Houses of Parliament; the elected Members of the Legislative Assemblies of the states; the elected Members of the Legislative Assemblies of the Union Territories of Delhi and Puducherry.

- Nominated members do not participate in the election of the President.
- When Assembly is dissolved, the members cease to be qualified to vote in the presidential election.
- Value of the vote of an MLA

$$= \frac{\text{Total Population of State}}{\text{Total Number of Elected MLAs}} \times \frac{1}{1000}$$

- Value of the vote of an MP

$$= \frac{\text{Total Value of Votes of all MLAs of All States}}{\text{Total Number of Elected MPs}}$$

The President's election is held in accordance with the system of proportional representation by means of the single transferable vote and the voting is through secret ballot.

- The candidate who gets 50% of votes is considered elected.

$$\text{Quota} = \frac{\text{Number of Votes Polled}}{2} + 1$$

In this method, each voter casts as many votes as there are candidates in the field by giving his preference. In the first phase, first preference votes are counted. In case a candidate secures the required quota, he is declared elected, otherwise the process of transfer of votes is set in motion.

- This process continues till a candidate secures the required quota. This procedure shows the majority of the elected President.
- All disputes regarding election of the President are adjudicated by the Supreme Court.
- Nomination for election of President must be supported by at least 50 electors as proposers and 50 electors as seconders.
- Security deposit for the nomination as President is ₹ 15000 in RBI.

Conditions of President's Office

Article 59 *of the Constitution lays down the following condition of the President's office*

- He should not be a member of either House of Parliament or a House of the State Legislature. If any such person is elected as President, he is deemed to have vacated his seat in that House on the date on which he enters upon his office as the President.
- He should not hold any other office of profit.
- He is entitled, without payment of rent, to the use of his official residence (the Rastrapati Bhavan).
- He is entitled to such emoluments, allowances and privileges as may be determined by Parliament.
- His emoluments and allowances cannot be diminished during his term of office.

Article 60 *Oath and affirmation of the President*

- The oath of the President is administered by Chief Justice of India and in his absence, the senior most Judge of the Supreme Court.
- Any person acting as the President also undertake similar oath.

Presidents of India

Name	Tenure		Important Facts
	From	To	
Dr Rajendra Prasad	26.01.1950	13.05.1962	• First President and also had the longest tenure (12 years)
Dr S Radhakrishnan	13.05.1962	13.05.1967	• Was also first Vice-President of India
Dr Zakir Hussain	13.05.1967	03.05.1969	• Shortest tenure; First Muslim President; First President to die in office
VV Giri	03.05.1969	20.07.1969	• First acting President of India
Justice M Hidayat-ul-lah	20.07.1969	24.08.1969	• Was also the Chief Justice of India and second Acting President
VV Giri	24.08.1969	24.08.1974	—
F Ali Ahmed	24.08.1974	11.02.1977	• Died in office
BD Jatti	11.02.1977	25.07.1977	• Acting President
N Sanjeeva Reddy	25.07.1977	25.07.1982	• Youngest President (64 years)
Giani Zail Singh	25.07.1982	25.07.1987	• First Sikh President
R Venkataraman	25.07.1987	25.07.1992	• Oldest President (76 years)
Dr SD Sharma	25.07.1992	25.07.1997	
KR Narayanan	25.07.1997	25.07.2002	• First Dalit President
Dr APJ Abdul Kalam	25.07.2002	25.07.2007	• First scientist to become President
Mrs Pratibha Patil	25.07.2007	25.07.2012	• First woman to become President
Pranab Mukherjee	25.07.2012	25.07.2017	—
Ramnath Kovind	25.07.2017	Till Date	—

Term of the President

Under Article 56, the President shall hold office for a term of 5 years from the date on which he enters upon his office.

- He may resign from his office by writing under his hand addressed to the Vice-President (he can communicate to the Speaker of the Lok Sabha).

Impeachment of the President

Under **Article 61**, President can be impeached from office for "violation of the Constitution".

- The impeachment can be initiated by either House of the Parliament.
- These charges should be signed by one-fourth members of the House (that framed the charges), and a 14 days' advance notice should be given to the President. After the impeachment motion is passed by a majority of two-thirds of the total membership of that House, it is sent to the other House, which should investigate the charges.
- The President has the right to appear and to be represented at such investigation. If the other House also sustains the charges and passes the motion by a majority of two-thirds of the total membership, the President to be removed from his office at that time and date.

Vacancy in the President's Office

- Under **Article 62** a vacancy in the President's office can occur in any of the following ways
- On the expiry of his tenure of 5 years. By his resignation.
- On his removal by the process of impeachment.
- By his death. Otherwise, e.g. when he becomes disqualified to hold office or when his election is declared void.
- An election to fill the vacancy (due to expiration of term) must be held before the expiry of the term.
- If the office fall vacant by resignation, removal, death or otherwise, then election to fill the vacancy should be completed **within 6 months** from the date of the occurrence of such a vacancy. The newly-elected President remains in office for a full term of 5 years from the date he assumes charge of his office.

Quick Digest

- In Presidential Election, VV Giri is the only person, who won the election of the President as an independent candidate in 1969.
- In July 1977, **Neelam Sanjeeva Reddy** was elected unopposed as no one else filled nomination for the post of the President.
- Justice **M Hidayat-ul-lah** is the only person to perform the function of the President two times in two different capacities, the first time in 1969, being the Chief Justice of the Supreme Court and the second time being the Vice-President of India in 1982.

Powers and Functions of the President

Powers and functions of the President can be categorised into

- Executive powers
- Legislative powers
- Financial powers
- Judicial powers
- Diplomatic powers
- Military powers
- Emergency powers

Executive Powers

- All executive actions of the Government of India are **formally** taken in the name of President.
- He can make rules specifying the manner in which the orders and other instruments made and executed in his/her name shall be authenticated.
- He appoints Prime Minister, other Ministers, Chief Justice and Judges of Supreme Court, High Courts, the Attorney-General of India, the Comptroller and Auditor General, Chairman and Members of UPSC, Chief Election Commissioner and other Members of Election Commission, Governors, Members of Finance Commission etc.
- He **can seek any information** relating to the administration of affairs of the union, and proposals for legislation from the Prime Minister.

Legislative Powers

- Summon or prorogue the Parliament and to dissolve the Lok Sabha.
- Summon a joint sitting of both the Houses of Parliament, which is headed by the Speaker of the Lok Sabha.
- Address the Parliament at the commencement of the first session after each general election and the first session of each year.
- He can appoint any member of the Lok Sabha to preside over its proceedings when the offices of both the Speaker and the Deputy Speaker fall vacant. Similarly, he can also appoint any member of the Rajya Sabha to preside over its proceedings when the offices of both the Chairman and the Deputy Chairman fall vacant.
- **Nominates 12 Members** in Rajya Sabha (from amongst person, who have special knowledge in respect of Literature, Science, Art and Social service) and **2 Members** of Anglo-Indian Community in the Lok Sabha.
- He decides the questions on disqualifications of Members of the Parliament, with consultation to the Election Commission.
- His prior recommendation or permission is needed to introduce certain types of bills in the Parliament, e.g. Money Bill, creation/recreation of new States Bill. When a bill is sent to the President after it has been passed by the Parliament, he can
  - give his assent to the bill or
  - withhold his assent to the bill or
  - return the bill (if it is not a Money Bill) for reconsideration of the Parliament. However, if the bill is passed again by the Parliament, with or without amendments, the President has to give his assent to the bill.
- He can **promulgate ordinances**, when the Parliament is not in session. The ordinances must be approved by the Parliament within 6 weeks from its reassembly. He can also withdraw an ordinance at any time (Article 123).
- He lays the reports of CAG, UPSC, Finance Commission etc before the Parliament.

Various Pardoning Powers of the President (Article 72)

- **Pardon** It removes both the sentences and the convictions and completely absolves the offender from all punishments and disqualifications.
- **Reprieve** It means a stay of execution of sentence pending a proceeding for pardon or commutation.
- **Remission** The power of remission reduces the amount of sentence without changing its character e.g. a sentence of rigorous imprisonment for 2 years may be remitted to regorous imprisonment for 1 year.
- **Respite** The power to grant respite means awarding a lesser sentence instead of the prescribed penalty in view of some special facts e.g. pregnancy of woman offender.
- **Commutation** It merely substitutes one form of the punishment for another of a lighter character. e.g. a death sentence may be commuted to rigorous imprisonment.

Financial Powers

- Money Bills can be introduced in the Parliament only with his prior recommendation.
- No demand for a grant can be made except on his recommendation.
- He through his representative, presents the **annual financial statement** before the Parliament. (*i.e,* the Union Budget).
- He can make advance out of the Contingency Fund of India to meet any **unforeseen expenditure**.
- He constitutes a **Finance Commission** after every five years to recommend the distribution of revenues between the Centre and the States.

Judicial Powers

- He appoints the Chief Justice and the Judges of Supreme Court and High Courts.

- He can seek **advice from the Supreme Court** on any question of law or fact. However, the advice tendered by the Supreme Court is not binding on the President (Article 143).

Diplomatic Powers

- The international treaties and agreements are negotiated and concluded on behalf of the President.
- Sends and receives diplomats like Ambassadors, High Commissioners, and so on.

Military Powers

- **Supreme Commander** of the defence forces of India. Appoints the Chiefs of the Army, the Navy and the Air Force.Declares war or concludes peace, subject to the approval of the Parliament.

Emergency Powers

The President of India can proclaim emergency in three conditions after getting the written recommendation of the Cabinet.

National Emergency (Article 352) arising out of war, external aggression or armed rebellion within the country.

Constitutional Emergency (Article 356) arising out of the failure of the constitutional machinery in the states. It is also known as **President's Rule**.

Financial Emergency (Article 360) arising out of a threat to financial stability or credit of India.

Emergency Declaration in India

- First emergency was declared in 1962, due to Chinese Aggression.
- Second emergency was declared in 1971, due to Indo-Pakistan War.
- Third emergency was declared in 1975, on grounds of internal disturbance.

Veto Power

- President of India is vested with three veto **Absolute, Suspensive** and **Pocket** veto. There is no **qualified veto** in the case of President of India.

Types of Veto

Absolute Veto Withholding of assent to the bill passed by the Legislature

Qualified Veto Sending back of a bill, which can be overridden by the Legislature with a higher majorty.

Suspensive Veto Sending back of a bill, which can be over sided by the Legislature with an ordinary majority.

Pocket Veto Taking no action on the bill passed by the Legislature.It was used in 1986 in the postal bill by the President of that time Giani Zail Singh.

POSITION OF INDIAN PRESIDENT

The Constitution of India has provided for a Parliamentary form of Government, and the President has been made only a nominal executive, the real executive being the Council of Ministers headed by the Prime Minister.

VICE-PRESIDENT

- **Article 63** There shall be a Vice-President of India. He occupies the second highest office in the country. The manner of election for Vice- President and President is same.
- Electoral college of Vice-President consists of elected and nominated members of both the Houses of Parliament.
- All disputes regarding election of Vice-President is adjudicated by the Supreme Court.

Qualifications

- Vise-President should be a citizen of India.
- He should have **completed 35 years** of age.
- He should be qualified for election as a Member of Rajya Sabha.
- He should not hold any office of profit.

Oath

Under **Article 69,** the oath of office of the Vice-President is administered by the President or some person appointed in that behalf by him.

Conditions of Office

- He should **not be a member** of either House of the Parliament or State Legislature.
- He should not hold any office of profit.

Term of Office

- He can resign from his office at any time by addressing the resignation letter to the President.
- He holds office for a **term of 5 years** from the date on which he enters upon his office.
- He can be removed by a resolution of the Rajya Sabha passed by an absolute majority and agreed by the Lok Sabha. [Article 67(b)]
- He can be elected for any number of terms.

Vacancy in Office

- A vacancy in the Vice-President's office can occur in any of the following ways
- On the expiry of his tenure, by his resignation, on his removal, by his death.
- When the vacancy is going to be caused by the expiration of the term of the sitting Vice-President, an election to fill the vacancy must be held before the expiration of the term. If the office falls vacant by resignation, removal, death or otherwise, then election to fill the vacancy should be held as soon as possible after the occurrence of the vacancy.
- The newly elected Vice-President remains in office for a full term of 5 years from the date he assumes charge of his office.
- **Emoluments** He draws his salary in his capacity as the Ex-officio Chairman of Rajya Sabha. His present salary is ₹ **125000** per month.

POWERS AND FUNCTIONS

- He acts as the *ex-officio* Chairman of Rajya Sabha. In this capacity, his powers and functions are similar to those of the Speaker of Lok Sabha.
- He acts as President when a vacancy occurs in the office of the President due to his resignation, removal, death or otherwise.
- He can act as President only for a maximum period of 6 months.
- While acting as President or discharging the functions of President, the Vice-President does not perform the duties of the office of Chairman of Rajya Sabha, those duties are performed by the Deputy Chairman of Rajya Sabha.
- If the offices of both the President and the Vice-President fall vacant by reason of death, resignation, removal etc the Chief Justice of India or in his absence the senior most judge of the Supreme Court acts as President.
- For the first time in 1969, when the President Dr Zakir Hussain died and the Vice-President V V Giri resigned, the Chief Justice M Hidayat-ul-lah acted as President.

Quick Digest

- **Krishna Kant** was the first Vice-President to die in office.
- When two Presidents, Dr Zakir Hussain and Fakruddin Ali Ahmed, died in office, the then respective Vice-Presidents, V V Giri and BD Jatti acted as President.
- The Vice-President **Dr S Radhakrishnan** discharged the functions of the President in June 1960, when the then President Dr Rajendra Prasad was on a 15 days tour to the USSR and again in July 1961, when Dr Rajendra Prasad was very ill.

List of Vice-Presidents

Name	Tenure	Notes
▪ Dr S Radhakrishnan	1952 to 1962	1st Vice-President; had the longest tenure (10 years, elected twice)
▪ Dr Zakir Hussain	1962 to 1967	
▪ VV Giri	1967 to 1969	Shortest tenure so far (2 years)
▪ GS Pathak	1969 to 1974	
▪ BD Jatti	1974 to 1979	
▪ Justice M Hidayat-ul-lah	1979 to 1984	
▪ R Venakataraman	1984 to 1987	
▪ Dr SD Sharma	1987 to 1992	
▪ KR Narayanan	1992 to 1997	
▪ Krishan Kant	1997 to 2002	Died in office
▪ Bhairon Singh Shekhawat	2002 to 2007	
▪ Mohammad Hamid Ansari	2007 to 2017	
▪ Venkaiah Naidu	2017 to till date	

PRIME MINISTER

- In the scheme of Parliamentary system of government, the President is the nominal executive authority (dejure executive) and **Prime Minister is the real executive** authority (de facto executive).
- Prime Minister is the Head of the Government while President is the Head of the State of the Republic of India. **Article 75** says that the Prime Minister shall be appointed by the President.

Oath, Term and Salary

- President administers to him the oaths of office and secrecy.
- The **term of the Prime Minister is not fixed** and he holds office during the pleasure of the President. However, this does not mean that the President can dismiss the Prime Minister at any time. So, long as the Prime Minister enjoys the majority support in the Lok Sabha, he cannot be dismissed by the President. However, if he loses the confidence of the Lok Sabha, he must resign or the President can dismiss him.
- The salary and allowances of the Prime Minister are determined by the Parliament from time to time.

Power and Functions

Prime Minister has following powers and functions

In Relation to Council of Ministers (CoMs)

The Prime Minister enjoys the following power as Head of Council of Ministers. He allocates and reshuffles various portfolios among the ministers.

He can ask a minister to resign or advise the President to dismiss him in case of difference in opinion.

He presides over the meeting of Council of Ministers and influences their decisions.

- He **guides, directs, controls, and coordinates** the activities of all the ministers.
- He can bring about the collapse of the Council of Ministers by resigning from office. When Prime Minister resigns or dies, the CoMs and other ministers cannot function because Prime Minister is the head of the CoMs.
- His resignation or death automatically dissolves the CoMs.

In Relation to the President

- Under **Article 78**, it is the duty of the Prime Minister :
- To communicate to the President, for **all decisions** of the Council of Ministers relating to the administration of the affairs of the Union and proposals for legislation;

'rime Ministers of India

Name	Tenure		Note
	From	To	
▪ Pandit Jawaharlal Nehru	15.08.1947	27.05.1964	First Prime Minister of India, died in office; also had the longest tenure (17 years)
▪ Gulzari Lal Nanda	27.05.1964	09.06.1964	First acting Prime Minister
▪ Lal Bahadur Shastri	09.06.1964	11.01.1966	Only Prime Minister to die abroad during an official tour
▪ Gulzari Lal Nanda	11.01.1966	24.01.1966	First to become acting Prime Minister twice
▪ Indira Gandhi	24.01.1966	24.03.1977	First woman Prime Minister of India; First Prime Minister to lose an election, first Rajya Sabha Member became PM
▪ Morarji Desai	24.03.1977	28.07.1979	Oldest Prime Minister (81 years) and the first to resign from office, first CM to become PM
▪ Charan Singh	28.07.1979	14.01.1980	Only Prime Minister, who did not face the Parliament
▪ Indira Gandhi	14.01.1980	31.10.1984	First Prime Minister to be assassinated
▪ Rajiv Gandhi	31.10.1984	01.12.1989	Youngest Prime Minister (40 years)
▪ VP Singh	21.12.1989	10.11.1990	First Prime Minister to step down after vote of no-confidence
▪ Chandra Shekhar	10.01.1990	21.06.1991	
▪ PV Narsimha Rao	21.06.1991	16.05.1996	First Prime Minister from Southern India
▪ Atal Bihari Vajpayee	16.05.1996	01.06.1996	Shortest tenure of a Prime Minister
▪ HD Deve Gowda	01.06.1996	21.04.1997	
▪ I K Gujral	21.04.1997	19.03.1998	
▪ Atal Bihari Vajpayee	19.03.1998	13.10.1999	
▪ Atal Bihari Vajpayee	13.10.1999	22.05.2004	
▪ Dr Manmohan Singh	22.05.2004	25.05.2014	First Sikh Prime Minister, Longest tenure after Jawahar Lal Nehru
▪ Narendra Modi	26.5.2014	Till date	First PM born after independence and also served as CM

- To furnish such information relating to the administration of the affairs of the Union and proposals for legislation as the President may call for and
- If the President requires, to submit for the consideration of the Council of Ministers any matter on which a decision has been taken by a minister but which has not been considered by the council.
- He **advices the President** with respect to the appointment of officials like CAG, Attorney-General of India, Chairman and members of UPSC, Election Commission, Finance Commission etc.

UNION COUNCIL OF MINISTERS

Appointment of Ministers

- Ministers are appointed by the President on the advice of the Prime Minister. It means only those persons can be appointed who are recommended by Prime Minister.
- The Prime Minister and other Ministers have to be members of either House of Parliament or should become members within 6 months of their appointment, failing, which they are removed.

Oaths and Salary of Ministers

President administers the oath to the minister. Salaries and allowances of ministers are determined by the Parliament from time to time.

Responsibility of Ministers

- **Collective Responsibility** Under Article 75, the CoMs is collectively responsible to Lok Sabha for all their acts. It means that the Cabinet decisions bind all Cabinet Ministers and other ministers even if they differed in the Cabinet meeting.
- It is a team and its member **sink and swim together** (Article 75).
- Article 75, also contains the principle of individual responsibility.
- **No Legal Responsibility** There is no provisions in the Constitution for a system of legal responsibility of a minister in India. While in Britain, there is legal responsibility of a minister.

Types of Minister

There are three types of Ministers

- **Cabinet Ministers** They are the real policy makers. The Cabinet's consent is necessary for all important matters.
- **Ministers of State** They can hold either independent charge or attached to a Cabinet Minister.
- **Deputy Ministers** They do not hold separate charge. There is another category of Ministers called Parliamentary Secretaries. However, no Parliamentary Secretary has been appointed since 1967.

DEPUTY PRIME MINISTER

- The post of Deputy Prime Minister is not mentioned in the Constitution, It is an extra constitutional body. Although seven persons have occupied this post since the inauguration of the Constitution.
- The Deputy Prime Minister occupies position next to the Prime Minister.

Name	Tenure
▪ Sardar Vallabhbhai Patel	1947-1950
▪ Morarji Desai	1967-1969
▪ Charan Singh and Jagjivan Ram (jointly)	1979-1979
▪ YB Chavan	1979-1980
▪ Devi Lal	1989-1990
▪ Devi Lal	1990-1991
▪ LK Advani	2002-2004

UNION LEGISLATURE

- The Constitution of India provides a Parliamentary form of government, both at the centre and in the states.
- The Parliament of India consists of the President, the Lok Sabha and the Rajya Sabha (Article 79).
- Although President is not a member of either House. He is an integral part of Parliament.
- Out of seven UTs, only two (Delhi and Puducherry) have representation in the Rajya Sabha.
- The population of other five are too small to have any representative in the Rajya Sabha.

Rajya Sabha (Article 80)

Rajya Sabha is a permanent body and **not subject to dissolution**. Its maximum strength is 250 (12 members nominated by the President having special knowledge or practical experience in the fields of science, literature, art and social service).

The total membership of the present Rajya Sabha is 245 however, one-third members retire every second year. Their seats are filled up by fresh elections and presidential nomination at the beginning of every third year.

- There are no seats reserved for SCs and STs in Rajya Sabha.
- Constitution has not fixed the term of office of members of the Rajya Sabha and left it to the Parliament.
- Representation of People Act (1951) provided the term of office of a member of the Rajya Sabha shall be **6 years**.

Lok Sabha (Article 81)

Lok Sabha is not a permanent body and subject to dissolution. Its maximum strength is 552, which includes 2 nominated members of Anglo-Indian Community, 530 members from states and 20 from Union Territories, Present strength of Lok Sabha is 545.

- Its **normal term is 5 years** from the date of its first meeting after the general elections, after which it automatically dissolves.
- The President is authorised to dissolve Lok Sabha at any time even before the completion of five years and this cannot be challenged in the Court of Law.
- Lok Sabha can be **extended** during the National Emergency by a law of Parliament for one year at a time for any length of time. But this extension cannot go beyond a period of 6 months after the emergency has ceased to operate.

Allocation of Seats in Parliament

S.N.	States/UTs	In Rajya Sabha	In Lok Sabha
1.	Andhra Pradesh	11	25
2.	Arunachal Pradesh	1	2
3.	Assam	7	14
4.	Bihar	16	40
5.	Chhattisgarh	5	11
6.	Goa	1	2
7.	Gujarat	11	26
8.	Haryana	5	10
9.	Himachal Pradesh	3	4
10.	Jammu and Kashmir	4	6
11.	Jharkhand	6	14
12.	Karnataka	12	28
13.	Kerala	9	20
14.	Madhya Pradesh	11	29
15.	Maharashtra	19	48
16.	Manipur	1	2
17.	Meghalaya	1	2
18.	Mizoram	1	1
19.	Nagaland	1	1
20.	Odisha	10	21
21.	Punjab	7	13
22.	Rajasthan	10	25
23.	Sikkim	1	1
24.	Tamil Nadu	18	39
25.	Tripura	1	2
26.	Uttarakhand	3	5
27.	Uttar Pradesh	31	80
28.	West Bengal	16	42
29.	Telengana	7	17

Union Territories			
1.	Andaman and Nicobar Island	—	1
2.	Chandigarh	—	1
3.	Dadra and Nagar Haveli	—	1
4.	Daman and Diu	—	1
5.	Delhi (The National Capital Territory of Delhi)	3	7
6.	Lakshadweep	—	1
7.	Puducherry	1	1
Nominated Members		12	2
Total		245	545

Members of Parliament

Qualification (Article 84)

The Constitution lays down the following qualifications for a person to be chosen as a Member of the Parliament.

- He must be a citizen of India.
- He must make and subscribe before the person authorised by the Election Commission an oath or affirmation according, to the form prescribed in the third Schedule. And must not be less than 30 years of age in the case of **Rajya Sabha** and not less than 25 years of age in the case of the **Lok Sabha**.
- He must possess other qualifications as prescribed by Parliament.

Disqualification (Article 102)

Under the Constitution, a person shall be disqualified for being elected as a Member of Parliament

- If he/she holds any office of profit under the Union or State Government (except that of a minister or any other office exempted by the Parliament).
- If he/she is of unsound mind and stands so declared by court.
- If he/she declared by court and stands so is undischarged insolvent.
- If he/she is not a citizen of India or has voluntarily acquired the citizenship of a foreign state or is under any acknowledgment of allegiance to a foreign state; and if he is so, disqualified under any law made by the Parliament.

Under the following conditions, a member of Parliament vacates his seat (Article 101)

- **Double Membership** (both Rajya Sabha and Lok Sahba).
- Disqualification, resignation.
- Absence (more than 60 days without permission).
- If his election is declared void by the court.
- If he/she is **expelled by the House**.
- If he/she is elected to the office of the President or Vice-President.
- If he/she is appointed as a Governor of a State.

Oath and Salary (Article 99)

- Every member has to make and subscribe to an oath or affirmation before the President or some other person appointed by him for this purpose.
- Salaries and allowances are determined by Parliament.

Speaker of Lok Sabha (Article 93)

- He/she is elected by Lok Sabha from amongst its members, as soon as, after the first meeting.
- The date of election is fixed by the President. Usually, the speaker remains in his office during the life of the Lok Sabha. He/she vacates office earlier in any of the following cases
- If he/she ceases to be member of Lok Sabha; if he/she resigns by writing to the Deputy Speaker; and

- If he/she is removed by a resolution passed by a majority of all the members of the Lok Sabha. Such a resolution can be moved only after giving 14 days advance notice.
- Under Resolution of removal, the Speaker cannot preside at the sitting of the House (he may be present). (Article 96)
- Whenever the Lok Sabha is dissolved, the Speaker does not vacate his office and continues till the newly elected Lok Sabha meets.

Role, Powers and Functions of Speaker

- He is the principal spokesman of the House, and his decision in all Parliamentary matters is final.
- He **maintains order and decorum** in the House for conducting its business.
- He adjourns the House to suspend the meeting in the absence of quorum (presence of only 1/10th of the total strength of the House). He does not vote in the first instance, but he can **exercise a casting vote** in the case of a tie (dead lock).
- He **presides over a joint sitting** of two Houses of the Parliament.
- He can allow a 'secret' sitting of the House.
- He certifies a Bill as Money Bill and his decision cannot be challenged.
- He appoints the Chairman of all the Parliamentary Committees of Lok Sabha. The speaker acts as the ex-offico Chairman of the Indian Parliamentary group of the Inter Parliamentary Union.

Speakers of Lok Sabha

Name	Tenure	
	From	To
GV Mavalankar	15.05.1952	27.02.1956
MA Ayyangar	08.03.1956	10.05.1957
MA Ayyangar	11.05.1957	16.04.1962
Hukam Singh	17.04.1962	16.03.1967
N Sanjeeva Reddy	17.03.1967	19.07.1969
Dr GS Dhillon	08.08.1969	19.03.1971
Dr GS Dhillon	22.03.1971	01.12.1975
Bali Ram Bhagat	05.01.1976	25.03.1977
N Sanjeeva Reddy	26.03.1977	13.07.1977
KS Hegde	21.07.1977	21.01.1980
Dr Balram Jakhar	22.01.1980	15.01.1985

Name	Tenure	
Dr Balram Jakhar	16.01.1985	18.12.1989
Rabi Ray	19.12.1989	09.07.1991
Shiv Raj Patil	10.07.1991	22.05.1996
PA Sangma	23.05.1996	23.03.1998
GMC Balyogi	24.03.1998	19.10.1999
GMC Balyogi	22.10.1999	03.03.2002
Manohar Joshi	10.05.2002	20.06.2004
Somnath Chatterjee	04.06.2004	31.05.2009
Meira Kumar	04.06.2009	04.06.2014
Sumitra Mahajan	06.06.2014	Till date

Deputy Speaker

- While the office of the Speaker is vacant due to any reason, the Deputy Speaker presides. (Article 95)
- **M. Ananthasayanam Ayyangar** was the First Deputy Speaker of Lok Sabha.
- At present **Mr M Thambidurai is Deputy Speaker** of Lok Sabha.

Chairman of Rajya Sabha

The **Vice-President** is the **Ex-officio Chairman** of Rajya Sabha. Article 89

As a presiding officer, the powers and functions of the Chairman of Rajya Sabha are similar to those of Speaker of Lok Sabha.

Deputy Chairman

- Elected by Rajya Sabha itself from amongst its members. Deputy Chairman is not subordinate to the Chairman. He is directly responsible to the Rajya Sabha.

Joint Session (Article 108)

- Joint sessions take place on the order of the President if
  (a) a Bill passed by one House, is rejected by another.
  (b) the amendments made by the other House are not acceptable to the House where the Bill originated.
- Joint session is presided over by the Speaker of the Lok Sabha. The deadlock over a Bill is resolved by a majority of the total numbers of the members of both the Houses present and voting.
- So far, joint-sittings have been held thrice in the history of Indian Parliament (1961, 1978 and 2002).

- Provision of joint sitting is applicable to ordinary bills or financial bills only and not to money bills or constitutional amendment bills.

Sessions of Parliament

- The Parliament generally meets in three sessions in a year i.e., Budget session (February-May) (longest session), Monsoon session (July- September), Winter session (November- December) (shortest session).
- There should not be a gap of more than 6 months between two sessions of Parliament.

Difference between Powers of Lok Sabha and the Rajya Sabha

- A Money Bill can be introduced only in the Lok Sabha and not in the Rajya Sabha. The **final power** to decide whether a particular bill is a Money Bill or not, is vested in the Speaker of the Lok Sabha.
- The Speaker of Lok Sabha presides over the joint sitting of both the Houses of Parliament.
- A resolution for the discontinuance of the National Emergency can be passed only by the Lok Sabha and not by the Rajya Sabha.
- The Rajya Sabha **cannot remove** the Council of Ministers by passing a no-confidence motion.
- This is because the Council of Ministers is collectively responsible only to the Lok Sabha. But, the Rajya Sabha can discuss and criticise the policies and activities of the government.

LEGISLATIVE PROCEDURE IN PARLIAMENT

- The legislative procedure is identical in both the Houses of Parliament. A Bill is a proposal for legislation and it becomes an Act or law when duly enacted.
- Bills may be classified under **four heads** *viz*, Ordinary, Money, Financial and Constitutional Amendment Bills. The Legislative procedure of government bills and private members bill is same.
- Money Bills cannot be introduced in the Rajya Sabha. The other bills can be introduced in either House.
- Every ordinary bill has to pass through five stages in the Parliament i.e. first Reading, second Reading, third Reading, Bill in the second House and Assent of the President. Finally, the Bill has to be notified by the Government to enable its implementation.

Stages of Bills

The different stages in the passage of Bills other than the Money Bills are as follows

Introduction of the Bill

- It involves introduction of Bill like provisions of the proposed law, accompanied by the 'Statement of Objects and Reasons'. Private member must give one month notice to introduce the Bill.
- After that it is published in the Gazette of India. The introduction of the Bill and its publication in the Gazette constitutes the **First Reading** of the Bill.

Special Powers of Rajya Sabha

Due to its federal character, the Rajya Sabha has been given two exclusive or special powers that are not enjoyed by the Lok Sabha.

- It can authorise the Parliament to make a law on a subject enumerated in the State List (Article 249).
- It can authorise the Parliament to create new All-India Services Common for both the centre and states (Article 312).

Second Reading of the Bill

- In the second reading principles of the Bill are discussed in details and the treasury and the opposition members give their views either in support or opposition of the Bill.
- The second reading is divided into two stages, (i) consists of a general discussion of the principles of the Bill and (ii) relates to discussion of clauses, schedules and amendments.
- If the Bill is referred to the Selected Committee or Joint Committee, it is expected to give its report within a specified date.
- The Bill then undergoes long discussions clause by clause and may undergo substantial change.

Third Reading of the Bill

- The third reading is the final reading. It is more or less a formal affair. The debate is confined to the acceptance or rejection of the Bill. The Bill is submitted to the vote of the House and has to be accepted or rejected altogether.

Bill in the Second House

- After the Bill has been passed by one House, it is transmitted to the other House, where it has to pass through the same process. The other House has four alternatives before it.
  1. It may pass the Bill as sent by the first House.
  2. It may pass the Bill with amendments and return it to the first House.
  3. It may reject the Bill altogether.
  4. It may not take any action and thus keep the Bill pending.
- In case the Bill is also passed by the second House or the first House agrees with the amendmendments made by the second house, the Bill is sent to the President for his assent.
- In case the Bill is rejected by the second House or it is kept by the second House with it for six months without any action or the first House disagrees with the amendments suggested by the second House, a deadlock is deemed to have taken place.

- To resolve a deadlock, the President may summon a joint-sitting of the two Houses under **Article 108**. If the majority of members present and voting at the joint-sitting pass the Bill, it is considered as passed by both Houses of Parliament and is sent for his assent.

Assent of the President

- After being passed by both Houses, when the Bill is presented to the President, *he has three options*
  1. He may assent to the Bill
  2. He may withhold his assent
  3. He may return the Bill for the reconsideration of the Houses.
- If the President gives assents to the Bill, it becomes an Act.
- If the President withholds his assent, the Bill ends.
- If the President returns the Bill for reconsideration and it is passed again by both the Houses, he has to give his assent after the second passage.
- Since, the Constitution provides no time limit for the President to give his assent, he may keep the Bill in his office without taking any action and prevent it from becoming an act.

Budget in Parliament

- The Constitution refers to the budget as the 'annual financial statement'. In other words, the term 'budget' has nowhere been used in the Constitution. 'Annual Financial Statement' has been dealt within Article 112 of the Constitution.
- The budget is a statement of the estimated receipts and expenditure of the Government of India in a financial year, which begins on **1st April** and ends on **31st March** of the following year.
- After introduction of the Budget, the Lok Sabha discusses the demands for grants of various ministries and departments. All expenditure after approval, charged on the consolidated fund of India, are then presented in the form of single Bill called the 'Appropriation Bill'. Proposals for taxation (to raise revenue) are presented in the form of 'Finance Bill'.
- The Government of India has two budgets, namely, the Railway Budget and the General Budget.
- From 2017, Railway Budget has been merged with the General Budget on the recommendation of Bibek Debroy Committee.

Consolidated Fund of India (Article 266)

- It is a fund to which all receipts are credited and all payments are debited. In other words,
  - all revenues received by the Government of India.
  - all loans raised by the government by the issue of treasury bills, loans or ways and means of advances.
  - all money received by the government in repayment of loans from the Consolidated Fund of India.
- All the legally authorised payments on behalf of the government are made out of this fund. No money out of this fund can be appropriated (issued or drawn) except in accordance with a Parliamentary law.

Contingency Fund of India (Article 267)

- **Article 267** of the Constitution authorised the Parliament to establish a 'Contingency Fund of India', into which amounts determined by law are paid from time to time. Accordingly, the Parliament enacted the Contingency Fund of India Act in 1950.
- This fund is placed at the disposal of the President and he can make advances out of it to meet unforeseen expenditure pending its authorisation by the Parliament.
- The fund is held by the finance secretary on behalf of President.

Public Account of India

- **Article 266** (2) provides that all other public moneys (other than those in the Consolidated Fund of India) received by or on behalf of the Government of India or the Government of a State shall be credited to the Public Account of India or the Public Account of the State, as the case may be. This account is operated by executive action and payments from it do not need Parliamentary approval.
- Moneys in this account include provident fund deposits, savings bank deposits, remittances etc.

Committee System

- Committees have been created so that members of Parliament can discuss and debate on the working of a certain department of the government.

- Most of the committees function under the direction of the **Speaker** and are essentially committees of the Lok Sabha.

- Committees are classified under two heads : Standing Committee and Adhoc Committees. **Adhoc Committees** are created for a temporary period.

- The **Standing Committees** are broadly classified into the following categories : Committees of Enquires, Committees to Scrutinise, Financial Committees, Committees of Administrative Character, Committees dealing with provision of facilities to members.

- The **Financial Committees** of Parliament are : Estimates Committee, Public Accounts Committee, Committee on Public Undertaking and 24 Departmental Related Committees.

- The **Public Accounts Committee** was set-up first in **1921** under the provisions of the Government of India Act of 1919. At present, it consists of 22 members (15 from the Lok Sabha and 7 from the Rajya Sabha). Since, 1967, a convention has developed whereby the Chairman of the Committee is selected invariably from the opposition.

- The origin of the Estimates Committee can be traced to the Standing Financial Committee set-up in **1921**. The first Estimates Committee was set-up in 1950. It has **thirty members**, all from the Lok Sabha only.

- The Committee on Public Undertakings was created in 1964 on the recommendations of the Krishna Menon Committee. It has 22 members (15 from the Lok Sabha and 7 from the Rajya Sabha).

- In 1993, 17 Department Related Standing Committees were set-up. In 2004, 7 more committees were set-up. Thus, total 24 committees exist as of today.

- Members of the Rajya Sabha are associated with all the committees except the Estimates Committee.

- The Chairman of all the committees (except the Joint Committee on salaries and allowances of MPs) are appointed by the Speaker from amongst the members of the committee.

- In case, Speaker is a member of a committee, he becomes **Ex-officio Chairman** of the committee.

SUPREME COURT

- Supreme Court stands at the apex of the 'Judicial System of India. It is the ultimate interpreter of the Consitution and the laws of the land.

- **Article 124** states the establishment and constitution of Supreme Court.

- Supreme Court was inaugurated on 28th January, 1950.

- At present, the Supreme Court consists of 31 judges (one Chief Justice of India (CJI) and 30 judges).

Appointment of Chief Justice

Only senior most Judge of the Supreme Court is appointed by the President as CJI. Other Judges of the Supreme Court are appointed by the President in consultation with the Chief Justice. He may also consult other Judges of the Supreme Court and High Court while appointing a Judge of the Supreme Court.

Acting Chief Justice

Under **Article 126**, The President can appoint a Judge of the Supreme Court as an acting CJI, when

- office of CJI is vacant; or
- the CJI is temporarily absent; or
- the CJI is unable to perform the duties of his office.

Qualifications

Under **Article 124 (3)**, a person to be appointed as a Judge of the Supreme Court should have the following qualifications

- He should be a citizen of India.

- He should have been a Judge of a High Court (or High Courts in succession) for five years. Or
- He should have been an advocate of a High Court (or High Courts in succession) for ten years. Or
- He should be a distinguished jurist in the opinion of the President.
- The Constitution does not prescribe a minimum age for appointment as a Judge of the Supreme Court.

Oath or Affirmation

Administered by the President or some person appointed by him for this purpose.

Tenure of Judges

The Constitution has not fixed the tenure of a Judge of the Supreme Court. *It makes the following provisions*

- Holds office **until he attains the age of 65 years.**
- Resign his office by writing to the President.
- Removed from his office by the President on the recommendation of the Parliament.

Removal of Judges or Impeachment

Under **Article 124** (4), a Judge of the Supreme Court shall not be removed from his office except by an order of the President passed after an address by each House of the Parliament **by special majority**. Judges can be removed only on the grounds of proved misbehaviour or incapacity.

Under **Article 124** (5) Parliament may by law regulate the procedure relating to the removal of a Judge of the Supreme Court. Under this Article Parliament provides the procedure for removal by the Judges Enquiry Act (1968).

- No Judge of the Supreme Court has been impeached so far. The first such case of impeachment is that of Justice V Ramaswami of the Supreme Court in Lok Sabha (1991-93). But, finally he could not be impeached.

- The second case of impeachment is that of **Justice Saumitra Sen** of the Calcutta High Court (became the first judge in Indian History, against whom an impeachment motion was passed in the Rajya Sabha). The BSP was the only party to oppose the motion to remove the judge. After this, he resigned and there was no need for impeachment.

Under **Article 217** (a), a Judge of the High Court "may by writing under his hand addressed to the President" resign his office.

Under **Article 124** (2) (a), a Judge of the Supreme Court "may by writing under his hand addressed to the President, resign his office".

Salaries and Allowances

Under **Article 125**, the salaries, allowances, privileges, leave and pension of the Judges of the Supreme Court are determined from time to time by the Parliament.

- Salary of Chief Justice of India is ₹ 1 lakh per month. Salary of other Judges of Supreme Court is ₹ 90000 per month.
- The retired Chief Justice and Judges are entitled to 50% of their last drawn salary as monthly pension.

Ad hoc Judges

Under **Article 127**, if at any time there is not a quorum of the Judges of the Supreme Court to hold or continue any session, CJI can appoint a Judge of the High Court as an Ad hoc Judge of the Supreme Court for a temporary period.

- He can do so only after consultation with the Chief Justice of the High Court concerned and with previous consent of the President.
- The judge so appointed should be qualified for appointment as the Judge of the Supreme Court.

Retired Judges

Under **Article 128**, at any time, the Chief Justice of India can request a retired Judge of the Supreme Court or a retired Judge of the High Court (who is duly qualified for appointment as a Judge of the Supreme Court) to act as a Judge of the Supreme Court for a temporary period.

> ### Seat of Supreme Court
> Under **Article 130**, the Constitution declares **Delhi as the seat of the Supreme Court**. But, it authorises the CJI to appoint any other place or places as seat of the Supreme Court. He can take this decision only with the approval of the President.

Procedure of the Court

The Supreme Court can, with the approval of the President, make rules for regulating generally the practice and procedure of the court.

Constitutional Bench A bench consisting of at least 5 judges. Constituted by the CJI to hear a case involving a substantial question of law.

Independence of the Judges

Independence of judges is ensured by following provisions

- Mode of appointment of CJI and Judges of the Supreme Court.
- **Security of tenure** (removed only by the President).
- Fixed service conditions (salary charged from Consolidated Fund of India).
- Conduct of judges cannot be discussed in Parliament or State Legislature.
- Ban on practice after retirement.
- Power to punish its contempt.
- Freedom to appoint its staff.
- Its jurisdiction cannot be curtailed.
- Difficult removal procedure.
- Separation from executive.

Jurisdiction and Powers of Supreme Court

- Original jurisdiction
- Writ jurisdiction
- Appellate jurisdiction
- Advisory jurisdiction
- A court of record
- Power of judical review
- Other powers

Original Jurisdiction (Article 131)

The Supreme Court decides the dispute between the centre and one or more states; the centre and any state or states on one side and one or more states on the other; or between two or more states.

- In the above disputes, the Supreme Court has exclusive original jurisdiction. They lie directly and exclusively with the Supreme Court.

Writ Jurisdiction (Article 32)

- Every individual has the right to move the Supreme Court directly by appropriate proceedings for the enforcement of his Fundamental Rights through the issuance of writs.

Appellate Jurisdiction (Article 132)

- The Supreme Court is primarily a court of appeal and hears appeals against the judgements of the lower courts. It enjoys a wide appellate jurisdiction, which can be classified under four heads
  (a) Appeals in constitutional matters.
  (b) Appeals in civil matters (Article 133).
  (c) Appeals in criminal matters (Article 134).
  (d) Appeal by special leave (Article 136.)

Advisory Jurisdiction

- The Constitution (Article 143) authorises the President to seek the opinion of the Supreme Court. It is duty bound to give its opinion, which is not binding on President.

Court of Record

As a Court of Record, Supreme Court has two powers

1. Judgments, proceedings and acts of Supreme Court are recorded for perpetual memory and testimony.
2. It can punish for contempt of court.

Power of Judical Review (Article 137)

- Judicial review is the power of the Supreme Court to examine the **constitutionality** of **legislative enactments** and executive order of both Central and State Government.
- On examination, if they are found to be violative of the Constitution, they can be declared as illegal, unconstitutional and invalid and they cannot be enforced by any authority.

- Judical review is needed for the reasons
- Uphold the supremacy of the Constitution
- Maintain federal equilibrium
- Protect the Fundamental Rights of the citizens

Some famous cases, in which the Supreme Court used the power of judical review are

- Golakanath Case (1967)
- Bank Nationalisation Case (1970)
- Privy Purse Abolition Case (1971)
- Kesavananda Bharati Case (1973)
- Minerva Mills Case (1980)

- **Article 141** Law declared by Supreme Court to be binding on all courts, within the territory of India.
- **Article 144** All authorities, civil and judicial in the Territory of India to act in aid of the Supreme Court.
- **Public Interest Litigation** (PIL) Any person can now initiate a proceeding on behalf of the aggrieved person (if the aggrieved persons cannot do so on their own) in either the High Court or the Supreme Court for the protection of greater public interest.

The National Judicial Appointment Commission Act, 2014

- The Bill has been introduced in conjuction with the Constitutional (121st Amendment) Bill, 2014, amends provisions related to appointment and transfer of judges to the higher judiciary.
- It establishes a National Judicial Appointment Commission (NJAC) to make recommendations to the President on appointment and transfer of judges to the higher judiciary.
- The NJAC Act, 2014 states that the NAC shall comprise : (i) the Chief justice of India (CJI), (ii) two other senior most judges of the Supreme Court (SC), (iii) the Union Minister for Law and justice, and (iv) two eminent persons to be nominated by the Prime Minister, the CJI and the Leader of Opposition of the Lok Sabha.
- The functions of the NJAC include making recommendations for appointments of the CJI, SC judges, Chief Justice and other High Court (HC) judges and transfer of HC judges.
- The NJAC shall elicit the views of the Governor and Chief Minister of the state before making recommendations.
- The NJAC shall not recommend a person for appointment if any two members of the Commission do not agree to such recommendation.

STATES EXECUTIVE

GOVERNOR

- The Governor is the Constitutional Head of the state and the same Governor can act as Governor of more than one state (Articles 153 and 154).
- Under **Article 155**, the Governor is appointed by the President. **Article 156** states that the Governor holds office during the pleasure of the President.

Qualification

Under **Article 158**, the Constitution lays down the following conditions for the Governor's office

- Must be citizen of India.
- Completed 35 years of age.
- Shall not be a member of both the Houses of Parliament or of a House of Legislative Assembly or Legislative Council (if any).
- Shall not hold office of profit.

Salary & Allowances

Use his official residence (Raj Bhawan) without payment of rent.

When same person is appointed as the Governor of two or more states, the emoluments and allowances payable to him are shared by states as determined by the President.

- Salary of the Governor is ₹ 1.1 lakh per month.

Oath

His oath is administered by the Chief Justice of the concerned State High Court and in his absence, the senior, most judge of that court.

Tenure of Governor

Under Article 156

(a) the Governor shall hold office during the pleasure of the President;

(b) may resign by writing under his hand addressed to the President;

(c) hold office for a period of 5 years.

Governor shall hold office until his successor enters upon his office.

Powers and Functions of Governor

Executive Powers

The executive power of the state shall be vested with the Governor and shall be exercised by him either directly or through officers subordinate to him in accordance with the Constitution. *These powers are as*

- All executive actions of the Government of a State are formally taken in his name. He can make rules for more convenient transaction of the business of a State Government.
- Appoints the Advocate General of a State (Article 165), State Election Commissioners, Chairman and members of the State Public Service Commission, VCs of Universities.
- He can seek any information relating to the administration of the affairs of the state and proposals for legislation from the Chief Minister.

Legislative Powers

- Governor is an integral part of the State Legislature. He has the right of addressing and sending messages and of summoning, proroguing and dissolving the State Assembly.
- He has the power to nominate one member of Anglo-Indian Community to the Legislative Assembly of the state.
- He nominates 1/6th members of Legislative Council.

Financial Powers

State budget is laid before the State Legislature by him. He constitutes a State Finance Commission after every five years to review the financial position of the Panchayats and the Municipalities.

Judicial Powers

- He can grant pardons, reprives, respites and remissions of punishment or suspend, remit and commute the sentence of any person convicted of any offence against any law relating to a matter, to which the executive power of the state extends.
- He cannot pardon a death sentence even if a State law provides for death sentence.

Emergency Powers

- The Governor has no emergency powers to counter external aggression or armed rebellion.
- He reports to the President, if the State Government is not running constitutionally and recommends to the Union Government, President's Rule (Article 356). When President's rule comes into force in any state, the Governor runs the state with the help of advisers on behalf of the President.

CHIEF MINISTER

Chief Minister is the Real Executive Head of the State Government. His position at the state level is analogous to the position of the Prime Minister at the centre.

Appointment

Article 164, says that Chief Minister shall be appointed by the Governor. This does not means that the Governor is free to appoint any one as a Chief Minister.

Oath, Term and Salary

- Oath of the office of Chief Minister is administered by the Governor or person appointed by him for this purpose.
- A person, who is not a member of State Legislature can be appointed, but he has to get himself elected within 6 months otherwise he is removed.
- The **term of the CM is not fixed** and he holds office during the pleasure of the Governor.

- He cannot be dismissed by the Governor as long as he enjoys the majority support in the Legislative Assembly.
- The salary and allowances of the Chief Minister are determined by the State Legislature.

Powers and Functions
in Relation to Council of Ministers (CoMs)

The CM as a head of the CoMs, enjoys the following powers

- The Governor appoints only those persons as ministers, who are recommended by the Chief Minister.
- He allocates and reshuffles the portfolios among ministers.
- He can ask a minister to resign or advise the Governor to dismiss him in case of difference of opinion.
- He presides over the meetings of the Council of Ministers and influences its decisions.
- He **aids, directs, controls** and **coordinates** the activities of all the ministers.

In Relation of the Governor

He is the **principle channel of communication** between the Governor and the Council of Ministers.

In Relation to State Legislature

- Advises the Governor with regard to summoning and proroguing the sessions of the State Legislature.
- Recommend the **dissolution** of the Legislative Assembly to the Governor at any time.

State Council of Ministers (CoMs)

- The CoMs headed by CM is the real executive authority in the Political-administrative system of the state.
- **Articles 163** and **164** deal with Council of Minister, in the states.

Oath and Salary

- **Oaths** of office and secrecy is administered by the Governor or person appointed by him for this purpose.
- **Salary and allowances** are determined by the State Legislature from time to time.

STATES LEGISLATURE

There is no uniformity in the creation of State Legislatures. Most of the states have unicameral system (single house), only 7 states Andhra Pradesh, Bihar, Jammu, Kashmir, Karnataka, Maharashtra, Uttar Pradesh and Telengana are having Bicameral (Double House). The Tamil Nadu legislative Council Act, 2010 has not come into force.

Legislative Assembly
(Article 170)

- The **Legislative Assembly** (Vidhan Sabha) consists of not more than 500 members and not less than 60 members. However, the Legislative Assembly of **Sikkim, Goa, Mizoram** Arunanchal Pradesh, Nagaland and **Puducherry** have less than 60 members.

Legislative Council (Article 171)

- As per **Article 169**, if the Legislative Assembly passes a resolution for abolishing or creating of the **Legislative Council** by a majority of the total membership of the assembly and by a majority of not less than two-third of the members present and voting, the Parliament may approve the resolution by a simple majority to create or abolish the Legislative Council.

Composition of Legislative Council

Of the total number of members of a Legislative Council

- **1/3rd** Elected from local bodies (municipalities and district boards).
- **1/12th** Elected by graduates of 3 years standing and residing in the state.

- **1/12th** Elected by teachers of 3 years standing in the state, not lower in standard than secondary school.
- **1/3rd** Elected by the members of the Legislative Assembly of the state from amongst person, who are not members of the assembly.
- **Rest** (1/6th) are nominated by the Governor from persons of special knowledge or practical experience of literature, science, art, cooperative movement and social service.
- **5/6th** of total number of members of Legistative Council are indirectly elected, and 1/6th are nominated by Governor.

Membership of the State Legislature

Qualification

Under Article 173, *they must fulfil the following conditions*

(a) He must be a citizen of India.

(b) He must make and subscribe before the person authorised by the Election Commission an oath or affirmation according to the form prescribed in the Third Schedule.

(c) He must be **not less than 30 years** of age in the case of the Legislative Council and **not less than 25 years** of age in the case of the Legislative Assembly.

(d) He must possess other qualifications prescribed by Parliament, under Representation of People Act (1951).

Oath or Affirmation It is administered by Governor or person appointed by him for this purpose.

Vacation of Seats (in cases of)

- Double membership
- Disqualification
- Resignation
- Absence (more than 60 days without permission)
  Other cases
  - if his election is declared void by the court, if he is expelled by the House,
  - if he is elected for the office of the President or office of Vice-President, if he is appointed to the office of Governor of a state.

Duration of the Two Houses

Legislative Assembly Same as Lok Sabha.
Leglislative Council Same as Rajya Sabha.

Presiding Officers of State Legislature

- Speaker/Deputy Speaker in Legislative Assembly (Article 178).
- Chairman/Deputy Chairman in Legislative Council (Article 182).

Speaker of Legislative Assembly

Speaker of Assembly is elected by the Assembly itself from amongst its members. He can vacate his office earlier in any of the *following three cases*

1. If he ceases to be a member of the Assembly;
2. If he resigns by writing to the Deputy Speaker; and
3. If he is removed by a resolution passed by a majority of all the members of the assembly. Such a resolution can be moved only after giving 14 days advance notice. (Article 179).

Powers and Duties of Speaker

- He **maintains order and decorum** in the Assembly for conducting its business and regulating its proceedings.
- He adjourns the Assembly or suspends the meeting in the absence of a quorum.
- He does not vote in the first instance. But, he can exercise a casting vote in the case of a tie.
- He can allow a **secret sitting** of the House at the request of the leader of the House.
- He decides whether **a bill is a Money Bill or not** and his decision on this question is final.
- He decides the questions of disqualification of a member of the Assembly, arising on the ground of defection under the provisions of the Tenth Schedule.
- He appoints the Chairman of all the committees of the Assembly and supervises their functions.

Chairman of Legislative Council

The Chairman is elected by the council itself from amongst its members. The Chairman vacates his office in any of *the following three cases*

1. If he ceases to be a member of the council,
2. If he resigns by writing to the Deputy Chairman; and
3. If he is removed by a resolution passed by a majority of all the members of the council. Such a resolution can be moved only after giving 14 days advance notice.

Legislative Procedure

- A Money Bill can be introduced only in the Legislative Assembly. The Assembly is not bound to accept any recommendation by the council, it may at the most withhold the bill for 14 days from the date of its receipt. (Article 198).
- In case of an Ordinary Bill, the Legislative Council can hold the bill for a maximum of three months. There is no provision for joint sitting in case of difference between the two Houses.

Powers of the State Legislature

- It participates in the election of the President.
- It can remove the Council of Ministers by passing a No-Confidence Motion.
- It controls the executive by various financial committees. It **ratifies certain Constitutional Amendments**, in which participation of half of the State Legislatures is required.

Strength of Legislative Assembly

S.N.	State/Union Territory	Number of Seats
I. States		
1.	Andhra Pradesh	175
2.	Arunachal Pradesh	60
3.	Assam	126
4.	Bihar	243
5.	Chhattisgarh	90
6.	Goa	40
7.	Gujarat	182
8.	Haryana	90
9.	Himachal Pradesh	68
10.	Jammu and Kashmir	87
11.	Jharkhand	81
12.	Karnataka	224
13.	Kerala	140
14.	Madhya Pradesh	230
15.	Maharashtra	288
16.	Manipur	60
17.	Meghalaya	60
18.	Mizoram	40
19.	Nagaland	60
20.	Odisha	147
21.	West Bengal	295
22.	Punjab	117
23.	Rajasthan	200
24.	Sikkim	32
25.	Tamil Nadu	235
26.	Telengana	119
27.	Tripura	60
28.	Uttarakhand	70
29.	Uttar Pradesh	403
II. Union Territories		
1.	Delhi	70
2.	Puducherry	30

Strength of Legislative Council

S.N.	Name of State	Number of Seats
1.	Uttar Pradesh	100
2.	Andhra Pradesh	58
3.	Karnataka	75
4.	Bihar	75
5.	Maharashtra	78
6.	Jammu and Kashmir	36
7.	Telengana	40

HIGH COURT

- Every High Court (whether exclusive or common) consists of a Chief Justice and such other judges as the President may from time to time deem necessary to appoint. Thus, the Constitution **does not specify the strength of a High Court** and leaves it to the discretion of the President.
- Accordingly, the President determines the strength of a High Court from time to time depending upon its workload.
- The Constitution of India provides a High Court for each state, but the 7th Amendment Act of 1956, authorised the Parliament to establish a common High Court for two or more states or a state and a union territory.
- The territorial jurisdiction of a High Court is co-terminus with the territory of a state.

Jurisdiction and Seats of High Courts

Name	Establis hed in the Year	Territorial Jurisdiction	Seat
Madhya Pradesh	1956	Madhya Pradesh	Jabalpur (Benches at Gwalior and Indore)
Bombay	1862	Maharashtra, Dadra and Nagar Haveli, Goa, Daman and Diu	Mumbai (Bench at Nagpur, Panaji and Aurangabad)
Calcutta	1862	West Bengal and Andaman and Nicobar islands	Kolkata (Circuit Bench at Port Blair)
Madras	1862	Tamil Nadu and Puducherry	Chennai
Allahabad	1866	Uttar Pradesh	Allahabad (Bench at Lucknow)
Karnataka	1884	Karnataka	Bengaluru
Patna	1916	Bihar	Patna
Orissa	1948	Odisha	Cuttack
Guwahati	1948	Assam, Nagaland, Mizoram and Arunachal Pradesh	Guwahati (Benches at Kohima and Aizawl and itanagar)
Rajasthan	1949	Rajasthan	Jodhpur (Bench at Jaipur)
Andhra Pradesh	1954	Andhra Pradesh and Telengana	Hyderabad
Kerala	1958	Kerala and Lakshadweep	Ernakulam
Jammu and Kashmir	1928	Jammu and Kashmir	Srinagar and Jammu
Gujarat	1960	Gujarat	Ahmedabad
Delhi	1966	Delhi	Delhi
Punjab and Haryana	1875	Punjab, Haryana and Chandigarh	Chandigarh
Himachal Pradesh	1971	Himachal Pradesh	Shimla
Sikkim	1975	Sikkim	Gangtok
Uttarakhand	2000	Uttarakhand	Nainital
Jharkhand	2000	Jharkhand	Ranchi
Chhattisgarh	2000	Chhattisgarh	Bilaspur
Manipur	2013	Manipur	Imphal
Meghalaya	2013	Meghalaya	Shillong
Tripura	2013	Tripura	Agartala

- At present, there are **24 High Courts** in the country. Out of them, three and seven are common High Courts for states and for both states and UTs respectively, Delhi is the only union territory that has a High Court of its own (since 1966).

Appointment of Judges

- Under **Article 217,** The judges of the High Court are appointed by the President.
- The Chief Justice of the High Court is appointed by the President after consultation with the Chief Justice of Supreme Court and Governor of the concerned state.

Qualification of Judges

- He should be a citizen of India.
- He should have held a judicial office in the territory of India for 10 years.

or

- He should have been an advocate of a High Court (or High Courts in succession) for 10 years.

Oath

Oath is administered by Governor or person appointed by him for this purpose.

Tenure

- He holds office until he attains the **age of 62 years**. Any questions regarding his age is to be decided by the President and is considered as final.

Removal

- He can resign his office by writing to the President.
- He can be removed from his office on the recommendation of the Parliament (same as Judge of SC).
- He vacates his office when he is appointed as a Judge of the Supreme Court or when he is transferred to another High Court.

Salaries and Allowances

- Determined by Parliament from time to time.
- Present salary of the Chief Justice of High Court is ₹ 90000 per month; and Judge of the High Court is ₹ 80000.

Independence of High Court

Following provisions are made to safeguard and ensure the independence of High Court

- Mode of appointment.
- Security of tenure.
- Fixed service conditions.
- Expenses charged on the consolidated fund of state.
- Conduct of judge cannot be discussed.
- Ban on practice after retirement.
- Power to punish for its contempt.
- Freedom to appoint its staff.
- Its jurisdiction cannot be curtailed.
- Separation from executive.

Jurisdiction and Powers of High Court

At present, a High Court enjoys the following jurisdiction and powers

- Original jurisdiction
- Writ jurisdiction (Article 226)
- Appellate jurisdiction
- Supervisory jurisdiction
- Control over subordinate courts.
- A court of record.
- Power of judicial review.

The Supreme Court can issue writ jurisdiction, only where a Fundamental Right has been infringed. High Court can issue these writs Under Article 226 not only in such cases, but also where an ordinary legal right has been infringed.

High Court does not have advisory power as in case of Supreme Court.

Subordinate Courts

Articles 233 to 237 in Part VI of the Contitution make the provisions to regulate the organisation of subordinate courts and to ensure their independence from the executive.

Appointment of District Judges

The appointment, posting and promotion of district judges in a state are made by Governor of the State in consultation with the High Court.

A person to be appointed as district judge should have the following qualifications

- He should not already be in the service of the Central or the State Government.

- He should have been an advocate or a pleader for seven years.
- He should be recommended by the High Court.

Appointment of Other Judges

Appointment of persons (other than district judges) to the judicial services of a state are made by the Governor of the State after consultation with the State Public Service Commission and the High Court.

NYAYA PANCHAYAT

The Nyaya Panchayats are the judicial bodies in village, which provide speedy and inexpensive justice for all petty civil suits. Usually, their domain of jurisdiction is limited to four to five villages only. They can impose only monetary fines at the most, as punishments are barred from the power to award imprisonment sentences (except Bihar).

Union-State Relations

The federal system adopted in India involves division of authority between the union and the states. *Relations between the union and states can be studied under the following parts.*

A. Legislative Relations (Art. 245-255)

- The Constitution divides the subjects into the Union List (100 subjects), the State List (61 subjects) and the Concurrent List (52 subjects). Enumerated in the Seventh Schedule under Article 246. Parliament has exclusive power to legislate on subjects mentioned in the Union List. This list contains subjects like defence, foreign affairs, atomic energy etc.
- State Legislatures have exclusive power to legislate on subjects mentioned in the State List. The State List contains subjects like health, sanitation, public order, agriculture etc. Both Parliament and State Legislatures can legislate on subjects mentioned in the Concurrent List. This list contains subjects like criminal law, forests, education, marriage and divorce etc.
- **Residual Powers** (i.e. subjects not included in any of the list) rest with Union Government.

Lok Adalat

- Lok Adalat (People's Courts), established by the government, settles disputes through conciliation and compromise. The first Lok Adalat was held in Gujrat on 14th March, 1982.
- The Lok Adalat is presided over by a sitting or retired judicial officer as Chairman, with two other member, usually a lawyer and a social worker. There is no court fee. If the case is already filed in a regular court, the fee paid is refunded if the dispute is settled at the Lok Adalat.
- Lok Adalat is very effective in settlement of money claims. Disputes, like partition suits, damages and matrimonial cases, can also be easily settled in Lok Adalat, as chances of compromise through give and take approach stand high in such cases.
- Lok Adalat is a boon to the litigant public, where they can get their disputes settled fast and free of cost.
- Lok Adalats have been given the status of a Civil Court and every award made by the Lok Adalat is final and binding on all parties and no appeals lies to any court against its award.

B. Administrative Relations (Art. 256-263)

The states are expected to comply with the Laws of the Parliament and not impede the exercise of the Executive Powers of the Union (Articles 256, 257). In this regard, the Union Government can issue necessary directives to the states. All disputes between states regarding the use, distribution or control of water are decided by the centre (Article 262).

C. Financial Relations (Art. 268-293)

- The states are greatly dependent on the Central Government for finance. The State Governments have been provided independent sources of revenue, but these are inadequate.
- The Union Government has the power to borrow from within India or outside, subject to the limits laid down by the Parliament, the borrowing power of the states is subject to several limitations and the cannot borrow from outside India.

Zonal Councils (Article 263)

- Six zonal councils have been established to discuss and advise on matters of common interest. The Union Home Minister has been nominated to be the common Chairman of all Zonal Councils. Set-up under State Reorganisation Act, 1956.
  - **Northern Zonal Council** Consist of Punjab, Rajasthan, Haryana, Jammu and Kashmir, Himachal Pradesh, Chandigarh and Delhi. Headquarters–New Delhi
  - **Central Zonal Counil** Uttar Pradesh, Uttarakhand, Chhattisgarh and Madhya Pradesh. Headquarters–Allahabad
  - **Eastern Zonal Council** Bihar, Jharkhand, West Bengal and Odisha. Headquarters–Kolkata
  - **Western Zonal Council** Maharashtra, Goa, Gujarat and UTs of Dadra and Nagar Haveli and Daman Diu. Headquarters– Mumbai
  - **Southern Zonal Council** Andhra Pradesh Tamil Nadu, Karnataka, Kerala and UT of Puducherry. Headquarters–Chennai
  - **North Eastern Council** It was created in 1971 by a separate Act of parliament for Assam, Manipur, Tripura, Meghalaya, Nagaland, Mizoram and Arunachal Pradesh. In 1994, Sikkim was included in it.

Punchhi Commission

In April, 2007, a new commission was set-up to re-examine centre-state relations. The commission was headed by former Chief Justice of India **MM Punchhi**.

The major recommendations of the Punchhi Commission can be summed up as follows

- There should be an **amendment in Articles 355** and **356** to enable the centre to bring specific trouble-torn areas under its rule for a limited period.
- **Inter-State Relation** An Inter- State Council can be established by the President under **Article 263** of the Constitution of India. The function of the Inter-State Council is to investigate and discuss subjects in which states and union have a common interest. It also makes recommendations for better co-ordination of policy and action with respect to a subject.
- Under **Article 262**, Parliament has constituted the Inter-State Water Disputes Tribunal for adjudication of disputes between states for the waters of any inter-state river or river valley.

- Inter-state river water disputes are excluded from the jurisdiction of all courts including the Supreme Court.
- The commission has proposed "localising emergency provision" under **Articles 355** and **356**, contending that localised areas either a district or part of a district be brought under government rule instead of the whole state.
- The commission supports the Governor's right to give sanction for the prosecution of ministers against the advice of the State Government.
- There should be **changes in the role of the Governor** including fixed five year tenure as well as their removal only through impeachment by the State Assembly.
- It has been proposed that the appointment of Governor should be **entrusted to a committee** comprising the Prime Minister, Home Minister, Speaker of the Lok Sabha and Chief Minister of the concerned state.

Sarkaria Commission

It was set-up in June, 1983, by the Central Government of India to examine the relationship and balance of power between states and centre. It was headed by Justice Rajinder Singh Sarkaria, a retired Judge of the Supreme Court of India.

Special Status of Jammu and Kashmir

- **Article 370** of the Indian Constitution accords special status to the State of Jammu and Kashmir. The Constitution specifically stipulates that the provisions with respect to the State of Jammu and Kashmir are of purely temporary nature. The prominent features of the special relationship of the State of Jammu and Kashmir with the Indian Union are as follows
  - The union has no power to make a proclamation of Financial Emergency with respect to state of Jammu and Kashmir under **Article 360**.
  - Jammu and Kashmir has its own Constitution, which was framed by a special Constituent Assembly and came into being on the 26th January, 1957.

- The Parliament cannot increase or decrease the area of the state or alter the name or boundary of the state without the consent of the State Legislature. The State Government shall be consulted by the centre before appointing a person as the Governor of Jammu and Kashmir.
- It has **dual citizenship**. Only the citizens of Jammu and Kashmir can take part in the election of the State Assembly and only he can buy immovable property in Jammu and Kashmir.
- The Parliament can make laws with regard to Jammu and Kashmir only on subjects meantioned in the Union List and not on the State List.

- The residuary powers in respect of Jammu and Kashmir rest with the State Government and not the Union Government.
- Besides the President's Rule, the Governor's Rule can also be imposed for a maximum period of six months, in case of constitutional breakdown in the state.
- The President of India can proclaim National Emergency on grounds of war and external aggression and not on grounds of armed rebellion.
- No preventive detention law made by the Parliament can have automatic extension to Jammu and Kashmir.

PANCHAYATI RAJ

PANCHAYATS

- Panchayats constitute functional institutions of grassroot governance in villages. The **Balwant Rai Mehta Committee**, January 1957, recommended that decision-making should be decentralised and elected local bodies should be established. However, the Panchayat Raj Institutions (PRIs) could not develop as it was expected to do so.
- In 1977, the government appointed the **Ashok Mehta Committee** to examine the measures to strengthen PRIs.
- The **LM Singhvi Committee** (1986) recommended Constitutional Status for local bodies.

73rd AMENDMENT ACT

- The Constitution 73rd Amendment Act,1992 inserted a new part IX into the Constitution.

The salient features of Part IX of the Constitution are as follows

- The term of the Panchayats is five years unless dissolved earlier. Seats shall be compulsorily reserved for Scheduled Castes and Scheduled Tribes. Seats to be reserved for backward classes is left at the discretion of the State Government.
- There is a provision of State Finance Commission to review the financial position of Panchayats and recommend grant-in-aids.

- **One-third** of the seats are reserved for women. A State Election Commission headed by the State Election Commissioner shall conduct elections for the Panchayats.
- The Constitution has provided for **three-tier system** of Panchayats at the village, intermediate and district levels.

Three Tier System

- The three-tier system of Panchayat Raj was first adopted by Rajasthan (Nagaur district on 2nd October, 1959) followed by Andhra Pradesh.

(a) Village Panchayat

- It consists of elected representatives of the people, its membership varies from 5-31. There is reservation for SC, ST and Women.
- Chairman, i.e. **Sarpanch** is elected in a manner as the State Legislature may provide directly or indirectly.
- Villages Panchayat has to answer Gram Sabha for all its actions.
- Gram Sabha comprises the residing adults of the Panchayat and it supervises the working of Panchayat.

(b) Block and Panchayat Samiti

- The Block consists 20-60 villages. It is governed by the elected members of Village Panchayat, which is called Panchayat Samiti.

- **Pradhan** is the head or Chairman of Panchayat Samiti.
- States with population less than 20 lakh need not constitute a Block Panchayat. Chairperson is elected form amongst the members.

(c) Zila Parishad

- Members of the Zila Parishad are elected from the district by direct election on the basis of adult franchise for a term of 5 years.
- Chairman of Zila Parishad is elected from amongst the members.

MUNICIPALITIES
(Articles 243P-243ZG)

- The Constitution of India provides the provision of local self government units in urban area by inserting Part IX-A through the 74th Amendment Act, 1992.
- The Constitution provides for three types of Municipalities. **Nagar Panchayat**, for areas in transition from rural to urban.
- **Municipal Council** is for smaller urban area.
- **Municipal Corporation** is for larger urban area. It is the biggest urban local government.
- The Constitution of Municipalities shall be determined by a Law of the State Legislature. Wards Committees shall be constituted in those Municipalities having a population of three lakh or more.
- Seats shall be reserved for Scheduled Castes and Scheduled Tribes.
- One-third of the seats shall be reserved for women.
- Municipalities will have the power to impose taxes, duties, tolls and fees in accordance with law. The Constitution provides for a State Finance Commission to review the financial position of the Municipalities and recommend measures to augment their funds.

- Under **Article 243 ZD, a District Planning Committee** shall be constituted to consolidate the plans prepared by the Panchayats and Municipalities in the district.
- Under **Article 243 ZE, a Metropolitan Planning Committee** shall be constituted to prepare a draft development plan for the metropolitan area as a whole.

OFFICIAL LANGUAGE

- **Part XVII** of the Constitution deals with the official language in **Articles 343** to **351**.
- Hindi written in **Devanagari Script** is to be the official language of the Union.
- In **1955**, the President appointed an official Language Commission under the **Chairmanship of BG Kher**.
- All proceeding in the Supreme Court and in every High Court are to be in **English Language** only.
- The authoritative texts of all bills, acts, ordinances, order, rules, regulation and by-laws at the central and state levels.
- Normally there were **fourteen** languages in Eighth Schedule, but **eight** were **added** during amendments, now 22 languages are there 1. Assamese 2. Bengali 3. Gujarati 4. Hindi 5. Kannada 6. Kashmiri 7. Konkani 8. Malayalam 9. Manipuri 10. Marathi 11. Nepali 12. Oriya 13. Punjabi 14. Sanskrit 15. Sindhi 16. Tamil 17. Telugu 18. Urdu 19. Santhali 20. Bodo 21. Maithili 22. Dogri.
- Sindhi was added by the 21st Amendment Act, 1967; Konkani, Manipuri and Nepali were added by the 71st Amendment Act, 1992; and Bodo, Dogri, Maithili and Santhali were added by the 92nd Amendment Act, 2003.
- The Constitution imposes a duty upon the centre to spread the development of the Hindi language so that it may become the 'lingua franca' of the composite culture of India.

MISCELLANEOUS

Comptroller and Auditor General of India

- The Constitution of India (Article 148) provides for an independent office of the Comptroller and Auditor General of India (CAG).
- He is the guardian of the public purse and audits the accounts of the government at both the levels- the centre and the state.
- His duty is to uphold the Constitution of India and laws of Parliament in the field of financial administration.
- **Article 148 to 151** of the Constitution deals with CAG's appointment, powers and audit reports.
- The CAG of India is appointed by the President for **six years or till sixty five years**, of age whichever is earlier.
- His removal process is similar to that of a Judge of the Supreme Court.
- **Shri V Narahari Rao**, was the first Comptroller and Auditor General of India (1948-1954).
- Rajiv Mehrishi is the present CAG of India.

Attorney General of India

- The Constitution (Article 76) has provided for the office of the Attorney General of India. He is the highest law officer in the country.
- The Attorney General of India must be a person, who is qualified to be appointed as a Judge of the Supreme Court. He is appointed by the President.
- The **term of office** of the Attorney General is **not fixed** by the Constitution. Further, the Constitution does not contain the procedure and grounds for his removal. He holds office during the pleasure of the President.
- The Attorney General's duty is to give advice to the Government of India upon such legal matters, which are referred to him by the President.

Advocate General of the State

- Article 165, has provided for the office of the Advocate General for the states. He acts as highest Law officer in the state, corresponding to the Attorney General of India.
- He is appointed by the Governor to give advice to state government on legal matters. And he also performs such other duties of a legal nature that are assigned to him by the Governor.

- The Attorney General appears before the Supreme Court and various High Courts in cases involving the Government of India.
- The Attorney General of India is **not a member of the Cabinet**.
- He has the Right to Speak in the either House of Parliament, but he has no Right to Vote.
- **KK Venugopal** is the present Attorney General of India.

Election Commission

- An independent Election Commission has been established under the Constitution in order to carry out and regulate the holding of elections in India. The Election Commission was established in accordance with the Constitution on 25th January, 1950.
- The Election Commission prepares, maintains and periodically updates the electoral roll, which shows who is entitled to vote, supervises the nominations of candidates, register political parties, monitors the election campaign.

Administrative Tribunals

- The 42nd Amendment Act of 1976 added a new Part XIV-A to the Constitution. This part is entitled as 'Tribunals' and consist of only two Articles, Article 323A dealing with administrative tribunals and Article 323B dealing with tribunals for other matters.
- The Central Administrative Tribunal (CAT) was set-up in 1985, with the principal bench at Delhi and additional benches in different states.

- It also organises the polling booths, counting of votes, and declaration of results, to ensure the orderly and fair manner of elections.

- At present Election Commission consists of Chief Election Commissioner and two Election Commissioners.
- The Constitution provides for an Independent Election Commission to ensure free and fair elections to the Parliament, the State Legislature and the offices of the President and Vice-President.
- The **Chief Election Commissioner** and other Election Commissioners are appointed by the President for **6 years or till 65 years**, whichever is earlier. (Article 324).

Chief Election Commissioners of India

Name	Tenure	
	From	To
Sukumar Sen	21.03.1950	19.12.1958
KVK Sundaram	20.12.1958	30.09.1967
SP Sen Verma	01.10.1967	30.09.1972
Dr Nagendra Singh	01.10.1972	06.02.1973
T Swaminathan	07.02.1973	17.06.1977
SL Shakdhar	18.06.1977	17.06.1982
RK Trivedi	18.06.1982	31.12.1985
RVS Peri Sastri	01.01.1986	25.11.1990
Smt VS Rama Devi	26.11.1990	11.12.1990
TN Seshan	12.12.1990	11.12.1996
MS Gill	12.12.1996	13.06.2001
JM Lyngdoh	14.06.2001	07.02.2004
TS Krishnamurthy	08.02.2004	15.05.2005
BB Tandon	16.05.2005	29.06.2006
N Gopalaswamy	30.06.2006	20.04.2009
Navin Chawla	21.04.2009	29.07.2010
SY Qureshi	30.07.2010	10.06.2012
VS Sampath	11.06.2012	15.01.2015
HS Brahma	16.01.2015	18.04.2015
Dr. Nasim Zaidi	19.04.2015	05.07.2017
Achal Kumar Joti	06.07.2017	22.01.2018
Om Prakash Rawat	23.01.2018	Till Date

Delimitation Commission

- Delimitation Commission or Boundary Commission of India is a commission, established by Government of India under the provisions of the Delimitation Commission Act. The main task of the commission is to redraw the boundaries of the various assemblies and Lok Sabha Constituencies based on a recent census. The representation from each state is not changed during this exercise. However, the number of SC and ST seats in a state are changed in accordance with the census.

- The commission is a powerful body, whose orders cannot be challenged in a court of law. The orders are laid before the Lok Sabha and the respective State Legislative Assemblies. However, modifications are not permitted.
- Delimitation Commissions have been set-up four times in the past, in 1952, 1963, 1973 and 2002, under Delimitation Commission Acts of 1952, 1962, 1972 and 2002.
- The delimitation commission was set-up on 12th July, 2002 after the 2001 Census with **Justice Kuldip Singh**, a retired Judge of the Supreme Court of India as its Chairperson.

The **assembly elections** in Karnataka, which were conducted in three phases in May, 2008 was the first one to use the new boundaries as drawn by the 2002 Delimitation Commission.

NOTA

The None Of The Above (NOTA) is an option on the Electronic Voting Machines (EVMs), through this peoples get the right of votes to reject all candidates contesting the elections. A 'NOTA' does not require the involvement of the presiding officer. The NOTA option was first used in the assembly election of five states in November 2013. The NOTA option would not impact the result of elections.

- The Chief Election Commissioner can be removed on ground similar to that of a Judge of the Supreme Court. The other Election Commis- sioners may be removed by the President on the recommendation of the Chief Election Commissioner.
- The general election is held on the basis of **Universal Adult Suffrage**.

Union Public Service Commission (UPSC)

- With the promulgation of the new Consitution for Independent India on 26th January, 1950, the Federal Public Service Commission was accorded a consitutional status as an autonomous entity and given the title Union Public Service Commission.

The Structure of UPSC

- The Chairman and other members of the UPSC are appointed by the President and they hold office for a term of **6 years** from the date of appointment or until they attain the age of **65 years**. They are independent of the Executive and Legislature in the same manner as the Judges of the Supreme Court.
- Age of retirement for a member of Public Service Commission of a State or Joint Commission is 62 years.

Removal of Members

- UPSC members can resign by addressing their letter of resignation to the President.
- President can remove them by issuing orders under the circumstances provided in the Constitution.

Functions of UPSC

- To conduct exams for appointment to services under the union. Advise the President (not obligatory on him) in matters relating to appointment, promotions and transfers from one service to another of civil servants.
- All disciplinary matters affecting person in the service of union.
- Matters regarding award of pension and awards in respect to injuries sustained during service under the government.

Central Information Commission (CIC)

- Right to Information became an act in 2005. The aim is to make the governments more transparent in its working. It came into operation on 12th October, 2005.
- Under the act, a Central Information Commission and State Information Commissions needs to be constituted.
- The Central Information Commission and State Information Commission hear complaints from any person, who has been denied information by any government authority.
- The Chief Information Commissioner and other Information Commissioners shall be **appointed by the President** on the **recommendation of a committee** consisting of the Prime Minister, the leader of opposition in Lok Sabha and a Union Cabinet Minister to be nominated by the PM. In its 6 years of working, the RTI Act has given citizens the power to make its government accountable. Increasingly citizens are using RTI Act to get access to information.

Planning Commission

The Planning Commission was an institution in the Government of India, which formulated India's Five-Year Plans. The Government has replaced Planning Commission with a new institution named NITI Aayog (National Institution for Transforming India).

NITI Aayog

- The institution will serve as '**Think Tank**' of the Government, a directional and policy dynamo.
- NITI Aayog will provide governments and the central and state levels with relevant strategic and technical advice across the spectrum of key elements of policy. This includes matters of national and international importance. PM is the ex-officio chairman of NITI Aayog.

Functions of NITI Aayog

- To foster cooperative federalism through structured support, initiatives and mechanisms with the states on a continuous basis, recognising that strong states make a strong nation.
- To develop mechanisms to formulate credible plans at the village level and aggregate these progressively at higher levels of government.
- To ensure, on areas that are specifically referred to it, that the interest of national security are incorporated in economic strategy and policy. To pay special attention to the sections of our society that may be at risk of not benefitting adequately from economic progress.
- To provide advice and encourage partnerships between key stakeholders and national and international like-minded Think Tanks, as well as educational and policy research institutions.
- To create a knowledge, innovation and entrepreneurial support system through a collaborative community of national and international experts, practitioners and other partners.

- To offer a platform for resolution of inter-sectoral and inter-departmental issues in order to accelerate the implementation of the development agenda.
- To actively monitor and evaluate the implementation of programmes and initiatives, including the identification of the needed resources so as to strengthen the probability of success and scope of delivery.

Members of NITI Aayog

- Prime Minister of India as the Chairperson.
- Governing Council comprising the Chief Ministers of all the States and Lt Governors of Union Territories.
- The Regional Councils will be convened by the Prime Minister and will comprise of the Chief Ministers of States and Lt Governors of Union Territories in the region. These will be chaired by the Chairperson of the NITI Aayog or his nominee. Experts, specialists and practitioners with relevant domain knowledge as special invitees nominated by the Prime Minister.
- The full-time organisational framework (in addition to the Prime Minister).
- **Vice-Chairperson:** To be appointed by the Prime Minister.
- **Members**: Full-time.
- **Part-time Members:** Maximum of 2 from leading universities research organisations and other relevant institutions in an ex-officio capacity. Part time members will be on a rotational basis.
- **Ex Officio Members :** Maximum of 4 members of the Union Council of Ministers to be nominated by the Prime Minister.
- **Chief Executive Officer:** To be appointed by the Prime Minister for a fixed tenure, in the rank of Secretary to the Government of India.
- Secretariat as deemed necessary.

Political Parties

- Political parties are voluntary associations or organised groups of individuals, who share the same political views and who try to gain political power through constitutional means and who desire to work for promoting the national interest.

Recognised National Political Parties

Party	Symbol	Year of Formation
Bahujan Samaj Party (BSP)	Elephant	1984
Bhartiya Janata Party (BJP)	Lotus	1980
Communist Party of India (CPI)	Ears of Corn and Sickle	1925
Communist Party of India-Marxist (CPM)	Hammer, Sickle and Star	1964
Indian National Congress (INC)	Hand	1885
Nationalist Congress Party (NCP)	Clock	1999
All India Trinamool Congress (AITC)	Flower and Grass	1998

- To be **recognised as a National Party,** a party needs to secure atleast 6% of the valid votes polled in any four or more states in a general election to the Lok Sabha or State Assembly. In addition to it, it has to win atleast four seats in the Lok Sabha from any state or states as well.
- For getting **recognition as a State Party**, a political party has to secure atleast 6% of the valid votes in the state during a general election, either to that of the Lok Sabha or the State Assembly. Apart from this, the party should also win minimum two seats in the assembly of the state concerned.

Anti-Defection Law

- The 52nd Amendment Act of 1985 provided for the disqualification of the Members of Parliament and the State Legislatures on the ground of defection from one Political Party to another.
- The 91st Amendment Act of 2003 made one change in the provisions of the Tenth Schedule. It omitted an exceptional provision i.e., disqualification on ground of defection not to apply in case of split.

- A member of a House belonging to any political party becomes disqualified for being a Member of the House
  (a) If he voluntarily gives up his membership of such political party; or
  (b) If he votes or abstains from voting in such House contrary to any direction issued by his political party without obtaining prior permission of such party and such act has not been condoned by the party within 15 days.
- An **independent member** of a House (elected without being set-up as a candidate by any political party) becomes disqualified to remain a member of the House, if he joins any political party after such election.
- A **nominated member** of a House becomes disqualified for being a member of the House, if he joins any Political Party after the expiry of six months from the date, on which he takes his seat in the House.

Recently, the Supreme Court in a significant ruling, held that a Member of Parliament or a State Legislature can be disqualified for defying a **whip** only on two counts, when voting against the government or not agreeing to policies and programmes of the government.

E-governance

- E-governance simply means electronic governance. Governments are providing various information on their website about their working, citizen's interaction with government becomes easier.
- The National E-governance Plan was approved by the cabinet in May 2005.
- Various E-governance projects of central government are MCA21 (Corporate Ministry), Pensions, Income Tax, Central Excise, Passport Seva Project, Aadhar, E-courts, E-procurement and e-office (Central secretariat).
- Besides, the Central Government, various State Governments are undertaking various projects for E-governance under the National E-governance plan.
- E-governance has the potential to change the way governments govern and its impact would be definetly felt by the citizens of India.
- Edistrict is a mission mode project under e-governance. Its objective under National E-governance Policy is computerisation of services. Under it, different programmes are conducted in following states
  - Jandoot Project – Madhya Pradesh
  - Compact 2020 – Andhra Pradesh
  - Land Programme – Kurnataka
  - Friends – Kerala
  - Dish – Haryana

Lokpal and Lokayuktas

The Lokpal and Lokayuktas Act, 2013 was made by the Parliament to provide for the establishment of body of Lokpal for the Union and Lokayukta for state to inquire into allegations of corruptions against certain public functionaries and for matters connecting them.

Salient Features of Lokpal and Lokayuktas Act

- Lokpal bill consists of a chairperson and a maximum of eight members of which 50% shall be judicial members. 50% of members of Lokpal shall be from SC/ST/OBCs, minorities and women.
- The selection of chairperson and members of Lokpal shall be through a selection committee consist of
  1. Prime Minister
  2. Speaker of Lok Sabha
  3. Leader of opposition in Lok Sabha
  4. Chief Justice of India or a sitting Judge of Supreme Court nominated by CJI.
  5. Eminent jurist on the basis of recommendations of the first four members of the selection committee. Prime Minister has been brought under the purview of the Lokpal.

National Human Rights Commission

- The National Human Rights Commission is a statutory body, constituted in 1993 under the Protection of Human Rights Act, 1993.
- The commission acts a watchdog of human rights in the country. It is a multimember body consisting of a chairman and four members. The chairman should be a retired Chief Justice of India, and members should be serving or retired Judges of supreme court and person having special knowledge or practical experience with respect to human rights.

National Commission for SCs and STs

- The National Commission for SCs and STs have been established under the Article 338 and 338-A respectively as a constitutional body.
- They investigate all matter related to constitutional and other legal safeguards for SCs and STs and report to the President on their working. And also advice on the planning process for socio-economic development of SCs and STs.

CONSTITUTIONAL AMENDMENTS

Under **Article 368**, of the Constitution, Parliament has the power of amending the Constitution.

There are three methods

- **Method of Simple Majority** The Constitution can be amended by simple majority in matters relating to citizenship, abolishing or creating second chambers in the states creation of states or alteration of boundaries of existing states etc. **By Special Majority** Constitutional Amendments must be passed by each House by a majority of the total membership of that House and by a majority of not less than two-thirds of the members of that House present and voting.
- **In the Third Method** In this method, apart from passing through a special majority in Parliament, it should also be passed by half the the state legislatures.

Basic Features

- The present position is that the Parliament under **Article 368** can amend any part of the Constitution including the Fundamental Rights, but without affecting the 'basic features' of the Constitution.
- However, the Supreme Court is yet to define or clarify as to what constitutes the 'basic feature' of the Constitution.
- From the various judgements, the following have emerged as 'basic features' of the Constitution: Supremacy of the Constitution, secular character of the Constitution, separation of powers between the Legislature, the Executive and the Judiciary, federal character of the Constitution, judicial review, rule of law, parliamentary system, free and fair elections, limited power of Parliament to amend the Constitution.

Important Constitutional Amendments

- **The First Amendment 1951,** to overcome certain practical difficulties related to Fundamental Rights. It made provision for special treatment of educationally and socially backward classes and added Ninth Schedule to the Constitution.
- **The Third Amendment 1954,** it substituted entry 33 of List III (Concurrent List) of the Seventh Schedule to make it correspond to Article 369.
- **The Seventh Amendment 1956,** was necessitated on account of reorganisation of States on a linguistic basis and changed First and Fourth Schedules.
- **The Eighth Amendment 1960,** extended special provision for reservation of seats for SCs, STs and Anglo-Indians in Lok Sabha and Legislative Assemblies for a period of 10 years from 1960 to 1970.
- **The Ninth Amendment 1960,** transferred certain territories to Pakistan following September, 1958, Indo-Pak Agreement.
- **The Tenth Amendment 1961,** incorporated the territories of Dadra and Nagar Haveli in Indian Union.
- **The Twelfth Amendment 1962,** incorporated the territories of Goa, Daman and Diu in Indian Union.
- **The Thirteenth Amendment 1962,** created Nagaland as a State of the Union of India.
- **The Fourteenth Amendment 1962,** incorporated former French Territory of Puducherry in Indian Union.
- **The Eighteenth Amendment 1966,** was made to facilitate reorganisation of Punjab into Punjab and Haryana and also created the UT of Chandigarh.
- **The Twenty-First Amendment 1967,** included Sindhi as the 15th regional language in the Eighth Schedule.
- **The Twenty-Second Amendment 1969,** created a sub-state of Meghalaya within Assam.

- **The Twenty-Third Amendment 1970,** extended the reservation of seats for SC/ST and nomination of Anglo-Indians for a further period of 10 years (upto 1980).

- **The Twenty-Seventh Amendment 1971,** provided for the establishment of the States of Manipur and Tripura, the formation of the Union Territories of Mizoram and Arunachal Pradesh.

- **The Thirty-First Amendment 1973,** increased elective strength of Lok Sabha from 525 to 545. Upper limit of representatives of state became 525 from 500.

- **The Thirty-Sixth Amendment 1975,** made Sikkim a state of the Indian Union.

- **The Forty-Second Amendment 1976,** provided supremacy of Parliament and gave primacy to Directive Principles over Fundamental Rights and also added 10 Fundamental Duties. New words-socialist, secular and integrity, were added in the Preamble.

- **The Forty-Fourth Amendment 1978,** restored the normal duration of Lok Sabha and Legislative Assemblies to 5 Years, Right to Property was deleted from Part III. It limited the power of the government to proclaim internal emergency.

- **The Forty-Fifth Amendment 1980,** extended reservation for SC/ST by 10 years (upto 1990).

- **The Fifty-Second Amendment 1985,** inserted the Tenth Schedule in the Constitution regarding provisions as to disqualification on the grounds of defection.

- **The Fifty-Fourth Amendment 1986,** enhanced salaries of Judges of Supreme Court and High Court.

- **The Fifty-Fifth Amendment 1986,** conferred statehood on Arunachal Pradesh.

- **The Fifty-Sixth Amendment 1987,** Hindi version of the Constitution of India was accepted for all purposes and statehood was also conferred on the UT of Goa.

- **The Sixty-First Amendment 1989,** reduced voting age from 21 to 18 years for Lok Sabha and Assemblies.

- **The Seventy-Third Amendment 1992,** (Panchayati Raj Bill) provided Gram Sabha in villages, direct elections to all seats in Panchayats and reservation of seats for the SC and ST, women and fixing of tenure of 5 years for Panchayats.

- **The Seventy-Forth Amendment 1992,** (Nagar Palika Bill) provided for Constitution of three types of municipalities, reservation of seats for SC and ST, women and the backward class.

- **The Seventy-Ninth Amendment 1999,** extended reservation for the SC/ST for further period of ten years, i.e. up to 25th January, 2010.

- **The Eightieth Amendment 2001,** certain changes were made to tax distribution provided under Articles 269, 270 and 272 of the Constitution.

- **The Eighty-Fourth Amendment 2001,** the number of representatives in the Lok Sabha and State Assemblies to freeze to current levels for the next 25th years (till 2026).

- **The Eighty-Fifth Amendment 2001,** provided for consequential seniority in case of promotion (with retrospective effect from 17th June, 1995) by virtue of the rule of reservation for government servants belonging to SCs/STs.

- **The Eighty-Sixth Amendment 2002,** the act deals with the insertion of a new Article 21A after Article 21. The new Article 21A deals with Right to Education "the state shall provide free and compulsory education to all children from the age of 6 to 14 years in such a manner as the state may, by law determine."

- **The Eighty-Eighth Amendment 2003,** provides for the insertion of a new Article 268A. Service tax levied by union and collected and appropriated by the union and the states. Amendment of Article 270, Amendment of Seventh Schedule.

- **The Eighty-Ninth Amendment 2003,** provides for the Amendment of Article 338. There shall be a National Commission for the SCs/STs.

- **The Ninety-First Amendment 2003,** amended the anti-defection laws and provided for Amendment of Article 75. The total number of Ministers, including the Prime Minister, and the Council of Ministers shall not exceed 15% of the total number of members of the House of the People.

- **The Ninety-Second Amendment 2003,** provided for the Amendment of Eigth Schedule by adding four new regional languages (Bodo, Maithili, Santhali and Dogri) thus, extending the list to 22 languages.

- **The Ninety-Third Amendment 2005,** (came into effect on 20th January, 2006) provided for special provision, by law, for the advancement of any socially and educationally backward classes of citizens or for the SCs/STs in so far as such special provisions relate to their admission to educational institutions including private educational institutions.

- **The Ninety-Forth Amendment 2006,** to provide for a Minister of Tribal Welfare in newly created Jharkhand and Chhattisgarh.

- **The Ninety-Fifth Amendment 2009,** extended reservation for the SC/ST for further period of ten years, that is upto 25th January, 2020.

- **The Ninety-Sixth Amendmant 2011** substituted 'Odia' for "Oriya'.

- **The Ninety-Seventh Amendment 2011,** provided for the Co-operative societies in Part IX B of the Constitution of India. It also amended Article 19 (1) (c) and inserted Article 43B.

- **The Ninety-Eighth Amendment Act, 2012**, Provided for special provisions for the Hyderabad-Karnataka region of the state of Karnataka.

- **The Ninety-Ninth Amendment Act, 2014**, regulates the procedure to be followed by the National Judicial Appointments Commission (NJAC) for appointment and transfer of chief Justice and Judges of Supreme Court and High Courts. But Supreme Court declared this unconstitutional and void.

- **The Hundredth Amendment Act, 2015**, deals with the acquiring of territories by India and transfer of certain territories to Bangladesh in pursuance of the agreements and its protocol between India and Bangladesh.

- **The Hundred and One Amendment 2017** deals with the Goods and Services Tax act. The GST is a comprehensive indirect tax levy on manufacture, sale and consumption of goods as well as services at the national level.

SOME PARLIAMENTARY TERMS

Quorum A Quorum is the minimum number of members of a deliberative assembly necessary to conduct the business of that group. Quorum for either House is 1/10th of the total number of members of each House including the presiding officer.

Penalty If a person sits or votes as a member of either House of the Parliament before he has complied with the requirements of Article 99 (oath) or when he knows that he is not qualified or that he is disqualified for membership thereof, he shall be liable in respect of each day on which he so sits or votes to a penalty of ₹ 500 to be recovered as a debt to the union.

Parliamentary Privileges Parliamentary privileges are special rights, immunities and exemptions enjoyed by the two Houses of Parliament, their committees and their members. Privileges are provided in Article 105 (Union Legislature) and Article 194 (State Legislature) of the Constitution.

Parliamentary privileges can be classified into two broad categories: collective privileges and individual privileges.

Collective Privileges *The privileges belonging to each House of Parliament collectively are*

- It can exclude strangers from its proceedings and hold **secret sittings** to discuss some important matters.
- It can make rules to regulate its own procedure and the conduct of its business and to adjudicate upon such matters.
- The courts are prohibited to enquire into the proceedings of a House or its committees.

Individual Privileges *The privileges belonging to the members individually are*

- They **cannot be arrested** during the session of Parliament and 40 days before the beginning and 40 days after the end of a session. This privilege is available **only in civil cases** and not in criminal cases.
- They have freedom of speech in Parliament. No member is liable to any proceedings in any court for anything said or any vote given by him in Parliament.

Question Hour The first hour of every sitting in both Houses (11 am to 12 pm). In this, questions are asked by members and answered by ministers. Question hour is an important mechanism through which Executive's accountability is brought about. *There are three types of questions*

(i) **A Starred Question** It requires oral answers. Supplementaries can be asked.

(ii) **An Unstarred Question** requires a written answer and hence, no supplementary questions can be asked.

(iii) **A Short Notice Questions** These are the ones which relates to matters of urgent public importance and can be asked by members with notice shorter than ten days prescribed for an ordinary question. It is answered orally.

Zero Hour the time gap between the question hour and the agenda is known as zero hour. This time is allotted everyday for miscellaneous business, call-attention notices, questions on official statements and adjournment motions. It has been in existence since 1962.

Motion It is a proposal brought before the House for its opinion or decision. *The different types of motions are*

Adjournment Motion It leads to setting aside the normal business of the Houses for discussing a definite matter of urgent public importance.

Call-Attention Motion A member (after permission from the speaker) calls the attention of the minister to any matter of 'urgent public importance'. There is no call-attention motion in the Rajya Sabha. Instead, there exists a motion called 'motion for papers'.

Censure Motion It can be moved only in the Lok Sabha and only by the opposition. It can be brought against the ruling government or against any minister for the failure of an act or seeking disapproval of their policy. A censure motion **must specify the charges** against the government for which it is moved.

No Confidence Motion It can be moved only in the Lok Sabha and only by the opposition. It needs the support of 50 members to be admitted. It can be brought only against the Council of Ministers and not against any individual minister. A No Confidence Motion, **need not to specify the reasons**, for which it has been moved. If it is passed, the Government has to resign.

Privilege Motion A resolution introduced by the opposition that a minister has mislead the House by giving wrong information.

Cut Motions They are **moved in the Lok Sabha only**. They are related to the budgetary process which seeks to reduce the amount for grants. The Cut Motion can be divided into three categories : policy cut, economy cut and token cut.

Lame Duck Session This refers to the last session of the existing Lok Sabha which is held after a new Lok Sabha has been elected after the general election.

Whip A directive issued by any political party to ensure the support of its members voting in favour or against a particular issue on the floor of the House. A person may lose the membership of the party and the legislature if he votes against the whip or abstains from voting.

Gerry Mandering It is the reorganisation of electoral districts attempted by the ruling party to gain some electoral advantage in the forthcoming elections.

Guillotine When due to lack of time, demand for grants are put to vote whether they are discussed or not in the House on the last day of the allotted time, it is called Guillotine and it concludes the discussion on demands for grants.

GLOSSARY

Address of President   The President of India addresses to both Houses of Parliament assembled together at the commencement of the first session after each general election to Lok Sabha and at the commencement of the first session of each year.

Adjournment of House   The Speaker of the Lok Sabha determines, when the sitting of the House is to be adjourned since die or to a particular day or to an hour or part of the same day. In the Rajya Sabha, Chairman decides when Rajya Sabha needs to be adjourned.

Breach of Privileges   If a person disregards the privileges, rights and immunities of the Members of Parliament, then he commits breach of privileges.

Closure   It is the Parlimentary procedure, by which debate is closed and the measure under discussion brought up for an immediate vote.

Contempt of Court   It is disobedience to or disregard of the rules, orders, process or dignity of a court , which has power to punish such offence committed.

Caretaker Government   It is the government in the interregnum, which comes into existence as soon as the Council of Ministers resigns or loses confidence, or the Prime Minister dies. It lasts till the next Council of Ministers is formed. It is a constitutional necessity under Article 74.

Delegated Legislation   The Parliament gives the Executive the Power to make rules and regulations regarding an act of the Parliament. Such rules are called delegated legislation.

Dissolution   Under Article 85, the President of India dissolves the House of the people as per the procedure fixed by the Constitution. The dissolution ends the very life of the existing House and fresh election is essential to form a new House.

Electoral Roll   It is commonly known as voter's list. It gives the names of all those people, who are eligible to vote.

Extradition   It is the surrender by a foreign state of a person accused of a crime to the state, where it was committed.

Floor Crossing   It refers to the defection of a Member of Parliament from the party he was elected, to another political party.

Hung Parliament   When in a general election, no political party or coalition of the political parties is in a position to form a majority government, such a Parliament is called a Hung Parliament.

Locus Standi   It means on what grounds can a person file a case. Earlier a person, who did not have locus standi, could not file a case on behalf of aggrieved person on his own. Later when the concept of Public Interest Litigation (PIL) started, locus standi was waived and any citizen could file a PIL and bring to court's notice, violation of rights of people.

Point of Order   It is an extra-ordinary process, which when raised, has the effect of suspending the business before the house and the member, who is on his legs gives way. This is meant to assist the Presiding Officer in enforcing the Rules, Directions and Provisions of the Constitution for regulating the business of the House.

Rule of Law   The rule of law theory was given by English jurist Dicey. It has three meanings. (a) absolute supremacy of law (b) equality before law (c) Consitution is the result of the ordinary law of the land.

Subordinate Legislation   The rules and regulations made by the government within the purview of the authority delegated by the Legislature are called Subordinate Legislation. It is the same as Delegated Legislation.

Untouchability   It means social disabilities historically imposed on certain classes of people by reason of their birth in certain castes.

Vote on Account   It is an estimate of an advance payment to enable government departments to carry on their work from the beginning of financial year till the passing of the Appropriation Act.

Vote of Credit   The Lok Sabha can grant vote of credit to meet an expenditure whose amount or details cannot be precisely stated on account of magnitude or the indefinite character of service.

FAQs (INDIAN POLITY)

1. When was the last meeting of the Constituent Assembly held?

2. Emergency provisions are enumerated in which part of the Constitution?

3. Land Reforms have been exempted from Judicial Scrutiny. Under which schedule have they been placed?

4. Which Vice President of India died while in office?

5. Department of official languages, comes under which Ministry?

6. How many members of Rajya Sabha are there in the Public Accounts Committee?

7. When was the First National Emergency declared?

8. Who was the first Speaker of the Lok Sabha?

9. When was the 42nd Constitutional Amendment Act enacted?

10. What is the minimum age required to be a member of the Rajya Sabha?

11. When did the Constituent Assembly adopt the National Flag?

12. What is the duration of the National Anthem "Jana Gana Mana"?

13. Under whom are the powers of the Union Executive as per the Constitution?

14. When was the Rajya Sabha first constituted?

15. Taxes on services, was enshrined in the Constitution by which amendment?

16. By which Constitutional Amendment was Delhi given the status of National Capital Territory?

17. Under which part of the Constitution are provisions of municipalities mentioned?

18. In which year, was the Constituent Assembly of India constituted?

19. Out of 389 members in the Constituent Assembly, how many were from the Provinces?

20. When President of India resigns from office, to whom does he address his resignation letter?

21. Who was Independent India's First Education Minister?

22. Provisions regarding anti-defection are mentioned in which Schedule of the Constitution?

23. After Independence, which state was the first to be established?

24. Freedom of Press is mentioned under which Article of the Constitution?

25. On which committee's recommendations was Fundamental Duties inserted in the Constitution?

26. Which Article of the Constitution has been described as "Heart and Soul of the Constitution" by Dr B R Ambedkar?

27. The Federation System in India has been borrowed from which country's Constitution?

28. In India, military and defence powers have been given to which authority?

29. Under which Article of the Constitution, has MGNREGA been brought?

30. Under which Article of the Constitution untouchability has been regarded as an offence?

31. Who determines the salary and emoluments of the Prime Minister?

32. Directive Principles of State Policy has been borrowed from which country's Constitution?

33. At present, how many members are there in the Rajya Sabha?

34. How much is the term of the Chief Election Commissioner of India?

35. Which committee of the Parliament examines the audit reports of the Comptroller and Auditor General of India?

36. Which amendment gave Constitutional Status to Panchayati Raj in India?

37. Disputes between centre and the states or between states themselves is decided by which court?

38. The election of the President of India is done by which process?

39. Who was the Viceroy of India, when the Shimla Conference took place?

40. The High Court can stop the proceedings of an inferior court on grounds of exceeding its jurisdiction. By which writ is this possible?

41. When was the First Amendment to the Constitution done?

42. Who is the head of the State Government?

43. How many members of the Muslim community were there in the Constituent Assembly?

44. The people of which State in India, have dual citizenship?

45. How are members of the Rajya Sabha elected?

46. Under which Article of the Constitution, the President's Pardoning Powers been enshrined?

47. Who was the Chairman of the Flag Committee?

48. Who was the Railway Minister in the Interim Cabinet (1946)?

49. Which party formed the government in Punjab Province in 1937?

50. Who was the Chairman of the Advisory Committee on Fundamental Rights, of the Constituent Assembly?

51. The provisions regarding Scheduled Areas and Scheduled Tribes has been mentioned in which Schedule of the Constitution?

52. Under which Article has "Right to Freedom of Religion" been mentioned?

53. Financial Emergency has been mentioned in which Article of the Constitution?

54. How many judges are there in the Supreme Court?

55. When and where was the First High Court established?

56. How many states of India have bicameral Legislature?

57. When was the Sarkaria Commission appointed?

58. Who is the Chairman of the 14th Finance Commission?

59. Under Jawaharlal Nehru, when was the Interim Government established?

60. Who was the Chairman of the Union Constitution Committee of the Constituent Assembly?

61. The republican form of Government, has been borrowed from which country's Constitution?

62. Who is the only President of India elected, as an independent candidate?

63. Who was the First Chief Justice of the Supreme Court of India?

64. Under which Constitutional Amendment, was the rights and privileges of rulers of Princely States taken away?

65. By which Constitutional Amendment, was the voting age reduced from 21 years to 18 years?

66. Who is the First Law Officer of India?

67. By which Article of the Constitution, UPSC has been created?

68. When did the Constitution of Jammu and Kashmir come into force?

69. Who has the powers to declare an area as scheduled area for the protection of Scheduled Tribes?

70. Which words were added to the Preamble by the 42nd Constitutional Amendment Act?

71. On what ground can the President be impeached?

72. Which President of India, won in the second counting of votes?

Answers

1. 24th January, 1950 2. Part XVIII 3. Ninth Schedule 4. Krishna Kant 5. Home Ministry 6. Seven 7. 26th October, 1962 8. GV Mavalankar 9. 1976 10. 30 years 11. 22nd July, 1947 12. 52 seconds 13. President of India 14. 3rd April, 1952 15. 88th Amendment 16. 69th Amendment 17. Part IX (A) 18. 1946 19. 296 20. Vice-President 21. Abul Kalam Azad 22. Tenth Schedule 23. 1953, Andhra Pradesh 24. Article 19. 25. Swaran Singh Committee 26. Article 32

27. Canada 28. President of India 29. Article 43 30. Article 17 31. Parliament 32. Ireland 33. 245 34. Six years or till 65 years whichever is earlier 35. Public Accounts Committee 36. 73rd Amendment 37. Supreme Court 38. Single Transferable Vote 39. Lord Wavell 40. Prohibition 41. 1951 42. Governor 43. 31 44. Jammu and Kashmir 45. By the members of Legislative Assemblies 46. Article 72 47. JB Kriplani 48. Asaf Ali 49. Unionist Party 50. Jawaharlal Nehru 51. 5th Schedule 52. Article 25 53. Article 360 54. 31 55. 14th May, 1862, Kolkata 56. Seven 57. 1983 58. Dr. YV Reddy 59. 1946 60. Jawaharlal Nehru 61. France 62. V.V. Giri 63. HL Kania 64. 26th Amendment 65. 61st Amendment 66. Attorney General 67. Article 315 68. 26th January, 1957 69. President of India 70. Socialist, Secular and Integrity 71. Violating the Constitution 72. V V Giri

INDIAN ECONOMY

INTRODUCTION OF ECONOMICS

The term economics comes from the ancient Greek word *oikonomia* mean management of a household. The term economic process refers to those activities, through which goods and services aimed at satisfying human needs, are produced, distributed and used.

Economics includes the study of labour, land and investments of capital, income and production and taxes and government expenditures. Adam Smith, regarded as the Father of Economics, defines Economics as, "The science relating to the laws of production, distribution and exchange."

Branches of Economics

The two chief branches are as follow:

Micro Economics

It examine the behaviour of basic elements in the economy, including individual agents (such as households and firms or as buyers and sellers) and market and their interaction.

Macro Economics

It studies the economy as a whole and its features like national income, unemployment, poverty, balance of payments and inflation.

It deals with formulation of models explaining relationship between factors such as consumption, inflation, savings, investment, national income and finance.

ECONOMY

It represents production, distribution or trade and consumption of goods and services in a given geographical area by different agents, which can be individuals, businesses, organisation or governments.

The study of economy of any country helps us to find out the financial condition of the population as well as the different working sectors of the economy.

The modern economy is a complex machine. Its job is to allocate limited resources and distribute output among a large number of agents mainly individuals, firms and governments allowing for the possibility that each agent's action can directly (or indirectly) affect other agent's actions. There are two major type of economies.

Open Economy

It refers to a market-economy, which is generally free from trade barriers and where exports and imports form a large percentage of the GDP.

No economy is totally open or closed in terms of trade restriction and all governments have varying degrees of control over movements of capital and labour.

Degree of openness of an economy determines a government's freedom to pursue economic policies of its choice and the susceptibility of the country to the international economic cycles:

Closed Economy

An economy in which no activity is conducted with outside economies. A closed economy is self-sufficient, meaning that no imports are brought in and no exports are sent out.

The goal of such economy is to provide consumers with everything that they need from within the economy's borders.

The degree of openness of an economy is decided by their respective governments by using policy controls like tariffs, import and export quotas, and exchange rate limits.

In India, since independence, the government has played a major role in planning economic activities.

Present Status of Indian Economy

- Indian economy is world's 6th largest economy or nominal GDP basis and the 3rd largest by Purchasing Power Party (PPP) in 2017.
- According to CSO-The growth in GDP during 2017-18 is estimated at 6.5% as compared to the growth rate of 7.1% in 2016-17.
- During each of the previous two year, 2014-15 and 2015-16, India's Gross Domestic Product (GDP) (Base year 2011-12) grew by 7.2% and 7.6% respectively per annum.
- From 1951 until 2013, India GDP Annual Growth rate averaged 5.8% reaching an all time high of 10.2% in December of 1988 and a record low of 5.2% in December of 1979.
- On a per capita income basis, India ranked 141th by nominal GDP and 126th by GDP (PPP) in 2017, according to the IMF.
- Purchasing Power Parity (PPP) is a theory, which states that exchanges rates between currencies are balanced, when their purchasing power is the same in each of the two countries.

Broad Sectors of Indian Economy

Primary Sector

The primary sector include production of raw material and includes agriculture, forestry and fishing.

Secondary Sector

Mining manufacturing, electricity, gas and water supply, construction. (also called manufacturing sector)

Tertiary Sector

Business, transport, telecommunication, banking, insurance, real estate, community and personnel services. (also called service sector)

Nature of Indian Economy

- **Mixed Economy** It is an economy, where both public and private sector co-exist. The nature of Indian economy is a mixed economy. The term Mixed economy was coined by JM Keynes.
- **Developing Economy** Following features shows that Indian economy is a developing economy
  - (a) Low per capita income.
  - (b) Occupational pattern is primary sector dominated.
  - (c) Heavy population pressure.
  - (d) Prevalence of chronic unemployment and underemployment.
  - (e) Steadily improving rate of capital formation.
  - (f) Low capital per head.
  - (g) Unequal distribution of wealth/assets.
- **Agrarian Economy** An agrarian economy is a type of economy that relies primarily on agricultural industry including livestock farming or corp production. It is form of economy whose major factor of production in the agricultural land.

NATIONAL INCOME OF INDIA

- National Income (NI) is the net value of all the final goods and services produced by s nationals during a financial year. It is a flow concept. In India, the financial year is from 1st April to 31st March. The national income is calculated annually.
- According to National Income Committee (1949). "A national income estimate measures the volume of commodities and service turned out during a given period counted without duplication".

- $NI = C + G + I + (X - M) + (R - P)$ − Depreciation − Indirect tax + Subsidies.

  C = Total Consumption Expenditure
  I = Total Investment Expenditure
  G = Total Government Expenditure
  X = Export
  M = Import
  (R-P) = Net Faction Income from abroad.

- When the National Income is measured at the base year price, it is called **national income at constant price**.

- When the national income is measured at the current year price, it is called national income at current year price.

- When NNP is calculated at Factor Cost (FC) it is called National Income. This measure is calculated by deducting indirect taxes and adding subsidies in NNP at Market Price (MP).

- $NNP_{FC} = NNP_{MP}$ − Indirect Taxes + Subsidies + Government surplus = National Income.

- $NI = NNP$ + Subsidies − Indirect taxes

- GNP − Depreciation − Indirect taxes + Subsidies.

- The CSO released the 'New series' of national accounts with base year 2011-12 instead of the base year 2004-05. The revisions happen every 5 years.

> - **National Income** is the measurement of the production power of an economic system in a given time period.
> - **National Wealth** is the measurement of the present assets available at a given time.

Methods of Measuring National Income

Product Method

In this method, net value of final goods and services produced in a country during a year is obtained, which is called total final product. This represents Gross Domestic Product (GDP). Net income earned in foreign boundaries by nationals is added and depreciation is subtracted from GDP.

Income Method

In this method, a total of net income earned by working people in different sectors and commercial enterprises is obtained. Incomes of both categories of people — paying taxes and not paying taxes are added to obtain national income. By income method, national income is obtained by adding receipts as total rent, total wages, total interest and total profit.

Consumption Method

It is also called expenditure method. Income is either spent on consumption or saved. Hence, national income is the addition of total consumption and total savings.

In India, a combination of production method and income method is used for estimating national income.

Estimates of National Income in India

- In 1868, the first attempt was made by Dadabhai Naoroji in his book 'Poverty and Un-British Rule in India'. He estimated the per capita annual income to be ₹ 20.

- The first scientific attempt to measure national income in India was made by professor VKRV Rao in 1931-32. He divided the Indian economy into 13 sectors.

- In 1949, National Income Committee under the Chairmanship of professor PC Mahalanobis was constituted. The other members were professor VKRV Rao and professor DR Gadgil.

- The Government of India appointed a National Income Committee under the Chairmanship of Dr PC Mahalanobis. This committee gave its first report in 1951 and final report New Series in 1954.

NATIONAL INCOME AGGREGATES

Gross Domestic Product (GDP)

It is the total money value of all final goods and services produced within the geographical boundaries of the country during a given period of time.

$$GDP = C + G + I$$

Where,

    C = Consumption expenditure

    G = Government expenditure

    I = Investment expenditure

But in closed economy, (R - P) = 0, then GDP = GNP where, (R - P) = Net factor income from abroad.

GDP At Market Price (GDP_{MP})

- It refers to the total value of all the goods and services at market price produced during a year within the geographical boundaries of the country.
- Market price refers to the actual transacted price and it includes indirect taxes such as Excise Duty, VAT, Service Tax, Customs Duty etc but it excludes government subsidies.

GDP at Factor Cost (GDP_{FC})

- GDP can be calculated at factor cost. This measure more accurately reveals the income paid to factors of production.
- The factor cost means the total cost of all factors of production consumed or used in producing a good or service. It includes government grants and subsidies, but it excludes Indirect Taxes.
- The difference between Market Price (MP) and Cost Price (CP) is because of the Indirect Taxes and Subsidies.
- GDP   = GDP   – Indirect Taxes + Subsidies
- In terms of value addition, the Gross Domestic Product of the economy is the sum total of the net value added and depreciation of all the firms of the economy.

Calculation of GDP

- GDP in a country is usually calculated by the National Statistical Agency, which compiles the information from a large number of sources.
- In case of India, it is Central Statistics Office (CSO), which estimates GDP. However, most countries follow established international standards for calculating GDP of their country.
- The international standards for measuring GDP are contained in the System of National Accounts (SNA), 1993, compiled by the International Monetary Fund (IMF), the European Commission (EC), the Organisation for Economic Cooperation and Development (OECD), the United Nations (UN) and the World Bank.

Source   Central Statistics Office   PE = Provisional Estimates (CSO)

Nominal GDP and Real GDP

Nominal GDP is evaluated at current market prices. Therefore, nominal GDP will include all of the changes in market prices that have occurred during the current year due to inflation or deflation. Real GDP is a better measurement of GDP, since it reflects the increase in quantity of goods and services by adjusting for any increase in prices. Real GDP is generally measured by using base year prices of goods and services.

Gross Value Added (GVA)

It is a measure of the value of goods and services produced in an area, industry or sector of an economy. It national accounts, GVA is output minus intermediate consumption, it is a balancing item of the national accounts' production account.

Gross National Product (GNP)

GNP refers to the money value of total output of production of final goods and services produced by the national residents of a country during a given period of time, generally a year.

Symbolically

$$GNP = GDP + (X - M) + (R - P)$$
$$GNP = C + G + I + (X - M) + (R - P)$$
$$X = Exports$$
$$M = Imports$$
$$(R - P) = Net\ factor\ income\ from\ abroad$$

Net National Product (NNP)

It is obtained by subtracting depreciation value (i.e. capital stock consumption) from GNP.

Symbolically, NNP = GNP − Depreciation

Personal Income (PI)

It is that income, which is actually obtained by the individual or nationals. *Symbolically,*

Personal Income = National Income − Undistributed profits of corporations − Payment for social security provisions − Corporate taxes + Transfer payments + Net interest paid by the government.

Personal Disposable Income (PDI)

When personal direct taxes are subtracted from personal income, the obtained value is called personal disposable income. *Symbolically,* PDI = PI − Direct taxes

National Statistical Organisation (NSO) was set-up on 1st June, 2005, for promoting statistical network in the country. It was then headed by professor SD Tendulkar. Gross Value Added (GVA) is a measure in economics of the value of goods and services produced in an area, industry or sector of an economy.

GVA = GDP + Subsidies − (direct, sales) taxes.

CSO and NSSO

- CSO (Central Statistical Organisation) was set-up in 1950, constituted to publish national income data.
- NSSO (National Sample Survey Organisation) was set-up in 1950, for conducting large scale sample survey to meet the data needs of the country for the estimation of national income and other aggregates.

Measurement of Growth and Development

Human Development Report

The Human Development Report (HDR), published by the UNDP since 1990, captures the essence of human development. Human development report rank countries based on their ranking on Human Development Index (HDI). HDI was devised by Pakistani economist Mahbub ul Haq along with Indian economist Amartya Sen.

In 2015 HDR, India has been placed at 130th position with 0.609 score in medium human development category. Norway, Australia and Switzerland occupies first three positions.

Meaning of HDI Value (2016 Report)

Very high Human development	=	0.800 and above
High Human development	=	0.701 and above
Medium Human development	=	0.550 and above
Low Human development	=	0.352 and above

Happy Planet Index (HPI)

HPI measures the ecological efficiency with which human well-being is delivered. It is calculated by multiplying indices of life satisfaction (estimated by compiling responses to international surveys) and life expectancy and dividing that product by ecological footprint.

Gross National Happiness (GNH)

The term Gross National Happiness was coined in 1972, by Bhutan's then King Jigme Singye Wangchuck.

GNH was designed in on attempt to define an indicator that measures quality of life or social progress in more holistic and psychological terms than the economic indicator of GDP.

Various Index of Human Development

Index	Variables	Country's Rank
Human Development Index (HDI) 2016	Life expectancy at birth index. Education index comprises mean year of schooling and expected year of schooling. GNI Per Capita (PPPUS $) Index for decent standard of living.	• Norway • Australia • Switzerland
Inequality adjusted HDI (IHDI) 2016	Introduced in HDR-2010.Measures the average level of human development after adjusting for inequality.If perfect equality, HDI = IHDIIf, inequality, HDI< IHDI Greater the inequality in society, greater the divergence between HDI and IHDI.	• Norway • Iceland • Australia
Gender Inequity Index (GII) 2016	Introduced in HDR-2010Gil exposes differences in the distribution. It measures gender inequality based on three dimensions and five indicators. **Indicators** • Maternal Mortality Ratio (MMR); • Adolescent Fertility Rate (AFR); • Educational attainment (secondary level and above); • Parliamentary representation; and • Labour force participation,	• Switzerland • Denmark • Netherland
Multidimensional Poverty Index (MPI)	• MPI launched by Oxford Poverty and Human Development Initiative (OPHI) and UNDP in July 2010. • It is a measure of serious deprivation in the dimesnsion of health, education and living standards that combines the number of deprived and intensity of their deprivation. **Indicators** Nutrition + Child Mortality (Health); Years of Schooling + Children enrolled (Education); Cooking fuel + Water + Toilet + Floor + Electricity + Assets (Standard of living).	

PLANNING COMMISSION

After independence in 1947, the Economic Programme Committee (EPC) was formed by All India Congress Committee with Nehru as its chairman. This committee was to make a plan to balance private and public partnership and urban and rural economies. In 1948, this committee recommended forming of a Planning Commission.

In March 1950, in pursuance of declared objectives of the government to promote a rapid rise in the standard of living of the people by efficient exploitation of the resources of the country, increasing production and offering opportunities to all for employment in the service of the community, the Planning Commission was set-up by a resolution of the Government of India as an advisory and specialised institution.

Jawaharlal Nehru was the first Chairman of the Planning Commission. Planning Commission was an extra constitutional body, charged with the reponsibility of making assessment of all resources of the country, augmenting deficient resources, formulating plans for the most effective and balanced utilisation of resources and determining priorities. Now, it has been replaced by a new institution named NITI Aayog.

NITI AAYOG

NITI Aayog or National Institution for Transforming India Aayog came into existence on 1st January, 2015. It is policy-making think-tank of government that replaces Planning Commission and aims to involve states in economic policy-making. It will provide strategic and technical advice to the Central and the State Governments.

Basic Structure of NITI Aayog

Chairperson	*Prime Minister*
Governing Council	Its members are Chief Minister and Administrators of the Union Territories
Special Invitees	Experts, Specialists and Practitioners with domain knowledge (nominated by Prime Minister)
Vice-President	Appointed by the Prime Minister
Full time Members	Their number is five.
Part time Members	Two ex-offcio members and university teacher
Ex-officio Members	Four Central Ministers
CEO	Secretary level officer from centre, who will be appointed for a fixed term.

National Development Council (NDC)

The NDC was constituted on 6th August, 1952, with Prime Minister as the Ex-officio Chairman and the Secretary of the Planning Commission as the Ex-officio Secretary of the NDC. Chief Minister of all the states and the members of the Planning Commission are the members of the NDC.

It is an extra-constitutional and non-statutory body (not formed by Act of Parliament).

STRATEGIES OF PLANNING

Harrod-Domar Strategy

- First Five Year Plan was based on this strategy.
- This strategy emphasised the role of capital accumulation's dual character, which on the one hand increases the national income (demand side role) and on the other hand increases the production capacity (supply side role).

Nehru-Mahalanobis Strategy

- Second Five Year Plan was based on this strategy.
- Based on Russian experience, this strategy is a two sector model, i.e. consumer good sector and capital good sector.
- The strategy emphasised investment in heavy industry to achieve industrialisation for rapid economic development.

Gandhian Strategy

- It was enunciated by Acharya SN Agarwal in his 'Gandhian Plan' in 1944. The basic objective of the Gandhian Model is to raise the material as well as cultural level of the masses so as to provide basic standard of life.

LPG Strategy

- Liberalisation, Privatisation and Globalisation (LPG) strategy of planning was introduced by the Finance Minister of that time, Dr Manmohan Singh under Narsimha Rao Government. The strategy ended the 'license permit raj' and opened the hitherto areas reserved for the public sector to private sector.

PURA Strategy

- PURA stands for providing Urban amenities in rural areas and was the brainchild of APJ Abdul Kalam.
- This strategy emphasises on three connectivities— physical, electronic, knowledge and thereby leading to economic connectivity to enhance the prosperity of cluster of villages in rural areas.

Five Year Plans (At a Glance)

Plan	Objectives	Assessment
First Plan (1951-56) (Harrod Domar Model)	• Highest priority accorded to agriculture in view of large import of foodgrains and inflation. • 31 % of total plan outlay on agriculture followed by transport and communication, social services, power and industry. • Economist KN Raj was the architect.	• Agriculture production increased dramatically. • National income went up by 18% and per capita income by 11%. • Target growth 2.1% and achieved 3.6%.
Second Plan (1956-61)	• Rapid industrialisation with particular emphasis on the development of basic and heavy industry, also called Nehru Mahalanobis Plan. • To increase national income by 25%, expansion of employment and reduction of inequality. • To increase the rate of investment from 7% to 11 % of GDP.	• Moderately successful, targeted growth rate was 4.5% but achieved 4.2%. • Durgapur (UK), Bhillai (USSR) and Rourkela (W Germany) steel plants set-up with foreign help. Atomic Energy Commission came into being in operation and TIFR was set-up. • Inflation and low agricultural production and Suez crisis.
Third Plan (1961-66) (Gadgil Yojana)	• Indian economy entered take off stage (WW Rostow). Self-reliant and self-generating economy was the goal. • To increase the national income by 30% and per capita income by 17%.	• Indo-China (1962) and Indo-Pakistan (1965) conflict diverted the resources from development to defence. • Targeted growth 5.6% achieved growth 2.72%. • The situation created by Indo-Pakistan Conflict (1965), two successive years of severe drought, devaluation of currency by 57%, general rise in prices and erosion of resources for plan delayed.
Annual Plans	• Due to the unfortunate failure of the third plan, the production in various sectors of the economy became stagnant. In 1966, the Government of India declared the devaluation of rupee, with a view to increase the exports of the country. So, the fourth plan was postponed and three annual plan were implemented. Some of the economists called this period i.e. from 1966 to 1969 as Plan Holiday.	
Fourth Plan (1969-74)	• Laid special emphasis on improving the condition of under privileged and weaker sections.	• First two years of the plan were successful with record foodgrain production on account of Green Revolution. • Targeted growth 5.7% however, achieved growth 3.3%. • The plan was failure on account of run way inflation (due to 1972 oil crisis or supply shock) huge influx of refugees from Bangladesh post 1972 Indo-Pak War.
Fifth Plan (1974-79)	• Original approach to plan prepared by C Subramaniam.However, final draft prepared by DP Dhar with objectives of removal of poverty (Garibi Hatao) and attainment of self-reliance. • Introduction of minimum needs programme.	• Targeted growth 4.4% and achieved growth 4.8%. • Fifth Plan terminated one year before the plan period in March 1978. • Brought to the core problem associated with coalition government making a mockery of formulation of Five Year Plan.

Plan	Objectives	
Annual Plan	Annual Plan (Gunar Myrdal) was brought out by Janata Party Government under Morarji Desai in 1978. The focus of the plan was enlargement of the employment potential in agriculture and allied activities to raise the income of the lowest income classes through minimum needs programme. Annual Plan period was 1979-80.	
Sixth Plan (1980-85)	Removal of poverty through strengthening of infrastructure for both agriculture and industry.The emphasis was laid on greater management, efficiency and monitoring of various schemes. Involvement of people in formulating schemes of development at local level.	Indian economy made an all round progress and most of the targets fixed by the plan was achieved. Targeted growth 5.2% and achieved growth 5.4%.
Seventh Plan (1985-90)	To accelerate foodgrains production To increase employment opportunities. To raise productivity.	Foodgrain production grew by 3.23% as compared to a long-term growth rate of 2.68% between 1967-68 and 1988-89.The Indian economy finally crossed the barrier of the Hindu rate of growth (professor Raj Krishna). Average annual growth rate was 6.0% as against the targeted 5.0% and average of 3.5% in the previous plans.
Annual Plan	The Eighth Plan could not take off due to fast changing political situations at the centre. Therefore, from 1990-1992, Annual Plans were formulated.	
Eighth Plan (1992-97)	Process of fiscal reforms and economic reforms initiated by Narsimhan Rao Government to prevent another major economic crisis. To increase the average industrial growth rate to 7.5%. To provide a new dynamism to the economy and improve the quality of life of the common man. Also called as Rao-Manmohan Singh Model. First indicative plan.	Higher economic growth rate of 6.6% achieved as against the targeted 5.6%. Improvement in current account deficit. Significant reduction in fiscal deficit.Agriculture growth and industrial growth increased. Unshackled private sector and foreign investment control was the prime reason for high growth. Overall socio-economic development indicators low.
Ninth Plan (1997-2002)	Growth with social justice and equality. Emphasis on seven Basic Minimum Services (BMSs), which included safe drinking water, universalisation of primary education, streamlining PDS among others. Pursued the policy of fiscal consolidation. Ensuring food and nutritional security to all. Empowerment of women, SC/STs/OBCs.	Global economic slow down and other factors led to revision of targeted growth rate from 7% to 6.5%, which too was not achieved. The economy grew at 5.4% only. Agriculture grew by 2.1% as against the target of 4.2% per annum.

Tenth Plan (2002-2007)	• The Tenth Plan aimed at achieving 8% GDP growth. • Assuming that ICOR (Incremental Capital Output Ratio will decline from 4.53% to 3.58%. • It aimed at increasing domestic saving rate from 23.52% to 29.4% of GDP and gross capital formation to 32.2% from 24.4% of GDP. • To improve the overall framework of governance. Agriculture was the core element.	• Increase in GDP growth to 7.5% compared to 5.4% in the Ninth Plan. The lower than targeted growth rate of 8% was due to low growth of 3% in the first year of Tenth Plan Increase in gross domestic saving and investment. • Reduction in ICOR to 4.2% though higher than targeted but less than Ninth Plan's ICOR of 4.53%. • Increase in foreign exchange reserves to US S 287 billion.
11th Plan (2007-2012)	• Average GDP growth of 8.1% per year. • Agricultural GDP growth of 4% per year. Generation of 58 million employment opportunities. • Sex ratio for age group 0-6 years to be raised to 935 by 2011-12 and to 950 by 2016-17.	• The growth rate during the 11th plan period was about 7.9%, which is higher than the 7.5% growth rate achieved in the 10th plan. • As against the target of 4% growth in the agricultural sector, the plan could register a growth of only 3% during 2007-12 period. • The services sector continued to register a growth rate of more than 10%. However, the industrial growth rate showed at 7.9%.
12th Plan (2012-2017)	• Real GDP growth rate of 8.2%. • Agriculture growth rate of 4.0%. • Manufacturing growth rate of 10%.	• The plan period was extended by six months.

15 Years Vision Document

The Ist 15 year vision document come into effect from 2017-18 after the end of the 12th five year plan. It will be formulated with centre objective of eradication of poverty. These will be framed keeping in mind the country's social goals and the sustainable development agenda. According to NITI Aayog, the issue was discussed at length and a decision was taken at the highest level 15 year Vision Documents divided into two parts

• **7-years National Development Agenda** The first 15-year vision document will start from 2017-18, along with a 7-year National Development Agenda which wll lay down the schemes, programmes and strategies to achieve the long-term vision.

• **3-years National Development Agenda** The long vision documents will comprise of three year mass economic framework. National Development Agenda will be reviewed after a gap of every three years to ensure that it was aligned with financial needs and requirements. For the first Development Agenda the review would be done in 2019-20, in line with the termination year of the 14th Finance Commission.

• 2017-18 to 2032-33 Vision Document
• 2017-18 to 2024-25 National Development Agenda
• 2017-18 to 2019-20 Review of Development Agenda (to be repeated after every three years).

Sectorial Growth Rate in Different Five Year Plans

Plan	Target Growth Rate	Agriculture	Industry	Services	Actual Growth Rate	Priority Areas/Achievements
First Plan	2.1	2.71	5.54	4.17	3.6	Development of agriculture and Allied sectors and Community Development Programme
Second Plan	4.5	3.15	5.59	4.94	4.21	Basic industries, Health sector
Third Plan	5.6	– 0.73	6.28	5.26	2.72	Food and Agriculture
Fourth Plan	5.7	2.57	4.91	3.22	3.3%	Agriculture and Irrigation, Self-reliance
Fifth Plan	4.4	3.28	6.55	5.66	4.83	Public health and Social welfare, Poverty elimination
Sixth Plan	5.2	2.25	5.32	5.41	5.4	Agriculture, Industry, Energy, Poverty Alleviation Programmes
Seventh Plan	5	3.47	6.77	7.19	6	Energy and Food
Eighth Plan	5.6	4.68	7.58	7.54	6.68	Human Resources Development
Ninth Plan	6.5	2.06	4.51	7.78	5.4	Social Justice, Human Development
Tenth Plan	8	2.34	8.9	9.4	7.5	Employment, Energy and Social reconstruction
Eleventh Plan	8.1	4	10.5	9.9	7.9	Rapid economic growth, Employment generation, Self-reliance and Education
Twelfth Plan	**8**	**04**	**10.9**	**10**	–	Faster, Sustainable and More inclusive growth

DEMOGRAPHY

Demography is the study of the size, territorial distribution and composition of population, change therein and the components of such changes.

Population Trend in India

- **1891-1921** Period of stagnant population
- **1921-1951** Period of steady growth
- **1951-1981** Period of high growth
- **1981-2011** Period of declining rate
- The year 1921 is known as the Year of Great Divide.

CENSUS 2011

The Census 2011, was the 15th National Census of the country. The census has covered 35 States and Union Territories, 640 Districts, 5767 Tehsils. 7742 Towns and more than 6 lakh villages.

- Top 5 States in Sex Ratio (0-6 age group) - Mizoram > Meghalaya > Andaman and Nicobar Islands > Puducherry > Chhattisgarh.
- Top 5 States of Population UP > Maharashtra > Bihar > West Bengal > Andhra Pradesh.
- Bottom 3 States of minimum population - Sikkim < Mizoram < Arunachal Pradesh.
- Top 5 States of literacy-Kerala > Mizoram > Goa > Tripura > Himachal Pradesh.

India	Census 2011
Total population	121,08,54,977
Males	623.7 million (51.54%)
Females	586.46 million (48.46%)
Population of 0-6 age group	16,44,78,150 (13.58%)
Population density (per sq km)	382
Literacy	73.0% (Male-80.9% and Female-64.6%)
Decadal Growth Rate	18,14,55,986 (17.7%)
Population Increase (2001-2011)	181 million
Sex Ratio	943 : 1000

National Population Policy

- Population policy refers to all those legal, administrative programmes and other government efforts, which aim at reducing birth rate and improving the quality of life.
- After independence, the Government of India adopted a national policy on population with the objective to check the increase in birth rate and improve the standard of living of people.
- This policy has been revised from time to time and its scope has been widened. It has been very effective in initiating measures for population control.

New National Population Policy (2000)

- The New National Population Policy (NPP) provides a policy framework to meet the reproductive and child health needs of the people of India for the next 10 years.

UIDAI

- The Unique Identification Authority of India is a statutory authority under provisions of the Aadhar (Targeted Delivery of Financial and other subsidies, Benefits and Services) Act, 2016 under the Ministry of Electronics and Information Technology. Earlier UIDAI was functioning as an attached office of erstwhile Planning Commission.
- It was created with the objective to issue Unique Identification numbers (UID), named as 'Aadhaar' to all residents of India.
- The numbers will be linked to the basic biometric information of the person, including photograph, iris and fingerprints.

Targets of World Population Prospects, 2000

- To achieve zero growth rate of population by 2045.
- To reduce Infant Mortality Rate below 30 per thousand live births by 2010.
- To reduce Maternal Mortality Rate to below 1 per thousand live births.

- To reduce birth rate to 2.1 per thousand by 2010.
- To reduce total fertility rate to 2.1 by 2010. It is estimated that the population of India will be 126.4 crores by 2016.

Main Features of WPP, 2000

- Appointment of a National Commission on population, presided over by the Prime Minister. The Chief Ministers of the States, Administrators of Union Territories and other related ministers to be its members.
- State Commissions on population headed by Chief Ministers. The new policy to be implemented by the Panchayats, municipalities and Non-Government Organisations.

Statewise Population Statistics (2011)

State/UT Territory	Total Population	Sex Ratio (per 1000 females)	Population Density (per km²)	Decadal Rate (growth rate)	Literacy Rate (in %)	Proportion of State/UT Population (in %)
Total India	1210569573	943	382	17.7	73.00	100
Jammu and Kashmir	12541302	889	56	23.6	67.2	1.04
Himachal Pradesh	6864602	972	123	12.9	82.8	0.57
Punjab	27743338	859	551	13.9	75.8	2.29
Chandigarh	1055450	818	9258	17.2	86	0.09
Uttarakhand	10086292	963	189	18.8	78.8	0.83
Haryana	25351462	879	573	19.9	75.6	2.09
Delhi	16787941	868	11320	21.2	86.2	1.39
Rajasthan	68548437	928	200	21.3	66.1	5.66
Uttar Pradesh	199812341	912	829	20.2	67.7	16.51
Bihar	104099452	918	1106	25.4	61.8	8.60
Sikkim	610577	890	86	12.9	81.4	0.05
Arunachal Pradesh	1383727	938	17	26	65.4	0.11
Nagaland	1978502	931	119	-0.6	79.6	0.16
Manipur	2570390	992	115	18.6	79.2	0.21
Mizoram	1097206	976	52	23.5	91.3	0.09
Tripura	3673917	960	350	14.8	87.2	0.30
Meghalaya	2966889	989	132	27.9	74.4	0.25
Assam	31205576	958	398	17.1	72.2	2.58
West Bengal	91276115	950	1028	13.8	76.3	7.54
Jharkhand	32988134	948	414	22.4	66.4	2.73
Odisha	41974218	979	270	14	72.9	3.47
Chhattisgarh	25545198	991	189	22.6	70.3	2.11
Madhya Pradesh	72626809	931	236	20.3	69.3	6.00
Gujarat	60439692	919	308	19.3	78	4.99

State/UT Territory	Total Population	Sex Ratio (per 1000 females)	Population Density (per km²)	Decadal Rate (growth rate)	Literacy Rate (in %)	Proportion of State/UT Population (in %)
Daman and Diu	243247	618	2172	53.8	87.1	0.02
Dadra and Nagar Haveli	343709	774	700	55.9	76.2	0.03
Maharashtra	112374333	929	365	16	82.3	9.28
Andhra Pradesh	84580777	993	308	11	67	6.99
Karnataka	61095297	973	319	15.6	75.4	5.05
Goa	1458545	973	394	8.2	88.7	0.12
Lakshadweep	64473	946	2049	6.3	91.8	0.01
Kerala	33406061	1084	860	4.9	94	2.76
Tamil Nadu	72147030	996	555	15.6	80.1	5.96
Puducherry	1247953	1037	2605	28.1	85.8	0.10

POVERTY

- Poverty is a social phenomenon where few section of society is unable to fulfil even basic necessities of life.
- Planning Commission (Now, NITI Aayog) is the authority, which publishes the poverty estimates based on various rounds of National Sample Survey Organisation (NSSO) on monthly per capita consumption expenditure. In India, the poverty line is defined on the basis of calorie intake. According to this, 2100 calories a day has been fixed for urban areas and 2400 calories in rural areas.
- Alternatively, in monthly per capita consumption expenditure terms, the poverty line is fixed at ₹ 454.0 for rural areas and ₹ 540.0 for urban are as in 2004-05.
- Since, NSSO 55th Round (1999), Planning Commission gives two poverty estimates based on Mixed Recall Period (MRP) and Universal Recall Period (URP).
- Mixed Recall Period, gives consumer expenditure data for five non-food items, namely clothing, footwear, durable goods, education and institutional medical expenses for 365 days and consumption data for remaining items are collected for 30 days period.
- Universal Recall Period, consumption data for all items are collected for a 30 days recall period.

Causes of Rural Poverty

- Rapid Population growth
- Lack of capital
- Lack of alternate employment opportunities other than agriculture
- Excessive population pressure on agriculture
- Illiteracy
- Regional disparities
- Joint family system
- Child marriage
- Lack of proper implementation of PDS (Public Distribution System)

Causes of Urban Poverty

- Migration from rural areas
- Lack of skilled labour
- Lack of housing facilities
- Limited job opportunities in cities
- Lack of vocational education/ training

New Definition of Slums

- As per the **Pranab Sen Committee's** new methodology, there has been increase in the urban slum population in 2011 to 93.06 million from 75.26 million estimated in 2001. This is an increase of 26.31%.
- As per the new definition, any compact housing cluster or settlement of atleast 20 households with a collection of poorly built tenements, which are mostly, temporary in nature . with inadequate sanitary, drinking water facilities and unhygienic conditions will be termed as slums.

Poverty and its Study in India

Various economists and organisations have studied the extent of poverty in India. *Some of them are as follows:*

Dandekar and Rath's Study of Poverty in India

Dr VM Dandekar and Mr Nilkantha Rath estimated the value of the diet with 2250 calories as the desired minimum level of nutrition.

They estimated that in 1968-69 about 40% of the rural population and a little more than 50% of the urban population lived below the poverty line.

Montek Singh Ahluwalia's Study of Rural Poverty (1977)

MS Ahluwalia studied the trends in incidence of rural poverty in India for the period 1956-57 to 1973-74. He used the concept of poverty line, i.e. an expenditure level of ₹ 15 in 1960-61 for rural areas and ₹ 20 per person for urban areas.

Estimate of Poverty by the Seventh Finance Commission (1978)

The Seventh Finance Commission made an attempt to have a more inclusive concept of poverty line.

Since, the NSS data cover only household consumer expenditure, thus, to get a more inclusive measure of welfare or deprivation, an estimate of the benefit of public expenditure was added to private consumer expenditure norm for calculating the augmented poverty line.

Tendulkar Committee Report

This committee moved away from just calorie criterion definition to a broader definition of poverty that also includes expenditure on health, education, clothing in addition to food. According to this report, 41.8% population in rural areas and 25.7% population in urban areas was living below poverty line.

Rangarajan Report on Poverty

The expert group under the Chairmanship of Dr C Rangarajan to review the Methodology for measurement of poverty in the country constituted by the Planning Commission in June, 2012 has submitted its report on 30th June, 2014. The report retained consumption expenditure estimates of NSSO as the basis for determining poverty. On the basis of this, it pegged the total number of poor in India at 363 million or 29.6% of the population. This is higher than 269.8 million poor people or 21.9% pegged by the Suresh Tendulkar Committee.

Highlights of the Report

The highlights of the report are as follows:

(i) The daily per capita expenditure is pegged at ₹ 32 for the rural poor and at ₹ 47 for the urban poor.

(ii) Poverty line based on the average monthly per capita expenditure is pegged at ₹ 972 for rural areas and ₹ 1407 for urban areas.

(iii) The percentage of people below the poverty line in 2011-12 was 30.95 in rural areas and 26.4 in urban areas.

Unemployment

Unemployment in India

- Unemployment occurs when a person who is actively searching for employment is unable to find a work. Unemployment is often used as a measure of the health of the economy. The most frequently cited measure of unemployment is unemployment rate. That is the number of unemployed persons divided by the number of people in the labour force.
- In India, a person working 8 hours a day for 273 days of the year is regarded as employed on a standard person year basis.

Estimation of Unemployment

- **B Bhagwati Committee** on unemployment estimates (1973) set-up by the Planning Commission gave three estimates of unemployment.

  These are as follows:

  - **Usual Principal Status** (UPS) Persons who remained unemployed for a major part of the year. This is also called 'open unemployment'.
  - **Current Weekly Status** (CWS) Persons who did not find even an hour of work during the survey week.
  - **Current Daily Status** (CDS) Persons who did not find work on a day or some days during the survey week. This is the comprehensive measure of unemployment, including chronic as well as underemployment.

TYPES OF UNEMPLOYMENT

Generally, unemployment can be classified into two types

Voluntary Unemployment

This type of unemployment is on account of people not interested to take the employment i.e. jobs are available but the persons are not interested in being employed.

It is psychological in nature. Therefore, such types of persons are not included in the category of unemployed.

Involuntary Unemployment

It refers to a situation in which the persons are interested to work but the jobs are not available. Such persons are included in the categories of unemployed persons. Under this there are various categories of unemployment. *They are as follow:*

Cyclical Unemployment

This type of unemployment is due to the recession in the economy. During recession, there is less requirement of man-power on account of the decrease in the level of economic activities and thus causes cyclical unemployment. This type of unemployment is prevalent in the developed countries. This is also known as Keynesian Unemployment.

Frictional Unemployment

This type of unemployment is caused by people taking time out of work, being between jobs or looking for a job.

The one cause of its evolution is decline of one industry and rise of the other and labour take some time before moving to the other industry. This type of unemployment is short-term in nature.

Seasonal Unemployment

It is an account of the seasonal nature of the productive activities, i.e., some productive activities are carried out only for certain duration of a year. Therefore, the persons employed in such activities are unemployed during off-season. This, generally, occurs in agro-based industries.

Disguised Unemployment

A situation in which more people are available for work then is shown in the unemployment statistics. It is also known as concealed unemployment and the discouraged worker effect.

Structural Unemployment

It refers to a mismatch of job vacancies with the supply of labour available, caused by shifts in the structure of the economy. Structural joblessness results from things like skills mismatches and policy to address such mismatches is inherently longer term in scope, involving education and encouraging innovation.

Technological Unemployment

Technology has always displaced some work and jobs. Thus, technological unemployment is a term used to describe the lack or loss of jobs due to technological changes or innovations. This type of unemployment typically comes from workers either being replaced by machines or having their jobs made easier and require fewer workers to accomplish the same task. It is one of the reasons of jobless growth.

12th Plan-Some Employment Related Ideas

Currently, India is passing through an unprecedented phase of demographic changes. The ongoing demographic changes are likely to contribute to an ever increasing size of labour force in the country. The census projection report shows that the proportion of population in the working age group (15-59 years) is likely to increase from approximately 58% in 2001 to more than 64% by 2021. But the overall population is not the issue the proportion of population in the working age group of 15-59 years will increase from 57.7% to 64.3%.

Employment, Poverty, Rural and Urban Development Programmes

Name of the Programmes	Year of Beginning	Objectives/Descriptions
Swarana Jayanti Shahari Rozgar Yojana (SJSRY), it has been revamped with effect from April 2009.	1997	To provide gainful employment to urban unemployed and under empoloyed poor through self-employment of wage employment.
Swaranajayanti Gram Swarozgar Yojana (SSGSY), it replaced IRPD, DWCRA, Ganga Kalyan Yojana (1997). Million Wells Scheme (1989) and Supply Improved Tolls kits to Rural Artisans (1992)	1st April, 1999	For elimination rurai property and unemployment and promoting self-employment through establishing micro enterprises in rural areas. Targets to cover 50% SCs/STs. 40% women, 15% minorities and 3% disabled.
Pradhan Mantri Gramodya Yojana (PMGY)	2000	Focus on village level development in 5 critical areas. i.e. primary health, primary education, housing, rural roads and drinking water and nutrition with the overall objective of improving the quality of life of people in rural areas.
Annapurna Scheme	2000	To ensure food security for all, create a hunger free India in the next five serve the poorest of the poor in rural and urban areas.
Food For Work Programme	2001	To give food through wage employment in the drought affected areas in 8 states. Wages are paid by the State Governments, partly in cash and partly in foodgrains.
Jai Prakash Narayan Rozgar Guarantee Yojana (JPNRGY)	Proposed in 2002-03 Budget	Employment guarantee is must poor districts.
MGNREGS (Mahatma Gandhi National Rural Employment Guarantee Scheme). The scheme was notified throughout the country with effect from 1st April, 2008. Renamed as MGNREGS from 2nd October, 2009. SGRY and Food for Work Programme merged into it.	2nd February, 2006	It aims at enhancing livelihood security of households in rural areas of the country by providing at least 100 days on guaranteed wage employment in a financial year to every household, whose adult members volunteer to do unskilled manual work. It also mandates 33% participation for women. The primary objective of the scheme is to augment wage employment.

Prime Minister's Employment Generation Programme (PMEGP)	2008	To generate employment opportunities in rural as well as urban areas through setting up of self-employment ventures/projects/ micro enterprises.
Nirmal Bharat Programme	2012	To eradicate practice of open defacation by 2020.
Direct Benefit Transfer	2013	Anti-Poverty Programme, aimed to transfer subsidies directly to the people living below poverty line.

Rural Development Programmes

Name of the Programmes	Year of Beginning	Objectives/Descriptions
Bharat Nirman Programme	2005	Development of rural infrastructure including six components : irrigation, water supply, housing, road, telephone and electricity.
Twenty Point Programme	1975	Poverty eradication and raising the standard of living.
Annapurna Scheme	2000	To ensure food security for all, create a hunger free India in the next 5 years and to reform and improve the Public Distribution System, so as to serve the poorest of the poor in rural and urban areas.
National Rural Drinking Water Programme (NRDWP) previously called Accelerated Rural Water Supply Programme	1st April, 2009	Aims to move forward from achieving habitation level coverage towards household level drinking water coverage through resorting to multiple sources like ground water, surface water etc.
Nirmal Gram Puruskar (NGP)	October, 2003	It is an incentive scheme to encourage PRIs to take up sanitation promotion.
Valmiki Ambedkar Aawas Yojana (VABAY)	December, 2001	Facilitates construction and upgradation of dwelling units for slum dwellers.
Jawaharlal Nehru Urban Renewal Mission (JNNURM), it has two components. (a) Basic services to urban poor; and (b) Integrated Housing and Slum Development Programme	3rd December 2005	To assist cities and towns in taking up housing and infrastructural facilities for the urban poor in 63 cities (now 65 cities) in the country.
Affordable Housing in Partnership (AHIP)	2009	Aims at constructing one million houses for the EWS/LIG/MIG with at least 25% for EWS category seeks to operationalise National Habitat Policy, 2007.

Women Empowerment Programmes

Name of the Programmes	Year of Beginning	Objectives/Descriptions
Support to Training and Employment Programme for Women (STEP)	2003-04	To increase the self-reliance and autonomy of women by enhancing their productivity and enabling them to take up income generation activities.
Rajiv Gandhi Scheme for Empowerment of Adolescent Girls (RGSEAG)- 'Sabla'	19th November, 2010	It aims at empowering adolescent girls of 11 to 18 years by improving their nutritional and health status, upgradation of home skills and vocational skills.
Rashtriya Mahila Kosh- (National Credit Fund for Women)	1993	It extends micro-finance services through a client friendly and hassle-free loaning mechanism for livelihood activities, housing micro enterprises, family needs etc for upliftment of poor women.

Indira Gandhi Matritva Sahyog Yojana (IGMSY)	2010	To improve the health and nutrition status of pregnant, lactating women and infants.
Swayam Siddha	2001	At organising women into Self-Help Groups to from a strong institutional base.
Dhan Laxmi	March 2008	Condition cash transfer scheme for the girl child to encourage families to educate girl children and to prevent child marriage.
Ujjwala	4th, December, 2007	A comprehensive scheme for prevention of trafficking with five specific components prevention, rescue, rehabilitation, reintegration and repatriation of victims.
National Mission for Empowerment of Women (NMEW)	2010	To achieve empowerment of women socially, economically and educationally by securing convergence of schemes.

Child Welfare Programmes

Name of the Programme	Year of Beginning	Objectives/Descriptions
Rajiv Gandhi National Creche Scheme for the Children of Working Mothers	2006	Overall development of children, childhood protection, complete immunisation, awareness generation among parents of malnutrition, health and education.
Integrated Child Protection Scheme (ICPS)	2009-10	Providing a safe and secure environment for comprehensive development of children who are in need of care and protection as well as children in conflict with law.
Scheme for Welfare of Working Children in Need of Care and Protection	2008-09	Provides for non-formal education vocational training etc to working children to facilitate their entry/re-entry into mainstream education.
Bal Bandhu Scheme	February, 2011	Provides for protection of children is areas of civil unrest. It is implemented by NCPCR with grant from PM's National Relief Fund.

Education Oriented Programmes

Name of the Programme	Year of Beginning	Objectives/Descriptions
Mid-Day Meal Scheme (largest feeding School programme in the world).	1995	Improving of the nutritional status of Children in classess I-VII in government, local body and government aided schools and EGS and AIE centeres with the end objective of enabling disadvantaged and poor children to attend school regularly.
Sarva Shiksha Abhiyan (SSA)	2001	All Children (6-14) complete 5 years of primary schooling by 2007; all children complete 8 years of elementary schooling by 2010 bridge all gender and social category gaps at primary stage by 2007 and at elementary education level by 2010; universal retention by 2010.
Kasturba Gandhi Balika Vidyalayas, (KGBVs) (with effect from) 1st April , 2007, merged with SSA)	2004	To set-up residential school at upper primary level for girls belonging to SC/ST/OBC/Minority communities. The scheme is being implemented in rural areas and urban areas with female literacy below 30% and national average respectively
National Programme for Education of Girls at Elementary Level (NPEGEL) important component of SSA	2003	Focused intervention to reach the 'Hardest to Reach' girls and provides for 'Model School' in every cluster with more intense community mobilisation and supervision of girls enrollment in schools.
Inclusive Education for the Disabled at Secondary Stage (IEDSS) replaced Integrated Education for Disabled Children (IEDS)	2009-10	Provides 100% central assistance for inclusive education of disabled children studying in class IX-XII in government, local body and goverment aided schools.

Name of the Programme	Year of Beginning	Objectives/Descriptions
Rashtriya Madyamik Shiksha Abhiyan (RMSA) or Scheme for Universalisation of Access for Secondary Education (SUCCESS)	March, 2009	Aims at raising the enrollment rate at secondary stage from 52.26% in 2005-06 to 75% in next 5 years by providing a secondary school within a reasonable distance of 5 km of any habitation: ensure universal access by 2017 and universal retention by 2020.
Saakshar Bharat	8th September, 2009	National Literacy Mission has been recast as 'Saakshar Bharat'. The aim is to cover all adults, is the age group of 15 and above, with its primary focus on women.

Health Oriented Programmes

Name of the Programme	Year of Beginning	Objectives/Descriptions
National Rural Health Mission (NRHM)	12th April, 2005	To provide effective healthcare to rural population with special focus on 18 States with weak health indices/infrastructure to raise public spending on health form 0.9% of GDP of 2.3% of GDP reduction of IMA and MMR and universal assess to health care with emphasis on women.
Janani Suraksha Yojana (JSY)	April, 2005	Focus on demand promotion for institutional deliveries in states and regions and targets lowering of MMR, it is conditional cash transfer programme to increase births in health facilities.
Pradhan Mantri Swasthya Suraksha Yojana (PMSSY)	2010	To correct regional imbalance in tertiary healthcare and augmenting facilities for quality medical education in the country; and setting up six AIIMS-like institution in phase-1 and in phase-2 two more AIIMS like institutions.

New Social Welfare Scheme

Some new social development schemes to address the critical issues of the country have been introduced.

- **Pradhan Mantri Krishi Sinchayee Yojana** The FM announced this programme in the budget as a measure to mitigate the risk to monsoon dependent irrigation. The scheme is aimed to give assured irrigation to farmers.
- **Swatchh Bharat Abhiyan** Total sanitation by 2019 is the slogan of programme. realising the importance of sanitation of government has sought the help of every citizen to achieve this goal. The year 2019 also marks the 150th Birth anniversary of Mahatma Gandhi.
- **Soil Health Card Scheme for Every Farmer** The government has initiated this scheme concerning the deterioration the soil health which leads to sub-optimal utilisation of farming resources. The government will initiate to provide every farmer a soil health card a in a mission mode. A sum of ₹ 100 crore is allotted.

- **A Dedicated TV Channel for Farmers** Kisan TV, dedicated to the interests of the agriculture and allied sector has been launched in the current financial year. This will disseminate real information to the farmers regarding new farming techniques, water conservation and organic farming etc.
- **Deendayal Upadhyaya Gram Jyoti Yojana** "Deendayal Upadhyaya Gram Jyoti Yojana" for feeder separation has been launched to augment power supply to the rural areas and for strengthening sub-transmission and distribution systems. Its long-term aim is to provide 24 ×7 uninterrupted power supply to all homes. A sum of ₹ 500 crores has been set aside for this scheme.
- **Van Bandhu Kalayan Yojana** For the welfare of the tribal people 'Van Bandhu Kalayan Yojana' is being launched with an initial allocation of ₹ 100 crore.
- **Beti Bachao, Beti Padhao Yojana** It was introduced for generating awareness and improving the efficiency of delivery of welfare services meant for women with an initial corpus of ₹100 crore. The

government would focus on campaigns to sensitise people of this country towards the concerns of the girl child and women. The process of sensitisation must begin early and therefore the school curriculum must have a separate chapter on gender main streaming.

- **National Heritage City Development Augmentation Yojana** The programme called Heritage City Development and Augmentation Yojana (HRIDAY), was launched for conserving and preserving the heritage characters of heritage cities. For the beginning programme is launched in the cities such as Mathura, Amritsar, Gaya Kanchipuram, Vellankani, Varanasi, Badami, Puri and Dwarka. The project will work through a partnership of Government, academic institutions and local community combining affordable technologies.

- **Shyama Prasad Mukherji Rurban Mission** It was launched to deliver integrated project based infrastructure in the rural areas. The scheme will also include development of economic activities and skill development. The preferred mode of delivery would be through PPPs while using various scheme funds. It is based on the example of Gujarat that has demonstrated successfully the urban development model of urbanisation of the rural areas, through which people living in the rural areas can get efficient civic infrastructure and associate services.

- **Neeranchal** To give an added impetus to watershed development in the country, a new programme called Neeranchal with an initial outlay of ₹ 2142 crores has been launched.

- **Pradhan Mantri Jan Dhan Yojana** Pradhan Mantri Jan Dhan Yojana is a scheme for comprehensive financial inclusion launched.

Account holders will be provided zero-bank account with rupay debit card.

Aim of scheme to tie every Indian in the rural or urban sector to the mainstream banking system. Scheme offers a life cover of ₹ 30000 and Accidental insurance of ₹ 200000. 100% financial inclusion. After six months of opening of the bank account, holders can avail ₹ 5000 overdraft from the bank.

- **Housing for All by 2022** Government has set-up a Mission on Low Cost Affordable Housing to be anchored in the National Housing Bank with a view to increase the flow of cheaper credit for affordable housing to the urban poor/EWS/LIG segment. The government has already outlined some other incentives such as easier flow of FDI in this sector and is willing to examine other positive suggestions. The government has included slum development in the list of Corporate Social Responsibility (CSR) activities to encourage the private sector to contribute more towards this activity.

- **USTAD Scheme** Union Minister Najma Heptullah launched a welfare scheme, Upgradation of Skills and Training in Ancestral Arts/Crafts for Development (USTAD) which aims at upgrading and promoting the skills of artisans from the minority community. It is launched from Varanasi in order to improve degrading conditions of world famous Banarasi Saree weavers who belong to minority communities. The programme is linked to the make in India campaign. It seeks to help weavers and artisans connect with buyers all over the world.

- **Deen Dayal Upadhyay Antyodaya Yojana** Union Government on 25th September, 2014 Deen Dayal Upadhyay Antyodaya Yojna will replace National Rural Livelihood Mission (Ajeevika) and National Urban Livelihood Mission. It is an overarching scheme for uplift of urban and rural poor through enhancement of livelihood opportunities through skill development and other means.

- **Smart Cities Mission** The objective of smart cities mission is to promote cities that provide core infrastructure and give a decent quality of life to its citizen, a clean and sustainable environment and application of 'smart' solutions. The mission is meant to set examples that can be replicated both within and outside the smart city, catalysing the creation of similar smart cities in various regions and parts of the country. The mission will cover 100 cities and its duration will be 5 years.

- **Amrut for 500 Cities** The Narendra Modi Government has renewed the 10 years old Jawaharlal Nehru National Urban Renewal Mission (JNURM) and named it after the first BJP Prime Minister.

  The renewed scheme is known as Atal Mission for Rejuvenation and Urban Transformation (AMRUT). AMRUT for 500 Tier 2 and Tier 3 cities will also be launched alongwith smart city project. For AMRUT as well, states have been asked to recommend cities which can be included under this scheme. Uttar Pradesh leads the pack, as it can nominate 64 cities under this project.

- **Startup Standup India** Startup India is a revolutionary scheme that has been started on August, 2015 to help the people who wish to start their own business. Standup India Scheme facilitates bank loan between ₹ 10 lakh and ₹ 1 Crore to at least one scheduled Caste (SC) or Scheduled tribe (ST) borrower and at least one woman borrower per bank branch for setting up a greenfield enterprise.

- **Pradhan Mantri Krishi Sinchai Yojana** The primary objectives of PMKSY are to attract investments in irrigation system at field level, develop and expend cultivable land in the country. The primary objective is to enhance ranch water use in order to minimise wastage of water, enhance crop per drop by implementing water saving technologies and precision irrigation.

- **Pradhan Mantri Ujjwal Yojana** Prime Minister Narendra Modi has launched Pradhan Mantri Ujjwal Yojana on 1st May, 2016 (Labour Day) at Ballia (UP) by providing cooking gas connections to 10 women.

The objective of the scheme is to provide cooking gas connections to 5 million beneficiaries below the poverty line in the next 3 years (till the year 2019).

- **Ujala Yojana** It was launched by Union Minister for State (IC) for Power, Coal and Renewable Energy Piyush Goyal in Bhopal, Madhya Pradesh on 30th April, 2016.

  The main motive of this policy is energy efficiency in the country. Consumers can buy the bulbs from distributor by showing any identification card.

- **Pradhan Mantri Fasal Bima Yojana** It is the new crop damage insurance scheme started on 18 Feb, 2016. It will replace the existing two crop insurance schemes National Agricultural Insurance Scheme (NAIS) and Modified NAIS.

- **Pradhan Mantri Garib Kalyan Yojana** The PMGKY notified along with other provisions of taxation laws (Second Amendment) Act, 2016 came into effect from 17 December, 2016. It provides for 50% tax and surcharge on declaration of unaccounted cash deposit in banks. Declarant must make mandatory deposit of 25% of undisclosed income in zero-interest PMGKY scheme 2016 with lock-in period of four years.

- **Pradhan Mantri Kaushal Vikas Yojana** It is a demand-driven, reward-based skill training scheme. PMKVY is formed to provide skill training to class 10 and 12 dropout youths across the country.

  Under the scheme, besides assessing and certifying 10 lakh youth for the skills they already possess, around 24 lakh youth will be skilled over the next year.

- **Atal Pension Yojana** The Atal Pension Yojana (APY) will focus on all citizens in the unorganised sector, who join the National Pension System (NPS) administered by the Pension Fund Regulatory and Development Authority (PFRDA) and who are not members of any statutory social security scheme. It is available to people between 18 and 40 year of age with bank accounts. The subscribers are required to opt for a monthly pension from ₹ 1000 to ₹ 5000.

- **Pradhan Mantri Jeevan Jyoti Bima Yojana** The PMJJBY is available to people in the age group of 18 to 50 and having a bank account. People who join the scheme before completing 50 years can, however, continue to have the risk of life cover upto the age of 55 years subject to payment of premium. Aadhar would be the primary **Know Your Customers** (KYC) for the bank account life insurance of ₹ 2 Lakh with a premium of ₹ 330 per year.

- **Pradhan Mantri Suraksha Bima Yojana** The scheme will be a one-year cover, renewable from year to year. It is available to people between 18 and 70 yr of age with bank accounts. It has an annual premium of ₹ 12 for ₹ 2 lakh accidental and ₹ 1 lakh full disability.

- **Varishtha Pension Bima Yojana** The Union Finance Minister Arun Jaitley re-launched Varishtha Pension Bima Yojana (VPBY) on 14th August, 2014 that will benefit the vulnerable section of society with limited resources as it will provide monthly pension ranging from ₹ 500 to ₹ 5000 per month to senior citizens of the country.

- **Pradhan Mantri Sahaj Bijli Har Ghar Yojana** The scheme aims electrifying all the households in rural and urban areas which are still living without power.

- **Rashtriya Vayoshri Yojana** To offer free-living assertive devices to senior citizens belong to BPL families.

- **UDAN Scheme** Udey Desh Ka Aam Nagrik scheme aims at regional air connectivity.

AGRICULTURE

IMPORTANCE OF AGRICULTURE

- Agriculture is the mainstay of the Indian economy despite emphasis on industrialisation in the last six decades.
- Its importance to the Indian economy can be gauged from the following facts.

Contribution to GDP

- According to the new series of national income released by CSO at 2011-12 prices, the share of agriculture in total GDP is 17% (Approx) in 2017-18.

Contribution to Employment

- Agriculture provides livelihood to more than half of the population.
- In 2011, it contributed 58% to the total employment in the country.

Contribution to Trade

- Although, the share of agricultural products in total trade of India is declining due to export diversification.
- Yet in 2009-10, it contributed 11% to the total exports and 13% to the total imports of the country.
- In addition to above, agriculture sector plays a crucial role in inclusive growth by directly attacking poverty and containing inflation. It is also an important source of raw material for a vast segment of industry.

Contribution of Agriculture in National Income

- Agricultural sector contributes a significantly large share to the national income of India, although it has come down from as high as 56% during the 1950s to 13.9 % in 2011-12 and is projected to go further in immediate future.

Agriculture and Five Year Plans

- The highest outlay on agriculture was during the First Plan, it was 31%.
- The Intensive Agricultural District Programme (IADP) followed by High Yielding Variety Programme (HYVP) was introduced during the Third Plan. First and Fifth Plan were the only plans, which achieved the set targets.
- Tenth Plan did not set any targets for crop production.
- The growth rate of agriculture during the Ninth and Tenth Plan were 2.4% and 2.3% respectively.

Agriculture in Eleventh Five Year Plan

- Eleventh Plan, recognising the importance of agriculture in promoting inclusive growth, fixed the agriculture growth rate of 4%. Actual outlay in the Eleventh Plan is estimated to be 18.5% of the total plan outlay. Contract farming was encouraged in fruits, vegetables and other crops.
- The average annual growth rate of GDP in agriculture and allied sectors during 11th plan was 3.7 per cent.

Agriculture in Twelfth Five Year Plan

- The approach paper aims at growth rate of 4% per annum in agriculture sector, with foodgrains growing at about 2% per year and non-foodgrains growing at 5.6%.
- The approach paper has emphasised on technology as the main vehicle for improving productivity in agriculture as natural resources are fixed. Severely indicting the public sector research in agriculture the Twelfth Plan encourages Public Private Partnership (PPP) in agriculture so as to bridge the gap in dryland areas and rapidly diversify agriculture.
- It emphasises on greater road connectivity, development of horticulture, dairying and other animal husbandry to further improve the market acces to the farmers.

Average Achievement in Agriculture in Five Year Plans (in percentage)

Five Year Plan	Growth Rate
First Five Year Plan (1951-52 to 1955-56)	2.71
Second Five Year Plan (1956-57 to 1960-61)	3.17
Third Five Year Plan (1961 -62 to 1965-66)	0.73
Annual Plan (1966-67 to 1968-69)	4.16
Fourth Five Year Plan (1969-70 to 1973-74)	2.57
Fifth Five Year Plan (1974-75 to 1978-79)	3.28
Sixth Five Year Plan (1980-81 to 1984-85)	2.52
Seventh Five Year Plan (1985-86 to 1989-90)	3.47
Annual Plan (1990-91 to 1991-92)	1.01
Eighth Five Year Plan(1992-93to1996-97)	4.68
Ninth Five Year Plan (1997-98 to 2001-02)	2.02
Tenth Five Year Plan (2002-03 to 2006-07)	2.3
Eleventh Five Year Plan (2007-08 to 2011-12)	3.6

Green Revolution

- It was a part of new agricultural strategy, which included, initially, the Intensive Agriculture District Programme (IADP) and later the High Yielding Varieties Programme (HYVP).
- It was launched in the year 1966 and was the brainchild of Norman Borlaug, though in India, it was made successful by Dr MS Swaminathan. The term 'Green Revolution' was coined by Dr William Gaud.
- The achievement of Green Revolution were rise in cereal production especially wheat and rice, change in cropping pattern in favour of wheat and increase in employment opportunities.
- The weaknesses of Green Revolution were growth of capitalistic farming, side tracked land reforms, widened income and regional disparities and environmental degradation.
- The Green Revolution demanded high yielding seed, increasing irrigation, pesticides in fertilizer.

Farmer's Commission

- A National Commission on farmers was appointed in 2004, under the Chairmanship of Dr MS Swaminathan, which interalia suggested an Agricultural Renewal Action Plan (ARAP).
- The ARAP comprised of soil health enhancement, irrigation water supply augmentation and demand management, credit and insurance, technological reforms and assured and remmunerative marketing.

Second Green Revolution

- The call for Second Green Revolution was given by then Prime Minister Manmohan Singh at the 93rd Science Conference in 2006.
- The Second Green Revolution seeks to build up on the achievements of first Green Revolution and bridge the regional and crop imbalance, which were not addressed by First Green Revolution.
- The Second Green Revolution seeks to cover dryland farming and concentrate on the small and marginal farmers. It seeks to raise the foodgrain production to 400 million tonnes by 2020.

Evergreen Revolution

- Concept given by renowned agricultural scientist Dr MS Swaminathan.
- The concept emphasises on 'organic agriculture' and 'green agriculture' with the help of integrated pest management, integrated nutrient supply and integrated natural resource management.
- The core of the evergreen revolution is 'sustainability'.

White Revolution

- White revolution is relates to phenomenal growth in milk production. To increase the pace of White Revolution, the operation flood was started. The father of operation flood was Dr Verghese Kurien. Operation flood was started by National Dairy Development Board in 1970.
- India ranks first in the world in milk production, which went up from 17 MT in 1950-51 to 146.3 MT in 2014-15. The per capita availability of milk in India has increased from 176 grams per day in 1990-91 to 322 grams per day by 2014-15. It is move than the world average of 294 grams per day during 2013.

Fisheries Sector

India is the third largest producer of fish and second largest producer of inland fish in the world. Fisheries constitute about 1 per cent of the GDP of the country and 5.08 per cent of agriculture GDP. The total fish production during 2014-15 was 10.46 MT.

Tricolour Revolution

The reference to a Tricolour Revolution was made by Prime Minister Narendra Modi. This phrase has three components.

These are as follows

- **Saffron Energy Revolution** for promotion and better utilisation of solar energy.

- **White Revolution** to ensure cattle welfare and further the goals of White Revolution.
- **Blue Revolution** for fishermen's welfare, cleansing rivers and sea and conserving water.

Food Security in India

- The need for food self-sufficiency was borne out on account of the experience gained from the PL-480 programme of the USA in the year 1966.
- Food security implies access by all people at all times to sufficient quantities of food to lead an active and healthy life. *Essentially, it involves*
  - quantitative dimension in term of food self-sufficiency;
  - qualitative dimension in form of nutritional requirement; and
  - purchasing power dimension so as to ensure access to all through employment generation programmes.

Major Agricultural Revolutions

Revolution	Production
Black Revolution	Petroleum Production
Blue Revolution	Fish Production
Brown Revolution	Leather/Non-conventional (India)/ Cocoa Production
Golden Fibre Revolution	Jute Production
Golden Revolution	Overall Horticulture Development/Honey Production
Green Revolution	Foodgrain (Cereals, Wheat and Leguminous plant) Production
Grey Revolution	Fertilizer Revolution
Pink Revolution	Onion production/ Pharmaceutical (India)/ Prawn Production
Rainbow Revolution	Holistic Development of Agriculture Sector
Red Revolution	Meat and Tomato Production
Round Revolution	Potato Revolution
Silver Fibre Revolution	Cotton Revolution
Silver Revolution	Egg/Poultry Production
White Revolution	Milk/Dairy Production (In India-Operation Flood)
Yellow Revolution	Oil Seeds Production
Evergreen Revolution	Increase in Productivity and Prosperity without Ecological Harm

Public Distribution System (PDS)

- PDS was envisaged in 1967 to act as a price support programme for the consumer during the periods of food shortage of the 1960's.
- The basic aim was to provide essential commodities such as rice, wheat, sugar, edible oil, soft coke and kerosene at subsidised prices. PDS is the largest distribution network of its kind in the world.
- Following the criticism of PDS, the government in June, 1997 replaced the PDS with Targeted Public Distribution System (TPDS). The system envisaged issuing special cards to BPL families and selling foodgrains to them at subsidised prices.

National Food Security Act, 2013

This act was notified with the objective to provide food and nutritional security in human life cycle approach, by ensuring access to adequate quantity of quality food at affordable prices to people. The act provide for coverage of upto 75% of the rural population and upto 50% of the urban population for receiving subsidised foodgrains under TPDS.

The eligible persons will be entitled to receive 5 kgs of foodgrains per person per month at subsidised prices of ₹ 3/2/1 per kg for rice/wheat/coarse grains. The existing Antyodaya Anna Yojana (AAY) households, which constitute the poorest of the poor, will continue to receive 35 kgs of foodgrains per household per month.

Agricultural Price Policy (APP)

- APP of the government seeks to ensure remunerative prices to the producers so as to encourage higher interest and production on the one hand, on the other, it safeguards the consumers interest by making food available at reasonable prices.

- To achieve this government announces **Minimum Support Prices** (MSPs) for 25 agricultural crops taking into accounts the recommendation of the Commission for Agricultural Cost and Prices (CACP). MSP is that price, at which government is ready to purchase the crop from the farmers directly, if crop price falls below the MSP.

- Commission for Agricultural Costs and Prices (CACPs) was set-up in 1965 with the name Agricultural Price Commission and was renamed as CACP in 1985.

- **Market Intervention Scheme** (MIS) is implemented for horticultural and agricultural commodities, generally perishable in nature and not covered under the Price Support Scheme (PSS).

- Economic cost is composed of three components; *viz* MSP, procurement incidentals and cost of distributing foodgrains.

Agriculture Credit

- There are two sources of credit available to farmers, *viz* institutional and private.

- **Institutional Credit** covers cooperative societies and banks, commercial banks, RRB and NABARD.

- **Non-Institutional/Private** sources of credit are moneylenders, traders and commission agents, relatives and landlords.

- Lead Bank Scheme (LBS) based on **area approach** was launched in 1969 on the recommendation of Dr Gadgil Committee and Narasimham Committee.

- Under the LBS, all the 14 nationalised banks and a few private sector banks were alloted specific districts and were asked to play the 'lead role' in coordinating credit deployment.

Regional Rural Banks (RRBs)

- **RRBs** formally launched in 2nd October, 1975 at Moradabad and Gorakhpur (Uttar Pradesh), Bhiwani (Haryana), Jaipur (Rajasthan) and Malda (West Bengal).

- The objective of the RRB was to provide credit and other facilities particularly to small and marginal farmers, agricultural labourers etc so as to develop agriculture.

- RRB's mobilise financial resource from rural/semi urban areas.

- It is jointly owned by GoI, the concerned State Government and sponsor banks.

Agriculture Insurance Company of India Limited (AIC)

- AIC was incorporated under the Companies Act, 1956 on 20th December, 2002 as a specialised insurer with the capital participation from GIC, four public sector General Insurance Companies and NABARD.

- The other specialised insurer is **Export Credit Guarantee Corporation** (ECGC). It was established in 1957.

NABARD

- National Bank for Agriculture and Rural Development (NABARD) was set-up in July, 1982 as the Apex Bank with a paid-up capital of ₹ 100 crore contributed equally by RBI and Government of India. Its headquarter is in Mumbai.
- The role of NABARD was to act as a refinance institution for all kind of production and investment credit to agricultural and village sector.
- The paid-up capital of NABARD was raised to ₹ 5000 crore on 23rd October, 2011 by the government. The RBI divested all of its stake from the NABARD to the government in October, 2010. Now, 99% shares of NABARD is with the government.
- Rural Infrastructure Development Fund (RIDF) was set-up in 1995-96, under NABARD for holistic rural development.

NAFED

National Agricultural Co-operative Marketing Federation of India Limited is the Apex Co-operative Organisation at the national level. It deals in procurement, distribution, export and import of selected agricultural commodities.

NCDC

National Co-operative Development Corporation was set-up in 1963, under an Act of Parliament. The object of NCDC is planning and promoting programmes for the production, processing, storage and marketing of agricultural produce and notified commodities through co-operative societies.

Quick Digest

- Kisan Credit Cards (KCCs) was introduced in 1998-99 by NABARD. The purpose of the KCC scheme is to facilitate short-term credit to farmers, Union-Budget 2012-13 has proposed to make KCC as smart cards and can be used at ATMs.
- Rehabilitation Package for Distressed Farmers was introduced in 2006 for 31 suicide prone-districts in the states of Andhra Pradesh, Karnataka, Kerala and Maharashtra.

Commodity Future Market

The commodity future market facilitates the price discovery process and provides a platform for price risk management in commodities. The market comprises 21 commodity futures exchanges, which include 5 national and 16 (commodity-specific) regional commodity exchanges.

Commodity Markets in India

- Commodity Exchange, **Mumbai**
- National Commodity and Derivatives Exchange, **Mumbai**
- Multi Commodity Exchange, **Mumbai**
- ACE Derivatives and Commodity Exchange Limited, **Ahmedabad**

Food Processing Industry

- India is the third largest producer of food in the world after China and the US.
- Food processing industry is the fifth largest industry in India in terms of production, consumption, exports and expected growth.

Mega Food Park Scheme

Mega Food Park Scheme was launched in 2008 that aims at providing a mechanism to link agricultural production to the market by bringing together farmers, processors and retailers so as to ensure maximising value addition, minimising wastage, increasing farmers' income and creating employment opportunities particularly in rural sector. Government provide financial assistance to set up modern infrastructure facilities for food processing. The 12th paln has targeted to set-up 50 mega food parks during the plan period.

Important portal and App

The **'Participatory Guarantee System'** portal will help small and marginal farmers engaged in organic farming to secure certificaton after checks for compliance to standards are carried out.

The **'Soil Health Card'** portal has been developed to register soil sample and record tests results along with fertiliser recommendations to create a national database on soil health for future use in research.

The **Fertiliser Quality Control System** portal will collate results of draw samples of imported fertilisers helping both consumers and importers with analysis reports.

Mobile app "AgriMarket Mobile"

This app has been developed with an aim to keep them abreast with crop prices around them. AgriMarket Mobile App can be used to get the market price of crops in the markets within 50 km of the device's location.

Mobile app "Crop Insurance"

It will help the farmers not only to find out complete details about insurance cover available in thier area, but also to calculate the insurance premium for notified crops, coverage amount and loan amount in case of a loaned farmer.

Soil Health Card Scheme

In February 2015, the Narendra Modi government had launched the Soil Health Card Scheme. Under this programme, the government plans to issue soil card to farmers to help them get a good harvest by studying the quality of soil.

The Soil Health Card studies and reviews the health of soil or rather we can say a complete evaluation of the quality of soil right from its functional characteristics, to water and nutrients content and other biological properties. Under this scheme Centre plans to target over 14 crore farmers in the next three years.

INDUSTRY

- Industry sector comprises of mining, manufacturing, electricity and gas and construction.
- Industry has a share of 28% in the overall GDP and its share in total employment increased from 16.2% in 1999-2000 to 26.7% in 2012-13.
- The long-term average annual growth of industries during the post-reform period between 1991-92 to 2011-12, averaged 6.7%.

Industrial Policies

- Industrial Policies were launched in 1948, 1956, 1977, 1980 and 1991.

- The Industrial Policy Resolution of 1948 marked the beginning of the evolution of the Indian Industrial Policy.
- The IPR 1956 called the **Economic Constitution** of India, gave the public sector a strategic role in the economy.
- The objective of the IPR 1956 was establishment of **socialistic pattern of the society** in the country.

New Industrial Policy, 1991

- Formed the basis for the economic reforms in India, which proved to be a watershed in the history of Indian economy.
- The main aim of the new industrial policy 1991 was to unshackle the Indian industries from the cobweb of unnecessary bureaucratic control;
- to introduce liberalisation with a view to integrate Indian economy with the world economy;
- to remove restrictions on FDI and to abolish MRTP Act, 1969; and
- to shed the load of the public enterprises.

Compulsory Licensing

- Distillation and brewing of alcoholic drinks.
- Cigars and cigarettes of tobacco and manufactured tobacco substitutes.
- Electronic, aerospace and defence equipment; all types.
- Industrial explosives including match boxes.
- Specific hazardous chemical *viz,* (a) Hydrocyanic acid; (b) Phosgene; and (c) Isocyanates and diisocyanates of hydrocarbon.

Disinvestment Policy

- The Industrial Policy Statement of 24th July, 1991 outlined the disinvestment of selected PSEs.
- Disinvestment is a process, through which privatisation could take place.
- The objective of pursuing disinvestment in India were unlocking resources trapped in non-strategic PSEs; reducing public debt and transferring commercial risk to the private sector.
- First Disinvestment Commission was set-up in 1996, under the Chairmanship of Mr EV Ramkrishna, which was later reconstituted in July, 2001, under Dr RH Patil.

Public Sector Enterprises

- As on 31st March, 2015, there were 298 Central Public Sector Enterprises (CPSEs). Out of 298 CPSEs, 235 were in operation and 63 were under construction.
- To measure the performance of management of PSEs at the end of the year in an objective and transparent manner, the concept of **Memorandum of Understanding** (MoU), on the recommendation of Arjun Sengupta Committee (1988), was started in 1991.

New Company Bill, 2013

- Six Decades Old Company Act, 1956 will be replaced by this act. In this act, it has been made mandatory for the companies to include provisions for social welfare. Till date, in the 54 years Old Company Act, 1956 has been amended 25 times.
- For companies having an annual turn over above ₹ 10 lakh, it has been made mandatory to appoint one third independent directors and at least appointment of one female director.

MAHARATNA

- In 2009, the government established the **Maharatna** status, which raised the PSEs investment ceiling from ₹ 1000 crore to ₹ 5000 crore.
- The Maharatnas firm can now decide on investments of upto 15% of their net worth.

Criteria for Maharatna

The six criteria for eligibility of Maharatna are as follows:

- Having Navratna status;
- Listed on Indian stock exchange;
- An average annual turnover of more than ₹ 25,000 crore during the last three years;
- An average annual net worth of more than ₹ 15,000 crore during the last three years; an average annual net profit after tax of more than ₹ 5000 crore during the last 3 years and should have significant global presence.

List of Maharatna

There are eight Maharatnas in India

- Oil and Natural Gas Corporation (ONGC)
- Gas Authority of India Limited (GAIL)
- Steel Authority India Limited (SAIL)
- Indian Oil Corporation (IOC)

- Bharat Petroleum Corporation Limited (BPCL)
- National Thermal Power Corporation (NTPC)
- Coal India Limited (CIL)
- Bharat Heavy Electricals Limited (BHEL)

NAVRATNA

To be qualified as a Navratna Company

- The company must obtain a score of 60 (of the total 100).
- The score is based on six parameters, which included net profit to net worth, total manpower cost to total cost of production, Profit Before Depreciation, Interest and Taxes (PBDIT) to capital employed, PBDIT to turnover, earning per share and inter-sectoral performance.
- The company must first be a Miniratna-I and must have four independent directors on its board. The Navratna status empowers a company to invest utpo ₹ 1000 crore or 15% of their net worth overseas without government approval.
- At present, there are **16 Navratnas**.

List of Navratna

- Bharat Electronics Limited
- Hindustan Aeronautics Limited
- Hindustan Petroleum Corporation Limited
- Mahanagar Telephone Nigam Limited
- National Aluminium Company Limited
- National Mineral Development Corporation
- Nevyeli Lignite Corporation Limited
- Oil India Limited
- Power Finance Corporation Limited
- Power Grid Corporation of India Limited
- Rashtriya Ispat Nigam Limited.
- Rural Electrification Corporation Limited
- Shipping Corporation of India Limited
- Engineers India Limited
- National Building Construction Corporation Limited
- Container Corporation of India Limited

MINIRATNA

- **Miniratna Category I** Public Sector Enterprises (PSEs) that have made profit continuously for the last three years or earned a net profit of ₹ 30 crores or more in one of three years. At present, there are 58 Miniratna I.
- **Miniratna Category II** PSEs that have made profit for the 1st three years and should have a positive net worth. At present, there are 15 Miniratna II.

Sick Industries

- A sick unit is one, which is in existence for atleast 5 years and 15% of its net worth has eroded. To combat industrial sickness particularly with regard to the crucial sectors and timely detection of sick and potentially sick industrial companies, **Sick Industrial Companies Act**, (1985) was enacted.
- SICA provisions were extended to public enterprises in 1993 so as to enable public sector enterprises to be referred to a quasi-judicial body **Board of Industrial and Finance Reconstruction** (BIFR) to take appropriate measures for revival and rehabilitation.

Small-Scale Industries

- A new thrust in favour of small scale industries was given in the Industrial Policy Resolution of 1977.
- With effect from 2nd October, 2006 government enacted the Micro, Small and Medium Enterprises Development Act.
- The **MSMED Act, 2006,** clearly defines, for the first time, not only the medium enterprises but also extends it to the services sector too.
- According to the Fourth Census (2009) of the MSME sector, 67% are manufacturing and 33% services enterprises.
- MSME sector contributes 8% to the GDP, 45% to the manufactured output, 40% to the exports and provides employment to 42 million people.
- SIDBI (Small Industries Development Bank of India) is a independent financial institution to finance the growth of MSME's.
- Abid Hussain Committee was set-up to look into the problems of small-scale industries.

Micro, Small and Medium Enterprises Policy, 2012

The policy was notified in March, 2012. The policy envisages that every Central Ministry/ PSU shall set an annual goal for procurement from the MSE sector with the objective of achieving minimum 20% of the total annual purchase from MSEs in a period of 3 years.

Enterprise	Manufacturing Sector	Service Sector
Large Enterprise	Investment in plant and machinery	Investment in Equipments
Micro Enterprises	Does not exceed ₹ 25 lakh	Does not exceed ₹ 10 lakh
Small Enterprises	More than ₹ 25 lakh, but does not exceed ₹ 5 crore	More than ₹ 10 lakh rupees, but does not exceed ₹ 2 crore
Medium Enterprises	More than ₹ 5 crore, but does not exceed ₹ 10 crore	More than ₹ 2 crore, but does not exceed ₹ 5 crore

LARGE SCALE INDUSTRIES

Iron and Steel Industry

- First steel industry at Kulti, West Bengal Iron Works Company was established in 1870.
- First large 'scale steel plant-TISCO at Jamshedpur (1907) was followed by IISCO at Burnpur (1919).
- The first public owned steel plant was Rourkela Integrated Steel Plant set-up in 1954 with the help of German Kmpp-Demag.
- India is the fourth largest producer of crude steel in the world after China, Japan and the USA in 2010. In 2009, India was ranked third.
- India is the largest producer of sponge iron since, 2002.
- Steel Authority of India Limited (SAIL) was established in 1974 for the development of the steel industry.

ron and Steel Plants in India

Location	Assistance
Rourkela (Odisha)	Germany
Bhilai (Chhattisgarh)	Russia
Durgapur (West Bengal)	Britain
Bokaro (Jharkhand)	Russia
Vishakhapatnam (Andhra Pradesh)	Russia

Cotton and Synthetic Textile Industry

- It is the largest industry in India accounting for about 20% of industrial output, provides employment to 20 million persons and contributes 33% to total export earnings. The first Indian modernised cotton cloth mill was established in 1818 at fort Gloster near Kolkata, but this was unsuccessful.
- The second mill was established in 1854 at Bombay by KGN Daber.
- The share of cotton in total cloth production declined from 65% to 50% in 2009-10. Whereas, that of fabrics rose from 27% to 50%.
- The organised textile industry comprises of (i) spinning mills; (ii) coarse and medium composite mills and (iii) fine and superfine composite mills.

Jute Industry

- It was started in 1855 at Rishra and India is the largest producer and second largest exporter of jute in the world. Jute Technology Mission was launched 2nd June, 2006.
- Government has enacted Jute Packing Materials (compulsory use in packing commodities) Act, 1997 to broaden the usage of jute.

Gems and Jewellery

- It is an important emerging sector in the Indian economy. According to the data released by the World Gold Council (WGC), India is the largest consumer of gold.
- India (especially, Surat and Mumbai) ranks among the 'big four' diamond cutting centres of the world, the other three being, Belgium (Antwerp), the USA (New York) and Israel (Ramat Gan).

Silk Industry

- India is the second largest (after China) silk manufacturer contributing to 18% of the total raw silk production.
- The majority of silk is produced mainly in Bhoodan Pochampally (also known as silk city), Kanchipuram, Dharamvaram and Mysore.

Sugar Industry

- India is the largest producer of sugar in the world with a 22% share.
- It is the second largest agro-based industry in the country.
- **BB Mahajan Committee** was set-up to study the sugar industry.
- The Sugar Development Fund was set-up in 1982, under the Sugar Cess Act.
- Dual price mechanism with partial control is applied to sugar industry. Under this, the government fixes the ratio of and free sale sugar quota in the ratio 28:72.

Cement Industry

- The foundation of stable Indian cement industry was laid in 1914, when the Indian Cement Company Limited manufactured cement at Porbandar in Gujarat.
- India is the second largest producer of cement in the world.
- The per capita consumption of cement in India is just 68 kg.

Automotive Industry

- India is the second largest manufacturer of motorcycle and fifth largest manufacturer of commercial vehicles in the world. In 2009, India was the fourth largest exporter of passenger cars after Japan, South Korea and Thailand.
- India is the largest manufacturer of tractors in the world. India is the ninth largest car manufacturer in the world.

Unorganised Sector and Informal Economy

- Unorganise informal workers refer to workers, who are not covered under any social security benefits irrespective of whether they work in organised or unorganised sector. 86% of the total workforce were in the unorganised sector in 2004-05.
- To look into the problems of unorganised sector, **National** Commission for Enterprises in the Unorganised Sector was set-up under the Chairmanship of **Dr Arjun Sengupta.**
- In accordance with the recommendation of the NCEUS, the Government of India enacted the **Unorganised Workers Social Security Act, 2008**.
- The act came into effect from 16th May, 2009. The act among other things provides for constitution of a National Social Security Board and State Social Security Board to recommend Social Security Schemes;
- Constitution of record keeping functions by the district administration.
- Constitution of a workers facilitation centre.
- A National Social Security Fund (NSSF) with initial allocation of ₹ 1000 crore for the unorganised sector workers has been set-up.
- A National Social Security Board (NSSB) has been constituted in 2009.

National Manufacturing Policy (NMP)

- The NMP was released by the government on 4th November, 2011 to bring about a qualitative and quantitative change with following objectives
- Increase manufacturing growth to 12-14% over the medium term;
- Enable manufacturing to contribute atleast 25% of GDP by 2022;
- Create 100 million additional jobs in the manufacturing sector by 2022;
- Provides for National Investment and Manufacturing Zone (NIMZ) on lands, which are degraded and uncultivable.

National Policy on Electronics (NPE), 2011

- NPE was released on 3rd October, 2011 providing for a roadmap for the development of the electronics sector in the country.
  The main objectives are as follow:
- To achieve a turnover of about US $ 400 billion by 2020;
- To create employment opportunities of around 28 million;
- To increase export from US $ 5.5 billion to US $ 80 billion 2020.

Make in India

Indian Prime Minister Narendra Modi on 25th September, 2014 launched the 'Make in India' (MIN) campaign with a high-pitch event held at New Delhi's Vigyan Bhawan. The campaign aims at reviving the job-creating manufacturing sector, which is being seen as the key to taking the Indian economy on a sustainable high growth path. 'Make in India' aims to take manufacturing sector, which is being seen as the key to taking the Indian economy on a sustainable high path. 'Make in India' aims to take manufacturing growth to 10% on a sustainable basis.

Digital India

Digital India is a major flagship programme of the Government of India, launched in August, 2014 aimed at transforming the country into a digitally empowered social and knowledge economy, as well as to revive the state of governance in the country. It is an 'Umbrella Programme' weaving together many existing schemes under multiple ministries and departments to ensure that its services are available to citizens electronically.

FOREIGN TRADE

Trade between two or more nations is called foreign trade or international trade. With the liberalisation of the economy in 1991 and adoption of 'export promotion' policy measures has led to substantial growth in exports and diversification of our exports.

- As per the World Trade Organisation (WTO), India's share in global export and imports increase from 0.8% and 1% respectively in 2004 to 1.7% and 2.5% in 2013. Its ranking in terms of leading exporters and importers is 19 and 12 respectively in 2014.

Balance of Payments (BOP)

- The balance of payments in a statical statement that systematically summarises, for a specific time period. The economic transactions of an economy with the rest of the world. BoP comprises of current account, capital account and omissions and changes in foreign exchange reserves.

Current Account

- Current account transactions are classified into merchandise (exports and imports) and invisibles.

  Invisibles Invisible transactions are *classified into three categories namely*
  1. Services travel 2. Income 3. Transfers

Capital Account

- Under capital account, capital inflows can be classified by instrument (debt/equity) and maturity (short/long-term).
- The main component of capital account include foreign investment, loans and banking capital.

Non-Debt Liabilities

Includes FDI and portfolio investment comprising of FIIs, ADRs/GDRs.

Debt Liabilities Includes External assistance, External Commercial Borrowings (ECBs), trade credit and banking capital (NRIs deposits).

Balance of Trade (BoT)

1. Balanced BOT i.e. Exports = Imports
2. Adverse BOT i.e. Exports < Imports
3. Favourable BOT, i.e. Exports > Imports

Foreign Exchange Reserves in India

These are the main Foreign Exchange Reserves in India
- Foreign Currency Assets (FCAs);
- Gold Stock of RBI;
- Special Drawing Rights (SDRs); and
- Reserve Tranche Position (RTP) in the IMF.

- **FERA** (Foreign Exchange Regulation Act), was enacted in 1973, to consolidate and regulate dealings in foreign exchange, so as to conserve the foreign exchange and utilise it to promote economic development.
- **FEMA** (Foreign Exchange Management Act) was enacted in 1999 to replace existing FERA. This act seeks to make offences related to foreign exchange civil offences.

SEZ Act, 2005
- Duty free import/ domestic procurement of goods for development, operation and maintenance of SEZ units.
- 100% Income Tax exemption an export income of SEZ units exemption from Central Sales Tax and Service Tax. Single window clearance mechanism for establishment of units.

Special Economic Zone (SEZ)

- A Special Economic Zone (SEZ) is a geographical region that has economic and other laws that are more free-market oriented than a country's typical national laws. Asia's first Export Processing Zone (EPZ) was set-up in **Kandla**, India in 1965. The first SEZ policy was announced in April, 2000, to make SEZ an engine of growth supported by quality infrastructure backed by attractive fiscal package.
- To overcome the short comings experienced on account of the multiplicity of controls and clearances and an unstable fiscal regime and with a view to attract foreign investments in India, SEZ Act, 2005 was enacted with effect from 10th February, 2005.

Foreign Trade Policy (FTP), (2015-20)

The Foreign Trade Policy, 2015-20 was finally announced by the Hon'ble Minister of Commerce and Industry, Smt Nirmala Sitharaman on 1st April, 2015.

The FTP has been announced in the backdrop of several measures initiated by the Government of India such as 'Make in India', 'Digital India' and 'Skills India', among others.

The focus of the new policy is to support both the manufacturing and services sectors, with a special emphasis on improving the 'ease of doing business'.

Features of FTP (2015-20)

Features of the foreign trade Policy are as follows:

- India to be made a significant participant in world trade by 2020.
- Merchandise Exports from India Scheme (MEIS) to promote specific services for specific markets Foreign Trade Policy.
- Service Exports from India Scheme has been replaced with Service Exports from India Scheme (SEIS).
- FTP would reduce export obligations by 25% and give boost to domestic manufacturing. FTP benefits from both MEIS and SEIS will be extended to units located in SEZs.
- Industrial products to be supported in major markets at rates ranging from 2% to 3%.

FOREIGN DIRECT INVESTMENT (FDI)

- FDI is a type of investment that involves the injection of foreign funds into an enterprises that operates in a different country of origin from the invester. FDI play an extraordinary and growing role in global business. It can provide a firm with new markets and marketing channels, cheaper production facilities, access to new technology, products, skill and financing.
- FDI occurs when a company invests in a business that is located in another country and it is investing not less than 10% of shares belonging to the foreign company. It is a non-debt capital flow. FII (Foreign Institutional Investment). Foreign portfolio investment occurs, when foreign investment in the form of shares, equities and bonds, is made by a foreign company.
- The three main institutions that handle FDI related issues in India are the Foreign Investment Promotion Board (FIPB), the Foreign Investment Implementation Authority (FIIA) and the Secretariat for Industrial Assistance (SIA) activities/sectors not opened to private sector, *viz* railways and atomic energy.
- Since, 20th May, 2011 FDI in **Limited Liability Partnership** (LLP) has been allowed.

FDI Limits in Various Sectors

Sector/Activity	Per cent of FDI/Equity	Entry Route
Defense Sector	100%	Automatic route
Telecom Services	100%	Automatic up to 49% government route beyond 49% and up to 100%
Tea Plantation, Animal Husbandry	100%	Automatic up to 49% government route beyond 49% and up to 100%
Asset Reconstruction Company	100%	Automatic up to 49% government beyond 49% and up to 100%
Petroleum and Natural Gas	49%	Automatic Route
Commodity Exchanges	49%	Automatic Route
Power Exchanges	49%	Automatic Route
Stock Exchanges/Clearing Corporations	49%	Automatic Route
Credit Information Companies, Pharma	74%	Automatic Route
Courier Services, e-commerce	100%	Automatic Route
Single Brand Product Retail trading, Multi Brand (food)	100%	Automatic up to 49% government route beyond 49% and up to 100%
Insurance Sector	49%	FIPB route (The CCEA* on 24th December, 2014; 49% FDI in Insurance).
Airlines	100%	100% FDI in scheduled airlines and upto 49% FDI airlines through automatic route.

* Cabinet Committee on Economic Affairs - CCEA.

THE INDIAN CURRENCY SYSTEM

- The present monetary system of India is based on inconvertible paper currency and is managed by the RBI. The present currency system is based on minimum reserve system of note issue. It was adopted in 1957, under the minimum reserve system, minimum of gold and foreign securities to the extent of ₹ 200 crore of which gold should be of value ₹ 115 crore and the balance in rupee securities is maintained.

- RBI Working Group on Money Supply headed by **YV Reddy** recommended for dropping of post office saving deposits. Accordingly, there are now only three monetary aggregates, *viz* M_1, M_2 and M_3.
  The revised monetary measure are as follow:

  M_1 = Coins and Notes + Demand Deposits + Other deposits with RBI.

  M_2 = M_1 + Time liabilities portion of saving deposits with banks + Certificates of deposits issued by banks + Term deposit maturing within a year.

  M_3 = M_2 + terms deposit with banks with maturity over 1 year + call/term borrowing of the banking system.

- *Coins are minted at four places, viz Mumbai, Kolkata, Hyderabad and Noida.*

Quick Digest

- The symbol of Indian rupee came into vague on 15th July, 2010.
- The new symbol is an amalgamation of Devanagri 'Ra' and the Roman 'R' without the stem.
- The new symbol designed by D Udaya Kumar, a post-graduate of IIT Bombay was finally selected by the Union Cabinet on 15th July, 2010.
- Though the symbol '₹' will not be printed or embossed on currency notes or coins, it would be included in the 'Unicode Standard' and major scripts of the world to ensure that it is easily displaced and printed in the electronic and print media.

Devaluation of Currency

- It means reducing the value of a currency by the fiscal authorities, so as to make exports cheaper and imports costlier and overcome balance of payments deficit. In India, devaluation has been resorted to four times.

  1. **First Devaluation** In June, 1949 (by 30.5%) (Finance Minister *Dr John Mathai*).

  2. **Second Devaluation** In June, 1966 (by 57%) (Finance Minister *Sachindra Chaudhry*).

  3. **Third Devaluation** On 1st July, 1991 (by 9%) (Finance Minister *Dr Manmohan Singh*).

  4. **Fourth Devaluation** On 3rd July, 1991 (by 11%) (Finance Minister *Dr Manmohan Singh*).

Printing of Securities and Minting in India

Security Press	Station	Related to
India Security Press (1922)	Nashik	Postal material, Postal stamps etc
Security Printing Press (Estd 1982)	Hyderabad	Union excise duty stamps
Currency Notes Press (1928)	Nashik	Bank notes from ₹ 1 to ₹ 100
Bank Notes Press (1974)	Dewas	Bank note of ₹ 20, ₹ 50, ₹ 100, ₹ 200, ₹ 500, ₹ 2000
Modernised Currency Notes Press (1995)	Mysore (Kar) Salbani (West Bengal)	
Security Paper (Estd 1967-68)	Hoshangabad	Banks and currency notes paper

Demonetisation

Currency demonetisation is a radical financial step in which a particular currency's status as a legal tender is declared invalid. On 9th December, 2016, Reserve Bank of India withdrew the old ₹ 500 and ₹ 1000 notes as official mode of payment. The reason for this move given was that it will help to tackle black money, help to eliminate fake currency and to lower cash circulation in the country.

INFLATION

It means a persistent rise in the general price level of goods and services leading to a fall in the currency's purchasing power.

Causes of Inflation

* Printing too much money. Increase in money supply in the economy.
* Increase in production cost.
* Tax rises. Decline in exchange rates.
* War or other events causing instability.

Effects of Inflation

It is economically disastrous for lenders. Balance of trade can become unfavourable. Severely impacts the common man by reducing their real income. Persistent high level of inflation leads to economic stagnation.

Measures to Control Inflation

* Increasing the bank interest rates.
* Regulating fixed exchange rates of the domestic currency.
* Controlling prices and wages.
* Providing cost of living allowances to citizens. Regulating black and speculative market. Supply side inflation can be controlled by increasing production of economy, specially foodgrains and by improving infrastructure.

Wholesale Price Index (WPI)

It measures the change in wholesale prices on weekly basis. On the basis of weekly indices, average annual WPI is worked out. Average annual wholesale prices of the current year are related to average annual wholesale prices of the base year (assumed as 100). The base year for WPI is 2004-05.

Consumer Price Index (CPI)

It measures the change in retail prices on monthly basis. On the basis of monthly indices, average annual CPI is worked out. Average annual retail prices for the current year are related to the average annual retail prices of the base year (assumed as 100).

Deflation A general decline in prices, often caused by a reduction in the supply of money or credit. Deflation can be also caused by a decrease in government, pesonal or investment spending. The unemployment since there is a lower level of demand in the economy, which can lead to an economic depression.

Stagflation When you have a slow economy with high inflation rates and unemployment, stagflation is usually resultant. When the economy does not grow and prices continue to rise have a stagflation cycle in the economy.

Banking in India

* The first bank of limited liability managed by an Indian was **Oudh Commercial Bank** established in 1881. Subsequently, **PNB** was established in 1894.
* The largest bank **Imperial Bank of India** was nationalised in 1955 and renamed as **State Bank of India** followed by formation of its 7 associates in 1959.
* The step toward 'Social Banking' was taken with the nationalisation of 14 Commercial Banks on 19th July, 1969. Six more Commercial Banks were nationalised on 15th August, 1980.
* As on March 2011, there were 4 non- Scheduled Commercial Banks in India.

Reserve Bank of India (RBI)

- RBI is the Central Bank of the country.
- RBI was set-up on the basis of Hilton Young Commission recommendation in April, 1935 with the enactment of RBI Act, 1934. Its first Governor was **Sir Osborne Smith**.
- The main purpose of creating RBI was to separate currency and credit from GoI.
- RBI was nationalised in 1949 and its first Indian Governor was **CD Deshmukh**.

Administration

- The headquarter of the RBI is in **Mumbai**.
- There are 14 Directors in Central Board of Directors besides the Governor, four Deputy Governors and one Government Official.
- Governor of RBI - Mr Urjit Patel.

Functions

The main functions of the RBI includes

- Monetary authority.
- Issue of currency. Banker and debt manager to government.
- Banker of Banks.
- Regulator of banking system.
- Manager of foreign exchange.
- Maintaining financial stability.
- Regulator and supervisor of the payment and settlement system.
- Since 1952, Monetary Policy of the RBI emphasise on twin goals.
  These are as follows:
    1. Economic growth
    2. Inflation control

Credit Control Instruments

Instrument of credit control can be divided into two namely Qualitative/ Selective credit control and Quantitative credit control.

Quantitative/General Credit Control

Quantitative credit control are used to control the volume of credit and indirectly to control the inflationary and deflationary pressures caused by expansion and contraction of credit.

The quantitative credit control consists of

- **Bank Rate** It is also called the rediscount rate. It is the rate, at which the RBI gives finance to Commercial Banks.
- **Cash Reserve Ratio** (CRR) It specifies the fraction of the total deposits of banks that they are obliged to keep with the RBI. Since 1962, the RBI has been empowered to vary the CRR requirement between 3% and 15% of the total demand and time deposits.
- **Statutory Liquidity Ratio** (SLR) It is the ratio of liquid asset, which all Commercial Banks have to keep in the form of cash, gold and unencumbered approved securities equal to not more than 40% of their total demand and time deposits liabilities. (ranges is 25-40%)
- **Repo Rate** It is the rate, at which RBI lends short-term money to the banks against securities. Repo rate injects liquidity in the market.
- **Reverse Repo Rate** It is the rate, at which banks park short-term excess liquidity with the RBI. Reverse Repo Rate withdraws liquidity from the market. This is always 100 base point 1% less than Repo rate.
- **Open Market Operations** Under OMOs, when the RBI sells G-secs in the market, it withdraws money liquidity from the market and thus, reduces volume of credit leading to control of inflation.

Qualitative/Selective/ Direct Credit Control

Qualitative measures are used to make sure that purpose, for which loan is given is not misused. It is done through

- credit rationing
- regulating loan to consumption etc.
- moral suation

SCHEDULED AND NON-SCHEDULED BANKS

- The scheduled banks are those, which are entered in the Second Schedule of the RBI Act, 1934. These banks have a paid-up capital and reserves of an aggregate value of not less than ₹ 5 lakh and satisfy the RBI that their affairs are carried out in the interest of their depositors.

- All Commercial Banks (Indian and foreign), Regional Rural Banks and State Cooperative Banks are Scheduled Banks. Non-Scheduled Banks are those, which are not included in the Second Scheduled of the RBI Act, 1934.

Structure of Banking in India

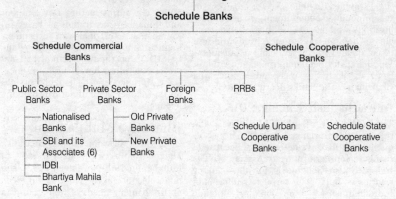

State Bank of India

- State Bank of India (SBI) was previously called **Imperial Bank of India** in 1921, which was created by amalgamation of 3 presidency banks *viz* **Bank of Bengal**, **Bank of Bombay** and **Bank of Madras**.
- It was nationalised in 1955.
- In 2017, the five associates of SBI and Bhartiya Mahila Bank were merged in State Bank of India. With this merger, SBI becomes one of the top 50 global banks.

PRIVATE SECTOR BANKS IN INDIA

- All those banks, where greater parts of stake or equity are held by the private shareholders and not by the government are called private sector banks.
- There are two categories of private sector bank old and new.
- Banking Regulation Act, 1949 was amended in 1993 and once again in 2001 to permit the entry of new private sector banks in the Indian banking sector; the objective was to instill greater competition in the banking system to increase productivity and efficiency.

Top Five Private Sector Banks
1. ICICI Bank, 1994 Vadodara
2. HDFC Bank, 1994 Mumbai
3. Axis Bank, 1994 Ahmedabad
4. Kotak Mahindra Bank, 1985 Mumbai
5. Yes Bank, 2004 Mumbai

Bank Board Bureau

The Bank Board Bureau (BBB) is constituted on 28th February, 2016. The Bureau is mandated to play a critical role in reforming the troubled public sector banks by recommending appointments to leadership positions and boards in those banks, and advise them on ways to raise funds and how to go ahead with mergers and acquisitions. Vinod Rai, former comptroller and Auditor General of India, was named the first Chairman of the Banks Board Bureau.

Indradhanush Scheme, 2015

The Public Sector Banks (PSBs) plays a vital role in Indian financial system. The assets quality of PSBs have deteriorated because of rising Non-Performing. Assets (NPA) Indradhanush Scheme is for the banking reforms in India. The seven Key reforms of Indradhanush mission include appointments, destressing, BBB, capitalisation, empowerment, frame work of accountablity and governance reforms.

RBI Grants New Bank Licence

The decade-long wait for new bank licences finally ended on 3rd April, 2014, with the Reserve Bank of India (RBI) deciding to issue permits to two of the 25 applicants. The ones to make the cut were **IDFC**, a diversified financial services firm with a special focus on infrastructure financing and **Bandhan,** the country's largest micro lender based in Kolkata.

RBI Guidelines for New Bank Licensing

While preparing guidelines, RBI recognises the need for an explicit policy on banking structure in India keeping in view the recommendations of the Narsimham Committee, Raghuram Rajan Committee and others view points.

New Bank

These new banks will be provided license under the Banking Regulation Act, 1949 (Section 22(1)), only after the fulfilment of these two conditions.

Bandhan Finance It is a microfinance company, based in West Bengal. It is headed by Shri Chandra Shekhar Ghosh and has a net worth of ₹ 1100 crore.

About 45 % of its branches in the rural areas. Bandhan Bank received the inprinciple approval of the RBI in April 2014, the banking regulator gave its final nod in June, 2015.

IDFC The Infrastructure Development and Finance Corporation is based in Mumbai. It is originally an investment finance company, headed by Shri Rajiv Lal. IDFC has the net worth of ₹ 21000 crore, but with a lower rural presence. IDFC started operating banking services on 1st October, 2015 under RBI Banking licence.

Bharatiya Mahila Bank

India's first all women bank, Bharatiya Mahila Bank was inaugurated in Mumbai on 19th November, 2013, The main objective of the bank was to focus on the banking needs of women and to promote their economic empowerment.

Usha Anantha Subramanian was appointed as the first Chairperson and Managing Director of public sector Bharatiya Mahila Bank (BMB). The BMB was based on the principle of : 'Women empowerment in India'. It has been the merged with State Bank of India in 2017.

Basel Norms

- These are set by Bank of International Settlement (BIS) headquartered in Basel, Switzerland. It prescribes for a set of minimum capital requirement for banks. 55 countries Central Banks are members of the BIS.

- In India Basel norms were introduced in 1988 by the RBI.

- So far two Basel norms *viz*, Basel-I and Basel-II have been implemented in India and third i.e., Basel-III norms became operational from 1st January, 2013.RBI issued guidelines in 1992 to maintain a capital adequacy ratio of 9% as mandatory for every Scheduled Commercial Banks (SCBs). Capital adequacy ratio is that ratio of the total capital of a bank to its risk weighted assets, which ensure's strength and stability of a bank to withstand reasonable degree of losses.

MUDRA Bank

Micro Units Development and Refinance Agency Bank (or MUDRA Bank) was launched on 8th April, 2015 with a corpus of ₹ 20000 crore and a credit guarantee corpus of ₹ 3000 crore.

It is a public sector financial institution in India. It provides loans at low rates to small entrepreneurs. MUDRA Bank will be set-up through a statutory enactment. It is a 100% subsidiary of SIDBI.

Classification of MUDRA Bank

MUDRA Bank has rightly classified the borrowers into three segments: the starters, the mid-stage finance seekers and the next level growth seekers. To address the three segments, MUDRA Bank has launched three loan instruments

- Shishu-covers loans upto ₹ 50,000 /-
- Kishor-covers loans above ₹ 50,000/- and upto ₹ 5 lakh
- Tarun-covers loans above ₹ 5 lakh and upto ₹ 10 lakh

All India Financial Institutions At a Glance

Financial Institution and their Headquarters	Purpose
Industrial Finance Corporation of India (IFCI) 1948, New Delhi	• To grant loans advances to industrial concerns and subscribe to debentures floated by them.
State Finance Corporations (SFCs) 1951	• To finance the needs of the small-scale and medium sized industries in respective states. 28 SFCs are in operations alongwith 28 State Industrial Development Corp (SIDC).
Industrial Credit and Investment Corporation of India (ICICI) 1955, Mumbai	• To stimulate the promotion of new industries and assist in modernisation of existing industries. • In 2002, ICICI merged with ICICI Bank no more a DFI.
Industrial Development Bank of India (IDBI) 1964 Mumbai	• To meet the financial needs of industrialisation and co-ordinate with all other agencies concerned with industrial development finance. • Wholly owned subsidiary of RBI till 1976. Merged with IDBI Bank in 2004.
Industrial Investment Bank of India (IIBI)1985	• To assist the industrial units in Eastern region.
Small Industries Development Bank of India (SIDBI), Lucknow	• To promote, finance and development industry in small scale sector.

Unit Trust of India (1964) (UTI)	• Set-up as an investment institution to stimulate and pool the savings of the middle and low income groups.
	• UTI bifurcated into two parts
	  (i) UTI Mutual Fund
	  (ii) Specified Undertaking of UTI (SUUTI)

National Housing Bank (NHB) 1988, New Delhi	• It is the apex institution of housing finance in India and is a wholly owned subsidiary of the RBI. • Launched RESIDEX for tracking prices of residential properties in India in 2007. At present, RESIDEX covers 15 cities in India. It is a refinance institution.
EXIM Bank (1982), Mumbai	• To finance, facilitate and promote foreign trade in India. • It is a specialised financial institution.
Tourism Finance Corporation of India Limited (TFCI)—1989, New Delhi	• Set-up on the recommendation of Yunhs Committee on Tourism. It is a specialised finance institution providing assistance to tourism related activities/projects.
Mutual Funds	• Mutual Funds are the most important among the newer capital market institutions. MFs functions is to mobilise the savings of the general public and invest them in stock market securities.
Venture Capital Funds	• Venture Capital Funds (VCFs) essentially give commercial support to new ideas and for the introduction and adaptation of new technologies.

Insurance Sector

- Insurance industry includes two sectors- **Life Insurance** and **General Insurance**.
- Life insurance in India was introduced by Britishers. A British firm in 1818 established the **Oriental Life Insurance Company** at Calcutta now Kolkata.
- Since the opening up, the number of participants in the Insurance Industry has gone up from 7 insurers (including LIC, four public sector general insurers, one specialised insurer and the GIC as the national re-insurer) in 2000 to 49 insurers as on 30th September, 2011.

Life Insurance Corporation (LIC)

- LIC was established on 1st September, 1956, which set the pace for nationalisation of life insurance under the Stewardship of CD Deshmukh. It has head office at Mumbai and eight zonal offices the most recent being at Patna.
- LIC is also operating internationally through branch offices in Fiji, Mauritius and UK and through joint venture companies in Bahrain, Nepal, Sri Lanka, Kenya and Saudi Arabia. In 2008, its wholly and subsidiary was opened in Singapore.

General Insurance Corporation (GIC)

- GIC was established on 1st January, 1973, *with its four subsidiaries, viz,*
  1. National Insurance Company Limited, Kolkata;
  2. The New India Insurance Company Limited, Mumbai;
  3. The Oriental Fire and General Insurance Company Limited New Delhi; and
  4. United India General Insurance Company Limited, Chennai.

- On 3rd November, 2000 GIC was renamed as GIC Re and approved as **Indian Reinsurer** and the four subsidiaries of GIC were separated from GIC and are functioning independently under Public Sector General Insurance Companies (GIPSA).
- GIC Reinsurer (Re) has branch offices in Dubai and London and a representative office in Moscow.

Insurance Regulatory and Development Authority of India (IRDAI)

- The Insurance Regulatory and Development Authority (IRDA) has changed its name to Insurance Regulatory and Development Athority of India (IRDAI). The change of name was effected in the Insurance Laws (Amendment) Ordinance, 2014 was promulgated by the President of India on 26th December, 2014.
- The ordinance contains certain amendments to the Insurance Regulation and Development Act, 1999 and inserted the words 'of India' after development authority.Insurance Regulatory and Development Authority of India(IRDA) is an autonomous apex statutory body which regulates and develops the insurance industry in India.
- It was constituted by a Parliament of India act called Insurance Regulatory and Development Authority Act , 1999 and duly passed by the Government of India. The agency operates from its headquarters at Hyderabad, Telangana where it shifted from Delhi in 2001. The FDI limit in insurance sector was raised to 49% in july, 2014.

Pension Sector

- New Pension System launched on 1st January, 2004.
- The NPS covers all employees of the Central Government and Central autonomous bodies, except armed forces 27 States have notified and joined the NPS.
- With effect from 1st November, 2009 the NPS was opened to all citizens.
- **NPS-Lite** is the lower cost version of NPS.

- **Swavalamban** Scheme was announced in the budget 2010. It is an incentive scheme for the NPS.
- Under this, any citizen in the unorganised sector, who fairs NPS in 2010-11 with a minimal annual contribution of annual ₹ 1000 and maximum of ₹ 12000 will receive a government contribution of ₹ 1000 in his NPS account.
- The National Securities Depositories Limited (NSDL) has been appointed as the Central Record Keeping Agency, for the NPS.
- The revised guidelines for NPS has raised the age from 55 years to 60 years. The Pension Fund Regulatory Development Authority was established on 23rd August, 2003.

Insurance Sector Schemes

Programme/ Schemes	Main Provisions
Janashree Bima Yojana (JBY)	• Launched on 10th August, 2000 by LIC. • JBY replaced Social Security Group Insurance Scheme (SSGIS) and Rural Group Life Insurance Scheme (RGLIC). • Provides for an insurance cover of ₹ 30000 on natural death, ₹ 75000 on permanent disability to accident and ₹ 37500 on partial disability. • The premium is ₹ 200 per member per annum. • 45 occupational groups having 25 members. • For both rural and urban people • For BPL and marginally above BPL people. • 50% of finance is met out of social security fund.
Universal Health Insurance Scheme (UHIS)	• Launched from the year 2003-04 for improving the healthcare access to the poor families. • Launched by four public sector general insurance company. • Export Credit Guarantee Corporation (ECGC) and the Agriculture Insurance Company (AIC) are the specialised insurers.
Rashtriya Swasthya Bima Yojana (RSBY)	• Launched on 1st October, 2007. • Provides smart-card based health insurance cover ₹ 30000 per family per annum to BPL families (a unit of five) in the unorganised sector. • The premium is shared in 75 : 25 between the centre and the states. • For BPL families (a unit of five). • For unorganised sector. • Its a smart card based cashless health insurance, cover ₹ 30000 per annum, of insurance or a family floats basis. • It also cover migrant workers. • It was for 5 years from 2008 to 2013. • It cover all pre-existing diseases, maternity benefit, transport cost. • It use IT application both private and public service providers for delivering the insurance package. • No age limit has been prescribed.
Aam Aadmi Bima Yojana (AABY)	• Launched on 2nd October, 2007 by LIC for rural landless households at Shimla. • Premium fixed at ₹ 200 per person per annum to be shared equally by centre and the states. • The age covered is 18 years to 59 years. • Death/permanent disability ₹ 75000, partial disability ₹ 37500 • For rural landless household. • Head of the family or one carring member in the family of rural landless. • Free add-on benefit for the children of the members of Aam Aadmi Bima Yojana. • For BPL families • Between 9th to 12th standard.
Universal Health Insurance Scheme	• For BPL families. • It gives reimbursement of medical expenses upto ₹ 30000 towards hospitalisation. • Include pre-existing diseases, maternal benefit. • Upto the age 70 years.

Indian Financial System

- Financial system refers to the borrowing and lending of funds for the demand and supply of funds of all individuals institutions, companies and of the government.
- The Indian Financial System consists of two parts, *viz*, Indian money market and the Indian capital market.

MONEY MARKET

- This is a market for 'near money' or it is the market for borrowing and lending of short-term funds.

Instruments of Money Market

- **T-Bills or treasury bills** are the government bonds, which are used to raise funds from the money market.
- **91 Days Treasury Bills** (T-bills) used by the government to raise funds from the market for short periods nothing but short-term government bond.
- **182 Days T-bills** introduced on the recommendation of Vaghul working groups, are variable interest bills sold through fortnightly auctions.
- **364 Days T-bills** introduced on the recommendation of Vaghul working group are long-dated bills, whose yields reflects the market conditions.
- **14 Days T-bills** introduced in April, 1997 by the RBI at a discount rate equivalent to the rate of interest on Ways and Means Advance (WMA) to the Government of India.
- **Dated Government Securities** are also type of treasury bills recommended by Chakravarty Committee on Monetary System (1988). These are 5 years and 10 years maturity government securities sold on an auction basis.
- **Certificate of Deposits** It is the certificate issued by bank/financial institute to other banks or financial institute, who give funds on short-term basis. Commercial Banks are a saving certificate entitling the bearer to receive interest. The maturity of a CoD varies from 3 months to 1 year.

- **Commercial Papers** It is an instrument to raise short-term funds by the corporate sector.
- It can be issued by a listed company with a working capital of almost 5 crore. The CP is issued in multiples of ₹ 25 lakh subject to a minimum issue of ₹ 1 crore. The maturity of CP is between 3 to 6 months.
- **Money Market Index** is an index, which helps investors to decide how much and where to invest in money market through providing information about prevailing market ratio.
- **Bankers Acceptance Rate** is the rate, at which the banker's acceptance is traded in secondary market.
- **LIBOR / MIBOR** London Inter-Bank Offered Rate/Mumbai Inter-Bank Offered Rate is the interest rate, at which bank borrows fund from other banks.

CAPITAL MARKET

- Capital market is concerned with provision of raising long-term funds of maturity 1 year or more.
- Capital market can be classified into debt market and equity market.
- In **debt market**, a company can acquire funds only by incurring debt and lender is guaranted of a fixed repayment e.g. bond.
- **Equity Market** Here, funds can be raised without incurring debt those, who finance the enterprise by purchasing equity instrument like shares.

SEBI

SEBI (Securities and Exchange Board of India) was **set-up** in **1988** and made a **statutory body** in 1992.

Main Functions

- To protect the interests of investor in securities. To promote the development of securities market and to regulate the securities market.

- For matters connected there with or incidental there to. To prohibit unfair trade practices in the market.
- Clause 49 of the Listing Agreement to the Indian stocks exchange relates to the improvement of corporate governance of all listed companies. It came into effect from 31st December, 2005.

New Law of SEBI

- In August 2014, the Securities Laws (Amendment) Act, 2014, gave SEBI additional powers, including to order the arrest of violators and seek call data records of individuals under investigation.
- The new law gave SEBI the powers to search and obtain information, including call records, about any suspected entity from within or outside the firm.

Stock Exchange in India

- Stock exchange or share market deals in shares, debentures and financial securities.
- There are 23 stock exchanges in India. Among them two are national level stock exchange namely Bombay Stock Exchange (BSE) and National Stock Exchange (NSE). The rest 21 are Regional Stock Exchanges (RSE).

Bombay Stock Exchange (BSE)

- It is a stock exchange located on Dalal Street, Mumbai, Maharashtra. It is the 11th largest stock exchange in the world by market capitalisation as on 31st December, 2012.
- Established in 1875, BSE Ltd (formerly known as **Bombay Stock Exchange Ltd**.), is the India's oldest Stock Exchange , one of **Asia's oldest** stock exchange and one of India's leading exchange groups.
- Over the past 137 years, BSE has facilitated the growth of the Indian corporate sector by providing it an efficient capital-raising platform. Popularly known as BSE, the bourse was established as 'The Native Share and Stock Brokers' Association" in 1875.

National Stock Exchange (NSE)

- It is the country's leading stock exchange located in the financial capital of Mumbai, India. National Stock Exchange (NSE) was established in the mid 1990s as a demutualised electronic exchange.
- NSE provides a modern, fully automated screen-based trading system, with over 2 lakh trading terminals, through which investors in every nook and corner of India can trade.
- NSE has played a critical role in reforming the Indian securities market and in bringing unparalleled transparency, efficiency and market integrity. NSE has a market capitalisation of more than US$989 billion and 1635 companies listed as on July 2013.

MCX SX Stock Exchange

- It is a private stock exchange head-quartered in Mumbai, which was founded in 2008. Now it is a MCX-SX Full Fledged Stock Exchange.
- Securities and Exchange Board of India (SEBI) on 10th July, 2012 granted permission to MCX Stock Exchange (MCX-SX) to operate as full-fledged stock exchange.
- MCX-SX would be able to offer additional asset classes, such as equity and equity F and O (Futures and Options) interest rate futures and wholesale debt segments.

Important Share Price Indexes of India

- **BSE SENSEX** This is the most sensitive share index of the Mumbai Stock Exchange. This is the representative index of 30 main shares. Its base year is 1978-79. BSE is the oldest stock exchange of India, founded in 1875.
- The barometer of Indian capital market. BSE sensitive index also referred to as BSE-30 is a free-float market capitali-sations-weighted stock market index of 30 well established and financially sound companies listed on Bombay Stock Exchange.

- The free-float market capitalisation of a company is determined by multiplying the price of its stocks by the number of shares issued by a company which is readily available for trading on the stock exchange. The base year/ period of SENSEX is 1978-79.
- **NSE-50** From 28th July, 1998, its name is S and P CNX Nifty. National Stock Exchange launched a new share Price Index, NSE-50 in place of NSE-100 in April, 1996. NSE-50 includes 50 companies shares. This stock exchanges was founded on **Ferwani Committees's** recommendation in 1994.
- The CNX Nifty covers 22 sectors of the Indian economy and offers investment managers exposure to the Indian market in one portfolio. The CNX Nifty index is a free float market capitalisation weighted index.
- The CNX Nifty Index was developed by Ajay Shah and Susan Thomas.

Global Indices

Index	Country
Hang Seng	Hong Kong
JCI	Indonesia
Nikkei 225	Japan
Kospi	South Korea
Kualalumpur Composite	Malaysia
TSEC Weighted Index	Taiwan
SSE Composite Index	China
SET	Thailand
FTSE 100	UK
NASDAQ Composite Index	US
STOXX	Europe
Dow Jones	US

Credit Rating Agencies

- It is a company that assigns credit ratings for issuers of certain type of debt obligation as well as the debt instrument, example of issuers are companies, State and Central Government etc.
- The credit rating represents the credit rating agency's evaluation of qualitative and quantitative information for a company or government; including non-public information obtained by the credit rating agencies analysts. The credit rating is used by individuals and entities that purchase the bonds issued by companies and governments to determine the likelihood that the government or company will pay its bond obligations.
- **CRISIL** set-up in 1988, is a credit rating agency. It undertakes the rating fixed deposit programmes, convertible and non-convertible debentures and also credit assessment of companies.
- **CRISIL 500** is the net share Price Index introduced by Credit Rating Agency. The 'Credit Rating Information Services of India Limited' (CRISIL) on 18th January, 1996.
- In some cases, the services of the underlying debt are also given ratings.

Credit Rating Agency	Established	Head-quarters
FITCH Group	1913	Paris
S and P Group	1860	New York
Moody's Investor Services	1909	New York

INDIAN FISCAL SYSTEM

It refers to the management of revenue and capital expenditure finances of the state.

FISCAL POLICY

It is the means by which a govrnment adjusts its spending levels and tax rates to monitor and influence a nations economy. It is the sister strategy to Monetary Policy through which a Central Bank influences a nations money supply.

These uses can affect the following macro economic variables in an economy

- Aggregate demand and the level of economic activity;
- The distribution of income;
- The pattern of resource allocation within the government sector and relative to the private sector.

Sources of Revenue

Main sources of revenue are customs duties, excise duties, service tax, taxes on property, corporate tax, income taxes.

Sources of Expenditure

Plan Expenditure includes agriculture, rural development, irrigation and flood control, energy, industry, minerals, transport and communications etc.

Non-Plan Expenditure It consists of interest payments, defence, subsidies and general services.

Public Debt

- Internal Debt It comprises loans raised from the open market treasury bills issued to the RBI, Commercial Banks etc.
- External Debt It consists of loans taken from World Bank, IMF, ADB and individual countries.

Deficits

In a budget statement, four types of deficits are mentioned

   (a) Revenue   (b) Capital

   (c) Fiscal   (d) Primary

Revenue Deficit

There are various ways to represent and interpret a government's deficit. The simplest is the revenue deficit which is just the difference between revenue receipts and revenue expenditures.

Revenue deficit = Revenue expenditure – Revenue receipts

Capital Deficit

An imbalance in a nation's balance of payments capital account in which payments made by the country for purchasing foreign assets exceed payments received by the country for selling domestic assets.

In other words, investment by the domestic economy in foreign assets is less than foreign investment in domestic assets. This is generally not a desirable situation for a domestic economy.

Capital deficit = Capital receipts – Disbursement on capital account

Fiscal Deficit

This is the sum of revenue and capital expenditure less all revenue and capital receipts other than loans taken.

This gives a more holistic view of the government's funding situation since it gives the difference between all receipts and expenditures other than loans taken to meet such expenditures.

Fiscal Deficit = Difference between country's expenditure and earnings

Fiscal deficit = Revenue receipts (Net tax revenue + Non-tax revenue) + Capital receipts (only recoveries of loans and other receipts) – Total expenditure (Plan and non-plan).

Primary Deficit

Amount by which a government's total expenditure exceeds its total revenue, excluding interest payments on its debt.

Primary deficit = Fiscal deficit – Interest payments.

UNION BUDGET

- The budget is an extensive account of the government's finances, in which revenues from all sources and expenses of all activities undertaken are aggregated.
- The Finance Minister presents the Union Budget every year in the Parliament that contains the Government of India's revenue and expenditure for one fiscal year, which runs from 1st April to 31st March.

Historical Preview

- The term 'Budget' is acutally derived from a French word 'Bougette', which means a sack or pouch. It was first used in France in 1803.
- In the Constitution of India the term Budget is nowhere used. It is rather mentioned as Annual Financial Statement under Article 112 comprising the revenue budget, capital budget and also the estimates for the next fiscal year called budgeted estimates.

Preparation of Budget

The budget is prepared by the budget division in the Ministery of Finance (MoF), after consulting with other ministries and the Planning Commission. The process majorly includes following steps which may be sequential or overlapping too.

Stages in Budget Enactment

The budget goes through the following six stages in the Parliament

- Presentation of the budget on the floor of the house before the Lok Sabha.
- General discussion on the budget.
- Scrutiny by departmentally related standing committees.
- Voting on demands for grants.
- Passing of Appropriation Bill (Article 114 of the Constitution of India).
- Passing of Finance Bill (under Rule 219 of the Lok Sabha).

Vote on Account

- Usually, the Appropriation Bill (expenditure part of budget) is passed by end of April, but government needs money from beginning of financial year, so government use vote-on-account to remove money from consolidated fund of India.

Types of Budgeting

Line Item Budgeting

If emphasises on the items (objects) of expenditure without highlighting its purpose. It gives object-wise (Line-item) classification in budget. Under this system, the amount granted by the legislature on a specific item should be spent on that item only.

Quick Digest

- **John Mathai** proposed the first budget of Republic of India in 1950 and also the creation of Planning Commission.
- Finance Minister **Morarji Desai** has given budget for the maximum number of times (10) followed by P Chidambaram, who has given 8 budgets.
- **CD Deshmukh** was the first Indian Governor of RBI to have presented the Interim Budget for the year 1951-52.
- **Mrs Indira Gandhi** is the only woman to hold the post of the Finance Minister and to have presented the budget in her capacity as the Prime Minister of India in 1978.
- The first such mini-budget was presented by TT **Krishnamáchari** on 30th November, 1956, in form of fresh taxation proposals through Finance Bills, demanded by the prevailing domestic and international economic situation.
- From 2017, the Railway Budget has been merged with the Central Budget on the recommendation of Bibek Debroy Committee.

Output Budgeting

It concentrate only on the quantitative aspect of expenditure.

Performance Based Budgeting

Its attempt to solve decision making problems based on a programmes ability to convert inputs to outputs and use inputs to affect certain outcomes. Performance may be judged by a certain programmes ability to meet certain objective that contribute to more abstract goal as calculated by that programmes ability to use resources efficiently by linking input to outputs.

Outcome Budgeting

This type of budgeting tries to ensure that budget outlays translate into concrete outcomes.

Zero-Based Budgeting

It is a method of budgeting, in which all budgetary allocations are set to nil at the beginning of a financial year.

Zero-based budgeting requires the budget request be re-evaluated thoroughly, starting from the zero-base. This process is independent of whether the total budget or specific line items are increasing or decreasing. Zero based budgeting also refers to the identification of a task or tasks and then funding resources to complete the task independent of current renouncing.

Gender Budgeting

It came into being in 2004-05. To contribute towards the women empowerment and removal of inequality based on gender, role of budgeting has been accepted through this step.

Programme Budgeting

It emphasis the planning aspect of budgeting for selecting the best out of a number of available programmes and for optimising the choice.

The Government has decided on 18 November, 2016 to merge Rail Budget with the Union Budegt from Budget year 2017-18.

TAX STRUCTURE IN INDIA

Tax is a compulsory payment by the citizens to the government to meet the public expenditure. It is legally imposed by the government on the taxpayer and in no case taxpayer can deny to pay taxes to the government.

Direct Tax

A direct tax is that tax, which is born by the person on whom it is levied. A direct tax cannot be shifted to other person. **Composition of Direct Taxes** Out of 56.3% of contribution of direct taxes to gross tax revenue in 2011-12, personal income tax contributed 19. 5% and corporation tax contributed 39.0%.

Structure of Taxes

Direct Tax	Indirect Tax
Personal Income Tax	Excise Duty
Corporation Tax	Custom Duty
Wealth Tax	Sales Tax
Gift Tax	Service Tax
Land Revenue	Value Added Tax
Profession Tax	Passenger Tax
Stamp Duty and Registration Charges	Entertainment Tax
Securities Transaction Tax	Electricity Duty
Banking Cash Transaction Tax	Motor Vehicles Tax

Indirect Tax

- These are those taxes, which have their primary burden or impact on one person. But that person succeeds in shifting his burden on to others. Indirect taxation is policy often used to generate tax revenue. Indirect tax is so called as it is paid indirectly by the final consumer of goods and services while paying for purchase of goods or for enjoying services.
- **Composition of Indirect Taxes** Out of 42.6% contribution of indirect tax to the total tax revenue in 2011-12, excise contribution was 16.7%, customs contribution was 13.4% and services tax contributed 9.3%.

GST (Goods and Services Tax)

The Goods and Service Tax (GST) has been implemented from July 1, 2017. It incorporates many of the indirect taxes levied by states and the Central Government. Some of the taxes GST replaced include Sales Tax, Central Excise, Duty, Octroi, Service Tax etc.

GST has three components

- CGST (Central Goods and Services act)
- SGST (State Goods and Services act)
- IGST (Integrated Goods and Services act)

FINANCIAL RELATIONS BETWEEN CENTRES AND STATES

- India possesses a federal structure, in which a clear distinction is made between the union and the state functions and sources of revenue.

- Our Constitution provides residual powers to the centre. Article 264 and Article 293 explain the financial relations between the Union and State Government. It makes a clear division of fiscal powers between the Centre and the State Government.

- Although, the states have been assigned certain taxes, which are levied and collected by them, they also have a share in the revenue of certain union taxes and there are certain other taxes, which are levied and collected by the Central Government, but whole proceeds are transferred to the states.

(A) **List I of Seventh Schedule of the Constitution Enlists the Union Taxes**

1. Taxes on income other than agriculture income.

2. Corporation tax.

3. Custom duties.

4. Excise duties except on alcoholic liquors and narcotics not contained in medical or toilet preparation.

5. Estate and succession duties other than on agricultural land.

6. Taxes on the capital value of assets agricultural land of individuals and companies.

7. Rates of stamp duties on financial documents.

8. Taxes other than stamp duties on transactions in stock exchanges and future markets.

9. Taxes on sales or purchases of newspapers and on advertisements there in.

10. Taxes on railway freight and fares.

11. Terminal taxes on goods or passengers carried by railways, sea or air.

12. Taxes on the sale or purchase of goods in the course of interstate trade.

(B) **List II of Seventh Schedule enlists the Taxes which are within the Jurisdiction of the States**

- Land revenue.

- Taxes on the sale and purchase of goods, except newspapers.

- Taxes on agricultural income.

- Taxes on land and buildings.

- Succession and estate duties on agricultural land. Excise on alcoholic liquors and narcotics.

- Taxes on the entry of goods into a local area.

- Taxes on the consumption and sale of electricity.

- Taxes on mineral rights (subject to any limitations imposed by the Parliament).

- Taxes on vehicles, animals and boats.

- Stamp duties except those on financial documents.

- Taxes on goods and passengers carried by board or inland water-ways.

- Taxes on luxuries including entertainments, betting and gambling.

- Tolls.

- Taxes on professions, trades, callings and employment.

- Capitation taxation.

- Taxes on advertisements other than those contained in newspapers.

(C) **Apart from taxes levied and collected by the state, the Constitution has provided for the revenues for certain taxes on the Union List to be allotted, partly or wholly to the states. These provision fall into various categories**

1. Duties, which are levied by the Union Government, but are collected and appropriated by the state. These include stamp duties, excise duties on medical preparations containing alcohol or narcotics.

2. Taxes, which are levied and collected by the Union, but the entire proceeds of which are assigned to the states, in proportion determined by the Parliament.
   These taxes include
   (i) Succession and estate duty.
   (ii) Terminal taxes on goods and passengers.
   (iii) Taxes on railway freight and fares.
   (iv) Taxes on transactions in stock exchange and future markets.
   (v) Taxes on sale and purchase of newspapers and advertisements therein.

3. Central taxes on income and union excise duties are levied and collected by the union, but are shared by it with the state in a prescribed manner.

4. Proceeds of additional excise duty on mill-made textiles, sugar and tobacco,

which are levied by the union, since 1957 in replacement of state relates taxes on these commodities, are wholly distributed among the state in a manner as to guarantee their former incomes from the displaced sales taxes.

FINANCE COMMISSION

Finance Commission is constituted to define financial relations between the centre and the state. Under the provision of Article 280 of the Constitution, the President appoint a Finance Commission for the specific purpose of devolution of non-plan revenue resources.

The functions of the commission are to make recommendations to the President in respect of the distribution of net proceeds of taxes to be shared between the union and the states and the allocation of share of such proceeds among the states. the principles, which should govern the payment of grants-in-aid by the centre to the states. any other matter concerning financial relations between the centre and the states.

Finance Commission in India

Finance Commission	Established in	Chairman	Operational Duration	Year of Submitting Report
I	1951	KC Niyogi	1952-57	1952
II	1956	K Santhanam	1957-62	1956
III	1960	AK Chanda	1962-66	1961
IV	1964	PV Rajamanar	1966-69	1965
V	1968	Mahaveer Tyagi	1969-74	1968
VI	1972	Brahma Nand Reddy	1974-79	1973
VII	1977	JM Shellet	1979-84	1978
VIII	1983	YB Chawan	1984-89	1983
IX	1987	NKP Salve	1989-95	1989
X	1992	KC Pant	1995-2000	1994
XI	1998	AM Khusro	2000-2005	2000
XII	2003	C Rangarajan	2005-2010	2004
XIII	2007	Vijay L Kelkar	2010-2015	2009
XIV	2012	Y Venugopal Reddy	2015-2020	2015
XV	2017	NK Singh	2020-2025	2017

Fourteenth Finance Commission

The 14th Finance Commission appointed under the chairmanship of Dr. YV Reddy gave its recommendation on principles which would govern the quantum and distribution of grant-in-aid along with other primary areas it deals with.

Recommendations

Major recommendations of the 14th *Finance Commission are as follows:*

- The Commission recommended increase in the share of states in the centre's tax revenue from the current 32% to 42%, the single largest increase ever recommended.
- In understanding the states' needs, it has ignored the plan and non-plan distinctions.
- According to the commission, the increased devolution of the divisible pool of taxes is a 'compositional shift in transfers' from grants to tax devolution.
- In recommending an horizontal distribution, it has used broad parameters—population (1971), changes in population since, then income distance, forest cover and area, among others.
- The 14th Finance Commission, headed by former RBI Governor YV Reddy, has endorsed the compensation road map for the goods and services tax finalised by the centre, but has called for an autonomous and independent GST compensation fund.
- It has recommended distribution of grants to states for local bodies using 2011 population data with weight of 90% and area with weight of 10%. Grants to states are divided into two. One, grant to duly constituted Gram Panchayats. Two, grant to duly constituted municipal bodies. And it has divided grants into two parts.
- The ratio of basic to performance grant is 90:10 for Panchayats; and 80:20 for municipalities.

INTERNATIONAL ECONOMIC ORGANISATIONS

INTERNATIONAL MONETARY FUND (IMF)

- IMF was conceived on 22nd July, 1944 and came into existence on 27th December, 1945, when 29 countries signed the agreement. It originally had 45 members. India is the founding member.

- IMF at present has 189 members and headquartered at Washington DC. The capital resources of the IMF comprise Special Drawing Rights (SDRs) and currencies that member pay under quotas calculated for them when they join the IMF.

- The quotas determine the amount of foreign exchange, a member may borrow from the IMF and its voting power on IMF policy matters. Quotas are denominated in SDRs.

- The member with largest quotas is USA followed by Japan and China. Tuvalu is the member with smallest quota. India with a quota share of 2.76% is now placed **eighth** largest quota holding country at the IMF.

- Based on noting share, India (together with Bangladesh) Bhutan and Sri Lanka are ranked **22nd** in the list of 24 constituencies.

- For India, Finance Minister is the Ex-officio Governor of the Board of Governors of the IMF. Governor of the RBI, is India's alternate Governor.

Special Drawing Rights

The SDRs were created in 1969 are supplementary foreign exchange reserves assets maintained by the IMF. SDRs are not a currency. Instead it represents a claim to currency held by IMF member countries. SDR, value is determined by weighted currency basket of five major currencies : the Euro, the US dollar, the British pound and Japanese Yen and Chinese Yuan. SDRs are also called **'paper gold'**.

WORLD BANK (WB)

- World Bank is the institution created at the **Bretton Woods Conference** in 1944. Along with the IMF, it constitutes **'twin-sister'** of Bretton Woods.

- World Bank has 189 members and is headquartered in Washington DC.

- The World Bank provides loans to developing countries for capital programme and its official goal is reduction of poverty.

- International Finance Corporation (IFC) was established in 1956, to provide loans to private industries of developing nations.

- International Development Association (IDA), known as the **soft loan window** of the World Bank was established on 24th September, 1960.

- International Centre for Settlement of Investment Disputes (ICSID) was established in 1966, to provide facilities for the conciliation and arbitration of investment disputes between member countries. It has 157 members.

- Multilateral Investment Guarantee Agency (MIGA) was founded in 1988 to promote foreign direct investment into developing countries. It has 175 members.

WORLD TRADE ORGANISATION

- It was constituted on 1st January, 1995, under the **Marrakesh Agreement** and took the place of GATT (General Agreement on Trade and Tariff) as an effective formal organisation. GATT was an informal organisation, which regulated world trade since, 1948.

- It is headquartered at Geneva. At present, it has 164 members. (Afghanistan has become the 164th WTO member).

Functions of WTO

- To oversee, implementation and administration of WTO agreements. To provide a forum for negotiations.
- To provide a dispute settlement mechanism. To provide facilities for implementation, administration and operation of multilateral and bilateral agreements of the world trade.
- The WTO is currently endeavouring to persist with a trade negotiation called Doha Development Agenda (DDA), which was launched in 2001, to enhance equitable participation of poor countries, which represent a majority of the world's population.
- **Singapore Issues** refer to transparency in government procurement, trade facilitation, trade and investment and trade and competition.
- **Swiss Formula** relates to NAMA (Non-Agricultural Market Access).

WTO Ministerial Conferences

Conference	Year	Place
First	1996	Singapore
Second	1998	Geneva
Third	1999	Seattle (USA)
Fourth	2001	Doha (Qatar)
Fifth	2003	Cancun (Mexico)
Sixth	2005	Hong Kong
Seventh	2009	Geneva
Eight	2011	Geneva
Nine	2013	Bali, Indonesia
Tenth	2015	Nairobi, Kenya
Eleventh	2017	Buenos Aires

ASIAN DEVELOPMENT BANK (ADB)

- It was established in December, 1966 with the aim to accelerate economic and social development in Asia and Pacific region. It is headquartered at **Manila**, Phillipines.
- The ADB offers hard loans from ordinary capital resources on commercial terms and the Asian Development Fund affiliated with the ADB extends soft loans from special fund resources with concessional conditions.
- At the end of 2014, Japan holds the largest proportion of shares at 15.7%. The United States hols 15.6%, China holds 6.5%, India holds 6.4% and Australia holds 5.8%. It has 67 member countries.

Asian Infrastructure Investment Bank (AIIB)

It is a Multilateral Development Bank (MDB) conceived for the 21st century. Chinese President Xi Jinping and Premier Li Keqiang announced the AIIB initiative during their respective visits to South-East Asian countries in October 2013.

By the deadline of March 31st for submission of membership applications, the Prospective Founding Members had increased to 57, and the 4th CNM was organised in Beijing in April 2015, after ratifications were received from 10 member states holding a total number of 50% of the initial subscriptions of the Authorised Capital Stock.

Committees on Various Sectors of Indian Economy

Committee	Sector
AC Shah Committee	Non-Banking Financial Company
Bimal Jalan Committee	Market Infrastructure Instruments
Malegam Committee	Functioning of Micro-Finance Institutions
Birla Committee	Corporate Governance
Kirith Parikh Committee	Rationalisation of Petroleum Product Prices
Chaturvedi Committee	Improving National Highways
SR Hashim Committee	Urban Poverty
Abhijit Sen Committee	Wholesale Price Index
C Rangarajan Committee	Services Prices Index and Financial Inclusion
Abid Hussian Committee	Development of Capital Markets
Damodaran Committee	Customer Service in Banks
Khandelwal Committee	Human Resource in Commercial Banks
Patil Committee	Corporate Debt
VK Sharma Committee	Credit to Marginal Farmers
Sarangi Committee	Non-Performing Assets
Khanna Committee	Regional Rural Banks
Dantawala Committee	Lead Bank Scheme
Gadgil Committee	Financial Inclusion
Thorat Committee	Deregulation of Small Saving Deposit Rates
Deepak Mohanty Committee	Monetary System in India
Raghuram Rajan Committee	Financial Sector Reform
Naresh Chandra Committee	Civil Aviation
Rakesh Mohan Committee	Railways
Kakodkar Committee	Rail Safety
Pitroda Committee	Rail Modernisation
JJ Irani Committee	Company Law Reforms
CB Bhave Committee	Disclosure Standards
Karve Committee	Small Scale Industry
Raja Mannar Committee	Banking Laws
LC Gupta Committee	Derivatives Trading
KR Chandratre Committee	Delisting of Shares

Glossary

Absolute Advantage   The ability to produce more units of a good or service than some other producer, using the same quantity of resources.

Aggregate Demand (AD)   A schedule (or graph) that shows the value of output (real GDP) that would be demanded at different price levels.

Aggregate Supply (AS)   A schedule (or graph) that shows the value of output (real GDP) that would be produced at different price levels. In the long run, the schedule shows a constant level of real GDP at all price levels, determined by the economy's productive capacity at full employment. In the short run, the aggregate supply schedule may show different levels of real GDP as the price level changes.

Automated Teller Machine (ATM)   A machine that provides cash and performs banking services (for deposits and transfers of funds between accounts,) automatically, when accessed by customers using plastic cards coded with Personal Indentification Numbers (PINs).

Balance of Payments Deficit   An imbalance in a nation's balance of payments, where more currency is flowing out of the country than is flowing in. This unequal flow of currency is considered unfavourable and can lead to a loss of foreign currency reserves.

Balance of Payments Surplus   An imbalance in a nation's balance of payments, in which more currency is flowing into the country than is flowing out. This unequal flow of currency is considered favourable and can lead to an increase in foreign currency reserves.

Balance of Trade   The part of a nation's balance of payments accounts that deals only with its imports and exports of goods and services. The balance of trade is divided into the balance on goods (merchandise) and the balance on services. If the value of a country's exports of goods and services is greater than its imports, it has a balance of trade surplus. If the value of a country's imports of goods and services is greater than its exports, it has a balance of trade deficit.

Balanced Budget   A financial plan, in which income is equal to expenses.

Blue Chip Stocks   Stocks in large, nationally known companies that have been profitable for a long time and are well-known and trusted.

Command Economy   An economy, in which most economic issues of production and distribution are resolved through central planning and controlling.

Consumer Price Index (CPI)   A price index that measures the cost of a fixed basket of consumer goods and services and compares the cost of this basket in one time period with its cost in some base period. Changes in the CPI are used to measure inflation.

Cost-Push Inflation   Inflation caused by rising costs of production.

Crowding-Out   Increased interest rates and decreased private investment caused by government borrowing.

Currency Devaluation   A government adjusts the value of the nation's currency so that it buys less of foreign currencies than before.

Current Account   Part of a nation's balance of payments accounts; records exports and imports of goods and services, net investment income and transfer payments with other countries.

Current Account Balance   The inflow of the goods, services, investment income and transfer accounts into the domestic country from foreign countries netted against the outflow of goods, services, investment income and transfer accounts from the domestic country to foreign countries.

Demand-Pull Inflation   Inflation caused by increasing demand for output or 'too much money chasing too few goods.'

Depreciation   A reduction in the value of capital goods over time due to their use in production.

Depreciation of Currency A decline in the price of one currency relative to another.

Depression A severe, prolonged economic contraction.

Fixed Exchange Rate An exchange rate that is set and therefore, prevented from rising or falling with changes in supply and demand for a nation's currency.

Flexible Exchange Rate An exchange rate that is determined by the international demand for and supply of a nation's money; a rate free to rise or fall (to float).

Hyperinflation A very rapid rise in the overall price level.

Imperfect Competition Any market structure, in which firms are not price takers, but instead must seek the price and output levels that maximise their profits.

Initial Public Offering (IPO) A company's first sale of stock to the public. When a company 'goes public', it sells blocks of stock shares to an investment firm that specialises in initial offerings of stock and resells them to the public.

Market Failures The systematic over production or underproduction of some goods and services that occurs, when producers or consumers do not have to bear the full costs of transactions they undertake. Usually related to externalities or the need for public goods.

Monopolistic Competition A market structure, in which slightly differentiated products are sold by a large number of relatively small producers and in which the barriers to new firms entering the market are low.

Monopoly A market structure in which there is a single supplier of a good or service. Also, a firm that is the single supplier of a good or service, for which there are no close substitutes; also known as a monopolist.

Monopsony A market situation, in which there is only one buyer of a resource. Also, a firm that is the only buyer of a resource; also known as a monopsonist.

Natural Monopoly An industry, in which the advantages of large-scale production make it possible for a single firm to produce the entire output of the market at a lower average cost than a number of firms each producing a smaller quantity.

Non-Price Competition Competition by firms trying to attract customers by methods other than reducing prices; examples include advertising and promotional gifts.

Oligopoly A market structure, in which a few, relatively large firms account for all or most of the production or sales of a good or service in a particular market and where barriers to new firms entering the market are very high. Some oligopolies produce homogeneous products; others produce heterogeneous products.

Open Market Operations The buying and selling of government bonds and securities by the federal Reserves to central bank reserve and the money supply.

Pegged Exchange Rate An exchange rate that is fixed within a certain range or against a major currency or basket of currencies.

Perfect Competition A market structure, in which a large number of relatively small firms produce and sell identical products and in which there are no significant barriers to entry into or exit from the industry.

Progressive Tax A tax that take a larger percentage of income from people in higher-income groups than from people in lower-income ones; the US federal income tax is an example.

Recession A decline in the rate of national economic activity, usually measured by a decline in real GDP for atleast two consecutive quarters (i.e. 6 months).

Regressive Tax A tax that takes a larger percentage of income from people in lower-income groups than from higher-income ones. Sales taxes and excise taxes are examples.

Velocity of Money Member The average number of times each dollar is spent on final goods and services in a year.

FAQs (Indian Economy)

1. The Indian economy should be developed on the socialistic pattern of society was enunciated, at which summit of the Indian National Congress?

2. In which plan did the Indian economy managed to cross the barrier of Hindu rate of growth of 3-3.5%?

3. How many Miniratnas Category-I companies are there at present?

4. What is the punch line of the Twelfth Five Year Plan?

5. Who headed the Committee on Rail Safety?

6. The CSO released the New Series of National Accounts with base year—instead of the base year 2004-05.

7. Which was the first insurance company in India?

8. Which were the two Five Year Plans when the set target for the foodgrain production was achieved during the overall plan period?

9. Which sector of the Indian economy is the second largest provider of the employment after agriculture?

10. What is the unemployment rate on Current Daily Status (CDS) basis as per the NSSO 66th Round (2009-10)?

11. Which state accounts for 9/10th of the natural rubber production in the country?

12. What is the rank of India in the recently released Human Development Report-2015?

13. Who gave the first scientific estimates of National Income in India?

14. When was the National Statistical Commission formed and who was the Chairman?

15. Which country is the largest foreign direct investor in India after in 2015?

16. Which country is the smallest holder of the quotas in the International Monetary Fund at present?

17. What is the present rank of India in terms of voting share in the IMF?

18. What is the present number of member nations of the World Trade Organisation?

19. What is the alternate name of the Bombay Plan prepared by some industrialists in 1944?

20. When was the dual exchange rate system adopted in India?

21. What is reverse repo rate and what is the present rate of repo?

22. Which are the four connectivities enunciated under the PURA model of growth in India?

23. Who is the present head of the Asian Development Bank and from where does he belong?

24. The Durgapur Steel Plant was set-up in collaboration with which country?

25. What was the rate of devaluation of rupee in June, 1966?

26. Which plan did not set any target for crop production?

27. The 'cafeteria approach' is associated with what?

28. Which state registered the maximum growth rate in population according to the Census 2011?

29. In India, for how many days in a year a worker should work to be called as a major worker or an employed person?

30. In which crop, India has the highest productivity in the world?

31. What is the core element of 'evergreen revolution' which has been envisaged for the rejuvenation of agriculture in India?

32. Who coined the term 'Green Revolution'?

33. Which year of the Five Year Plans in India is referred to as "Second Green Revolution"?

34. With which is the Colin Clark thesis associated?

35. Rolling Plan was adopted in India, in which year?

36. What is the percentage of tax proceeds which need to be shared with the States by the centre as per the recommendation of the 13th Finance Commission?

37. Is Good and Services Tax (GST) a sales tax or Value Added Tax? (VAT)

38. What is the main goal of the World Bank?

39. In order to arrive at Gross National Product at factor cost from Gross National Product at market prices, what needs to be deducted?

40. Which concept among the various concepts of National Income is referred as Real National Income?

41. Which Indian Bank has the maximum number of branches outside India?

42. How many Zonal offices does Life Insurance Corporation (LIC) have at present?

43. Who spearheaded the nationalisation of insurance industry in India and in which year?

44. How many associate banks does SBI have at present?

45. Who headed the committee on micro finance institutions reforms?

46. Which industrial policy for the first time recognised the role of small-scale industry?

47. As per the MSME Act, 2006, what is the investment limit of the medium enterprises in the manufacturing sector?

48. What are the essential components of inclusive growth?

49. How money multiplier is arrived at?

50. Which measure of money supply in India is also called the narrow money?

51. Who was the first Governor of RBI?

52. Agriculture in India is associated, with which type of unemployment?

53. What is the present rate of saving and investment in India?

54. When was Banking Ombudsman Scheme implemented in India?

55. Who gave the concept of Physical Quality of Life Index (PQLI)?

56. What is the rank of India in terms of Green House Gases (GHGs) emissions in absolute terms in the world?

57. The National Solar Mission has set the target of generating 20000 MW electricity through solar power, by which year?

58. The National Manufacturing Policy, 2011 seeks to generate, how much additional employment by 2022?

59. What does NIMZ stands for?

60. What is the decadal growth rate of population from 2001 to 2011?

61. What is the present system, which is adopted by the RBI in the management of currency in India?

62. Who is the Vice-Chairman of newly form NITI Aayog?

Answers

1. Avadi Summit 2. Seventh Plan
3. 54 4. Faster, sustainable and inclusive growth 5. Dr Anil Kakodkar
6. 2011-12. 7. Oriental Life Insurance Company, in 1818 8. First and Fifth Plan 9. Services sector provides 29% employment followed by Industry sector 10. 6.6%
11. Kerala 12. 130 13. Professor V K R V Rao 14. 2005, Professor SD Tendulkar 15. Mauritius 16. Tuvalu
17. 8th 18. 157 19. Plan of Economic Development for India
20. 1992 21. Reverse Repo Rate is the rate, at which RBI allows Commercial Banks to park surplus fund with the RBI. It withdraws liquidity form the market. The present Repo Rate is 7.75%.
22. Physical, electronic, knowledge and economic 23. Takehiko Nakao, Japan 24. The UK 25. 57.5%
26. Tenth Plan 27. Family Planning
28. Bihar 29. 273 30. Pulses
31. Sustainability 32. Dr William Gaced 33. 1983-84 34. Structural change in the economy 35. 1978
36. 32.5% 37. Both 38. Reducing poverty 39. Net indirect tax 40. Net National Product at factor cost
41. State Bank of India 42. 8 43. C D Deshmukh, 1956 44. 5 45. Y H Malegam 46. Industrial Policy, 1977
47. ₹ 5 crore to ₹ 10 crore
48. Poverty reduction, agriculture, social sector development, reduction in regional disparities and protecting environment 49. Broad Money (M3)/Reserve Money (M_0) 50. M1
51. Sir Osborne Smith 52. Disguised unemployment 53. 36.8% and 38.1%
54. 2006 55. Morris D Morris 56. 3rd
57. 2020 58. 100 million
59. National Investment and Manufacturing Zone 60. 17.64%
61. Minimum Reserve System, 1957
62. Arvind Panagriya.

GENERAL SCIENCE

PHYSICS

Physics is the study of nature and its laws. The word physics has been derived from a Greek word *physis* which means nature. Physics is one of the academic disciplines, perhaps the oldest through its inclusion of astronomy.

Units

Measurement of any physical quantity involves comparison with a certain basic arbitrarily chosen and widely accepted reference standard called **unit**.

SI SYSTEM

It is based on the following seven basic units and two supplementary units

Name of Quantity	Name of Unit
Basic Units	
▪ Length	metre
▪ Mass	kilogram
▪ Time	second
▪ Electric current	ampere
▪ Thermodynamic temperature	kelvin
▪ Luminous intensity	candela
▪ Amount of substance	mole
Supplementary Units	
▪ Plane angle	radian
▪ Solid angle	steradian

Important Derived Units

Physical Quantity	Definition	SI Unit
Area	Length square	m^2
Velocity	Displacement per unit time	ms^{-1}
Force	Mass x acceleration	$kgms^{-2}$

Greatest Units

$$1 \text{ light year} = 9.46 \times 10^{15} \text{ m}$$
$$1 \text{ parsec} = 3.086 \times 10^{16} \text{ m} = 3.26 \text{ ly}$$
$$1 \text{ AU} = 1.5 \times 10^{11} \text{m}$$
$$1 \text{ metric tonne} = 10^3 \text{ kg}$$
$$1 \text{ quintal} = 10^2 \text{ kg}$$

Dimensions of Physical Quantities

Dimensions of a physical quantity are the powers, to which the fundamental quantities must be raised to represent that quantity completely. There fore, the dimensional formula of a quantity is expressed in terms of fundamental quantities, commonly mass M, length L and time T. Any physical quantity is either a scalar or a vector.

e.g. Force = $[MLT^{-2}]$, Density = $[ML^{-3}]$

Scalar Quantities

Physical quantities which have magnitude only and no direction are called scalar quantities. e.g. mass, speed, volume, work, time, power, energy etc.

Vector Quantities

Physical quantities which have both magnitude and direction and also obey triangle law of vector addition are called vector quantities.

e.g. displacement, velocity, acceleration, force, momentum, torque etc.

KINEMATICS

It is the branch of mechanics, which deals with the motion of object.

Distance

- The length of the actual path covered by a body in a particular time interval is called distance. It is always positive.
- It is a scalar quantity.
- Its unit is metre.

Displacement

- The difference between the final and the initial position of an object is called displacement. It may be positive, negative or zero.
- It is a vector quantity. Its unit is metre.
- The magnitude of displacement may or may not be equal to the path length traversed by an object.

$$|\text{Displacement}| \leq |\text{Distance}|$$

Speed

- Speed is the distance covered by a moving body in per unit of time interval.
- It is a scalar quantity. It is always equal to or greater than magnitude of the velocity.
- The **average speed** of a particle for a given interval of time is defined as the ratio of total distance travelled to the total time taken.

Average speed

$$= \frac{\text{Total distance travelled}}{\text{Total time taken}}$$

- If the body covers first half distance with speed v_1 and next half with speed v_2, then

$$\text{Average speed} = \frac{2v_1 v_2}{v_1 + v_2}$$

Velocity

The rate of change of displacement of a body is called velocity.

$$\text{Velocity} = \frac{\text{Displacement}}{\text{Time}}$$

- Velocity is a vector quantity.
- It may be positive or negative.
- Average velocity

$$= \frac{\text{Total displacement}}{\text{Total time}}$$

- If the body covers first half distance with velocity v_1 and next half with velocity v_2, then

$$\text{Average velocity} = \frac{2v_1 v_2}{v_1 + v_2}$$

- If a body travels with uniform velocity v_1 for time t_1 and with uniform velocity v_2 for time t_2, then

Average velocity

$$= \frac{v_1 t_1 + v_2 t_2}{t_1 + t_2}$$

- If a body is moving on a circular path, then after completing one complete cycle, its average velocity is zero.

Uniform Velocity

An object is said to be moving with uniform velocity if it undergoes equal displacements in equal intervals of time.

Non-Uniform Velocity

An object is said to be moving with non-uniform or variable velocity if it undergoes unequal displacements in equal intervals of time.

Relative Velocity

When two bodies are moving in the straight line, the speed (or velocity) of one with respect to another is known as its relative speed (or velocity).

v_{AB} = velocity of A with respect to B

$$= \mathbf{v}_A - \mathbf{v}_B$$

Acceleration

- It is the rate of change of velocity. Its SI unit is m/s^2. It is a vector quantity.
- When the velocity of a body increases with time then its acceleration is positive and if velocity decreases with time then its acceleration is negative and is called retardation or deceleration.
- Acceleration of an object is zero, if it is at rest or moving with uniform velocity.

Average acceleration,

$$a = \frac{v_2 - v_1}{\Delta t}$$

$$= \frac{\Delta v}{\Delta t}$$

MOTION/REST

If the position of a body or a system of bodies does not change with time, it is said to be at rest.

On the other hand, if the position change with time, it is said to be in motion.

A particle in rest does not have the speed and acceleration, while a particle in the motion has its speed and also may have some acceleration, if the speed changes with respect to time.

Equation of Motion

For motion on a straight line with constant acceleration a

(i) $v = u + at$ (ii) $s = ut + \frac{1}{2}at^2$

(iii) $v^2 = u^2 + 2as$

Equation of Motion Under Gravity

(a) **Downward Direction**

(i) $v = u + gt$ (ii) $h = ut + \frac{1}{2}gt^2$

(iii) $v^2 = u^2 + 2gh$

where, s = displacement travelled

h = height, t = time

u = initial velocity

v = final velocity

a = acceleration,

g = acceleration due to gravity

for retardation a will be replaced by $-a$

(b) **Upward Direction** If velocity of a body is decreasing instead of increasing, then equation of motion are

$$v = u - gt$$
$$h = ut - \frac{1}{2}gt^2$$
$$v^2 = u^2 - 2gh$$

(c) Distance travelled by a body in nth second s_{nth}

$$s_{nth} = u + (2n-1)\frac{a}{2}$$

- If the body is thrown upwards, then it will rise until its vertical velocity becomes zero. Then, the maximum height attained is $h = \dfrac{u^2}{2g}$.

Graphical Representation of Motion

Displacement-Time Graph

If a body moves with a uniform velocity then displacement - time graph is a straight line. The slope or gradient of the straight line is speed.

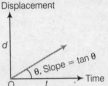

Velocity-Time Graph

1. **Constant Acceleration** If a body moves with a constant velocity, velocity-time graph is a straight line.

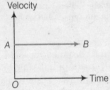

2. **Uniformly Accelerated Motion** The velocity-time graph is a straight line.

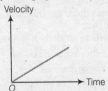

Two Dimensional Motion

In this motion of a body is described in a rectangular co-ordinate axis.

Projectile Motion

- When a particle is projected so that it makes certain angle with horizontal then the motion of the particle is said to be projectile. Path of a projectile is parabolic in nature.

- The initial velocity u of the projectile can be *resolved into two components*

   (i) $u \cos \theta$ (horizontal direction)

   (ii) $u \sin \theta$ (vertical direction)

For the Projectile Motion

Maximum Height It is the maximum vertical distance travelled by a body.

It is given by $(H) = \dfrac{u^2 \sin^2 \theta}{2g}$

Horizontal Range The distance between projecting and landing point.

It is given by $(R) = \dfrac{u^2 \sin 2\theta}{g}$

Time of Flight Time taken in reaching the landing point from projecting point. It is given by

$(T) = \dfrac{2u \sin \theta}{g}$

- For maximum range $\theta = 45°$. Therefore, a long jumper takes jump at an angle of 45°.
- For maximum height $\theta = 90°$.
- The horizontal range is the same when the body is projected at θ or $(90° - \theta)$.
- When a body is dropped freely from the top of the tower and another body is projected horizontally from the same point, both will reach the ground at the same time.
- When two balls of different masses are projected horizontally they will reach ground at same time.

Circular Motion

- When an object moves along a circular path, then its motion is called circular motion e.g. motion of top etc. If an object moves along a circular path with uniform speed, its motion is called uniform circular motion. It is accelerated even if the speed of the body is constant. The motion of a satellite is an accelerated motion.
- The acceleration is directed towards the centre and is given by $a = \dfrac{v^2}{r}$, where v is the speed and r is the radius. This is called **centripetal acceleration**.

FORCE

Force is a push or pull which can change the position or direction of a body.

Centripetal Force

A body performing circular motion is acted upon by a force which is always directed towards the centre of the circle. This force is called centripetal force. Any of the forces found in nature (such as frictional force, gravitational force, electrical force, magnetic force etc) may act as a centripetal force.

- **Cyclist** bends his body towards the centre on a turn while turning to obtain the required centripetal force.
- Generally, **in rain** the scooter slips at the turning of a road because the friction between tyre and road is reduced. Due to this, necessary centripetal force is not provided. Roads are banked at turns to provide the required centripetal force for taking a turn.

Centrifugal Force

Pseudo Force When we in a non-inertial frame of reference to apply Newton's laws, we have to apply a force on the object equal to mass times in opposite direction of acceleration or retardation of the frame. Centrifugal force is such a Pseudo force. It is always equal and opposite to centripetal force.

Cream separator, centrifugal drier etc work on the principle of centrifugal force.

NEWTON'S LAWS OF MOTION

First Law

- "Every body retains its state of rest or state of uniform motion, until an external force is applied on it." This law is also known as law of inertia or **law of Galileo**
- First law gives the definition of inertia. **Inertia** is the virtue of a body due to which it tries to retain its state.

Inertia is of three types

    Inertia of rest

    Inertia of motion

    Inertia of direction

- A person sitting in a moving car falls forward, when the car stops suddenly. This is because the feet of the passenger comes to the rest along with the car, but the upper part of his body, tends to remain in motion due to inertia of motion.

- The dust particle come out from a carpet, when it is beaten with a stick due to their inertia of rest.

Inertial Frame Whenever the frame of reference is moving with uniform velocity or is at rest.

- **Non-Inertial Frame** Whenever the frame of reference is accelerating or retarding or rotating is called non-inertial frame of reference.

Second Law

- "The force applied on a body is equal to the product of mass of the body and the acceleration produced in it e.g. $F = ma$."
- The second law of motion gives the definition of force.
- A force is any influence that causes an object to undergo a certain change, either concerning its movement, direction and geometrical structure.
- SI unit of force is **Newton** (N).

Linear Momentum

- The product of the mass and the velocity of a body is called the linear momentum of the body.
- It is a vector quantity. Its unit is kg-m/s.
  $\therefore$ Linear momentum = **Mass** $\times$ **Velocity**
- A heavier body has a larger linear momentum than a lighter body moving with the same velocity.
- In the absence of external forces, the total linear momentum of the system remains conserved.

Application of Conservation of Linear Momentum

- When a man jumps from a boat to the shore, the boat slightly moves away from the shore. Rocket works on the principle of conservation of momentum.
- When a bullet is fired from a gun, the gun recoils or gives a sharp pull in backward direction.

Impulse

- If a force acts on a body for a very short time Δt, then the product of force and time is called the impulse.

- Impulse = Change in momentum
  = **Force** $\times$ Time interval
- Its SI unit is N-s or kg-m/s.

Concept of Impulse

- A cricketer moves his hands backwards while catching a ball.
- A person jumping from a height on a 'concrete' floor receives more injury than when jumping on a spongy floor.
- Vehicles like cars, buses and scooters are provided with shockers.
- Bogies of the trains are provided with buffers to avoid severe jerks during shunting of trains. Buffers increase the time-duration of jerks during shunting. This reduces the force with which bogies push or pull each other and thus severe jerks are avoided.

Third Law

- "Every action have equal and opposite reaction." Action and reaction always act on the different bodies.
- On firing the bullet, the gunner is pushed in backward direction.
- When the boatman is jumped from the boat, the boat is pushed back.
- In a rocket, gases are ejected with a great speed from the rocket backwards and rocket is pushed forwards.
- While swimming, a person pushes the water backwards (action). The water pushes the swimmer forward with the same force (reaction).

Equilibrium

- If the resultant of all the forces acting on a body is zero, then the body is said to be in equilibrium. If a body is in equilibrium, it will be either at rest or in uniform motion. If it is at rest, the equilibrium is called static, otherwise dynamic.
- *Static equilibrium is of the following two types*
  - (i) **Stable Equilibrium** If on slight displacement from equilibrium position a body has tendency to regain its original position, it is said to be in stable equilibrium.

(ii) **Unstable Equilibrium** If on a slight displacement from equilibrium position, a body moves in the direction of displacement and does not regain its original position, the equilibrium is said to be unstable equilibrium. In this equilibrium, the centre of gravity of the body is at the highest position.

Neutral Equilibrium

If on slight displacement from equilibrium position a body has no tendency to come back to its original position or to move in the direction of displacement, it is said to be in neutral equilibrium.

• In neutral equilibrium, the centre of gravity always remains at the same height.

Condition for Stable Equilibrium

For stable equilibrium of a body, *the following two conditions should be fulfilled*

(i) The centre of gravity of the body should be at the minimum height.

(ii) The vertical line passing through the centre of gravity of the body should pass through the base of the body.

Centre of Mass Centre of mass of a body (system of particles) is a point where the entire mass of the body is supposed to be concentrated. We can define position of centre of mass r by

$$X = \frac{m_1 \mathbf{r}_1 + m_2 \mathbf{r}_2 + \dots\dots + m_n \mathbf{r}_n}{m_1 + m_2 + \dots\dots + m_n}$$

where, $\mathbf{r}_1, \mathbf{r}_2, \dots\dots \mathbf{r}_n$ are position vectors of constituent particles.

FRICTION

• If we slide or try to slide a body over a surface, the motion is resisted by a bonding between the body and the surface. This resistance is called frictional force.

• The opposite force that comes into play when one body tends to move over the surface of another body but actually motion has yet not started is called **static friction**.

• The maximum value of the static frictional force which comes into play when a body just begins to slide over the surface of another body is called **limiting frictional force**.

• When two bodies actually roll on each other (as in case of ball bearing), the **rolling friction** comes into play.

• When two bodies actually slide over each other, **sliding friction** comes into play.

• When a body moves over the other body, then the force of friction acting between two surfaces in contact in relative motion is called Kinetic Friction.

• $\mu_s > \mu_\kappa > \mu_r$, here μ_s, μ_κ and μ_r are called coefficient of static, kinetic and rolling friction respectively.

Advantages and Disadvantages of Friction

• Walking is possible due to friction.

• The transfer of motion from one part of a machine to other part through belts is possible by friction.

• Brake works on the basis of friction.

• Friction causes wear and tear of the parts of machinery in contact. Thus, their lifetime gets reduced.

Methods of Reducing Friction

• By polishing, by lubrication, by proper selection of material and by using ball bearing friction can be reduced to some extent.

Work, Energy and Power

WORK

When a body is displaced by applying a force on it, then work is said to be done. If a body is displaced by a distance s on applying a force F on it, then work done $W = F \cdot s = Fs \cos \theta$, where '$\theta$' is the angle between the force and the direction of displacement. It is a scalar quantity. Its unit is joule (J).

Positive Work Done

- Positive work means that force is applied along the direction of displacement. e.g. when a horse pulls a cart on a level road, when a body falls freely under gravitational pull.

Negative Work Done

Negative work means that force is opposite to displacement. e.g. when a positive charge is moved towards another positive charge, when a body is made to slide over a rough surface.

Zero Work Done

If the force is perpendicular to the displacement and if either the force or the displacement is zero, work done is zero. e.g. when a body is moved along a circular path with the help of a string, when a coolie travels on a platform with a load on his head and when a person does not move from his position but he may be holding any amount of heavy load.

ENERGY

- It is defined as capacity of doing work. Its unit is joule in SI and erg in CGS system.
- Mechanical energy is in two forms; kinetic energy and potential energy.

Kinetic Energy

- It is the energy possessed by a body by virtue of its motion.
- If a body of mass m is moving with velocity v, then kinetic energy

$$KE = \frac{1}{2} mv^2 = \frac{p^2}{2m}$$

where, p is the linear momentum.

- When momentum is doubled, kinetic energy becomes four times.
- **Kinetic energy** of air is used to run wind mills.
- Kinetic energy of **running water** is used to run the water mills.
- A **bullet** fired from a gun can pierce a target due to its kinetic energy.
- If a body is moving in horizontal circle then its kinetic energy is same at all points, but if it is moving in vertical circle, then the kinetic energy is different at different points.

Potential Energy

- It is the energy possessed by a body by virtue of its position.
- Suppose a body is raised to a height h above the surface of the earth, then potential energy of the body $= mgh$.
- When a body is falling downwards, then its potential energy goes on changing to kinetic energy.
- The potential energy of the **wound spring** of a clock is used to drive the hands of the clock.
- The potential energy of water in dams is used to run turbines in order to produce electric energy using the generators.

Conservative and Non-conservative Forces

A non-dissipative force is known as conservative force e.g. gravitational force, electrostatic force. Non-conservative forces are dissipative forces e.g. frictional forces, viscous force.

Law of Conservation of Energy

- According to the law of conservation of energy, "Energy can neither be created nor be destroyed but it can only be transformed from one form to another."
- The sum of all kinds of energies in an isolated system remains constant at all times.

Transformation of Energy

- In a heat engine, heat energy changes into mechanical energy.
- In the electric bulb, the electric energy is converted into light energy.
- In burning coil, oil etc., the chemical energy changes into heat energy.
- In solar cell, solar energy changes into electrical energy.
- In playing sitar, mechanical energy changes into sound energy.
- In microphone, sound energy changes into electrical energy.
- In loud speaker, electrical energy changes into sound energy.
- In battery, chemical energy changes into mechanical energy.
- In electric motor, electrical energy changes into mechanical energy.
- In candle, chemical energy changes into light and heat energy.

POWER

- Rate of doing work by a body is called **power**.

  i.e. $\text{Power} = \dfrac{\text{Work done}}{\text{Time taken}}$

  $P = \dfrac{W}{t}$

- SI unit of power is watt (W) or joule per second and it is a scalar quantity.

  $$1 \text{ W} = 1 \text{ J/s}$$
  $$1 \text{ kW} = 10^3 \text{ W}$$
  $$1 \text{ MW} = 10^6 \text{ W}$$

  1 Horse Power (HP) = 746 W
  1 watt/second (W-s) = 1 J
  1 watt/hour (W-h) = 3600 J
  1 kilowatt hour (kW-h) = 3.6×10^6 J

Torque

- The turning effect of a force on a body is known as **the moment of the force or torque**. Torque is a vector quantity.
  i.e. Torque, $Z = F \cdot d$
  Where, $F = $ force
  $d = $ perpendicular distance of force from the axis of rotation.

Simple Machines

- It is based on moment of force.
- Lever, inclined plane, screw guage etc. are simple machine.
- Scissors, sea saw, brakes of cycle, hand pump, plass are lever of first kind.
- Nut cracker and waste carrying machine are lever of second kind.
- Tong, man's hand and tiller are lever of third kind.

GRAVITATION

In 1686, Newton stated that in the universe each particle of matter attracts every other particle. This universal attractive force is called *gravitation*.

Gravitational Force

- It is always attractive in nature.
- It is the weakest force but is a long range force.
- Mathematically it is represented as

  $$F_G = \frac{GMm}{r}$$

  where, F_G is gravitational force, G is gravitational constant, M is the mass of first particle, m is the mass of second particle and r is the distance between them.
- This is called **Newton's universal law of gravitation.**
- The value of G is 6.67×10^{-11} N-m^2/kg^2

Gravity

- It is the force by which the Earth attracts a body towards its centre.
- The acceleration due to gravity is the rate of increase of velocity of a body falling freely towards the Earth. It is represented by

  $$g = \frac{GM_e}{R_e^2}$$

  where, M_e is the mass of the Earth and R_e is the radius of Earth.
- The value of g at the surface of Earth is 9.8 m/s^2.
- The Earth is surrounded by an atmosphere of gases due to gravity. The value of g on the Moon is 1/6th of that on the Earth surface.

Variation in the Value of g

- When we go above the surface of the Earth, the acceleration due to gravity goes on decreasing.
- When we go below the surface of the Earth, the acceleration due to gravity goes on decreasing and becomes zero at the centre of the Earth.
- Decreasing the rotational motion of Earth, the value of g increases.
- When we go from the equator towards the poles, the value of g goes on increasing.
- If Earth stops its rotation about its own axis, then at the equator the value of g increases and consequently the weight of body lying there increases.
- The value of g is maximum on the surface of the Earth.

Centre of Gravity

- The centre of gravity of a body is that point at which the whole weight of the body appears to act.
- It can be inside the material of the body or outside it.
- For regularly shaped body, the centre of gravity lies at its geometrical centre.

Mass

- The mass of a body is the quantity of matter contained in it. It is a scalar quantity and its SI unit is kg.
- Mass is measured by an ordinary equal arm balance.
- Mass of body does not change from place-to-place and remains constant.

Weight

- The weight of a body is the force with, which it is attracted towards the centre of the Earth. It is a vector quantity and its SI unit is Newton (N).
- It is measured by a spring balance.
- It is not constant and it changes from place to place.

Weight of a Body in a Lift

- If lift is stationary or moving with uniform speed (either upward or downward), the apparent weight of a body is equal to its true weight.
- If lift is going up with an acceleration, the apparent weight of a body is more than the true weight. If lift is going down with an acceleration, the apparent weight of a body is less than the true weight.
- If the cord of the lift is broken, then it falls freely. In this situation, the weight of a body in the lift becomes zero. This is the situation of weightlessness.
- While going down, if the acceleration of lift is more than acceleration due to gravity, a body in the lift goes in contact of the ceiling of lift.

SATELLITE

- The heavenly body which revolves around the planets is called satellite. Moon is a natural satellite of Earth.
- The speed of a satellite does not depend upon the mass of the satellite.
- A satellite revolving very close to Earth's surface has a period of revolution about 84 min and its speed is nearly 8 km/s.
- Every body inside the satellite is in a state of weightlessness. Total energy of the satellite is negative.
- *Artificial satellites are of two types* Geostationary and Polar satellites

  (i) The satellite whose time period is 24 h, is called **geostationary satellite**. It is used to reflect TV signals and telecast TV programs from one part of the world to another. This satellite revolves around the Earth at a height of 36000 km. INSAT-2B and INSAT-2C are geostationary satellites of India.

  (ii) **Polar satellites** revolve around the earth in polar orbits at a height of approximately 800 km. The time period of these satellites is approximately 84 minute. These satellites are used in weather forecasting, in studying upper region of the atmosphere, in mapping etc. PSLV Series Satellites are Polar Satellites of India.

Escape Velocity

- The minimum velocity that should be given to the body to enable it to escape away from Earth's gravitational field is called escape velocity. It is given by

$$v_e = \sqrt{\begin{array}{l} 2 \times acceleration \\ due\ to\ gravity \times Radius\ of \\ the\ Earth \end{array}}$$

  Its value on the Earth's surface is 11.2 km/s.

- The value of the escape velocity of a body does not depend on its mass. Its value on the moon surface is 2.38 km/s. So, there is no atmosphere around the moon.
- Escape velocity is $\sqrt{2}$ times the orbital velocity.
- Satellites are launched with the escape velocity as needed.

Kepler's Laws

- All planets move around the Sun in elliptical orbits having the Sun at one foci of the orbit.
- The areal speed of a planet around the Sun is constant.
- The square of the period of revolution (T) of any planet around the Sun is directly proportional to the cube of its mean distance from the Sun (a) i.e. $T^2 \propto a^3$.

Quick Digest

- The Earth rotates on its axis from West to East. This rotation makes the Sun and the stars appear to be moving across the sky from East to West.
- The response of plants to gravity is called geotropism.
- We are able to see a live telecast of cricket matches or other programmes with the help of a communication satellite, which is a geostationary satellite.

General Properties of Matter

Matter It is the substance that occupies definite space and mass which is perceptible to sense.

ELASTICITY

- It is that property of the material body by virtue of which the body opposes any change in its shape or size when deforming forces are applied to it, and recovers its original state as soon as the deforming forces are removed.
- Steel is more elastic than rubber.
- **Elastic Limit** The maximum limit of the external force upto which elasticity of the body is maintained.

Plasticity

- The property of a body by virtue of which it does not regain its original configuration even after the removal of deforming force is called plasticity.
- Putty, paraffin wax are nearly perfectly plastic bodies.

Stress

The internal restoring force acting per unit area of cross-section of the deformed body is called stress. Its unit is N m^2 or pascal.

Strain

- The change in length, volume, shape of the body per unit of the original value under the application of the deforming force is called strain. Strain is unit less quantity.
- **Hooke's law and Modulus of Elasticity** The ratio of stress to strain is a constant for the material and is called modulus of elasticity.

$$E = \frac{\text{Stress}}{\text{Strain}}$$

- It is also called **Hooke's law,** which states that within the limit of elasticity the strain produced in a body is directly proportional to the stress applied to it.
- **Young's Modulus** If strain is longitudinal, then the modulus of elasticity is called Young's modulus.
- **Bulk Modulus** If under the effect of uniform pressure, the volume of the body changes it is called the bulk modulus of elasticity.
- **Modulus of Rigidity** The ratio of tangential stress to shearing strain is called modulus of rigidity.

MECHANICAL PROPERTIES OF FLUIDS

PRESSURE

- It is defined as force acting normally on unit area of the surface.

$$\text{Pressure} = \frac{\text{Normal force}}{\text{Area}}$$

- Its unit is N/m^2 also called pascal. It is a scalar quantity.
- Pressure in a liquid is given by $p = h\rho g$ where, h is the height, (ρ) is density of the liquid and g is acceleration due to gravity.
- Atmospheric pressure of 1 atm

$$= 1.01 \times 10^5 \ N/m^2 = 760 \text{ torr}$$

- Atmospheric pressure decreases with altitude. This is why (i) it is difficult to cook on the mountain, (ii) the fountain pen of a passenger leaks in aeroplane at height.
- Atmospheric pressure is measured by barometer. The slow rise in the barometric reading is the indication of clear weather.
- Sudden fall in barometric reading is the indication of storm.
- Slow fall in barometric reading is the indication of rain.

DENSITY AND RELATIVE DENSITY

- The density of a substance (ρ) is defined as the ratio of its mass (M) to its volume (V).

i.e. $\text{Density} = \dfrac{\text{Mass}}{\text{Volume}}$

Its unit is kg/m^3.
- Density of water is maximum at $4°C$.
- The **relative density** is defined as the ratio of the density of the substance to the density of water at $4°C$ i.e.

Relative density

$$= \frac{\text{Density of substance}}{\text{Density of water at } 4°C}$$

- Relative density has no unit.
- Relative density is measured by hydrometer.
- Ice floats on water surface as its density $(0.92 \ g/cm^3)$ is lesser than the density of water $(1 \ g/cm^3)$.
- The density of human body is less than the density of water but the density of head is greater than the density of water.

- Therefore, during swimming a person displaces the water with hands and legs and thus total weight of displaced water becomes equal to the weight of the body.
- If ice floating in water in a vessel melts, the level of water in the vessel does not change.
- The density of sea water is more than that of normal water. This explains why it is easier to swim in sea water.

Pascal's Law

- The pressure exerted anywhere at a point of confined fluid is transmitted equally and undiminished in all directions throughout the liquid.
- Hydraulic lift, hydraulic press, hydraulic brake work on the basis of Pascal's law.

BUOYANCY

- The upward force exerted by a fluid on the immersed body is called buoyant force or upthrust. The upthrust acts at the centre of gravity of the liquid displaced by the submerged part of the body that is called the **centre of buoyancy**.
- Buoyant force depends on the density of the fluid and not on the density of body and acts on centre of gravity of displaced fluid.

Archimedes' Principle

- When a solid body is immersed wholly or partially in a liquid, then there is some apparent loss in its weight. This loss in weight is equal to the weight of the liquid displaced by the body.

Law of Floatation

- Whenever a solid body is dipped into a fluid, the fluid exerts force of buoyancy on it, if the force of buoyancy equals to weight of the solid, the solid will remain in equilibrium. This is called **floatation**.
- If density of material of body is equal to density of liquid, the body floats fully submerged in liquid in neutral equilibrium.

- When body floats in neutral equilibrium, the weight of the body is equal to the weight of displaced liquid. The centre of gravity of the body and centre of gravity of the displaced liquid should be on one vertical line for the condition.

SURFACE TENSION (T)

- It is the force (F) acting normally to an unit length (l) of an imaginary line drawn on the surface of liquid.

i.e. $$T = \frac{F}{l}$$

- Its unit is N/m.
- **Cohesive force** It is the intermolecular force of attraction acting between the molecules of the same substance.
- **Adhesive force** It is the intermolecular force of attraction acting between the molecules of different substance.
- The surface tension decreases with rise in temperature and becomes zero at the critical temperature.
- Due to the surface tension, rain drops are spherical in shape.
  - **Warm soup** is tasty because at high temperature its surface tension is low and consequently the soup spreads on all part of the tongue.
  - When **kerosene** oil is sprinkled on water, its surface tension decreases.

Some Phenomena Based on Surface Tension

- Small drops of **mercury** are spherical, while large ones are flat.
- Formation of **lead shots**.
- Floatation of needle on water.
- Dancing of camphor on water.
- Bigger bubbles can be formed from the soap solution easily than from water.
- Detergent helps in cleaning the clothes.

CAPILLARITY

- **Capillary tube** A long glass tube of very fine (hair like) bore is called capillary tube.
- The phenomenon of rise or fall of liquids in a capillary tube is called capillarity.
- The liquids which wet glass and for which the angle of contact is acute rise up in the capillary tube, while those which do not wet glass, for which the angle of contact is obtuse are fall down in the capillary tube.

Note *The angle of contact is zero for pure water and clean glass. It is 90° for water and silver, 8° for ordinary water and glass and 135° for mercury and glass.*

Some Practical Examples of Capillarity

- The **kerosene oil** in a lantern and the melted wax in a candle, rise in the capillaries formed in the cotton wick and thus they are burnt.
- **Writing nib** is split in the middle so that a fine capillary is formed in it. When it is dipped in ink the ink rises in the capillary.
- The **water** given to the fields rises in the innumerable capillaries formed in the stems of plants and trees and reaches the branches and the leaves.
- The farmers **plough their fields** after rains so that the capillaries formed in the soil are broken and the water remains in the lower layers of the soil.

VISCOSITY

- It is the property of the liquid by virtue of which it opposes the relative motion between its adjacent layers.
- Viscosity of an ideal fluid is zero.
- Viscosity is the property of both liquids and gases. With rise in temperature, viscosity of liquids decreases and that for gases increases.
- Viscosity of gases is much less than that of liquids.
- Viscosity of liquid increases with increase in pressure.
- Viscosity of a fluid is measured by its coefficient of viscosity. Its SI unit is ($N sm^{-2}$) or pascal-second (Pa-s).

Terminal Velocity

- When a body falls in a viscous medium, its velocity first increases and finally becomes constant. This constant velocity is called terminal velocity.
- Terminal velocity of a **spherical body** falling in a viscous medium is proportional to the square of radius of the body.
- When a **liquid flow** through a pipe, its speed is maximum near axis and minimum near the walls of the pipe.
- According to the equation of continuity the speed of **fluid flow** becomes faster in the narrow pipe.
- **Stream Line Flow or Steady Flow** In this flow velocity at every point in the fluid will remains constant.
- **Turbulent Flow** In this flow, the speed of water is quite high, then the flow becomes irregular.
- **Critical Velocity** The limiting velocity of a liquid above which flow will become turbulent.
- **Principle of Continuity** For a tube of flow, between two points having area of cross-section A_1 and A_2 and velocities v_1 and v_2, between two points $Av =$ Constant, $\Rightarrow$ $A_1v_1 = A_2v_2$

Bernoulli's Theorem

- When an incompressible and non-viscous liquid (or gas) flows in streamlined motion from one place to another, then at every point of its path the total energy per unit volume (pressure energy + kinetic energy + potential energy) remains constant.

  i.e. $p + \rho g h + \frac{1}{2}\rho v^2 = $ constant

  where, $p=$ pressure, $\rho =$ density of fluid, $v=$ velocity of flow, $h=$ height of the tube of flow
- Venturimeter, Pitot tube, Bunsen's burner, atomizer, filter pump and magnus effect are based upon the Bernoulli's theorem.

SIMPLE HARMONIC MOTION

- If a body moves to and fro on a straight line about a fixed position, then its motion is called simple harmonic motion.

  When a particle executing SHM passes through the mean position, then

- no force acts on the particle.
- velocity is maximum.
- acceleration is zero.
- kinetic energy is maximum.
- potential energy is zero.

When a particle executing SHM is at the extreme end, then

- velocity of particle is zero.
- acceleration of the particle is maximum.
- kinetic energy of particle is zero.
- potential energy is maximum.
- restoring force acting on the particle is maximum.

Note

- *In case of spring block system the restoring force $F = -kx$*

  where, x is displacement of the block from mean position and k is spring constant.
- *In case of spring block system, time period of oscillation is given by $T = 2\pi \sqrt{\dfrac{m}{k}}$, where m is mass of the block.*

Periodic Motion

- Any motion which repeats itself after a regular interval of time is called **periodic** or **harmonic motion** and the period of repetition is called **time period**.
- Motion of hands of a clock, motion of Earth around the Sun, motion of the needle of a sewing machine are the examples of periodic motion.

Oscillatory Motion

- If a particle repeats its motion after a regular time intervals about a fixed point, motion is said to be oscillatory or vibratory.
- Motion of piston in an automobile engine, motion of balance wheel of a watch are the examples of oscillatory motion.

Simple Pendulum

- It is a heavy point mass suspended from a rigid support by means of an elastic inextensible string.

- Time period of simple pendulum

$$T = 2\pi \sqrt{\frac{\text{length of pendulum}}{\text{acceleration due to gravity}}}$$

where, l is the length of simple pendulum and g is the acceleration due to gravity.
- The maximum time period of a simple pendulum is 84.6 min.
- A pendulum clock goes slow in summer and fast in winter.
- If a simple pendulum is suspended in a lift descending down with acceleration, then time period of pendulum will increase. If lift is ascending, then time period of pendulum will decrease.
- If a lift falling freely under gravity, then the time period of the pendulum will be infinite. At Moon, the time period of simple pendulum increases, because acceleration due to gravity at Moon decreases.

Resonance

- It is a phenomenon that occurs when a vibrating system or external force drive another system to oscillate with greater amplitude at a specific preferential frequency.

Wave Motion

WAVES

- A wave is a disturbance which propagates energy from one place to the other without the transport of matter.
- These are of two types
  (i) Mechanical waves
  (ii) Electromagnetic waves

Mechanical Waves

- The waves which require material medium (solid, liquid or gas) for their propagation are called mechanical waves or elastic waves.
- *These are of two types*
  1. Longitudinal waves
  2. Transverse waves

Longitudinal Waves

- If the particles of the medium vibrate in the direction of propagation of wave motion, the wave is called longitudinal wave. Waves on springs or sound waves in air are examples of longitudinal waves.

Transverse Waves

- If the particles of the medium vibrates perpendicular to the direction of propagation of wave, the wave is called transverse wave. Waves on strings under tension, waves on the surface of water are examples of transverse waves.

Electromagnetic Waves

- The wave which do not require medium for their propagation i.e. which can propagate even though the vacuum are called electromagnetic wave. They propagate as transverse wave.
- The wavelength range of electromagnetic wave is 10^{-4} m to 10^4 m.
- Cathode rays, canal rays, α-rays, β-rays are not electromagnetic waves. Light and heat waves are examples of electromagnetic waves.

Important Terms Related to Waves

- **Amplitude** Maximum displacement of a vibrating particle of medium from its mean position is called amplitude.
- **Phase** The position of a point in time (instant) on wave form cycle.
- **Wavelength** Wavelength is the distance between any two nearest particle of the medium, vibrating in the same phase.
- **Frequency** Frequency of vibration of a particle is defined as the number of vibrations completed by the particle in one second.

$$\text{Frequency } (f) = \frac{1}{\text{Time Period } (T)}$$

- Velocity of wave (v)

$$= \text{Frequency } (f) \times \text{Wavelength } (\lambda)$$

SOUND WAVE

- It is longitudinal mechanical waves.
- The longitudinal mechanical waves which lie in the range 20 Hz to 20,000 Hz are called **audible** or **sound waves**.
- These are sensitive to human ear.
- The longitudinal mechanical waves having frequencies less than 20 Hz, called **infrasonic**.
- These are produced by earthquakes, volcanic eruption, ocean waves and elephants and whales.
- The longitudinal mechanical waves having frequencies greater than 20000 Hz are called **ultrasonic waves**.
- Human ear cannot detect the ultrasonic waves. But certain creatures like dog, cat, bat, mosquito can detect these waves. Bat produce ultransonic waves.
- Ultrasonic waves are used for sending signals, measuring the depth of sea, cleaning clothes and machinery parts of clocks, removing lamp shoot from chimney of factories and in ultrasonography.

Speed of Sound

- Speed of sound is maximum in solids and minimum in gases.
- Speed of sound in air is 332 m/s, in water is 1483 m/s and in iron is 5130 m/s. Speed of sound basically depends upon elasticity and density of medium.
- When sound enters from one medium to another medium, its speed and wavelength changes but frequency remains unchanged.
- Speed of sound remains unchanged by the increase or decrease of pressure.
- The speed of sound increases with the increase in temperature of the medium. The speed of sound in air increases by 0.61 m/s when the temperature is increased by 1°C.
- The speed of sound is more in humid air than in dry air because the density of humid air is less than the density of dry air.

- The speed of sound in air is very slower as compared to the speed of light in air. Therefore, in rainy season, the flash of lightning is seen first and the sound of thunder is heard a little later.
- The speed of sound in a medium is given by $v = \sqrt{\dfrac{E}{\rho}}$, where, E is modulus of elasticity of the medium, ρ = density

For gases, $v = \sqrt{\dfrac{\gamma p}{\rho}}$

Where, p is pressure and γ is ratio of specific heats.

Characteristics of Sound Waves

Intensity

- Intensity of sound at any point in space is defined as amount of energy passing normally per unit area held around that point per unit time. SI unit of intensity is W/m^2.
- Intensity of sound at a point is inversely proportional to the square of the distance of point from the source and directly proportional to square of amplitude of vibration, square of frequency and density of the medium.
- The loudness depends on intensity as well as upon the sensitivity of the ear.

Pitch

- It is that characteristic of sound which distinguishes a sharp sound from a grave sound.
- Pitch depends upon frequency of sound waves.
- The pitch of female voice is higher than the pitch of male voice.
- The pitch of sound produced by roaring of lion is lower, whereas the pitch of sound produced by mosquito whisper is high.

Quality

It is that characteristic of sound which enables us to distinguish between sounds produced by two source having the same intensity and pitch.

Shock Waves

- A body moving with supersonic speed in air leaves behind it a conical region of disturbance which spreads continuously. Such a disturbance is called shock wave.
- These waves carry huge energy and may even make cracks in window panes or even damage a building.
- The speed of supersonic wave is measured in **mach number**. One **Mach number** is the ratio of speed of source to the speed of sound.

$$\text{Mach number} = \frac{\text{Velocity of source}}{\text{Velocity of sound}}$$

- If Mach number > 1, body is called supersonic.
- If Mach number > 5, body is called hypersonic.
- If Mach number < 1, body is said to be moving with subsonic speed.

Reflection of Sound Wave

- When sound waves incidence on any rigid surface, it returns to its original medium, this is called reflection of sound wave.

Echo

- The repetition of sound due to reflection of sound waves, is called an echo. To hear echo, the minimum distance between the observer and reflector should be 17.2 m. Persistence of ear is 1/10 s.
- At the Moon the echo is not heared due to absence of atmosphere.
- A group of soldiers **on a bridge** are advised not to walk in steps because **their movement** causes the bridge to vibrate. If they walk in step, the frequency of vibration may match the natural frequencey of the bridge structure and thus causing resonance. This resonance of frequencey can cause the bridge to collapse.
- When a gun is fired at a visible distance, the sound heard a little after the smoke is seen because the velocity of light is much higher than that of sound.

Sonar

- It stands for sound navigation and ranging. It is used to measure the depth of a sea, to locate the enemy submarines and shipwrecks .
- The transmitter of a sonar produces pulses of ultrasonic sound waves of frequency of about 50000 Hz.
- The reflected sound waves are received by the receiver.

DOPPLER'S EFFECT

- If there is a relative motion between source of sound and observer, the apparent frequency of sound heard by the observer is different from the actual frequency of sound emitted by the source. This phenomenon is called Doppler's effect.
- When the distance between the source and observer decreases, the apparent frequency increases and *vice-versa*.

Uses

(i) By police to check over speeding of vehicles.

(ii) At airport to guide the aircraft.

(iii) To study heart beats and blood flow in different parts of the body.

HEAT

- It is a form of energy which flows from hotter to colder body by virtue of temperature difference.
- It is due to the kinetic energy of the molecules constituting the body.
- Its units are calorie (cal), kilocalorie (kcal) or joule (J).
- 1 cal = 4.18 J, 1 kcal = 1000 cal

TEMPERATURE

- It is the measurement of hotness or coldness of a body.
- An instrument used to measure the temperature of a body is called a thermometer.
- The normal temperature of a human body is 37° C or 98.4°F.
- − 40° is the temperature at which Celsius and Fahrenheit thermometers read same.

- The clinical thermometer reads from 96°F to 110°F.
- Triple point is the state at which all the three states of matter coexist. The triple point of water is 273.16 K.
- Scales of temperature measurement

$$\frac{C}{5} = \frac{F-32}{9} = \frac{R}{4} = \frac{K-273}{5}$$

- The temperature at which Celsius and Reaumur scale read the same is zero.
- Freezing point of mercury is $-39°C$. Hence, to measure temperature below this temperature, alcohol thermometer is used. Freezing point of alcohol is 115°C.

Pyrometer

- Pyrometer measures the temperature of a body by measuring the radiation emitted by the body.
- It cannot measure temperature below 800°C because at low temperature emission of radiation is very small and cannot be detected.

SPECIFIC HEAT

- It is the amount of heat required to raise the temperature of a unit mass of the substance by 1°C. Its unit is J/kg-°C.
- It is given by $S = \dfrac{Q}{m\Delta\theta}$, where m is the mass Q is amount of heat given to the substance and $\Delta\theta$ is change in temperature.
- Specific heat of water is 4200 $Jkg^{-1}°C^{-1}$ or $1 cal g^{-1}\,°C^{-1}$ which is high in comparison to most other substances. Therefore, water is used as coolant in radiator of vehicle.
- For most substances, the specific heat increases with rise in temperature and assumes a constant value at high temperature.
- The specific heat of water, however decreases with rise in temperature from 0°C to about 4°C after which it increases with temperature.
- Mercury has low specific heat.
- **Latent Heat of Vaporisation** It is the amount of heat required to change the phase of the substance at constant temperature.

- Hot water burns are less severe than that of steam burns because steam has high latent heat.
- Latent heat of fusion of ice is 80 cal/g.
- Latent heat of vaporisation of steam is 536 cal/g.
- Its SI unit is J/kg. Ice at 0°C appears colder than that water at 0°C, because ice takes more heat.
- **Molar Heat Capacity at Constant Pressure** (C_P) It is the amount of heat required to raise the temperature of 1 mole of gas by 1 K at constant pressure.
- **Molar Heat Capacity at Constant Volume** (C_V) It is the amount of heat required to raise the temperature of 1 mole of gas by 1 K at constant volume.

$$C_P - C_V = R \quad \text{(Mayer's relation)}$$

where, R is gas constant = 2 cal $mol^{-1}K^{-1}$

$\gamma = \dfrac{C_P}{C_V}$ = ratio is of specific heat capacities

Thermodynamics

- **Zeroth law of Thermodynamics** If two bodies A and B are separately in thermal equilibrium with the third body C, then A and B will be in thermal equilibrium with each other.
- **First Law of Thermodynamics** The amount of heat given to a system is used up in two ways, first to increase the internal energy and second to do the external work.
- i.e. $dQ = dU$ (internal energy) + dW (work done).
- **Second Law of Thermodynamics** The second law of thermodynamics is the outcome of human experience under which heat energy can be converted into mechanical energy.
- **Kelvin-Planck's Statement** It is impossible to construct a device which operates in a cycle that will take heat from a body and convert it completely into the work without producing any other effect.
- **Clausius Statement** It is impossible to construct a self acting device which operates in a cycle that will transfer heat from a cold body to a hot body without expenditure of work.
- Change in entropy at temperature T. When ΔQ amount of heat exchanged is $\Delta s = \dfrac{\Delta Q}{T}$ its SI unit is J/K.

Thermal Expansion

- It is the increase in size of the body on heating.
- A solid can undergo *three types of thermal expansions*
    1. Linear expansion (expansion in length).
    2. Superficial expansion (expansion in area).
    3. Cubical expansion (expansion in volume).

Note *Almost every liquid expands with the increase in temperature. But when temperature of water is increased from 0°C to 4°C, its volume decreases, after this its volume increases.*

Relation between the coefficients of linear, superficial and cubical expansions: $\alpha : \beta : \gamma = 1 : 2 : 3$

Practical Applications of Thermal Expansions

- **Telephone wires** are given enough gap to allow the wires for contraction in winter.
- An ordinary **pendulum clock** runs faster in winter but slower in summer, because in summer the length of pendulum increases, while in winter it decreases.
- In the **construction of bridges**, ends of steel girders are not fixed but placed on rolls to allow free expansion and contraction in summer and winter respectively to avoid any damage to the bridge.
- A gap is provided between the **iron rails** of the railway track so that rails can easily expand during summer and do not bend.

Humidity

- The amount of water vapour in air is called as humidity.
- The amount of water vapour present in 1 m^3 air is called its absolute humidity.
- The ratio of amount of water vapour (m) actually present in a certain volume of air at a given temperature to the amount of water vapour (M) required to saturate it, is called **Relative Humidity** (R_H).
- Relative humidity is measured by **hygrometer**.
- Relative humidity increases with the increase of temperature.

Transmission of Heat

Transfer of heat from one place to other place is called transmission of heat. There are three processes, by which transmission of heat takes place.

- Conduction
- Convection
- Radiation

Conduction

- In this process heat is transferred without actual movement of the particles of medium.
- In this process path of heat transfer is irregular. In solid, transmission of heat takes place by **conduction process**.
- Mercury though a liquid is heated by conduction and not by convection.

Convection

- In this process, heat is transferred by the actual movement of particles of the medium due to difference in densities of different parts of the medium.
- In liquid and gases transmission of heat takes place by **convection process**. This process is also slow.
- The chimney used in kitchen or in a factory is based on the convection. In rooms ventilators are provided to escape the hot air by the process of convection.

Radiation

It is the quickest way of transmission of heat in which there is no need of medium for transfer of heat. Heat from the Sun reaches the Earth by radiation. In this process, heat is transferred at the speed of light.

Kirchhoff's Law

- Kirchhoff's law signifies that good absorbers are good emitter.
- If a shining metal ball with some black spot on its surface is heated to a high temperature, the shining ball becomes dull but the black spots shines brilliantly because black spot absorbs radiation during heating and emit in dark.

Perfectly Black Body

- A perfectly black body is one which absorbs completely all the radiations falling on its surface, whatever be the wavelength.

Note *Since perfectly black body is a perfect absorber, hence according to Kirchhoff's law, it will also be a perfect radiator.*

Stefan's Law

- The radiant energy emitted by unit area of perfectly black body per unit time is directly proportional to the fourth power of its absolute temperature.

$$E \propto T^4 \Rightarrow E = \sigma T^4$$

where, σ is Stefan's constant and its value is $5.67 \times 10^{-8} \ Wm^{-2}K^{-4}$

Newton's Law of Cooling

- The rate of loss of heat by a body is directly proportional to the difference in temperature between the body and its surrounding.
- **Cooking utensils** are made of aluminium, brass and steel because these substances have low specific heat and high conductivity.
- **In deserts** day temperature are very high and night temperature are extremely low because the specific heat of sand is very low. Therefore it absorbs the heat readily and its temperature raises by a large degree during the day. At night sand radiates the heat equally readily making the temperature loss.
- **Human breath** is visible in winter but not in summer because in winter air is cold and so water vapours present in the human breath condense, making it visible.
- **A thick glass tumbler** often cracks when very hot liquid is poured into it because the inner surface of the thick glass tumbler coming in contact with the hot liquid expands more in comparison with the outer surface which has relatively lower temperature. This unequal expansion of inner and outer surfaces causes the tumbler to crack.
- **Water from a hand pump** is warm in winter and cold in summer because in winter outside temperature is low and in summer outside temperature is higher as compared to the temperature of water obtained from underground which remains practically unchanged due to Earth being bad conductor of heat.

LIGHT

- It is the radiation which makes our eyes able to see the object. Its speed is $3 \times 10^8 \ m/s$.
- It is the form of energy. It is a transverse wave.
- It takes 8 min 19 s to reach on the Earth from the Sun.
- The light reflected from Moon takes 1.28 s to reach Earth.
- It represents the phenomenon of reflection, refraction, interference, differaction, scattering and polarisation.

Reflection of Light

- The return of light into the same medium after striking a surface is called reflection.

Laws of Reflection

There are two laws of reflection

   (i) The angle of incidence is always equal to angle of reflection.

   (ii) The incident ray, normal and reflected ray all lie in the same plane at point of incidence.

Reflection from Plane Mirror

- Size of image is always equal to size of object.
- The image in a plane mirror appears as far behind the mirror as the object is infront of it.
- If the object is displaced by a distance a towards or away from the mirror, then its image will be displaced by a distance a towards or away from the mirror.
- The minimum size of the mirror required to see the full image of an observer is half the height of the observer.
- If the plane mirror is rotated in the plane of incidence by an angle θ, then the reflected ray rotates by an angle 2θ.

- Focal length of plane mirror is infinity. i.e. power of the plane mirror is zero.
- Linear magnification produced by plane mirror is 1.
- When two plane mirrors are kept facing each other at an angle θ and an object is placed between them, then
  (a) Number of images,
  $$n = \left(\frac{360°}{\theta} - 1\right),$$
  if $\frac{360°}{\theta}$ is even or the object lies symmetrically.
  (b) Number of image,
  $$n = \left(\frac{360°}{\theta}\right), \text{ if } \frac{360°}{\theta} \text{ is odd or the}$$
  object lies asymmetrically.

Reflection at Spherical Surface

- Spherical mirrors are the mirrors in which reflecting surface side is spherical.

There are two types of spherical mirrors
  (i) Convex mirror
  (ii) Concave mirror
  Mirror formula is given by $\frac{1}{v} + \frac{1}{u} = \frac{1}{f}$
  u = object distance,
  v = image distance
  f = focal length of the mirror
  Magnification (m)
  $$= \frac{\text{Length (height) of image}}{\text{Length (height) of object}} = \frac{-v}{u}$$

Uses of Mirrors

1. Plane mirrors are used as looking glass.
2. Concave mirror is used as shaving mirrors, used by doctors, shades of table lamp, for search lights.
3. Convex mirror is used as back view mirrors in vehicles, in street lamps etc.

Refraction of Light

- When a ray of light passes from one medium to other, it bends from its path. This phenomenon of bending of light ray is called as refraction of light.
- When a ray of light travels from one medium to another the wavelength and velocity of light changes, but the frequency does not change.

Laws of Refraction

There are two laws of refraction
  (i) The incident ray, the refracted ray and the normal at the point of incidence all lie on the same plane.
  (ii) The ratio of the sine of the angle of incidence to the sine of the angle of refraction is a constant for a given medium
  $$\frac{\sin i}{\sin r} = {}_1\mu_2 = \frac{\mu_2}{\mu_1}$$

where, ${}_1\mu_2$ is called **refractive index** of second medium with respect to first medium.

Image Formation by Concave Mirror

Position of Object	Position of Image	Size of Image	Nature of Image
At infinity	At F	Highly diminished	Real and inverted
Between infinity and C	Between F and C	Diminished	Real and inverted
At C	At C	Same size	Real and inverted
Between F and C	Between infinity and C	Enlarged	Real and inverted
At F	At infinity	Highly enlarged	Real and inverted
Between F and P	Behind the mirror	Enlarged	Virtual and erect

where, C is centre of curvature, P is pole of the mirror and F is focus.

Image Formation by Convex Mirror

Position of Object	Position of Image	Size of Image	Nature of Image
At infinity	At F	Highly diminished	Erect and virtual
Between infinity and pole	Between F and P	Diminished	Erect and virtual

where, F is focus, P is pole and C is centre of curvature.

- **Twinkling of stars** is based upon refraction.
- **Due to refraction**, rivers appear shallow, coin in a beaker filled with water appears raised, pencil in the beaker appear broken.
- At sunset and sunrise, due to refraction, **Sun appears above horizon**, while it is actually below horizon.
- The duration of day appears to be increased by nearly 4 min due to **atmospheric refraction**.
- Writing on a **paper appears lifted** when a glass slab is placed over the paper.
- The refractive index of a medium is maximum for violet colour of light and minimum for red colour of light.
- Refractive index decreases with rise in the temperature.

Total Internal Reflection of Light

- When a light ray goes to rarer medium from denser medium, then as we increase the angle of incidence, angle of refraction also increases. The angle of incidence for which the angle of refraction becomes 90° is called **critical angle**.
- If the angle of incidence in denser medium is greater than critical angle (C), then the ray is reflected back into the denser medium, this phenomenon is called **total internal reflection**. It is necessary for the total internal reflection of light to occur that the light ray should go to rarer medium from denser medium.
- Angle of incidence in denser medium should be greater than critical angle.
- In desert, the phenomena of **mirage** occurs due to total internal reflection.
- The **air bubbles** in glass paper weight appear silvery white due to total internal reflection. **Sparkling of diamond** is due to multiple total internal reflection taking place inside the diamond.

Scattering of Light

- When light ray passes through a medium in which particles are suspended, whose sizes are of the order of wavelength of light, then light on striking these particles, deviated in different directions.

This phenomenon is called scattering of light.

- Red colour of light is scattered least and violet colour of light is scattered most. Therefore, danger signals are of red colour.
- Blue colour of sky is due to scattering of light. The brillant red colour of rising and setting Sun is due to scattering of light.
- Clouds appear white due to scattering of light.

Optical Fibre

It is a device based on total internal reflection by which a light signal can be transferred from one place to the other with a negligible loss of energy.

It is used in testing the internal organs of human body i.e. endoscopy.

Lenses

- Lens is a transparent medium bounded by two curved surfaces. *Lenses are of two types*
  (i) Concave or divergent lens.
  (ii) Convex or convergent lens.

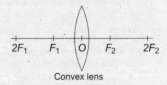

Convex lens

where, O = optical centre
F_1 = first focus
F_2 = second focus

Lens formula is given by $\dfrac{1}{v} - \dfrac{1}{u} = \dfrac{1}{f}$

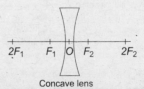

Concave lens

Magnification (m)

$$= \frac{\text{Length (height) of image}}{\text{Length (height) of object}} = \frac{v}{u}$$

Image Formation by a Convex Lens

Position of Object	Position of Image	Size of Image	Nature of Image
At infinity	At F_2	Highly diminished	Real and inverted
Beyond $2F_1$	Between F_2 and $2F_2$	Diminished	Real and inverted
At $2F_1$	At $2F_2$	Same size	Real and inverted
Between $2F_1$ and F_1	Beyond $2F_2$	Enlarged	Real and inverted
At F_1	At infinity	Highly enlarged	Real and inverted
Between F_1 and lens	Behind the object, on the same side of the object	Enlarged	Virtual and erect

Image Formation by a Concave Lens

Position of Object	Position of Image	Size of Image	Nature of Image
At infinity	At F_2	Diminished	Erect and virtual
Between infinity and lens	Between F_2 and lens	Diminished	Erect and virtual

- If the lens is immersed in a medium having refractive index more than that of lens, then the nature of the lens changes i.e. convex lens behaves as convave lens and *vice-versa*.
- If the lens is immersed in a medium having refractive index equal to that of the lens, the lens behaves as a plane glass plate.
- An air bubble in water behaves as a concave lens.

Power of Lens

- It is the reciprocal of focal length of lens. It is measured in metre.

$$P = \frac{1}{f(m)}$$

- Its unit is dioptre (D).

Prism

- It is a uniform transparent refracting medium bounded by two plane surfaces inclined at certain angle.

Dispersion of Light

- When a narrow beam of light is incident on a prism, the emergent beam is not only deviated, but at the same time splits up into a coloured band of seven colours. This phenomenon is called dispersion of light.
- The seven colours of band are violet, indigo, blue, green, yellow, orange and red.
- Violet colour deviates through maximum angle and red colour deviates through the minimum angle.
- Red, green and blue are called primary colours or basic colours.

Mixing of Colours

- Red + Green + Blue = White
- Red + Blue = Magenta
- Blue + Green = Peacock blue (or Cyan)
- Red + Green = Yellow
- If all the colours of white light are reflected back from the object, then it appears white.
- And if all the colours of white light is absorbed by an object, then it appears black.
- **Polarisation** is the only phenomenon which proves that light is a transverse wave.
- The layer of kerosene oil over water surface appear coloured in the presence of sunlight due to proper **interference of light**.

HUMAN EYE

- It is an optical instrument just like a photographic camera. It forms the real image of the object on retina of the eye.
- For the normal eye, the range of vision is from 25 cm to infinity.

Defects of Vision Myopia

- In this case, the person cannot see the distant object clearly.
- Image is formed before the retina. Concave lens is used for correcting myopia.

Hypermetropia

- In this case, the person cannot see near object clearly.
- Image is formed behind the retina.
- Convex lens is used for correcting hypermetropia.

Astigmatism

- In this case, the curvature of cornea becomes irregular and image is not clear. Cylindrical lens is used for correcting astigmatism.

Presbyopia

- In old age the power of accommodation of the eye lens decrease, therefore, neither near nor distant objects are clearly seen. Presbyopia can be removed by using bifocal lenses.

Cataract

- In this defect, an opaque, white membrane is developed on cornea due to which a person loses power of vision partially or completely.
- This defect can be removed by removing this membrane through surgery.

SIMPLE MICROSCOPE

- It consists of a convex lens of short focal length.
- It is used to see the magnified images of very small objects.

$$\text{Magnifying power} = 1 + \frac{D}{f}$$

Compound Microscope

- It consists of two convex lenses.
- In a compound microscope the focal length of the objective lens is short and that of the eyepiece is slightly greater than it. The final image formed by the compound microscope is inverted, magnified and virtual.

$$\text{Magnifying power} = \frac{v_0}{u_0}\left(1 + \frac{D}{f_e}\right)$$

where,

v_0 = distance of image from the objective

u_0 = distance of object from the objective

Telescope

- It is used to see the magnified images of the distant objects.
- There are two types of telescopes
  - (i) Astronomical telescope
  - (ii) Galilean telescope
- In an astronomical telescope, the objective lens is a convex lens of large focal length, but eye-piece is a convex lens of short focal length.

$$\text{Magnifying power} = \frac{f_0}{f_e}\left(1 + \frac{f_e}{D}\right)$$

- In Galilean telescope, the objective lens is a convex lens of large focal length, but the eye-piece is a concave lens of short focal length.

Electricity

Electric Charge

- It is something that a body attains when it loses or gains the electrons.
- The positive and negative labels and sign for electric charges were chosen arbitrarily by **Benjamin Franklin**.
- Similar charges repel each other while opposite charges attract each other.
- Charge is a scalar quantity and its SI unit is coulomb C.
- Electricity is associated with the charge.
- The proton possesses positive charge $(+e)$ and electron possesses an equal negative charge $(-e)$,

where, $e = \pm 1.6 \times 10^{-19} C$

- **Conductors** are those substances which allow passage of electrical charge to flow through them and have very low electrical resistance.
- Metals like silver, iron, copper are conductors.
- Human body and Earth act like a conductor. Silver is the best conductor.
- **Insulators** are those substance which do not allow passage of charge through themselves. Rubber, wood, mica, glass, ebonite are insulators.

Coulomb's Law

The force of attraction or the force of repulsion acting between the two point charges is proportional to the product of the magnitudes of the two charges and inversely proportional to the square of the distance between them.

i.e. $F = \dfrac{1}{4\pi\varepsilon_0}\dfrac{q_1 q_2}{r^2}$

Electric Field

- The region around an electric charge in which the electric effect can be experienced is called the electric field.

Electric Field Intensity (E)

The electric field intensity at any point is the force experienced by a unit positive charge placed at that point.

i.e. Electric field intensity $(E) = \dfrac{F}{q_0}$

where, q_0 is positive test charge

- Electric field intensity inside a charged hollow conductor is zero.
- **Electric Field Lines of Force** Electric field at a place is pictorially represented by these lines. These originate at positive charge and terminate at negative charge.

Electric Potential

- Electric potential at any point of the electric field can be measured by the amount of work done in bringing a unit positive charge from infinity to that point.
- Its unit is volt and it is a scalar quantity.
- The electric potential inside a spherical surface is same at each point and is equal to the potential on the surface.
- Electrical potential on Earth is considered to be zero.
- Work done in bringing a unit positive charge from one point to other point is the **potential difference** between the two points.
- The work done in moving charge on equipotential surface is zero, because potential remains same throughout the surface.

ELECTRICAL CAPACITY

- When a conductor is given a charge, its potential rises in proportion to the charge given, the constant of proportionality is called **capacitance** (C) i.e. $C = \dfrac{Q}{V}$
- Its SI unit is coulomb (C)/volt (V) called **Farad** (F) For capacitances $C_1, C_2, C_3 \ldots$ are in parallel, equivalent capacitance is given by $C = C_1 + C_2 + \ldots + C_n$

  For capacitances in series

  $$\dfrac{1}{C} = \dfrac{1}{C_1} + \dfrac{1}{C_2} + \ldots + \dfrac{1}{C_n}$$
- **Potentiometer** is used to measure the exact potential difference between two points of an electric circuit or to measure the electromotive force (emf) of a cell.

Electric Current

- It is amount of charge that flows per second through a cross-sections of conductor. Current is scalar quantity. Its unit is ampere (A).

Ohm's Law

- It states that the physical conditions (temperature, mechanical strain etc) remaining unchanged, the current (I) flowing through a conductor is always directly proportional to the potential difference. (V) across its two ends.

  i.e. $I \propto V$

  $\Rightarrow \qquad V = IR$

  where, R is a constant called resistance of circuit.

  $$\dfrac{V}{I} = R$$
- SI unit is ohm (Ω).

Resistance

- The ability of material to oppose the electric current through it, is known as its electrical resistance.
- The resistance of a conductor is directly proportional to its length and inversely proportional to its cross-sectional area (A),

  i.e. $R \propto \dfrac{l}{A} \Rightarrow R = \rho\dfrac{l}{A}$.

  where, ρ is the resistivity of material.
- On increasing the temperature of the metal, its resistance increases.

- On increasing the temperature of semi- conductor, its resistance decreases.
- On increasing the temperature of electrolytes, their resistance decreases.
- For resistances in series
$$R = R_1 + R_2 + \ldots + R_n$$
- For resistances in parallel
$$\frac{1}{R} = \frac{1}{R_1} + \frac{1}{R_2} + \ldots + \frac{1}{R_n}$$

Resistivity

- **Specific resistance** or **resistivity** depends only on the material of conductor and its temperature. Resistivity increases with temperature.
- Resistivity of a conductor change with impurity.
- Resistivity of an alloy is greater than the resistivity of its constituents.
- If a wire is stretched or doubled on itself, its resistance will change, but its specific resistance will remain unaffected.

Galvanometer

- It is a device used to detect and measure electric current in a circuit. It can measure current up to 10^{-6} A.
- A galvanometer can be converted into a voltmeter by connecting a very high resistance in its series.

   Note Shunt is a low resistor connected in parallel with a circuit or device that reduces the amount of electric current flowing through it.

Ammeter

- It is a device which is used to measure electric current in a circuit.
- It is connected in series in the circuit.
- The resistance of an ideal ammeter is zero.

Voltmeter

- It is a device used to measure the potential difference between two points in a circuit.
- It is connected in parallel in the circuit.
- The resistance of an ideal voltmeter is infinite.

Important Points

- A lightning conductor is fixed to tall building to protect them from the distructive effect of the lightning.
- The filament of an electric bulb is made of tungston because it has a high melting point and can be heated to a high temperature to emit light.
- An electric bulb makes a bang when it is broken because there is a vacuum inside the electric bulb, when the bulb is broken air rushes in at great speed from all sides to fill the vacuum. The rushing of air produces a noise generally referred to as the bang.

Electric Power

- It is the electric work done by the electric instruments per unit time, i.e. $P = \dfrac{W}{t}$. Its unit is watt.

Kilowatt Hour (kWH)

- It is the unit of energy and is equal to the energy consumed in the rate of 1 kilowatt (1000 J/s) for 1 hour.
- 1 kilowatt hour $= 3.6 \times 10^6$ joule.

Electric Fuse

- It is a small conducting wire of alloy of copper, tin and lead having low melting point and high resistance.
- It is a protective device used in series to prevent the damage due to excess flow of current.
- All electric appliances like bulbs, fans etc are connected in parallel across the live wires and the neutral wires.

Electric Cell

- Electrical cell is a device which converts chemical energy into electrical energy.
- *Electrical Cells are basically of two types*
   (i) Primary cell   (ii) Secondary cell

Primary Cell

- In primary cell electrical energy is obtained from the irreversible chemical reaction taking place inside the cell. After complete discharge, primary cell becomes unserviceable.
- e.g. Voltaic cell, Leclanche cell, Daniel cell, Dry cell etc.

Secondary Cell

- Secondary cells can be charged again and again. Acid and alkali accumulators are the types of secondary cells.

TRANSFORMER

- Transformer is a device which converts low voltage AC into high voltage AC and high voltage AC into low voltage AC. It is based on electromagnetic induction.
- Microphone converts sound energy into electrical energy and works on the principle of electromagnetic induction.
- DC motor is a device which converts electrical energy into mechanical energy. Step-up transformer converts a low voltage of high current into a high voltage of low current. Step-down transfomer converts a high voltage of low current into a low voltage of high current.

> **AC Dynamo** (or generator) is a device used to convert mechanical energy into electrical energy. It works on the principle of electro-magnetic induction.

MAGNETS

- The material which can attract the magnetic substances (such as cobalt, iron and nickel) is called a magnet and the property of attracting the magnetic substance by a magnet is called magnetism.
- The magnets which do not lose their magnetism with normal treatment are called permanent magnets.
- The materials which retain their magnetism for a long time are called hard magnetic materials. When a magnet is freely suspended, it aligns itself in the geographical North-South direction.
- The permanent magnets are made of certain alloys of nickel, cobalt and alloys of iron with some carbon. They are made in various shapes such as bar, rod, disc, ring etc.
- When poles of two magnets are brought close together, they exert force on each other.
- Similar poles repel each other and dissimilar poles attract each other.
- The area surrounding the magnet in which, another magnet experience a force on it is called **magnetic field**. The unit of magnetic field is newton/ampere- metre or weber/ metre^2 or tesla.
- **Magnetic lines of force** are imaginary lines in the magnetic field, which shows the direction of magnetic field continuously.
- The magnetic lines of force outside the magnet always travel from North pole to South pole and inside the magnet from South pole to North pole.

Characteristics of Substance

Diamagnetic Substance	Bismuth, zinc, copper, silver, gold, diamond, mercury, etc.
Paramagnetic Substance	Aluminium, platinum, manganese, sodium, oxygen etc.
Ferromagnetic Substance	Iron, cobalt, nickel, ferric chloride etc.

Permanent Magnet

They are made of steel and temporary magnet or electromagnets are made of soft iron.

The soft iron can be magnetised or demagnetised easily.

Curie Temperature

- As temperature increases, the magnetic property of ferromagnetic substance decreases and above a certain temperature the substance changes into paramagnetic substances. This temperature is called Curie temperature.
- For soft iron, Curie temperature is 1000 K.
- **Magnetic Flux** (ϕ_m) The number of magnetic lines of force crossing a surface normally

$$\phi_m = BA$$

where, B is magnetic field strength and A is area normal to the field lines. Its SI unit is weber.
- **Electromagnetic Induction** The rate of change of magnetic flux through a coil is called induced emf.
- The direction of induced emf will be such that it opposes the cause.

Atomic and Nuclear Physics

Cathode Rays

- Cathode rays are the stream of high speed negatively charged particles moving from cathode to anode in a discharge tube.
- Cathode rays are used in cathode ray oscilloscope and in production of X-rays.

Properties of Cathode Rays

1. Cathode rays travel in straight lines.
2. Cathode rays can ionise the gases.
3. Cathode rays can produce X-rays.
4. Cathode rays can produce fluorescence.
5. Cathode rays can penetrate through thin metal foils
6. Cathode rays are deflected in magnetic field.
7. Cathode rays are deflected in electric field.

Anode Rays or Positive Rays or Canal Rays

- Positive rays are moving positive ions of the gas filled in the discharge tube. The mass of these particles is nearly equal to the mass of the atoms of gas.

Properties of Positive Rays

- These rays travels in straight line.
- These consists of fast moving positively charged particle.
- These rays are deflected in magnetic field and electric field.
- Speed of positive rays is less than that of cathode rays. These rays can affect the photographic plate.
- These rays penetrate through the thin aluminium foil.
- These rays can produce fluorescence and phosphorescence.

X-Rays

These rays were discovered by Roentgen. These rays are electromagnetic in nature.

Properties of X-Rays

- X-rays travels in straight line.
- Speed of X-rays is equal to speed of light. These are not deflected by electric and magnetic fields.
- X-rays produce illumination on falling on fluorscent substances.
- X-rays ionise the gas through which they pass.
- X-rays penetrate through different depth into different substances.
- X-rays shows photoelectric effect.
- X-rays are used in surgery, radio-therapy, engineering department and searching.
- The intensity and the penetrating power of X-rays can be controlled independently.

Photoelectric Effect

The phenomenon of emission of electrons from a metal surface when light of appropriate frequency is incident on it, is called photoelectric effect. The electrons emitted during photoelectric current, are called photoelectrons.

Applications of Photoelectric Cells

- In reproduction of sound in cinema, television and photo telegraphy.
- To control the temperature in furnace and in chemical processes.
- In automatic doors.
- In photoelectric counters.
- In automatic switches for street lights.
- In photoelectric sorters.

Photoelectric Cell

- It is a device based on phenomena of photoelectric effect which converts light energy directly into electric energy.
- Photoelectric effect is based on the law of conservation of energy.

Fluorescence and Phosphorescence

- Fluorescence is the phenomena of emission of light of low frequency from a substance when some light from a source is incident on it.

- While in phosphorescence the substance can emit light for some time even after the source is removed.
- Zinc sulphide exhibit the phenomena of phosphorescence.

RADIOACTIVITY

- **Henry Becquerel**, **Madame Curie** and **Pierre Curie** discovered the phenomenon of radioactivity in 1896 and for this they jointly won Noble prize.The rays emitted by radioactivity were first recognized by Rutherford.
- Radioactivity is a nuclear phenomenon. It is spontaneous emission of radiation from the nucleus.
- The nucleus having protons 83 or more are unstable. They emit α, β particles and γ rays to become stable. The elements of such nucleus are called radioactive elements and the phenomenon of emission of α, β particles and γ rays is called **radioactivity**.
- The penetrating power for α-particle is minimum and for γ-rays is maximum.

Important Points

- The effect on the mass number and atomic number with the emission of α, β and γ rays is decided by Soddy-Fajan law. Radioactivity is detected by G M counter.
- When a radioactive atom emits one α-particle then atomic number of resultant atom decreases by 2 unit and mass number decreases by 4 unit.
- When a radioactive atom emits one β-particle then atomic number of resultant atom increases by 1 unit and mass number remains same.
- When a radioactive atom emits γ-rays the mass number and atomic number remain unchanged.
- **Half-life** of a radioactive material cannot be changed by physical or chemical processes. The percentage of atoms left after one mean life time is equal to 37%.
- **Radioactive carbon-14** is used to measure the age of fossils and plants. In radio carbon dating age is decided by measuring the ratio of $_6C^{12}$ and $_6C^{14}$.

- **Madame Curie** and her husband **Pierre Curie** discovered a new radioactive element radium and found that an ore of uranium is much more radioactive than the pure Uranium. The end product of all natural radioactive element after emission of radioactive rays is lead.

- **Nuclear Fission** The process of the splitting of a heavy nucleus into two or more lighter nucleus is called nuclear Fission.
- **Nuclear Fusion** The process of combining of two lighter nucleus to form one heavy nucleus, is called nuclear fusion. Hydrogen bomb is based on nuclear fusion and it is more destructive than an atom bomb.

Mass-Energy Relation

- Albert Einstein establised a relation between mass and energy on the basis of special theory of relativity in 1905. According to this mass can be converted into energy and *vice-versa.*
  i.e. $E = mc^2$
  where, c is the velocity of light and E is the energy equivalent of mass m.

SEMICONDUCTOR

- The substance in which electric conduction is not possible at a low temperature but on increasing the temperature, electric conduction becomes possible are called the semiconductor.
- At absolute zero kelvin, semiconductor behaves like a perfect insulator.
- The electrical conductivity of a semiconductor increases with the increase in temperature.
- Germanium and silicon are two important semiconductors.
- A pure semiconductor is called **intrinsic semiconductor** and to increase its conductivity a chemical process is performed on it which is called doping.
- In pure semiconductors, impurity must be less than 1 in 10^8 parts of semiconductor.
- An impure semiconductor is called **extrinsic semiconductor**. *These are of two types*
  1. *n*-type   2. *p*-type

n-type Semiconductor

- If pentavalent impurity atom (such as antimony, arsenic, phosphorus etc.) is added to the pure germanium or silicon crystal, the crystal so obtained is called the n-type semiconductor.
- Pentavalent impurities are called donor.

p-type Semiconductor

- If trivalent impurity atom (such as aluminium, boron, gallium etc.) is added to the pure germanium or silicon crystal, the crystal so obtained is called p-type semiconductor.
- Trivalent impurities are called accepter.

p-n Junction

- An arrangement consisting a p-type semiconductor brought into a close contact with n-type semiconductor, is called a p-n junction.
- Rectifier is a device which converts **alternating voltage into direct voltage** or current. Diode valve acts a **rectifier**.
- LEDs are specially designed diode made of GaAsP, GaP and are used in electronic gadgets as indicator light.
- Zener diode is a highly doped p-n junction diode which is not damaged by high reverse current.

Noble Prize

- **2016** The Noble Prize in Physics 2016 was awarded to David J. Thouless, F. Duncan, M. Haldane and J. Michael Kosterlitz for "theoretical discoveries of topological phase transitions and topological phases of matter."
  These theoretical discoveries revealed the possibility of a bizarre world where matter can take on different and strange stages.
- **2015** The Nobel prize is Physics 2015 was jointly awarded to Takaaki Kajita and Arthur B. MC.Donald "for the discovery of neutrino oscillations, which shows that neutrinos have mass".
- **2014** The Noble prize in Physics 2014 was awarded jointly to Isamu Akasaki, Hiroshi Amano and Shiji Nakamura, for inventing a new energy efficient and environment friendly light source-the blue Light Emitting Diode (LED).

TRANSISTOR

It is a combination of two p-n junctions joined in series. Transistors are of two types : n-p-n junction transistor and p-n-p junction transistor

- Triode valve can be used as amplifier, oscillator, transmitter and detector.

- Air bubble rises up in water because of upthrust and its potential energy decreases.
- When **two protons** are brought towards each other they repel each other being similar charges, thus work is done by us in bringing them close. So, potential energy increases.
- When the energy of the **satellite is negative**, it moves in either a circular or an elliptical orbit. When the energy of **satellite is zero,** it escapes away from its orbit and its path becomes parabolic.
- When the energy of a **satellite is positive**, it escapes from the orbit following a hyperbolic path. When the **height of the satellite is increased,** its potential energy increases and kinetic energy decreases.

NANOTECHNOLOGY

- **Nanotechnology** is the study of manipulating matter on an atomic and molecular scale. Generally nanotechnology deals with strcutures sized between 1 to 100 nanometre in at least one dimension, and involves developing materials or devices within that size.
- The term nanotechnology was defined by **Tokyo University of Science** Professor Norio Taniguchi in a 1974 paper as follows: "Nanotechnology mainly consists of the processing, separation, consolidation, and deformation of materials by one atom or by one molecule."
- **Molecular nanotechnology** sometimes called molecular manufacturing, describes engineered nanosystems (nanoscale machines) operating on the molecular scale. Molecular nanotechnology is especially associated with the molecular assembler, a machine that can produce a desired structure or device atom-by-atom using the principles of mechnosynthesis.

- **Spintronics** a technology that exploits the intrinsic spin of the electron and it associated with magnetic with moment, in addition to its fundamental electronic charge, in solid-state devices.
- **Diamondoids** Non-scale molecules with characteristic diamond structure isolated from petroleum.
- Grey Goo is hypothetical end-of-the-world scenario involving molecular nanotechnology in which out of control self- replicating robots consume all matter on earth, while building more of themselves.
- Carbon nanotubes and nanofibers are molecular-scale tubes of graphitic carbon with outstanding properties.
- Nano computing is the technique of computing by using the various nano components.

Units of Measurement

Quantity	Unit (SI)	Quantity	Unit (SI)
Volume	Cubic metre	Heat	Joule
Acceleration	Metre/second^2	Absolute temperature	Kelvin
Density	Kilogram/metre^3	Resistance	Ohm
Momentum	Kilogram metre/second	Electromotive force	Volt
Work	Joule	Electrical conductivity	Mho/metre
Energy	Joule	Electric energy	Kilo watt hour
Pressure	Pascal or Newton/metre^2	Electric power	Kilo watt or watt
Frequency	Hertz	Magnetic intensity	Orsted
Power	Watt	Charge	Coulomb
Weight	Newton or Kilogram	Magnetic induction	Gauss
Impulse	Newton-second	Intensity of sound	Decibel
Angular velocity	Radian /second	Power of lens	Dioptre
Viscosity	Poise	Depth of sea	Fathom
Surface tension	Newton/metre		

Important Laws/Theories and their Scientist

Laws/Theories	Scientist
Gravitational Law, Laws of Motion	Newton
Theory of Relativity	A. Einstein
Discovery of X-ray	WC Rontgen
Principle of Lever, Relative Density	Archimedes
Kinetic Theory of Temperature	Kelvin
Theory of an Atom	Dalton
Laws of Electrolysis	M Faraday

Important Scientific Instruments

Instrument	Use
Altimeter	It measures altitudes and is used in aircrafts.
Ammeter	It measures strength of electric current (in ampere).
Audiometer	It measures intensity of sound.
Barometer	It measures atmospheric pressure.
Binocular	It is used to view distant objects.

Instrument	Use
▪ Calorimeter	It measures quantity of heat.
▪ Cardiogram	It traces movements of the heart, recorded on a cardiograph.
▪ Chronometer	It determines longitude of a place kept on board ship.
▪ Cinematography	It is an instrument used in cinema making.
▪ Dynamo	It converts mechanical energy into electrical energy.
▪ Dynamometer	It measures electrical power.
▪ Electrometer	It measures electricity.
▪ Electroscope	It detects presence of an electric charge.
▪ Endoscope	It examines internal parts of the body.
▪ Fathometer	It measures the depth of the ocean.
▪ Galvanometer	It measures the electric current of low magnitude.
▪ Hydrometer	It measures the specific gravity of liquids.
▪ Hygrometer	It measures humidity in air.
▪ Hydrophone	It measures sound under water.
▪ Lactometer	It determines the purity of milk.
▪ Manometer	It measures the pressure of gases.
▪ Mariner's compass	It is an instrument used by the sailors to determine the direction.
▪ Microphone	It converts the sound waves into electrical vibrations.
▪ Microscope	It is used to obtain magnified view of small objects.
▪ Odometer	It is an instrument by which the distance covered by wheeled vehicles is measured.
▪ Phonograph	It is an instrument for producing sound.
▪ Photometer	This instrument compares the luminous intensity of the source of light.
▪ Periscope	It is used to view objects above sea level (used in sub-marines).
▪ Radar	It is used for detecting the direction and range of an approaching plane by means of radio microwaves.
▪ Radiometer	It measures the emission of radiant energy.
▪ Seismograph	It measures the intensity of earthquake shocks.
▪ Salinometer	It determines salinity of solution.
▪ Spectrometer	It is an instrument for measuring the energy distribution of a particular type of radiation.
▪ Speedometer	It is an instrument placed in a vehicle to record its speed.
▪ Sphygmomanometer	It measures blood pressure.
▪ Spherometer	It measures the curvatures of surfaces.
▪ Stereoscope	It is used to view two dimensional pictures.
▪ Stethoscope	An instrument which is used by the doctors to hear and analyse heart and lung sounds.
▪ Stroboscope	It is used to view rapidly moving objects.
▪ Tachometer	An instrument used in measuring speeds of aeroplanes and motor boats.
▪ Telescope	It views distant objects in space.
▪ Thermometer	This instrument is used for the measurement of temperatures.
▪ Thermostat	It regulates the temperature at a particular point.
▪ Voltmeter	It measures the electric potential difference between two points.

Inventions and Discoveries

Invention	Year	Inventor	Country
Adding machine	1642	Pascal	France
Aeroplane	1903	Orville & Wilbur Wright	USA
Air conditioning	1902	Carrier	USA
Airplane (Jet engine)	1939	Ohain	Germany
Airship (Non-rigid)	1852	Henri Giffard	France
Atomic bomb	1945	J Robert Oppenheimer	USA
Ball-point pen	1888	John J Loud	USA
Barometer	1644	Evangelista Torricelli	Italy
Battery (Electric)	1800	Alessandro Volta	Italy
Bicycle	1839-40	Kirkpatrick Macmillan	Britain
Bicycle tyres (Pneumatic)	1888	John Boyd Dunlop	Britain
Bifocal lens	1780	Benjamin Franklin	USA
Bleaching powder	1798	Tennant	Britain
Bunsen burner	1855	R Willhelm von Bunsen	Germany
Burglar alarm	1858	Edwin T Holmes	USA
Camera (Kodak)	1888	Walker Eastman	USA
Car (Steam)	1769	Nicolas Cugnot	France
Car (Petrol)	1888	Karl Benz	Germany
Carburetor	1876	Gottlieb Daimler	Germany
Cassette (Videotape)	1969	Sony	Japan
Cement (Portland)	1824	Joseph Aspdin	Britain
Cinema	1895	Nicolas & Jean Lumiere	France
Clock (Mechanical)	1725	I-Hsing & Liang Ling-Tsan	China
Clock (Pendulum)	1656	Christian Huygens	Netherlands
Compact disc	1972	RCA	USA
Compact disc player	1979	Sony, Philips	Japan, Netherlands
Computer (Laptop)	1987	Sinclair	Britain
Computer (Mini)	1960	Digital Corp	USA
Diesel engine	1895	Rudolf Diesel	Germany
Dynamo	1832	Hypolite Pixii	France
Electric flat iron	1882	H W Seeley	USA
Electric lamp	1879	Thomas Alva Edison	USA
Electric motor (DC)	1873	Zenobe Gramme	Belgium
Electric motor (AC)	1888	Nikola Tesla	USA
Electric iron	1882	Henry W Seely	USA
Electric washing machine	1906	Alva J Fisher	USA
Electro-magnet	1824	William Sturgeon	Britain
Electron	1897	Thomson J	Britain
Electroplating	1805	Luigi Brugnatelli	Italy
Electronic computer	1824	Dr Alan M Turing	Britain

Invention	Year	Inventor	Country
▪ Facsimile machine	1843	Alexander Bain	Britain
▪ Fibre optics	1955	Kepany	Britain
▪ Film (Moving outlines)	1885	Louis Prince	France
▪ Film (Talking)	1922	J Engl, J Mussolle & H Vogt	Germany
▪ Galvanometer	1834	Andre-Marie Ampere	France
▪ Gramophone	1878	Thomos Alva Edison	USA
▪ Helicopter	1924	Etienne Oehmichen	France
▪ Hydrogen bomb	1952	Edward Teller	USA
▪ Intelligence testing	1905	Simon Binet	France
▪ Jet engine	1937	Sir Frank Whittle	Britain
▪ Laser	1960	Theodore Maiman	USA
▪ Launderette	1934	J F Cantrell	USA
▪ Lift (Mechanical)	1852	Elisha G Otis	USA
▪ Lighting conductor	1752	Benjamin Franklin	USA
▪ Loudspeaker	1900	Horace Short	Britain
▪ Machine gun	1918	Richard Gatling	Britain
▪ Magnetic recording tape	1928	Fritz Pfleumer	Germany
▪ Microphone	1876	Alexander Graham Bell	USA
▪ Microscope (Comp.)	1590	Z Janssen	Netherlands
▪ Microscope (Elect.)	1931	Ruska Knoll	Germany
▪ Microwave oven	1947	Percy LeBaron Spencer	USA
▪ Motor cycle	1885	G Daimler	Germany
▪ Movie projector	1893	Thomas Edison	USA
▪ Neon lamp	1910	Georges Claude	France
▪ Neutron bomb	1958	Samuel Cohen	USA
▪ Optical fibre	1955	Narinder Kapany	Germany
▪ Pacemaker	1952	Zoll	USA
▪ Photoelectric cell	1893	Julius Elster, Hans F Geitel	Germany
▪ Photography (On metal)	1826	J N Niepce	France
▪ Photography (On paper)	1835	WH Fox Talbot	Britain
▪ Photography (On film)	1888	John Carbutt	USA
▪ Piano	1709	Cristofori	Italy
▪ Pistol, revolver	1836	Colt	USA
▪ Radar	1922	AH Taylor & Leo C Young	USA
▪ Radiocarbon dating	1947	Libby	USA
▪ Radio telegraphy	1864	Dr Mohlon Loomis	USA
▪ Radio telegraphy (Trans Atlantic)	1901	G Marconi	Italy
▪ Rayon	1883	Sir Joseph Swan	Britain
▪ Razor (Electric)	1931	Col Jacob Schick	USA
▪ Razor (Safety)	1895	King C Gillette	USA
▪ Refrigerator	1850	James Harrison, Alexander catlin	USA

Invention	Year	Inventor	Country
Rubber (Latex foam)	1928	Dunlop Rubber Co	Britain
Rubber (Tyres)	1846	Thomas Hancock	Britain
Rubber (Vulcanised)	1841	Charles Goodyear	USA
Rubber (Waterproof)	1823	Charles Macintosh	Britain
Safety pin	1849	Walter Hunt	USA
Ship (Steam)	1775	I C Perier	France
Ship (Turbine)	1894	Hon Sir C Parsons	Britain
Steam engine	1698	Thomas Savery	Britain
Steam engine (Piston)	1712	Thomas Newcomen	Britain
Steam engine (Condenser)	1765	James Watt	Britain
Steel (Stainless)	1913	Harry Brearley	Britain
Stethoscope	1819	Laennec	France
Submarine	1776	David Bushnell	USA
Super computer	1976	JH Van Tassel	USA
Tank	1914	Sir Emest D Swington	Britain
Tape recorder	1899	Fessenden Poulsen	Denmark
Telegraph	1787	M Lammond	France
Telegraph code	1837	Samuel F B Morse	USA
Telephone (Cellular)	1947	Bell Labs	USA
Telephone (Imperfect)	1849	Antonio Meucci	Italy
Telephone (Perfected)	1876	Alexander Graham Bell	USA
Telescope	1608	Hans Lippershey	Netherlands
Television (Mechanical)	1926	John Logie Baird	Britain
Television (Electronic)	1927	PT Farnsworth	USA
Television (Colour)	1928	John Logie Baird	Britain
Transformer	1831	Michael Faraday	Britain
Transistor	1948	Bardeen, Shockley & Brattain	USA
Transistor radio	1955	Sony	Japan
Uranium Fission (Atomic reactor)	1942	Szilard Fermi	USA
Vacuum cleaner (Elec.)	1907	Spangler	USA
Video tape	1956	Charles Ginsberg	USA
Washing machine (Elec.)	1907	Hurley Machine Co	USA
Watch	1462	Bartholomew Manfredi	Italy
Wireless (Telegraphy)	1896	G Marconi	Italy

CHEMISTRY

MATTER AND ITS STATES

MATTER

- Matter is anything which has mass and occupies space.
- It exists in five states, *viz*, solid, liquid, gas, plasma and Bose-Einstein condensate. Out of which the former three are commonly seen.

States of Matter

The five states of matter are discussed below

Solids

- They have definite volume and definite shape.
- They are incompressible and have strongest intermolecular interactions.
- They are very dense as compared to liquid and gas. *e.g.,* wood, stone, iron, etc.

Melting Point

- It is a temperature at which a substance converts from its solid state to liquid state. Melting point of ice is $0°\,C$.
- Melting point decreases in the presence of impurity.

Sublimation

- It is the process of conversion of a substance from the solid state to the gas state without passing through an intermediate liquid phase.
- It is used to separate a sublimate (substance undergoing sublimation like camphor, naphthalene, ammonium chloride, etc) from non-sublimate.

Liquids

- They have definite volume but no definite shape. They take the shape of the vessel in which they are kept.
- They can flow, hence, considered as fluids e.g., milk, water, mercury, etc.

Boiling Point

- It is a temperature at which vapour pressure of a liquid becomes equal to atmospheric pressure and at which a substance converts from its liquid state to gaseous state.
- It is different at different places.
- Boiling point of water at normal conditions is $100°C$.
- It usually decreases at high altitudes, that's why, at high altitudes, the boiling point of water is less than $100°C$ and more time is required to cook a food.
- Boiling point of water in pressure cooker is high due to high pressure and hence, less time is required to cook the food.
- Boiling point increases in the presence of impurity.

Evaporation

- It is the process of conversion of a liquid into vapours at any temperature below its boiling point. It increases with increase in surface area and temperature.
- It produces cooling. That's why we feel cool when some nail polish remover or spirit is kept on our palm.

Gases

- They have neither definite volume nor definite shape. They take the shape and volume of the container in which they are filled.
- They are highly compressible.
- They can flow so considered as fluids, e.g., air, oxygen and nitrogen.

Condensation

- It is the process of conversion of gas into liquid or liquid into solid
- Solids, liquids and gases are inter convertible by changing the conditions of temperature and pressure.

$$\text{Solid} \underset{\text{cool}}{\overset{\text{heat}}{\rightleftharpoons}} \text{Liquid} \underset{\text{cool}}{\overset{\text{heat}}{\rightleftharpoons}} \text{Gas}$$

Plasma

- The fourth state of matter is called plasma. This state contains ionised gas with super energetic and super excited particles.
- Fluorescent tube contains helium (He) gas and neon (Ne) gas. Sign bulb contains neon (Ne) gas.

Bose-Einstein Condensate

- In 1924-25, Satyendra Nath Bose and Albert Einstein gave the information about Bose-Einstein condensate. It is a state of matter of a dilute gas of boson cooled up to temperature which is very close to absolute zero or -273.15°C. In fact, it is a fifth state of matter.

Particles of Matter

Atoms

- It is the smallest particle of matter that takes part in chemical reactions. (by Dalton's atomic theory).
- It can neither be created nor destroyed (law of conservation of mass given by Lavoisier).
- It does not exist in free state and has a fixed atomic mass e.g., iron (Fe), gold (Au), silver (Ag), etc.

Molecules

- These are the smallest part of the matter that exist in free state.
- They are formed by the joining of two or more atoms in fixed ratio (law of multiple proportions given by Dalton).
- They have fixed molecular mass which is obtained by adding the atomic masses of all the atoms present in a molecule, e.g., water (H_2O), ammonia (NH_3), carbon dioxide (CO_2), etc.

Pure Substances

A substance is said to be pure if all the constituent particles of that substance are the same in their chemical nature. e.g., all the elements and compounds are pure substances.

Elements

- They contain only single type of atoms. Elements combine to give molecules.
- Examples of elements are sulphur, phosphorus, oxygen etc.
- Elements known at present are 118. Out of which 94 are natural. Elements which are liquid at room temperature are mercury (Hg) and bromine (Br).
- Elements which become liquid at a temperature slightly above the room temperature (303 K) are gallium (Ga) and caesium (Cs).
- Elements have the following order of abundance in earth crust : Oxygen > silicon > aluminium > iron > calcium.
- Elements have the following order of abundance in human body : Oxygen > carbon > hydrogen > nitrogen.

Compounds

- These contain more than one kind of atoms. These cannot be separated into constituent atoms by simple physical methods.
- Their examples are silica (SiO_2), water (H_2O), sugar ($C_{12}H_{22}O_{11}$), salt (NaCl), etc.

Impure Substances

A substance is said to be impure, if all the constituent particles of that substance are not same in their chemical nature.

Mixtures

- These are obtained by mixing two or more substances in any proportion.
- Mixtures can be homogeneous, *i.e.*, have uniform composition throughout (*e.g.*, salt solution, sugar solution, air, true solutions, etc) or heterogeneous, *i.e.*, have non-uniform composition (e.g., mixture of salt and sugar, colloidal solutions, etc).

Solutions or True Solutions

- These are homogeneous mixtures of two or more substances.
- A solution contain two components : solute (in less quantity) and solvent (in more quantity). Examples of solutions are sugar solution, tincture of iodine (solution of iodine in alcohol), aerated drinks like soda water, air, alloys, etc.
- Concentration of solution may be expressed by percentage, mole fraction, parts per million, gram per litre, molarity molality, normality, etc.

Colloidal Solutions

These are heterogeneous mixtures.

These contain two phases, i.e., dispersed phase and dispersion medium.

- These can scatter light because of the presence of large solute particles, i.e., they show **Tyndall effect** and **Brownian movement**.
- **Blue colour of sky** is also due to scattering of light by dust particles suspended in air.
- They are separated by special technique like centrifugation.
- Colloidal solutions are coagulated by adding an electrolyte.
- Colloidal solutions are purified by dialysis, which is also used in the purification of blood with the help of artificial kidney machine.
- **Coagulation** found its use in purification of water by alum, stop bleeding by $FeCl_3$, formation of delta at the junction of sea and river.
- They are of following types on the basis of dispersed phase and dispersion medium.

Dispersed phase	Dispersion medium	Type of colloid	Examples
Liquid	Gas	Aerosol	Fog, clouds, mist
Solid	Gas	Aerosol	Smoke, automobile exhaust
Gas	Liquid	Foam	Shaving cream
Liquid	Liquid	Emulsion	Milk, face-cream
Solid	Liquid	Sol	Milk of magnesia, mud
Gas	Solid	Foam	Foam, rubber, sponge, pumice stone
Liquid	Solid	Gel	Jelly, cheese, butter
Solid	Solid	Solid sol	Coloured gemstone, milky glass

Separation of Mixtures

A number of physical and chemical methods are used to separate the number of mixtures. *Some important methods are discussed below*

Centrifugation

- It is based upon the principle that the denser particles are forced to the bottom and the lighter particles stay at the top when spun rapidly.
- It is used in diagnostic laboratories for blood and urine tests, in dairies and home to separate butter from cream, in washing machine to squeeze out water from wet clothes, etc.

Distillation

- It is a method of separating mixtures based on differences in volatilities of components in a boiling liquid mixture.
- It is used to separate mixtures of ether and toluene, benzene and aniline, etc.

Fractional Distillation

- It is used to separate liquids having very less difference in their boiling points.
- It is used to obtain pure diesel, petrol, kerosene oil, coaltar, etc from crude oil or mineral oil.
- It is used to separate a mixture of acetone (329 K) and methyl alcohol (338 K).

Vacuum Distillation

- It is also known as distillation under reduced pressure.
- It is used for the substances which decomposes below their boiling point.
- It is used to obtain glycerol and H_2O_2 and to concentrate sugarcane juice in sugar industry.

Steam Distillation

- It is used to separate a steam volatile compound from non-volatile or non-steam volatile compounds.
- It is used to purify sandalwood oil, terpentine oil, aniline, nitrobenzene, etc.

Crystallisation

- It is used to separate a mixture of inorganic solids with the help of suitable solvent.
- Their examples include separation of a mixture of sugar and salt by using ethyl alcohol.

Chromatography

- It is the modern technique used for separation and purification of organic compounds. It was discovered by Tswett.
- It is used for the separation of coloured pigments from a plant.

Reverse Osmosis

- It is a technique in which solvent molecules move from the solution of higher concentration to the solution of lower concentration when these are separated by semipermeable membrane and excess pressure is applied to the solution of higher concentration.
- It is used for desalination of sea water.

Physical Change

- It is the change which only affect the physical properties like colour, hardness, density, melting point, etc., of matter.
- It does not affect the composition and chemical properties of matter.
- Examples of physical changes are crystallisation, sublimation, boiling, vaporisation, cutting of trees, dissolving common sugar in water, etc.

Chemical Change

- These affect the composition as well as chemical properties of matter and result in the formation of a new substance.
- Their examples are burning of fuel, burning of candle, electrolysis of water, burning of paper, photosynthesis, ripening of fruits, etc.

Mole Concept

It states that the number of molecules present in 12 g of C-12 is called one mole. *i.e.,* $1 \text{ mol} = 6.023 \times 10^{23}$

$$= \text{Avogadro's number } (N_A)$$

e.g., 1 mole of atom =
$$= \text{gram atomic weight}$$
$$= 6.023 \times 10^{23} \text{ atoms}$$

Number of moles
$$= \frac{\text{Mass (in gram)}}{\begin{array}{c}\text{Atomic weight}\\\text{(or molecular weight)}\end{array}}$$

GAS LAWS

Mass (m), Volume (V), pressure (p) and temperature (T) of a gas are the measurable properties. The laws which inter-relate these properties are called gas laws.

Boyle's Law

- At constant temperature, the pressure of a fixed amount of gas (number of moles) is inversely proportional to its volume.
- The mathematical equation is

$$p \propto \frac{1}{V} \quad or \quad pV = k \quad or \quad p_1V_1 = p_2V_2$$

$$p = \text{Pressure of the gas},$$
$$V = \text{Volume of the gas},$$
$$k = \text{Constant}$$

Charles' Law

- At constant pressure, volume of a fixed mass of a gas is directly proportional to its absolute temperature.
- This law can be written as $V \propto T$

where, V is the volume of the gas,
T is the absolute temperature.

Gay Lussac's law

At constant volume, pressure of a fixed amount of a gas varies directly with temperature, i.e. $p \times T$ or $\frac{p}{T} = K$ or $\frac{P_1}{T_1} = \frac{P_2}{T_2}$

(K = constant).

Combined Gas Law or Ideal Gas Equation

- It is a gas law which combines Charles' law, Boyle's law and Gay-Lussac's law.
- This law can be stated mathematically as,

$$\frac{pV}{T} = R \; ; \; pV = RT$$

where, R = Universal gas constant

For n moles of the gas, $pV = nRT$

Avogadro's Law

- It states that equal volumes of all gases at the same temperature and pressure contains the equal number of molecules.
- It is stated mathematically as,

$$V \propto n \text{ or } V = kn$$

  V = Volume of the gas,

  n = Number of moles of the gas,

  k = Proportionality constant

Graham's Law of Diffusion

According to this law, "the rate of diffusion of a gas is inversely proportional to the square root of its density."

$$\frac{r}{r} = \sqrt{\frac{d_2}{d_1}} = \sqrt{\frac{M_2}{M_1}}; \quad \left(d = \frac{M}{V}\right)$$

where, r_1 is the rate of diffusion for the first gas (volume or number of moles per unit time).

r_2 is the rate of diffusion for the second gas.

d_1 is the density of gas 1.

d_2 is the density of gas 2.

M_1 is the molar mass of gas 1.

M_2 is the molar mass of gas 2.

Dalton's Law of Partial Pressures

It states that the total pressure exerted by a gaseous mixture of two or more non-reacting gases is equal to the sum of the partial pressures of each individual component in the gas mixture.

$$p_{total} = p_1 + p_2 + \quad + p_n$$

Ideal and Real Gases

- Ideal gases follow gas laws in all conditions of temperature and pressure.
- Real gases follow gas laws only at high temperature and low pressure.

Critical Temperature

- It is the temperature above which a gas cannot be liquefied.

  At STP,

$$p = 1 \text{ atm} = 760 \text{ mm Hg}$$
$$T = 273 \text{ K} = 0°C$$

- Volume of one mole of all the gases

  $= 22.40 \text{ L} = 22400 \text{ mL}$

ATOMIC STRUCTURE

Modern Atomic Theory

According to this theory, 'atom is made up of three fundamental particles called electrons, protons and neutrons.'

Discovery of Cathode Rays and Electrons ($_{-1}e^0$)

- These rays were discovered by Sir Julius Plucker.
- These originate from cathode and travels in a straight line towards anode.
- Cathode rays cause mechanical motion, i.e., they consists of material particles.
- These rays carry negative charge and generate X-rays.
- Electron was discovered by JJ Thomson. [It's antiparticle is positron ($_{+1}e^0$)].
- It has mass 9.1×10^{-31} kg or 0.00054 u.
- It has charge -1.6×10^{-19} C (by Millikan's oil drop experiment).

Discovery of Anode Rays and Protons ($_1H^1$ or P)

- These rays were discovered by Goldstein (also called positive rays).
- These do not originate from anode.
- These are positively charged and have velocity less than cathode rays.
- Proton was discovered by Rutherford.
- It is positively charged.
- It is present in the nucleus.
- It has charge $+1.6 \times 10^{-19}$ C and mass 1.672×10^{-27} kg or 1.00727 u.
- It has mass 1836 times than that of the electron.

Discovery of Neutron ($_0n^1$)

- It was discovered by Chadwick.
- It has zero charge and 1.674×10^{-27} kg or .00867u mass.
- It is present inside the nucleus. Its antiparticle is antineutrino.
- **Hydrogen** is the only atom in which neutrons are not present.
- **Electromagnetic forces** bind electrons with the nucleus.

- Atoms having same number of electrons and protons are neutral. If electrons are less than proton, the atom carries positive charge and if electrons are more than proton, the atom carries negative charge.

Discovery of Nucleus

- The model known as Rutherford's Model, was based upon α-particle scattering experiment and suggests that most of the part of an atom is empty.
- It also suggests that the entire mass of an atom is concentrated on its centre at the nucleus. The nucleus is surrounded by electrons that move around the nucleus with a very high speed in circular paths called orbits.
- It contains protons and neutrons which are collectively called nucleons.

Characteristics of Atom
Atomic Number (Z)

- It is equal to the number of protons.
- It is equal to the number of electrons in neutral atom.
- It is written as a subscript to the left of the symbol of the atom, e.g., $_6C$ here 6 is the atomic number of carbon (C).

Mass Number

- It is equal to the sum of number of protons and number of neutrons.
- It is written as a superscript to the right of the symbol of the atom, e.g., C^{12} here 12 is the mass number of carbon (C).

> Mass number = Number of protons + Number of neutrons = Atomic number + Number of neutrons = Number of electrons + Number of neutrons (in case of neutral atom)

Different Atomic Species
Isotopes

- These have same atomic number but different mass number. e.g., isotopes of hydrogen e.g., $_1H^1$, P (protium), $_1H^2$ or (deuterium) and $_1H^3$ or T (tritium). T is radioactive.
- Isotopes of polonium are maximum.
- **Hydrogen** (H-1) is the lightest isotope and lead-208 is the heaviest isotope (with mass 207.974).

Isobars

- These have the same mass number, but different atomic number.
- $_{18}Ar^{40}$, $_{19}K^{40}$, $_{20}Ca^{40}$ are isobars.

Isotones

These have same number of neutrons, e.g., $_1H^3$ and $_2He^4$ as both have two neutrons.

Various Models and Theories
Niels Bohr Model

This model suggests that the electrons are confined into clearly defined, quantised orbits and could jump between these, but could not freely spiral inward or outward in intermediate states.

Planck's Quantum Theory

According to this theory

1. Atoms and molecules could emit or absorb energy only in the form of discrete packets of energy called quanta.
2. The energy of quantum (E) is proportional to its frequency (v),

   e.g., $E = hv$

   where, h = Planck's constant
   $(6.626 \times 10^{-34}$ Js)

3. The energy is quantised (multiple of nhv)

de-Broglie Concept

It suggests that matter possesses dual nature, *i.e.*, has wave nature as well as particle nature. It also suggests that wavelength (λ) of electron is inversely proportional to its momentum (p) *i.e.*,

$$\lambda = \frac{h}{p} = \frac{h}{mv}$$

where, m = mass of electron
and v = velocity of electron

Heisenberg's Uncertainty Principle

This principle states that it is impossible to determine simultaneously the exact position and exact momentum (velocity) of an electron. It is given as

$$\Delta x \cdot \Delta p \geq \frac{h}{4\pi}$$

where, Δx is the uncertainty in position and Δp is the uncertainty in momentum

Orbits and Subshell

- According to quantum mechanical model, the orbits contain subshell which in turn contain orbitals.
- Four subshells are defined in different atoms, i.e., s, p, d and f.
- s-subshell contains one orbital, p-subshell contains 3-orbitals, d-subshell contains 5-orbitals and f-subshell contains 7-orbitals.
- An orbital can accommodate only maximum of 2-electrons.

The distribution of subshells in different orbits is as follows

Orbits	Subshell
1	s
2	s, p
3	s, p, d
4	s, p, d, f
5	s, p, d, f
6	s, p, d
7	s, p

The names of these subshells are taken as including the orbital name with the subshell name, e.g., the s-subshell of 5th orbital is termed as $5s$, $6d$, etc.

Electronic Configuration

- It is the arrangement of electrons in various shells, subshells and orbitals in an atom.
- It is written as 2, 8, 8, 18, 18, 32

  or

- It is written as nl^x (where, n indicates the principal quantum number, l indicates the azimuthal quantum number or subshell and x is the number of electrons).
- Number of electrons in n shell = $2n^2$ e.g., in second shell the number of electrons $= 2 \times 2^2 = 8$ exceptions of normal rule.

Electronic configuration of some elements are tabulated below

Elements	Configuration	
	2, 8, 8... **type**	**nl^x type**
Sodium ($_{11}$Na)	2, 8, 1	$1s^2, 2s^2, 2p^6, 3s^1$

Elements	Configuration	
*Chromium ($_{24}$Cr)	2, 8, 13, 1	$1s^2, 2s^2, 2p^6, 3s^2,$ $3p^6, 3d^5, 4s^1$
Iron ($_{26}$Fe)	2, 8, 14, 2	$1s^2, 2s^2, 2p^6, 3s^2,$ $3p^6, 3d^6, 4s^2$
*Copper ($_{29}$Cu)	2, 8, 18, 1	$1s^2, 2s^2, 2p^6, 3s^2,$ $3p^6, 3d^{10}, 4s^1$

Aufbau Principle
(building up, construction)

- It is used to determine the electronic configuration of an atom.
- According to it, orbitals are filled in order of their increasing energies, starting with the orbital of lowest energy. Increasing order of energies of various orbitals is,

  $1s < 2s < 2p < 3s < 3p < 4s < 3d < 4p$
  $< 5s < 4d < 5p < 6s < 4f < 5d < 6p < 7s$
  $< 5f < 6d < 7p$

Hund's Rule of Maximum Multiplicity

It states that if two or more orbitals of equal energy are available, electrons will occupy them singly before filling them in pairs.

Quantum Numbers

These show the position and energy of electrons in an atom. *These are four in numbers*

Principal Quantum Number, n

- It describes the energy of electron and is always a positive integer (electron shell).
- It is represented by $K, L, M, N, \ldots$ or 1, 2, 3, 4, ...
- It shows the distance of outer electron from the nucleus.

Azimuthal Quantum Number, l

- It describes the subshells and orbital angular momentum of each electron.
- It shows the shapes of orbitals, e.g., s-orbital is spherical, p-orbital is dumb-bell shape, d-orbital is double dumb-bell shape and f-orbitals have complicated structure.
- It has values 0 to $n - 1$.
- l equal to 0 shows s-orbital, 1 shows p-orbital, 2 shows d-orbital and 3 shows f-orbital.

Magnetic Quantum Number, **m**

It shows the orbital of a subshell or orientation of electron and has values from $-l$ to $+l$ including zero.

Spin Quantum Number, **s**

- It describes the spin of each electron (spin up or spin down).
- The value of s can be $+\frac{1}{2}$ or $-\frac{1}{2}$.

RADIOACTIVITY

- It was discovered by Henry Becquerel but term radioactivity was given by Madam Curie. It is the process of spontaneous disintegration of nucleus and is measured by Geiger counter.
- It is a nuclear phenomenon, thus remains unaffected by external factors like temperature, pressure, etc.

Radioactive Rays

Radioactivity involves emission of α, β and γ rays or particles and has units Curie, Becquerel, Rutherford.

Alpha (α) Rays

- These rays consist of positively charged helium nuclei (He^{++}). They have $+2$ unit charge and 4 u mass.
- They have low penetrating power but very high ionising power and kinetic energy.
- An α-emission reduces the atomic mass by 4 and atomic number by 2, thus, the new nuclei formed occupy a position two places left to the parent nuclei in the periodic table (Soddy Fajans group displacement law).

Beta (β) Rays

- These rays consist of negatively charged electrons ($_{-1}e^{0}$) and have -1 unit charge and zero mass.
- These are more dangerous than α-rays.
- These have high penetrating power as compared to α-rays.
- A β-emission increased the atomic number by one with no change in atomic mass, thus, the new nuclei obtained

Pauli Exclusion Principle

- It is the quantum mechanical principle which states that no two identical fermions (particles with half-integer spin) may occupy the same quantum state simultaneously.

or

- Only two electrons may exist in the same orbital but these electrons must have opposite spin.

occupy a position one place right to the parent nuclei in the periodic table (Soddy Fajans group displacement law).

Gamma (γ) Rays

- These are electromagnetic radiation and have very high penetrating power.
- These have low ionising power and kinetic energy.
- Their emission does not affect the position of nuclei in the periodic table.

Half-Life Period

It is the time in which a radioactive substance remains half of its original amount.

Nuclear Fission

- It is a process in which a heavy nucleus is broken down into two or more lighter fragments.
- It is usually accompanied with the emission of neutrons and large amount of energy. It is used in nuclear reactor and atom bomb.

Atom Bomb

It is based on uncontrolled nuclear fission. It contains ^{235}U or ^{239}Pu as fuel.

Nuclear Reactor

- It is a device that is used to produce electricity and permits a controlled chain nuclear fission.
- It contains fuels e.g., $_{92}U^{235}$, moderator (e.g., graphite and heavy water, D_2O) to slow down neutrons and control rods (made up of boron steel or cadmium) to absorb neutrons.

- It may also contain liquid sodium as coolant.

Nuclear Fusion

- It is a process which involves fusion of two or more lighter nuclei to give a heavier nuclei.
- It occurs only at extremely high temperature ($> 10^6$K), so also called thermonuclear reactions.
- It is used in hydrogen bomb. Energy of Sun is also a result of a series of nuclear fusion reactions.

Hydrogen Bomb

It contains a mixture of deuterium oxide (D_2O) and tritium oxide (T_2O) in a space surrounding an ordinary atom bomb.

Radiocarbon Dating

It is used in determining the age of carbon bearing materials such as wood, animal fossils, etc. It is based on the concentration of C_{14} and C_{12} isotopes.

Uranium Dating

It is used to determine the age of earth, minerals and rocks.

Uses of Radioisotopes

1. **Iodine-131** is employed to study the structure and activity of thyroid gland. It is also used in internal radiation therapy for the treatment of thyroid disease.
2. **Iodine-123** is used in brain imaging.
3. **Cobalt-60** is used in external radiation therapy for the treatment of cancer.
4. **Sodium-24** is injected along with salt solution to trace the flow of blood.
5. **Phosphorus-32** is used for leukemia therapy.
6. **Carbon-14** is used to study the kinetics of photosynthesis.

CHEMICAL BONDING

- It is formed by elements to complete eight electrons in their outer shell i.e., to complete their octet.
- It results in decrease in energy and increase in stability.

Ions

These are of two types : cation and anion. Cations are formed by the loss of electrons and carry positive charge, e.g., Na^+, Mg^{2+}. **Anions** are formed by the gain of electrons, and carry negative charge e.g., Cl^-, F^-, etc.

Electrovalent Bond or Ionic Bond

- It is a type of chemical bond formed through an electrostatic attraction between two oppositely charged ions.
- It is formed between a cation, which is usually a metal, and an anion, which is usually a non-metal, e.g.,

$$Na + \overset{\times\times}{\underset{\times\times}{\times Cl \times}} \longrightarrow [Na^+][\overset{\times\times}{\underset{\times\times}{\overset{\bullet}{\times} Cl \overset{\times}{}}}]$$

2, 8, 1   2, 8, 7   sodium chloride

Ionic Compounds

- They can conduct electricity in molten state or in solution, but not in solid state.
- They have a high melting point and tend to be soluble in water. Examples of such compounds are limestone ($CaCO_3$), common salt (NaCl), lime (CaO), magnesium oxide (MgO), etc.
- The energy required to separate the ions of an ionic compound is called **lattice energy**.

Covalent Bond

- It is a type of chemical bond that is characterised by the sharing of electrons between two atoms.
- It may be a single bond (—), formed by sharing of two electrons i.e., one electron from each atom, double bond (=), formed by sharing of four electrons i.e., two electrons from each atom, or triple bond (≡), formed by sharing of six electrons i.e., three electrons from each atom.
- The geometry of few covalent molecule H_2O (water) – Bent, NH_3 (ammonia) – pyramidal, CH_4 (methane)–tetrahedral, CO_2 (carbon dioxide) – linear.
- Single bond contains only 1 σ-bond; double bond contains 1 σ and 1π-bond; and triple bond contains 1σ and 2π-bonds.

Covalent Compounds

1. They are non-conductor of electricity.
2. They have low thermal conductivity.
3. They are insoluble in water, but soluble in non-polar solvents like benzene, acetone, ether, etc.
4. They have low melting and boiling points (diamond and graphite have very high melting point.)
5. They are directional. So, have definite geometry.

Coordinate or Dative Bond

- It is a special type of covalent bond in which both the electrons for sharing (i.e., shared pair of electrons) are given by only one atom.
- Coordinate compounds have properties in between the ionic and covalent compounds.
- Examples of coordinate compounds are

$$\left[\begin{array}{c} H \\ | \\ H-N\rightarrow H \\ | \\ H \end{array} \right]^+ \quad ; C \equiv\!\!\equiv N, \text{ etc}$$
(Ammonium ion)   (Cyanide ion)

Hydrogen Bond

- It is the attractive interaction of a hydrogen attached to highly electronegative atom (such as N, F, O) with another electronegative atom, such as nitrogen, oxygen or fluorine.
- It is stronger (has energy 5 to 30 kJ/mol) than a van der Waals' interaction.
- It occurs in both inorganic molecules such as water and organic molecules such as DNA.
- Ethanol, amine (except 3° amine), etc., can form **H-bond** with water, so these are soluble in water although these are **covalent compounds**.

---

van der Waals' Interaction/Force

The attractive forces among the non-polar molecules in solid or liquid states. These are relatively weaker compared to normal chemical bonds.

The ability of Geckos which can hang on a glass surface using only one toe-to climb on sheer surfaces has been attributed to the van der Waals' forces between these surfaces and spatulae or microscopic projections, which cover the hair-like setae found on their footpads.

CHEMICAL REACTION

The process in which substances (reactants) react to form new compounds (products), is known as chemical reaction.

Types of Chemical Reactions

Chemical reactions are of following types

Combination Reactions

In such reactions, two or more substances combine to give a single substance, e.g.,

$$\underset{\substack{\text{Calcium} \\ \text{oxide}}}{CaO} + \underset{\text{Water}}{H_2O} \longrightarrow \underset{\substack{\text{Calcium} \\ \text{hydroxide}}}{Ca(OH)_2}$$

Decomposition Reactions

These are those irreversible reactions in which, a molecule decomposes into two or more simpler molecules e.g.,

$$\underset{\substack{\text{Potassium} \\ \text{chlorate}}}{2KClO_3} \overset{\Delta}{\longrightarrow} \underset{\substack{\text{Potassium} \\ \text{chloride}}}{2KCl} + \underset{\text{Oxygen}}{3O_2}$$

Dissociation Reactions

These are those reversible reactions in which a molecule dissociates into two or more simple molecules, *e.g.*,

$$\underset{\substack{\text{Hydrogen} \\ \text{iodide}}}{2HI} \rightleftharpoons \underset{\text{Hydrogen}}{H_2} + \underset{\text{Iodine}}{I_2}$$

Reversible Reactions

Reversible reactions are those which occurs in forward as well as in backward direction but never go to completion.

Irreversible Reactions

Irreversible reactions occur only in forward direction and go to completion.

Displacement Reactions

In such reactions, an atom or a group of atoms of a molecule is replaced by another atom or group of atoms e.g.,

$$CuSO_4 + Fe \longrightarrow FeSO_4 + Cu$$

Copper   Ferrous
sulphate   sulphate

Double Displacement Reactions

These involve exchange of ions between two compounds. e.g.,

$$NaCl + AgNO_3 \longrightarrow AgCl + NaNO_3$$

Reactions occurring between the ions or ionic compounds are very fast.

Exothermic Reactions

These are those reactions in which energy is released, e.g., burning of natural gas, respiration, decomposition of vegetable matter into compost, combustion reactions etc.

Endothermic Reactions

These are those reactions in which energy is consumed, e.g., digestion, photosynthesis, evoporation of water, melting of an ice, etc.

Redox Reactions

In such reactions, oxidation and reduction occurs, simultaneously. These are called disproportionation reaction when the same element is oxidised as well as reduced.

Oxidation

- It involves addition of oxygen or any other electronegative element like fluorine (F), chlorine (Cl), nitrogen (N), etc.
- It involves removal of hydrogen (H) or any other electropositive element like sodium (Na). It involves loss of electrons *i.e.*, increase in the positive charge of ion.

Reduction

- It involves addition of hydrogen or any other electropositive element.
- It involves removal of oxygen or any other electronegative element. It involves gain of electron, *i.e.*, decrease in oxidation state.

Oxidising Agent or Oxidant

These are the substances that have the ability to **oxidise** other substances, *e.g.*, H_2O_2, MnO_4^-, CrO_3, $Cr_2O_7^{2-}$, OsO_4^{2-} or elec- tronegative elements (O_2, F_2, Cl_2, Br_2) etc.

Reducing Agent or Reductant

These are the substances that have the ability to **reduce** other substances, transfer electrons to another substance; *e.g.*, electropositive element, metals such as lithium, sodium, magnesium, iron, zinc, and aluminium, hydride transfer reagents, such as $NaBH_4$ and $LiAlH_4$, etc.

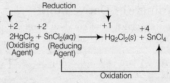

Catalysis

- It was discovered by Berzelius.
- It is a term, used for the reactions/ processes which occur in the presence of certain substances that increase the rate of the reaction without being consumed. Such substances are called **catalysts**.
- Catalysis is called **homogeneous** when reactant and catalyst are in same phase e.g., for the manufacture of sulphuric acid.

$$SO_2(g) + \frac{1}{2}O_2(g) \xrightarrow{NO(g)} SO_3(g)$$

- Catalysis is called **heterogeneous**, when reactant and catalyst are in different phase, e.g., Haber's process for the synthesis of ammonia.

$$N_2(g) + 3H_2(g) \xrightarrow{Fe(s)} 2NH_3 (g)$$

- Catalysis is called **autocatalysis**, when one of the product increases the rate of the reaction i.e., acts as catalyst. e.g.,

$$CH_3COOC_2H_5 + H_2O \longrightarrow$$
$$CH_3COOH + C_2H_5OH$$

PERIODIC TABLE

- It is a tabular display of the chemical elements, organised on the basis of their properties.
- It contains **horizontal rows** called **periods** and **vertical columns** called **groups**.

Mendeleef's Periodic Law

It states that, 'the physical and chemical properties of elements are the periodic function of their atomic masses.'

Modern Periodic Law

It states that, "physical and chemical properties of the elements are periodic functions of their atomic numbers".

Long Form of Periodic Table

It is just graphical representation of Aufbau principle. It is based on the electronic configuration of elements and contains 118 elements. *It is divided into four blocks*

s-Block

- It contains 1 and 2 group, *i.e.*, hydrogen and alkali metals (Li, Na, K, Rb, Cs, Fr) and alkaline Earth metals (Be, Mg, Ca, Sr, Ba, Ra). General electronic configuration of these elements is ns^{0-2}.
- These elements are soft metals, electropositive and form basic oxides.

p-Block

- It comprises the last six groups (13-18).
- General electronic configuration of this block elements is $ns^2 np^{1-6}$.

- It is the only block which contain metals, non-metals and metalloids.
- Heavier elements show inert pair effect. s and p-block elements are collectively called **representative elements**.

d-Block

- It comprises 10 groups (3 to 12). These elements are called transition elements.
- General electronic configuration of d-block elements is $(n-1)d^{1-10}ns^{1-2}$.
- Elements of this block contain unpaired electrons and are paramagnetic.
- These elements are generally coloured and used as catalyst.
- Hg, Zn, Cu, Sc, etc., are d-block elements, but not the **transition elements**.

f-Block

- It usually offset below the rest of the periodic table, comprises two rows of 14 elements, called the lanthanides and actinides respectively.
- General electronic configuration of this block elements is $(n-2)f^{1-14}(n-1)d^{1-10}ns^{1-2}$.

There are two series in this block $4f$ and $5f$ series. $4f$ series elements are called lanthanides and $5f$ series elements are called actinides. Elements of this block are called **inner-transition elements** and present in IIIB (3) group only.

Period → Group	s-block															p-block					
	IA (1)	IIA (2)														IIIA (13)	IVA (14)	VA (15)	VIA (16)	VIIA (17)	0 (18)
1	H 1						d-block or transition elements														He 2
2	Li 3	Be 4											B 5	C 6	N 7	O 8	F 9	Ne 10
3	Na 11	Mg 12	(3) IIIB	(4) IVB	(5) VB	(6) VIB	(7) VIIB	(8)	(9) VIIIB	(10)	(11) IB	(12) IIB	Al 13	Si 14	P 15	S 16	Cl 17	Ar 18
4	K 19	Ca 20	Sc 21	Ti 22	V 23	Cr 24	Mn 25	Fe 26	Co 27	Ni 28	Cu 29	Zn 30	Ga 31	Ge 32	As 33	Se 34	Br 35	Kr 36
5	Rb 37	Sr 38	Y 39	Zr 40	Nb 41	Mo 42	Tc 43	Ru 44	Rh 45	Pd 46	Ag 47	Cd 48	In 49	Sn 50	Sb 51	Te 52	I 53	Xe 54
6	Cs 55	Ba 56	La 57	Hf 72	Ta 73	W 74	Re 75	Os 76	Ir 77	Pt 78	Au 79	Hg 80	Tl 81	Pb 82	Bi 83	Po 84	At 85	Rn 86
7	Fr 87	Ra 88	Ac 89	Rf 104	Db 105	Sg 106	Bh 107	Hs 108	Mt 109	Ds 110	Rg 111	Cn 112	Uut 113	Fl 114	UUp 115	Lv 116	Uus 117	Uuo 118

Ce 58	Pr 59	Nd 60	Pm 61	Sm 62	Eu 63	Gd 64	Tb 65	Dy 66	Ho 67	Er 68	Tm 69	Yb 70	Lu 71
Th 90	Pa 91	U 92	Np 93	Pu 94	Am 95	Cm 96	Bk 97	Cf 98	Es 99	Fm 100	Md 101	No 102	Lr 103

→ f-block or inner-transition elements

Newly Discovered Element

Ununseptium, recently discovered, a superheavy chemical element with atomic number 117, is a member of group-17 in the periodic table below the five halogens (fluorine, chlorine, bromine, iodine and astatine). Its synthesis was claimed in Dubna, Russia by a joint Russian-American collaboration. In 2014, the GSI Helmholtz Centre for Heavy Ion Research in Germany also claimed to have successfully repeated original experiment. Ununseptium is a temporary systematic name that is intended to be used before a permanent one is established. It is commonly called element-117, instead of ununseptium.

Periodic Properties and their Trends

Periodic properties are those which shows a regular trend along a period and a group.

Atomic Size

- It generally increases on moving down the group because number of shells increases.
- It decreases along a period from left to right. Thus, size of alkali metal is largest and that of halogens is smallest in a period.
- Smallest atom is hydrogen and largest atom is cesium.
- Most poisonous metal is plutonium.

Valency

- It is the combining capacity of an element.
- It increases from 1 to 7 along a period with respect to oxygen whereas with respect to hydrogen, it first increases from 1 to 4 and then decreases to 0.
- For alkali metal (i.e., sodium, potassium, etc.,) it is 1, for alkaline Earth metals (i.e., magnesium, calcium, etc.,) is 2, for aluminium, it is 3 and for nitrogen it is 3. It remains the same in a group.
- For s-block elements, all the elements in a group have same valency.

- For p-block elements, they show variable valencies [P(3, 5), S(4, 6) but tendency to show higher valency decreases when we move down in a group due to inert pair effect.
- For d-block elements Fe(2, 3), Cu (1, 2) the elements of same group may have different valencies, and the element itself exhibit different valencies.

Oxidation State

- It is the hypothetical charge that an atom would have if all bonds of atoms of different elements were removed.
- It is typically represented by integers, which can be positive, negative or zero.
- It is $+1$ for hydrogen, -2 for oxygen (except in peroxide i.e., -1 and in F_2O i.e., $+2$), $+1$ for sodium and potassium and $+2$ for magnesium (Mg), calcium (Ca), strontium (Sr).
- It is -1 for fluorine (always).
- It is zero for a neutral molecule.

Example : Calculation of oxidation number of Mn in $KMnO_4$.

Let the oxidation number of Mn is X.
$$KMnO_4 = 1 + X + 4(-2) = 0$$
Therefore, the oxidation number of Mn in $KMnO_4$ is $+7$.

Metallic Character

- It is the tendency of an element to form cation by the loss of electrons.
- It decreases along a period from left to right and increases in a group on moving downwards.

Ionisation Energy

- It is the energy required to remove an electron from the outermost shell of an isolated gaseous atom.
- It generally increases along a period from left to right but ionisation energy of Be, Mg, Ca, Sr is larger than the ionisation energy of B, Al, In, Tl, respectively. Moreover, ionisation energy of N, P is larger than ionisation energy of O, S respectively.
- It generally decreases in a group on moving downwards.

Electron Affinity (EA)

- It is defined as the energy liberated when an extra electron is added to an atom.

- It increases across a period from left to right but EA of II(2), 15 group and 0 group is 0 or positive.
- It decreases on moving down a group.
- It is highest for chlorine.

Electronegativity

It is the tendency of an atom in a molecule to attract the shared electrons towards itself. It increases regularly along a period from left to right and decreases on moving down a group. It is highest for fluorine.

Metals and their Properties

- These are the elements which are hard, lustrous, ductile, malleable, sonorous and conductor of heat and electricity in their solid as well as molten state.
- These form oxide with air. These oxides are generally basic, but oxides of zinc and aluminium are amphoteric, *i.e.,* have acidic as well as basic properties.
- These evolve hydrogen gas when reacts with water and acids.
- Metals which are highly reactive displace the less reactive metals from their salts. The order of reactivity is : potassium (K) > calcium (Ca) > sodium (Na) > magnesium (Mg) > aluminium (Al) > zinc (Zn) > iron (Fe) > lead (Pb) > hydrogen (H) > copper (Cu) > mercury (Hg) > silver (Ag) > gold (Au) (Thus, gold is less reactive metal).

e.g., When iron nails are kept in copper sulphate solution (blue), iron being more reactive displaces the copper from copper sulphate solution and thus, the blue colour of solution disappears.

- Mercury (metal) is liquid at room temperature.
- Metal with lowest density is lithium.
- Tungsten is the metal having highest melting point.
- Reactivity of metals increases while that of non-metals decreases on moving down the group.
- Sodium and potassium are soft and highly reactive metals. These react with air and water. That's why these are kept in kerosene oil. Silver, gold and platinum do not react with air even on strong heating.

- Sodium and potassium burn in water while calcium floats over it.
- Copper (Cu) is the first metal used by man.
- Pb (lead) is a bad conductor of electricity.
- Ti (Titanium) is called strategic metal.

Non-Metals and their Properties

- These may be solid, liquid or gas (bromine is the only liquid non-metal).
- These are soft, non-lustrous, brittle, non-sonorous and non-conductor of heat and electricity.
- These have low melting and boiling points.
- These form oxides with oxygen which are generally acidic.
- Examples are noble gases [i.e., helium (He), neon-(Ne), argon (Ar), krypton (Kr), xenon (Xe) and some other *p*-block elements].
- Diamond is the hardest substance known. Iodine is lustrous. Melting point is very high for diamond and graphite.
- The order of hardness of some substances is : diamond > corundum > topaz > quartz.

Helium

- It is a noble gas (discovered by Lockyear and Janssen).
- It is used for filling balloons and other lighter aircrafts. Helium, when mixed with Oxygen, is used by deep-sea divers for breathing and for respiratory patients.
- It is used as a heat transfer agent in gas cooled nuclear reactors.

Neon

It was discovered by Ramsay and Travers. It is used in neon signs.

Argon

It was discovered by Rayleigh and Ramsay. It is used to generate inert atmosphere for welding and to fill incandescent light bulbs. A mixture of mercury vapours and argon gas is filled in tube lights.

Xenon

It is called stranger gas. Xe, when mixed with Kr, used in high intensity, short exposure photographic flash tubes.

Uses of Some Important Metals and Non-Metals

- **Ferrous Oxide** (FeO) is used to prepare ferrous salts and green glass.
- **Ferric Oxide** (Fe_2O_3) is used in jeweller's rouge.
- **Silver Nitrate** ($AgNO_3$) is called lunar caustic and is used to prepare the ink used during voting.
- **Silver Iodide** (AgI) is used for artificial rain.
- **Mercuric Chloride** ($HgCl_2$) is used to prepare calomel and as a poison.
- **Hydrogen Peroxide** (H_2O_2) is used as an oxidising agent, bleaching agent, as an insecticide and for washing old oil paintings.

Metalloids

These have properties of metals as well as non-metals. They are present only in *p*-block. Their examples are arsenic, antimony, germanium, tellurium, silicon and boron.

Minerals

These are the substances in the form of which metal is found in nature.

- The main **constituent of pearl** is calcium carbonate ($CaCO_3$).
- **Ruby and sapphire** are chemically aluminium oxide, Al_2O_3.
- In haemoglobin and myoglobin, **iron** is present as Fe^{2+}.

Ores

- These are the minerals from which metal can be obtained conveniently and beneficially.
- All ores are minerals but all minerals are not ores.

Gangue or Matrix

These are the impurities associated with the ore.

Ores of Some Important Metals

Metals	Ores
Sodium (Na)	Chile salt petre ($NaNO_3$)
	Common salt or brine ($NaCl$)

Metals	Ores
Aluminium (Al)	Bauxite ($Al_2O_3 \cdot 2H_2O$)
	Corundum (Al_2O_3)
	Cryolite (Na_3AlF_6)
	Feldspar ($KAlSi_3O_8$)
Potassium (K)	Nitre (KNO_3)
	Carnalite ($KCl \cdot MgCl_2 \cdot 6H_2O$)
Magnesium (Mg)	Magnesite ($MgCO_3$)
	Dolomite ($MgCO_3 \cdot CaCO_3$)
	Epsom salt ($MgSO_4 \cdot 7H_2O$)
Calcium (Ca)	Calcite ($CaCO_3$)
	Flurospar (CaF_2)
Copper (Cu)	Cuprite (Cu_2O)
	Copper glance (Cu_2S)
	Copper pyrites ($CuFeS_2$)
Silver (Ag)	Ruby silver ($Ag_2S \cdot Sb_2S_3$)
	Horn silver ($AgCl$)
Zinc (Zn)	Zinc blende (ZnS)
	Calamine ($ZnCO_3$)
	Zincite (ZnO)
Mercury (Hg)	Cinnabar (HgS)
Tin (Sn)	Cassiterite (SnO_2)
Lead (Pb)	Galena (PbS)
	Cerrusite ($PbCO_3$)
Iron (Fe)	Haematite (Fe_2O_3)
	Magnetite (Fe_3O_4)
	Siderite ($FeCO_3$)
Uranium (U)	Pitch blende (kernatite) (U_3O_8)
Thorium (Th)	Monazite

METALLURGY

It is the process of extraction of metal from its ores.

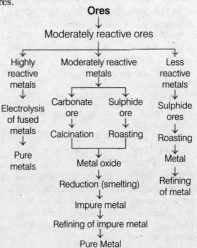

Calcination

- It is the process of heating the concentrated ore in absence or in limited supply of air below its melting point. It is done for hydroxide or carbonate ore.
- It is done in reverberatory furnace.

Roasting

- It is the process of heating the concentrated ore in excess of air.
- It is used for sulphide ores.
- It is done in reverberatory furnace.

Smelting

It is the process of heating the oxides of elements with coke and flux above their melting point.

Flux and Slag

- These are the substances which converts infusible impurities into fusible substances called slag.
- These are of two types : Acidic flux such as SiO_2 (used to remove basic impurities) and basic flux such as CaO, MgO (used to remove acidic impurities).

Electrolytic Refining

In electrolytic refining, anode is made up of impure metal and cathode is made by thin strip of pure metal.

Alloys

These are mixtures of two metals or a metal and a non-metal. They have properties different from the main metal. An alloy of mercury is called amalgam.

Alloys and their Uses

Alloy	Composition	Uses
Brass	Copper (70%)+Zinc (30%)	In making utensils
Bronze	Copper (90%)+Tin (10%)	In making coins, bell, utensil
Gun metal	Copper (88%)+ (10%) Tin+Zinc (2%)	In making gun, barrels, gears and bearings
German silver	Copper (60%)+Zinc (20%)+Nickel (20%)	In making utensils
Solder	Lead (50%)+Tin (50%)	For soldering
Bell metal	Copper (80%)+Tin (20%)	For casting bells, statues
Munz metal	Copper (60%)+Zinc (40%)	In making coins
Magnalium	Aluminium (95%)+Magnesium (5%)	For frame of aeroplane
Duralumin	Aluminium (94%)+Copper+Magnesium and manganese	For making automobile parts
Type metal	Lead (80%)+Antimony (15%)+Tin (5%)	In printing industry
Stainless steel	Iron (75%)+Chromium (15%), Nickel (10%)+Carbon (0.5%)	For making utensils and surgical cutlery
Babbit metal	Tin (89%)+Antimony (9%)+Copper (2%) Nickel+Chromium	In making heater coil

ACIDS, BASES AND SALTS

Arrhenius Concept

According to this concept, "acids are those substances which give H^+ ions in their aqueous solution and bases are those substances which give $\overline{OH}$ ions in their aqueous solution."

$$HCl\,(aq) \longrightarrow H^+ + \overline{Cl}$$
$$NaOH\,(aq) \longrightarrow Na^+ + \overline{OH}$$

Bronsted Lowry Concept

According to this concept, "acids are proton donors and bases are proton acceptors."

$$\underset{\text{Acid}}{CH_3COOH} + \underset{\text{Base}}{H_2O} \longrightarrow \underset{\substack{\text{Conjugate}\\\text{Base}}}{CH_3CO\overline{O}} + \underset{\substack{\text{Conjugate}\\\text{acid}}}{H_3O^+}$$

$$H_2O + H_2O \rightleftharpoons \overline{OH} + H_3O^+$$
$$NH_3 + NH_3 \rightleftharpoons \overline{N}H_2 + NH_4^+$$

Lewis Concept

According to this concept, "Acids are electron pair acceptors and bases are electron pair donors."

$$:NH_3 + BF_3 \rightarrow H_3N{:}\rightarrow BF_3$$
$$\qquad\qquad\quad \text{Base}\quad\text{Acid}$$

Properties of Acids and Bases

- Acids have sour taste and turns blue litmus red. While, bases have bitter taste and turns red litmus blue.
- Acids reacts with metal to liberate hydrogen gas.
  Acid + Metal $\longrightarrow$ Salt + Hydrogen gas.
- Bases also reacts with some metals to liberate hydrogen gas.
  e.g., $Zn + 2NaOH \longrightarrow Na_2ZnO_2 + H_2$
- Acid and base reacts together to form salt and water and the reaction is called **neutralisation reaction**.
  Acid + Base $\longrightarrow$ Salt + H_2O.
  $HCl(aq) + NaOH(aq) \longrightarrow$
  $\qquad\qquad\qquad NaCl(aq) + H_2O\,(l)$
- Acids reacts with metallic oxides to give salt and water which shows that metallic oxides are basic in nature. Whereas, bases reacts with non-metallic oxides to give salt and water which shows that non-metallic oxides are acidic in nature.
- When dissolved in water, acids release H^+ ions and bases (or especially alkalies) releases OH^- ions.
  $$HA + H_2O \longrightarrow H_3O^+ + A^\ominus$$
  $$BOH + H_2O \longrightarrow B^+ + OH^\ominus$$
  Acids like HCl, HNO_3 H_2SO_4, etc., and bases like NaOH, KOH, etc., are good conductors of electricity in their aqueous solutions.

Some Important Points

- Aqua Regia is a mixture of conc HCl and conc. HNO_3 in a ratio of 3 : 1 and is used to dissolve noble metals like gold, platinum, etc.
  Pickles are always kept in glass jar because acid present in them reacts with metal of metallic pot.

- **Acidity** is the number of replaceable OH^- ions, e.g., it is 1 for NaOH, 2 for $Ca(OH)_2$. Whereas **Basicity** represents the number of replaceable H^+ ions, e.g., it is 1 for HCl, 2 for H_2SO_4.

Sources of Some Naturally Occurring Acids

Acids	Sources
Citric acid	Lemon, orange, grapes
Maleic acid	Unripe apple
Tartaric acid	Tamarind
Acetic acid	Vinegar
Lactic acid	Milk
Hydrochloric acid	Stomach
Oxalic acid	Tomato

Uses of Some Acids and Bases

Acids	Uses
Nitric acid, oxalic acid	photography
Sulphuric acid	petroleum exploration
Hydrochloric acid	leather industry
Benzoic acid, formic acid, citric acid, acetic acid	preservation for food stuff

Bases	Uses
Calcium hydroxide calcium oxide	manufacturing of bleaching powder
Magnesium hydroxide	antacid, in sugar industries
Sodium hydroxide	manufacture of hard soaps and drugs, paper and textile industry, petroleum refining
Potassium hydroxide	manufacture of soft soaps

pH Value

- It is a measure of acidity or basicity of a solution.
- It is defined as the negative logarithm of the concentration in mol/L of hydrogen ions which it contains, i.e.,

$$pH = -\log[H^+] = \log\frac{1}{[H^+]}$$

or $[H^+] = 1 \times 10^{-pH}$

- It is 7 for neutral solution, greater than 7 for basic solution and less than 7 for acidic solution.

- pH of some common substances are:

Substance	pH	Substance	pH
Gastric juice	1.0-3.0	Rain water	6.0
Soft drinks	2.0-4.0	Tears	7.4
Lemon	2.2-2.4	Sea water	8.5
Vinegar	2.4-3.4	Milk of magnesia	10.5
Urine (human)	4.8-8.4	Milk (cow)	6.3-6.6
Saliva (human)	6.5-7.5	Blood plasma (human)	7.30-7.42

Indicators

- These are the substances which give different colours in acidic and basic solutions.
- Some indicators and their colour in acidic and basic medium are:

Indicators	Colour	
	In Acid	In Base
Phenolphthalein	Colourless	Pink
Methyl orange	Orange	Yellow
Methyl red	Red	Yellow
Phenol red	Yellow	Red

Salts

These are the product of neutralisation reaction between an acid and a base e.g.,

$$HNO_3\,(aq) + \underset{base}{KOH\,(aq)} \longrightarrow$$
$$\underset{salt}{KNO_3\,(aq)} + \underset{water}{H_2O\,(l)}$$

These are of the following types :

Mixed Salt

These are obtained by neutralisation of an acid by two base or a base by two acids. e.g., bleaching powder $(CaOCl_2)$.

Double Salt

It is obtained by mixing two or more salt, e.g.,
Alum $(K_2SO_4 \cdot Al_2(SO_4)_3 \cdot 24H_2O)$,
Mohr Salt $(FeSO_4 \cdot (NH_4)_2SO_4 \cdot 6H_2O)$.

Important Salts
Common Salt

- It is sodium chloride (NaCl).
- It is obtained from sea water.
- It is also known as table salt.

Baking Soda

- It is sodium hydrogen carbonate $(NaHCO_3)$. It is a mild non-corrosive base.
- When mixed with a mild edible acid such as tartaric acid it is called baking powder and is used to make bread or cake soft and spongy.
- It is used as mild antiseptic for skin infections, in soda-acids and as fire extinguishers.
- Ant or bee sting contains methanoic or formic acid. Due to which victim feel pain and irritation. Use of a mild base like baking soda is a remedy for it.

Washing Soda

It is chemically sodium carbonate decahydrate $(Na_2CO_3 \cdot 10H_2O)$ and is used in glass, soap and paper industries and also for removing permanent hardness of water.

Bleaching Powder

- It is chemically $Ca(OCl)Cl$ or $CaOCl_2$.
- It is used for bleaching cotton and linen in the textile industry, for bleaching wood pulp in paper factories.
- It is used for disinfecting drinking water.

Plaster of Paris

- It is chemically calcium sulphate hemihydrate $\left(CaSO_4 \cdot \frac{1}{2} H_2O\right)$ and obtained by heating gypsum $(CaSO_4 \cdot 2H_2O)$. It contains half molecule of water of crystallisation.
- It is a white powder and on mixing with water, changes into a hard solid mass, called gypsum.
- It is used to plaster fractured bones, for making toys, materials for decoration and for making smooth surfaces.

Copper Sulphate (Blue Vitriol)

Copper sulphate when anhydrous, is white and when associated with water of crystallisation (i.e., $CuSO_4 \cdot 5H_2O$), is blue, so it is called blue vitriol. It is used to test the presence of water.

Lime

- It is chemically calcium oxide (CaO) and also called quicklime.
- It is used in the manufacture of glass, cement, etc., and for drying ammonia and alcohol.
- Excessive use of fertilizers makes the soil more acidic. To neutralise it, quicklime is added to soil as acidic soil is not good for growth of the plant.

Potassium Nitrate

It is used as fertiliser, in gun powder $(C + S + KNO_3)$, in matchsticks, etc.

Magnesium hydroxide

It is used as a **remedy for hyper acidity in stomach**.

ELECTROCHEMISTRY

It is the study of production of electricity from energy released during spontaneous chemical reactions and use of electrical energy to carry out non-spontaneous chemical transformations.

ELECTROLYSIS

The process in which a non-spontaneous reaction is carried out by using electrical energy.

It is used

- in production of oxygen for space craft and nuclear submarines.
- in layering metals to fortify them.
- in production of hydrogen for fuel.
- in electrolytic etching of metal surfaces like tools or knives with a permanent mark or logo.
- **Electrometallurgy** is the process of reduction of metallic compound into pure metal by electrolysis.
- **Anodisation** is an electrolytic process that makes the surface of metals resistant to corrosion.
- Electrolysis of brine (the water, saturated or nearly saturated with salt, usually sodium chloride) gives hydrogen and chlorine. The products are gases.

$$2NaCl + 2H_2O \longrightarrow 2NaOH + H_2 + Cl_2$$

Faraday's Laws of Electrolysis

First Law of Electrolysis

It states that the quantity of elements separated by passing an electric current through a molten or dissolved salt is proportional to the quantity of electric charge passed through the circuit.

$$w \propto Q \; ; \quad w = ZQ = Z\,it$$

(Charge (Q) = Current (i) × Time (t))

Second Law of Electrolysis

The amount of different substances liberated at the electrodes by the same quantity of electricity passing through the electrolytic solution are proportional to their chemical equivalent weights.

$$W \propto E \quad \text{or} \quad \frac{W_1}{W_2} = \frac{E_1}{E_2}$$

Electrochemical Cell

- It is a device that produces an electric current from energy released by a spontaneous redox reaction (in short which converts chemical energy into electrical energy). This kind of cell includes the galvanic cell or voltaic cell.
- It has two conductive electrodes, *i.e.*, anode (at which oxidation occurs) and cathode (at which reduction occurs).
- It contains an electrolyte in between the electrodes, which contains ions that can move freely.

BATTERY

- It is an arrangement of one or more cells connected in series.
- It is basically a galvanic cell.

These are of two types
1. **Primary batteries** (non-rechargeable) e.g., dry cell, mercury cell etc.
2. **Secondary batteries** (rechargeable) e.g., lead storage battery, nickel- cadmium battery.

Lechlanche Cell or Dry Cell

- It consists of a zinc container that acts as anode and carbon (graphite) rod surrounded by powdered manganese dioxide and carbon which acts as cathode. It contains a paste of NH_4Cl and $ZnCl_2$ in between the electrodes.
- It is used in transistors and clocks.
- It has a potential of 1.5 V.

Mercury Cell

- It is suitable for the low current devices like hearing aids and camera, etc.
- It consists of zinc-mercury amalgam as anode and a paste of HgO and carbon as cathode. The electrolyte is a paste of KOH and ZnO.
- It has potential of 1.35 V. This potential remains constant during its whole life.

Lead Storage Battery

- It is a secondary battery.
- It acts as electrochemical cell during discharging (i.e.,during use) and as electrolytic cell during charging.
- It is used in automobiles and invertors.
- It consists of lead as anode and a grid of lead packed with lead dioxide (PbO_2) as cathode. A 38% solution of sulphuric acid is used as an electrolyte.
- It consists of a series of six identical cells assembled in series. Each cell may produce a potential of 2 V, hence overall voltage produced is 12 V.
- $PbSO_4$ is formed when lead storage battery is in use and lead dioxide are formed when it is charged.

Fuel Cell

These are galvanic cells which use energy of combustion of fuels like hydrogen (H_2), methane (CH_4), methanol (CH_3OH), etc., as the source to produce electrical energy. e.g., hydrogen-oxygen fuel cell.

Corrosion

- It is the process of oxidative deterioration of a metal surface by the action of environment to form unwanted products.
- *e.g.,* conversion of iron into rust [$Fe_2O_3 \cdot x\, H_2O$], tarnishing of silver (due to the formation of Ag_2S), development of green coating of $Cu(OH)_2 \cdot CuCO_3$ (basic copper carbonate)] on copper and bronze. It is basically an electrochemical process.
- Corrosion of iron is called **rusting**. It is accelerated by the presence of impurities i.e. H^+, electrolytes such as NaCl, gases such as CO_2, SO_2, NO, NO_2, etc.
- **Formation of a layer** of aluminium oxide over aluminium surface protects the metal from further corrosion.
- **A sliced apple** turns brown if kept open for some time due to the oxidation of iron present in the apple.

It is prevented by the following methods
- By electroplating.
- By surface coating (i.e., coating of surface with oil, grease, paint and varnish), by alloying, by galvanisation of iron (process of deposition of a thin layer of zinc over iron surface).

CARBON AND ITS COMPOUND

Carbon

It is a member of group 14 in the Periodic Table, with symbol C and atomic number 6.

It has three crystalline allotropes

Graphite

- It is opaque and black.
- It is a very good conductor of electricity.
- It is soft enough to form a streak on paper.
- It is used for thermal insulation (i.e. firebreaks and heat shields).
- It is a very good lubricant.

Diamond

- It is highly transparent.
- It is the hardest material known.
- It is an electrical insulator.
- Under normal conditions, it has the highest thermal conductivity of all known materials.
- It is an ultimate abrasive.

Fullerenes

- C_{60} looks like a soccer ball (or bucky ball).
- It contains 20 six membered rings and 12 five membered rings of carbon atoms.
- It acts as a wonderful lubricant and the alkali metal compounds of C are used as superconducting substance at the temperature range of 10-40 K.

Graphene

Graphene is an allotrope of carbon. Its structure is one-atom-thick planar sheets of carbon atoms that are densely packed in a honeycomb crystal lattice. The term graphene was coined as a combination of graphite and the suffix-ene by Hanns-Peter Boehm, who discovered single-layer carbon foils in 1962.

Organic Compounds

- These are the compounds of mainly carbon and hydrogen or compounds of carbon and hydrogen with other elements like phosphorus, oxygen, nitrogen, sulphur, halogens etc.

- **Urea** It is the first synthesised organic compound (discovered by Wholer).
- **Acetic Acid** It was the first organic compound synthesised in the laboratory from its elements.

Hydrocarbons

- These are the compounds of only carbon and hydrogen.

These are of three types

Saturated Hydrocarbons

- These compounds contain only single bonds.
- These are also called alkanes or paraffins and have general formula C_nH_{2n+2} where, $n = 1, 2, 3 \ldots$ Methane is the first member of this group.

Unsaturated Hydrocarbons

- These have atleast one double ($=$) or triple ($\equiv$) bond and are called alkene and alkynes, respectively.
- These have general formula C_nH_{2n} for alkene and C_nH_{n-} for alkynes.
- **Ethylene** (C_2H_4) It is the first member of alkene and acetylene (C_2H_2) is the first member of alkyne.

Aromatic Hydrocarbons

- These have ring structure with alternate double bonds and obey $(4n + 2) \pi e^-$ (Huckel's rule).
- Benzene is the first member of aromatic hydrocarbons.

Functional Group

- It is an atom or group of atoms in a molecule, which is responsible for the chemical properties of the molecules.
- —OH is alcoholic group, —CHO is aldehyde group, >C=O is keto group, —COOH is carboxylic acid group, —O— is ether group.

Homologous Series

- It is a series of compounds in which adjacent members differ by a —CH_2— unit (14 unit mass).
- All members of a **homologous series** have same functional group and same chemical properties.

Isomerism

Compounds having the same molecular formula, but different structure are called isomers and the phenomenon is called isomerism. e.g., C_2H_6O can have the following structures CH_3OCH_3 and C_2H_5OH.

Uses of Some Important Organic Compounds

Methane (CH_4)

It is used to manufacture printer ink, methyl alcohol and to obtain light and energy.

Ethylene (C_2H_4)

It is used to prepare mustard gas (war gas) and for ripening of fruits.

Glycol ($C_2H_6O_2$)

It is used as an antifreeze mixture in car radiator and prevent the freezing of fuel in space crafts.

Acetylene (C_2H_2)

It is used to generate light, to weld metals as oxy-acetylene flame and to prepare synthetic rubber (neoprene).

Methyl Alcohol (CH_3OH)

It is used as a fuel with petrol, used to synthesise varnish and polish, used to denature ethanol.

Chloroform ($CHCl_3$)

It is used as an anaesthetic and to preserve substances obtained from plants and animals. It converts into poisonous phosgene ($COCl_2$), when exposed to sunlight. So, it is kept in dark bottles.

Glycerine ($C_3H_8O_3$)

It is used to synthesise explosive nitroglycerine, stamp ink and boot polish.

Formic Acid (HCOOH)

It is used as a preservative for fruits and juices, in leather industry and in coagulation of rubber.

Acetic Acid (CH_3COOH)

It is used in vinegar, medicines and act as a solvent.

Oxalic Acid ($C_2H_2O_4$)

It is used in printing of clothes, in photography and in the synthesis of coaltar.

Glucose ($C_6H_{12}O_6$)

It is used for the synthesis of alcohol and as a preservative for fruit juice.

Benzene (C_6H_6)

It is used as a solvent for oil fat and in dry cleaning. Sodium benzoate is a food preservative.

Toluene ($C_6H_5CH_3$)

It is used to synthesise explosive TNT, for dry cleaning and for the synthesis of medicines like chloramine.

Phenol (C_6H_5OH)

It is used to synthesise explosive, 2, 4, 6-trinitro-phenol (picric acid) and bakelite.

Ethyl Alcohol (C_2H_5OH)

It is used for drinking as a liquor, in medicine to prepare tincture and as an insecticide and as a fuel with petrol.

Name	Rum	Brandy	Whisky	Beer	Champagne	Cider
Alcohol %	45-55%	40-50%	40-50%	3-6%	10-15%	2-6%
Raw material	Molasses	Grapes	Barley	Barley	Grapes	Apple

ENERGY RESOURCES

Natural Resources

These resources are obtained by nature like air, water, mineral, sunlight, etc.
These are of two types

Renewable Natural Resources

These are available in excess amount e.g., air, sunlight, etc.

Non-Renewable Natural Resources

These resources are available in limited quantity, e.g., minerals, coal, petroleum, natural gas, etc.

Fuels

These are the substance which produce heat and light on combustion.

Coal

- It is believed to formed by the slow carbonisation of vegetable matter buried underneath the Earth from centuries ago, in limited supply of air under high temperature and pressure prevailing there.
- It is available in different varieties : Peat (60% C), lignite or brown coal (70% C), bituminous coal (80% C) and anthracite (90% C).

- Bituminous is the most common variety of coal. Coal is used for the synthesis of water gas and producer gas.

Petroleum

- It is a dark coloured oily liquid with offensive odour. It is also called rock oil, mineral oil, crude oil or black gold.
- When subjected to fractional distillation, it gives different products at different temperatures.

Liquefied Petroleum Gas (LPG)

It is a mixture of *n*-butane, *iso*-butane and some propane.

- It is easily compressed under pressure as liquid and stored in iron cylinders.
- A strong foul smelling substance called ethyl mercaptan, is added to LPG which detect the gas leakage.

Compressed Natural Gas (CNG)

- It consists mainly of methane (95%) which is a relatively unreactive hydrocarbon and makes its nearly complete combustion.
- It has octane rating of 130.

Different Fuels, their Composition and Source

Fuel	Composition	Source
Water gas	Carbon monoxide (CO) + hydrogen (H_2)	By passing steam over red hot coke
Producer gas	Carbon monoxide (CO) + nitrogen (N_2)	By passing insufficient air over red hot coke
Oil gas	Methane (CH_4) + ethylene (C_2H_4) + acetylene(C_2H_2)	By destructive distillation of kerosene
Coal gas	Hydrogen (H_2) + methane (CH_4) + ethylene + acetylene + CO	By fractional distillation of wood
Natural gas	Methane (83%) + ethane	From petroleum
LPG	Butane (C_4H_{10}) + propane (C_3H_8)	From oil wells
Biogas or Gobar gas	Methane (CH_4) + carbon dioxide (CO_2) + hydrogen (H_2) + nitrogen (N_2)	From organic wastes

Different Fractions Obtained by Fractional Distillation of Petroleum

S.No.	Fraction	Boiling Range	Uses
1.	Uncondensed gases	room temperature	Fuel gases, refrigerants, production of carbon black, hydrogen
2.	Crude naphtha (It gives on refractionation)	30-150°	
	(i) petroleum ether	30-70°	Solvent
	(ii) petrol or gasoline	70-120°	Motor fuel, dry cleaning, petrol gas
	(iii) benzene derivatives	120-150°	Solvent, dry cleaning
3.	Kerosene	150-250°	Fuel, illuminant, oil gas
4.	Gas oil		
5.	Fuel oil	250-350°	As a fuel for diesel engines converted to gasoline by cracking
6.	Diesel oil		
7.	Lubricating oil	350-450°	Lubrication
8.	Paraffin wax	> 500° C	Candles, boot polish, wax paper
9.	Vaseline	> 500° C	Ointments, lubrication paints, road surfacing as fuel

Some Important Physical Quantities

Calorific Value

- It is defined as the heat obtained when 1 g of a fuel is burnt in excess of oxygen and is expressed in kcal/g.

Calorific value of some important fuels are as follow

Fuel	Calorific Value (kJ/g)
Coal	25-32
Kerosene oil	48
Petrol	50
Diesel	45
Bio gas	35-40
LPG	50
Wood	17
Cow dung	6-8
Ethanol	30
Methane	55
Hydrogen	150
Natural gas	35-50

- **Hydrogen** is the fuel of future.
- Alcohol, when mixed with petrol, is called power alcohol. It is an alternative source of energy.
- For the **combustion of a substance**, its ignition temperature should be low.

Note Substances that are used to reduce the knocking property are known as anti-knocking compounds. e.g., Totra Ethyl Lead (TEL)

Octane Number

- Octane number is the percentage of *iso-*octane in the mixture of *iso-*octane and *n*-heptane which has same knocking properties as the fuel sample.
- It is a measure of quality of petrol (gasoline). It is zero for heptane and 100 for *iso-*octane. (2, 2, 4-trimethyl pentane).
- Higher the octane number, better is the fuel.

Cetane Number

- Cetane number is the percentage of cetane in the mixture of cetane and α-methyl naphtalene which has same knocking properties as the fuel sample.
- It is a measure of quality of diesel. It is 100 for Cetane and 0 for α-methyl naphthalene.

Flame

It is the hot part of fire and has three parts

1. **Innermost Region of Flame** It is black because of the presence of unburned carbon particles.
2. **Middle Region** It is yellow luminous due to partial combustion of fuel.
3. **Outermost Region** It is blue (non-luminous) due to complete combustion of fuel.

It is the hottest part of flame and is used by the Goldsmith to heat the gold.

Fire Extinguisher

In case of **electric fires** and **oil fires**, water cannot be used as an extinguisher as it is a conductor of electricity and oil being lighter comes above the water. Such fires are extinguished by carbon dioxide.

Safety Match Stick

Safety match stick contains a mixture of antimony trisulphide and potassium chlorate at its one end. Its box side contains a mixture of powdered glass and red phosphorus.

Man-Made Materials

Soaps

These are sodium and potassium salts of higher fatty acids. e.g., sodium palmitate, sodium stearate, etc.

Detergents

- These are sodium or potassium salts of long chain alkyl or aryl sulphonates or sulphates e.g., sodium alkyl sulphonate, sodium alkyl benzene sulphonate, etc.
- These are also called **soapless soap**.
- Detergents form **lather with** hard water.
- Detergents cause pollution but straight chain alkyl group containing detergents are biodegradable and do not cause pollution.
- The cationic detergents are used as fabric softeners and germicides while non-ionic detergents are used as liquid dish washing detergents.

Fertilisers

- These substances increase the fertility of soil by providing elements essential for the growth of plants like nitrogen, phosphorus and potassium. e.g., basic calcium nitrate $[CaO \cdot Ca(NO_3)_2]$, ammonium sulphate $[(NH_4)_2SO_4]$. These two chemicals increases the acidity of soil which can be removed by adding lime.
- Other examples are calcium cyanamide or nitrolim $(CaCN_2)$, Urea or carbamide (it does not effect the pH of soil), calcium super phosphate or super phosphate of lime $[Ca(H_2PO_4)_2 + 2CaSO_4 \cdot 2H_2O]$.

Glass

- It is an amorphous or transparent solid, also called **supercooled liquid**.
- It contains mainly silica (SiO_2).

It can be of the following types

1. **Soda or Soft Glass** is sodium calcium silicate $(Na_2O \cdot CaO \cdot 6SiO_2)$ It is the ordinary glass and used for making bottles, window panes, etc.
2. **Potash Glass or Hard Glass** contains potassium (from K_2CO_3). It has higher softening temperature. It is used for making chemical apparatus such as beakers, flasks, funnel, etc.
3. **Crown Glass** contains potassium oxide (K_2O), barium oxide (BaO), boric oxide (B_2O_3) and silica (SiO_2). It is used for optical apparatus.
4. **Flint Glass** contains lead oxide (PbO) and used in optical instruments like lenses, prisms.
5. **Crook's Glass** contains cesium oxides. It is used for spectacles as it absorbs UV rays.
6. **Jena Glass** contains B_2O_3 and alumina. It is stronger and more resistant to acids and alkalies, that's why used for making laboratory bottles, for keeping acids and alkalies.
7. **Milky Glass** is prepared by adding tin oxide (SnO_2), calcium phosphate $[(Ca_3(PO_4)_2]$ or cryolite (Na_3AlF_6) to the melt glass.
8. **Glass Laminates** is made by fixing polymer sheets between layers of glass. It is used to make windows and screens of cars, trains and aircraft. Specially manufactured glass laminates are used as bulletproof material.

Different Substances gives Different Colours to Glass

Colour	Substance Added
Red	Copper (I) oxide (Cu_2O)
Green	Chromium oxide (Cr_2O_3)
Violet	Manganese oxide (MnO_2)
Blue	Cobalt oxide (CoO)
Brown	Iron oxide (Fe_2O_3)

Cement or Portland Cement

- It is a complex material containing the silicates and aluminates of calcium with small amount of gypsum.
- *It has the following composition*
  Calcium oxide (CaO) = 50–60%
  Silica (SiO_2) = 20 – 25%
  Alumina (Al_2O_3) = 5 –10%
  Magnesium oxide (MgO) = 2 – 3%
- It is manufactured from limestone and clay. If cement contains excess lime, cracks during settings can occur and if lime is less, cement is of weak strength.
- Gypsum decreases the rate of setting of cement.
- A paste of sand, cement and water is called **mortar** and is used for joining bricks and plastering walls.
- A mixture of stone chips (gravel), sand, cement and water is known as **concrete** and is used for flooring and making roads.
- Concrete with steel bars and wires is called **Reinforced Concrete** (*R*C) and used for constructing roofs, bridges and pillars.

Medicines

These are the chemicals used for the treatment of diseases and reduce suffering from pain. *These are classified as*

- **Analgesics** are used to reduce pain. e.g., aspirin, paracetamol, morphine, etc.
- **Antipyretics** is used to reduce body temperature during high fever, e.g., paracetamol, aspirin, phenacetin, analgin and novalgin.
- **Tranquilisers** are used to treat stress, mild and severe mental disease. These are also called psychotherapeutic drugs. e.g., equanil, valium, veronal, serotonin, chlorodiazepoxide, meprobamate, etc.
- **Antiseptics** prevent the growth of microorganisms or kill them but are not harmful to living tissues. e.g., dettol, savlon, iodine tincture, boric acid, hydrogen peroxide, etc.

- Dettol is a mixture of chloroxylenol and α-terpineol. Chloroxylenol is responsible for its antiseptic property.
- **Antibiotics** are obtained from microorganisms and used to destroy the other microorganisms e.g., penicillin, (discovered by A. fleming in 1929) ampicillin, amoxycillin (all are narrow spectrum), ofloxacin, tetracycline, chloramphenicol (all are broad spectrum).
- **Antimalarial** are used to treat malaria. e.g., chloroquine.
- **Sulpha drugs** are alternatives of antibiotics, e.g., sulphanilamide, sulphadiazine, etc.
- **Antacids** are used as a remedy for acidity. e.g., magnesium hydroxide, sodium bicarbonate (baking soda), etc.
- **Pesticides** are used to destroy the organisms that harm the crop.
  These are of the following types
  1. **Insecticides** e.g., DDT, aluminium phosphate, gammexane.
  2. **Fungicide** e.g., bordeaux mixture.
  3. **Herbicides** e.g., benzipram, benzadox.
  4. **Rodenticides** e.g., aluminium phosphide.

Polymers

They are made up of many repeating units known as monomers. Some important polymers such as plastics, fibres and rubber are discussed below.

Plastics

- These are cross-linked polymers (a substance having high molecular weight and repeating unit) and are very tough.
- **Lac** is a natural plastic (polymer).

These are of two types

1. **Thermoplastics** are the polymers which can be easily softens on heating and hard on cooling e.g., polythene, polystyrene, polyvinyl chloride, teflon etc.
2. **Thermosetting plastics** are the polymers which undergo permament change on heating due to excessive cross-linking. These cannot be reused, e.g., bakelite.

Some Important Polymers and their Monomers

Polymer	Monomer
Polyethylene	Ethylene
Polystyrene	Styrene
Polyvinyl chloride (PVC)	Vinyl chloride
Polytetrafluoro ethylene (PTFE) or teflon	Tetrafluoro ethene
Bakelite	Formaldehyde + Phenol
Urea formaldehyde resin	Urea + Formaldehyde
Melmac	Melamine + Formaldehyde

Fibres

These have strong intermolecular forces like hydrogen bonding. e.g., nylon-66, dacron, orlon, etc.

Natural Rubber

It is an elastomer. It is a polymer of isoprene (2-methyl-1, 3 butadiene). It is also called *cis*-polyisoprene. Synthetic rubber (neoprene) is a polymer of chloroprene.

- It is insoluble in water, dilute acids and alkalies, absorbs a large amount of water and has low tensile strength and elasticity.
- It is heated with sulphur compounds at 373K in the presence of ZnO to improve the properties. This process is called vulcanisation of rubber.
- If it is vulcanised with 5% S, it is used for making tyres and if with 30% sulphur, it is used in making battery cases.
- *Trans*-polyisoprene is called *gutta-purcha*.
- Thiokol rubber is a polymer of ethylene chloride and sodium polysulphide and is used in the manufacture of hoses, tank lining, engine gaskets and rocket fuel.

Explosives

Some examples of explosives are trinitrotoluene (TNT), nitroglycerine or trinitroglycerine (TNG), cyclotrimethylene trinitroamine (RDX, also called cyclonite).

AIR, WATER

Air or Atmosphere

- Air is a homogeneous mixture of different gases.
- It has the following composition : 78% nitrogen; 21% oxygen, 0.03-0.05% carbon dioxide (CO_2), argon, etc.
- An atmosphere is a layer of these gases surrounding a planet or other material body of sufficient mass that is held in place by the gravity of the body.

Constituent of Atmosphere

It has different density at different heights from sea level. Thus, several layers are formed. *These layers are*

Troposphere

- It is the lowest layer of atmosphere, extend upto a height of 18 km from sea level.
- It is a turbulent and dusty zone which contains air (N_2, O_2, CO_2) much water vapours and clouds.

Stratosphere

- It lies between 18-60 km above sea level.
- It is the layer which contains ozone layer (protects us from harmful UV rays coming from the Sun), so called ozonosphere.

Mesosphere

- It extends from 60-85 km above sea level.
- Its temperature decreases with height and reaches to $-100°$C. That's why when any meteors enter in mesosphere, it burns up.

Thermosphere

- It extends up to 10-50 km above sea level.
- In this region, the temperature can rise to 1500°C, a person would not feel warm because of the extreme low pressure.
- The international space station orbit is also in thermosphere.

Exosphere

- It lies between 500-1600 km above sea level.
- This region contains ionised gases.
- Beyond this region, interstellar space is present.

Major Gases in Air

Oxygen (O_2)

- It was discovered by K Scheele.
- It is obtained during photosynthesis.
- It is colourless, odourless, neutral gas which gets adsorbed over alkaline pyrogallol.
- It is non-combustible, but helps in combustion. It form oxides with metals and non-metals.
- It is used for artificial respiration and in oxy-hydrogen flame and, oxygen-ethylene flame and oxygen-acetylene flame (used for welding) and as a rocket fuel.
- **Metal oxides** are generally basic but alumina (Al_2O_3), zinc oxide (ZnO) and tin oxide (SnO_2) are amphoteric oxides.
- **Carbon dioxide** (CO_2) is acidic while carbon monoxide (CO) is neutral.

Ozone (O_3)

- It is an allotrope of oxygen.
- It is used as an insecticide, in purification of water, to preserve food, to synthesise artificial silk and camphor, act as a bleaching agent.

Nitrogen (N_2)

- It was discovered by Rutherford (in 1771).
- It is a colourless, odourless, non-combustible, non-poisonous gas.
- It is neutral and lighter than air containing N_2.
- It is filled in sealed packets and bulbs to create inert atmosphere.
- Living beings die in an environment of nitrogen.
- Soil contains several pores filled with air containing N_2. At the time of raining these pores get filled with water. That's why earthworm come at the surface to breath.

Carbon Dioxide (CO_2)

- It is used by plants for photosynthesis.
- It is 1.5 times heavier than water.
- It turns the lime water milky which disappears in the excess of CO_2 due to conversion of milky calcium carbonate $(CaCO_3)$ into soluble calcium bicarbonate.
- It is used to extinguish fire and for artificial respiration when mixed with oxygen (carbogen).
- It is dangerous to have **charcoal fire** burning in a closed room because it produces carbon monoxide gas, which is suffocating.
- **Plants respire** at night and releases CO_2 which reduces oxygen content of air required for breathing, so it is dangerous to sleep under trees at night.
- **Eno** (fruit salt) produces effervescence if dissolved in water due to evolution of CO_2 gas.

Water (H_2O)

- It contains two elements : hydrogen and oxygen (H_2O). It constitute about 70% part of Earth.
- It is a universal solvent and maintains the body temperature due to its high specific heat.
- It has boiling point ° and freezing point ° Its density is maximum at 4°C.

Types of Water

There are different types of water

Soft water Soft water easily form lather with soap due to absence of soluble salts, calcium and magnesium.

Hard water It does not form lather with soap due to presence of Calcium and magnesium salts.

It is of two types

Temporary Hard Water

- It contains bicarbonates of calcium and magnesium.
- It is converted into soft water by boiling or by adding calculated quantity of calcium hydroxide (Clark's process).

Permanent Hard Water

- It contains sulphates and chlorides of calcium and magnesium.
- It is converted into soft water by adding sodium carbonate (Na_2CO_3), or calgon or zeolite.

Heavy Water

It is deuterium oxide, D_2O (molecular mass 20). It is used as a moderator in nuclear reactors, in the study of mechanisms of chemical reactions involving hydrogen and its compounds, etc.

POLLUTION

Pollution is the contamination of material particles or energy into the natural environment. It causes adverse effects on the ecosystem.

Types of Pollution

Air Pollution

- It occurs when any harmful gases, dust, smoke enters into the atmosphere and make it difficult for plants, animals and humans to survive.
- Common respiratory diseases such as asthma, bronchitis can occur.

Water Pollution

- It is due to the presence of foreign substances like sewage, algae, soluble salts, etc., in water.
- It can also be due to presence of metals in water. This pollution causes following diseases.

Metal	Disease
Chromium and Arsenic	Cancer
Cadmium	Itai-itai disease
Mercury	Minamata disease

- For a healthy aquatic life, dissolved oxygen (DO) is 5-6 ppm.
- For clean water, BOD (biochemical oxygen demand) is less than 5 ppm while for highly polluted water, it is 17 ppm or more.

Soil Pollution

It is alteration in soil. It is caused by pesticides, insecticides (e.g., DDT, BHC etc) herbicides (e.g., sodium chlorate), fungicides (e.g., organomercury compounds).

Hazardous Effect of Pollution

Greenhouse Effect

It is the heating of Earth and its objects because of the trapping of IR radiations by carbon dioxide (CO_2), methane (CH_4), nitric oxide (NO), ozone (O_3), chlorofluoro carbons (CFCs) and water vapours.

Global Warming

- It is a result of increased concentration of greenhouse gases.
- It may result in melting of ice caps and glaciers, spreading of several infectious diseases like malaria, sleeping sickness, etc.

Acid Rain (By Robert Augus)

- It has pH less than 5. It is due to the presence of oxides of nitrogen and sulphur in air that dissolve in rain water and forms nitric acid and sulphuric acid.
- It damages the buildings and other structures made up of limestone and results in several diseases such as skin infections.
- pH of normal rain water is 5.6.

Pollutants

These are the substances that contaminate the environment and of two types

Primary Pollutants

These persist in the environment in the form in which they are produced e.g., sulphur dioxide (SO_2), nitrogen dioxide (NO_2), etc.

Secondary Pollutants

- These are the products of reaction of primary pollutants e.g., PAN (Perocyacylnitrates), ozone (O_3), aldehyde, etc.
- The **order of different pollutants** to cause pollution is carbon monoxide (CO), SO_2 > hydrocarbon > particulates > nitrogen oxides.

Carbon Monoxide (CO)

- It is formed by incomplete combustion.
- It is a colourless, odourless gas.
- It contain a triple bond and are fairly polar, resulting in a tendency to bind permanently to haemoglobin molecules, displacing oxygen, which has a lower binding affinity.

Particulates

These are minute solid particles and liquid droplets dispersed in air. e.g., mists, dusts, smoke, fumes, etc.

Disease	Cause
Pneumoconiosis	Due to inhalation of coal dust.
Silicosis	Due to inhalation of free silica (SiO_2).
Black lung disease	Found in workers of coal mines.
White lung disease	Found in textile workers.
Byssinosis	Due to inhalation of cotton fibre dust.

Smog

It is a consequence of particulate pollution and is of two types

Classical Smog

- It is also called London type smog.
- It is reducing in nature.

- It is formed in cool humid climate when carbon soot particles combine with gaseous oxides of sulphur.

Photochemical Smog

- It is also called Los Angeles smog.
- It occurs in warm, dry and sunny climate by the action of sunlight on unsaturated hydrocarbons and nitrogen oxide.
- It is oxidising in nature.

Tropospheric Pollution

Presence of undesirable solid or gaseous particles in the air. Gaseous air pollutants are S, N and C, H_2S, hydrocarbons, ozone and other oxidants. Particulate pollutants are dust, mist, fumes, smoke, smog, etc.

Stratospheric Pollution

- Stratospheric pollution means depletion of ozone layer (ozone hole) by certain compounds like chlorofluorocarbons (CFCs), oxides of nitrogen (which are released into upper atmosphere from engines of supersonic transport planes).
- CCl_4, halons and methyl chloroform also **deplete ozone layer**.
- Depletion of ozone layer can cause skin cancer, sunburn, ageing of skin, cataract or even blindness and also increases the evaporation of surface water.

Industrial Names of Some Important Compounds

Industrial Name	Chemical Name and Formula
Alum	Potassium aluminium sulphate ($K_2SO_4 \cdot Al_2(SO_4)_3 \cdot 24\ H_2O$)
Alcohol	Ethyl alcohol (C_2H_5OH)
Baking powder	Sodium bicarbonate ($NaHCO_3$)
Blue vitriol	Copper sulphate ($CuSO_4 \cdot 5H_2O$)
Bleaching powder	Calcium hypochlorite ($CaOCl_2$)
Borax	Sodium tetraborate decahydrate ($Na_2B_4O_7 \cdot 10H_2O$)
Brine or salt	Sodium chloride (NaCl)
Calomel	Mercurous chloride (Hg_2Cl_2 or HgCl)
Caustic potash	Potassium hydroxide (KOH)
Caustic soda	Sodium hydroxide (NaOH)
Chile salt petre	Sodium nitrate ($NaNO_3$)
Chloroform	Trichloromethane ($CHCl_3$)
Dry ice	Solid carbon dioxide (CO_2)

Industrial Name	Chemical Name and Formula
Epsum	Magnesium sulphate ($MgSO_4 \cdot 7H_2O$)
Glauber's salt	Sodium sulphate decahydrate ($Na_2SO_4 \cdot 10H_2O$)
Green vitriol	Ferrous sulphate ($FeSO_4 \cdot 7H_2O$)
Gypsum	Calcium sulphate ($CaSO_4 \cdot 2H_2O$)
Hypo	Sodium thiosulphate pentahydrate ($Na_2S_2O_3 \cdot 5H_2O$)
Laughing gas	Nitrous oxide (N_2O)
Litharge	Lead oxide (PbO)
Lunar castic	Silver nitrate ($AgNO_3$)
Magnesia	Magnesium oxide (MgO)
Marble or chalk or pearl	Calcium carbonate ($CaCO_3$)
Marsh gas	Methane (CH_4)
Mohr's salt	Ferrous ammonium sulphate, $(NH_4)_2SO_4 \cdot FeSO_4 \cdot 6H_2O$
Mosaic gold	Stannous sulphide (SnS_2)
Muriatic acid	Hydrogen chloride (HCl)
Pearl ash	Potassium carbonate (K_2CO_3)
Plaster of Paris	Calcium sulphate hemihydrate $\left(CaSO_4 \cdot \frac{1}{2} H_2O \right)$
Quicklime	Calcium oxide (CaO)
Red lead	Lead peroxide (Pb_3O_4)
Rock salt	Sodium chloride ($NaCl$)
Ruby or sapphire	Aluminium oxide, (Al_2O_3)
Sand	Silicon dioxide (SiO_2)
Sal ammoniac	Ammonium chloride (NH_4Cl)
Slaked lime	Calcium hydroxide [$Ca(OH)_2$]
Spirit	Methyl alcohol (CH_3OH)
Soda ash	Sodium carbonate (Na_2CO_3)
Vinegar	Acetic acid (CH_3COOH)
Vermilion	Mercuric sulphide (HgS)
Washing soda	Sodium carbonate decahydrate ($Na_2CO_3 \cdot 10H_2O$)
White vitriol	Zinc sulphate ($ZnSO_4 \cdot 7H_2O$)

Important Points

A candle blows off when covered because it does not get oxygen which helps in burning.

Phosphorus catches fire if kept in air but it is unreactive with water, so it is kept in water.

When **sugar is heated** above 200°C, it decomposes into carbon and water. Therefore, gets charred.

While **making ice cream**, salt is mixed with ice to reduce freezing temperature from 0°C to 5°C, This helps to freeze the cream.

Lactose content of milk undergoes fermentation and changes into lactic acid which on reaction with lactose forms curd.

Zinc phosphide is used for killing rats and zinc chloride is used for coating furniture to prevent termites.

Calcium hydride (CaH) is called hydrolith. In flash bulb, magnesium wire is kept in atmosphere of nitrogen gas.

Barium sulphate is used in X-rays of abdomen as barium meal.

Silver and copper are best conductor of electricity. Gold and silver are the most malleable metal.

Iron pyrites (FeS_2) is known as fool's gold.

Zinc oxide (ZnO) is known as flower of zinc or chinese white and is used as white paint.

Silver spoon is not used in egg food as it turns black.

Mercury is stored in iron pot.

Radium is extracted from pitch blende.

Phosphine gas is used in Holme's signals.

Sea weeds contain iodine. Bones contain 57% calcium phosphate.

Artificial perfumes are prepared from ethyl acetate.

Chlorine is used for the purification of water, for synthesis of baking powder, etc.

Na and K are highly **reactive**. They react with air and water that's why, they are kept in kerosene oil.

The Nobel Prize in Chemistry (2014) Eric Betzig, Stefan W Hell, William E Moerner won the Nobel Prize in Chemistry (2014), for the smart work of surpassing the limitations of the light microscope, which has brought optical microscopy into the nano dimension. By this achievement, scientists can visualise the roadways of individual molecules in the living cells. Now this can be seen that how molecules produce synapses between nerve cells in the brain. Also they can find proteins involved in different diseases like Parkinson, Alzheimer and Huntington as well as in fertilised eggs.

The Nobel Prize in Chemistry (2015) was awarded jointly to Tomas Lindahl, Paul Modrich and Aziz Sancar. "for mechanistic studies of DNA repair".

They have mapped, at a molecular level, how cell repair damaged DNA and safeguard the genetic information. Their work has provided fundamental knowledge of how a living cell function and can be used for the developments of new cancer treatment.

Nobel Prize in Chemistry 2016

The Nobel Prize in chemistry for 2016 has been awarded to Jean-pierre. Sauvage, sir J. Fraser Stoddart and Bernars L. Feringa for *developing molecular machines*.

"Molecular machines will most. Likely to be used in the development of things such as were materials, sensors and energy storage systems."

BIOLOGY

INTRODUCTION

- Biology is a natural science concerned with the study of life and living organisms, *i.e.*, plants and animals. It is classified into two part: Botany and zoology.
- Study of plants is called **Botany** and study of animals is called **Zoology**. Zoology and Botany are collectively called **Biology**. The term 'Biology' was coined by **Lamarck** and **Treviranus**.
- The scientist who gave his thought for the first time about the life of plants and animals was **Aristotle**. That's why he is known as the *Father of Biology*. He is also known as the *Father of Zoology*.
- Theophrastus is known as *Father of Botany*.

CHARACTERISTIC OF LIVING ORGANISMS

- They have cellular organisation and also respire, *i.e.*, take in O_2 and evolve CO_2.
- Metabolism is one of the most important characteristic feature of living organism. It comprises two phases that are anabolism (constructive phase) and catabolism (destructive phase.)
- They take nutrition for their growth.
- They have tendency to reproduce.
- They have the ability to respond to changes in both internal and external environment *i.e.*, they have sensitivity. Their survival chances are maximum.
- They move from place to place as animals or some bacteria. Plants cannot move but some movement can occur in plants.

The Cell

- The Cell is the basic structural and functional unit of all known living organisms. It is the smallest unit of life and is often called the building block of life.
- The branch of biology which deals with the study of cell, is called **Cytology**.
- **Robert Hooke** coined the term *cell* when he saw honey-comb like structure in the section of cork. However, he only discovered *cell wall*.
- The first living cell was discovered by **Leeuwenhoek**.

Types of Cells
These are of two types

1. **Prokaryotic Cells**
   (*Pro*=primitive, *karyos*=nucleus) These are primitive cells, lacking a well defined nucleus and most of the other cell organelles, *e.g.*, bacterial cell.

2. **Eukaryotic Cells** (*Eu* = true, *karyos* = nucleus) These have a well defined nucleus and membrane bound cell organelles. These are present in unicellular and multicellular plant and animal cells.

Differences between Prokaryotic and Eukaryotic Cell

Prokaryotic Cell	Eukaryotic Cell
Simplest and primitive in nature.	Developed and comparatively complex in nature.
Lacks nuclear envelope	Nucleus is present with elaborate nuclear envelope
Membrane bound cell organelles are absent.	Membrane bound cell organelles are present.
Single naked chromosome present.	Many chromosomes are present.
Cell division is direct.	Cell division occurs by mitosis or meiosis.

Facts about Cell

- The largest known cells are unfertilised Ostrich egg cells (size 6 inch diameter).
- The smallest cell is of PPLO (*Mycoplasma gallisepticum* of size 0.1-0.3 μm).
- **Human nerve cell** is the longest animal cell.
- Largest unicellular plant is *Acetabularia* (10 cm) and animal is *Amoeba* (1 mm).
- The largest human cell is the **female ovum** and the smallest human cell is the **red blood cell**.

Parts of Cell and their Functions

A typical cell consists of cell wall and protoplasm.

Protoplasm of Cell

It is the living fluid matter present inside the plasma membrane. The fluid present outside the nuclear membrane is called **cytoplasm** and the fluid present inside the nuclear membrane is called **nucleoplasm**. Deutoplasm is the non-living matter of the cell.

Cell Wall

It is present in plant cells, bacteria, fungi, algae and some archaea. It is composed of cellulose in plants and chitin in fungi. It is non-living. Its main function is to provide shape and rigidity to the cell.

Plasma Membrane

The cell is enclosed by a thin membrane called the **cell membrane** or **plasmalemma**. It is composed of proteins and phospholipid molecules. It is elastic, living and selectively permeable, *i.e.*, provide passage for various substances.

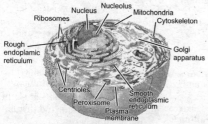

Structure of the Cell

Mitochondria

- It was discovered by **R Altman** in 1880 and the term **mitochondria** was coined by **Carl Benda**.
- It is bounded by a double membrane. The inner membrane has many folds, called the **cristae**. Fluid (called matrix) is present on interior, which contains many enzymes and coenzymes. It is a semi-autonomous (can form its own copies) organelle and is called **power house of the cell** because in it, stepwise oxidation of fuel occurs which results in release of chemical energy. This energy is stored in the form of ATP.

Plastids

- These are present only in plant cells and are of three types– chloroplasts (green), leucoplasts (white) and chromoplasts (of various colours except green). Chloroplast is the site of photosynthesis as it contains chlorophyll, while leucoplasts are storage plastids. Chloroplast is called the **kitchen of the cell**.
- The red colour of tomatoes is due to the presence of lycopene pigment, *i.e.*, chromophore.
- The colour of carrot is due to carotene pigment.

Endoplasmic Reticulum

It was discovered by **KR Porter**. These are hollow membranous system having ribosomes (thus called Rough ER) or no ribosomes (thus called Smooth ER).

Rough endoplasmic reticulum is the site of protein synthesis, while smooth endoplasmic reticulum is the site of synthesis of steroids and detoxification.

Golgi Apparatus

It was discovered by **Camillo Golgi**. It is made up of sac-like flattened structures and play an important role in secretion, transportation and acrosome formation.

Nobel Prize in Physiology and Medicine 2013

The Nobel Prize in Physiology or medicine 2013 was awarded jointly to James E Rothman, Randy W Schekman and Thomas C Sudhof for their discoveries of machinery regulating vesicle traffic, a major transport system in our cells. In general, we call it Golgi body. Randy Schekman discovered a set of genes that were required for vesicle traffic. James Rothman discovered machinery that allows vesicle to fuse with their targets to deliver the stored matter..

Ribosomes

Ribosomes were discovered by **GE Palade**. These are minute, non-membranous particles, composed of RNA and protein. 70 S type of ribosomes are found in prokaryotes, while 80 S type in eukaryotes. These are the site of protein synthesis.

Lysosomes

- Lysosomes were discovered by **de Duve**. These are polymorphic organelles having hydrolytic enzymes. These enzymes function at (acidic) pH ~ 5. These are sometimes called **suicidal bags of the cell**.
- Lysosome helps in carcinogenesis, *i.e.*, conversion of a normal cell into cancerous cell.

Centrosome

It was discovered by **T Boveri**. It is composed of two set of centrioles and participate in the formation of mitotic spindle during cell division.

Vacuoles

These are non-living reservoir, bounded by a membrane called tonoplast. Pigment anthocyanin is present in the cell vacuole, which provide colour to flowers. It stores toxic metabolic waste and helps in osmoregulation.

Nucleus

It was discovered by **Robert Brown**. It contains nucleoplasm, nucleolus and chromatin material. Nucleolus is rich in protein and RNA. All this material is covered up by a nuclear membrane. Chromatin is the **controlling centre of cell** as it form chromosomes.

Chromosome

Chromosome is thread-like structure, found in the nucleus. Bead-like structures found on chromosome are called **genes**, which are made up of DNA and are the carrier of genetic information from generation to generation. Chromosomes are units of inheritance. In some viruses *e.g.* retrovirus, RNA is the genetic material.

Differences between Plant and Animal Cell

Plant Cell	Animal Cell
It has cell wall.	Cell wall is usually absent.
Plastids are found.	Plastids are usually absent.
Centrioles and centrosome are absent.	Centrioles and centrosomes are found in all cells.
A big vacuole is present.	Vacuole is absent or very small in size.

Nucleic Acids

These contain the genetic instructions used in the development and functioning of all known living organisms.
These are of two types : DNA and RNA.

Deoxyribonucleic Acid (DNA)

- DNA was discovered by **James D Watson** and **Francis Crick**, who got Nobel Prize for this discovery.
- It is a long polymer made from repeating units called nucleotides.
- Each nucleotide consists of a nucleoside (i.e. nitrogenous base and deoxyribose sugar) and a phosphate group, joined together by phosphodiester bonds.
- It has four bases, *i.e.* adenine, guanine, cytosine and thymine.
- Adenine and guanine are the **purine** bases; cytosine and thymine are **pyrimidine** bases.

Ribonucleic Acid (RNA)

- It is also made up of a long chain of nucleotides.
- Each nucleotide consists of a nitrogenous base, a ribose sugar, and a phosphate group.
- It contains uracil in place of thymine.
- RNA is of three types—
    - mRNA (messenger RNA)
    - rRNA (ribosomal RNA)
    - tRNA (transfer RNA)

These three RNA's take part in protein synthesis.

Cell Division

- It is the process by which a cell increase in number. It is essential for the growth, development and repair of the body.

- It is of two types – *Mitosis and Meiosis*

(i) **Mitosis** It occurs in unicellular organism during asexual reproduction. Each mitotic cell division results in the formation of two daughter cells having number of chromosomes equal to the parent cell.

   Tumour or cancer is a result of uncontrolled mitosis.

(ii) **Meiosis** It occurs in reproductive cells and is called reduction division because of the presence of single set of chromosomes (*i.e.*, half of the parent chromosomes). It results in the formation of four daughter cells.

- Exchange of genetic material occurs between chromatids (branches of chromosome) of a diploid set during pachytene stage of meiosis and is known as crossing over.

Differences between DNA and RNA

DNA	RNA
It usually occurs inside nucleus and in some cell organelles like mitochondria and chloroplast.	Very little RNA occurs inside nucleus. Most of it is found in the cytoplasm.
DNA is the genetic material except in some viruses.	RNA is not the genetic material except in certain viruses, *e.g.*, HIV, reovirus.
It is double stranded with the exception of some viruses like $\phi \times 174$.	RNA is single stranded with the exception of some viruses, *e.g.*, double stranded in T_2, T_4, T_6 bacteriophage.
DNA shows regular helical coiling.	There is no regular coiling except in parts of RNA.
It contains deoxyribose sugar.	It contains ribose sugar.
Nitrogen base thymine occurs in DNA along with other three i.e. adenine, cytosine and guanine.	Thymine is replaced by uracil in RNA. The other three are adenine, cytosine and guanine.
It replicates to form new DNA molecules.	It cannot replicate itself except in RNA-RNA viruses.
DNA controls heredity, evolution, metabolism, structure and differentiation.	RNA controls only protein synthesis.

BIOMOLECULES

Biomolecules are the substances that are essential for a living being to perform the basic functions, *e.g.*, carbohydrates, proteins, lipids (fats), nucleic acids and vitamins.

Carbohydrates

- It was believed that these are the organic compounds which have carbon, hydrogen and oxygen in the ratio of $1 : 2 : 1$ but starch $(C_6H_{10}O_5)_n$ and

some others are exceptions. So this definition has been changed. According to modern definition, these are the polyhydroxy aldehydes and ketones or their derivatives.

- These are the source of energy and about 50-75% energy is obtained by the oxidation of carbohydrates.

- The main end product of carbohydrate digestion is glucose, which is called **blood sugar**. It oxidises to give energy along with CO_2 and H_2O.

- 1 gm glucose provides about 17 kJ energy or 4.2 kcal energy.
- Carbohydrates are better fuel as compared to proteins and fats as they readily decompose to give energy.
- Main sources of carbohydrates are wheat, maize, rice, potato etc.

The carbohydrates are categorised into following three types

Monosaccharides

- These are simple sugars, which cannot be hydrolysed further, *e.g.,* ribose, glucose, fructose, galactose etc.
- In human beings, blood glucose level is 100-120 mg/mL. Extra glucose, if any, is converted into glycogen in the liver by a process called **glycogenesis**.
- **D-fructose** is the sweetest of all sugars and is found in fruit juice, honey etc.

Oligosaccharides

- They release 2-10 monosaccharides on hydrolysis, like disaccharides, e.g. sucrose, lactose maltose etc and trisaccharides, like raffinose etc.
- Sucrose is also called **invert sugar**. It gives glucose and fructose when subjected to hydrolysis.

Polysaccharides

- They release more than ten monosaccharides on hydrolysis. These are non-sugars, *i.e.,* do not have sweet taste, *e.g.,* cellulose, glycogen and starch.
- Cellulose is found in plant cell wall and is digested by ruminants (like cow, goat, buffalo, etc), but not by carnivorous or omnivorous animals like human beings. Thus, it acts as roughage in case of human beings.

Function of Carbohydrates

- Carbohydrates provide energy, that acts as reserve food, help in the synthesis of nucleic acid and form exoskeleton of animals. Excessive intake of carbohydrate results in digestive problems and obesity.

Proteins

These are found in all living cells. These are the compounds of carbon (C), hydrogen (H), oxygen (O), nitrogen (N) and sulphur (S). These form 15% part of human body. Snake venom, ricin of castor and bacterial toxins are proteinaceous in nature. Main sources of protein are groundnuts, soyabean, pulses, fish etc.

Function of Proteins

- These are important for the growth and repair of the body (75% of our body is protein only). However, in the deficiency of carbohydrates, these acts as the source of energy. Protein also control the development of genetic characters.
- Deficiency of protein causes **Kwashiorkor** (a disease in which hands and legs of children get slimmed and the stomach comes out) and **Marasmus** (a disease in which muscles of children are loosened). Kwashiorkor occurs in children between 1 to 5 years of age and marasmus in children below 1 year.

Lipids (Fats)

- These are also the compounds of carbon (C), hydrogen (H) and oxygen (O). Chemically, these are the ester of glycerol and fatty acids. These are present in cytoplasm, cell wall etc.
- The main source of fats are ghee, butter, almond, cheese, egg yolk, meat, soyabean etc.
- Fats are digested by enzymes called lipases in the small intestine. Generally, at 20°C, these are in solid state but if their state is liquid at this temperature, these are termed as oils.
- Fatty acids are of two types- Saturated and Unsaturated. Saturated fatty acids are found in coconut oil and palm oil, while unsaturated fatty acids are found in fish oil and vegetable oil.
- Excess of saturated fats raises the level of blood cholesterol and may cause arteriosclerosis. This may lead to heart attack.

Function of Lipids

The main functions of lipids are

- These provide twice the energy than that from carbohydrates.
- These remain under the skin and prevents the loss of heat from the body.

Malnutrition Effects

- Deficiency of fat results in dryskin and weight loss.
- If fat is in excess, the body gets fatty and result in several heart diseases and high blood pressure.
- The skin fat, in case of whales and seals, forms a thick layer called the blubber. It acts as reserve food and also maintains the body temperature.

Vitamin

- It was first discovered by **FG Hopkin**. However, the term vitamin was coined by **C Funk**.
- Vitamin is an organic compound, which cannot be synthesised in sufficient quantities by an organism and must be obtained from the diet.
- They provide no calories, they only regulate chemical reactions occurring in the metabolism of the body.

These are divided into two groups

1. **Fat soluble vitamin**, *viz*. vitamin-A, D, E and K.
2. **Water soluble vitamin**, *viz*. vitamin-B and C.
- Vitamin-B_{12} contains cobalt. Vitamin-D is synthesised in our skin by the action of ultraviolet rays of the sunlight. Vitamin-K is synthesised in our colon by the bacteria.
- Water soluble vitamins normally do not show hypervitaminosis (this disease occurs due to excess intake of vitamins) as excess of these vitamins is normally excreted through urine.
- In balanced diet, all the important nutrients (like carbohydrate, protein, fats, vitamins etc.) are available in sufficient quantity.

Vitamins, their Deficiency Diseases and Sources

Vitamin	Chemical Name	Deficiency Disease	Source
Vitamin-A	Retinol, carotenoids	Night-blindness(Nyctalopia), Hyperkeratosis, Keratomalacia	Orange, green vegetables, carrots, pumpkin, squash and spinach.
Vitamin-D	Calciferol	Rickets and Osteomalacia	Fish, eggs, liver and mushrooms.
Vitamin-E	Tocopherols, tocotrienols	Infertility	Many fruits and vegetables.
Vitamin-K	Phylloquinone	Non-clotting of blood	Green vegetables
Vitamin-B_1	Thiamine	Beri-beri, Wernicke-Korsakoff syndrome	Oatmeal, rice, vegetables, cauliflower, potatoes, liver and eggs.
Vitamin-B_2	Riboflavin	Cracking of skin, reddish eye, cracking of tongue	Dairy products, bananas, popcorn and green beans.
Vitamin-B_3	Niacin and nicotinic acid	Pellagra, Glossitis	Meat, broccoli and avocados.
Vitamin-B_5	Pentothenic acid	Premature greying of hair (Achromotrichia),	Meat, fish, eggs, many vegetables, mushrooms.
Vitamin-B_6	Pyridoxine	Dermatitis, anaemia, mental disorder	Meat, vegetables, tree nuts and bananas.
Vitamin-B_7	Biotin	Dermatitis, enteritis and anaemia	Raw egg yolk, liver, peanuts and vegetables.
Vitamin-B_9	Folic acid, folinic acid	Megaloblastic anaemia and birth defects.	Leafy vegetables, pasta, bread, cereal and liver.
Vitamin-B_{12}	Cyanocobalamin (contains cobalt)	Pernicious anaemia	Meat and other animal products.
Vitamin-C	Ascorbic acid	Scurvy (Sailer's disease)	Peppers, citrus fruits.

Biological Evolution

Origin of Universe

- The universe is made up of matter and energy. Scientists believe that it was formed about 10 to 13 billion years ago as a vast, dense, red-hot and rotating gaseous cloud of cosmic dust called the "primaeval matter or 'ylem'.
- Two hypothesis *i.e.*, Big -Bang (universe formation through a very big explosion) and Nebular (universe formation by the condensation of gaseous cloud) were given to explain origin of Earth.

ORIGIN OF LIFE

- Life originated on Earth about 3.5 billion years ago. Some philosophical theories like special creation, spontaneous generation, Biogenesis, panspermia (life originated in the form of pansperms from some unknown part of the universe) or cosmozoic and catastrophism (life orginated suddenly from inorganic matter) were given to explain origin of life.
- The first scientific account of the origin of life was given by Russian scientist AI Oparin in his book 'Origin of life'.
- The primitive atmosphere contained hydrogen, methane, ammonia and water vapour. In it, oxygen and ozone were absent. Thus, it was believed that life is originated from inorganic substances by a series of complex reaction.
- Hydrogen atoms were most numerous and most reactive in the primitive atmosphere. First, these combined with all available oxygen atoms, forming water and leaving no free oxygen atoms. Thus, the primitive atmosphere was 'reducing' unlike the present 'oxidising' atmosphere. This was also supported by **Miller** and **Urey** in 1953.
- In Miller-Urey experiment, a mixture of water, hydrogen, methane and ammonia was cycled through an apparatus and the organic compound, amino acids were obtained.

Organic Evolution

More and more creation of organism by gradual changes from low category animal to higher animal is called **organic evolution**.

There are several evidences regarding organic evolution.

Evidences from morphology and anatomy

On the basis of morphology (outer appearance) and anatomy (inner structure), several evidences have been described as follows

Homologous Organs

- The organs which are similar in basic structure and origin but dissimilar in function are called homologous organs, *e.g.*, wings of bat; cat's paw, front foot of horse, human's hand and wings of birds.
- These show divergent evolution.

Analogous Organs (Homoplastic)

- The organs which are similar in shape and function but dissimilar in their origin and development. *e.g.*, wings of insects, birds and bats, eyes of octopus and mammals.
- They show convergent evolution.

Vestigial Organs

- These are degenerate, non-functional organs which were functional earlier.
- Human body has been described to possess about 90 vestigial organs. Some of these are muscles of ear pinna, canine teeth and third molar teeth, body hairs, vermiform appendix, nictitating membrane of eye, caudal vertebral (coccyx or tail bone) etc.

Atavism *or* Reversion

It is the sudden reappearance of some ancestral features. Appearance of thick body hair, large canines, monstral face, short temporary tails, extra nipples etc are examples of atavism.

Evidence from Connecting Links

Connecting link is one which exhibit characteristics of more than one groups.

Intermediate Forms between Two Groups of Organisms

Organism	Connecting Link Between
Virus	Living and non-living
Euglena (Protozoa)	Plants and animals
Proterospongia (Protozoa)	Protozoa and Porifera
Peripatus (Arthropoda)	Annelida and Arthropoda
Neopilina (Mollusca)	Annelida and Mollusca
Balanoglossus (Chordata)	Non-chordata and Chordata
Dipnoi (Lung fish)	Pisces and Amphibia
Archaeopteryx (Aves)	Reptiles and Aves
Prototheria (Mammalia)	Reptiles and Mammalia

THEORIES OF EVOLUTION

Lamarckism (1809)

- Jean-Baptiste de Lamarck gave the idea that an organism can pass on characteristics that it acquired during its lifetime to its offspring (also known as heritability of acquired characteristics).
- Lamarck's theory of evolution was published in *Philosophie Zoologique* and had four propositions, *viz*
  1. Living organisms and its parts tend to increase in size due to internal force of life.
  2. Formation of new organs is the result of a new need and new involvement.
  3. Individuals lose characteristics that they do not require (or use) and develop characteristics that are useful.
  4. Individuals inherit the traits of their ancestors.

Darwinism (1859)

- Darwin's theory of evolution *was Origin of Species* by Natural Selection.
- The theory consists of five propositions, they are
  1. Overproduction or enormous fertility
  2. Struggle for existence
  3. Variation and heredity
  4. Survival of the fittest or natural selection
  5. *Origin of species*.

Mutation Theory

- Hugo de Vries proposed the theory of mutation, while working on *Oenothera lamarckiana* plant.
- Mutations are discontinuous variations.
- Mutations are due to changes in chromosomes, genes and DNA.
- These may or may not be inherited.

Synthetic Theory

According to it, the five basic factors are

1. Gene mutation
2. Changes in chromosome structure and number
3. Genetic recombination
4. Natural selection
5. Reproductive isolation

First three factors are responsible for genetic variablity.

- Devonian period is known as Age of fishes.
- Mesozoic era is known as Age of Reptiles.
- Coenozoic era is known as Age of Mammals.

Classification of Organisms

In Linnaeus time, a two kingdom system of classification with Plantae and Animalia kingdom was developed. The system did not distinguish between the eukaryotes and prokaryotes, unicellular and multicellular and photosynthetic organisms.

Five Kingdom System

RH Whittaker (1969) proposed a five kingdom classification. The kingdom named were Monera, Protista, Fungi, Plantae and Animalia.

Classification of Animalia Kingdom

Storer *and* Usinger *classified animals into following phylums*

Characteristics of the Five Kingdoms

Character	Monera	Protista	Fungi	Plantae	Animalia
Cell type	Prokaryotic	Eukaryotic	Eukaryotic	Eukaryotic	Eukaryotic
Cell wall	Non-cellulosic	Present in some	Present	Present	Absent
Nuclear membrane	Absent	Present	Present	Present	Present
Body organisation	Cellular	Cellular	Multicellular/ loose tissue	Tissue/ organ	Tissue/ organ/organ system
Mode of nutrition	Autotrophic and heterotrophic	Autotrophic and heterotrophic	Heterotrophic	Autotrophic	Heterotrophic
Examples	Bacteria archaebacteria cyanobacteria and some primitive fungi	Amoeba Euglena Dinoflagellates	Acholrophyllus, heterotrophic fungi	Multicellular eukaryotic plants	Multicellular animals

Phylum–Protozoa

- These are unicellular animals, *i.e.*, made up of only one cell.
- In these, all the metabolic activity like digestion, respiration, excretion and reproduction takes place in unicellular body.
- Respiration and excretion take place through diffusion.

e.g., Amoeba, Plasmodium, Euglena etc.

Phylum–Porifera

- These are found in marine water and have porous body. The pores are called **ostia**. These are multicellular animals.
- Their skeleton is made up of minute calcareous or siliceous spicules.

e.g., Sycon, Sponge etc.

Phylum–Coelenterata

- These are aquatic animals, have thread-like structures called tentacles around the mouth which help in holding the food.
- They have specialised cnidoblast cell to help in catching the food.
- Phenomenon of polymorphism (many forms) and metagenesis (alternation of generation) are associated with coelentrates.

e.g., Hydra, Jelly fish, Sea Anemone etc.

- *Hydra* has a tendency of regeneration of body organs.

Phylum– Platyhelminthes

- Animals of this phylum have alimentary canal with single opening, anus is absent.
- Excretion takes place by flame cells.
- There is no skeletal system such as, respiratory system, circulatory system etc.
- These are hermaphrodite animals (males are not separated from females).

e.g., Planaria, Liver fluke, Tape worm etc.

Phylum–Aschelminthes

- These are long, cylindrical, unsegmented worms.
- Their alimentary canal is complete in which mouth and anus both are present.
- There is no circulatory and respiratory system but nervous system is developed. Excretion takes place through **protonephridia**.
- They are unisexual.
- Most forms are parasitic but some are free living in soil and water.

e.g., Ascaris, Threadworm, etc.

- Threadworm is found mainly in the anus of child. Due to which children feel itching and often vomits. Some children urinate on the bed at night.

Phylum-Annelida

- Their body is long, thin, soft and metamerically (truly) segmented.
- Alimentary canal is well-developed.
- These are the first to have proper organ systems.
- Nervous system is normal and blood (called haemolymph) is red (iron rich haemoglobin).
- Their blood flows in closed vessels.
- Like in earthworm, there are five pairs of blood vessels called as heart.
- They respire through skin, in some animals respiration takes place through coelom.
- Excretion by nephridia.
- They move through setae made up of chitin.

e.g. Earthworm, *Nereis,* Leech etc.

Phylum–Arthropoda

- Arthropoda is the largest phylum (contains maximum number of animals and its existence is recorded for maximum period over the Earth).
- Jointed leg is their main feature.
- Their body is divided into three parts–head, thorax and abdomen.
- Circulatory system is open type. Cockroach's heart has 13 chambers.
- Trachea or book lungs, body surface are respiratory organs.

e.g., Cockroach, Prawn, Crab, Bug, Fly, Mosquito, Bees, etc.

- Insects generally have six feets and four wings.
- Ant is a social animal which reflects division of labour.
- Termite is also a social animal which lives in colony.

Phylum–Mollusca

- Their body is soft and divided into head and muscular foot.
- Mantle is always present in it, which secretes a hard calcareous shell.
- Their alimentary canal is well-developed.
- Respiration takes place through gills or **ctenidia**. Blood is colourless.

- Excretion takes place through kidneys.

e.g., *Pila, Aplysia* (Sea rabbit), *Doris* (Sea lemon), *Octopus* (Devil-fish), *Sepia* (Cuttle-fish).

- Eyes of octopus are similar to chordate eyes.

Phylum– Echinodermata

- All the animals in this group are marine. They have **water vascular system**. Brain is not developed in nervous system.
- They have a special capacity of regeneration.
- These are the only invertebrate animals which contain proper bone like structures (ossicles).

e.g., Star fish, Sea urchin, Sea cucumber etc.

Phylum-Chordata

- They have notochord. A dorsal hollow tubular nerve cord and paired pharyngeal gill slits at some stage of their life span.
- In advanced forms, notochord changes to vertebral column, nerve cord develops to brain and spinal cord and pharyngeal gill slits to structures of jaw attachment.
- This phylum is sub-divided into two sub-phylum, i.e., Protochordata and Vertebrata.

Some main classes of phylum– Chordata are as follows

Pisces

- These are aquatic animals (cold-blooded animals). Their heart pumps only impure blood and have two chambers.
- Respiration takes place through gills.

e.g., *Trygon, Scoliodon, Torpedo etc.*

Amphibia (First land vertebrates)

- These are found both on land and water. All of them are cold-blooded.
- Respiration takes place through gills, skin and lungs.
- They have three chambered heart.

e.g., Frog, *Necturus*, Toad, *Icthyophis, Salamander*.

Reptilia (First true land vertebrates)

- These are crawling animals.
- These are cold-blooded and contains two pair of limbs.
- The skeleton is completely flexible.
- Respiration takes place through lungs.
- They have $3\frac{1}{2}$ chambered heart (four chambered in crocodile).
- Their eggs are covered with shell made up of calcium carbonate.

  e.g., Lizard, Snake, Tortoise, Crocodile, Turtle, *Sphenodon etc.*

  - Cobra is the only snake which makes nests.
  - *Heloderma* is the only poisonous lizard.
  - Sea snake is also called *Hydrophis belcheri*. It is the world's most poisonous snake.

Aves (Aerial Vertebrates Birds)

- The animals of this group are warm-blooded tetrapod vertebrates with flight adaptation.
- Their fore-feet are modified into wings to fly.
- They respire through lungs.
- Birds have no teeth, beak helps in feeding.
- They have a single ovary and pneumatic bones. *e.g.,* Crow, Peacock, Parrot etc.

  - Flightless birds are Kiwi and Emu.
  - Largest bird is Ostrich.
  - Smallest bird is Humming bird.
  - Largest zoo in India is Alipur (Kolkata) and the largest zoo of the world is Cruiser National Park in South Africa.

Mammalia

- These are warm-blooded animals.
- Tooth comes twice in these animals **(diphyodont)**.
- There is no nucleus in their red blood cells (except in camel and llama).
- Skin of mammals contains hair.
- External ear is present.

Mammalia is divided into three sub-classes

- **Prototheria** It lays eggs, *e.g.,* Echidna.
- **Metatheria** It bears the immature child, *e.g.,* Kangaroo.
- **Eutheria** It bears the well developed child, *e.g.,* Humans.
  They give birth to young ones, but *Echidna* and *Platypus* are the egg laying mammals.

SYSTEMS OF HUMAN BODY

Integumentary System

The human skin (integumentary) is composed of a minimum of three major layers of tissue, the **epidermis, dermis** and **hypodermis**.

Epidermis

The top layer of skin is made up of epithelial cells and does not contain blood vessels.

Dermis

- It gives elasticity to the integument, allowing stretching and conferring flexibility, while also resisting distortions, wrinkling and sagging.
- Nails grow 1 mm per week on an average.
- Protein, keratin stiffens epidermal tissue to form finger nails.

Hypodermis

- It is made up of adipose tissue.

  It performs several important functions
  1. Protect against invasion by infectious organisms.
  2. Protect the body from dehydration.
  3. Maintain homeostasis.
  4. Act as a receptor for touch, pressure, pain, heat and cold.
  5. Protect the body against sunburns by secreting melanin.
  6. Generate vitamin-D through exposure to ultraviolet light.
  7. Store water, fat, glucose and vitamin-D.

Animal Nutrition and Digestion

Animals are not able to synthesise their own food, therefore they obtain it from outside environment for their nutritional requirements.

Mineral Nutrients

- These are metals, non-metals and their salts other than the four elements—carbon, hydrogen, nitrogen and oxygen and constitute about 4% of total body weight.
- Milk, eggs, meat, fruit, food, vegetables etc are the sources of minerals.

Minerals are of two types

1. **Macronutrients** These are required in large amount, *e.g.*, calcium (Ca), phosphorus (P), potassium (K) etc.
2. **Micronutrients** These are required in very small amount (less than 1 g), *e.g.*, iodine (I), iron (Fe), zinc (Zn) etc.

Minerals and their Functions in the Body

Mineral	Major Food Source	Uses	Deficiency Disease
Macronutrients			
Calcium (Ca)	Milk, cheese, bread and vegetables.	Muscle contraction, nerve action, blood clotting and the formation of bone.	Tetany and rickets.
Phosphorus (P)	Cheese, eggs, pea nuts and most foods.	Bone and tooth formation, energy transfer from foods, DNA, RNA and ATP formation.	Tetany and rickets.
Sulphur (S)	Dairy products, meat, eggs and broccoli.	Formation of thiamine, keratin and coenzymes.	Disturbed protein metabolism
Potassium (K)	Potatoes, meat and chocolate.	Muscle contraction, nerve action, active transport.	Nervous disorder, poor muscles leading to paralysis.
Sodium (Na)	Any salted food, meat, eggs and milk.	Muscle contraction, nerve action and active transport.	Nervous, depression, muscular cramps, pH disbalance
Chlorine (Cl)	Salted food and seafood.	Anion/cation balance and gastric acid formation.	Loss of appetite muscle cramps.
Magnesium (Mg)	Meat, chocolate and green vegetable	Formation of bone, formation of coenzymes in cell respiration.	Irregularity of metabolism.
Micronutrients (Trace Elements)			
Iron (Fe)	Liver, kidney, red meat, cocoa powder and water cress	Formation of haemoglobin, myoglobin and cytochromes.	Anaemia and low immunity.
Fluorine (F)	Water supplies, tea, sea food, meat, liver and beans.	Resistance to tooth decay.	Weak teeth (if present in excess causes mottling of (teeth)
Zinc (Zn)	Meat, liver and beans.	Enzyme activation and carbon dioxide transport.	Anaemia, retarted growth, weak immunity and fertilty.
Copper (Cu)	Liver, meat and fish.	Enzyme, melanin and haemoglobin formation.	Anaemia, weak blood vessels and connective tissues.
Iodine (I)	Seafood, iodised salt and fish.	Thyroxine production	Goitre
Manganese (Mn)	Tea, nuts, spices and cereals.	Bone development and enzyme activation.	Irregular growth of bones and connective tissues.
Chromium (Cr)	Meat and cereals.	Uptake of glucose.	Irregular metabolism.
Cobalt (Co)	Meat and yeast.	Synthesis of vitamin-B_{12}, formation of red blood cells	Anaemia

Water

About 70% of the human body consists of water. Two-third of water exists inside cells, the other one-third is outside the cells in tissue fluid and blood plasma. It is essential for digestion, transportation, excretion and to regulate body temperature.

Many factors affects the health of human body. One of them is adulteration.

Food Adulteration

Addition of undesirable, cheap and harmful substances in the food is called food adulteration.

Indian Standards Institution (ISI) Mark and Agmark (Agricultural marketing) are given by the Bureau of Indian Standards after testing the purity and quality of material and food respectively.

Some Common Adulterants in Food

Food Item/Stuff	Adulterant
Milk, curd and cheese	Water and urea
Sweets	Saccharin, harmful colour
Ghee	Vanaspati and animal fats
Cereals	Stones, sand and grit
Dhania powder	Powdered horse dung
Haldi powder	Lead chromate
Pulses	Metanil yellow
Edible oils	Argemone oil
Black pepper	Papaya seed

HUMAN DIGESTIVE SYSTEM

The human digestive system consists of alimentary canal and digestive glands. The alimentary canal consists of mouth, (having teeth and tongue) oesophagus, stomach, small intestine and large intestine.

Teeth

- With the help of teeth the food is chewed. *Teeth are of four types*
  Incisors (for cutting)
  Canines (for tearing)
  Premolars (for chewing)
  Molars (for chewing and grinding)

- The number of teeth are different in different animals. These are represented by dental formula as
  I C Pm M – Upper half jaw
  I C Pm M – Lower half jaw
  Where, I – Incisors, C – Canines,
  Pm – Premolars and M – Molars.

- Premolars and molars are called **cheek teeth**. Milk teeth do not include molar teeth.

- In humans, first teeth come in between 6 and 8 months. By the age of 6, milk teeth are gradually replaced by permanent teeth.

- Hardest part in the body is tooth enamel.

- In elephants, the tusks are the incisors of upper jaw.

- Maximum number of teeth are present in horse and pig.

Dental Formulae of Some Mammals

Mammal	Dental Formula	Total Number of Teeth
Man (child)	2102/2102 × 2	20
Man (adult)	2123/2123 × 2	32
Horse	3143/3143 × 2	44
Dog	3142/3143 × 2	42
Cow and Sheep	0033/3133 × 2	32
Cat	3131/3121 × 2	30
Rabbit	2033/1023 × 2	28
Mouse	1003/1003 × 2	16

Tongue

- Saliva, secreted by the salivary glands, is mixed with the chewed food by the tongue.

- Tongue also contains taste buds due to which we sense bitter, sour, salty or sweet taste.

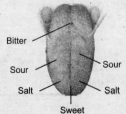

Taste Areas on the Human Tongue

Functions of the Digestive System

Splitting of complex food materials into simpler molecules by hydrolysis so that they can be easily absorbed by the intestine is the main function of digestive system.

- Man and other animals have holozoic nutrition *i.e.*, solid form of food.

Complete digestion process takes place in following four steps

Ingestion of Food

- Ingestion takes place in buccal cavity.
- Saliva lubricates the food and binds the food particles together to form bolus.
- Salivary gland have starch spitting enzyme **ptyalin**.
- Parotid gland is the largest salivary gland.

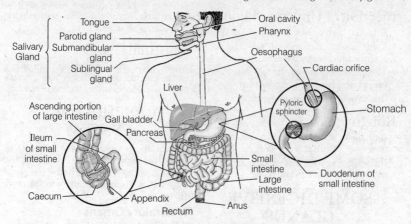

Human Digestive System

Digestion of Food

Digestion in Mouth

In mouth, salivary amylase acts on starch.

$$\text{Starch} \xrightarrow{\text{Ptyalin}} \text{Maltose}$$
$$\text{(Complex form)} \qquad \text{(Simple form)}$$

Digestion in Stomach

- The food passes down through the oesophagus into stomach.
- Now food is mixed with gastric juice and hydrochloric acid which disinfect the food and creates acidic medium.
- Pepsin digests proteins and converts them into peptones.
- Rennin convert milk into curd.
- Digested food now is called **chyme**.

Digestion in Duodenum

- Chyme moves to duodenum.
- Food is mixed with bile (liver) to breakdown fats into smaller globules.
- Trypsin acts upon proteins and break them into polypeptides. Amylase converts starch into simple sugar.
- Lipase convert fats into fatty acids and glycerol.

Digestion in Intestine

- Food passes into ileum and mixes with intestinal juice, where
  - Maltase converts maltose into glucose
  - Lactase converts lactose into glucose and galactose
  - Sucrase converts sucrose into glucose and fructose
  - Trypsin digests the peptides into amino acids

Absorption and Assimilation of Digested Food

- Ileum's internal surface has finger-like folds called **villi**.
- It helps in absorption of food.
- Intestinal juice is alkaline in nature.
- pH of saliva, gastric juice, pancreatic juice and intestinal juice is respectively 6.8, 2.0, 7.0 and 8.5.

Ejection of Unwanted Food

- Digested food passes into large intestine.
- Large intestine cannot absorb food, but absorbs much of the water.
- The remaining semi solid waste is called **faeces** and is passed into rectum.
- It is expelled out through anus.

Roughage

- Roughage is another term for dietary fibres e.g., Natural food, dalia etc.
- It does not provide energy but only helps in retaining water in the body.

SOME DIGESTIVE GLANDS

Liver

- It is the largest gland of the human body and secretes bile juice, which is stored in gall bladder.
- It regulates the quantity of glucose in the blood by converting extra glucose (if any) into glycogen or glycogen (during deficiency of glucose) is converted into glucose.
- It destroys dead RBC and regulates body temperature. It converts excess of amino acid into ammonia (which is converted into urea by Ornithine cycle). Urea comes out from the body through kidney.
- If there is any obstruction in bile duct, liver cells stop taking bilirubin from the blood, consequently it spreads throughout the body which is called **jaundice**.
- Liver is an important body organ in investigation of a person's death that has been due to poison in food.

Pancreas

- It is the second-largest gland of the human body and contains islets of Langerhans and exocrine part secreting enzymes for carbohydrate, protein and nucleic acid digestion.
- The most common is the β-cells, which secretes insulin, a hormone deficiency of which causes diabetes melitus.
- Excess of insulin causes hypoglyaemia, in which one loses the reproducing capacity and vision.

Intestinal Glands

Crypts of Lieberkuhn and Brunner's glands are intestinal glands and secrete intestinal juice which is alkaline in nature.

RESPIRATORY SYSTEM

Respiration is a catabolic process in which the respired oxygen is used in the oxidation of food resulting in the release of energy. It is brought about by respiratory organs.

Respiratory Organs of Some Animals

Respiratory Organ	Animal
Lungs	Reptiles like lizards, mammals like man, camel, cattle, etc.
Skin	Frog, earthworm and leeches
Gills	Fishes, tadpoles and prawns
Trachea	Insects, centipedes and millipedes.
Body surface	Amoeba, Euglena, Chlamydomonas, Spirogyra, Hydra, etc.
Book lungs	Spider, scorpion, ticks and mites.
Book gills	King crab, prawn, cray fish and Daphnia.
Air bladder	Lung fish and bony fishes(e.g., Labeo).
Air sacs/lungs	Birds

Human Respiratory System

- Overall passage of air in humans is as follows:

  Nostrils → Pharynx → Larynx → Trachea → Bronchi → Bronchioles → Alveoli → Cells → Blood.

- The human respiratory system is shown in the following diagram.

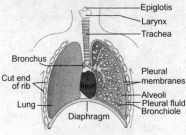

Human Respiratory System

Types of Respiration
Aerobic Respiration

- The respiration taking place in the presence of oxygen is known as aerobic respiration.
- This respiratory oxygen oxidises the substance into carbon dioxide, water and energy, as follows

  $$Glucose + O_2 \longrightarrow Carbon\ dioxide + Water + Energy.$$

- In this process, each glucose molecule is converted into two molecules of pyruvic acid by the process, called **glycolysis**. It takes place in the cytoplasm of the cell. The pyruvic acid formed, releases energy with the formation of carbon dioxide and water (in Kreb's cycle which occur in mitochondria).

Anaerobic Respiration

- The respiration taking place in the absence of oxygen is known as anaerobic respiration.
- It is found in endoparasites like roundworm. In this process, the respiratory substances are incompletely oxidised to carbon dioxide and alcohol.

$$Glucose \xrightarrow{yeast} Carbon\ dioxide + ethyl\ alcohol$$

$$Glucose \xrightarrow{\quad muscles + Energy\ (in\ plants)\quad} Lactic\ acid + Energy\ (in\ animals)$$

PHASES OF AEROBIC RESPIRATION

External Respiration
(Breathing or Ventilation of Lungs)

- It involves inspiration and expiration of air.
- **Inspiration** is the process of intake of air. During inspiration, muscles of the diaphragm contract and diaphragm flattens.
- The lower ribs are raised upward and outwards. The chest cavity enlarges, the air pressure in the lungs gets decreased and air rushes into the lungs.
- **Expiration** is breathing out of air. During expiration, relaxation of muscles of the ribs and diaphragm takes place.
- Diaphragm again become dome-shaped. Chest cavity is reduced and air is forced outwards through nose and trachea.
- Breathing rate in humans is 18 - 20 times per min.
- The exchange of gases, *i.e.*, oxygen and carbon dioxide takes place due to the difference in their partial pressures.

Internal Respiration
(Oxidation of Food)

- It is a complex process in which food is broken down to release energy.
- Transportation of oxygen takes place by haemoglobin of blood. Whereas transportation of only 10-20% carbon dioxide takes place by haemoglobin of blood.
- Approximately 400 ml water is lost through breathing everyday.

- Respiration being a catalytic process, also **reduces the weight** of the body.
- **Larynx** or voice box or Adam's apple produces sound. It has a small flap of cartilage called the epiglottis, which prevents the food from entering the trachea.
- **Purring sound** in cats is due to the vibration of false vocal cord.
- In hippopotamus, true vocal cord is absent.
- **Total Lung Capacity** (TLC) = 6000 mL
- **Residual Volume** (RV) = 1200 mL
- **Tidal Volume** (TV) = 500-600 ml

CIRCULATORY SYSTEM

- It is a transport system that supplies the useful material and removes the waste from the body cells.
  It consists of heart, blood vessels and blood.

HEART

- Heart is a thick, muscular, contractile, automatic pumping organ of blood vascular system.
- The chamber which receives the blood from body tissues are called **auricles** and the chambers of heart which pump blood to body tissues are called **ventricles**.
- There is a thin two layered sac around the heart known as **pericardium**, filled with a watery fluid called pericardial fluid, which allows frictionless movements of heart and protects it from mechanical shocks.

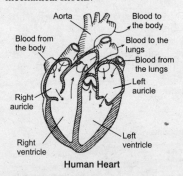

Human Heart

- **Fishes** have only two-chambered heart (one auricle and one ventricle).
- In **amphibians**, **heart is three-chambered.**
- In **crocodile**, **birds** and **mammals**, the heart is divided into four chambers (two auricles and two ventricles).
- **Reptilian heart** is structurally three-chambered but is functionally four-chambered (*i.e.*, incomplete four-chambered) except in crocodile.
- A **new born baby's** heart weight is about 20 g.
- The **average weight** of heart in men is 280-340 g, while in women is 230-280 g.

Diseases of Heart

Angina pectoris	Pain in heart muscles, appearing as chest pain. It is caused due to obstruction in coronary artery.
Tachycardia	Increased rate of heartbeat.
Bradycardia	Decreased rate of heartbeat.
Heart attack	Breathlessness, palpitations, pain in the chest, unconsciousness appear suddenly (**Nitroglycerine** is used for the treatment).
Heart block	When heart beat is not passed to the ventricles properly. This is the defect of conducting system of the heart.
Coronary thrombosis	Due to the formation of clot in coronary artery.
Myocardial infarction	It is the death of a part of heart muscle following cessation of blood supply to it. It is acute heart attack.

- The circulation of blood through the whole body can be shown as

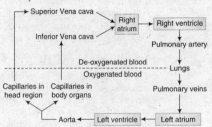

Circulation of Blood through the Whole Body

- To pump out blood, the heart chamber undergoes alternate contraction called **systole** and relaxation called **diastole**. The regular sequence of these systole and diastole causes the heart sound **Lub** and **Dub**.
- Arteries carry **pure blood** from the heart while veins carry **impure blood** to the heart.
- Human heart beat is myogenic in nature, *i.e.*, initiated by a patch of modified heart muscles itself without requiring an external stimulation. This patch is called **SA node** (sino-auricular node) or **pacemaker**.
- When SA-node becomes defective, *i.e.*, it does not generate cardiac impulses, it can be cured by surgical grafting of an artificial pacemaker (an electric device) in the chest of the patient. It stimulate the heart electrically at regular intervals.
- The normal **rate of heartbeat** at rest is about 70-72 times per minute. In a newly born baby, heartbeat rate is about 140 per minute.
- During **heavy exercise** it may be high as 170-200 times per minute.

BLOOD

- Blood is a fluid connective tissue and composed of blood corpuscles, plasma and platelets.
- It is slightly alkaline is nature (pH 7.4).
- Its volume in an adult is 5.8 L.
- The oxygenated or pure blood is bright red while the deoxygenated blood is purple coloured (Darker shade of red).

- People who live at high altitudes have more blood than those who live in low regions. This extra blood supplies additional oxygen to body cells.
- During blood clotting fibrinogen changes into fibrin by thrombin which is obtained from thromboplastin in the presence of Ca^{2+}.
- The haemoglobin content of adult female varies from 13.5-14.5% whereas in adult male its amount varies from 14.5-15.5% Haemoglobin count is highest in the foetus and is about 23 g per 100 mL of blood at birth.

Blood Vessels

Blood vessels are of three types

Arteries

- These are thick walled blood vessels which carry the blood away from the heart to various body parts. These are deep seated in the body and have no valves in them.
- These carry oxygenated blood except the pulmonary artery which carries deoxygenated blood to the lungs. In arteries, blood flows at a high pressure and a higher speed.

Veins

- These are thin walled blood vessels and carry blood away from various body parts towards the heart. These have valves in them to prevent back flow of blood in them. Blood flows at low pressure and at a lower speed.
- These carry deoxygenated blood except the pulmonary vein which carries oxygenated blood to the heart.

Capillaries

- These are the thinnest blood vessels and connect arteries to the veins.
- These help in exchange of materials like the nutrients, gases, waste products etc., between blood and cells.

Blood Type of Parent and their Children

Blood Type of Parent (Homo or Heterozygous)	Possible Blood Type of Children
O × O	O
O × A	O, A
O × B	O, B
O × AB	A, B
A × A	A, O
A × B	O, A, B, AB
A × AB	A, B, AB
B × B	B, O
B × AB	A, B, AB
AB × AB	A, B, AB

Blood Cells
Erythrocytes (RBCs)

- Red blood cells contain the blood's haemoglobin and distribute oxygen.
- RBCs are the most abundant cells.

- Mature red blood cells lack a nucleus and organelles in mammals. However, in camel and llama it is nucleated.
- One RBC contains about 280 haemoglobin molecules.

Leukocytes (WBCs)

These are part of the body's immune system; they destroy and remove old or aberrant cells and cellular debris, as well as attack infectious agents and foreign substances. These are much less in number than RBCs (1 : 600).

Thrombocytes (Platelets)

It is responsible for blood clotting (coagulation). It changes fibrinogen into fibrin.

Comparison between Plasma and Lymph

Plasma	Lymph
It contains 92% water, 8% blood plasma proteins and trace amounts of other materials	Lymph contains a variety of substances including proteins, salts, glucose, fats, water and WBCs.
It is cell free part of blood, contain salts, considerable amount of proteins as well as more or less all constituents of body.	It is modified tissue fluid, contains cells like lymphocyte and monocytes, salt and small amount of proteins. It is colourless.
It flows within blood vessels.	It flows within lymphatic vessels.
It takes part in nutrition, excretion, respiration, etc., by transporting various materials and helps in the defence mechanism of the body by producing antibodies.	It supplies nutrition to tissue devoid of blood supply, takes part in fat absorption and defence mechanism of the body.
It can coagulate because it contains fibrinogen and prothrombin.	It can coagulate but very slowly because it contains these two in small quantities.

Blood Pressure (BP)

- The pressure created by the blood on the walls of the blood vessels due to the repeated pumping of heart is called **blood pressure**. It is measured by **sphygmomanometer**.
- It can be felt at certain places in our body *viz.*, wrist of the hands etc.
- Blood pressure is recorded as systolic/diastolic. Blood pressure in a normal person is 120 / 80 mmHg. Factors affecting blood pressure are age, cardiac output, total peripheral resistance etc.

- If a person has persistent high blood pressure then it is called **hypertension** and persistent high blood pressure is 150/90 mm Hg. Factors responsible are over eating, fear, worry, anxiety, sorrow etc. **Hypotension** is condition of low blood pressure, *i.e.*, persistent 100/50 mm Hg.
- **Electrocardiograph** (ECG) is used to check proper working of heart by using electrodes.

SKELETAL SYSTEM

The human skeleton consists of both fused and individual bones supported and supplemented by ligaments, tendons, muscles and cartilage.

It is divided into two parts

Axial Skeleton (80 Bones)

- It includes skull, vertebral column and bones of chest (ribs and sternum).
- Vertebral column is responsible for the upright position of the human body.
- Most of the body weight is located at the back of the vertebral column. It provides flexibility to the neck and protection to spinal cord.

Appendicular Skeleton (126 Bones)

Their function is to make locomotion possible and to protect the major organs of locomotion, digestion, excretion and reproduction.

Important Bones in the Body

Body Part	Name of the Bones	Total Number
Skull (29)	Facial	14
	Cranium	8
	Hyoid	1
	Ear ossicles (maleus, Incus, stapes)	6
Vertebral column(26)	Cervical	7
(Note-The total number of bones in vertebral column, initially is 33 and after development, it reduces to 26)	Thoracic	12
	Lumbar	5
	Sacrum	1(5)
	Coccyx	1(4)
Bones of chest (25)	Sternum	1
	Ribs	24 (12 pairs)
Shoulder (Pectoral girdle)	Scapula Clavicle	4
Upper arm	Humerus	2
Fore arm	Radius-ulna	4
Wrist	Carpals	16
Palm	Metacarpals	10
Fingers	Phalanges	28
Hips (Pelvic girdle)	Ilium, ischium, Pubis (Innominate)	2
Thigh	Femur	2
Knee	Patella	2
Shank	Tibia-Fibula	4
Ankle	Tarsal	14
Sole	Metatarsal	10
Toes	Phalanges	28

Joints

The structural arrangements of tissues by which bone and bone or bone and cartilage joined together.

They are of following types

Joint Name	Location
Immovable	Bones of skull
Slightly movable	Pubic bones of pelvic girdle
Hinge	Ankle, Knee, elbow
Ball and Socket	Shoulder and hip
Pivot	Radius and humerus
Saddle	Metacarpal and carpal
Gliding	Vertebra, radio-ulna and carpals

- **Tendons** join the muscles and bones.
- The muscles which join bone to bone are called **ligaments**.

Diseases of Skeletal System

- Hard tissue deposits over articular cartilage along with higher secretion of synovial fluid causing pain and stiffness lead to **rheumatoid arthritis**. (An auto immune disease).
- Tearing of articular cartilage and development of bony lumps at places causing pain, stiffness and permanent bending lead to **osteoarthritis**.
- **Osteoporosis** is loss of bone density due to excessive absorption of calcium and phosphorus from the bone.
- **Osteopetrosis** is a hereditary disease marked by abnormally dense bone and by the common occurrence of fractures of affected bone.
- Birds have spongy bones with air filled spaces, called **pneumatic bones**.
- **Rigor mortis** is the state of body stiffening after death.

- **Chronic fatigue** is the inability of a muscle to contract due to depletion of its chemicals and lactic acid accumulation by repeated contraction. A completely fatigued muscle refuses to respond to nervous stimuli.

Muscular System

- Human body has about 639 types of muscles.
- Muscles specialised to contraction are of three types, i.e., striated, unstriated and cardiac.
- **Striated muscles** Also called skeletal muscles or voluntary muscles. They are present in limbs, tongue, pharynx etc.
- **Unstriated muscles** These are involuntary muscles and present in urinary bladder, in walls of large blood vessels and alimentary canal.
- **Cardiac muscles** They are involuntary, striated and non-fatigued fibres which are found in the wall of heart, where they form myocardium. They generate their own wave of excitation.

EXCRETORY SYSTEM

The process of removal of nitrogenous wastes from the body is called excretion. The organs of excretion are called excretory organs.

Excretory Organs of Some Animals

Excretory Organ	Animal
Contractile vacuole	Amoeba
Flame cells/solenocytes	Tapeworm
Renette cell	Ascaris
Nephridia	Earthworm
Malpighian tubules	Cockroach
Coxal glands	Scorpion
Green glands	Prawn

Excretory Products
Ammonotelic Animals

These animal excrete nitrogen in the form of ammonia, e.g., aquatic invertebrates Amoeba, Hydra, Prawn, Pila, and freshwater fishes, bony fishes, Frog's tadpole.

Ureotelic Animals

They excrete nitrogen in the form of urea, e.g., mammal (man), frogs, toads, other amphibians and cartilaginous fishes like sharks.

Uricotelic Animals

They excrete the nitrogenous wastes in the form of uric acid, e.g., Reptiles, snakes, lizards, crocodiles and birds.

Human Excretory System

The human excretory system includes—the kidneys (two), ureters (two), urinary bladder (one) and urethra (one).

Kidney

- It is bean-shaped, chocolate brown organ lying in the abdomen, one on each side of the vertebral column just below the diaphragm.
- The left kidney is placed a little higher than the right kidney (but reverse in rabbit).
- These form the urine and controls osmotic pressure within the organism with respect to external environment.
- Nephrons are the functional and structural unit of kidney. Each nephron is made up of Bowman's capsule and renal tubule. Renal tubule is made up of Proximal Convolutid Tubule (PCT), Henle's loop, Distal Convoluted Tubule (DCT) and Collecting Tubule (CT).

Ureters

These bring the urine downward and open into urinary bladder.

Urinary Bladder

- It temporarily stores the urine.
- It can hold about 0.5-1.0 L of urine.
- It is absent in birds. In both reptiles and birds, ureters and rectum, opens into a common sac called **cloaca**.

Urethra

- It is a muscular and tubular structure which extends from neck of bladder to outside. In females, this tube is small and serves as a passage of urine only.
- In males, it is long and functions as a common passage for urine and spermatic fluids.

Urine

- It is a pale yellow coloured fluid due to presence of **urochrome** pigment.
- It is acidic in nature (pH 6.0) and is slightly heavier than water.
- It has a faint aromatic odour due to urinoid. Daily urine output in normal adult is 1.5-1.8 L.
- Chemical composition of urine : water is 95-96%, urea is 2% and some other substance like uric acid, creatinine, etc., are 2-3%.
- The urine on standing gives a pungent smell. It is due to conversion of urea into ammonia by bacteria.
- **Haemodialysis** is the process of removal of excesss urea from the blood of patient using artificial kidney.
- Kidney stone are generally calcium oxalate crystals.

NERVOUS SYSTEM

- The nervous system provides the fastest means of communication within the body so that suitable response to stimuli can be made at once.
- Nervous system is found only in animals and absent in plants.
- In most animals, the nervous system consists of two parts—central and peripheral nervous system.

Central Nervous System (CNS)

Brain

- Brain lies in the cranium of skull.
- Cerebrospinal fluid is present in brain and spinal cord.

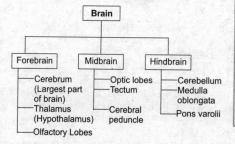

The functions of brain parts are as follows

Forebrain

- **Cerebrum** leads to consciousness, storage of memory having information.
- **Thalamus** deals with touch, visual system, sleep and wakefulness.
- **Hypothalamus** deals with water balance in body, behavioral patterns of sex, sleep, stress emotions etc. It also regulates pituitary hormones and metabolism of fat, carbohydrate water and maintain body temperature (homeostasis).

Midbrain

It deals with visual analysis, auditory etc.

> **Broca's area** is present in brain and is related with speech production, while **Wernick's area** of brain is related with understanding of speech.

Hindbrain

- **Cerebellum** controls coordination of accurate movements and balancing.
- **Medulla oblongata** is long connecting part of brain to spinal cord. It deals with control of heart beats, blood vessels, breathing, salivary secretion and mostly reflex and involuntary (uncontrolled) movements.

> **Nobel Prize in Medicine 2016**
>
> The Nobel Prize in physiology or medicine 2016 was awarded to Yoshinori Ohsumi "for his discoveries of mechanisms for autophagy.
>
> The word 'autophagy' originates from the Greek words *auto,* meaning 'self and phageil meaning to 'eat'. It is an evolutionarily conserved process in which the eukaryotic cell can recycle part of its own content.

Spinal Cord

Deals with impulses to and from the brain and is the centre for reflex actions like blinking of the eye when an object comes near to our eyes suddenly, rapid withdrawal of hand while coming near to heat, knee jerk reflex etc.

Acquired reflex action is also called conditioned reflex as dependent on past experience, training and learning.

It was first demonstrated by Ivan Petrovich Pavlov e.g. learning, dancing, cycling, swimming, singing and driving etc are controlled by spinal chord. It is under cerebral control during learning.

Peripheral Nervous System (PNS)

- It is a collective term for the nervous system structures that do not lie within the **CNS**.
- It is composed of cranial and spinal nerves. There are **10 pairs** of cranial nerves in fishes and amphibians and **12 pairs** in rest of the higher chordates.
- There are **10 pairs of spinal nerves** found in fishes and amphibians and **31 pairs in humans**.
- The PNS is divided into two divisions: Somatic Nervous System (SNS) and Autonomous Nervous System (ANS).
- It is a part of peripheral nervous system that relays impulses from the CNS to skeletal muscles.

Autonomous Nervous System (ANS)

It is also a part of peripheral nervous system that transmits impulses from the CNS to involuntary organs and smooth muscles of the body. *Autonomic nervous system consists of two divisions*

1. **Sympathetic Nervous System** increases defence system of body against adverse conditions. It is active in stress condition, *e.g.*, pain, fear and anger.

2. **Parasympathetic Nervous System** provides relaxation, comfort, pleasure at the time of rest. It helps in the restoration and conservation of energy.

- **Electroencephalogram** (EEG) is a test that measures and records the electrical activity of our brain.

SENSE ORGANS

Eye

Eyes are the sensitive detectors of light. The human eye can distinguish about 10 million colours. *It consists of three parts*

Sclerotic Layer

It is the outermost, bony layer, which includes

- **Cornea** the clear, dome-shaped tissue, covering the front of the eye.
- **Conjunctiva**, the continuation of upper eyelid.

Choroid Layer

It is the middle layer and consists of

1. **Pupil** is the black hole in the centre of the iris. It changes size as the amount of light changes.
2. **Ciliary muscles** regulates the lens curvature.
3. **Iris** is the coloured part of the eye. It controls the amount of light that enters the eye by changing the size of the pupil.
4. **Lens** is a biconvex transparent circular solid located just behind the iris. It focuses light onto the retina.

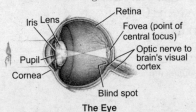

The Eye

Retina

- Light sensitive tissue that lies at the back of the eye. It contains millions of photoreceptors (rods and cones) that convert light rays into electrical impulses that are relayed to the brain *via* the optic nerve.
- The image formed on retina is real and inverted.

- **Rods** are highly sensitive to dim light and contain a reddish purple pigment called rhodopsin. Night vision involves mostly rods (not cones).
- **Cones** are sensitive to bright light, hence differentiate the colours.
- The **fovea centralis** is the area of sharpest vision due to high concentration of cones.
- The **blind spot** (optic disc) has no rods and cone cells, hence no image is form in this region.

Eye Defects

Nearsightedness (Myopia)

- A condition in which nearby objects are seen more clearly than distant objects because light is focused in front of the retina, not on it. It can be corrected by using concave glasses.

Farsightedness (Hypermetropia)

- A condition in which distant objects are seen more clearly than nearby objects because light is focused behind the retina, not on it.
- It can be corrected by using convex glasses.

Astigmatism

- A condition in which the lens is warped, causing images not to focus properly on the retina.
- The cylindrical glass can correct the defect.
- Colour blindness also called Daltonism is caused due to deficiency of cones. While night blindness is due to deficiency of rhodopsin in rods.
- **Retina of Owl** contains only rods while fowl contains only cones.
- The **eyes of carnivores** like cat, dog, iron sea etc, glow in night due to tapetum lucidum. Eyes are **most sensitive** to yellow green colour. Bees can see ultraviolet light.

Presbyopia

- It is a reduction in pupil size and the loss of accommodation or focusing capability with age, leading to a substantial decrease in light received at the retina.
- Bifocal lens can correct the defect.
- **Conjunctivitis** is an inflammation of conjunctiva by bacteria.

Correspondence between Camera and Eye

Part of Camera	Corresponding Part of Eye
Box	Sclera
Black inner paint	Choroid
Shutter	Eye lids
Diaphragm	Iris
Light hold	Pupil
Lens	Lens
Light sensitive film plate	Retina

Ear

- Ears are meant for both balancing and hearing.
- It can be divided into three parts as **External ear** (pinna + external auditory canal), **Middle ear** (tympanic cavity) and **Internal ear** (bony and membranous labyrinth).
- Hearing is controlled by auditory area of temporal lobe of cerebral cortex.
- Human ear can receive the sound ranging between 60-80 decibel.
- Human ear is sensitive to sounds frequency 50-20,000 cycles/sec.
- Defects of ear are : **Otalgia ear, ache** (Pain in ear); **Othitis media** (Acute infection of middle ear) **Labyrithine** disease (malfunction of inner ear).

Nose

- Nose is a sense organ for smell or olfaction. *It contains*
  1. **Olfactory cells** which are more chemosensitive than taste cells.
  2. **Olfactory stimuli** such as, chloroform and ammonia are irritating and can cause tearing.
- Dogs have an acute olfactory sense. They can trace people because they can distinguish between the odours of different persons.

REPRODUCTIVE SYSTEM

- The process by which new individuals are produced from their parents is called **reproduction** and the organs which are used for this process, collectively constitute the **reproductive system**.
- Reproduction is of two types, *i.e.*, asexual and sexual.
- In **asexual reproduction**, only one parent is involved and sex cells are not involved.
- In **sexual reproduction**, two parents are involved and formation and fusion of gametes takes place.

Modes of Reproduction in Different Organisms

Mode of Reproduction	Organism
Fission (asexual)	*Amoeba*, bacteria, flatworm etc.
Budding (asexual)	*Hydra*, yeast and sponge etc.
Syngamy (sexual)	Cockroach, frog and human being etc.

Male Reproductive System

- The various organs which constitute the male reproductive system and their functions are tabulated below:

Reproductive Organ	No	Function
Testes	2	Produce sperm and testosterone
Sperm duct	2	Conduct the sperm from the testes to urethra
Seminal vesicles	2	Secrete seminal plasma
Epididymis	2	Temporarily store sperm and provides mobility.
Urethra	1	Conduct urine and sperms.
Prostate gland	2	Secrete an alkaline fluid to neutralise the acidity of urethra and make the sperm more active.
Cowper's gland	2	Secrete an alkaline white lubricating fluid.
Penis (have rich blood supply)	2	Pass urine and deposit sperm in female genital tract.

- Males can produce spermatozoa (sperm) throughout their life from age of 13-14 years. The growth of hairs on body is due to masculine hormones.

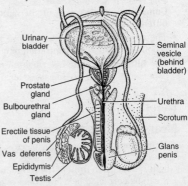

Male Reproductive System

Female Reproductive System

Female reproductive system includes *following organs which are tabulated below*

Reproductive Organ	No	Function Performed
Ovaries	2	To produce ova and hormones.
Oviducts	2	To move the ovum towards uterus.
Uterus	1	To provide space for developing child.
Vagina	1	To receive the sperms.

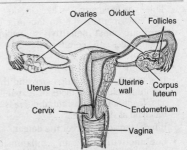

Female Reproductive System

- If sperm is present, the egg will be fertilised in the ampullary isthmic junction of Fallopian tube.

- After maturity the ovary releases an ovum (egg cell) after every 28 days.
- The connection between developing embryo and mother is made by **placenta**. It supplies blood, organic and inorganic nutrients, hormones, antibodies etc.
- The embryo develops for nine months in uterus. It is called **gestation period**.
- Child is delivered after its development and mother produces milk to nourish the child (lactation).
- The first milk which comes out from the mother's mammary gland just after child birth is called **colostrum**.
- This milk is rich in protein, antibodies which imparts immunity to new born baby.

Menstrual Cycle

- Reproductive period of a human female extends from puberty (10-14 years) to menopause (40-50 years).
- The release of the first menstrual flow or period is called **menarche**.
- **Menarche** marks the onset of reproductive life and onset of puberty in females.
- **Menopause** is stopping of ovulation and menses. It normally occurs between the age of 45 to 55. This stage onwards, woman lose the ability to reproduce.
- The periodic vaginal bleeding during menstrual cycle is called **menstruation**.
- On an average menstural cycle is completed in 28 days.
- It is absent during pregnancy, may be suppressed during lactation and permanently stops at menopause. About 13 mature eggs are released from two ovaries of female in a year.
- Menstrual cycle is controlled by FSH, LH, oestrogen and progesterone hormones.

Birth Control Methods *or* Contraception Methods

- The prevention of union of sperm and ovum is known as **contraception**. The various methods used for it are diaphragm, contraceptive pills, tubectomy, vesectomy, copper-T etc.

- **Amniocentesis** or amniotic fluid test is technique of finding out sex and disorder of foetus.

Gestation Periods of Some Animals

Animal	Gestation Period	Animal	Gestation Period
Buffalo	310 days	Horse	340 days
Elephant	610 days	Leopard	105 days
Lion	120 days	Tiger	103 days
Whale	365 days	Squirrel	40 days

ENDOCRINE SYSTEM

- It includes endocrine or ductless glands. Their secretion is known as **hormones**.
- *Different types of hormones are*
- **Steroids**, *e.g.*, oestradiol, testosterone, androsterone, aldosterone, cortisol and cortisone.
- **Peptides**, *e.g.*, insulin, glucagon, pituitary hormones, parathormone and relaxin.
- **Amino acid derivatives**, *e.g.*, adrenaline, noradrenaline and thyroid hormones.

Various glands are:

Hypothalamus

It is a part of forebrain and regulates the pituitary glands and maintains body temperature (homeostasis).

Pituitary Gland *or* Hypophysis

- It governs other endocrine glands like thyroid, adrenal and gonads.
- Pituitary gland is also known as **master gland**.

Thyroid Gland

- It is the largest endocrine gland and located in neck region.
- It is the **'pace setter'** of the endocrine system. *It secretes*
  1. **Thyroxine,** which regulates BMR (Basal Metabolic Rate), physical, mental and sexual development.
  2. **Thyrocalcitonin** secreted by the C-cells and regulates the calcium homeostasis (lowers calcium level).

Pancreas

It is both an exocrine and endocrine gland. The **islet of Langerhans** (endocrine) have *three major types of cells*

1. **Alpha-Cells** secretes glucagon hormone which increases blood sugar level.
2. **Beta-Cells** secretes insulin, which decreases the amount of sugar in the blood.
3. **Delta-Cells** secretes somatostatin which is an anti-growth factor.

Adrenal Gland

- It is also known as **emergency gland**.
  - (a) **Cortex** (outer layer)
  - (b) **Medulla** (inner layer) It secretes two important hormones— Epinephrine or adrenaline and nor-epinephrine or noradrenaline
- It increases the blood glucose level, blood pressure and cardiac output.

Pineal Gland

- It is situated in the brain and also known as **clockwork gland**.
- It regulates the ovaries and has an effect on the biological rhythm.

GONADS

These secrete steroid hormones.

Ovarian Hormones (Oestrogens)

It helps in the development of primary and secondary sexual characters (oestradiol, oestriol and estrogen). Hypersecretion of androgenic steroids in female results in stopping of menstruation, hairs on face and breasts.

Testicular Hormones (Androgens)

These are produced by Leydig cells of testes.It stimulate growth, maturation and maintenance of male gonads and development of secondary sexual characters, *e.g.*, testosterone, androsterone etc.

HEALTH

Health is the functional or metabolic efficiency of a living being. In human, it is the general condition of a person's mind, body and spirit, usual meaning, to be free from illness, injury or pain.

DISEASES

It is a condition of the body or its part in which functions are disturbed. The diseases may be broadly classified into two types, *i.e.*, congenital and acquired.

Congenital Diseases

These are anatomical or physiological abnormalities present from birth.
They may be caused by

- A single gene mutation (alkaptonuria, phenylketonuria, albinism, sickle-cell anaemia, haemophilia and colour blindness).
- Chromosomal aberrations (Down's syndrome, Klinefelter's syndrome and Turner's syndrome).
- Environmental factors (cleft palate and harelip). Unlike the gene and chromosome induced congenital defects, environmentally caused abnormalities are not transmitted to the children.

Acquired Diseases

These diseases develop after birth. They are further of two types, *i.e.*, communicable and non-communicable.

1. **Communicable** (infectious) diseases are caused by pathogenic micro-organisms, such as bacteria, viruses, parasites or fungi; the diseases can be spread, directly or indirectly, from one person to another. Infectious diseases, are also known as transmissible diseases.
2. **Non-communicable** (non-infectious) diseases are not passed by organisms among people, but come from genetic or lifestyle factors.

COMMUNICABLE DISEASES

These are the diseases which may pass or carried from one human or animal to other.

Communicable diseases are illness caused by germs such as bacteria, viruses and spread by an infected person, animals or object to other persons.

Viral Diseases

Viruses are parasitic and causes a number of diseases.

Bird Flu (H_5N_1)

Bird flu (Avian influenza) is a disease caused by an influenza virus-A, that primarily affect birds.

The following persons may be on higher risk for developing the bird flu

- Farmers and others, who work with poultry.
- Travellers, visiting affected countries.
- Those who have touched an infected bird.
- Those who eat raw or undercooked poultry meat, eggs from infected birds.

Symptoms

Fever, cough, sore throat, muscle aches and eye infection (conjunctivitis).

Treatment

Treatment with the antiviral medication oseltamivir (tamiflu) or zanamivir (relenza) may make the disease less severe. Oseltamivir may also be prescribed for persons, who live in the same house as those diagnosed with avian flu.

Severe Acute Respiratory Syndrome (SARS)

It is a serious form of pneumonia. It is caused by a virus that was first identified in 2003. Infection with the SARS virus causes acute respiratory distress (severe breathing difficulty) and sometimes death.

Symptoms

Cough usually starts 2-3 days after other symptoms like Fever, headache and muscle aches.

Treatment

Antibiotics to treat bacteria that cause pneumonia. Antiviral medications. High doses of steroids to reduce swelling in the lungs. Oxygen, breathing support (mechanical ventilation) or chest therapy.

Hepatitis

Hepatitis is a swelling and inflammation of the liver. It is not a condition, but is often used to refer a viral infection of the liver.

Hepatitis can be caused by

- Immune cells in the body attacking the liver and causing autoimmune hepatitis. Infections from viruses (such as hepatitis-A, B or C), bacteria or parasites. Liver damage from alcohol, poisonous mushrooms or other poisons.
- Medications, such as an overdose of acetaminophen, can cause harm or death also.

Symptoms

Abdominal pain or distention. Breasts development in males. Dark urine and pale or clay coloured stools. Fatigue, general itching, fever, usually low-grade jaundice (yellowing of the skin or eyes) and loss of appetite, nausea, vomiting and weight loss.

AIDS

Acquired Immuno Deficiency Syndrome (AIDS) is a disease of the human immune system caused by the Human Immunodeficiency Virus (HIV). AIDS was first recognised by the Centres for Disease Control and Prevention (CDC) in 1981.

HIV Infection

AIDS is a condition caused by HIV infection. The condition gradually destroys the immune system, which makes it harder for the body to fight infections.

Transmission

HIV can be spread by the following

- Through sexual contact i.e. oral, vaginal and anal sex.
- Through blood transfusions, accidental needle sticks or needle sharing.

- From mother to child: A pregnant woman can transmit virus to her foetus through their shared blood circulation or a nursing mother can pass it to her baby through breast's milk.

Test for AIDS

- Enzyme Linked Immunosorbent Assay/ Enzyme Immuno Assay (ELISA/EIA)
- Radio Immuno Precipitation Assay/ Indirect Fluorescent Antibody Assay (RIP/IFA)
- Polymerase Chain Reaction (PCR)
- Western Blot Confirmatory Test.

NON-COMMUNICABLE DISEASES

There are various kinds of non-communicable diseases, which affect the health of human beings. *Some of the common non- communicable diseases are*

Diabetes

Diabetes is a long-term condition caused by too much glucose (sugar) in the blood. *There are two main types of diabetes*

Type 1

Diabetes occurs when the body doesn't produce enough insulin to function properly or the body's cells don't react to insulin. This is known as insulin resistance.

Type 2

Diabetes is far more common than type 1 diabetes, which occurs when the body doesn't produce any insulin at all.

Symptoms

Symptoms common to both types of diabetes include

(i) Feeling very thirsty.

(ii) Urinating frequently, particularly at night.

(iii) Feeling very tired.

(iv) Weight loss and loss of muscle bulk.

Cancer

It is uncontrolled growth of abnormal cells in the body. Some diseases cause emergence of tumours in body. These are called neoplastic diseases. This includes from a minor role to a lethal cancer.

Causes of Cancer

- Cancer is induced by physical, chemical and biological factors or agents. These are called carcinogens or cancer causing agents. Ionising radiations such as X-rays, γ-rays and non-ionising radiations such as ultraviolet (UV) damage the DNA leading to neoplastic transformation.
- Tobacco smoke contains chemical carcinogens that causes lung cancer. Viruses also cause cancer. These are called oncogenic viruses as they have genes called viral oncogenes.

Cancer Detection and Diagnosis

Leukaemia or blood cancer can be detected based on biopsy and histopathological studies of the tissue and blood and bone marrow tests for increased cell counts. Cancers of internal organs are detected using techniques such as Radiography Computed Tomography (RCT) and Magnetic Resonance Imaging (MRI).

Cancer Therapy

- **Cryo Surgery** It is the technique of using extreme rapid cooling that freeze tissues, thereby destroy them. Rapid cooling to temperature below freezing point produces irreversible cell damage and cell death occurs at 20°C to – 90°C.
- **Proton Therapy** It is a type of particle therapy, which uses a beam of protons to irradiate diseased tissue, most often in the treatment of cancer.
- **Radiation Therapy** Radiation therapy is a cancer treatment. Its goal is to kill cancer cells and shrink tumours.
- **Stem Cell Transplantation** Stem cell transplants can be an effective treatment for people with certain forms of cancer, such as leukaemia and lymphoma.
- **Peripheral Blood Stem Cell Transplantation (PBSCT)** It is also called peripheral stem cell support. This procedure restore stem cells that has been destroyed by high doses of chemotherapy.

Heart Diseases

Some heart diseases are as follow

Angina Pectoris

Human with angina, experience pain in the centre of the chest. The chest can feel constricted and tight, but the pain can also be oppressive, as if something is crushing your chest. Pain starts in the centre of the chest behind the breast bone (sternum) or on the left side of the front of the chest. It can spread out to other parts of your body like your arms and stomach.

Myocardial Infarction

- It is commonly known as **heart attack**, results from the interruption of blood supply to a part of the heart, causing heart cells to die.
- This is most commonly due to occlusion (blockage) of a coronary artery following the rupture of a vulnerable atherosclerotic plaque, which is an unstable collection of lipids (cholesterol and fatty acids) and white blood cells (especially macrophages) in the wall of an artery.
- The result is ischemia (restriction in blood supply) and ensuing oxygen, if left untreated for a sufficient period of time, can cause damage or death (infarction) of heart muscle tissue (myocardium).

Heart Arrest

- It occurs when the heart is unable to provide sufficient pump action to distribute blood flow to meet the needs of the body. Heart arrest can cause a number of symptoms including shortness of breath, leg swelling and exercise intolerance.
- The condition is diagnosed with echocardiography and blood tests. Treatment commonly consists of lifestyle measures such as smoking cessation, light exercise including breathing protocols, decreased salt intake and other dietary changes and medications.

Arthritis

- It affects the musculoskeletal system, specifically the joints. It is the main cause of disability among people over 55 years of age in industrialised countries.
- **Rheumatoid Arthritis (RA)** It is a long-term disease that leads to inflammation of the joints and surrounding tissues. It can also affect other organs.

Osteoarthritis

It is a joint inflammation that results from cartilage degeneration. It can be caused by ageing, heredity and injury from trauma or disease. The most common symptom of osteoarthritis is pain in the affected joint(s) after repetitive use.

Gout

Gout is a kind of arthritis. It can cause an attack of sudden burning pain, stiffness and swelling in a joint, usually a big toe. These attacks can happen over and over unless gout is treated. Overtime, they can harm your joints, tendons and other tissues. Gout is most common in men.

Sexually Transmitted Diseases

- **Gonorrhoea** It is caused by bacteria *Neisseria gonorrhoeae*. Anyone who has any type of sexual contact can catch gonorrhoea. The infection can be spread by contact with the mouth, vagina, penis or anus.
- **Syphilis** It is a sexually transmitted infection caused by the spirochete bacterium *Treponema pallidum* sub-species *pallidum*. The primary route of transmission is through sexual contact; it may also be transmitted from mother to foetus during pregnancy or at birth, resulting in congenital syphilis.
- **Genital herpes** It is a Sexually Transmitted Infection (STI) caused by the Herpes Simplex Virus (HSV).
- **Trichomoniasis** It is a sexually transmitted infection caused by the parasite *Trichomonas vaginalis*.

Mental Disorder

A mental disorder or mental illness is a psychological pattern or anomali, potentially reflected in behaviour, that is generally associated with distress or disability and which is not considered part of normal development of a person's culture. This may be associated with particular regions or functions of the brain or rest of the nervous system, often of the context in a social

Alzheimer's Disease

It is a progressive mental deterioration that can occur in middle or old age, due to generalised degeneration of the brain. It is the commonest cause of premature senility.

DRUGS

A drug is a substance, which when taken in, alters the body functions. Repeated use of drugs particularly for obtaining quick pleasure is called drug abuse.

Some Simple Drugs

Below are the types of simple drugs

Analgesic (Pain Killers)

These drugs act in various ways on the peripheral and central nervous system; they include paracetamol (acetaminophen), the non-steroidal anti-inflammatory drugs (NSAIDs) such as the salicylates, narcotic drugs such as morphine, synthetic drugs with narcotic properties such as tramadol and various others.

Anaesthetic

An anaesthetic is used to temporarily reduce or take away sensation, usually so that painful procedures or surgery can be performed.

There are two types of anaesthetics

- **General** which make the patient unconscious.
- **Local** which numb the part of the body that would otherwise feel pain.

Antibiotics (Bactericidal)

These are powerful medicines that fight bacterial infections. When used properly, antibiotics can save lives. They either kill bacteria or stop them for reproducing.

Antihistamines

These are medicines that can be used to relieve severe itching and help in breaking histamine cycle. It leads to thickening and weeping of the skin and generally makes the eczema worse and more likely to become infected because scratching breaks the skin.

Tranquiliser

It is a drug that induces tranquility in an individual. The minor tranquilisers induce a feeling of calm and relaxation. Depending on the medication and dosage, this can range from feeling of mild euphoria to states of drowsiness, confusion and lightedness.

Sedative

It is a substance that induces sedation by reducing irritability or excitement. At higher doses it may result in slurred speech, staggering gait, poor judgment and slow, uncertain reflexes.

Doses of sedatives such as benzodiazepines, when used as a hypnotic induce sleep, tend to be higher than amounts used to relieve anxiety, whereas only low doses are needed to provide a peaceful and calming sedative effect.

Narcotic

It is originally referred medically to any psychoactive compound with any sleep-inducing properties.

Antipyretics (Temperature Reduction)

These are drugs or herbs that reduce fever. Antipyretics cause the hypothalamus to over ride an interleukin-induced increase in temperature. The body then works to lower the temperature, resulting in a reduction of fever.

- Bacteria of cholera and TB was discovered by Robert Koch.

Disorders Caused by Hormonal Irregularities

Disorders	Hormone	Quantity	Gland
Dwarfism	GH	Deficiency	Pituitary
Gigantism	GH	Excess	Pituitary
Acromegaly	GH	Excess	Pituitary
Simmond's disease	GH	Deficiency	Pituitary
Diabetes insipidus	ADH	Deficiency	Pituitary
Cretinism	Thyroxine	Deficiency	Thyroid
Simple goitre	Thyroxine	Deficiency	Thyroid
Myxoedema	Thyroxine	Deficiency	Thyroid
Exophthalmic goitre	Thyroxine	Excess	Thyroid
Tetani	Parathyroid	Deficiency	Parathyroid
Plummer's disease	Thyroxine	Deficiency	
Addison's disease	Mineralocorticoids (aldosterone) and glucocorticoids (cortisol)	Deficiency	Adrenal cortex
Crohn's disease	Mineralocorticoids	Excess	Adrenal cortex
Cushing disease	Corticosteroid	Excess	Adrenal cortex

Bacterial Diseases in Human Beings

Disease	Pathogen	Affected Organ	Symptom
Tuberculosis	Mycobacterium tuberculosis	Lungs	Repeated coughing, high fever.
Diphtheria	Corynebacterium diphtheriae	Respiratory tract	Difficulty in respiration (mainly in child of age 2-5 yrs).
Whooping cough or pertussis	Bacillus pertussis	Respiratory system	Continuous coughing.
Cholera	Vibrio cholerae	Intestine	Vomiting, acute diarrhoea, muscular cramps, dehydration etc.
Leprosy or Hansen's disease	Mycobacterium leprae	Chronic infection of skin and nerve	Ulcers, nodules, scaly scabs (the infected part of the body becomes senseless).
Tetanus (lock jaw)	Clostridium tetani	Central nervous system	Painful contraction of neck and jaw muscles followed by paralysis of thoracic muscles.
Pneumonia	Diplococcus pneumoniae	Lungs	Sudden chill, chest pain, cough, high and fever.
Typhoid	Salmonella typhi	Intestine	High fever, diarrhoea and headache
Anthrax	Bacillus anthracis	Skin and intestine	—
Plague (i) Bubonic plague	Pasteurella, Yersinia pestis	Blood disease	High fever, weakness and haemorrhage which turn black.
(ii) Pneumonic plague	"	Lungs	Haemorrhage of bronchi, lungs.
(iii) Septicemic plague	"		Anaemia, fever, chills leading to death with in two days.
Gonorrhoea (sexual disease)	Neisseria gonorrhoea	Urinary tract	Swelling in urinary tract

Viral Diseases in Human Beings

Disease	Pathogen	Affected Part	Symptom
Measles (*Rubella disease*)	Rubella virus	Whole body	Loss of appetite, reddish eruption on the body.
Chicken pox	Varicella virus	Whole body	High fever, reddish eruption on body.
Small pox	Variola virus	Whole body	Light fever, eruption of blood on body
Polio or poliomyelitis	Polio virus	Throat, backbone and nerve	Fever, backbone and intestine wall cells are destroyed. It leads to paralysis.
Influenza (flu)	Influenza virus	Whole body	Inflammation of upper respiratory tract, nose throat and eyes.
Rabies (*hydrophobia*)	RNA virus called rabies virus	Nervous system	Encephalitis, fear of water, high fever, headache, spasm of throat and chest leading to death.
Hepatitis (*Epidemic Jaundice*)	Hepatitis virus	Liver	Loss of appetite, nausea, whitish stool and jaundice.
(i) Hepatitis-A	Hepatitis-A virus		Not fatal
(ii) Hepatitis-B	Hepatitis-B virus		Fatal
Dengue fever	RNA containing dengue virus	Whole body, particularly head, eyes and joints	High fever, backache, headache, retro-orbital pain behind the eye ball.
AIDS (*Acquired Immuno Deficiency Syndrome*)	HIV (Human Immuno Deficiency Virus)	White blood cells	Weak immune system.
Herpes	Herpes virus	Skin	Swelling of skin.
Ebola virus disease	Ebola Virus (filovirus)	Whole body	Fatal hemorrhagic fever, liver and kidney disfunction vomiting, headache.
Swine influenza (flu)	H_1N_1 flu virus	Whole body (muscles)	Headache, tiredness, sore throat, Vomiting, breathing problems.

Protozoan Diseases, their Vectors and Affected Part

Disease	Pathogen (Causative agent)	Vector	Parts Affected and Symptoms
Pyorrhoea	*Entamoeba gingivalis*	None, infection by lip kissing.	Bleeding of gums.
African trypanosomiasis	*Trypanosoma gambienes*	Tse-tse fly (*Glossina palpalis*)	Blood and nervous tissue. Man feels sleepy, may cause death.
Amoebic dysentery (*Amoebiasis*)	*Entamoeba histolytica*	None, Infection by contamination.	Colon (intestine). Develop loose motion with blood, pain in abdomen
Diarrhoea	*Giardia*	None, infection by contamination	Digestive system causes loose motions, vomitting.
Kala azar or dumdum fever	*Leishmania donovani*	Sand flies (*Phlebotomus*)	Spleen and liver enlarge and high fever develops.
Filaria or elephantiasis	*Wuchereria bancrofti*	*Culex* mosquito	Swelling of legs, testes and other body parts.
Malaria	*Plasmodium* sp.	Female *Anopheles* mosquito	Periodical attacks of high fever, pain in joints accompanied by chill, heavy perspiration and fast pulse.

- Fishes like cat fish, *Gambusia* and aquatic birds eat mosquito larvae.
- Quinone, a product of *Cinchona* tree, is administered for malaria.

Fungal Diseases in Human Beings

Disease	Pathogen (fungi)	Symptoms
Asthma or aspergillosis	Aspergillus fumigatus	Obstruction in the functioning of lungs.
Athlete's foot	Tinea pedis	Skin disease, cracking of feet.
Scabies	Acarus scabiei	Skin itching and white spot on the skin.
Ringworm	Tricophyton Verrucosum	Round red spot on skin.
Baldness	Tinea capitis	Hair fall.

Some Immunological Tests and Diseases

Test	Disease	Test	Disease
Ames test	Carcinogenecity	Widal test	Typhoid
Dick test	Scarlet fever	Wayson stain test	Plague
Montoux test	Tuberculosis	Tourniquet test	Dengue fever
Rose-Waaler test	Rheumatoid fever	ELISA test	AIDS
Wassermann test	Syphilis		

Some Viral Diseases in Animals

Animal	Virus	Disease
▪ Cow	Variola vera	Small pox
▪ Buffalo	Pox virido orthopox	Small pox
▪ Cow	Blue tongue virus	Blue tongue
▪ Cow	Herpes virus	Herpes
▪ Dog	Street rabies virus	Rabies

Vaccination

- It is the process of artificial introduction of germs or the germ substance called **antigen** into the body for developing resistance to a particular disease. The material introduced into the body is called **vaccine**.
- A vaccine is a dead or weakened microbes. They are unable to produce disease as they are less in number but they stimulate the body to produce antibodies.
- World Health Organisation (WHO) in 1974 officially launched a global vaccination programme to protect children from six fatal diseases. Diphtheria, pertussis, tetanus, polio, TB (Tuberculosis) and measles. It was launched in India in 1985.
- BCG (Bacillus Calmette Guerin) vaccine is given to protect against TB (Tuberculosis).
- DPT (diphtheria, Pertussis and Tetanus) vaccine is given to babies within first 6 weeks of their birth.

Some Vaccines and their Doses

Age	Vaccination	Dose
Birth to 12 months	▪ DPT (triple vaccine, against diptheria, whooping cough/pertussis and tetanus)	▪ Three doses (commonly oral) at intervals of 4-6 weeks.
	▪ Polio (Sabin's oral, previously Salk's injectible)	▪ Three doses at intervals of 4-6 weeks.
	▪ BCG (Bacillus Calmette Guerin)	▪ Intradermal and one vaccine
9-15 months	▪ Measles vaccine (MMR or Measles, Mumps and Rubella)	▪ One dose

Age	Vaccination	Dose
8-24 months	▪ DPT ▪ Polio (oral) ▪ Cholera vaccine (can be repeated every year before summer)	▪ Booster dose ▪ Booster dose ▪ One
5-6 years	▪ DT (Bivalent vaccine against diphtheria and tetanus) ▪ TAB (vaccine against *Salmonella typhi*, S. *paratyphi* A *and* S *paratyphi* B) or Typhoid Paratyphoid vaccine	▪ Booster dose ▪ Two doses at intervals of 1-2 months
10 years	▪ Tetanus, TAB (typhoid)	▪ Booster dose
16 years	▪ Tetanus, TAB	▪ Booster dose

Human Body (At a Glance)

▪ Total number of muscles in the body	639
▪ Total number of bones in the human body	206
▪ Largest organ of human body	Skin
▪ Number of cells in body	75 trillion
▪ Longest bone	Femur (Thigh bone)
▪ Smallest bone	Ear–ossicle and stapes
▪ Weight of brain	1424 g
▪ Blood volume	6.8 L (in 70 kg body)
▪ Normal BP	120/80 mm Hg
▪ Hb content in body	500-700 gm
▪ Blood platelets	200000-400000 per cubic mm
▪ Universal blood donor	O Rh–(ve)
▪ Universal blood recipient	AB
▪ Blood clotting time	2-5 minutes
▪ Normal body temperatue	98.4° F or 37°C
▪ Breathing rate	16-20/minute
▪ Dental formula	Adult : 2123/2123 = 32 Child : 2120/2120 = 20 milk teeth
▪ Largest endocrine gland	Thyroid
▪ Largest muscle in the body	Gluteus maximus (Buttock muscle)
▪ Greatest regeneration power	In liver
▪ Menopause age	40-50 years
▪ Minimum regeneration power	In brain cells
▪ Minimum distance for proper vision	25 cm
▪ Pulse rate	72/minute
▪ Normal sperms count	200-350 million/ejaculation
▪ ESR (Erythrocyte Sedimentation Rate)	4-10 min/h
▪ Thinnest skin	Conjunctiva

Human Genetic Disorders

The important human genetic disorders can be categorised as follows

Human Genetic Disorder due to Autosomal Abnormalities

Disorder	Chromosome Complement	Effect
Down's syndrome	Trisomy 21 (extra chromosome number)	Short stature, epicanthus, small round head, protruding lower lip, flattened nasal bridge, mental retardation, short life, daffiness.
Edward's syndrome	Trisomy 18 (extra chromosome number)	Long but narrow skull, small face, short digits, webbed neck, corneal opacity, mental retardation.
Cri-du-chat syndrome	Deletion is short arm of chromosome 5	Microcephaly, encrusted distance between eyes, moon face, severe mental deficiency, cat like cry of neonate.
Patau's syndrome	Trisomy 13 (extra chromosome number)	Left plate and lip, polydactyl, mental retardation, anomalies in dermal pattern, heart viscera and genitalia.

GENETICS

It is the study of heredity and variations. The term 'Genetics' was coined by W Bateson in 1905. Gregor Johann Mondel (commonly called Father of Genetics) *proposed three laws*

(a) **Law of Dominance** It states that crossing of plant with red and white flower produced plants only with red flower *i.e.,* dominant trait appear and recessive disappeared.

(b) **Law of Segregation** It states that allele of a gene separate during gamete formation. It is also called law of purity of genetics or law of splitting of hybrids. It gives 3 : 1 ratio in F_2 generation.

(c) **Law of Independent Assortment** It states that two or more genes assort independently during inheritance. It gives 9 : 3 : 3 : 1 ratio in F_2 generation. Linkage is an exception to this law.

- **Test Cross** The cross between heterozygous F_1 and homozygous recessive is called test cross. In test cross, the monohybrid ratio is 1 : 1 and dihybrid ratio is 1:1:1:1.

- **Back Cross** The cross between heterozygous F_1 hybrid and homozygous dominant allele is called back cross.

Some Important Genetic Terms

- **Phenotype** It is the physical appearance of an individual.

- **Genotype** It is the entire genetic complement of an individual organism.

- **Alleles** The two individual genes in a particular gene pair that occupies same locus (position) on homologous pair of chromosome.

- **Dominant and Recessive Traits** (inherited character) The traits may be dominant or recessive depending upon the fact that on crossing the individuals (which are homozygous for a particular trait of same character the trait which appears in the F_1 generation is called dominant and the other one is recessive.

- **Hybrid** An offspring, which is obtained from a cross between two genetically different parents.

- **Linkage** The phenomenon of genic inheritance in which genes of a particular chromosome show their tendency to inherit together, *i.e.,* tendency to retain their parental combination even in the offsprings is known as linkage.

- **Mutation** It is a sudden change of a gene (gene mutation) or chromosome (chromosomal mutation) from one form to another, which are passed to the daughter cells.

- **Heteroploidy** It is the variation in chromosome number.

- **Pleiotropy** It occurs when one gene influences multiple phenotypic traits.

Human Genetic Disorder due to Abnormalities in Sex-Chromosome Number

Name	Chromosomes Complement	Effect
Turner's syndrome	44+XO (45)	Phenotypically female, sterile due to undifferentiated gonads, webbed neck, low posterior hair line increased carrying angle of elbow, short stature.
Noonan's syndrome	44+ YO (45)	Phenotypically male, short stature, webbed neck, drooping upper eyelid, little development of gonads.
Super males	44+XYY (45)	Male, tall, excess testosterone secretions, subnormal intelligence.
Super females	44+XXX(47) 44+XXXX(48)	Female, mental retardation, low fertility but genitalia normal.
Klinefelter's syndrome	44+XXY(47) 44+XXYY(48)	Male tall with long legs, some with gynecomastia, small testes, azospermia, infertile, increased excretion of gonadotropin.

Human Genetic Disorder due to Gene Mutations in Autosomes
(Chromosome that is not a sex chromosome)

Disorder	Dominant/ recessive	Autosomal/ Sex-linked	Symptoms	Effect
Phenylketonuria	Recessive	Autosomal (chromosome 12)	Failure of brain to develop infancy mental retardation.	Defective form of enzyme phenyl alanine hydroxylase.
Sickle-cell anaemia	Recessive	Autosomal (chromosome 11)	Aggregation of erythrocytes, more rapid destruction of erythrocytes leading to anaemia.	Abnormal haemoglobin in RBCs
Haemophilia A/B	Recessive	Sex-linked (X-chromosome)	Failure of blood to clot.	Defective form of blood clotting factor VIII/IX.
Colour blindness	Recessive	Sex-linked (X-chromosome)	Failure to discriminate between red and green colour.	Defect in either red or/and green cones.
Huntington's disease	Dominant	Autosomal (chromosome 4)	Gradual degeneration of brain tissue in middle ages.	Production of an inhibitor of brain cell metabolism.
Cystic fibrosis	Recessive	Autosomal (chromosome 7)	Mucus clogging in lungs, liver and pancreas anomalies.	Failure of chloride ion transport mechanism.

Biotechnology

It deals with technique of using live micro-organisms, their parts or processes for the manufacture of useful or commercial substances. It has two core techniques *i.e.,* genetic engineering and technique to facilitate the growth and multiplication of only desired microbes. In genetic engineering (also called recombinant DNA technology) restriction endonucleases are very useful. They cleave the DNA at specific locations called restriction sites.

- Vectors are organisms or their parts used to transfer the desired DNA from one organism to another. The common vectors are bacteriophage, **cosmids**, phagemids, plasmids etc.
- **Polymerase Chain Reaction** (PCR) developed by **Kary Mullis** (1983) can clone or amplify the small amount of DNA. It involves denaturation, primer annealing and polymerisation in the definite sequence.

Applications of Biotechnology

A number of transgenic plants, medicines, acids are produced through genetic engineering.

Bt Cotton

It was developed to reduce the heavy reliance on pesticides. The bacterium *Bacillus thuringiensis* (Bt) naturally produces a chemical harmful only to a small fraction of insects.

Bt Brinjal

It is a transgenic brinjal (also known as an egg plant or aubergine) created by inserting a crystal protein gene (*Cry* IAc) from the soil bacterium *Bacillus thuringiensis* into the genome of various brinjal varieties.

Bacillus thuringiensis (*Bt*)

It is Gram positive, soil-dwelling bacterium, commonly used as a biological pesticide. The *Cry* toxin found in the bacterium is extracted and used as a pesticide. It also occurs naturally in the gut of caterpillars of various types of moths and butterflies, as well as on the dark surfaces of plants.

Golden Rice

- It is a variety of *Oryza sativa (rice)* produced through genetic engineering to biosynthesise beta-carotene, a precursor of pro-vitamin-A in the edible parts of rice. Golden rice was developed as a fortified food to be used in areas, where there is a shortage of diet having vitamin-A.
- **Golden Rice 2** produces up to 23 times more beta-carotene than the original variety of golden rice. Golden rice was created by Ingo Potrykus of the Institute of Plant Sciences at the Swiss Federal Institute of Technology, working with Peter Beyer of the University of Freiburg.
- Carotene impart orange colour to carrots and is the reason why genetically modified rice is golden. For the golden rice to make beta-carotene, three new genes are inserted: two from daffodils and the third from a bacterium.

Flavr Savr

By the use of antisense RNA technology the enzyme polygalacto-uronase, which causes damage to pectin is deactivated and the tomato is kept fresh for longer duration.

Canola

It is either of rape seed (*Brassica napus* L) or field mustard (*Brassica campestris* L or *Brassica rapavar*). Its nodes are used to produce edible oil suitable for consumption by humans and livestock. The oil is also suitable as biodiesel.

Dairy Products

- Cheese is prepared by the coagulation of casein and other minor milk proteins (curdling of milk) by an enzyme rennin extracted from calf gastric mucosa.
- *Streptococcus* and *Lactobacillus* species are involved in the manufacture of most cheese.

- In cheese manufacture, micro-organisms are important in both souring and ripening processes.
- Semisoft blue **Roquefort cheese** of France is produced using the mold *Penicillium roqueforti*.
- **Yoghurt** is a preserved milk product having a distinct taste and a thick texture than milk.
- Yoghurt is made by fermenting whole milk with a mixture of *Lactobacillus bulgaricus, Streptococcus lactis* and S. *thermophilus* at 40° to 46°C.

Vitamins

- **Vitamin C was the first vitamin to be produced** by a fermentation process using *Acetobacter*, a wild bacterium.
- Bacteria used for industrial production of **vitamin-B_{12}** are *propionibacterium shermanii, P. freundenreichii* and *Pseudomonas denitrificans*.
- Vitamin-B_2 (Riboflavin) is synthesised by many micro-organisms including bacteria, yeasts and fungi. The fungus, *Ashbya gossypii* is **used for the microbial production of vitamin-B_2**.

Biotechnologies in Human Health

- **Monoclonal antibodies** are made outside the body by the hybrid cell cultures known as **hybridomas**.
- Monoclonal antibodies (mAb) are antibodies that are identical because they were produced by one type of immune cell and are all clones of a single parent cell.
- **A biochip** is a discrete collection of gene fragments on a stamp-sized chip that can be used to screen for the presence of particular gene variants.

- Biochips allow rapid screening of gene profiles, a tool that promises to have a revolutionary impact on medicine and society.
- Biochips can **help in identifying precise forms of cancer**.
- **Gene therapy** is the treatment of disease by replacing, altering or supplementing a gene whose absence or abnormality is responsible for the disease. Gene therapy is unique as it employs the genetic material, i.e. DNA, itself as the means of treatment.

DNA finger printing is the technique, in which the banding pattern of DNA fragments is compared and can be used in many species, including human, to indicate relativity. (used for rape victim, paternity, other criminals).

- **Human insulin** or **humulin** is the first genetically engineered pharmaceutical product, developed by Eli Lilly and company in 1982.
- **Genentech**, a California-based company, have produced **human growth hormone** (hGH) from genetically engineered bacteria.
- **Somatostatin** is the first polypeptide, which was expressed in *E coli* as a part of the fusion peptide.
- **BST** or **Bovine Somatotropin** is produced in a large quantity from milk production in cows.
- In 1997, a transgenic cow **'Rosie'** produced human alpha-lactalbumin protein enriched milk (2.4 grams per litre).
- It is possible to cure **phenylketonuria** disease by using recombinant DNA techniques in early period of pregnancy.
- **Urokinase** is involved in dissolution of blood clots. It has been synthesised in huge quantity by using genetically engineered bacteria with urokinase genes.

Organic Acids Synthesised by Various Microbes

Organic Acid	Micro-organism
Lactic acid	Lactobacillus delbreukii, L bulgaricus, Streptococcus lactis and Rhizopus species
Acetic acid (vinegar)	Acetobactor aceti
Citric acid	Aspergillus niger, Penicillium sp and Mucor sp.
Gluconic acid	Aceobacter aceti, Aspergillus niger, Penicillium and Chrysogenum
Propionic acid	Propionibacterium
Butyric acid	Clostridium acetobutylicum
Oxalic acid	Aspergillus sp.
Gallic acid	Aspergillus niger
Some amino acids	Escherichia coli

Types of Antibiotic with their Source and Action

Antibiotics	Source	Action
Penicillin	Penicillium chrysogenum, P notatum + Phenyl Acetic Acid	Tonsilitis, Sore Throat, Gonorrhea, Rheumatic Fever, some Pneumonia types
Griseofulvin	Penicillium griseofulvum	Antifungal, especially for Ringworm
Nystatin	Streptomyces noursei	Antifungal for Candidiasis and overgrowth of Intestinal Fungi during excessive antibiotic treatment.
Hamycin	Streptomyces pimprina	Antifungal Antibiotic
Fumagillin	Aspergillus fumigatus	Broad spectrum antibacterial especially against Salmonella and Shigella.
Bacitracin	Bacillus licheniformis	Syphilis, Lymphonema or Reticulosis.
Streptomycin	Streptomyces griseus	Meningitis, Pneumonia, Tuberculosis and Local Infection. Toxic in some, through eighth cranial nerve.
Chloramphenicol Chloromycetin	Streptomyces venezuelae, S. lavendulae	Typhoid, Typhus, Whooping cough, Atypical Pneumonia, Bacterial Urinary Infections.
Tetracyclines/ Aureomycin	Streptomyces aureofaciens	Viral pneumonia, Osteomyelitis, Whooping Cough. Eye infections.
Oxytetracycline/ Terramycin	Chlorotetracycline → Hydrogenation Streptomyces rimosus	Intestinal and Urinary Infections (Spirochaetes, Rickettsia, Viruses)
Erythromycin	Streptomyces erythreus (= S. erythraeus)	Typhoid, Common Pneumonia, Diphtheria, Whooping Cough etc.
Gentamycin	Micromonospora purpurea	Effective against Gram (+) bacteria
Polymixin	Bacillus polymyxa	Antifungal

* Milk is pasteurised (preserved) by boiling it at 62.8° for 30 minutes (Low Temperature Holding method or LTH) or at 71.7.°C for 15 seconds (high temperature holding method). These treatments kill all bacteria.

Botany

- It is the branch of biology which deals with plants, which are considered as multicellular ulcerates. The cells of these organisms contain a cell wall made up of cellulose and other polysaccharides. Plants have the ability to synthesise their own food (autotrophic) in the presence of sunlight, *via* the process of photosynthesis.

- Plants have two main groups *i.e.,* **cryptogams** (lower plants without well defined flowers and seeds) and **phanerogams** (higher plants with well defined flowers and seeds).

- **Cryptogams** further contains thallophytes and pteridophytes with bryophytes in between. Here, thallophytes means those plants which have thallus like body *i.e.,* without roots, leaves and stem *e.g.,* algae, fungi, bacteria etc.

- All the plants of cryptogams are considered as primitive as these do not have well defined features of plants like presence of **phloem** (a tissue for food transport) and presence of **xylem** (a tissue for water transport etc).

- **Phanerogams** are well defined advanced plants with proper roots, leaves and stem and well differentiated tissue system. These can be categorised as **Gymnosperms** (Naked Seed) and **Angiosperms** (Covered seed) plants.

- Algae like *Nostoc, Anabaena* etc are used as manure.
- *Sphagnum* a genus of mosses is used as fuel and antiseptic.

- Some plants catch insects to fulfill their nitrogen requirement. Such plants are called insectivorous plants.

PLANT MORPHOLOGY

Plant morphology represents a study of the development, form and structure of plants and by implication, an attempt to interpret these on the basis of similarity of plan and origin.

Classification of Plants

- Plant classification is the placing of known plants into groups or categories to show their relationship.

- Thus, plants are classified into group having same characteristics.

- **Thallophyta** A phylum of plants of very diverse habit and structure, *e.g.,* Algae, fungi and lichens.

- **Bryophytes** Have stems and leaves but lack true vascular tissue and reproduce by spores *e.g.,* Mosses, hornworts, liverworts etc.

- **Pteridophytes** Vascular plants with leaves, stems and roots, but lack both seeds and flowers, *e.g.,* Ferns, *Lycopodium*, horsetails etc.

- **Gymnosperms** Group of seed producing plants. A plant that has seeds unprotected by an ovary or fruit, *e.g.,* Conifer, cycads, pine tree etc.

- **Angiosperms** (Vascular plants) A major group of flowering plants. Their characteristics are the possession of protected seeds or fruits, *e.g.,* Rose, tulip, tomatoes etc.

Virus

The term virus was given by Pasteur. Virus was discovered by Iwanowski in the extract of diseased tobacco plant. Virus is a nucleoprotein entity which do not have machinery of its own but can utilise the synthetic machinery of living cell of other organisms for its multiplication. Virus is considered to be a cellular, i.e. without a cell.

Bacteria

Basically, bacteria are unicellular prokaryotes. Their cell wall is generally, made up of peptidoglycans and polysaccharides. Genetic material is not organised into nucleus, i.e. a primitive nucleus is present (without a nuclear membrane). All membrane bound cell organelles are absent.

Flagella, if present is single-stranded, made up of protein flagellin.

Gamete formation is absent.

PARTS OF A PLANT

Different parts of a plant perform different function. Accordingly they are divided into root, stem, leaves, flower, fruits and seeds.

Root

It is that part of plant body, which develops from radicle and grows down into the earth. It gives secondary and tertiary roots.

Plants have two types of root systems

1. **Tap root** develop from radicle, normally found in dicot plants.
2. **Adventitious root** with a main tap root that is larger and grows faster than the branch roots.

Modification of Tap Roots

Conical This type of root is thickened towards base but thin near the side of the plant, *e.g.,* Carrot.

Napiform This type of root is very broad at the top and tapering like a tail at the bottom, *e.g.,* turnip, beet root etc.

Fusiform This type of root is inflated in the middle portion, while thin towards bottom and top, *e.g.,* Radish.

Pneumatophores This type of root is found in salty soil near the sea and for the respiratory activities, it undergoes toward negative geotropism, *e.g., Rhizophora,* plant sundari etc.

Mycorrhizal These roots are known from 90% of plant species and are mutualistic association of a fungus with plant root tissue. Most plants require specific mycorrhizal fungi without, which they are unable to absorb sufficient quantities of P, Zn and Mn.

The fungus takes the place of root hairs and may penetrate the cortex completely (endomycorrhizae) or remain on the surface of the root (ectomycorrhizae).

Functions of Root

- Keeps the plants static.
- Transports water and mineral salts to the stem and ultimately to the leaves.
- Absorbs water and mineral salts from the soil.

Stem

It is the ascending organ of the plant, which is formed by the elongation of plumule. Thus, stem is that part of the plant, which originates from plumule and goes towards sunlight opposite to the gravity.

Underground Modifications

In the adverse conditions underground stems store their food and become thickened and tuberous.

Various types of modifications can be described as

Stem tuber Potato

Bulb Onion, garlic, tulips, lilies etc.

Corm Gladiolus, *Crocus sativus* or saffron etc.

Rhizome Ginger, turmeric, arrow root etc.

Subaerial Modifications

There are various types of modifications exists in such types of stem

Runner Grass root, *Mereilia* etc.

Stolon Mint, jasmine, strawberry etc.

Offset Water hyacinth, *Pistia* etc.

Sucker Pudira, *chrysanthemum* etc.

Aerial Modifications

Various aerial modifications are:

Stem tendril Grape

Stem thorn Lemon, roses, jujube plum or Chinese date

Phylloclade Cactus

Bulbils *Ruscus.*

Leaf

It is a green part, its main function is to make food through photosynthesis and respiration. *Leaves are mainly of two types*

1. **Simple Leaf** A leaf having one blade but blade is not divided, *e.g.,* mango.
2. **Compound Leaf** A leaf with more than one blade. All blades are attached to a single leaf stem, *e.g.,* Rose, orange etc.

Parts of a Typical Leaf

Leaf Base   It is the lowermost part of the leaf, borne onto the node of the stem or its branches.

Petiole   The stalk of leaf that connects the lamina with the stem or its branch is called petiole.

Lamina   It is the terminal, flattened, green and conspicuous part of a leaf and is specialised to manufacture food (photosynthesis).

Differences between Stem and Root

Stem	Root
Cuticle or cutinised outer walls of epidermal cells present.	Cuticle or cutinised outer walls absent.
Epidermis is protective in function.	Epidermis (young) is absorptive in function. It is called epiblema or rhizodermis.
Stomata is present in epidermis.	Stomata is absent in epiblema.
Stem hairs are additional cells, *i.e.*, they do not arise as outgrowths of epidermal cells.	Root hairs are tubular outgrowths of the epiblema (epidermal) cells.
Chloroplasts may be present in some outer cells of the cortex.	Chloroplast almost absent.
Cortex narrow.	Cortex broad.
Endodermis is inconspicuous.	Endodermis is conspicuous.
Pericycle not involved in secondary growth.	Pericycle actively involved in root branches formation and in secondary growth.
Xylem characteristically endarch.	Xylem characteristically exarch.
Xylem and phloem fibres present.	Xylem and phloem fibres usually absent.
Secondary growth, if occurs, takes place by primary cambium, which is both interfascicular and intrafascicular.	Secondary growth, if present, takes place by secondary cambium, the conjunctive parenchyma and pericycle start meristematic activity and participate.

Inflorescence

The arrangement of flowers on a floral axis is called inflorescence. The portion of stem that bear cluster of flowers is called peduncle and the stalk of individual flower is called pedicel. The inflorescence has been classified into five distinct types according to modes of branching and modification of peduncle.

Solitary

Racemose

Cymose

Mixed

Specialized

Out of four, two types are most important.

Racemose Inflorescence

In racemose inflorescence, the main axis is capable of continuous growth. The flowers show acropetal succession on the main axis.

Cymose Inflorescence

In cymose inflorescence, the main axis ends in a flower, since the peduncle stops growing. The flowers show basipetal succession.

Common Racemose Inflorescence *and* their Presence

Inflorescence	Presence
Spike	Adhatoda
Spikelet	Grasses
Catkin	Morus
Spadix	Banana and maize
Corymb	Iberis amara (candy tuft)
Capitulum (head)	Sunflower
Special	Inflorescence and their presence
Cyathium	Euphorbiaceae family
Verticillaster	Ocimum and Leucus
Hypanthodium	Ficus

FLOWER

It is a modified shoot that consists of accessary whorls (calyx and corolla) and essential whorls (androecium and gynoecium). The plant, which bears both male and female flower is called **monoecious**, while separate plants with one type of flower are called **dioecious**.

Calyx

The outermost whorl consisting of units called sepals; these are typically green and enclose the rest of the flower in the bud stage, however, they can be absent or prominent and petal-like in some species.

Corolla

The next whorl toward the apex, composed of units called petals, which are typically thin, soft and coloured to attract animals that help the process of pollination.

Androecium

The next whorl, consisting of units called stamens. It consist of two parts–a stalk called a filament, topped by an anther, where pollen is produced by meiosis and eventually dispersed.

Gynoecium

- The innermost whorl of a flower, consisting of one or more units called **carpels**. The carpel or multiple fused carpels form a hollow structure called an **ovary**, which produces ovules internally.
- Ovules are megasporangia and they in turn produce megaspores by meiosis, which develop into female gametophytes. These give rise to egg cells.
- The gynoecium of a flower is also described using an alternative terminology, wherein the structure one sees in the innermost whorl (consisting of an ovary, style and stigma) is called a **pistil**.
- A pistil may consist of a single carpel or a number of carpels fused together. The sticky tip of the pistil, the stigma, is the receptor of pollen. The supportive stalk, the style, becomes the pathway for pollen tubes to grow from pollen grains adhering to the stigma.

Pollination

Transfer of pollens from stamens to stigma is called pollination.

It is of two types

Self-pollination

Transfer of pollen from stamen to the stigma of same flower or different flower of the same plant.

Cross–pollination

In this, pollen reach from anther of one flower to the stigma of different flower of same species. This is done with the help of air, water, insects or animals (agents of pollination). In most flowers, maximum pollination occurs by the method of anemophily (by mind). In this mode, pollen-loss is maximum.

Fruits

It is ripened ovary of flower. The fruit may be true (formed from ovary alone) or false (developed from other part of flower except ovary). These are of three main types, *i.e.*, simple, aggregate and composite.

Simple Fruit

A simple fruit always develops from a single ovary containing one or more carpels and may or may not include additional modified accessory floral (perianth) structures. In addition, a simple fruit is either fleshy or dry. Fleshy fruits are edible and are seen in the fresh fruit and vegetable section of your local super market.

Aggregate Fruits

These are groups of simple fruits, developed from multicarpellary or polycarpellary, apocarpous ovary of a flower. These are etaerio of follicle, etaerio of achenes, etaerio of berries and etaerio of drupes.

Composite Fruits

A composite or multiple fruit develops from the complete inflorescence. *These are of two types*

Sorosis A multiple fruit derived from just the pistils of many unisexual flowers of an inflorescence, *e.g.*, Mulberry, jackfruit, pineapple etc.

Syconus A multiple fruit derived from numerous ovaries borne on the inside of the fleshy receptacle of an inflorescence. Also in accessory fruit, the fleshy portion of the fruit is formed by the hollow peduncle of the (inside-out) inflorescence, *e.g.*, peepal, gular.

Seeds

Seed is a fertilised mature ovule that possesses an embryonic plant.

There are two types of seeds

Non-endospermic seeds non-albuminous seed Endosperm is absent in this seed and stores their food material in cotyledons, *e.g.*, Gram, pea.

Endospermic or albuminous seed These possess endosperm and store their food in it, *e.g.*, Castor, maize, rice.

AGRICULTURE

- Agriculture is derived from Latin words *Ager* and *Cultura*. *Ager* means land or field and *Cultura* means cultivation. Therefore, the term *Agriculture* means cultivation of land, *i.e.*, the science and art of producing crops and livestock for economic purposes.
- It was the key development in the rise of sedentary human civilisation, whereby farming of domesticated species created food surpluses that nurtured the development of civilisation.

AGRONOMY

The branch of agriculture that deals with field crop production and soil management. Agronomists generally work with crops that are grown on a large scale (*e.g.*, small grains) and that require relatively little management. Agronomic experiments focus on a variety of factors relating to crop plants, including yield, diseases, cultivation and sensitivity to factors such as climate and soil.

Cropping Pattern

Crop Rotation

It is the practice of growing a series of dissimilar types of crops in the same area in sequential seasons. It confers various benefits to the soil.

Crop rotation also mitigates the build-up of pathogens and pests that often occurs, when one species is continuously cropped and can also improve soil structure and fertility by alternating deep-rooted and shallow-rooted plants.

Intensive Cropping

It refers to efficient use of water, nutrients and tillage. The interdependence of and synergies among water, nutrients and energy in regard to increasing crop performance is generally preferred.

Main Crops for Rotations	
One yearly	Paddy and wheat
Two yearly	Maize and cotton
Three yearly	Tomato and lady's finger
Four yearly	Cotton and wheat

Zero Tillage

It is a way of growing crops from year to year without disturbing the soil through tillage.

No-till is an agricultural technique, which increases the amount of water and organic matter (nutrients) in the soil and decreases erosion. It increases the amount and variety of life in and on the soil.

It has two distnctive features

- **Sole Cropping** It is to cultivate a pure variety of crop.
- **Monoculture** Planting a sole crop in a field regularly but harvest it single in a year.

Companion Planting/Cropping

It is the planting of different crops in proximity on the theory that they assist each other in nutrient uptake, pest control, pollination and other factors necessary in increasing crop productivity.

Intercropping

It is the practice of growing two or more crops in proximity. It is particularly important not to have crops competing with each other for physical space, nutrients, water or sunlight.

The most common goal of intercropping is to produce a greater yield on a given piece of land by making use of resources that would otherwise not be utilised by a single crop.

Multiple Cropping

It is the practice of growing two or more crops in the same space during a single growing season.

It can take the form of double-cropping, in which a second crop is planted after the first has been harvested or relay cropping, in which the second crop is started amidst the first crop before it has been harvested.

Farming System

Mixed Farming

It is one in which crop production is combined with the rearing of livestock. The livestock enterprises are complementary to crop production, so as to provide a balance and productive system of farming.

Ranching

It is the practice of raising the grazing livestock such as cattles, sheep or poultry. The area is known as **ranch** and the practice is called *ranching*. The ranching and cowboy tradition originated in Spain. During the Reconquista in middle ages the Spanish nobles got huge lands on grants.

Terrace Farming

It is a piece of sloped land, which has been landscaped in such a way that, the practice of farming can be easily carried out.

Generally, this type of farming is done in the mountain regions along the slope. The land is cutout along the slope and terraces are made. This system is more common in North-Eastern hilly tracts of India.

Truck Farming (Marketing Gardening)

It is a horticultural practice of growing fruits, vegetables, etc., on commercial basis, in trucks for direct delivery to big restaurants, hotels and motels. This technique was evolved by the english speaking farmers, who referred them as truck farms in 19th century.

Organic Farming

Organic agriculture means a process of developing a viable and sustainable agroecosystem. It is an agricultural practice that relies on crop rotation, green manure, compost and biological pest control.

Organic farming uses fertilisers and pesticides but strictly limits the use of synthetic fertilisers, pesticides, plant growth regulators such as hormones, livestock antibiotics, food additives and genetically modified organisms.

Blanching

In it, the young shoots of a plant are covered to exclude light to prevent photosynthesis, which would produce chlorophyll and thus, remain pale in colour. Blanched vegetables have a more delicate flavour and texture than unblanched.

SEED SCIENCE

- It is a basic and most important input of agriculture. A good quality seed is one, which is free from adulterants, diseased or insect-pest infestations, which hinder or reduce the quality of a seed.
- The era of hybridisation of seeds started after 1930. The hybrid seeds are the cross breeded seeds, which are artificially developed so as to have the desirable characters. While developing a hybrid seed, it goes through the various developmental stages.
- *These are*
  - **Nuclear Seed** It is initial pure seed of an improved variety available with the breeder.
  - **Breeder's Seed** It is the seed obtained from the progeny (generation) of nucleus seed.
  - **Foundation Seed** The breeder seeds grown on State Government farms and agriculture universities under scientific observations and check.
  - **Registered Seed** The seeds grown from nucleus, breeder's and foundation seeds.
  - **Certified Seed** The seeds certified before release as a new variety having all the desirable characters.

Synthetic and Composite Seed Varieties

- **Synthetic variety:** It is a variety developed by selecting a number of inbred lines with good General Combinig Ability (GCA). Synthetic varieties can be developed by using clones or inbreeds, *e.g.,* ICMS 7703.
- **Composite variety:** It is a variety that is developed by mixing of seeds of various outstanding inbred lines, which have similar characteristics. So, the exact reconstitution of composite variety is not possible, *e.g.,* Sona, Shakti, African tall etc.

Hybrid Seed

- It is produced by cross-pollinated plants. In hybrid seed production, the crosses are specific and controlled. The advantage of growing hybrid seed compared to inbred lines comes from heterosis.
- To produce hybrid seed, elite inbred varieties are crossed with well-documented and consistent phenotypes (such as yield) and the resulting hybrid seed is collected.

Artificial Seed

It is encapsulated plant propagule (somatic embryo/shoot bud) in a suitable matrix, containing substances like nutrients, growth regulators, herbicides, insecticides, fungicides and mycorrhizae, which will allow and help it to grow into a complete plantlet.

Genetically Modified Seeds

It is that they have been altered or modified, through biotechnology to have their genetic structure changed. This is usually accomplished by either adding or taking away genes of the original.

Terminator Seed

The term *Terminator seeds* as it applies to the area of agriculture can be defined as a descriptive term used by some for seeds that have been genetically engineered to produce a crop whose first generation produces sterile seeds, thus preventing a second generation from being grown from seeds saved from the first.

Traitor Technology

In this technology, to make the induced gene active, certain chemicals are used. Many Multi National Corporations (MNCs) are trying to bring this in India and environmentalists are opposing it.

Crop Diversification

It is intended to give a wider choice in the production of a variety of crops in a given area so as to expand production related activities on various crops and also to lessen risk. Crop diversification in India is generally viewed as a shift from traditionally grown less remunerative crops to more remunerative crops.

AGROFORESTRY

It is an integrated approach of using the interactive benefits from combining trees and shrubs with crops and/or livestock. It combines agricultural and forestry technologies to create more diverse, productive, profitable, healthy and sustainable land-use systems. A narrow definition of agroforestry is trees on farms.

Vermicomposting

It is a method of using worms to transform organic waste into a nutrient-rich fertiliser. It is a healthy and clean way to eliminate wastes going into our landfills, which improves the environment. Vermicomposting is inexpensive and only takes two to three months to produce results.

Plant Preservation

Like other organisms plants can also be infected with the disease. All these disease causing agents are called **Pests**. Main causative agents are virus, bacteria and fungi. As *for example*, wheat is infected with rust and smut. In paddy, generally blast is found, which is spread by Gandhi bug. In cotton, bollworm causes disease.

Keeping fruits and vegetables fresh for a longer period without hampering its physical and chemical properties, is called fruits and vegetables preservation. Essential Commodities Act, 1955 has Part-3 for its revelation.

Methods of Preservation

Various methods of preservation are

Low Temperature

Microbes become inactive at low temperature. We can keep them in freezer.

Pasteurisation

It is a mild heating treatment at temperatures up to 100°C (which is the boiling point of water at elevations up to 300 metres above sea level). This method causes only a slight decrease in taste and nutritional value. Pasteurised products therefore spoil faster than sterilised products.

Canning

There are two primary methods of canning A hot water bath and pressure canning which ever method you use, be sure to use jars with lids made specifically for that technique. Glass canning jars, which are reusable, come in various sizes (most are single pints or quarts), so choose one that best suits your canning needs.

Integrated Pest Management (IPM)

It is an ecological approach to agricultural pest control that integrates pesticides/herbicides into a management system incorporating a range of practices for economic control of a pest. *An IPM system is designed around six basic components*

Acceptable Pest Levels

- The emphasis is on control, not eradication. IPM programmes first work to establish acceptable pest levels, called action thresholds and apply controls if those thresholds are crossed. IPM holds that wiping out an entire pest population is often impossible and the attempt can be expensive and environmentally unsafe.
- These thresholds are pest and site specific, meaning that it may be acceptable at one site to have a weed such as white clover, but at another site it may not be acceptable.
- By allowing a pest population to survive at a reasonable threshold, selection pressure is reduced. This stops the pest gaining resistance to chemicals produced by the plant or applied to the crops. By not killing all the pests there are some un-resistant pests left that will dilute any resistant genes that appear.

Preventive Cultural Practices

Selecting varieties best for local growing conditions and maintaining healthy crops is the first line of defence, together with plant quarantine and cultural techniques such as crop sanitation (e.g., removal of diseased plants to prevent spread of infection).

Monitoring

Regular observation is the cornerstone of IPM. Observation is broken into two steps, first inspection and second, identification. Visual inspection, insect and spore traps and other measurement methods and monitoring tools are used to monitor pest levels.

Since, insects are cold-blooded, their physical development is dependent on the temperature of their environment. Many insects have had their development cycles modelled in terms of degree days. Monitor the degree days of an environment to determine when is the optimal time for a specific insect's outbreak.

Responsible Pesticide Use

Synthetic pesticides are generally used as required and often only at specific times in a pest life cycle.

Locust Control and Research

On seeing the grave situation of locust attack, a warning centre as, locust warning organisation has been created, at Jodhpur. It has locust surveillance and monitoring through 5 circle offices and 23 outposts.

Mechanical Controls

They include simple hand-picking, erecting insect barriers, using traps, vacuuming and tillage to disrupt breeding.

Biological Controls

The main focus for biological control is on promoting beneficial insects that eat target pests. Biological insecticides, derived from naturally occurring microorganisms (*e.g.*, Bt, entomopa-thogenic fungi and entomo- pathogenic nematodes).

Animal Husbandry

The rearing of animals for specific purposes is called domestication and such animals are called domestic animals. Domestication of animals started during the hunting and gathering phase of human civilisation.

BUFFALOES

Bubalus bubalis is its scientific name. Generally, it is assumed that India is place of its origin. *There are two types breeds of buffaloes*

Exotic or Marshy

These are generally found in Myanmar, Philippines, Malaysia, Thailand, Singapore, Indonesia, China. These are used for cart mainly. Its breeds are Jerangi, Kuhzestani, Ongole, Sinhala, Manofi, Suinue and Walede.

Aquatic or Indian

These are heavy or light weighted and generally preferred to stay in water. It has low heat-tolerancce capacity.

These are again categorised into two types

Heavy Weight Buffaloes

It includes three breeds

- **Jaffrabadi** Its place of origin is supposed to be at Junagarh, Kutch and Jamnagar of Gujarat. It gives 15-18 L milk per day. Its milk contains 7-9% fat.
- **Murrah** It found generally in Punjab, Haryana, Delhi, Rajasthan, Uttar Pradesh etc. It generally gives about 25 L milk per day.
- **Nili Ravi** It is found mainly in Ferozpur of Punjab. Horns are small, white spots on mouth and head. Gives on an average 1500-1800 L milk per year.

Light Weight Bufffaloes

It includes following breeds

- **Bhadawari** It is generally found in Etawah, Agra, Gwalior and surrounding areas. It gives 4.5 L milk per day. 12-14% fat is found in its milk. Male buffaloes are used as load carrying cattle.

- **Mehsana** It is found in Mehsana, Sabar Kantha, Palanpur and Banaskatha. It gives 8-9 L milk per day. 8-13% fat is present in its milk. It is considered as a hybrid of Murrah and Surti breeds.
- **Surti** It found in Gujarat, South-West part, Anand, Nadiad and Vadodara. It gives on an average 1700 L milk per year. 8-12% fat is available in its milk.
- **Nagpuri or Ellichpuri** It found in Nagpur, Akola and Amrawati. It gives on an average 1000-1200 L milk per year. 7-8% fat is present in its milk.
- **Tarai** It found in Tarai belt of Ramnagar, Tanakpur. It gives about 900-1200 L milk in a year.
- **Manda** It found in the boundary of Mondosa and Parlakimedi mountain. Male is used for carrying heavy loads.
- **Toda** It found on the Nilgiri mountain in Tamil Nadu. It gives about 4-8 L milk per day.

COWS

Scientific name of cow is *Bos indicus* and *Bos taurus*. In India, 30 varieties of cows are present. Rearing of cow and bull is preferred in India. 16% of the world cow and bull are present in India.

Varieties of Cows

Some varieties of cows are as follows

Humped Indian Breeds

These are high milk-yielding and their calves are not used for agricultural purposes.

Following are its important breeds

Sahiwal Actually found in Mont-Gomari in Pakistan. In India, it is found in Punjab, Delhi, Uttar Pradesh, Madhya Pradesh and Bihar. It gives around 2150 L milk in a year. 4-6% is content of fat in its milk.

Red Sindhi Found in Allahabad, Guwahati, Bengaluru. It gives around 5440 L milk in a year.

Gir Generally found in Junagarh, Kathiawad, Mumbai, Pune, Ahmedabad, Hyderabad. Oxen are very strong. It gives 1746 L milk on an average. Fat content is 4-5% in its milk.

Deoni Similar to Gir breed. It gives 1600-1650 L milk in a year. Fat content is 4-5% in its milk.

Dual Purpose Breeds

These breeds give more milk along with its calf is very useful in ploughing. *Following are its breeds*

- **Haryana** It found in Rohtak, Haryana. It give 1000-1100 L milk in a year. Maximum milk yielding capacity is 3178 kg/yr Calf is best for ploughing activities.
- **Nimari** It mainly found in Khargaun. Oxen are very strong.
- **Tharparkar** It mainly found in Kutch, Marwar and in Northern Mumbai. It is also known as Thari. Its average milk yielding capacity is 1474 kg.

Load Carrying Breeds

- **Nageri** Main place of origin is believed to be Rajasthan. Now maximum found in Haryana, Uttar Pradesh and Punjab. Famous for fast walk and heavy load.
- **Malvi** Main place of origin is Uttar Pradesh, now also found in Madhya Pradesh and in Rajasthan.
- **Amritmahal** It found in Mysore of Karnataka. These breeds are fast running and quick.
- **Gangatiri** Main place of origin is Uttar Pradesh. These are very useful for agricultural practices.
- **Siri** It basically a hilly breed. Found in Darjeeling and Sikkim. Used in carrying heavy loads.

Without Humped Cows (Exotic Breeds)

Milk Yielding Breeds

- **Jersey** Its colour is almond and body is, spotted, milk yielding capacity is 4500 L per year 5% fat content in its milk.
- **Brown Swiss** It mainly found in Switzerland. It gives 5200 L milk in a year. Fat content is 4%.

SHEEP

There are many breeds of sheep (*Ovis aries*) in our country. Today sheeps are raised in all parts of the world. Sheep provides us with wool, skin and mutton. A sheep lives for about 13 years.

Exotic Breeds of Sheep

- **Merino** This is the main representative of the Merino breed in Australia and is found in extremely high number throughout New South Wales, Queensland, Victoria and Western Australia.
- **South Devon** The South Devon is a longwool and meat breed which originated in South Devon and Cornwall in England. They are of the English Longwool type and are similar to Devon Longwoolled but are larger. Both sexes are polled and are naturally hornless.
- **Lincoln** It is found in England and it is useful for wool and meat.
- **Corriedale** It is mainly found in New Zealand and Australia. It is useful for wool and meat.
- **Romney Marshy** The Romney Marshy are found in England. Romney wool has the finest fibre diameter of all the longwool breeds. These are mainly used for wool production.

Shearing of Wool

It is essential to promote the health of sheep. The removal of hairs (wool) from the recommended periods for shearing of wool are winter (February-March) and rainy (August- September) season when rich grazing ground is available.

The sheeps are washed properly before the removal of hairs. The manufacture of wool from sheep hairs is a complicated process consisting of cleaning, drying, bleaching, dyeing, spining and twisting.

GOAT

There are many breeds of goat (Capra capra) in our country. Goat provide us milk, meat, skin and hair. The fine soft wool called Pashmina is the underfur of Kashmir and Tibet goats.

Noori

World's first Pashmina goat clone, produced in Kashmir has been named Noori and Arabic word referring to light. Funded by world bank, the clone project was a jointy worked on Skaust and Nari Karnal.

The clone has come as good news for fine fibre producing Pashmina goats, which are only spotted at an altitude of 14,000 feet in **Ladakh**.

Asom Hilly Breeds

These are smaller dwarf breeds of goats found in the hilly tract of Asom and other Eastern states.

Important Breeds of Indian Goats

Breeds	Distribution
Gaddi and Chamba	Himachal Pradesh
Kashmiri and Pashmina	Himachal Pradesh, Kashmir and Tibet
Jamunapari	Uttar Pradesh and Madhya Pradesh
Beetal	Punjab
Marwari	Rajasthan
Berari	Maharashtra
Malabari	Kerala
Bengal	Bihar and Odisha

Exotic Breeds of Goat

Exotic breeds of Goats are

- Saahen
- Nubian
- Boer
- Sudan Nubian

- Toggenburg
- Baluchi

- Alpine
- Angora
- Mubende
- Kambing Katjang
- Khursani
- Anglo Nubian

PIGS

- It is also called hog or swine and is an omnivorous, non-ruminant, gregarious mammal of genus *Sus.*
- All breeds of pigs have descended from the European wild boar *Sus scrofa* or a crossbreed of this and the Asiatic species, *S. indicus.* The care and management of pigs is called piggery.
- Pigs are the most prolific breeders and quick growers among the domestic animals.
- A group of 10 sows (female hog) and one boar may produce over 160 piglets in a year.
- Pigs are most useful domestic animals, especially of lower classes of society. They are most economical source of meat and animal fat.

Breeds of Pig

Domesticated	Distribution
Indigenous Pigs	
Ghori	Manipur, Asom, Meghalaya and Arunachal Pradesh
Desi	Uttar Pradesh, Bihar, Punjab and Madhya Pradesh
Exotic Pigs	
Landrace	Switzerland and Denmark
Large White Yorkshire	UK
Berkshire	UK

CAMELS

The camel is a large, horn less, ruminant mammal of genus *Camelus.* It is popularly called the **ship of the desert** because of its great travelling power in a desert.

It is a valuable beast carrying burden in hot desert and semi-desert regions as it can live on minimum food and water when travelling with load. *There are two types of camels*

1. **Arabian camels** (*Camelus dromedarius*) With a single hump, short hair and found in North Africa to India. It does not occur in wild form.

2. **Turkish or Bactrian camels** (*Camelus bactrianus*) With two humps, long hair and found in Gobi desert of Central Asia. It occurs in wild form also.

COMPUTER

INTRODUCTION

The word computer has been derived from the Latin word 'COMPUTARE', which means to compute or to calculate.

A computer can be defined as an electronic device used to calculate and manipulate the data (i.e. input) and generates an output in the form of useful information by following a set of procedural instructions.

British scientist **Charles Babbage** is considered as the Father of Computer. He invented the first mechanical computer in early 19th century and further in 1833, he conceived a automatic analytical engine for performing arithmetic functions.

Alan Mathison Turing is widely regarded as the Father of Modern Computers or Father of theortical computer science and Artificial Intelligence (AI).

Characteristics of Computer

- Speed
- Accuracy
- Diligence
- Versatility

Applications of Computer

- Education
- Hospitals
- Business
- Weather forecasting
- Entertainment
- Organisations

Generations of Computer

The history of computers is discussed in terms of different generations of computer.

Generation	Technology Used	Features	Processing Speed	Examples	Languages
First (1940-1956)	Vacuum Tubes or Valves	■ Magnetic drum for primary storage ■ Punch card used as secondary storage	Measured in miliseconds	Mark-I, UNIVAC, ENIAC	Machine language
Second (1956-1963)	Transistor	■ Magnet core memory used as internal storage ■ Magnet tapes used as secondary storage	Measured in microseconds	IBM-700, IBM 1401	Assembly language and HLL (FORTRAN, COBOL)
Third (1964-1971)	IC (Integrated Circuit)	■ Semiconductor memory used as primary storage ■ Magnetic disks were used as secondary storage	Measured in nanoseconds	IBM 360 series, ICL 1901	HLL (SNOBOL, BASIC)
Fourth (1971-Present)	VLSI or Microprocess	■ Massive use of magnetic and optical storage devices	Measured in picoseconds and beyond.	IBM PC, Pentium PC, APPLE, Macintosh.	HLL (ORACLE, EDA)
Fifth (Present & Beyond)	Bio-chips & ULSI	■ Artificial intelligence will make computer intelligent and knowledge based	Very high speed	Robotics	Natural Language

Types of Computer

Computer can be classified on three basis

On the Basis of Functions

- **Analog Computers** This is a type of computer that reads data using measurement and some program scale. It calculates by measuring continuous changes in the physical quantities. e.g. Mechanical integrators, nomogram, speedometer etc.
- **Digital Computers** This is a computer that performs calculations and logical operations with quantities represented as binary digits. e.g. Desktop, mainframe etc.
- **Hybrid Computers** These computers are the combination of both analog and digital computers. It works by measuring quantity and calculating logical operations. e.g. ECG monitors, HRS-100 etc.

On the Basis of Purposes

- **General Purpose Computers** This type of computers are designed in order to work in all environments. They are versatile computers but are not efficient and also consume a large amount of time in generating the results. e.g. ENIAC, desktops etc.
- **Special Purpose Computers** They are designed to perform only a specified task. They are not versatile and their speed and size depends on the task. They are efficient and consume less time in generating results. e.g. ATM, aircraft controllers etc.

On the Basis of Size and Capability

- **Micro Computers** It is a digital computer used by individuals and is also considered as an acronym for Personal Computers (PCs). They are small in size. They are usually used at homes, in schools and offices etc. e.g. Laptop, Palmtop, Notebook, Desktop etc.

- **Mini Computers** This type of computers are more powerful than micro computers, but less powerful than mainframe computers. They are also termed as mid-range computers.

It is a multiprocessing system capable of supporting 4 to about 200 users simultaneously. e.g. IBM mid range computers, K-202, SDS-92 etc.

- **Mainframe Computers** It is a very large computer and is used for handling major applications in large business organisations. They can also be used as centralised computers with several terminal users connected to it. They can contain large databases and are also known as super servers.

They can handle huge amount of input/output (I/O) operations at the same time. They are very expensive. e.g. Fujitsu's ICL VME, Hitachi's Z800 etc.

- **Super Computers** It can be defined as the most powerful computer in terms of performance and storage capacity. They are highly expensive and are employed for specialised applications such as for weather forecasting, several scientific researches etc.

NASA (National Aeronautics for Space Administration) uses super computers for launching space shuttles, controlling them and for space exploration purpose.

PARAM is the first super computer in India. It is a series of gigaflops developed by the Centre of Development of Advanced Computing (C-DAC), Pune.

Super Computers Developed in India

Super Computers	Year	Mft Company
Pratyush	2017	IITM, Pune
PARAM Kanchenjunga	2016	C-DAC and NIT Sikkim
PARAM ISHAN	2016	C-DAC and IIT Guwahati
Aaditya	2013	Indian Institute of Tropical Meteorology
PARAM YUVA II	2013	C-DAC, PUNE
SAGA-220	2011	ISRO
ANUPAM-Adhya	2010-11	BARC
PARAM YUVA	2008	C-DAC, PUNE
EKA	2007	Computational Research Laboratories, PUNE
PARAM SARITA	2007	C-DAC, PUNE

Top 10 Super Computers of World as on 2016

Name	Manufactured Company	Country	Operating System	Memory	Speed
Sunway Taihu Light (2016)	National Super computing center	China	Linux	1.31 PB	105 Peta flops
Tianhe-2 (2013)	Sun Yat-Sen University	China	Kylin Linux	1,375 TB	33.86 Petaflops
Titan (2012)	Oak Ridge National Laboratory (Cray)	America	Linux	693.5 TB	17.59 Petaflops
Sequoia (2011)	IBM	America	Linux	1,572,864 GB	12 Petaflops
K-computer (2011)	Fujiter	Japan	Linux	1,410,048 GB	10.5 Petaflops
Mira (2010)	IBM	America	Linux	—	8.16 Petaflops
Piz Diant (2009)	Cray INC	Switzerland	Linux	—	6.2 Petaflops
Stampede (2008)	Dell	America	Linux	192,192 GB	5.2 Petaflops
JU Queen (2007)	IBM	Germany	Linux	458,752 GB	5 Petaflops
VULCAN (2005)	IBM	America	Linux	393,216 GB	4.3 Petaflops

Components of Computer

The computer system comprises of the following four main components

1. Input Unit

It consists of those devices through which user can enter the data into a computer. It links a computer to the external environment. It translates the data into computers understandable form. Some input devices are

- Keyboard is used to enter data or information, which may be in numeric form or alphabetical form, in a computer system.

- Mouse is a pointing device which provides a means to input data and commands in graphic form by selecting through moving an arrow called pointer.

- Trackball is another pointing device which is an alternative to a mouse.

- Joystick is an input device that moves in all directions and controls the movement of the cursor.

- Scanner is an optical input device and uses light as an input source to convert an image into an electronic form that can be stored on the computer.

- Touch Screen is an electronic visual display that can detect the presence and location of a touch within the display area.

2. Output Unit

This unit contains those devices that provide the desired output (results) in the human acceptable format.

Some output devices are

- Monitor is also known as Visual Display Unit (VDU). The monitor is provided along with the computer to view the display result. The popular types of monitor are

  - LCD (Liquid Crystal Display), a special type of liquid is sandwiched between two plates. It is a thin, flat and light weight screen made up of any number of colour or monochrome pixels arranged in front of a light source.

  - LED (Liquid/Light Emitted Diode) is an electronic device that emits light when electrical current is passed through it.

  - TFT (Thin Film Transistor) is a LCD with active-matrix displays, each pixel is controlled by one to four transistors that can make the screen faster, brighter, more colorful than passive-matrix and capable of being viewed at different angles.

  - 3-D Monitors describe an image that provides the perception of length. When 3-D images are made interactive then user feel involved with the scene, and this experience is called virtual reality.

- Printer prints information and data from the computer onto a paper. It can print documents in colour as well as in black and white.

- Plotter is a special kind of output channel, like a printer, that produces images on paper. They are mainly used to produce large drawings or images.

- Speaker is an output device that receives sound in the form of electric current. It needs a sound card connected to a CPU, that generates sound.

3. CPU (Central Processing Unit)

CPU is considered as the 'Brain of Computer'. It is responsible for all the manipulations and processing of the data provided to the computer. It is further categorised basically into two main components

- **Arithmetic Logical Unit** (ALU) This unit performs both arithmetical and logical operations. Arithmetic operations involves addition, subtraction, multiplication, division etc and the logical operations involves AND, OR, NOT, NOR, NAND etc.

- **Control Unit** (CU) It is an important part that instructs, maintains and controls the flow of information but does not store the data. It tells the memory, ALU and I/O devices that how they have to respond to the program's instructions.

4. Memory Unit

This unit stores the data and instructions, intermediate results or the processed data and thus, provides the relevant information whenever required by the other units of computer.

It consists of two types

- **Primary Memory** It is considered to be the main memory of computer that stores the data which is currently in use by the computer.

  Types of Primary Memory:
  - RAM (Random Access Memory) is a volatile memory, which losses the data when the power gets switched OFF. There are basically two types of RAM: Static RAM and Dynamic RAM.

- ROM (Read Only Memory) is a non-volatile memory, which retains the data even when the power gets switched OFF.

  Program and data that cannot be altered are stored in ROM. There are basically three types of ROM: Programmable ROM(PROM), Erasable PROM(EPROM) and Electrically EPROM(EEPROM).

- **Secondary Memory** The computer system uses secondary memory to store data, program instruction and information. It stores the data permanently. User can access or retrieve the data whenever required. Types of Secondary Memory:
  - Magnetic Tape (sequential access)
  - Magnetic Disk (Floppy Disk, Hard Disk)
  - Optical Disc (CD, DVD, Blu-ray Disc)
  - Solid State drive (Flash drive, SD cards)

Cache Memory

It is a type of memory used to hold the frequently used data. It acts as a buffer between the CPU and the main memory. It consumes less access time as compared to main memory and thus, is used to match up the speed of fast running processor.

Registers

These are defined as the special memory units used by the CPU to speed up the rate of accessing information. There are some special type of registers used for specific work.

e.g. Program Counter (PC) is used to hold the address of the next instruction for execution. Some other examples are Accumulator, Memory Buffer Register (MBR), Instruction Register (IR) etc.

Hardware

It can be defined as the physical components of a computer i.e. the parts that can be seen and touched.

The four main categories of hardware are
- Input devices e.g. keyboard, mouse etc.
- Output devices e.g. printer, monitor etc.
- Storage devices e.g. hard disk, floppy disk etc.
- Processing devices e.g. CPU etc.

Software

The term software can be defined as the set of programs and procedures that enable a computer to perform a specific task or to process the information. Software can be classified into three types:

System Software

It is a set of one or more programs designed to control the operations of a computer system including hardware components and implementations of application software.

Types of System Software are

- **Operating System** It is a system software, consisting of an integrated set of programs that controls computer resources (CPU, memory, I/O devices, etc) and provides common services for efficient execution of various application software.
- **Language Translator** It helps in converting programming languages to machine language. There are three kinds of language translator
  - **Assembler** It converts program written in assembly language into machine language.
  - **Interpreter** It converts a high level language into machine language by converting it line by line.
  - **Complier** It also converts high level language program into machine language at one go.

Utility Software

It is a type of system software, which is used to support, secure and enhance the existing programs and data in the computer system. It is also used to debug the software errors. e.g. antivirus software, backup software etc.

Programming Language

It is a set of keywords, symbols and a system of rules for constructing statements, by which human can communicate, to be executed by a computer.

Programming languages are mainly categorised into two parts:

Low Level Languages These languages are designed to operate and handle the entire hardware and instruction set architecture of a computer system directly. It is divided into two parts:

- **Machine language**, referred to as machine code or object code, is a collection of binary digits or bits that the computer reads and interprets.
- **Assembly language** uses structured commands as substitutions for numbers, allowing humans to read the code easier.

High Level Languages These languages are not limited by the computer, designed for a specific task and are easier to read, write and understand. e.g. BASIC, C, FORTRAN, JAVA etc.

Application Software

It is a set of one or more programs designed to carry out operations for a specific application. It cannot run on itself, but it is dependent on system software to get executed. It is written in high level language.

Application Software	What Does It Do?	Examples
Word Processor	Virtually all personal computers are equipped with a word-processing program, which has the same function as a type-writer for writing letters, reports or other documents and printings.	Microsoft Word, WordPerfect
Spreadsheet	A table containing text and figures, which is used to perform calculations. Spreadsheets are usually used for budgets, statistics and so on.	Microsoft Excel, Lotus 1-2-3
Database Management System	Used for storing information, e.g. the names and addresses of the clients.	Microsoft SQL Server, Oracle
Accounting Program	They generate extensive financial reports, produce invoices and statements to customers, handle accounts payable and receivable, print payroll checks and payroll reports and track inventories.	Tally (all versions)
Presentation Tool	To create presentations by allowing one to produce slides or handouts.	Microsoft PowerPoint

Application Software	What Does It Do?	Examples
Desktop Publishing	For creating magazines, newsletters, books and so on.	QuarkXPress, Adobe Pagemaker
Multimedia Application	Used for creating multimedia presentations. e.g. Websites, animations and videos.	Dreamweaver, Flash, Premier
Telecommunication Software	A program that helps a user to connect and transfer information and files to and from the Internet. It is often a part of operating system or system software.	Dial-up Networking, Open Transport

NETWORKING

Computer networking relates to the communication between a group of two or more computers linked together. When we communicate on a network, we share information or data through a communication medium. E-mailing, instant messaging and web pages all are dependent on communication that take place across an underlying computer network.

Benefits of Networking

- Data and Fill sharing
- Software sharing
- Hardware sharing
- Reliability

Network Devices

These are required to amplyfy the signal to restore the original strength of signal and to provide an interface to connect multiple computers in a network. Many types of Network Devices

- **Repeater** is a device that amplifies the signals when they are transported over a long distance so that the signal can be as strong as the original signal.
- **Hub** is like a repeater with multiple ports used to connect the network channels.
- **Gateway** is an interconnecting device, which joins two different network protocols together.
- **Switch** forwards a data packet to a specific route by establishing a temporary connection between the source and the destination.
- **Bridge** reduces the amount of traffic on a LAN by dividing it into two segments.
- **Modem** is a device that converts digital signal to analog signal and vice-versa.

Types of Computer Network

- **Local Area Network (LAN)** In this, computers can be connected with a geographical area spread over 1 km to 10 km or we can say within a same building. All the terminals are connected to a main computer called server.
- **Metropolitan Area Network (MAN)** It is a data network designed for a town or city. Its main purpose is to share hardware and software resources among the various users.
- **Wide Area Network (WAN)** In this, the computers are farther apart and are connected by radiowaves. Such a network may spread over countries.

Communication Media

Communication media of a network refer to the transmission media or the connecting media used in the network. Transmission media can be divided into two broad categories; guided and unguided media.

- **Guided Media or Wired Technologies** It consists of a cable composed of metals like copper, tin or silver. Basically, these are divided into three categories
  - **Ethernet Cable or Twisted Pair** A type of cable that consists of two independently insulated wires twisted around one another. The use of two wires twisted together helps to reduce crosstalk and electromagnetic induction.
  - **Coaxial Cable** A type of wire that consists of a center wire surrounded by insulation and then a grounded shield of braided wire. The shield minimizes electrical and radio frequency interference.

* **Fiber-Optic Cable** A type of wire that containing one or more optical fibers that are used to carry light. The optical fiber elements are typically individually coated with plastic layers and contained in a protective tube suitable for the environment.

* **Unguided Media or Wireless Technologies** When the computers in a network are interconnected and data is transmitted through waves, then they are said to be connected through unguided media. Some commonly used unguided media of transmission are

  * **Radio Wave Transmission** There are two principal ways in which electromagnetic (radio) energy travels from a transmitting antenna to a receiving antenna. One way is by GROUND WAVES that are radio waves that travel near the surface of the Earth (surface and space waves) and the other is by SKY WAVES that are radio waves that are reflected back to Earth from the ionosphere.

  * **Microwave Transmission** It is the transmission of information or energy by electromagnetic waves whose wavelengths are conveniently measured in small numbers of centimeter; these are called microwaves.

  * **Satellite Communication** It provides communication links between various points on Earth. It covers a vast range of area. It is very useful in television transmission.

  * **Infrared Wave Transmission** It refers to energy in the region of the electromagnetic radiation spectrum at wavelengths longer than those of visible light, but shorter than those of radio.

  * **Bluetooth** It is a wireless technology standard for exchanging data over short distances from fixed and mobile devices and to create a Personal Area Networks (PANs).

Network Related Terms
Topology

It is defined as the way in which several nodes of the network are linked together. It represents the physical path between the connected nodes. e.g. Bus, Ring, Star, Tree, Mesh etc.

Network Interface Card (NIC)

It is a hardware component that connects a computer to a computer network as it contains the physical address of a computer. It is also known as network adaptor.

Public Switched Telephone Network (PSTN)

It is the world's collection of inter connected voice oriented public telephone networks. It provides landline phone service to residence and many other establishments. Thats why is also referred as Plain Old Telephone Service (POTS).

Value Added Network (VAN)

It provides Electronic Data Interchange (EDI) facility. It acts as a regional post office that examines the from and to information. It subscribes services like invoices sale purchase order etc.

Integrated Service Digital Network (ISDN)

It is a set of communication standards for digital transmission of voice, videos and other data services. It combines both circuit switching and packet switching for the purpose of transmitting data.

Firewall

It is a combination of both software and hardware based devices to permit or deny network transmission based on a set of rules. It is frequently used to protect network from unauthorised access while permitting legitimate communication to pass.

INTERNET

Internet is defined as network of networks that consists of millions of private and public computer networks linked together and sharing information using client server relationship. Data is shared by packet switching through standardised Internet Protocol Suite (TCP/IP).

Important Protocols Used over Internet

HyperText Transfer Protocol (HTTP)

It is a set of rules for transmitting files such as text, images, sound, videos etc, on the World Wide Web (WWW). As soon as a web user opens the web browser, the user is indirectly making use of HTTP. Its primary function is to establish a connection with the server.

Transmission Control Protocol/ Internet Protocol (TCP/IP)

It is a combination of two separate protocols TCP and IP, which are used together. TCP ensures the reliability of data transmission across the Internet connected networks while IP ensures how packets of information are sent out over networks.

Point to Point Protocol (PPP)

It is dial account which puts the computer directly on the Internet. Using this protocol each computer on the server has its own name and IP address.

File Transfer Protocol (FTP)

It is a type of transfer protocol that enables the user to transfer their files from one computer to another in a network environment and develop a communication. e.g. E-mails etc.

Telnet

It is a network protocol that allows a user on one computer to log into another computer that is part of the same network. It is an underlying TCP/IP protocol for accessing remote computers.

Terminology Related to Internet

World Wide Web (WWW)

It is a collection of connected documents by hypertext links, enabling the user to search for information by moving from one document to another; usually accessed by web browsers *via* Internet.

Web Server

It is a program that serves the files to the web user with the use of client server model approach and WWW's http. It contains the web pages corresponding to the website available on the Internet.

Client Server

It is a network architecture which separates the client from the server. Each instance of the client software can send request to server.

Webpage

It is a resource on WWW, usually written in HTML/XHTML with hypertext links that enable navigation from one page to another.

Website

It is a collection of web pages, grouped under a same domain name on the WWW or Internet.

Web Browser

It is an application software that runs over the client computer connect it with the server or to access the Internet and the WWW. e.g. Opera, Internet Explorer, Mozilla Firefox etc.

Uniform Resource Locator (URL)

Web address is a synonym for URL. It is basically a string of characters or an addressing scheme used by WWW browsers to locate sites on the Internet. e.g. http://www.google.com/services/index.htm

Domain Name

It is a way to identify and locate computers connected to the Internet. It always have two or more parts, separated by dots(.). e.g. google.com, yahoo.com etc.

Wireless Application Protocol (WAP)

WAP is a technical standard for accessing information over a mobile wireless network. A WAP browser is a web browser used by the mobile devices that are based on this protocol.

IP Address

Along with the physical address stored in NICs, Internet requires and additional addressing that identifies the connection of a host to its network which is known as the IP address. No two hosts on the Internet can have the same IP address. Each IP address consists of 4 bytes i.e. 32 bits defining 3 fields: Class, Network ID and Host ID.

Internet Service Provider (ISP)

It is an organisation that provides the Internet connection services to the people, who want to used Internet.

Communication through Internet

E-mail (Electronic Mail)

It is a service provided by the Internet that allows the exchange of digital messages through a network. It provides a communication medium through which people can communicate with each other.

Instant Messaging

There are several applications (apps) provided for instant messaging such as Viber, WeChat, Line, WhatsApp etc. Among all, WhatsApp is considered to be the most globally popular messaging app. It was bought by facebook in 2014. The messengers are only available for Android, Black berry, iOS and Windows phone mobile operating system.

Social Networking Sites (SNS)

It is a platform to build social networks or social relations among people who share interests, activities, events etc., within their individual networks. e.g. Facebook, Twitter, LinkedIn, Instagram etc.

- **Facebook** It is a very popular social networking site among the users. It allows the users to share their ideas, activities, images, videos, events etc., within their individual network.
- **LinkedIn** It is available in multilingual languages. It is mainly for students or professionals. It enables users to connect with colleagues, looking for a job or business relationships and get answers to industry questions.

WIRELESS COMMUNICATION

The origin of wireless communication goes back to 1896, when Marconi invented the wireless telegraphy. Wireless communication is the transfer of information over a distance without the use of electrical conductors or wires. The distance involed may be short or long. e.g. GPS units, wireless computer mice, keyboards and headsets, satellite television etc.

Generations of Wireless Communication

1G (The First Generation)

It is a wireless telephone technology and mobile telecommunication introduced in 1980s. 1G networks use analog signals as opposed to digital signals used by all the successive generations. In this, voice calls were generally modulated to a higher frequency typically 150 MHz and up.

2G (The Second Generation)

It was commercially launched for the GSM (Global System for Mobile Communication) standard in 1991 by Radiolinja in Finland. It was allowed for enhanced data services and also introduced the Short Messaging Services (SMSs).

3G (The Third Generation)

It was introduced by NTT DoCoMo in Japan in 2001. Its data transfer rates are 384 K bit/sec to 2M bits/sec. So, it allows for never before services like video calls, video conferencing, mobile, TV etc.

4G (The Fourth Generation)

TeliaSonera was the first operator in the world to commercially launch 4G in late 2009 in the City Centre of Stockholm and Oslo and a year later it was launched in Finland.

Bharti Airtel had launched 4G on mobiles in Bangalore, thus becoming the first in India to offer such a service on 14th February 2014.

5G (The Fifth Generation)

It will be a successor for 4G. It is a term used in some research papers and projects to denote the next major phase. Alliance feels that 5G should be rolled out by 2020 to meet business and consumer demands.

Security Threats

Phishing

It is characterised by the attempts to fraudulently acquire sensitive information such as passwords, credit card details etc. by masquerading as a trustworthy person.

Intruders

The attacker who would constantly find their way for breaking and entering into a secured system to access confidential or users information are called intruders.

Virus

It is defined as a program or a piece of code that gets loaded onto the computer without users knowledge and replicates itself. Various kinds of virus are Boot sector virus, Macro virus, Resident virus, Polymorphic virus, Direct action virus etc.

e.g. Creeper, Stuxnet, Melissa, Conficker, Code red, SQL Slammer, Nimda (derived from the word 'Admin') etc.

- Creeper is generally accepted to be the first computer virus written by Bob Thomas at BBN (Bolt Beranak and Newman) in 1971.

Worm

It is a self replicating computer program, similar to a virus. It is a self contained program and does not need to be a part of another program to propagate itself.

Spam

It is an unsolicited message sent over the Internet in the form of E-mails, to a large number of users for the purpose of spreading malware, advertising phishing etc.

Spyware

It is a type of malicious software installed on computers and collects information about users without their knowledge and may send such information to another entity. It can assets control over the computer without the consumer's knowledge.

Malware

A software which is specifically designed to disrupt or damage a computer system. It is a superset of computer viruses, worms, spyware, trojan horses and other malicious or unwanted software.

Botnet

It is a number of Internet computers that have been set-up to forward transmissions including spam and viruses to the other computers on the Internet without the knowledge of their owners. It is also known as Zombie Army.

Antivirus

It is a software consisting of computer programs that attempt to identify, detect and prevent the malware from the computer. It typically uses two different techniques to accomplish this

- Examining files to look for known viruses by means of a virus dictionary.
- Identifying suspicious behaviour from any computer program which might indicate infection.

  e.g. Kaspersky, Norton, AVG, Avast, McAfee etc.

Some Famous Personalities

Bill Gates

Bill Gates is an American Business magnate, computer programmer, Philanthrophist, inventor and co-founder of Microsoft (the software company) with Paul Allen. He acquired the posts like CEO, Chairman and Chief Executive Architect. He stepped down in Febrauary, 2014 and now is one of the Board of Members of Microsoft.

Steve Jobs

Steve Jobs was an American businessman, inventor and industrial designer and the co-founder of Apple Inc with Stephen Wozniak. He was the Chairman and CEO of Apple Inc.

Mark Elliot Zuckerberg

Mark Elliot Zuckerberg is an American computer programmer and Internet entrepreneur best known as one of the co-founders of the famous social networking site 'Facebook'. He is considered as one of the youngest billionaires as on April, 2013. He is the Chairman and Chief-Executive of Facebook. Recently facebook bought Whatsapp (an instant messenger) by paying $ 19 billion.

Tim Cook

Tim Cook is the CEO of Apple Inc. He has filled the seat of Steve Jobs. He is the decision maker in a company that has revolutionized the way humans see and use technology.

Tim Berners Lee

Tim Berners Lee also known as Tim BL is a British computer scientist and the inventor of the World Wide Web (WWW). He implemented the first successful communication between a Hypertext Transfer Protocol client and server via the Internet.

Jan Koum

Jan Koum founded a proprietary, cross-platform instant messaging service for Smartphones with Brian Acton, which is called WhatsApp in 2009. It is one of the most popular mobile messaging application. Jan Koum is the CEO and co-founder of WhatsApp Incorporation.

Smart Facts Related to CS & IT

iOS (iphone OS) It is the Apple's, mobile operating system developed originally for the iphone and later deployed on the iPod Touch and iPad as well.

Apple It is a prominent hardware and software company best known for its series of PCs, iPods, iPads, iphones etc. It was founded by Steve Jobs and Stephen Wozniak.
Recently, Apple has launched large screen iPhone 6 and 6 Plus, which has advanced features including health control apps, 4.7 and 5.5 inches display, better image quality and good battery backup.

Android It is designed primarily for touchscreen mobile devices such as smartphones and tablet computers. It is the most widely used mobile OS and, as of 2013, the highest selling OS overall.

CAPTCHA (Completely Automated Public Turing test to tell Computers and Humans Apart) It is a type of challenge response test used in computing as an attempt to ensure that the response is generated by a human being.
The process usually involves a computer asking a user to complete simple test which the computer is able to grade the user.

Rail Radar It is an online application that was launched by the CRIS (Centre for Railway Information Systems) on 10th October 2012 to find out the location of a large no of trains.

E-mail Triage It is a structured technique for processing E-mail. It is helpful for the user in order to make rapid, effective decisions about the mails stored in the Inbox of the user. At the end of the process, user is left with only the bits that require attention.

Deep Blue It was a chess playing super computer developed by IBM. This computer is able to do the work equivalent to the work of 32 computers and can think 20 crore steps of chess in one second. This was the computer which had defeated world chess champion Garry Kasparov in 1997.

HP, Google, Microsoft and Apple have one thing in common that all of them were started in garages.

Wanna Cry Ransomware It was a worldwide cyber-attack by the Wanna Cry Ransomware Cryptoworm in 2017 which targeted computers running the Microsoft Windows operating system.

Robot Sophia It is a social humanoid robot developed by Hong-Kong company Hanson Robotics.

Glossary

- **Algorithm** It is a finite set of step-by-step, well defined instructions for accomplishing desired actions or results.

- **Animation** It is the optical illusion of motion created by the consecutive display of images of static elements.

- **Artificial Intelligence** It is a branch of science that deals with helping machines find solutions to complex problems in a more human like fashion.

- **Basic Input/Output System** (BIOS) It is also known as ROM BIOS. It is a consistent way for application programs and operating system to interact with input/ouput devices.

- **Biometric Device** A device used for user authentication that verifies some physical characteristics of a user such as the person's appearance, finger print etc.

- **Blu-ray Disc** It can be defined as a digital optical disc data storage medium, storing high definition video resolution. It contains 25 GB per layer and 50 GB dual layer. It is a plastic disc with 120 mm diameter and 1.2 mm thickness, the same size as of DVDs and CDs.

- **Camcorder** It is a video camera recorder. It is a portable electronic device capable of recording live motion video and audio, for later playback.

- **Cloud Computing** It is a general term for the delivery of hosted services over the Internet whereby shared resources, softwares and information are provided to computers and devices as a utility over the network.

- **Cookies** These are often used to store information on the computer system to track the browsing pattern on a particular site.

- **Cryptography** It is a method of storing and transmitting data in a particular coded form so that only those can read and process it, for whom it is intended. It includes encoding and decoding of data.

- **Firmware** It is defined as the program that has been written on to ROM.It cannot be changed or deleted by an end user. They are in the non-volatile memory. Firmware is the combination of both software and hardware.

- **Flow Chart** It is the graphical representation formed with specified symbols (fig) and shows the flow of data, operations performed and the sequence of their execution.

- **Microprocessor** It is the controlling element in a computer system and is sometimes referred to as the chip. e.g. Intel, Dual core, Pentium-IV etc. Intel 4004 was the first microprocessor.

- **Motherboard** The biggest piece of silicon housed in the system unit of a computer is motherboard. All the other electronic devices and circuits of computer system are attached to this board like, processor, ROM, RAM, expansion slots and USB ports. It also includes controllers for devices like the hard drive, keyboard and mouse.

- **Multimedia** It refers to the use of several medias such as text, audio, graphics, video etc, to convey information. It simply means, being able to communicate in more than one way.

- **Robot** It is a system that contains sensors, control systems, manipulators, power supplies and software all working together to perform a task.

- **Robotics** It is the branch of technology that deals with the design, construction, operation, structural disposition, manufacture and application of robots and computer systems for their control, sensury feedback and information processing.

Abbreviations

ANSI	American National Standard Institute
ALGOL	Algorithmic Language
ASCII	American Standard Code for Information Interchange
ARPANET	Advanced Research Projects Agency Network
BASIC	Beginner's All Purposes Symbolic Instruction Code
BIOS	Basic Input Output System
BPS	Bits Per Second
CAD	Computer Aided Design
CGI	Common Gateway Interface
COBOL	Common Business Oriented Language
DSL	Digital Subscriber Lines/Domain-Specific Language
ENIAC	Electronic Numerical Integrator And Computer
EDI	Electronic Data Interchange
FAX	Far Away Xerox
FORTRAN	Formula Translation
GPS	Global Positioning System
GIF	Graphic Interchange Format
IBM	International Business Machine
ISDN	Integrated Services Digital Network
LIPS	List Processing
MICR	Magnetic Ink Character Recognition
MMS	Multimedia Messaging Service
MODEM	MODulator DEModulator
MIDI	Musical Instrument Digital Interface
NICNET	National Information Centre Network
OMR	Optical Mark Reader
OOP	Object Oriented Programming
RISC	Reduced Instruction Set Computer
SNOBOL	String Oriented Symbolic Language
SMTP	Simple Mail Transfer Protocol
SQL	Structured Query Language
TDMA	Time Division Multiple Access
TRAI	Telecom Regulatory Authority of India
UPS	Uninterruptible Power Supply
USB	Universal Serial Bus
WiMAX	World Wide Interoperability for Microwave Access
Wi-Fi	Wireless Fidelity
WLAN	Wireless Local Area Network
XHTML	Extensible HyperText Markup Language
ZIP	Zone Information Protocol

GENERAL KNOWLEDGE

First in World (Male)

First Secretary-General of United Nations	Trygve Lie (Norway)
First President of United States of America	George Washington
First President of the Republic of China	Dr Sun Yat Sen (1912)
First Prime Minister of Great Britain	Robert Walpole (1715)
Pakistan's first Governor-General	Mohammed Ali Jinnah
First Ethnic-Indian Prime Minister of Fiji	Mahendra Choudhary
First American President to visit India	Dwight David Eisenhower
First Russian (Soviet) Prime Minister to visit India	Nikolai Bulganin
First European invader of Indian soil	Alexander The Great
First man to go into space	Major Yuri Gagarin (USSR)
First man to walk in space	Alexey Leonov (Russia)
First space tourist	Dennis Tito (USA)
First man to set foot on the Moon	Neil Armstrong (USA)
First man to fly an aeroplane	Wright Brothers
First man to reach North pole	Robert Peary
First man to reach South pole	Roald Amundsen
First man to climb Mount Everest	Sherpa Tenzing Norgay and Sir Edmund Hillary (29th May, 1953)
First man to climb Mount Everest twice	Nawang Gombu (1965)
First blind man to scale Mount Everest	Erik Weihenmayer (25th May, 2001)
First person to sail around the world	Ferdinand Magellan
First deaf and dumb to cross the Strait of Gibralter	Taranath Shenoy (India)
First European to visit China	Marco Polo
First man to draw the map of Earth	Anexemander
First man to compile encyclopaedia	Aspheosis (Athens)
First man to win Nobel Prize for Literature	Sully Prudhomme (France)
First man to win Nobel Prize for Peace	Henry Dunant (Switzerland) and Frederic Passy (France)
First man to win Nobel Prize for Physics	WK Roentgen (Germany)
First man to win Nobel Prize for Chemistry	Jacobus H Van't Hoft (Holland)
First man to win Nobel Prize for Medicine	AE Von Behring (Germany)
First man to win Nobel Prize for Economics	Ragnar Frisch (Norway) and Jan Tinbergen (Holland)
First and only black man ever to win singles Wimbledon Trophy	Arthur Ashe (USA)
First Asian to head the International Cricket Council	Jagmohan Dalmiya
First man to hit double century in One Day International Match	Sachin Tendulkar (India)

First in World (Female)

First woman President of UN General Assembly	Vijaya Lakshmi Pandit (1953)
First woman President of a country	Maria Estela Peron (*Argentina*)
First woman Prime Minister of a country	S Bhandarnayake (*Sri Lanka*)
First woman Prime Minister of England	Margaret Thatcher
First woman Prime Minister of any Muslim country	Benazir Bhutto (*Pakistan*)
First woman cosmonaut in space	Valentina Tereshkova (*USSR*)
First woman space tourist	Anousheh Ansari (*Irani American*)
First woman to reach the North pole	Frances Phipps
First woman to set foot on the North pole	Ann Bancroft, USA
First woman to reach Antarctica	Caroline Michaelson
First woman to climb Mount Everest	Junko Tabei (*Japan*)
First woman in the world to cross the Strait of Gibralter	Sophie Psilolignou (*Greek*)
First woman to chair US Central Bank 'Federal Reserve'	Janet Yellen
First UN Deputy Secretary-General	Louise Frechette (*Canada*)
First female Amputee to climb Mount Everest	Arunima Sinha

First in World (Miscellaneous)

First country to make a Constitution	United States of America
First country to appoint Lokpal	Sweden
First country to ban capital punishment	Venezuela
First country to give voting right to woman	New Zealand
First country to impose carbon tax	New Zealand
First country to start VAT (Value Added Tax)	Brazil and Germany
First country to issue plastic currency	Australia
First country to issue paper currency	China
First country to give constitutional status to animal rights	Switzerland
First country to implement family planning	India
First country to start Civil Services Competition	China
First country to make education compulsory	Prussia (*Germany*)
First country to print books	China
First country to sign nuclear agreement with India	France
First country to send human to Moon	United States of America
First space ship landed on Mars	Viking-I 20th August, 1975
First space shuttle launched	Columbia
First country to launch satellite into space	Russia (*former USSR*)
First country to launch radio telescope satellite into space	Japan
First city to be attacked with Atom Bomb	Hiroshima (*Japan*)
First country to win the Football World Cup	Uruguay (1930)
First country to host the Modern Olympic Games	Greece
First lamb created using DNA from an adult sheep	Dolly
First heart bypass operation by a Robot, carried out in	Germany
First cloned human baby	Eve
First religion of the world	Sanatan Dharma
First university of the world	Taxila University

Superlatives of the World
Largest, Biggest, of the Smallest, Longest, Highest, Tallest etc)

Continent	Smallest—Australia Largest—Asia
Country	Largest (in area)—Russia Largest (in population)—China
Mountain Range	Longest—Andes (South America) Highest—Himalayas
Mountain Peak	Highest—Mount Everest (*Nepal*) (8848 m)
Desert	Largest Hot Desert—Sahara, Africa Largest Cold Desert—Gobi (Mongolia)
River	Longest—Nile (6690 km) Busiest—Rhine (Germany) Largest—Amazon (South America)
Basin	Largest—Amazon
Gorge	Largest—Grand Canyon, on the Colorado river, USA
Waterfall	Highest—Salto Angel Falls (*Venezuela*)
Delta	Largest—Sundarbans, India
Gulf	Longest—Gulf of Mexico
Island	Largest—Greenland (*renamed Kalaallit Nunaat*)
Bay	Largest—Hudson Bay, Canada
Peninsula	Largest—Arabia
Volcano	Largest—Mauna Loa (Hawaii Islands), Highest-ojos del Salado, Andes, Argentine-Chile (6885 m)
Sea (*Inland*)	Largest—Mediterranean
Ocean	Deepest and Biggest—The Pacific
Lake	Deepest—Baikal (*Siberia*) Highest—Titicaca (*Bolivia*) Largest (Fresh Water)—Lake Superior, USA Largest (Artificial)—Lake Kariba (*between Zabia and Zimbabwe*)
World's Rainiest Spot	*Mawsynram (Meghalaya)*
Sea Port	Largest— Shanghai (*China*)
Airport	Largest—King Fahd International Airport, Saudi Arabia (by area) Highest—Daocheng Yading Airport, Garzi, Tibet (*China*)
Airliner	Largest— Airbus A380
Dam	Tallest—Jinping-I Dam (*China*) Longest—Hirakud Dam (*Odisha*), India Biggest (Water storage capacity)— Kariba Dam, Zimbabwe Largest (Concrete)—Grand Coulee Dam (USA)
Coral formation	Largest—The Great Barrier Reef (*Australia*)
Cruise ships	Largest—Royal Caribbean
Canal	Longest—Beijing-Hangzhou Grand Canal
Animal	Most Intelligent—Chimpanzee Fastest—Cheetah
Acrhipelago	Largest (area)—Malay Archipelago Largest (number)—Norway Archipelago
Asteroid Impact Zone	Largest—Australia
Nation with boundary	Largest—Canada

Plateau	largest—Pamir Plateau (Asia)
Road	Highest—Leh-Manali Road (India, NH1-A)
Country Sharing border with others	Maximum—China (14)
Country with population Density	Highest—Macau
Bird	Largest—Ostrich Largest (Sea)—Albatross Fastest—Needle-tailed swift Smallest—Humming bird
Mammal	Largest—Blue whale Smallest—Bumblebee bat
Park	Largest—National Park, Greenland
Railway	Longest—Trans-Siberian Railway
Railway Platform	Longest—Gorakhpur, India Largest—Grand Central Terminal, New York (USA)
Tunnel	Longest and Largest (Canal)—Le Rove Tunnel (South of France) Longest (Railway)—Gotthard Base Tunnel (Switzerland)
Bridge	Longest—Danyang-Kunshan Grand Bridge (Beijing-Shanghai High-speed Railway)
Building	Tallest—Burj Khalifa, Dubai (828 m)
Minar (Free standing)	Tallest—Great Hassan II Mosque, Casablanca, Morocco
Statue	Tallest—Spring Temple Buddha, China
Tower	Tallest—Tokyo Sky Free, Tokyo (Japan)
Mosque	Largest—Masjid at Haram (Mecca)
Temple	Largest—Angkor Vat (Combodia)
Church	Largest—Basilica of St Peter, Vatican City, Rome (Italy)
Museum	Biggest—Smithsonian Institution, Washington DC
Place	Coldest—Verkhoyansk (Siberia), Temperature —85°C Hottest—Al-Aziziyah (Libya, Africa), 136°F Driest—Atacama Desert, Chile (South America)
Stadium	Largest—Strahov Stadium in Prague (the Czech Republic)
Wall	Longest—Great Wall of China
Capital City	Highest—La Paz (Bolivia)
City	Highest—Wen Chuan (Tibet, China) Largest (in population)—Tokyo Biggest (in area)—Hulunbuir, China
Day	Longest—21st June (in Northern hemisphere) Shortest—22nd December (in Southern hemisphere)
Substance	Hardest—Wurtzite boron nitride
Metal	Lightest—Lithium Heaviest—Osmium Costliest—Californium 252 ($ 27 million per gram)
Diamond	Largest—The Cullinan (over 1.5 lb) Largest (Mine)—Kimberley (South Africa)
Melting Point	Highest—Tungsten, 34100°C
Gas	Lightest—Hydrogen

Countries with Capitals and Currencies

Country	Capital	Currency
Afghanistan	Kabul	Afghani
Albania	Tirana	Lek
Algeria	Algiers	Algerian Dinar
Angola	Luanda	New Kwanza
Antigua and Barbuda	Saixt John's	East Caribbean dollar
Argentina	Buenos Aires	Peso
Armenia	Yerevan	Dram
Australia	Canberra	Australian Dollar
Austria	Vienna	Euro
The Bahamas	Nassau	Bahamian dollar
Bangladesh	Dhaka	Taka
Barbados	Bridgetown	Barabados dollar
Belarus	Minsk	Belorussian ruble
Belgium	Brussels	Euro
Bhutan	Thimphu	Ngultrum
Bostwana	Gaborone	Pula
Brazil	Brasilia	Real
Cambodia	Phnom-Penh	Riel
Canada	Ottawa	Canadian Dollar
Chile	Santiago	Peso
China	Beijing	Yuan, Renminbi
Colombia	Bogota	Peso
Denmark	Copenhagen	Krone
Djibouti	Djibouti	Djiboutian Franc
East Timor	Dili	US Dollar
Egypt	Cairo	Egyption Pound
Ethiopia	Adis Ababa	Birr
Finland	Helsinki	Euro (Formerly Morka)
France	Paris	Euro (Formerly French Franc)
Georgia	Tbilisi	Lari
Germany	Berlin	Euro
Greece	Athens	Euro
Iceland	Reykjavik	Krona
India	New Delhi	Rupee
Indonesia	Jakarta	Rupiah
Iran	Tehran	Riyal
Iraq	Baghdad	Dinar
Israel	Jerusalem	Shekel
Italy	Rome	Euro
Jamaica	Kingston	Jamaican dollar

Country	Capital	Currency
Japan	Tokyo	Yen
Kazakhstan	Astana	Tenge
Kenya	Nairobi	Shilling
Kuwait	Kuwait City	Kuwait Dinar
Latvia	Riga	Euro
Liberia	Monrovia	Liberian Dollar
Libya	Tripoli	Libyan Dinar
Mauritius	Port Louis	Rupee
Mongolia	Ulan Bator	Tugrik
Morocco	Rabat	Dirham
Mozambique	Maputo	Metical
Myanmar	Naypyidaw	Kyat
Namibia	Windhoek	Namibian Dollar
Nepal	Kathmandu	Rupee
Netherlands	Amsterdam	Euro
Nigeria	Abuja	Naira
North Korea	Pyongyang	Won (WPW)
Norway	Oslo	Krone
Pakistan	Islamabad	Rupee
Phillippines	Manila	Peso
Poland	Warsaw	Zloty
Porfugal	Lisbon	Euro
Qatar	Doha	Riyal
Russia	Moscow	Ruble
Saudi Arabia	Riyadh	Riyal
Singapore	Singapore	Dollar
Somalia	Mogadishu	Somali Shilling
South Africa	Pretoria	Rand
South Korea	Seul	Won (KRW)
South Sudan	Juba	Sudanese Pound
Spain	Madrid	Euro
Sri Lanka	Colombo	Rupee
Sudan	Khartoum	Pound
Sweden	Stockholm	Krona
Switzerland	Bern	Swiss Franc
Taiwan	Taipei	Taiwan New Dollar
Thailand	Bangkok	Baht
Turkey	Ankara	Lira
Uganda	Kampala	Uganda Shilling
UK	London	Pound Sterling
Ukraine	Kiev	Hryvnia
US	Washington DC	Dollar
Zimbabwe	Harare	Dollar

TOP 5

Largest and Smallest Countries

Largest Country (Area-wise)	Largest Country (Population-wise)	Smallest Country (Area-wise)	Smallest Country (Population-wise)
Russia	China	Vatican City	Dominica
Canada	India	Monaco	Marshall Islands
US	USA	Nauru	Saint Kitts and Nevis
China	Indonesia	Tuvalu	Monaco
Brazil	Brazil	San Marino	Liechtenstein

Languages and Religions

Languages Spoken

Language	Speaker
Mandarin Chinese	882 million
Spanish	392 million
English	312-380 million
Arabic	206-422 million
Hindi	310 million

Religions of the World

Religion	Member	Percentage
Christianity	2.1 billion	33.0%
Islam	1.5 billion	21%
Hinduism	900 million	14%
Buddhism	376 million	6%
Sikhism	23 million	0.36%

Geographical Epithets

Geographical Epithet	Location	Geographical Epithet	Location
Blue Mountains	Nilgiri Hills	Island of Pearls	Bahrain (Persian Gulf)
City Beautiful	Chandigarh	Key to the Mediterranean	Gibraltar
City of Golden Gate	San Francisco	Land of Lakes	Scotland
City of Magnificent Buildings	Washington (USA)	Land of Golden Fleece	Australia
City of Palaces	Kolkata	Land of Maple	Canada
City of Seven Hills	Rome	Land of Morning Calm	South Korea
City of Skyscrapper	New York (USA)	Land of the Midnight Sun	Norway
Cockpit of Europe	Belgium	Land of the Rising Sun	Japan
Dark Continent	Africa	Land of the Thunderbolt	Bhutan
Eternal City of Hopers	Rome	Land of Thousand Lakes	Finland
Forbidden City	Lhasa (Tibet)	Land of White Elephant	Thailand
Windy City	Chicago	Pearl of the Antilles	Cuba
Land of Golden Pagoda	Myanmar	Pearl of the Pacific	Guayaquil Port of Ecuador
Garden City	Chicago	Roof of the World	The Pamirs, Central Asia
Gift of the Nile	Egypt		
Granite City	Aberdeen	Spice Garden of India	Kerala
Hermit Kingdom	North Korea	Sugar Bowl of the World	Cuba
Holy Land	Palestine	Whiteman's Grave	Guinea coast of Africa
Island Continent	Australia	Playground of Europe	Switzerland
Island of Cloves	Zanzibar	Land of Kangaroo	Australia

Geographical Discoveries

Discovery	Discoverer	Discovery	Discoverer
America	Christopher Columbus	North Pole	Robert Peary
China	Marco Polo	South Pole	Amundsen
Australia	James Cook	Mount Everest	Edmund Hillary
Newfoundland	Cabot Sebastian	Sailed around the World	Magellan
Hudson Bay	Henry Hudson	Sea route to India *via* Cape of Good Hope	Vasco da Gama
Tasmania Island	Abel Tasman	Planets	Kepler
Hawaian Island	James Cook	Solar System	Copernicus
Cape of the Good Hope	Bartolomew Dias		

National Monuments of Major Countries

Monument	Country	Monument	Country
Statue of Liberty (*New York*)	USA	Kinder Disk	Denmark
Kremlin (*Moscow*)	Russia	Christ the Redeemer	Brazil
The Great Wall of China	China	Machu Picchu	Peru
Emperial Palace (*Tokyo*)	Japan	Taj Mahal (*Agra*)	India
Eiffel Tower (*Paris*)	France	Tugu Negara (*Kuala Lumpur*)	Malaysia
Leaning Tower of Pisa	Italy	The Great Sphinx (*Giza*)	Egypt
Opera House (*Sydney*)	Australia	Pyramid (*Giza*)	Egypt

Major News Agencies of the World

Agency	Country
Associated Press (AP)	USA
Novosti	Russia
Interfax	Russia
China News Service, Xin Hua	China
Allgemeiner Deutschar Nachrichtendienst	Germany
Deutsche Presse Agentur	Germany
Agence France Presse (AFP)	France
Agence Parisienne de Presse	France
Kyodon Tsushin	Japan
Reuters	UK
Exchange and Telegraph Company	UK
Australian Associated Press	Australia
Australian United Press	Australia
Agenzia Nazionale Stampa Associate (ANSA)	Italy
Europa Press	Spain
Algemeen Nederlands Persbureau	Netherlands
Associated Israel Press (AIP)	Israel
Press Trust of India (PTI)	India
United News of India (UNI)	India
Islamic Republic News Agency	Iran
Petra	Jordan
WAFA	Palastine
Middle East News Agency	Egypt
Anadol Ajansi	Turkey
Antara	Indonesia
Malaysian National News Agency	Malaysia
Associated Press of Pakistan	Pakistan
Bangladesh Sangbad Sangstha	Bangladesh
Indonesian National News Agency	Indonesia
Kenya News Agency	Kenya

National Emblem of Major Countries

Country	Emblem
Australia	Kangaroo
Bangladesh	Water Lily
Canada	White Lily, Maple Leaf
Chile	Candor and Huemul
Denmark	Beach
France	Lily
Germany	Corn Flower
India	Lion Capital of Ashoka
Iran	Perso Arabic Script of Arabic word 'Allah'

Country	Emblem
Italy	White Lily
Japan	Chrysanthemum
Netherlands	Lion
New Zealand	Southern Cross, Kiwi, Fern
Norway	Lion
Pakistan	Crescent and Star
Spain	Eagle
UK	Rose
USA	Bald eagle, Golden Rod

Legislatures of the World

Country Name	Legislature Name
Afghanistan	Shora
Albania	People's Assembly
Algeria	National People's Assembly
Australia	Parliament/Federal Parliament
Austria	National Assembly
Bangladesh	Jatia Sansad
Bhutan	Tasongadu
Botswana	National Assembly
Brazil	National Congress
Britain	Parliament (House of Commons and House of Lords)
Canada	Parliament
China, Mainland	National People Congress
China, National	Yuah (National Assembly)
Colombia	Congress
Denmark	Folketing
Egypt	People's Assembly
France	National Assembly
Germany	Bundestag
India	Sansad (Parliament)
Indonesia	People's Consultative Assembly
Iran	Majilis
Iraq	National Assembly
Ireland	Orieachtas

Country Name	Legislature Name
Israel	Knesset
Japan	Diet
Kenya	National Assembly
Korea (North)	Supreme People's Assembly
Korea (South)	National Assembly
Libya	General People's Congress
Malaysia	Parliament (Dewan Rakyat, Dewan Negara)
Mongolia	Great People's Khural
Nepal	Rashtriya Panchayat
Netherlands	State General
New Zealand	Parliament (House of Representatives)
Norway	Storting
Pakistan	National Assembly
Romania	Grand National Assembly
Russia	Duma
South Africa	Parliament
Spain	Cortes Generales
Switzerland	Federal Assembly
Syria	People's Council
Turkey	Grand National Assembly
USA	Congress
Zambia	National Assembly

Political Parties of Major Countries

Country	Political Party
Australia	Liberal Party, Labour Party
Bangladesh	Bangladesh Nationalist Party, Awami League, Jatiya Party
China	Communist Party of China
France	Socialist Party, National Front, Union for French Democracy
India	Bahujan Samaj Party (BSP), Bhartiya Janta Party (BJP), Communist Party of India (CPI), Communist Party of India (Marxist) (CPM), Indian National Congress (INC), Nationalist Congress Party (NCP), Aam Admi Party (AAP)
Iraq	Ba'ath Party
Israel	Labour Party, Likud Party, Hamas Party, Shas Party
Nepal	Nepali Communist Party, Nepali Congress Party, Madhesi Jana Adhikar Forum
Pakistan	Muslim League, Pakistan People Party
Russia	Liberal Democratic Party, Democratic Choice of Russia, United Russia Party
South Africa	African National Congress, National Party, Inkatha Freedom Party
Sri Lanka	United National Party, Freedom Party
UK	Conservative Party, Labour Party, Liberal Democratic Party
USA	Republican Party, Democratic Party

Major Newspapers of the World

Newspaper	Country	Newspaper	Country
The Sydney Morning Herald	Australia	People's Daily	China
The Age	Australia	Mainichi Daily News	Japan
Globe and Mail	Canada	The New Zealand Herald	New Zealand
The Gazette	Canada	The Press	New Zealand
Le Monde Dawn	Paris (France)	The Scotsman	UK
Dawn	Pakistan	The Guardian	UK
Die Welt	Germany	The Herald	UK
The Times	Britain	The Courier	UK
The Sun	Britain	Merdeka	Indonesia
New York Times	USA	Pravada	Russia
Washington Post	USA	The Hindu	India

Official Books of Major Countries

Blue Book	An official report of the British Government
Green Book	An official publications of Italy and Iran
Grey Book	An official report of the Government of Japan and Belgium
Orange Book	An official publication of the Government of Netherlands
White Book	An official publication of China, Germany and Portugal
Yellow Book	French official book
White Paper	An official paper of the Government of Britain and India on a particular issue
Joint Paper	The point report of two or more than two governments

Some Important Symbols or Signs

Pen	Symbol of culture and civilisation
Lotus	Culture and civilisation
Red Cross	Medical aid and hospital
Red Flag	Revolution; also sign of danger
Black Flag	Symbol of protest
Yellow Flag	Flown on ships or vehicles carrying patients suffering from infectious diseases
White Flag	Sign of truce, Symbol of Peace
Flag flown upside down	Symbol of distress
Flag flown at half mast	Symbol of national mourning
Pigeon or Dove	Symbol of peace
A blind folded woman holding a balanced scale	Symbol of justice
Black strip on face arm	Sign of mourning or protest
One skull on two bones crossing each other diagonally	Sign of danger
Wheel (*Chakra*)	Symbol of progress
Olive Branch	Symbol of peace

Fathers of Various Fields

Field	Father	Field	Father
Atom Bomb	Dr Robert Oppenheimer	Anatomy	Andreas Vesalius
Aviation	Alberto Santos Dumont	Nuclear Physics	Ernest Rutherford
Railways	George Stephenson	Modern Physics	Galileo Galilei
Chemistry	Robert Boyle	Sanskrit Grammar	Panini
Modern Chemistry	Antoine Lavoisier	Geometry	Euclid
Economics	Adam Smith	Mathematics	Archimedes
Geography	Eratosthenes	Internet	Vint Cerf and Bob Kahn
Sociology	Auguste Comte	Robotics	Al-Jazari
Political Science	Aristotle	Computers	Charles Babbage
Philosophy	Rene Descantes	Artificial Intelligence	John Mc Carthy
Modern Psychology	Wilhelm Maximilian Wundt	Modern Observational Astronomy	Galileo Galilei
English Poetry	Geoffrey Chaucer	Science	Galileo Galilei
Greek Tragedy	Aeschylus	Modern Science	Galileo Galilei
Immunology	Edward Jenner	Indian Nuclear Science	Homi Jahangir Bhabha
Genetics	Gregor Johann Mendel	Nanotechnology	Richard Errett Smalley
Biology	Aristotle		
Microbiology	Antonie Van Leeuwenhock		

Intelligence/Detective Agencies of the World

Detective Agency	Country	Detective Agency	Country
Central Intelligence Agency (CIA),Federal Bureau of Investigation (FBI)	USA	Research and Analysis Wing (RAW), Intelligence Bureau (IB)	India
KGB/GRU	Russia	National Intelligence Agency	South Africa
Central External Liaison Department	China	Australian Security and Intelligence Organisation	Australia
Naicho Capitalize	Japan	Sazamane Etelaat Va Amniyate Kechvar (SAVAK)	Iran
Director General de la Securite Exterieure (DGSE)	France	General Security Directorate	Iraq
Military Intelligence (MI-5) and 6, Special Branch, Joint Intelligence Organisation	UK	AL-Mukhabarat AL-Ammah	Egypt
MOSSAD	Israel	Inter Services Intelligence (ISI)	Pakistan

The Seven Wonders of the World

Ancient World	Medieval World	Modern World
Colossus of Rhodes	Colossus of Rome	Great Pyramid of Giza
Lighthouse of Alexandria	Catacombs of Alexandria	Hagia Sophia (Istanbul)
Hanging Gardens of Babylon	The Great Wall of China	Leaning Tower of Pisa (Italy)
Temple of Artemis at Ephesus	The Pagoda of Nanking	Taj Mahal (Agra, India)
Great Pyramid of Giza	Leaning Tower of Pisa	Washington Monument
Mausoleum at Halicarnassus	Sancta Sophia of Constantinople	Eiffel Tower (Paris, France)
Statue of Zeus at Olympia	Stonehenge	Empire State Building

The 'New' Wonders of Modern World

Chichen Itza, Mexico	Petra, Jordan
Christ Redeemer, Brazil	The Roman Colosseum, Italy
The Great Wall of China	The Taj Mahal, India
Machu Picchu, Peru	

Longest Bridges in the World

Name	Length metres (ft)	Country
Danyang-Kunshan Grand Bridge Beijing	164800 m (540700 ft)	China
Tianjin Grand Bridge Beijing	113700 m (373000 ft)	China
Weinan Weihe Grand Bridge Zhengzhou-Xian	79732 m (261588 ft)	China
Bang Na Expressway	54000 m (177000 ft)	Thailand
Lake Pontchartrain Causeway	38442 m (126122 ft)	United States
Manchac Swamp Bridge	36710 m (120440 ft)	United States
Yangcun Bridge Beijing-Tianjin Intercity Railway	35812 m (117493 ft)	China
Hangzhou Bay Bridge	35673 m (117037 ft)	China

First in India (Male)

First Governor-General of India	William Bentinck (1833-35)
Governor-General of Independent India	Lord Lewis Mountbatten
First and Last Indian Governor-General of Free India	C Rajagopalachari (1948-1956)
The first Muslim President of India	Dr Zakir Hussain

The first Prime Minister of India who resigned before the full term	Morarji Desai
First person to stay in Rashtrapati Bhawan	Lord Irwin
President of National Congress	Womesh Chandra Bannerjee
The first Home Minister of India	Sardar Vallabhbhai Patel
The first Indian Judge of International Court of Justice	Dr Nagendra Singh
Indian Managing Director of World Bank	Gautam Kazi
Governor of Reserve Bank of India	Sir Osborne Smith
The first Indian to join the ICS	Satyendra Nath Tagore
The first Field Marshal of India	SHFJ Manekshaw
The first Indian Commander-in-Chief of India	General KM Karippa
The first Indian Naval Chief	Vice Admiral RD Katari
The first Indian to win the Nobel Prize	Rabindranath Tagore (1913)
The first Indian to get Nobel Prize in Physics	CV Raman
The first Indian to receive Nobel Prize in Economics	Amartya Sen
The first person of Indian origin to get Nobel Prize in Medicine	Hargobind Khurana
The first Indian to receive Bharat Ratna Award	Dr Radhakrishnan
Sportsperson to receive Bharat Ratna	Sachin Tendulkar
The first person to receive Magsaysay Award	Acharya Vinoba Bhave
First cricketer to get Padma Bhushan	CK Nayudu
First Indian to get the Grammy Award	Pandit Ravishankar
The first person to receive Stalin Peace Prize	Saifuddin Kitchlew
The first person to receive Jnanpith Award	Sri Shankar Kurup
The first Indian pilot	JRD Tata (1929)
First Indian to swin across the English channel	Mihir Sen
First Indian to score triple century in Test Cricket	Virender Sehwag
First Ex-CJI appointed as Governor	P Sathasivam, as Governor of Kerala
First Viceroy of India	Lord Canning (1858-62)
First Minister of Education in India	Dr. Abul Kalam Azad
First speaker of Lok Sabha	G.V. Mavalankar
First Indian member of British House of Commons	Dadabhai Naoroji
First Indian Cricketer to score a Test Century	Lala Amarnath (1933)
First Chief Election Commissioner of India	Sukumar Sen

First in India (Female)

The first woman Prime Minister	Indira Gandhi
The first woman Minister in Government	Rajkumari Amrit Kaur
The first woman Judge in Supreme Court	Fathima Beevi
The first woman Chief Justice of High Court	Leela Seth
First Woman Lawyer to appear before a High Court in India and first to preside over the Rajya Sabha	Violet Alva
The first woman President of United Nations General Assembly	Vijaya Laxmi Pandit
The first woman Chief Minister of an Indian state	Sucheta Kripalani
The first woman Governor of a State in free India	Sarojini Naidu
The first woman Chairman of Union Public Service Commission	Rose Millian Bethew
The first woman Director General of Police	Kanchan C Bhattacharya

The first woman IPS Officer	Kiran Bedi
The first woman President of Indian National Congress	Annie Besant
The first woman Judge	Anna Chandy
The first woman Barrister	Cornelia Sorabjee
The first woman Honours Graduate	Kamini Roy
The first woman Chairperson of Indian Airlines	Sushma Chawla
The first woman to receive Nobel Prize	Mother Teresa
The first woman Airline Pilot	Durga Banerjee
The first woman to receive Bharat Ratna	Indira Gandhi
The first woman to receive Jnanpith Award	Ashapurna Devi
The first woman to receive Ashoka Chakra	Nirja Bhanot
The first woman Asian Games Gold Medal Winner	Kamaljit Sandhu
The first woman Olympic Medal Winner	Karnam Malleswari
The first woman to climb Mount Everest	Bachhendri Pal
The first woman to climb Mount Everest twice	Santosh Yadav
The first woman to cross English channel	Aarti Saha
First Woman Doctor	Kadambini Ganguly
First Test Tube Baby	Durga (Kanupriya Agarwal, 1978)
First woman to participate in Olympics	N. Polley (1924, Tennis)
First woman Chief Election Commissioner of India	V.S. Ramadevi (1990)
First woman Speaker of Lok Sabha	Meira Kumar (2009)
First woman to win Wimbledon from India	Sania Mirza
First woman to go into Space	Kalpana Chawla
First woman to win Silver in Olympics	PV Sindhu
First woman wrestler to win Olympic Medal	Sakshi Malik
First woman President	Pratibha Patil
First Indian woman to become member of International Olympic Committee	Nita Ambani

First in India (Miscellaneous)

The first Bank	Bank of Hindustan (1770)
First general post office of India	Madras (GPO 1786)
India's first plane to be hijacked	Fokker Friendship Plane (1971)
First telephone line introduced in India	1851
First talkie film of India	Alam Ara (1931)
First battle tank of India	Arjun
First satellite of India	Aryabhatta
The first Indian state to implement the Panchayati Raj System	Rajasthan
District to become India's first totally electrified district	Palakkad (Kerala)
City to have an e-court	Ahmedabad
First Indian to win individual Olympic gold	Abhinav Bindra
First lunar probe	Chandrayaan-I (October 2008)
First dedicated military Satellite	Rukmini (01G-SAT-7)
First Mars Orbiter Mission	5th November, 2013
First Central Agricultural University	Imphal (Manipur)
First state to Attain 100% Primary Literacy Level	Kerala
First district with complete rural Broadband coverage	Idukki (Kerala)

Superlatives India
(Biggest, Highest, Largest, Longest, Smallest, Tallest, etc)

The longest river	The Ganga (2525 km)
The longest river of Southern India	Godavari
The longest canal	Indira Gandhi Canal or Rajasthan Canal (*Rajasthan*)
The longest dam	Hirakud dam (*Odisha*)
The longest sea beach	Marina beach (*Chennai*)
The highest lake	Devtal lake (Uttarakhand)
The highest dam	Bhakhra Nangal dam on Sutlej river (*Punjab*)
The largest lake	Wular lake (*Jammu and Kashmir*)
The largest saline water lake	Chilka lake (*Odisha*)
The largest fresh water lake	Wular lake (J & K)
The largest artificial lake	Govind Sagar (*Rihand dam*)
The largest river island	Majuli, Brahmaputra river (*Assam*)
The highest waterfall	Kunchikal falls, Shimoga (*Karnataka*)
The deepest river valley	Bhagirathi and Alaknanda
The longest river bridge	Bhupen Hazarika Bridge, Lohit River (9.15 Km)
The longest sea bridge	Bandra-Worli Sea link
The largest cantilever bridge	Rabindra Setu or Howrah Bridge (*Kolkata*)
The state with longest coastline	Gujarat
The longest river without delta	Narmada
The longest railway platform	Gorakhpur
The longest road	Grand Trunk Road (*Kolkata to Delhi*)
The highest road	Road at Khardungla (*in Leh-Manali sector*)
The longest corridor	Corridor of Ramnathswami Temple at Rameshwaram (*Tamil Nadu*)
The highest airport	Leh Airport (*Ladakh*)
The largest desert	Thar (*Rajasthan*)
The largest delta	Sunderbans (*West Bengal*)
The largest zoo	Zoological Garden (*Kolkata*)
The biggest stadium	Yuva Bharti (*Salt lake*) Stadium (*Kolkata*)
The tallest TV tower	Pitampura (*New Delhi*)
The largest gurudwara	Golden temple, (*Amritsar*)
The largest cave temple	Kailash temple (*Ellora, Maharashtra*)
The highest peak	Godwin Austin, K-2 (8611 m)
The largest mosque	Jama Masjid (*Delhi*)
The longest tunnel	Jawahar Tunnel, Banihal Pass (*Jammu and Kashmir*)
The largest animal fair	Sonepur (*Bihar*)
The largest cave	Amarnath (*Jammu and Kashmir*)
The highest gate way	Buland Darwaza, (*Fatehpur Sikri, UP*)
The tallest statue	Veera Abhaya Anjaneya Hanuman Swami (Andhra Pradesh)
The most populous city	Mumbai (*Maharashtra*)
The oldest church	St Thomas Church at Palayur, Trichur (*Kerala*)
The biggest church	Saint Cathedral at old Goa (*Goa*)
The longest national highway	NH-7 (*Varanasi to Kanyakumari*)
The highest award	Bharat Ratna
The highest gallantry award	Param Vir Chakra

Famous Sobriquets of Important Persons

Person	Nickname
Abdul Gaffar Khan	Badshah Khan; Frontier Gandhi
Bal Gangadhar Tilak	Lokmanya
CF Andrews	Deenabandhu
CN Annadurai	Anna
CR Das	Deshabandhu
C Rajagopalachari	Rajaji
Dadabhai Naoroji	Grand Old Man of India
Jawaharlal Nehru	Chacha, Panditji
Jayaprakash Narayan	Loknayak
Lal Bahadur Shastri	Man of Peace
Lala Lajpat Rai	Punjab Kesari; Lion of Punjab (Sher-i-Punjab)

Person	Nickname
MK Gandhi	Bapu; Mahatma, Father of the Nation
MS Golwalkar	Shri Guruji
Madan Mohan Malaviya	Mahamana
Rabindranath Tagore	Gurudev
Rajinder Singh	Sparrow
Sarojini Naidu	Nightingale of India
Sheikh Mohammad Abdullah	Lion of Kashmir (Sher-i-Kashmir)
Sheikh Mujibur Rahman	Bangabandhu
Subhash Chandra Bose	Netaji
T Prakasam	Andhra Kesari
Vallabhbhai Patel	Iron Man of India, Bismarck of India

Crematorium of Famous Person (India)

Crematorium	Persons
Samata Sthal	Jagjeevan Ram
Karma Bhumi	Dr Shankar Dayal Sharma
Mahaprayan Ghat	Dr Rajendra Prasad
Raj Ghat	Mahatma Gandhi
Vijay Ghat	Lal Bahadur Shastri
Kisan Ghat	Chaudhary Charan Singh
Smriti Sthal	IK Gujral

Crematorium	Persons
Veer Bhumi	Rajiv Gandhi
Ekta Sthal	Giani Zail Singh, Chandra Shekhar, PV Narasimha
Uday Bhoomi	KR Narayanan
Shanti Van	Jawaharlal Nehru
Shakti Sthal	Indira Gandhi

Some Great Works Associated with Famous Persons (India)

Father of Sanskrit Grammar	Panini
Founder of Anand Van	Baba Amte
Founder of 'Auroville Ashram' (Puducherry)	Aurobindo Ghosh
Founder of Shantiniketan	Rabindranath Tagore
Founder of Vishwabharati	Rabindranath Tagore
Founder of Paunar Ashram	Vinoba Bhave
Founder of Bhudan Movement	Vinoba Bhave
Founder of Golden Temple	Guru Arjan Dev
Founder of Khalsa Panth	Guru Gobind Singh

Major Newspapers in India

Newspaper	Published From	Language
Economic Times	Mumbai, Delhi	English
Hindustan Times	Delhi, Patna	English
Deccan	Bengaluru	English
Mid Day	Mumbai	English
National Herald	Lucknow, Delhi, Kolkata	English
Pioneer	Lucknow, Delhi, Kanpur	English
Search Light	Patna	English
The Hindu	Bengaluru, Chennai, Coimbatore	English
The Indian Express	Delhi, Mumbai, Chennai, Lucknow, Madurai, Ahmedabad	English
The Statesman	Kolkata, New Delhi	English
The Times of India (*Largest English circulating newspaper in the world*)	New Delhi/Mumbai/ Ahmedabad	English
The Tribune	Ambala, Chandigarh	English
Aaj	Kanpur, Varanasi	Hindi
Amar Ujala	Allahabad/Agra/Jhansi/ Meerut	Hindi
Hindustan	Delhi/Patna	Hindi
Nav Bharat Times	New Delhi/Mumbai	Hindi
Amrit Bazar Patrika	Kolkata	Bengali
Anand Bazar Patrika	Kolkata	Bengali
Yugantar	Kolkata	Bengali
Matrabhoomi	Cuttack	Odiya
Akali Patrika	Jallandhar	Punjabi
Tej	Delhi	Urdu
Dinamani	Madurai	Tamil

Renamed Indian Cities

Old Name	Changed Name	Old Name	Changed Name
Vizagapatam	Vishakhapatnam	Avantika	Ujjain
Bezawada	Vijayawada	Bhelsa	Vidisha
Masulipatam	Machilipatnam	Bombay	Mumbai
Gauhati	Guwahati	Yanaon	Yanam
Baroda	Vadodara	Koyamutthoor	Coimbatore
Broach	Bharuch	Madras	Chennai
Simla	Shimla	Cape Comorin	Kanyakumari
Trivandrum	Thiruvananthapuram	Conjeevaram	Kanchipuram
Cochin	Kochi	Cawnpore	Kanpur
Calicut	Kozhikode	Benares	Varanasi
Palghat	Palakkad	Calcutta	Kolkata

UNESCO World Heritage Sites in India

Year of Inclusion	Sites
1983	Ajanta Caves (Maharashtra)
1983	Ellora Caves (Maharashtra)
1983	Taj Mahal (Uttar Pradesh)
1983	Agra Fort (Uttar Pradesh)
1984	Sun Temple, Konark (Odisha)
1985	Mahabalipuram Temples (Tamil Nadu)
1985	Manas Wildlife Sanctuary, Bharatpur (Rajasthan)
1985	Kaziranga National Park (Assam)
1985	Keoladeo National Park, Bharatpur (Rajasthan)
1986	Churches in Goa (Goa)
1986	Khajuraho Temples (Madhya Pradesh)
1986	Fatehpur Sikri (Uttar Pradesh)
1986	Hampi Temples (Karnataka)
1987	Sundarbans National Park (West Bengal)
1987	Elephants Caves (Maharashtra)
1987	Pattadakal Temples (Karnataka)
1988	Nanda Devi National Park (Uttarakhand)
1989	Sanchi Stupa (Madhya Pradesh)
1993	Humayun's Tomb (Delhi)
1993	Qutub Minar (Delhi)
1999	Darjeeling Himalayan Railway (West Bengal)
2002	Mahabodhi Temple (Bodh Gaya) (Bihar)

Year of Inclusion	Sites
2003	Rock Shelters of Bhimbetaka (Madhya Pradesh)
2004	Brihadeshwara Temple (Gangaikondacholapuram, Tamil Nadu)
2004	Victoria Terminus (CST), Mumbai
2004	Airavatesvara Temple, Darasuram (Tamil Nadu)
2004	Champaner-Pavagadh Archaeological Park (Gujarat)
2005	Valley of Flowers (Uttarakhand)
2005	Nilgiri Mountain Railway (Tamil Nadu)
2007	Red Fort (Delhi)
2008	Kalka-Shimla Railway (Himachal Pradesh)
2010	Jantar Mantar, Jaipur (Rajasthan)
2012	Western Ghat
2013	Hill forts of Rajasthan
2014	Rani ki Vav (Gujarat)
2014	Great Himalayan National Park (Himachal Pradesh)
2016	Nalanda Mahavihara (Bihar)
2016	Khangchendzonga National Park (Sikkim)
2016	The Architectural work of Le corbusier (Chandigarh)
2017	Historic city of Ahmadabad (Gujarat)

Foundation Day of Some States

1st January	Nagaland Day
21st January	Manipur, Meghalaya and Tripura Day
6th February	Jammu and Kashmir Day
20th February	Mizoram and Arunachal Pradesh Day
11th March	Andaman and Nicobar Islands Day
22nd March	Bihar Day (Bihar Diwas)
30th March	Rajasthan Day
1st April	Utkal (Odisha) Day
14th April	Tamil Nadu Day
15th April	Himachal Pradesh Day
1st May	Gujarat and Maharashtra Day
16th May	Sikkim Day
1st November	Chattisgarh
09th November	Uttaranchal (Now Uttarakhand) Day
15th November	Jharkhand Day (Jharkhand Diwas)
2nd June (2014)	Telangana Day

Famous Tourist Spots of India

Site	Location	Founder
Aram Bagh	Agra (Uttar Pradesh)	Babur
Anand Bhawan	Allahabad (Uttar Pradesh)	Moti Lal Nehru
Adhai Din Ka Johpda	Ajmer (Rajasthan)	Qutub-ud-din Aibak
Ajanta Caves	Aurangabad	Gupta Rulers
Akbar's Tomb	Sikandera (Uttar Pradesh)	Jahangir
Bibi Ka Maqbara	Aurangabad (Maharashtra)	Aurangzeb
Bharatpur Fort	Bharatpur (Rajasthan)	Raja Surajmal Singh
Bundi Fort	Bundi (Rajasthan)	Qutub-ud-din Aibak
Bada Imambada	Lucknow (Uttar Pradesh)	Nawab Asaf-ud-daulah
Belur Math	Kolkata	Swami Vivekanand
Botanical Garden	Shibpur (West Bengal)	—
Chhatra Mahal	Bundi Fort	Rani Chhatrasal
Chenna Keshab Temple	Belur (Karnataka)	Vishnu Vardhan
Char Temple	Konark (Odisha)	Narasing Dev I
Chasma-Shahi	Jammu and Kashmir	Ali Mardan Khan
Charar-e-Sarif	Srinagar (Kashmir)	Jainul Abedin
Choota Imambada	Lucknow (Uttar Pradesh)	Mohammad Ali Shah
Cochin Fort	Kerala	Portuguese
Dewan-e-Khas	Agra Fort (Uttar Pradesh)	Shah Jahan
Dilwara Jain Temple	Mount Abu (Rajasthan)	Vastu Pal Tejpal
Deeg Palace	Deeg (Rajasthan)	Raja Badan Singh
Dhar Fort	Dhar (Madhya Pradesh)	Mohammad Bin Tughlaq
Etamad-ud-daulah's Tomb	Agra (Uttar Pradesh)	Noor Jahan
Ellora Caves	Aurangabad	Rashtrakuta Dynasty
Elephanta Caves	Mumbai	Rashtrakutas
Fatehpur Sikri	Agra (Uttar Pradesh)	Akbar
Firoz Shah Kotla	Delhi	Firoz Shah Tughlaq
Fort William	Kolkata	Lord Clive
Fateh Sagar	Udaipur (Rajasthan)	Maharana Fateh Singh
Gateway of India	Mumbai	British Government
Golconda Fort	Hyderabad (Andhra Pradesh)	Qutubshahi Dynasty
Gol Ghar	Patna (Bihar)	British Government
Humayun's Tomb	Delhi	Hameeda Bano Beghum
Hauz Khas	Delhi	Ala-ud-din Khilji
Hajratbal Masjid	Srinagar (Kashmir)	—
Harmandir Sahib	Patna (Bihar)	Maharaja Ranjit Singh
Junagarh	Bikaner (Rajasthan)	Raja Jai Singh
Jama Masjid	Delhi	Shah Jahan
Jantar-Mantar	Delhi and Jaipur	Sawai Jai Singh
Jodhpur Fort	Jodhpur (Rajasthan)	Rao Jodha Ji
Jaku Temple	Kolkata	Rani Ras Moni
Jagannath Temple	Puri (Odisha)	Chola Gang Dev

Site	Location	Founder
Jama Masjid	Agra (Uttar Pradesh)	Shah Jahan
Khas Mahal	Agra (Uttar Pradesh)	Shah Jahan
Kankaria Lake	Ahmedabad	Sultan Qutub-ud-din
Khirki Masjid	Delhi	Ghiyas-ud-din Tughlaq
Kandaria Mahadev	Khajuraho (Madhya Pradesh)	Chandela Kings
Kanheri Caves	Mumbai	Buddhists
Laxman Temple	Chhatarpur (Madhya Pradesh)	Chandela Rulers
Laxmi Narayan Temple	Delhi	Birla Family
Laxman Jhula	Rishikesh (Uttarakhand)	—
Moti Masjid	Agra Fort (Uttar Pradesh)	Shah Jahan
Moti Masjid	Delhi Fort	Aurangzeb
Mrignayani Palace	Gwalior (Madhya Pradesh)	Raja Man Singh Tomar
Madan Palace	Jabalpur (Madhya Pradesh)	Raja Madan Shah
Mecca Masjid	Hyderabad (Andhra Pradesh)	Kuli Kutub Shah
Nahargarh Fort	Jaipur (Rajasthan)	Raja Jai Singh
Nishaat Bagh	Jammu and Kashmir	Asaf Ali
Nakhuda Masjid	Kolkata	—
Old Fort (Purana Quila)	Delhi	Sher Shah Suri
President House	Delhi	British Government
Pichhola Lake	Udaipur (Rajasthan)	—
Pathar Ki Masjid (Naev Masheed)	Patna (Bihar)	Parvez Shah
Padari Ki Haveli	Patna (Bihar)	Father Capuchin
Patthar Ki Masjid	Jammu and Kashmir	Noor Jahan
Prince of Wales Museum	Mumbai	George V
Rani Ki Badi	Bundi (Rajasthan)	Rani Nathvati
Red Fort	Delhi	Shah Jahan
Sheesh Mahal	Agra (Uttar Pradesh)	Shah Jahan
Safdarjung ka Maqbara	Delhi	Shuja-ud-daulah
Sabarmati Ashram	Ahmedabad	Mahatma Gandhi
St Geogre Fort	Chennai (Tamil Nadu)	East India Company
		Vimal Shah
Shalimar Bagh (Garden)	Srinagar (Kashmir)	Jahangir
Sunset Point	Mount Abu (Rajasthan)	—
Sher Shani Masjid	Patna (Bihar)	Parvez Shah
Sher Shah's Tomb	Sasaram (Bihar)	Islam Shah Suri, Son of Sher Shah
Taj Mahal	Agra (Uttar Pradesh)	Shah Jahan
Tughlakabad	Delhi	Ghiyas-ud-din Tughlaq
Umaid Palace	Jodhpur (Rajasthan)	Maharaj Ummed Singh
Vijay Stambh	Chittorgarh (Rajasthan)	Rana Kumbha
Victoria Memorial	Kolkata	—
Vishnupad Temple	Gaya (Bihar)	Rani Ahilya Bai

Agriculture and Animal Husbandry Institutions

Indian Agriculture Research Institute	New Delhi
Central Rice Research Institute	Cuttack
Central Sugarcane Research Institute	Coimbatore
Central Tobacco Research Institute	Rajahmundry
Central Potato Research Institute	Kufri, Shimla
National Centre of Organic Farming	Ghaziabad
National Plant Protection Training Institute	Hyderabad
Central Frozen Semen Production and Training Institute	Hissar Ghatta (Karnataka)
Central Sheep Breeding Farm	Hissar
Indian Veterinary Research Institute	Izzatnagar, Bareilly (Uttar Pradesh)
Animal Health Institute	Jalandhar
Central Institute of Fisheries, Nautical and Engineering Training	Kochi
Integrated Fisheries Project	Kochi
Central Island Agriculture Research Institute (ICAR)	Port Blair
Central Institute of Cotton Research	Nagpur
Central Institute of Agricultural Engineering	Bhopal
Central Institute of Fisheries Education	Mumbai
Central Institute of Fisher Technology	Cochin
Central Institute of Fresh Water Agriculture	Bhubaneswar
Central Soil Salinity Research Institute	Karnal
Central Inland Fisheries Research Institute	Barrackpore
Locust Warning Organisation	Jodhpur
National Institute of Agricultural Marketing	Jaipur
Random Sample Poultry Performance Testing Centre	Gurgaon
National Institute of Animal Health	Baghpat (Uttar Pradesh)
Disease Investigation Laboratory	Pune
Institute of Animal Health & Veterinary Biologicals	Bengaluru (Karnataka)
Indian Council of Agricultaural Resarch (ICAR)	New Delhi
National Sugar Research Institute	Kanpur

Commerce Industrial Regulatory Boards

Rubber Board	Kottayam	Spices Board	Kochi
Coffee Board	Bengaluru	Indian Institute of Foreign Trade	New Delhi
Tea Board	Kolkata	Indian Institute of Packaging	Mumbai
Tobacco Board	Guntur (*Andhra Pradesh*)	Indian Diamond Institute	Surat
Animal Welfare Board of India	Chennai	Central Pollution Control Board	New Delhi

Institute of Communication

Bharat Ratna Bhim Rao Ambedkar Institute of Telecom Training	Jabalpur
Tele Communication Engineering Centre	New Delhi
National Academy of Telecom Finance and Management	Secunderabad, Hyderabad
Advanced Level Telecom Centre	Ghaziabad
Indian Institute of Telecom Management (IITM)	Pune
Indian Railways Institute of Signal Engineering and Telecommunications	Secunderabad
Telecom Centres of Excellence (TCOE) India	New Delhi

Education

Central Institute of Indian Languages	Mysore
Central Institute of English and Foreign Languages	Hyderabad
Rashtriya Sanskrit Sansthan	New Delhi
Rashtriya Sanskrit Vidyapeetha	Tirupati
Indian National Academy of Engineering	New Delhi
High Altitude Training Centre	Shillaru (*Himachal Pradesh*)
Fire Training Centre	New Delhi
Maharishi Sandipani Rashtriya Veda Vidya Prathisthan	Ujjain
Indian School of Business	Hyderabad
Indian Statistical Institute	Kolkata
National Law School	Bangalore
Indian Institute of Space Science and Technology	Thiruvananthapuram (*Kerala*)
Indian Institute of Public Administration	New Delhi
Indira Gandhi Institute of Development Research	Mumbai

Energy

National Power Training Institute	Faridabad
Centre for Wind Energy Technology	Chennai
National Solar Energy Federation of India (NSEFI)	New Delhi

Environment

Centre for Environmental Education (CEE)	Ahmedabad
Centre for Mining Environment (CME)	Dhanbad
GB Pant Institute of Himalayan Environment and Development	Almora (Uttarakhand)
Centre for Ecological Sciences (CES)	Bengaluru
National Biodiversity Authority (NBA)	Chennai
CPR Environmental Education Centre (CEEC)	Chennai
Animal Welfare Board of India (AWBI)	Chennai
Forest Survey of India (FSI)	Dehradun
Indian Council of Forest Research and Education (ICFRE)	Dehradun
Indira Gandhi National Forest Academy (IGNFA)	Dehradun
Wildlife Institute of India (WIT)	Dehradun
Indian Institute of Chemical Technology (IICT)	Hyderabad
Central Soil and Material Research Station (CSMRS)	New Delhi
National Mangrove Genetic Resource Centre (NMGRC)	Odisha
National Coral Reef Research Centre (NCRRC)	Port Blair
National Institute of Hydrology (NIH)	Roorkee
National Environmental Engineering Research Institute	Nagpur

Forest

Centre for Social Forestry and Eco-rehabilitation (CSFE)	Allahabad
Indian Plywood Industries Research and Training Institute (IPIRTI)	Bengaluru
Indian Institute of Forest Management (IIFM)	Bhopal
Institute of Forest Genetics and Tree Breeding (IFGTB)	Coimbatore
Forest Research Institute (FRI)	Dehradun
Tropical Forestry Research Institute (TFRI)	Jabalpur

Arid Forest Research Institute (AFRI)	Jodhpur
Rain Forest Research Institute (RFRI)	Jorhat, Assam
Institute for Forest Productivity (IFP)	Ranchi
Himalayan Forest Research Institute (HFRI)	Shimla
Advanced Research Centre for Bamboo and Rattans (ARCBR)	Aizawal
Centre for Forestry Research and Human Resource Development (CFRHRD)	Chhindwara

Food and Civil Supplies

Bureau of Indian Standards	Delhi
Indian Grain Storage Management and Research Institute	Hapur
National Institute of Training for Standardisation	New Delhi
National Agricultural Cooperative Marketing Federation of India Ltd (NAFED)	New Delhi
Food Corporation of India (FCI)	New Delhi

Government Industrial Undertakings

Bharat Electronics Ltd	Jalahalli (Bengaluru)
Heavy Engineering Corporation Ltd	Ranchi
Heavy Machine Building Plant	Ranchi
Heavy Vehicles Factory	Avadi (Chennai)
Hindustan Aeronautics Ltd	Bengaluru
Hindustan Aircraft Factory	Bengaluru
Hindustan Prefab Limited	New Delhi
Hindustan Teleprinters Ltd	Chennai
Integral Coach Factory	Perambar (Tamil Nadu)
Security Paper Mill	Hoshangabad (Madhya Pradesh)
Neyveli Lignite Corporation Ltd	Neyveli (Tamil Nadu)
Hindustan Organic Chemicals Ltd	Mumbai (Maharashtra)
Hundustan Photo Films Manufacturing Company Ltd	Ooty (Tamil Nadu)
Hindustan Zinc Ltd	Udaipur (Rajasthan)

Health and Family Welfare

National Academy of Medical Science	New Delhi
National Institute of Ayurveda	Jaipur
National Institute of Unani Medicines	Bengaluru
National Institute of Homeopathy	Kolkata
National Institute of Naturopathy	Pune
National Institute of Siddha	Chennai
Morarji Desai National Institute of Yoga	New Delhi

Health and Medicinal Research Centres in India

School of Tropical Medicine	Kolkata
Central Leprosy Training and Research Institute	Chengalpattu (Tamil Nadu)
PGI Medical Education and Research	Chandigarh
National Institute of Nutrition	Hyderabad
National Institute of Occupational Health	Ahmedabad
King Institute of Preventive Medicine	Guindy (Chennai)
All India Institute of Hygiene and Public Health	Kolkata
All India Malaria Research Institute	New Delhi
All India Institute of Medical Sciences	New Delhi

National Tuberculosis Institute	Bengaluru
Indian Cancer Research Centre	Mumbai
Institute of Ayurvedic Studies and Research	Jamnagar (Gujarat)
Vallabhbhai Patel Chest Institute	Delhi
Haffkine Institute	Mumbai
National Institute of Communicable Diseases	Delhi
Indian Council of Medical Research	New Delhi

Industry

Sardar Vallabhbhai Institute of Textile Management	Coimbatore
Institute of Pesticide Formulation Technology	Gurgaon
Central Institute of Plastic Engineering and Technology	Chennai

Justice and Law

National Judicial Academy	Bhopal
Sardar Vallabhbhai Patel National Police Academy	Hyderabad
National Institute of Criminology and Forensic Science	New Delhi
National Law School of India University	Bengaluru

Labour

V V Giri National Labour Institute	Noida (Uttar Pradesh)
National Instructional Media Institute	Chennai
Central Staff Training and Research Institute	Kolkata

Laboratories

Central Scientific Instrument Organisation	Chandigarh
Central Leather Research Institute	Chennai
Indian Institute of Petroleum	Dehradun
Central Mining Research Station	Dhanbad
Central Fuel Research Institute	Dhanbad (Jharkhand)
National Geophysical Research Institute	Hyderabad
National Metallurgical Laboratory	Jamshedpur
Central Glass and Ceramic Research Institute	Kolkata
National Botanical Research Institute	Lucknow
Central Drug Research Institute	Lucknow
Central Institute of Medical and Aromatic Plants	Lucknow
Central Food Technological Research Institute	Mysore
National Environment Engineering Institute	Nagpur
National Physical Laboratory	New Delhi
Pulses Research Laboratory	Pachmarhi (Madhya Pradesh)
National Biological Laboratory	Palampur (Himachal Pradesh)
National Institute of Oceanography	Panaji (Goa)
Central Electronic Engineering Research Institute	Pilani (Rajasthan)

Mass Communication

Film and Television Institute of India	Pune
Satyajit Ray Film and Television Institute	Kolkata
Indian Institute of Mass Communication	New Delhi

Nuclear and Space Research Centres in India

Research Centre	Place
Indian Rare Earths Limited (IREL)	Alwaye (Kerala)
Uranium Corporation of India Limited	Jadugora (Jharkhand)
Atomic Energy Commission (AEC)	Mumbai
Electronics Corporation of India Limited	Hyderabad
Bhabha Atomic Research Centre (BARC)	Trombay (Mumbai)
Radio Astronomy Centre	Ootacamund (Tamil Nadu, Ooty)
Tata Institute of Fundamental Research	Mumbai
Saha Institute of Nuclear Physics	Kolkata
Centre of Earth Science's Studies	Thiruvananthapuram (Kerala)
Physical Research Laboratory	Ahmedabad
Space Commission	Bengaluru
Vikram Sarabhai Space Centre	Thiruvananthapuram
Indian Space Research Organisation (ISRO)	Bengaluru
Space Application Centre	Ahmedabad
Thumba Equatorial Rocket Launching Station	Thumba (Kerala)
College of Satellite Communication Technology	Ahmedabad

Social Welfare Institutes

Institute for Empowerment of Persons with Multiple Disabilities	Chennai
National Institute of Rehabilitation Training and Research	Cuttack
National Institute for the Visually Handicapped	Dehradun
National Institute for Orthopaedically Handicapped	Kolkata
Ali Yavar Jung National Institute for the Hearing Handicapped	Mumbai
Institute of Physically Handicapped	New Delhi
National Institute of Public Cooperation and Child Development	New Delhi
National Institute for Mentally Handicapped	Secunderabad (Telangana)

Science and Technology Research Institutes

Physical Research Laboratory	Ahmedabad
Jawaharlal Nehru Centre for Advanced Scientific Research	Bengaluru
Indian Institute of Astrophysics	Bengaluru
The National Centre for Biological Science	Bengaluru
Raman Research Institute	Bengaluru
Institute of Life Sciences	Bhubaneswar
National Institute of Ocean Technology	Chennai
Central Marine Research Station	Chennai
Wadia Institute of Himalayan Geology	Dehradun
National Centre for Antarctic and Ocean Research	Goa
High Altitude Research Laboratory	Gulmarg (Kashmir)
The Survey Training Institute	Hyderabad
Centre for DNA Finger Printing and Diagnostics	Hyderabad
Indian National Centre for Ocean and Information Services	Hyderabad

Institute of Microbial Technology	Hyderabad
Institute of Bio-resources and Sustainable Development	Imphal
The Centre for Marine Living Resource and Ecology	Kochi
S N Bose National Centre for Basic Sciences	Kolkata
National Brain Research Centre	Manesar (Haryana)
Indian Institute of Geomagnetism	Mumbai
Indian Cancer Research Centre	Mumbai
Visvesvaraya National Institute of Technology	Nagpur
National Environmental Engineering Research Institute	Nagpur (Maharashtra)
Indian National Academy of Engineering	New Delhi
National Institute of Immunology	New Delhi
Indian National Science Academy	New Delhi
National Seismological Database Centre	New Delhi
National Centre for Plant Genome Research	New Delhi
National Centre for Cell Science	Pune
Indian Institute of Tropical Meteorology	Pune
Indian Lac Research Institute	Ranchi
SV National Institute of Technology	Surat
Shri Chitra Tirunal Institute for Medical Science and Technology	Thiruvananthapuram

Transport

Rail Wheel Factory	Bengaluru
Chittaranjan Locomotive Works	Chittaranjan (West Bengal)
The National Institute of Aviation Management and Research	Delhi
Indira Gandhi Rashtriya Uran Akademi	Fursatganj (Uttar Pradesh)
National Institute of Water Sports	Goa
The Indian Institute of Tourism and Travel Management	Gwalior
Rail Coach Factory	Kapurthala
Diesel Locomotives Work	Varanasi
LBS College of Advance Maritime Studies and Research	Mumbai
Marine Engineering and Research Institute	Mumbai
Fire Service Training School	Narayanpur (Kolkata)
Integral Coach Factory	Perumbur (Chennai)
Maritime Training Institute	Powai (Mumbai)

Water Resources

The Central Soil and Material Research Station	New Delhi
The Central Water and Power Research Station	Pune
The National Institute of Hydrology	Roorkee

Youth Affairs and Sports

Netaji Subhash National Institute of Sports	Patiala
The Rajiv Gandhi National Institute of Youth Development	Sriperumbudur (Tamil Nadu)

Important Dates and Days of the Year

January

1 Army Medical Corps Establishment Day
4 Louis Braille Day
8 African National Congress Foundation Day
9 NRI Day (Pravasi Bhartiya Diwas)
10 World Hindi Day
11 World Laughter Day
12 National Youth Day (Birthday of Swami Vivekanand)
15 Army Day
21 Manipur, Meghalaya, Tripura Diwas
23 Netaji Subhash Chandra Bose's birth anniversary
24 Rashtriya Balika Divas, Giri Child Day
25 National Tourism Day, Voter's Day, International Customs and Excise Day, Voters Day
26 Indian Republic Day, International Customs Day
30 Martyr's Day (Mahatma Gandhi's Martyrdom), World Leprosy Eradication Day

February

1 Indian Coast Guard Day
2 World Wetlands Day
4 National Day of Sri Lanka
5 Kashmir Day (Organised by Pakistan)
13 World Radio Day
20 World Social Justice Day
21 International Mother Tongue Day
24 Central Excise Day
28 National Science Day

March

3 National Defence Day, World Wildlfie Day
4 National Security Day
8 International Women's Day
11 Andaman Nicobar Day
13 World Kidney Day
15 World Consumer Rights Day, World Disabled Day
16 National Vaccination Day
18 Ordnance Manufacturing Day
21 World Forestry Day, International Day for the Elimination of Racial Discrimination
22 World Water Day
23 World Meteorological Day
24 World TB Day
26 Bangladesh Liberation Day
27 World Theatre Day

April

2 World Autism Awareness Day
5 National Maritime Day, International Day for Mine Awareness
7 World Health Day
10 World Homeopathy Day
13 Jallianwala Bagh Massacre Day (1919)
14 BR Ambedkar Remembrance Day; Fire Extinguishing Day
17 World Haemophilia Day
18 World Heritage Day, Azad Hind Fauz Day
21 Civil Services Day
22 World Earth Day
23 World Book and Copyright Day
24 Panchayat Divas
25 World Malaria Day
26 World Intellectual Property Day

May

1 International Labour Day (May Day), Maharashtra Day, Gujarat Day
2 World Asthma Day
3 World Press Freedom Day, International Energy Day
8 World Red Cross Day
11 National Technology Day
12 International Nurses Day
15 International Family Day
17 World Telecommunications Day
21 Anti-Terrorism Day, Rajiv Gandhi Death Anniversary
22 World Biodiversity Day
24 Commonwealth Day
31 World Anti-Tobacco Day

June

1	Global Day of Parents
5	World Environment Day
20	World Refugee Day
21	International Yoga Day
23	International Widow Day, International Olympic Day
29	National Statistics Day

July

1	Doctor's Day, State Bank of India Foundation Day
4	American Independence Day
7	International Day of Co-operatives
11	World Population Day
18	International Nelson Mandela Day
26	Kargil Victory Day
28	World Nature Conservation Day, World Hepatitis Day

August

1	World Breast Feeding Day
6	Hiroshima Day (World Peace Day)
9	Kranti Divas, Nagasaki Day, Quit India Day, International Day of word's Ingenious People
12	International Youth Day
15	India's Independence Day
19	World Photography Day
20	Sadbhavna Diwas
29	National Sports Day (Dhyanchand's birthday)
30	Small Industry Day

September

5	Teachers' Day, Dr Radhakrishnan's Birthday
8	International Literacy Day (UNESCO)
14	World First Aid Day
15	Engineers Day, International Day of Democracy
16	World Ozone Day
18	Biosphere Day, World Alzheimer's Day
20	Railway Police Force Foundation Day
21	International Day of Peace
24	World Deaf Day, World Heart Day
27	World Tourism Day

October

1	International Day for the Elderly (UN)
2	International Non-violence Day, Lal Bahadur Shastri and Mahatma Gandhi's Birthday
3	World Habitat Day
4	World Animal Welfare Day
5	World Teacher's Day
8	Indian Air Force Day
9	World Postal Day
10	World Mental Health Day; National Post Day
11	International Girl Child Day
13	World Calamity Control Day (UN)
14	World Standards Day
15	World White Cane Day (Guiding the blind)
16	World Food Day
17	International Poverty Eradication Day
20	National Solidarity Day (China attacked India on that day)
21	World Iodine Shortage Day
22	World Energy Day
24	United Nations Day, World Polio Day
31	World Thrift Day, National Integration Day

November

7	Infant Protection Day; National Cancer Awareness Day
10	Transport Day, Malala Day (by UN)
11	National Education Day
14	Children's Day, World Diabetics Day
16	National Press Day
17	National Epilepsy Day
18	World Adult Day
19	World Citizen Day, National Integration Day, World Toilet Day
20	Universal Children's Day (UN), Africa Industrialisation Day
21	World Fisheries Day
25	World Non-veg Prevention Day
26	Law Day, National Milk Day, Samvidhan Diwas

December

1	World AIDS Day
2	International Day for the Abolition of Slavery, World Computer literacy Day

3	World Disabled Day
4	Navy Day
5	International Volunteers Day
7	Armed Forces Flag Day
10	Human Rights Day
11	UNICEF Day
14	National Energy Conservation Day
16	Vijay Divas
19	Goa's Liberation Day
23	Kisan Divas (Farmer's Day)
25	National Good Governance Day, X-Mas Day
29	International Biodiversity Day

Important UNO Decades

1991-2000	UN Decade against Drug Abuse
1995-2004	Decade for Human Rights Education
1997-2006	Decade for the Eradication of Poverty
2003-2012	UN Literacy Decade : Education for All
2005-2014	UN Decade of Education for Sustainable Development
2005-2015	International Decade for Action 'Water for Life'
2006-2016	Decade of Recovery and Sustainable Development of the Affected Regions
2008-2017	Second UN Decade for the Eradication of Poverty
2010-2020	UN Decade for Deserts and Fight against Desertification
2011-2020	Decade of Action for Road Safety
	UN Decade on Biodiversity
	Third UN International Decade for the Eradication of Colonialism

UN International Year

2017	International Year of Sustainable Tourism for Development
2016	International Year of Pulses
2015	International Year of Soils
2015	International Year of Light and Light-based Technologies
2014	International Year of Small Island Developing States
2014	International Year of Crystallography
2014	International Year of Family Farming
2013	International Year of Water Cooperation
2013	International Year of Quinoa
2012	International Year of Cooperatives
2012	International Year of Sustainable Energy for All
2011	International Year of Chemistry
2011	International Year of Forests
2011	International Year of Youth
2010	International Year for the Rapprochement of Cultures
2010	International Year of Biodiversity

Abbreviations

A

ABM	Anti Ballistic Missile
AD	Anno Domini (After the birth of Jesus)
ADF	Asian Development Fund
AERE	Atomic Energy Research Establishment
AFSPA	Armed Forces Special Power Act
AGOC	Asian Games Organising Committee
AIDS	Acquired Immuno Deficiency Syndrome
ALH	Advanced Light Helicopter
APPLE	Ariane Passenger Payload Experiment
ASAT	Anti-Satellite Weapon
ASEAN	Association of South-East Asian Nations
ASCI	Advanced Strategic Computing Initiative
ASCII	American Standard Code for Information Interchange
ATM	Automated Teller Machine
APEC	Asia Pacific Economic Cooperation
ASSOCHAM	Associated Chamber of Commerce and Industry of India
ASLV	Augmented Satellite Launch Vehicle
ASI	Archaeological Survey of India
AVES	Acute Viral Encephalitic Syndrome
AWACS	Airborne Warning And Control System

B

BC SBI	Banking Codes and Standard Board of India
BARC	Bhabha Atomic Research Centre
BBC	British Broadcasting Corporation
BC	Before Christ (Before the birth of Jesus Christ)
BCG	Bacillus Calmette Guerin (Anti-Tuberculosis Vaccine)
BCTT	Banking Cash Transaction Tax
BCCI	Board for Control of Cricket in India
BHEL	Bharat Heavy Electricals Limited
BHIM	Bharat Interface for Money
BIMSTEC	Bay of Bengal Initiative for Multi-Sectoral Technical and Economic Cooperation
BIS	Bureau of Indian Standards
BIT	Binary Digit (Basic unit of information in computing and telecommunication)
BMDS	Ballistic Missile Defence System
BRO	Border Roads Organisation
BRT	Bus Rapid Transit

C

CAA	Civil Aviation Authority
CABE	Central Advisory Board of Education
CAG	Comptroller and Auditor General
CAD	Computer Aided Design
CAIR	Centre for Artificial Intelligence and Robotics
CAPES	Computer-Aided Paperless Examination System
CAZRI	Central Arid Zone Research Institute
CAT	Central Administrative Tribunal
CBI	Central Bureau of Investigation
CECA	Comprehensive Economic Cooperation Agreement
CERT	Computer Emergency Response team
CHOGM	Commonwealth Heads of Government Meeting
CISF	Central Industrial Security Force
CITES	Convention on International Trade in Endangered Species
CLASS	Computer Literacy and Studies in School
CNG	Compressed Natural Gas

COLA	Cellular Operator Association of India
CPCB	Central Pollution Control Board
CPRI	Central Power Research Institute
CSIR	Council of Scientific and Industrial Research
CVC	Central Vigilance Commission

D

DAVP	Directorate of Advertising and Visual Publicity
DDT	Dichlorodiphenyl Trichloroethane
DFDR	Digital Flight Data Recorder (Black Box)
DIG	Deputy Inspector General
DPSA	Deep Penetration Strike Aircraft
DPT	Diphtheria Pertussis Tetanus
DRDO	Defence Research and Development Organisation

E

ECG	Electro Cardiogram
ECT	Electro Concvulsive Therapy (electric shock treatment)
EEG	Electro-Encephalography
EET	Exempt Exempt Taxation
ELISA	Enzyme Linked Immuno Sorbent Assay (used for testing AIDS)
EXIM Bank	Export -Import Bank of India
ECGC	Export Credit Guarantee Corporation
ESCAP	Economic and Social Commission for Asia and the Pacific
EVM	Electronic Voting Machine
EPZ	Export Processing Zone

F

FDI	Foreign Direct Investment
FII	Foreign Institutional Investor
FBI	Federal Bureau of Investigation
FERA	Foreign Exchange Regulation Act
FEMA	Foreign Exchange Management Act
FICCI	Federation of Indian Chambers of Commerce and Industry
FRIBA	Fellow of the Royal Institute of British Architects
FLAG	Fibre Optic Link Around the Globe

G

GAIN	Global Alliance for Improved Nutrition

GATS	General Agreement on Trade in Services
GATT	General Agreement on Tariffs and Trade
GEF	Global Environment Fund
GMPS	Global Mobile Personal Communications System
GMT	Greenwich Mean Time
GNSS	Global Navigation Satellite System
GPS	Global Positioning System
GSLV	Geosynchronous Satellite Launch Vehicle

H

HAC	Hindustan Aluminium Corporation
HAL	Hindustan Aeronautics Limited
HIV	Human Immunodeficiency Virus
HRIDAY	National Heritage City Development and Augmentation Yojana.
HYVS	High Yield Variety Seeds

I

IAAI	International Airport Authority of India
IAEA	International Atomic Energy Agency
IBRD	International Bank for Reconstruction and Development
ICAO	International Civil Aviation Organisation
ICAR	Indian Council of Agricultural Research
ICMR	Indian Council of Medical Research
ICRC	International Committee of the Red Cross
IDPL	Indian Drugs and Pharmaceuticals Limited
IMO	International Maritime Organisation
INSAS	Indian Small Arms System
INSAT	Indian National Satellite
IPC	Indian Penal Code
IPCC	Intergovernmental Panel on Climate Change

IRBM	Intermediate Range Ballistic Missile
IRSS	Indian Remote Sensing Satellite
ISCS	Integrated Smart Card System
ISRO	Indian Space Research Organisation

J,K,L

JNNURM	Jawaharlal Nehru National Urban Renewal Mission
KYC	Know Your Customer
KG	Kinder Garten
LCA	Light Combat Aircraft
LOC	Line of Control
LOAC	Line of Actual Control
LTA	Light Transport Aircraft
LIGO	Laser Interferamenter Gravitational-wave Observatory

M

MAT	Minimum Alternative Tax
METSAT	Meteorological Satellite
MMS	Multimedia Message Service
MRTS	Mass Rapid Transit System
MTCR	Missile Technology Control Regime

N

NACO	National AIDS Control Organisation
NADA	National Anti-Doping Agency
NAFTA	North American Free Trade Agreement
NASA	National Aeronautics and Space Administration
NATA	Natural Aptitude Test for Architecture
NATO	North Atlantic Treaty Organisation
NCEP	National Committee on Environmental Planning
NeGP	National e-Governance Plan
NEP	National Education Policy
NEPA	National Environment Protection Act
NTPC	National Thermal Power Corporation

O

OCI	Overseas Citizen of India
OAS	Organisation of American States
OAU	Organisation of African Unity
ODS	Ozone Depletion Substances

OIC	Organisation of Islamic Countries
OSCE	Organisation for Security and Cooperation in Europe
OROP	One Rank One Pension

P

PURA	Provision of Urban Amenities in Rural Areas
PATA	Pacific Asia Travel Association
PIB	Press Information Bureau
PN	Participatory Note
POTA	Prevention of Terrorism Act
PSLV	Polar Satellite Launch Vehicle
PWD	Public Works Department

Q,R

QIB	Qualified Institutional Buyer
QIP	Qualified Institutional Placement
RAF	Rapid Action Force
RBI	Reserve Bank of India
RCC	Reinforced Cement Concrete
RDSS	Radio Determination Satellite Service
RLV	Reusable Launch Vehicle
RTGS	Real Time Gross Settlement System

S

SAFTA	South Asian Free Trade Area
SAIL	Steel Authority of India Limited
SAPTA	SAARC Preferential Trading Agreement
SATNAV	Satellite Navigation
SAVE	SAARC Audio Visual Exchange
SCO	Shanghai Cooperation Organisation
SCOPE	Standing Commitiee of Public Enterprises
SEBI	Securities and Exchange Board of India
SIDBI	Small Industries Development Bank of India
SMART	Simple Moral Accountable Responsive and Transparent
SPIN	Software Process Improvement Networks
STARS	Satellite Tracking and Ranging Station
STARTS	Strategic Arms Reduction Treaty Station

SWIFT	Society for Worldwide Interbank Financial Telecommunications

T

TADA	Terrorist and Discruptive Activities (Prevention) Act
TAPS	Tarapur Atomic Power Station
TIN	Tax Identification Number
TNT	Tri Nitro Toluene (high explosive)
TRAI	Telecom Regulatory Authority of India
TRIPS	Trade Related Intellectual Property Rights

U

UAV	Unmanned Aerial Vehicle
UNCTAD	United Nations Conference on Trade and Development
UNDP	United Nations Development Programme
UNEP	United Nations Environment Programme
UNFPA	United Nations Fund for Population Activities

V

VAT	Value Added Tax
VLSI	Very Large Scale Integration
VOIP	Voice Over Internet Protocol
VSAT	Very Small Aperture Terminals

W

WADA	World Anti-Doping Agency
WAVE	Wireless Access for Virtual Enterprise
WFP	World Food Programme
WFTU	World Federation of Trade Unions
WLL	Wireless in Local Loop
WWF	World Wide Fund for Nature

X,Y

YMCA	Young Men's Christian Association
YWCA	Young Women's Christian Association

Z

ZSI	Zoological Survey of India
ZIP	Zone Improvement Plan

Books and their Authors

Famous Books of Foreign Writers

Authors	Books
William Shakespeare	• King Lear • All's Well That Ends Well • Twelfth Night • Comedy of Errors • Romeo and Juliet • Antony and Cleopatra • The Tempest • Macbeth • Julius Caesar • Othello
Charles Dickens	• A Tale of Two Cities • Oliver Twist • David Copperfield • Great Expectations
George Bernard Shaw	• Back to Methuselah • Man of Destiny • Arms and the Man • Man and Superman
Leo Tolstoy	• Resurrection • War and Peace • Anna Karenina
Barack Obama	• Dreams from My Father : A Story of Race and Inheritance • The Audacity of Hope: Thoughts on Reclaiming the American Dream
TS Eliot	• Murder in the Cathedral • The Wasteland, and other poem
HG Wells	• The War of the Worlds • The Time Machine • Invisible Man
George Eliot	• Mill on the Floss • Middle March
John Milton	• Paradise Regained • Paradise Lost
Jane Austen	• Pride and Prejudice • Sense and Sensibility
Lewis Carroll	• Through the Looking Glass • The Hunting of Snark
Rober Louis Stevenson	• Kidnapped • Treasure Island
Abdul Salam Zaeef	• "My Life With the Taliban"
Adam Gilchrist	• True Colour : My life (Autobiography)

Authors	Books
Javier Moro	• A Dramatised Biography of, Sonia Gandhi • The Red Sari
Salman Khurshid	• The Other Side of the Mountain.
Adam Smith	• Wealth of Nations
AG Noorani	• "India—China Boundary Problems, 1846 to 1947"
Al Gore (former US Vice President)	• "An Inconvenient Truth"
Andy Marino :	• Narendra Modi : A Political Biography
Arthur Conan Doyle	• Adventures of Sherlock Holmes
Arthur I Miller	• Empire of the Stars
Arthur Stanley Eddington	• Expanding Universe
Anna Jeon Mayhew	• The Dry Glass of August
Alan Shapiro	• Night of the Republic
Benazir Bhutto	• Reconciliation : Islam Democracy and the West
Catherin O' Flynn	• The News Where you are
Charles Darwin	• Descent of Man, Origin of Species
Cherie Blair	• Speaking for Myself
Chester Bowles	• A View from Delhi
Dan Brown	• The Lost Symbol
David Loshak	• Pakistan Crisis
Desmond Tutu	• No Future Without Forgiveness
DH Lawrence	• Sons and Lovers • Lady Chatterley's Lover
Dominque Lapierre	• "A Rainbow in the Night-Nelson Mandela and the Tumultuous Birth of South Africa"
Domingo Martinez	• Thy Boy Kings of Taxas
Dould Maraniss	• Barack Obama: The Making of the Man
Doniel Silva	• Moscow Rules
E M Forster	• A Passage to India
Edited by Michele Kelley, Deepika D´Souza	• "The World Bank in India—Undermining Sovereignty, Distorting Development"

Authors	Books
Edward Gibbon	Decline and Fall of the Roman Empires
Eric Segal	Love Story
Ernest Hemingway	The Old Man and the Sea
Fyodor Dostoevsky	The Idiot
GB Shaw	Apple Cart
Gabrielle Hamilton	Blood, Bones and Butter
George Co Bush	Decision Point (Autobiography)
George Orwell	Ninteen Eighty Four
Goethe	Faust
HB Stowe	Uncle Tom's Cabin
Herschele Gibbs	To the Point (Autobiography)
Herta Muller	The Appointment
Homer	Odyssey
Isaac Newton	Principia Mathematica
Jasper F Forde	Shades of Grey
Jean Paul Sartre	Iron in the Soul
Jeffrey Archer	First Among Equals
JK Rowling	The Tales of Beedle the Barol
John Masefield	Nine Days Wonder
John Ruskin	Unto this Last
Jonathan Swift	Gulliver's Travels
Joy Adamson	Born Free
Jules Verne	Around the World in 80 days
Karl Marx	Das Kapital
Katherine Mayo	Mother India
Kim Edwards	Lake of Dreams
L Fischer	A Week with Gandhi
Lapierre and Collins	Freedom at Midnight
Larry Collins Sdomininique lapierre	Mountbatten and Independent India
Lord Byron	Don Juan
Lord Curzon	Problems of The East
M Veerappa Moily	"Shree Ramayana Mahanveshanam"
Machiavelli	The Prince
Margaret Mitchell	Gone with the Wind

Authors	Books
Mark Twain	Adventures of Tom Sawyer
Martin Amis	The Pregnant Widow
Mathew Arnold	Sohrab and Rustum
Maxim Gorky	Mother
Michael Jackson	Moon Walk (Autobiography)
Michael Phelps	No Limits : The Will to Succeed
Nandan Nilekani	Imaging India : Ideas for a New Century
Nelson Mandela	The Conversations with Myself
Oliver Goldsmith	She Stoops to Conquer
Oscar Wilde	Importance of Being Earnest
Pallava Bagla	"Destination Moon-India's quest for the Moon, Mars and Beyond"
Parvez Musharraf	"In the Line of Fire"
Pearl S Buck	The Rainbow
Philip Pullmen	The Good Man Jesus and The Scoundrel Christ
Plato	The Republic
Robert TS Mickles Sr	Blood Kin, A Savannah Story
Rudyard Kipling	Jungle Book
Ruskin Bond	Notes from a Small Room
R M Lala	For the Love of India : The Life and Times of Jamsetji Tata
Shoaib Akhtar	Controversially Yours (Autobiography)
Sydney Sheldon	The Naked Face
Syyed Amir Ali	The Spirit of Islam
TC Boyle	Wild Child
Thomas Moor	Utopia
Toni Morrison	What Moves at the Margin : Selected Non-Fiction
Thomos Weber	Gandhi at First Sight
Tony Blair	A Journey
U Thant	View from the UN
Willam Alexander	Goblin Secrets
Walter Scott	Ivanhoe
Winston Churchill	Gathering Storm
ZA Bhutto	If I am Assassinated, The Myth of Independence

Famous Books by Indian Writers

Authors	Books	Authors	Books
Dr APJ Abdul Kalam	• Ignited Minds : Unleashing the Power within India, • You Are Born to Blossom, My Journey, • India 2020-A vision for the New Millennium, • Wings of Fire	Sarat Chandra Chattopadhyay	• Devdas • Parineeta
		Sarojini Naidu	• The Golden Threshold • The Bird of Time
		Munshi Prem Chand	• Rang Bhoomi • Godan
Amitabh Ghosh	• The Great Derangement: Climate Change and the Unthinkable	Rammohan Roy	• Precept of Jesus • A Gift to Monotheists
Mulk Raj Anand	• The Village, • Seven Summers, • Two Leaves and a Bud, • Coolie	Mahatma Gandhi	• My Experiments with Truth • Hind Swaraj
		Amartya Sen	• Development as Freedom • The Idea of Justice
Amrita Pritam	• Kora Kagaz, • Death of a City, • Kagaz Te Kanwas, The Revenue Stamp	Abul Kalam Azad	• India Wins Freedom
		AL Basham	• Wonder That was India
		Amit Chaudhuri	• The Immortals
		Annie Besant	• Wake up India
Ramachandra Guha	• Makers of Modern India • India after Gandhi : The History of the World's Largest Democracy, • Environmentalism : A Global History, • The States of Indian Cricket	Anuradha Roy	• The Folded Earth
		Aravind Adiga	• The White Tiger
		Arundhati Roy	• The God of Small Things • The ministry of Utmost Happiness
		Asha Purna Devi	• Subarnalata
		Aurobindo Ghosh	• Life Divine
Jawaharlal Nehru	• Bunch of Old Letters, Glimpses of World History, • Letters from a Father to his Daughter, • The Discovery of India	Balwant Gargi	• Naked Triangle
		BG Tilak	• Gita Rahasya
		BR Ambedkar	• What Congress and Gandhi have done to Untouchables
		Brig John Dalvi	• Himalayan Blunder
Khushwant Singh	• The Sunset Club, • Sahibs Who Loved India, • Why I Supported the Emergency, Truth, Love and A Little Malice, • We Indians, • A Bride for the Sahib, Maharaja in Denims	Dadabhai Naoroji	• Poverty and Unbritish Rule in India
		Daisy Hason	• The To-Let House
		Din Bandhu Mitra	• Neel Darpan
		Dr Radha Krishnan	• Hindu View of Life
		Dr Rajendra Prasad	• India Divided
RK Narayan	• Guide, Dark Room, • The Vendor of Sweets	VD Savarkar	• Indian War of Independence
Chetan Bhagat	• One Night @ the Call Centre, • Revolution 2020, Love, Corruption, Ambition, What young India Wants Making India Awesome, • Half Girlfriend, • One Indian Girl	Edited by Pranab Mukherjee	• The Congress and The Making of Indian Nation
		Fyodor Dostoevsky	• The Idiot
		Gen Ayub Khan	• Friends not Master
		Gopal Krishna Gandhi	• Of a Certain Age : Twenty Life Sketches
Bankim Chandra Chattopadhyay	• Devi Chaudharani • Anand Math	Gopinath Mohanty	• Moti Mahal
		Hamid Ansari	• Travelling Through Conflict
Maithili Sharan Gupt	• Saket • Yashodhara	IK Gujral	• Matters of Discretion (Autobiography)
JP Narayan	• Prison Diary • To all Fighters of Freedom, Why Socialism?	Imran Hashmi	• The Kiss of Life
		Indira Gandhi	• My Truth
		Janardan Thakur	• All the Prime Minister's Men

Authors	Books
aswant Singh	Jinnah—India, Partition, Independence
yotiba Phule	Ghulam Giri and other Stories
K Natwar Singh	One life is not enough 'My China Diary'
Kapil Dev	Straight from the Heart
Kapil Sibal	I Witness—Partial Observation
Khan Abdul Ghaffar Khan	Pakhtoon
Kingshuk Nag	The Namo Story : A Political Life
KM Munshi	I Follow the Mahatama
Kuldip Nayar	The Judgement
Kailash Sathyarthi	Azad Bachpan Ki Or
KP Mathur	The Unseen Indira Gandhi
Kishalay Bhattacharya	Blood or My Hands; Confession of stated Encounters .
Kartar Lahani	The Making of India
Lal Krishna Advani	My Country My Life
Lala Lajpat Rai	Unhappy India
Mahadevi Verma	Yama
Maj HPS Ahluwalia	Face of Everest
Manohar Malgaonkar	A Bend in the Ganges
Meghnad Desai	The Rediscovery of India
MJ Akbar	Nehru : The Making of India
Morarji Desai	A Minister and his Responsibilities
Narayan Lakshman	Patrons of the Poor : Caste Politics and Policy Making in India
Narayan Shehgal	A Voice of Freedom
Narendra Modi	"Convenient Action : Gujarat's Response to Climate Change"
Nilanjan Mukhopadhyay	Narendra Modi: The Man, The Times
Nirad C Choudhary	An Unknown Indian
NR Narayan Murthy	A Better India A Better World
PM Nayar	The Kalam Effect: My Years with the President
PVR Rao	Defence Without Drift
Rabindranath Tagore	Chitra
Raghunath Mashelkar	"Timeless Inspirator—Reliving Gandhi"
Rajmohan Gandhi	The Good Boat Man : A Portrait of Gandhi
Ramdhari Singh Dinkar	Rashmirathi

Authors	Books
Rashika Chaube and Chhaya Mahajan	An Inspirational Journey: Pratibha Devi Singh Patil; The First Women President of India
Ramesh Chandra Dutta	Economic History of India
Ravi Shankar	My Music, My Life
Ronald Segal	Crisis of India
Saniya Mirza	Ace Against Odse
Ruskin Bond	A little book of Happiness
S Nihal Singh	My India
SC Bose	The Indian Struggle
Shashi Tharoor	The Elephant, the Tiger and the Cell Phone : Reflections on India in the 21st century India Shastra', Pax Indica
Shashi Tharoor and Shaharyar Khan	Shadows Across the Playing Field : 60 years of India-Pak Cricket
Shobha De	Superstar India : From Incredible to Unstoppable
Shyam Bhatia	Good Bye Shahzadi (A Biography of Benazir Bhutto)
Sir Syyed Ahmed Khan	Causes of the Indian Mutiny
SK Nandi	Ramacharit
Sri Aurobindo Ghosh	Savitri
Subramanian Swamy	"Electronic Voting Machines—Unconstitution al and Tamperable"
Sunil Gavaskar	Sunny Days
Surjit Singh Barnala	My Other Two Daughters
Swami Dayanand	Satyarth Prakash
TS Krishnanmurthy	The Miracle of Democracy : India's Amazing Journey
Upinder Singh	A History of Ancient and Early Medieval India from Stone Age to the 12th Century
V V Giri	Voice of Conscience
Veerappa Moily	Unleashing India
Vinita Kamte	To the Last Bullet
Vinod Mehta	Lucknow Boy (Autobiography)
Virat Kohli	Driven
YV Reddy	Global Crisis Recession and Uneven Recovery
Jairam Ramesh	Indira Gandhi : A Life in Nature
DG Tendulkar	Gandhi in Champaran

Award Winning Authors of Indian Origin and their Writings

Author	Writings	Award
Salman Rushdie	- Midnight Children - Shame - The Moor's Last Sigh - Fury - The Satanic Verses - Two years, at Month and Twenty-at Night	Booker Prize 1981 (Midnight Children)
Vikram Seth	- The Golden Gate - A Suitable Boy - An Equal Music - Summer Requiem - Two Lives	Padma Shri in Literature and Education 2007
Arundhati Roy	- The God of Small things - The Algebra at Infinite Justice	Booker Prize 1997 (The God of Small Things)
Rohinton Mistry	- Such a Long Journey - Family Matters - A Fine Balance	Booker Prize 1991 (Such a Long Journey)
VS Naipaul	- A House for Mr Biswaas - India : a Wounded Civilization - An Area of Darkness - India : a Million Mutinies now - The Masque of Africa - A Bend in The River	Nobel Prize in Literature 2001 (for having united perceptive narrative and incorruptible scrutiny in works that compel)
Amitav Ghosh	- The Circle of Reason - River of Smoke - The Glass Palace - Shadow Line - The Calcutta Chromosome - Flood of Fire - The Hungry Tide - Sea of Poppies - In an Antique Land	Padma Shri by Government of India 2007 (for his best work in English Language) Crossword Book Prize in 2008 for Sea of Poppier
Jhumpa Lahiri	- The Namesake - The Interpreter of Maladies - The Unaccustomed Earth	Pulitzer Prize 2000 (The Namesake)
Shashi Tharoor	- The Great Indian Novel - Show Business - India : From Midnight to Millenium - India Shastra: Reflections on the Nation in our time	Common Wealth Writer's Prize (The Great Indian Novel)
Upamanyu Chatterjee	- The Mammaries of the Welfare State - English - August - Way to 90	Sahitya Akademi Award 2004 (The Mammaries of the Welfare State)
Kiran Desai	- The Inheritance of Loss	Man Booker Prize 2006

Books Awarded with Prizes

Books	Authors	Year
Pulitzer Prize		
▪ The Road	Cormac McCarthy	2007
▪ The Looming Tower : Al-Qaeda and The Road to 9/11	Lawrence Wright	2007
▪ The Brief Wondrous Life of Oscar Wao	Junot Diaz	2008
▪ The Years of Extermination : Nazi Germany and The Jews, 1939-1945	Saul Friedlander	2008
▪ Olive Kitteridge	Elizabeth Strout	2009
▪ Slavery by Another Name : The Re-Enslavement of Black Americans from The Civil War to World War II	Douglas A Blackmon	2009
▪ The Dead Hand : The Untold Story of The Cold War Arms Race and its Dangerous Legacy	David E Hoffman	2010
▪ Tinkers	Paul Harding	2010
▪ A Visit from the Goon Squad	Jennifer Egan	2011
▪ The Emperor of All Maladies : A Biography of Cancer	Siddhartha Mukherjee	2011
▪ The Orphan Master's Son (Fiction)	Adam Johnson	2013
▪ Disgraced (Drama)	Ayad Akhtar	2013
▪ 3 Sections (Poetry)	Vijay Seshadri	2014
▪ The Goldfinch (Fiction)	Donna Tartt	2014
▪ Digest (Poetry)	Gregory Pardlo	2015
▪ Sympathizer (Fiction)	Viet Thanh Nguyen	2016
▪ Underground Railroad (Fiction)	Colson Whitehead	2017
Man Booker Prize		
▪ The Gathering	Anne Enright	2007
▪ The White Tiger	Aravind Adiga	2008
▪ Wolf Hall	Hilary Mantel	2009
▪ The Finkler Question	Howard Jacobson	2010
▪ Troubles	JG Farrell	2010
▪ The Sense of an Ending	Julian Barnes	2011
▪ Bring up the Bodies	Hilary Mantel	2012
▪ The Luminaries	Eleanor Catton	2013
▪ The Narrow Road to the Deep North	Richard Flanagan	2014
▪ A Brief History of Seven Killings	Marlon James	2015
▪ The Sellout	Paul Beatty	2016
▪ Lincoln in the Bardo	George Saunders	2017
Sahitya Akademi Award		
▪ Hajar Churashir Maa	Mahasweta Devi	1996
▪ Mahabharata An Inquiry in the Human Condition	Chaturvedi Badrinath	2009
▪ Hawa me Hastakshar	Kailash Vajpeyi	2009
▪ Book of Rachel	Esther David	2010
▪ Mohan Das	Uday Prakash	2010
▪ India After Gandhi	Ramachandra Guha	2011
▪ Rehan Per Ragghu (Novel)	Kashinath Singh	2011
▪ Pathar Fenk Rara Hoon (Poetry)	Chandrakant Devtale	2012
▪ Miljul Man (Novel)	Mridula Garg	2013
▪ Trying to Say Goodbye (Poetry)	Adil Jussawala	2014
▪ Vinayak (Novel)	Ramesh Chandra Shah	2014
▪ Aag ki Hansee	Ramdash Mishra	2015
▪ Parijat	Nasrina Sharma	2016
▪ The Black Hill (Novel)	Mamang Dai	2017

Books	Authors	Year
Saraswati Samman		
▪ Kayakalap	Lakshmi Nandan Bora	2008
▪ Lafzan di Dargah	Surjit Paatar	2009
▪ Mandra	SL Bhyrappa	2010
▪ Irama Kathaiyum Iramayakalum	AA Manavalan	2011
▪ Manalezhuthu	Sugathakumari	2012
▪ Dhool Paudho Par	Govind Mishra	2013
▪ Ramayana and Mahanveshanam	Veerappa Moily	2014
▪ Chitt-Chete	Padma Sachdev	2015
▪ Hawthan	Mahasalcohwar Sail	2017
Orange Prize		
▪ Half of a Yellow Sun	Chimamanda Ngozi Adichie	2007
▪ The Road Home	Rose Rose Tremain	2008
▪ Home	Marilynne Robinson	2009
▪ The Lacuna	Barbara Kingsolver	2010
▪ Serious Men	Manu Joseph	2010
▪ The Sly Company of People Who Care	Rahul Bhattacharya	2011
▪ Home Boy	HM Naqvi	2011
▪ The Tiger's Wife	Tea Obreht	2011
▪ The Song of Achilles	Maleline	2012
▪ May We Be Forgiven	AM Homes	2013
▪ How to Be Both	Ali Smith	2015
▪ The Glorious Heresies	Lisa Mcinerney	2016
▪ The Power	Naomi Alderman	2017

United Nations

The United Nations (UN) is an international organisation, whose stated aims are facilitating cooperation in international law, international security, economic development, social progress, human rights and achievement of world peace.

The United Nations Day is celebrated on 24th October each year. Presently, there are **193** member states of the United Nations.

Principle Organs

There are six principle organs of the United Nations, they are

1. General Assembly
2. The Security Council
3. The Economic and Social Council
4. The Trusteeship Council
5. The International Court of Justice
6. The Secretariat

General Assembly

- It is also called as the town meeting of the world.
- The General Assembly meets at least once in a year and the session commences on the first Tuesday of September.
- It appoints the Secretary General of UN Secretariat on the recommendation of the Security Council.
- The presidency of the Assembly rotates each year among the five geographical groups of the countries *viz* Asia, African, Latin America, East European and West European and other states.
- Consist of all member states of the UN.
- Each member nation can send five delegates, but each nation has only one vote.
- The headquarters of General Assembly is at New York (US).

Security Council

- The main aim of Security Council is the maintenance of the international peace and security.
- The Security Council originally consisted of eleven members, but increases to fifteen in 1965.
- Security Council comprises of five permanent members namely **China, UK, Russia, France** and **USA** and 10 non-permanent members, elected for a term of 2 years by a two-third majority of the General Assembly, five non- permanent members retire every year. Retiring members cannot be re-elected immediately.
- Permanent member have Veto Power, which can be cast against any decision supported by the majority members.
- The headquarters of Security Council is at New York (US).

Economic and Social Council (ECOSOC)

- Its main aim is to promote social progress and better standards of life.
- ECOSOC comprises 54 members, 18 (one third) of whom are elected every year by the General Assembly of UN, to serve a 3-years term. The retiring members as well as the President are eligible for immediate re-elections. The headquarters of ECOSOC is at New York (US).

The Trusteeship Council

- The United Nations Trusteeship Council was established to help ensure that trust territories were administered in the best interests of their inhabitants and of international peace and security.
- Trusteeship Council was formed in 1945.

- The headquarters of Trusteeship Council is at New York (US).
- The trusteeship council suspended operation on 1st November, 1994. With the independence of Polau, the last remaining United Nations trust territory, on 1st October, 1994.

The International Court of Justice (ICJ)

- The International Court of Justice (ICJ) is the primary judicial organ of the United Nations.
- Its main functions are to settle legal disputes submitted to it by states and to provide advisory opinions on legal questions submitted to it by only authorised international organs, agencies and the UN General Assembly. The headquarters of ICJ is at Hague (Netherland).
- The ICJ was established in 1945.
- It consists of 15 judges. The judges of the court are elected by the General Assembly along with the Security Council for a 9-years term.

The Secretariat

- The United Nations Secretariat is one of the principle organs of the United Nations, an inter governmental organisation charged with the promotion of aiding states to collectively maintain international peace and security. It serves as a forum for member-states to discuss and resolve pressing issues in the international field through primarily diplomatic resources.
- The Secretariat is composed of a Secretary General, assisted by a staff of international civil servants worldwide. The Secretary General is appointed by the General Assembly upon the recommendation of the Security Council.
- The Secretary General of the UN is elected for 5-years and eligible for re-election, although, none so far has held office for more than two terms.

Secretary Generals Till Date

Name	Resignation/Retirement
Trygve Lie (1946-1952)	On November, 1952, resigned
Dag Hammarskjold (1953-1961)	Died in plane crash in Northern Rhodesia (now Zambia)
U Thant (1961-1971)	Declined to consider a third term

Name	Resignation/Retirement
Kurt Waldheim (1972-1981)	China voted against his third term
Javier Perez (1982-1991)	Refused to be considered for a third term
Boutros- Boutros Ghali (1992-1996)	The United States voted against his second term
Kofi Annan (1997-2006)	Retired after two full term
Ban ki- Moon (1st January, 2007-2016)	Retired after two full term
Antonio Guterres (1st January 2017-Present)	

Important United Nation Agencies

Name of Agency	Estd in	Headquarters	Objective
Universal Postal Union (UPU)	1874	Bern, Switzerland	The UPU is a specialised agency of the United Nations that coordinates postal policies among member nations, in addition to the worldwide postal system.
International Labour Organisation (ILO)	1919	Geneva	To improve conditions and living standard of workers.
International Monetary Fund (IMF)	1945	Washington DC	Promotes international monetary cooperation.
Food and Agricultural Organisation (FAO)	1945	Rome	To improve living conditions of rural population.
International Bank for Reconstruction and Development (IBRD)	1944	Washington DC	To provide funds from different sources, offers loans to middle income developing countries.
United Nations International Children's Emergency Fund (UNICEF)	1946	New York	To promote children's welfare all over the world.
United Nations Educational, Scientific and Cultural Organisation (UNESCO)	1945	Paris	To promote collaboration among nations through education, science and culture.
International Telecommunication Union (ITU)	1865	Geneva	Sets international regulations for radio telegraph, telephone and space radio communications.
International Civil Aviation Organisation (ICAO)	1944	Montreal, Canada	It codifies the principles and techniques of international air navigation and fosters the planning and development of international air transport to ensure safe and orderly growth.
World Health Organisation (WHO)	1948	Geneva	Attainment of highest possible level of health by all people.
International Atomic Energy Agency (IAEA)	1957	Vienna	To promote peaceful uses of atomic energy.
International Development Association (IDA)	1960	Washington DC	An affiliate of the World Bank, aims to help under-developed countries raise living standards.
United Nations Development Programme (UNDP)	1965	New York	Helps developing countries increase the wealth producing capabilities of their natural and human resources.
United Nations Environmental Programme (UNEP)	1972	Nairobi	Promotes international cooperation in human environment.
World Trade Organisation (WTO)	1995	Geneva	Setting rules for world trade to reduce tariffs.

International Organisations and Groups

Organisation and HQ	Member	Objective
Red Cross Estd in 1863 (Geneva, Switzerland)	190	International Humanitarian Movement for relief of suffering in time of war/disaster.
International Olympic Committee (IOC) Estd in 1894 (Switzerland)	98	To promote the Olympic ideals and administer olympic games.
International Criminal Police Organisation (INTERPOL) Estd in 1923 (Lyon, France)	190	To promote international cooperation among criminal police authorities.
The Commonwealth (London) formally estd by London Declaration 28th April, 1949	53	It was originally known as 'The British Commonwealth of Nations'. It is an association of sovereign and independent states which formally made up the British empire.
Arab League (AL) Estd in 1945 [Cairo (Egypt)] Syria suspended following the 2011 uprising	22	To promote economic, social, political and military cooperation.
International Organisation for Standardisation (ISO) Estd in 1947 (Switzerland)	162	To promote the development of international standards.
North Atlantic Treaty Organisation (NATO) Estd in 1949 (Brussels)	28	Mutual defence and cooperation
Colombo Plan Estd in 1950 (Sri Lanka)	27	To promote economic development in South and South-East Asia.
South-East Asia Treaty Organisation (SEATO) Estd in 1954 (Bangkok)	8	To provide for collective and economic cooperation in South-East Asia.
Organisation of Petroleum Exporting Countries (OPEC) Estd in 1959 [Vienna (Austria)]	13	Attempts to set world prices by controlling oil production and also pursues member interest in trade and development.
World Wildlife Fund For Nature (WWF) Estd in 1961 (Switzerland)	–	To save the wildlife from extinction.
Amnesty International (AI) Estd in 1961 (London)	–	To keep a watch over human rights violation worldwide. Got Nobel Prize in 1977 for Peace.
Non-Aligned Movement (NAM) Estd. in 1961	120	Political cooperation and establishment of separate identity from both USA and USSR (in the Cold-War era).
Organisation for Economic Co-operation and Development (OECD) Estd in 1961 (Paris, France)	34	To stimulate economic progress and world trade.
Group of Seventy Seven (G-77) Estd in 1964	134	To promote economic cooperation among developing nations.
European Union Formally estd by Treaty of Maastricht in 1993 [Brussels (Belgium)]	28	To create a United Europe in which member countries would have such strong economic and political bonds that war would cease to be a recurring fact.

Organisation and HQ	Member	Objective
Asian Development Bank (ADB) Estd in 1966 (Manila)	67	To promote socio-economic development in Asia.
Association of South-East Asian Nations (ASEAN) Estd in 1967 (Jakarta)	10	Regional economic Social and cultural cooperatino among the non-communist countries of South-East Asia.
Group of 8 (G-8) on 24 March. 2014, Russia was suspended, due to association with crimean crises, 2014 summit took place in Brussels.	8	To promote Cooperation among major non-communist economic power.
Organisation of Islamic Cooperation (OIC) Estd in 1969 (Saudi Arabia)	57	To promote Islamic solidarity among member states and to consolidate cooperation among members.
World Economic Forum (WEF) Estd in 1971 (Geneva) Annual meeting 2015- Davos, Switzerland	–	To improve the state of the world by engaging leaders in partnerships to shape global, regional and industry agendas.
Gulf Cooperation Council (GCC)Estd in 1981	6	It is a political and economic union of the Arab states.
Nordic Council Estd in 1952	8	Geo-political, inter-parliamentary forum for cooperation among Nordic countries.
South Asian Association for Regional Cooperation (SAARC) Estd in 1985 (Kathmandu)	8	To promote economic, social and cultural cooperation in South Asia.
Group of 15 (G-15) Estd in 1989	17	To promote economic cooperation among developing nations.
Asia Pacific Economic Cooperation (APEC) Estd in 1989 (Singapore)	21	To promote trade and investment in the Pacific basin.
Commonwealth of Independent States (CIS) Estd in 1991 [Minsk (Belarus)]	9	To coordinate inter-common wealth relations and to provide a mechanism for the orderly dissolution of the USSR.
Sanghai Cooperation Organisation (SCO) Estd in 1996 (Beijing, China)	6	To develop mutual cooperation.
Group of Twenty (G-20) Estd in 1999 2014 summit-Brisbane	20	For cooperation and consultation or matters pertaining to the International Financial System.
African Union OAU charter–1963 AU founded–2002	54	To accelerate the political and socio-economic integration of the continent.
BRICS (Brazil, Russia, India, China and South Africa) First formal summit-Yekaterinburg, 2009	5	To improve the economical condition of the country.
Arctic Council Estd. in 1996	8	Try to keep Arctic area clean and safe.
BASIC Estd in 2009	4	To coordinate the policies of developing countries regarding climate change.
European Union	28	To create a United Europe in which member countries would have some strong economic and political bonds that war would lease to be a recurring fact.

Sports

OLYMPICS

- The Olympic Games were held for the first time by the Greeks in 776 BC on Mount Olympus, in honour of the Greek God, Zeus. They were stopped by a royal order of the Roman Emperor Theodosius in AD 394.
- These games were revived in 1894 by the efforts of a French Baron **Pierre de Coubertin** and the first modern Olympic Games were started in Athens the capital of Greece on 6th April, 1896. Separate winter Olympic Games began in 1924. Women have been participating in the Olympics since 1912.
- The Olympic Games are organised after every 4-years.

Founder and Governing Body

- In 1894, Baron Pierre de Coubertin founded the International Olympic Committee (IOC) to govern the Olympic Movement (comprising International Sports Federations (ISF's), National Olympic Committees (NOCs) and Organising Committees for each specific games).
- IOC chooses the host city and the games to be contested organisation and funding is made by the host city.
- International Sports Federation (ISF) determines the qualification rules for each Olympic.
- The Head office of International Olympic Committee (IOC) is at **Lausanne** (Switzerland).

Olympic Symbol

- It contains five rings or circles linked together to represent the sporting friendship of all people. Each ring is of a different colour *i.e.*, blue, yellow, black, green and red. The rings are meant to represent five continents *viz* Africa (Black), America (Red), Asia (Yellow), Australia (Green) and Europe (Blue).

Olympic Flag

- The Olympic Flag was created in 1913 at the suggestion of Baron Pierre de Coubertin. It was adopted in Paris in June, 1914, but it was raised over an Olympic stadium for the first time at the Antwerp games (Belgium) in 1920. There is also a second Olympic Flag, which is used for the Winter games. These flags are made of white silk and contain five interwined rings of the Olympic Emblem.
- From left to right the rings are Blue (Europe), Yellow (Asia), Black (Africa), Red (America) and Green (Australia). Atleast one of these colours is found on the flag of every country.
- The flag is 3 m long and 2 m wide. The emblem placed in the center is 2.06 m by 60 cm.

Olympic Motto

Olympic Motto 'Citius, Altius, Fortius' is the Latin motto meaning 'Faster, Higher and Stronger' composed by Father Didon in 1897.

The motto was introduced in 1924 at the Olympic Games in Paris.

Olympic Flame

The Olympic flame symbolises the continuity between ancient and modern games. It was at the Amsterdam Games in 1928 that for the first time an Olympic flame was ceremonially lighted and burned in a giant torch at the entrance of the stadium. The modern version of the flame was adopted in 1936 at the Berlin Games.

Olympic Medals

Olympic champions are rewarded with medals and certificate. The winning athlete or sports persons receive a Gold Medal which, is 60 mm in diameter and 3 mm thick and is made of 92.5% silver plated with 6 gm of gold.

Olympic Mascot

- The Olympic Mascot(s) is/are a character, usually an animal native to the area or occasionally human figures, who represents the cultural heritage of the place, where the Olympic and Paraolympic Games are taking place.
- Since the 1968, Winter Olympics in Grenoble, France the Olympic Games have had a mascot. The first major mascot in the Olympic Games was Misha in the 1980 Summer Olympics in Moscow. The 2016 summer olympic's mascot is vinicius, a representation of Brazilian wildlife.

Olympic Gold Order

- It is presented by the International Olympic Committee for distinguished services in the development of the Olympic Movement.

Olympics : Quick Digest

- 'Norman Pritchard' was the first Indian player to participate in Olympic (2nd Olympic Games in 1900) and won two Silver Medals in athletics.
- **Marrie Lila Rao** is 1st Indian woman participant in the Olympics after Independence.
- India officially participated in the Olympics for the first time in the Sixth Olympic Games (1920) at Antwerp Belgium.
- The **Indian Olympic Association** was established in 1927. Sir Dorabji Tata was its first President.
- **Sonia Denoncourt** (Canada) was the 1st woman referee in football in Atlanta Olympics.

The Winter Olympic Games are a major international sporting event that occours once every 4 years. Unlike the Summer Olympics, the Winter Olympics feature sports practiced on snow and ice. The first Winter Olympics, the 1924 Winter Olympics, was held in Chamonix, France. The games were held every 4 years from 1924 until 1936, after which they were interrupted by World War II.

The Olympics resumed in 1948 and was again held every 4 years. Until 1992, the Winter and Summer Olympic Games were held in the same years, but in accordance with a 1986 decision by the International Olympic Committee (IOC) to place the Summer and Winter Games on separate 4 year cycles in alternating even-numbered years, the next Winter Olympics after 1992 was in 1994.

The last Olympic games were held in 2014 at Sochi, Russia. It is scheduled to be held in 2018 at Pyeongchang, South Korea.

Summer Olympic Games

Year	Venue
1896	Athenes, Greece
1900	Paris, France
1904	St Louis, France
1906	Athenes, Greece (Games were not recognised by IOC)
1908	London, Great Britain
1912	Stockholm, Sweden
1916	Games not held due to World War I
1920	Antwerp, Belgium
1924	Paris, France
1928	Amsterdam, Netherlands
1932	Los Angeles, USA
1936	Berlin, Germany
1940	Games not held due to World War II
1944	Games not held due to World War II
1948	London, Great Britain
1952	Helsinki, Finland
1956	Melbourne, Australia
1960	Rome, Italy
1964	Tokyo, Japan
1968	Mexico City, Mexico
1972	Munich, West Germany
1976	Montreal, Canada
1980	Moscow, Russia
1984	Los Angeles, USA
1988	Seoul, South Korea
1992	Barcelona, Spain
1996	Atlanta, USA
2000	Sydney, Australia
2004	Athenes, Greece
2008	Beijing, China
2012	London, Great Britain
2016	Rio de Janeiro, Brazil
2020	Tokyo, Japan (Scheduled)

India's Performance in Olympics

Discipline	Year	Performance
Wrestling	1952	KD Jadhav won Bronze Medal in men's 52-57 kg Freestyle
	2008	Sushil Kumar won Bronze Medal in men's 66 kg Freestyle
	2012	Sushil Kumar won Silver Medal in men's 66 kg Freestyle
	2012	Yogeshwar Dutt won Bronze Medal in men's 60 Kg Freestyle
	2016	Sakshi Malik won Bronze Medal in women's 58 Kg Freestyle
Hockey	1928	Won Gold Medal
	1932	Won Gold Medal
	1936	Won Gold Medal
	1948	Won Gold Medal
	1952	Won Gold Medal
	1956	Won Gold Medal
	1960	Won Silver Medal
	1964	Won Gold Medal
	1968	Won Bronze Medal
	1972	Won Bronze Medal
	1980	Won Gold Medal
Shooting	2004	Rajyavardhan Singh Rathore won Silver Medal in double trap
	2008	Abhinav Bindra won Gold Medal in Men's 10 m air rifle
	2012	Vijay Kumar won Silver Medal in 25 Rapid Fire Pistol
	2012	Gagan Narang won Bronze Medal in 10m Air Rifle
Athletics	1900	Norman Pritchard won two Silver Medals in (200 m) and (200 m hurdle) events
	1960	Milkha Singh-fourth in 400 m final Zora Singh- eighth in 50 km walk
	1964	Gurbachan Singh Randhawa -fifth in 100 m hurdles (final)
	1976	Sriram Singh-seventh in 800 m final Shivnath Singh-eleventh in the marathon
	1980	Sriram Singh-Semifinalist in 800 m
	1984	PT Usha-fourth in 400 m hurdles
Football (Soccer)	1956	Semi-finals
Tennis	1996	Leander Paes won Bronze Medal in men's singles event
Weightlifting	2000	Karnam Malleshwari won Bronze Medal in women's 69 kg category
Boxing	2008	Vijender Singh won a Bronze Medal (75 kg)
	2012	Mary Kom won a Bronze Medal in Women's flyweight
Badminton	2012	Saina Nehwal won a Bronze Medal in Women's singles
	2016	PV Sindhu won a Silver in women's singles
Gymnastics	2016	Dipa Karmakar 4th place in the vault Final.

Commonwealth Games

- The Commonwealth Games are a festival of sports of the Commonwealth countries. The first Commonwealth Games were held in 1930 in Hamilton, Canada.
- The 2010 Commonwealth Games were held in New Delhi, India.
- Since 1930, the games have been conducted every 4-years except for 1942 and 1946.
- The Commonwealth Games Federation (CGF) is the organisation, which is responsible for the direction and control of the Commonwealth Games.
- There are currently 53 members of the Commonwealth of Nations and 71 team participate in the games.
- 20th Commonwealth Games of 2014 were held in Glasgow (Scotland, UK).
- The 2018, Commonwealth Games will be held in Australia.

Asian Games

- The Asian Games, also called the Asiad, are a multisport event held every 4-years among athletes from all over Asia.
- The games are regulated by the Olympic Council of Asia (OCA), under the supervision of the International Olympic Committee (IOC).
- The first Asian Games were held in 1951 in New Delhi (India). The 2014 Asian Games were held in Incheon, South Korea. 2018 Asian Games will be held in Jakarta (Indonessia).
- The AGF (Asian Games Federation) adopted 'Ever Onward', given by Pt Jawaharlal Nehru, as the motto of the Asian Games, which continues till today.
- The emblem is a bright full rising Sun with interlocking rings. The King of Patiala presented the Torch and the Flag for the first Asian Games and since then they have been carried from country to country.

South Asian Federation (SAF) Games

- Like the Commonwealth Games, the South Asian Federation (SAF) Games is a sports festival of South Asian countries. The governing body of these games is South Asian sports Council formed in 1983.
- The first South Asian Federation Games were held at Kathmandu (Nepal) in 1984. SAF Games, 2016 were held in India.
- The eight participating countries are India, Pakistan, Sri Lanka, Bangladesh, Nepal, Bhutan, Afghanistan and Maldives. The games form a part of the SAARC programme. The motto of the SAF Games is 'peace, prosperity and progress'.
- No SAF Game were staged in 1986 as it was the year of commonwealth and Asian Games.
- The SAF Games have been rechristened South Asian Games on 2nd April, 2004. Afghanistan joined the games in 2006.

Afro-Asian Games

- The first-ever Afro-Asian Games were held in 2003 at Hyderabad (India). 2007 in Algiers (Cancelled).
- The official mascot of the 2003 games was 'Sheroo' (a cartoon representation of the Royal Bengal Tiger) and the message was 'two continents-one spirit'.

Cricket

- The first Cricket World Cup was organised in England in 1975. A separate women's Cricket World Cup has been held every 4-years since 1973.
- The Cricket World Cup Tournament is organised by the International Cricket Council (ICC). The ICC was founded in 1909 and its headquarters is located in Dubai, United Arab Emirates.
- In 1877, the first Cricket Test Match was played in Melbourne between England and Australia.
- The first One Day International Cricket Match was played in the year 1971 between England and Australia in Melbourne.
- The Board of Control for Cricket in India (BCCI) was formed in 1927.

List of Cricket World Cup

1975	Lord's, England	West Indies beat Australia
1979	Lord's, England	West Indies beat England
1983	Lord's, England	India beat West Indies
1987	Kolkata, India	Australia beat England
1992	Melbourne, (Australia)	Pakistan beat England
1996	Lahore, Pakistan	Sri Lanka beat Australia
1999	Lord's, England	Australia beat Pakistan
2003	Johannesburg, South Africa	Australia beat India
2007	Bridgetown, West Indies	Australia beat Sri Lanka
2011	Mumbai, India	India beat Sri Lanka
2015	Australia/New Zealand	Australia beat New Zealand
2019	England and Wales	Scheduled

Women's Cricket World Cup

The ICC Women's Cricket World Cup is the premier international championship of women's One Day International Cricket. The event is organised by the sport's governing body, the International Cricket Council (ICC). It was originally administered by the International Women's Cricket Council until the two associations merged in 2005. The first tournament was held in England in 1973, 2-years before the first men's tournament.

Women's Cricket World Cup Venus

Year	Place	Won
1982	New Zealand	Australia
1988	Australia	Australia
1993	England	England
1997	India	Australia
2000	New Zealand	New Zealand
2005	South Africa	Australia
2009	Australia	England
2013	India	Australia
2017	England	London
2021	New Zealand	Scheduled

Important Facts

Administrator	International Cricket Council
Format	Women's ODI
First tournament	1973, England
Last tournament	2013, India
Next tournament	2017, England
Current champion	Australia
Most successful	Australia (6 titles)
Most runs	Debbie Hockley (1501)

Twenty-20 World Cup

- It is organised by the International Cricket Council (ICC). It is held every 2-years.

ICC Twenty-20 Cricket World Cup

Year	Host Nations	Final Venue	Winner	Runner-up
2007	South Africa	Johannesburg	India	Pakistan
2009	England	Lord's, London	Pakistan	Sri Lanka
2010	West Indies	Barbados	England	Australia
2012	Sri Lanka	R Premdasa Stadium, Colombo	West Indies	Sri Lanka
2014	Bangladesh	Sher-e Bangla Cricket Stadium, Dhaka	Sri Lanka	India
2016	India	Eden Garden Kolkata, India	WestIndies	England
2020	Australia	—	—	—

Women's Twenty-20 Cricket

- Women's Twenty-20 cricket is the newly emerging use of the Twenty-20 match format in women's cricket. While both women's cricket and Twenty-20 have themselves enjoyed recent success, women's Twenty-20 has only been an international cricket game format since 2004. In June, 2009, the ICC held the first Women's World Twenty-20 in England, the hosts became the first World Twenty-20 champion.
- Australia won their third consecutive tittle in Women's World Twenty-20 after defeating England.
- In 2016, West Indies won the T-20 Women's World Cup after defeating Australia.

Football World Cup

- The Football World Cup is organised by FIFA (Federation of International Football Association).
- The headquarters of FIFA is located in Zurich, Switzerland.
- The World Cup is called 'Jules Rimet Cup' named after the name of FIFA President Jules Rimet.
- The first Football World Cup was organised in Uruguay in 1930.
- In 1942 and 1946, the Football World Cup was not played because of the World War II.
- Brazil is the only nation to have participated in every World Cup so far.
- 20th FIFA World Cup 2014 held in Brazil. Germany defeated Argentina in the final. FIFA appoints Russia as host for 2018 World Cup and Qatar for 2022 World Cup.

Hockey World Cup

- The Hockey World Cup is organised by the International Hockey Federation (FIH) once in 4-years. The headquarters of FIH is located in Lausanne, Switzerland. The first Hockey World Cup was organised in Barcelona (Spain) in 1971 and winner is Pakistan. Women's Hockey World Cup has been held since 1974.
- The 2010 Hockey World Cup was held in New Delhi and winner was Australia.
- The 13th Hockey World Cup (men's and women's edition both) were held in Hague (Netherlands) in 2014. Australia won the men's tournament after defeating Netherland. Netherland won the women's tournament after defeating Australia.
- The 14th Hockey World Cup will be held in India in 2018.

Lawn Tennis

- It was invented in 1870 by Major Wing Field in Wales. Wimbledon championship started in 1877 for men only. For women it was introduced in 1884.
- The four Grand Slam tournaments are considered to be the most prestigious tennis tournaments in the world. They are held annually and include, in chronological order, the Australian Open, the French Open, Wimbledon and the US Open. Apart from the Olympic Games, Davis Cup, Fed Cup and Hopman Cup, they are the only tournaments regulated by the International Tennis Federation (ITF).
- The Association of Tennis Professionals or ATP was formed to protect the interests of male professional tennis players is now known as the ATP World Tour.

Grand Slam Tournaments

Tournament	Date	Location	Surface	First Held
Australian Open	January	Melbourne	Hard (Plexicushion)	1905
French Open	May-June	Paris	Clay	1925
Wimbledon	June-July	London	Grass	1877
US Open	August-September	New York City	Hard (Decco Turf)	1881

Other Sports

Table Tennis

Table Tennis was introduced in the Olympic Games in 1988 at Seoul (South Korea).

Billiard

Cue sports also known as billiard sports, are a wide variety of games of skill generally played with cue stick, which is used to strike billiard balls, moving them around a cloth-covered billiards table bounded rubber cushions.

Polo

Polo (Chowgan) is a team sport played on horseback, in which the objectives is to score goals against an opposing team. Sometimes called, 'The sport of kings' it was highly popularised by the British. It is not an Olympic sport.

Wrestling

Wrestling is a form of combat sport involving grappling types techniques such as clinch fighting, throws and take downs, joint locks, pins and other grappling holds.

Formula One (F1) Race

- Formula one, also known as Formula 1 or F1 and referred to officially as the FIA Formula One World Championship, is the highest class of single seater auto racing sanctioned by the Federation International Automobile (FIA).
- It was started in 1950.
- The first Formula One World Championship was won by Italian Giuseppe Farina in Alfa Romeo in 1950. The first F1 race in India was held at the Buddha International Circuit in Greater Noida, UP (2011).

Badminton

The modern name in 1873 of Badminton came from the Badminton House, the International Badminton Fedration was establisment in 1934, the new name is Badminton World Federation.

Cycling

- The Tour de France tournament is an annual bicycle race held in France and nearby countries. First staged in 1903, the race covers more than 3600 km and last three weeks. This is organised every year in month of July.
- The 2002 Summer Olympics will be the first, at which men and women complete in the some number of events in all cycling disciplines.

Swimming

- Swimming is a water based sport governed by the Federation Internationals de Natation (FINA) and is formed in 1908. FINA is the International Federation (IF) recognised by the International Olympic Committee (IOC) for administering international competition in the aquatic sports.
- Its headquarters is at Lausanne, Switzerland.

Shooting

- Shooting sports have been contested at every Summer Olympic Games since the birth of the modern Olympic Movement at the 1896 Summer Olympics except at the 1904 and 1928 editions.

Marathon

The marathon is a long-distance runing event with on official distance of 42.195 km (26 miles and 385 yards), that is usually run as a road race.

The event was instituted in commemoration of the fabled run of the Greek Soldier Phedippiddes, a messenger from the Battle of Marathon to Athens.

Specific Names of Playing Areas

Sport	Name of Playing Area	Sport	Name of Playing Area
Badminton	Court	Golf	Link, Green**
Baseball	Diamond	Lawn Tennis	Court
Boxing	Ring	Ice Skating	Rink
Cricket	Pitch*	Wrestling	Ring, Arena

* Pitch in fact is the space between the wickets and not the entire cricket field.
** It is the area around the hole only.

Important Sport Terms

Sport	Terms
Basketball	Dunk, front court, lay up, held ball, pivot, rebound, steal
Cricket	Bye, draw, googly, topspin, over throw, duck, hit wicket
Football	Bend dribble, dissent, dummy, feint, free kick, header, red card, throwins
Hockey	Bully, striking, circle, post back
Chess	Castle, diagonaes, files, pawns, peices, promote, gambit, pawn
Boxing	Jab, laying on knock, second out habbit punch, upper cut
Badminton	Loab, let, drive, drop, love
Polo	Chuker, bunker
Baseball	Diamond, home run, put out, strike, ant-rubber.
Rifle Shooting	Target, muzzle fulb, bulls eye
Wrestling	Half, nelson, hold sager, rebuts
Golf	Fore some, stymie, T, put hole, caddy, nib lick, iron, the green, bunkeer
Billiards	Jigger, pot, break pot, in off, cans, bolting, long, hazard, cue
Swimming	Breast stroke, twist, butterfly, crawl, spring board
Volley Ball	Antennae, attack hit, libero, service, set-up, blocking, dribbling
Lawn Tennis	Advantage, ace, dence, volley, foot foult, smash, grand-slam, slice, love
Table Tennis	End line, flat hit, foil, service, phnholder grip, reverse, top-spin, couter-hitting, let

Important Cups and Trophies

Sport	Cup and Trophy
Cricket	Irani Trophy, Dilip Trophy, Ranji Trophy, Vijay Hazare Trophy, Asia Cup, Deodhar Trophy, CK Naidu Trophy, Cooch-Behar Trophy, Gandhi-Mendela Series, the Ashes Series, etc
Football	Durand Cup, Nizam Gold Cup, Rovers Cup, Sanjay Gold Cup, Santosh Trophy, Subroto Mukherjee Cup, Vittal Trophy, Nehru Gold Cup
Hockey	Agha Khan Cup, Azlan Shah Cup, Nehru Trophy, Dhyanchand Trophy, Beighton Cup, Scindia Gold Cup, Modi Gold Cup, Indira Gandhi Gold Cup, Rangaswami Cup, Khan Abdul Gaffar Cup
Golf	Canada Cup, Muthian Gold Cup, Ryder Cup, Walker Cup
Table Tennis	Corbillion Cup (women), Jayalaxmi Cup (women), Swaythling Cup (men)
Lawn Tennis	Davis Cup, Hamlet Cup, Australian Open, French Open, Wimbledon, US Open, Hopman Cup
Badminton	Thomas Cup (men), Uber Cup (women), Narang Cup, All England Open
Boxing	Aspy Adjania Trophy
Rowing	Wollington Trophy
Bridge	Ruia Trophy
Polo	Ezra Cup, Winchestor Cup, Radha Mohan Cup

Sports Organisations

FIDE	Federation International Des Echecs (*World Chess Federation*)	Chess
FIFA	Federation International de Football Association	Football
IHF	Indian Hockey Federation	Hockey
ICC	International Cricket Council	Cricket
ITTF	International Table Tennis Federation	Table Tennis
BWF	Badminton World Federation	Badminton

Measurements of Sports Fields and Instruments

Cricket	*Ball*	155.9 gm to 163 gm in weight
	Bat	96.5 cm in length and 10.8 cm width (Maximum)
	Pitch	20.12 m
	Length of the Stumps	71.1 cm (28 inch)
	Length of the Crease	1.22-1.83 (4 ft)
Football	*Field*	100 × 64 m to 110 × 75 m
Hockey	*Field*	100 yards × 60 yards
	Weight of the Ball	155-163 gm
	Colour of the Ball	White
	Weight of Hockey Stick	280 gm
Lawn Tennis	*Court*	23.77 m × 8.23 m (Singles)
	Ball	6.35 cm to 6.67 cm (in diameter) 56.7 gm to 2.53 gm (Weight)
Volley Ball	*Field*	18 m × 9 m
	Net	1 m deep and 9.50 m long 2.43 m (for men) and 2.24 m for women (Height)
	Ball	Circumference 66 cm + 1 cm Weight 270 gm + 10 gm
Badminton	*Court*	13.40 m × 5.18 m or 44×20 ft.
	Net	Top 1.524 m in height from the floor
	Shuttle	4.73 to 5.50 gm in weight and shall have 14 to 16 feathers fixed in Court
Kabaddi	*Field*	13 m × 10 m (According to Kabaddi Federation of India)
Kho-Kho	*Field*	34 × 16 m
Derby Course	*Length*	1.5 miles
Marathon Race	*Length*	26 miles, 385 yards
Polo	*Field Length*	300 yards
	Field Width	150 yards
	Distance between the Goals	250 yards
	Distance between the Goal post	8 yards
Chess		64 Squares on chessboard
	Colour	Black and White
	Nos. of same colour chess	16
Baseball	*Distance of each case*	90 ft
	Base distance along with hypotenuse	127 ft
Boxing	*Length and Width of the Ring*	4.9 × 4.9 m^2 to 6.1 × 6.1 m^2

Famous Sports Stadiums

Stadium	Sports	Place
Brookland	Football	England (UK)
Twickenham	Rugby Football	England (UK)
Putney Mart Lake	Boat Race	England (UK)
Yankee Stadium	Boxing	New York (USA)
Brooklyn	Baseball	New York (USA)
Forest Hill	Tennis	USA
Sendy Lodge	Golf	Scotland
Flemington	Horse Racing	Melbourne (Australia)
Headingley Manchester	Cricket	England (UK)
Lords, Oval, Leeds	Cricket	England (UK)
Black Heath	Rugby Football	London (UK)
Wimbledon	Lawn Tennis	London (UK)
Wembley Stadium	Football	London (UK)
Shivaji Stadium	Hockey	Delhi
National Stadium	Hockey	Delhi
National Stadium	Hockey and others	Mumbai
Wankhede Stadium	Cricket	Mumbai
Brabourne Stadium	Cricket	Mumbai
Eden Garden	Cricket	Kolkata
Green Park Stadium	Cricket	Kanpur
Keenan Stadium	Cricket	Jamshedpur
Trent Bridge	Cricket	England (UK)
White City	Dog race	England (UK)
Hurlington	Polo	England (UK)
Henlay Regatta	Regata	England
Brisbance, Melbourne, Perth, Sydney	Cricket	Australia
Indraprastha Stadium	Indoor Games	Delhi
Jawaharlal Nehru Stadium	Athletics	Delhi
Ferozeshah Kotla Ground	Cricket	Delhi
Ambedkar Stadium	Football	Delhi
Nehru, Chepauk Stadium	Cricket	Chennai
Barabati Stadium	Cricket	Cuttack
Aintree, Doncaster Epsom	Horse Racing	England (UK)

Players and their Associated Games

Players	Game	Country	Players	Game	Country
Jhansher Khan	Squash	Pakistan	Soma Biswas	Athletics	India
Jaspal Rana	Shooting	India	Arjun Singh Atwal	Golf	India
Geet Sethi	Billiards	India	Narayan Karthikeyan	Formula One	India
Ian James Thorpe	Swimming	Australia			
Anju B George	Long Jump	India	Tiger Woods	Golf	USA
Michael J Jordan	Basket Ball	USA	Andi Murray	Tennis	Scotland
Pankaj Arjan Advani	Snooker	India	Kim Clijster	Tennis	Belgium
Saina Nehwal	Badminton	India	Caroline Wozniaciki	Tennis	Den Mark
Surya Sekhar Ganguly	Chess	India			
Shikha Tandon	Swimming	India	Victoria Anzarenka	Tennis	Belarush
Ignace Tirkey	Hockey	India	Sania Mirza	Tennis	India

Nickname of Players

Player	Nickname
• Major Dhyanchand	Hockey ka Jadoogar
• Milkha Singh	Flying Sikh
• PT Usha	Payyoli Express, Golden Girl
• Shoaib Aktar	Rawalpindi Express
• Rahul Dravid	The Wall
• Harbhajan Singh	Bhajji, The Turbanator
• Javagal Srinath	Mysore Express
• Paes and Bhupati	Indian Express

National Sports

Country	National Sport
• Australia	Cricket
• Canada	Lacrose (Ice Hockey)
• China	Table Tennis
• England	Cricket
• India	Hockey
• Japan	Sumo
• Malaysia	Badminton
• Scotland	Ring by Football
• Spain	Bull Fighting
• USA	Baseball

Players and their Books

Player	Book
Balvir Singh	Golden Hatrick
Viswanathan Anand	My Best Game of Chess
David Beckham	My Side
Major Dhyanchand	Goal
Sunil Gavaskar	Sunny Days, Idols
Tiger Woods	How I Paly Golf
Kapil Dev	Cricket My Style
Sachin Tendulkar	Playing It My Way
Yuvraj Singh	The Test of My Life

National Games of India

The National Games of India is a sporting event held in India. It comprises various disciplines in which sportsmen from the different states of India participate against each other.

It was in 1924, in erstwhile Punjab, that the Indian chapter of the Olympic movement was born. The same year, the country's first Olympic Games, now christened as National Games, were organised in Lahore, the then capital of undivided Punjab. National Games are held once in 2 years, But took Guwahati 5 years to conduct the games after the National Games in 2002 are organised in Andhra Pradesh.

List of National Games from 1985

Year	Host	Duration	Top Placed Team
1985	New Delhi	19-26 November	Maharashtra
1987	Cannanore, Calicut, Trichur, Quiton & Allepey	20-28 December	Kerala
1994	Mumbai & Pune	16-25 January	Maharashtra
1997	Bengaluru and Mysura	31 May-11 June	Karnataka
1999	Imphal	14-25 Feb	Manipur
2001	Ludhiana, Patiala, Jalandhar, Chandigarh, Anandpur Sabih, Mohali	19 Nov-1 Dec	Punjab
2002	Hyderabad, Secunderabad, Visakhapatnam	13-22 Dec	Andhra Pradesh
2007	Guwahati	9-18 Feb	Services
2011	Ranchi, Jamshedpur & Dhanbad	12-26 Feb	Services
2015	Thiruvananthapuram, Kollam, Alapuzha, Ernakulam, Kozhikode, Thrissur, Kannur	31 Jan-14 Feb	Services
2016	Goa	November	Goa
2018	Uttarakhand	November	

Principle Languages of India

India has 22 languages which have been given the offficial language status

Assamese	It is an Indo-Aryan language and is the official language of Assam.
Bengali	It is one of the leading Indo-Aryan language and is the official language of West Bengal.
Gujarati	It is an Indo-Aryan language and is the official language of Gujarat.
Hindi	The largest spoken Indo-Aryan language. It is the official language of the Government of India. Various dialects of Hindi are Khariboli, Brajbhasha, Bundeli, Awadhi, Marwari, Maithili and Bhojpuri. In 6 states and UTs, Hindi is the official language.
Kannada	It belongs to the Dravidian family and is the official language of Karnataka.
Kashmiri	It is an Indo-Aryan language. It is often mistaken as the official language of Jammu and Kashmir.
Konkani	It is the official language of Goa and is spoken by thousands of Konkanis in Maharashtra, Karnataka and Kerala. It was added in 1992 by 71st Amendment. It is an Indo-Aryan language.
Malayalam	Belong to the Dravidian family and is the official language of Kerala.
Manipuri	It is the official language of Manipur. It was added in 1992 by 71st Amendment. It is a sino-Tibetan language.
Marathi	It is an Indo-Aryan language and is the official language of Maharashtra.
Nepali	It is spoken in parts of Uttar Pradesh, Bihar, West Bengal, Assam, etc. It was added in 1992 by 71st Amendment. It is an Indo-Aryan language.
Oriya	It is an Indo-Aryan language and is the official language of Odisha.
Punjabi	It is an Indo-Aryan language and is the official language of Punjab.
Sanskrit	It is one of the earliest languages of the world. Early Sanskrit is known as **Vedic Sanskrit** and covers the period between 2000 and 500 BC.
Sindhi	It is an Indo-Aryan language. It was added in 1967 by 21st Amendment.
Tamil	It is the oldest of the Dravidian languages and is the official language of Tamil Nadu.
Telugu	It is numerically the biggest of the Dravidian languages and is the official language of Andhra Pradesh.
Urdu	It is the official language of Jammu and Kashmir. It is an Indo-Aryan language. Modern Urdu developed due to the efforts of Sir Sayyed Ahmed Khan (1817-1898).
Dogri	It is generally spoken in Himachal Pradesh and Jammu. It is a combination of ancient Sanskrit and Pahari Dogri languages. It has been added by the 92nd Constitutional Amendment Act, 2003.
Maithili	It is chiefly spoken in the Maithilianchal region of Bihar. It is the second state language of Bihar. It has been added by the 92nd Constitutional Amendment Act, 2003.
Santhali	It is chiefly spoken in the area of Chota Nagpur Plateau in Jharkhand and Bihar. It has been added by the 92nd Constitutional Amendment Act, 2003.
Bodo	It is chiefly spoken in Assam and its adjoining North-East States. It has been added by the 92nd Constitutional Amendment Act, 2003. It belongs to the Sino-Tibetan family of languages.

National Insignia of India

Emblem The National Emblem of India is an adaptation of the Buddhist Lion Capital of Ashoka at Sarnath, near Varanasi in Uttar Pradesh.

Animal The Tiger is the National Animal of India. It is the symbol of India's wealth of wildlife. The magnificent tiger, *Panthera tigris*, is a striped animal.

Bird The Peacock (*Pavo cristatus*), is the National Bird of India. It is symbol of qualities like beauty and grace.

Flag The National Flag is a horizontal tricolour of deep saffron (kesari) at the top, white in the middle, dark green at the bottom and a blue wheel (chakra) with 24 sticks at the centre.

Fruit The Mango (*Mangiferra indica*) is the National Fruit. It has been cultivated in India since time immemorial.

Tree The National Tree of India is The Banyan (*Ficus bengalensis*) Tree. This huge tree towers over its neighbours and has the widest trunk.

Sport Field Hockey, in which India has an impressive record with eight Olympic medals, is considered as the National Sport. However, Home Ministry has said that officially, no sport has been accorded, the status of National Sport.

Anthem Jana-Gana-Mana.... The song was composed originally in Bengali by Rabindranath Tagore, adopted in its Hindi version is our National Anthem.

Song The song **Vande Mataram**, composed in Sanskrit by Bankimchandra Chatterji, is our National Song.

Calendar The National Calendar based on the Saka Era with Chaitra as its first month and a normal year of 365 days was adopted from 22nd March, 1957.

Flower Lotus scientifically known as *Nelumbo nucifera* is the National Flower of India

Other National Symbols

National Sentence	Satyamev Jayate
National Language	Hindi in Devnagiri Script
Father of the Nation	Mahatma Gandhi
National Foreign Policy	Non-Alignment
National Information Letter	White Letter
National Currency	Rupee (₹)
National Festivals	– Republic Day (26th January) – Independence Day (15th August) – Gandhi Jayanti (2nd October)
National River	Ganga
National Aquatic Animal	Ganga Dolphin (*Platanista gangetica*)
National Heritage Animal	Elephant

Indian Defence

Indian Army Commands

Command	HQ Location
Central Command	Lucknow
Eastern Command	Kolkata
Northern Command	Udhampur
Southern Command	Pune
SW Command	Jaipur
Western Command	Chandimandir
Training Command (ARTRAC)	Shimla

Indian Air Force Commands

Command	HQ Location
Central Air Command	Allahabad
Eastern Air Command	Shillong
Southern Air Command	Thiruvananthapuram
South Western Air Command	Gandhi Nagar
Western Air Command	New Delhi
Training Command	Bengaluru

Indian Navy Commands

Command	HQ Location
Western Naval Command	Mumbai
Eastern Naval Command	Visakhapatnam
Southern Naval Command	Cochin

Indian Defence Training Institutions

Training Institution	Place	Estd in
Rashtriya Indian Military College (RIMC)	Dehradun	1922
Army Cadet College (ACC)	Dehradun	
Indian Military Academy (IMA)	Dehradun	1932
High Altitude Warfare School (HAWS)	Gulmarg	1948
National Defence Academy (NDA)	Khadakwasla	1949
National Defence College (NDC)	New Delhi	1960
Officers Training Academy (OTA)	Chennai	1963
Counter-Insurgency and Jungle Warfare School	Vairengte (Mizoram)	1970
College of Defence Management	Secunderabad	1970
College of Combat/Army War College	Mhow (MP)	1971
Army Air Defence College (AADC)	Gopalpur (Odisha)	1989
Army School of Physical Training (ASPT)	Pune	

Ranks of Commissioned Officers

Army	Air Force	Navy
Field Marshal	Marshal of the IAF	Admiral of the Fleet
General	Air Chief Marshal	Admiral
Lt General	Air Marshal	Vice Admiral
Major General	Air Vice Marshal	Rear Admiral
Brigadier	Air Commodore	Commodore
Colonel	Group Captain	Captain
Lt Colonel	Wing Commander	Commander
Major	Squadron Leader	Lt Commander
Captain	Flight Lieutenant	Lieutenant
Lieutenant	Flying Officer	Sub-Lieutenant

Paramilitary and Reserve Forces

Name	Established
Assam Rifles (AR)	• It was established in 1835 called Cachar Levy. It is the oldest paramilitary force in the country. • Its main objective is to keep vigilance of international borders in North-East and countering insurgency operations in Arunachal Pradesh, Manipur, Mizoram and Nagaland.
Intelligence Bureau (IB)	• It was set-up in 1920. • Its objective is to collect secret information relating to country's security. • It was originally set-up as Central Special Branch (CSB) in 1887 and renamed IB in 1920.
Central Reserve Police Force (CRPF)	• It was set-up in 1939. • Its main objective is to assist the State/Union Territory Police in maintenance of law and order.
National Cadet Corps (NCC)	• It was established in 1948. • Its main objective is to stimulate interest among the youth in the defence of the country in order to build up a reserve manpower to expand armed forces.
Territorial Army (TA)	• It was established in 1948. • It is a voluntary, part-time force (between 18 and 42 years), not of professional soldiers, but civilians, who wish to assist in defence of the country.
Indo-Tibetan Border Police (ITBP)	• It was established in 1962, after the Chinese attack. • It is basically employed in the Northern borders for monitoring the borders and also to stop smuggling and illegal immigration.
Home Guard	• It was established in 1962, to assist the police in maintaining security, to help defence forces and to help local authorities in case of any eventuality.
Central Bureau of Investigation (CBI)	• It was established in 1941 and renamed CBI on 1963. • Its objective is to investigate cases of misconduct by public servants, cases of cheating, embezzlement and fraud. • CBI is also entrusted with the investigation of international crime cases in collaboration with Interpol.
Border Security Force (BSF)	• It was established in 1965. • It keeps a vigil over the international borders against the intrusion in the country.
Central Industrial Security Force (CISF)	• It was set-up in 1969 after the recommendations of Justice B Mukherji. • Its objective is to monitor the industrial complexes of Central Government.
Indian Coast Guard	• It was set-up in 1978. • Its objective is to protect the maritime and other national interests in the maritime zones of India.
National Security Guards (NSG)	• It was established in 1984 to counter the surge of militancy in the country. • It is a highly trained force which deals with the militants effectively.
National Crime Records Bureau (NCRB)	• It was established in 1986. • Its objective is to collect crime statistics at the national level, information of inter-state and international criminals to help investigation agencies.
Rapid Action Force (RAF)	• It was established in 1991. • Under the operational command of CRPF, 10 battalions of the CRPF have been reoriented for tackling communal riots in the country.

Defence Research in India

Defence Research and Development Organisation (DRDO)

It is an agency of the Republic of India, responsible for the development of technology for use by the military, headquartered in New Delhi, India.

It was formed in 1958, by the merger of Technical Development Establishment and the Directorate of Technical Development and Production with the Defence Science Organisation.

Integrated Guided Missile Development Programme (IGMDP)

The IGMDP was launched in 1983, for the development of a comprehensive range of missiles including the intermediate range, Agni Missile (surface-to-surface) and short range missiles such as the Prithvi Ballistic Missile (surface-to-surface), Akash Missile (surface-to-air), Astra Missile (air-to-air), Trishul Missile (surface-to-air) and Nag Missile (anti-tank).

Indian Missiles

Name	Range
Agni-I	It is a medium-range ballistic missile with a range of 700-800 km.
Agni-II	It is an intermediate-range ballistic missile with a range of 2000-3000 km.
Agni-III	It is an intermediate-range ballistic missile with a range of 3000-5000 km.
Agni-IV	It is an intermediate-range ballistic missile with a range of at a distance upto 4000 km.
Agni-V	It is an intercontinental ballistic missile with a range of 5000-8000 km.
Prithvi	Prithvi is a tactical surface-to-surface Short-Range Ballistic Missile (SRBM). It has three versions.
Prithvi-I (SS-150)	Army Version (150 km range with a payload of 1000 kg).
Prithvi-II (SS-250)	Air Force Version (250 km range with a payload of 500 kg).
Prithvi-III (SS-350)	Naval Version (350 km range with a payload of 1000 kg).
Dhanush (SS-350)	Dhanush is reportedly a naval version of Prithvi-III, which can be launched from ships. It can carry 500 kg of conventional or nuclear warhead, to a distance of 600 km.
Astra	Astra is Beyond Visual Range (BVR) air-to-air missile. Astra is designed to be capable of engaging targets at varying range and altitudes allowing for both short-range targets (upto 20 km) and long-range targets (upto 80 km) using alternative propulsion modes.
Akash	▪ Akash is a medium range surface-to-air missile defence system developed by DRDO and BEL as part of the IGMDP. The missile can target aircraft up to 30 km away, at altitudes of 18000 m. Akash can be fired from both tracked and wheeled platforms. ▪ Akash is said to be capable of both conventional and nuclear warheads, with a reported payload of 60 kg.
Trishul	Trishul is a short range surface-to-air missile. The range of the missile is 12 km and is fitted with a 15 kg warhead. The weight of the missile is 130 kg.
Nag	Nag is India's third generation 'Fire-and-Forget' anti-tank missile. It is an all weather, top attack missile with a range of 3 to 7 km.
Sagarika	K-15 Sagarika is a nuclear-capable submarine launched ballistic missile with a range of 750 km. It belongs to the K Missile family. The latest test of the K-15 Missile was done on 11th March, 2012.
Agni VI	It is an intercontinental ballistic missile with a range of 8000-12000 km.

Name	Range
Brahmos	▪ Brahmos is a stealth supersonic cruise missile that can be launched from submarines, ships, aircraft or land. It is a joint venture between Republic of India's DRDO and Russian Federation's NPO Mashinostroyeniya, who have together formed Brahmos Aerospace Private Limited.
	▪ It is the world's fastest cruise missile in operation. The missile travels at a speed of mach 2.8 to 3.0. It has a range of 290 km. It can carry 300 kg of conventional or nuclear warhead.
	▪ It is a hypersonic cruise missile with a range of 290 km. It is under development.
Shaurya	▪ The Shaurya Missile is a short-range surface-to-surface ballistic missile developed by DRDO for use by the Indian Army capable of hypersonic speeds, it has a range of 600 km and is capable of carrying a payload of one-tonne conventional or nuclear warhead.
	▪ Shaurya Missile is a land version of the under-water launched K-15 Missile, Sagarika.
Nirbhay	▪ Nirbhay is a long range, subsonic cruise missile being developed in India. The missile will have a range of 1000 km. The missile will have a speed of 0.8 mach. The Nirbhay will be able to launched from multiple platforms on land, sea and air.

Indian Military Aircrafts

Aircraft	Origin	Type	Versions
Il-76 Phalcon	Russia	Airborne Early Warning	Il-76
Sukhoi Su-30 MKI	Russia, India	Multirole Air Superiority Fighter	Su-30 MKI
Antonov An-32 Cline	Soviet Union	Cargo Aircraft	An-32
HAL Tejas	India	Fighter	Mark I
SEPECAT Jaguar	France, United Kingdom	Ground-Attack	SI
Mikoyan-Gurevich Mig-27	Soviet Union	Ground-Attack	MIG-27 ML
Mil Mi-35 Hind-E	Soviet Union	Attack Helicopter	Mi-35
Mi-17	Soviet Union	Transport Helicopter	Mi-17
HAL Dhruv	India	Utility Helicopter	Dhruv
Nishant	India (DRDO)	Unmanned Aerial Vehicles (UAV)	—
HTT40	India (HAL)	Replacement of HPT-32	—

Indian Military Radars

Naval	▪ Super Vision-2000 3D airborne naval surveillance radar.
	▪ Revathi 3D Naval medium range radar derived from the 3D CAR.
Land-based and Airborne	▪ Swordfish Long Range Tracking Radar.
	▪ INDRA series of 2D radars, low level radar to search and track low flying cruise missiles, helicopters and aircraft for the Indian Army.
	▪ BFSR-SR 2D short range battlefield surveillance radar for the Indian Army.
	▪ Rajendra Radar 3D medium range fire control radar for Akash SAM.
	▪ Central Acquisition Radar (3D-CAR) planar array tracking radar for all branches of the Indian armed forces. Air force version known as the Rohini Naval Version known as Revathi.
	▪ 3D AESA Long Range Tracking Radar tracking high speed ballistic missile targets.
	▪ Low Level Lightweight Radar (LLLR) 2D low level aircraft tracking radar.
	▪ Gadanki Ionospheric Radar Interferometer (GIRI) 30 MHz radar system for Ionospheric, meteor and space weather research.

List of Combat Vehicles

Name	Type	Origin
Arjun MBT mk-1	Main Battle Tank	India
T-90 S 'Bhishma'/T-90 M	Main Battle Tank	Russia, India
T-72 M1 'Ajeya'	Main Battle Tank	Soviet Union
T-55	Main Battle Tank	Soviet Union
BMP-2 'Sarath'	Infantry Fighting Vehicle	Soviet Union
BMP-1	Infantry Fighting Vehicle	Soviet Union
NAMICA (Nag Missile Carrier)	Tank Destroyer	India
CMT (Carrier Mortar Tracked)	Mortar Carrier	India
FV 432	Armoured Personnel Carrier	United Kingdom
OT-64 SKOT	Armoured Personnel Carrier	Czechoslovakia, Poland
BRDM-2	Reconnaissance Vehicle	Soviet Union
Ferret	Reconnaissance Vehicle	United Kingdom
PRP-3	Battlefield Surveillance System	Soviet Union

Indian Naval Aircrafts

Aircraft	Origin	Type	Version
Dornier Do 228	Germany	Utility Transport	Do 228-101 Do 228-201
HAL Dhruv	India	Utility Helicopter	
HAL HJT-16 Kiran	India	Trainer	
Aerospatiale SA 316 Alouette III	India	Utility Helicopter	SA 316 B SA 319
HAL HPT-32 Deepak	India	Basic Trainer	
Kamov Ka-31 Helix-B	Russia	AEW (Airborne Early Warning)	
Tupolev Tu-142 Bear	Russia	Maritime Patrol	Tu-142 M
Ilyushin Il-38 May	Russia	Maritime Patrol	Il-38 SD
Mikoyan MiG-29 K	Russia	Multi-Role Fighter Trainer	MiG-29 K, MiG-29 KUB
Kamov Ka-25 Hormone	Russia	Naval Helicopter	
Kamov Ka-28 Helix-A	Russia	Anti Submarine Naval Helicopter	
BAE Sea Harrier	UK	Fighter Trainer	FRS 51 T4
Westland Sea King	UK	Anti-Submarine Warfare Search and Rescue, Utility Transport	
Sikorsky SH-3 Sea King	USA	Anti-Submarine Warfare Utility Helicopter	UH-3 H

Sub-marines of the Indian Navy

INS Vibhuti	- It was India's first indigenously built missile boat launched at Mazgaon Docks in Mumbai. - It is a veer class corvette.
INS Savitri	- It was India's first warship fabricated at Hindustan shipyard Limited in 1990. - It is a Sukanya class patrol vessel of the Indian Navy.

INS Shakti	• It was India's first indigenously built submarine. • The ship is one of the largest in the Indian Navy as it is 175 m in length and 32 m in width. It is a Deepak-class fleet tanker.
INS Chakra	• The INS Chakra II (K-152 Nerpa) is a 8140 tonne project 518 (NATO Akula II) type nuclear-powered attack submarine. • Constituted in 1993, but suspended due to lack of funding. • K-152 Nerpa was launched in October 2008 and entered service with the Russian Navy in late 2009. • The submarine was leased to the Indian Navy in 2011 and was formally commissioned into service as the INS Chakra II at a ceremony in Vishakhapatnam on 4th April, 2012.
INS Arihant	• It is a class of nuclear powered ballistic missile submarines. • It is India's first indigenously designed and built nuclear submarine. • It is currently under sea-trial.
INS Kalvari	• It is the first of Indian Navy's six Kalvari class sub-marine being build in India. It is a diesal-electric attack sub-marine, which is designed by French naval defence and energy company DCNS and being manufactured at Mazagon Dock Limited in Mumbai.
INS Arighat	• It is the second Arihant-class submarine and the second nuclear-powered ballistic missile submarine being built by India. It was launched on 19th November, 2017.
INS Khanderi	• It is the second of the Indian Navy's six Kalvari-class submarines being built in India. It is a diesel-electric attack submarine. It was launched on 12th January, 2017.

Warships/Base of the Indian Navy

INS Vikrant	• The first Aircraft carrier of Indian Navy was INS Vikrant. • India purchased the INS Vikrant from the United Kingdom in 1957.
INS Viraat	• INS Viraat is a centaur class aircraft carrier currently in service with the Indian Navy. • The Viraat was completed and commissioned in 1959, as the Royal Navy's HMS Hermes and transferred to India in 1987.
INS Prahar	• It is world's fastest missile ship commissioned in 1997. It is a veer-class Corvette.
INS Delhi	• It is India's largest and most sophisticated indigenously built warship. • It was launched in 1991 at Mazgaon Docks and Commissioned in 1997. • It is the leadship of her class of guided Missile destroyers.
INS Mysore	• It is a Delhi class guided missile destroyer currently in active service with the Indian Navy. INS Mysore was built at Mazgaon Dock Limited in Mumbai and it was commissioned in 1999.
INS Prabal	• It is a veer class corvette, currently in active service with the Indian Navy. • It was built at Mazgaon Dock Limited and Commissioned in 2002.
INS Talwar	• It is the leadship of the Talwar class frigates of the Indian Navy. • Its name means 'Sword' in English. • It was built in Russia and commissioned into the Indian Navy in 2003.
INS Beas	• It is a Brahmaputra class frigate of the Indian Navy. • It was built at the Garden Reach Shipbuilders and Engineers (GRSE) Kolkata, and it was commissioned in 2005.
INS Kadamba	• It is India's largest naval base located near Karwar in Karnataka. • It was commissioned in 2005, under the project Seabird.
INS Vikramaditya	• It is India's biggest ship, aircraft carrier. • It was acquired from Russia. • It entered into Service with the Indian Navy in 2013.
INS Kolkata	• It is the lead ship of the Kolkata class guided missile destroyers of Indian Navy. • It was handed over to the Navy on 10th July, 2014.

INS Visakhapatnam	• It is the lead ship of the Visakhapatnam–class stealth guided-missile destroyers of the Indian Navy.
	• It is being constructed at Mazagon Dock Limited (MDL) and has been launched on 20th April, 2015. The ship is expected to get commissioned by 2018.
INS Kavaratti	• It is an anti-submarine warfare corvette of the Indian Navy.
	• It is the last of four komodo class corvettes under various stages of induction with the Indian Navy.
	• The ship was built by Garden Reach Shipbuilders and Engineers, Kolkata and launched on 19th May, 2015.
INS Kochi Start	• It is the second ship of the Kolkata–class destroyers built for the Indian Navy.
	• It is built at Mazagon Dock Limited, Mumbai. She was commissioned to Indian Navy on 30th September, 2015.
	• It has been built under the code name of project 15 Alpha.

India's Atomic Research

India's atomic energy research started with the establishment of the Atomic Energy Commission on 10th August, 1948. Department of Atomic Energy (DAE) was established in 1954, for implementation of atomic energy programmes.

Bhabha Atomic Research Centre (BARC) It was set up in 1954, as the Atomic Energy establishment at Trombay, near Mumbai and in 1967, was renamed as BARC in the memory of its founder Dr Homi Bhabha. It is the premier national centre for Research and Development (R & D) work in nuclear energy and related disciplines. At present, *BARC houses three research reactors*

1. Apsara, a one MW Swimming pool type reactor.
2. Cirus, a 40 MW reactor.
3. Dhruva, a 100 MW high power nuclear research reactor.

Earlier, there were two more research reactors at BARC

1. Zerliana (zero energy, natural uranium)
2. Purnima I-III (fuel: plutonium/ uranium-233)

The centre has built two Synchrotron Radiation Sources (SRSs) called Indus I and Indus II and developed versatile lasers for various applications.

Indira Gandhi Centre for Atomic Research (IGCAR) It was set-up in 1971, at Kalpakkam in Chennai for research and development of fast breeder technology. IGCAR designed Fast Breeder Test Reactor (FBTR), which uses indigenous mixed fuel with a plutonium and natural uranium base. IGCAR also developed the country's first neutron reactor, Kamini, which is a 30 MW reactor and uses uranium fuel.

Atomic Mineral Directorate (AMD) It is located in Hyderabad and carries out surveys, exploration and evaluation of the resources required for the atomic energy programmes of the country.

Variable Energy Cyclotron Centre (VECC) It was set-up in 1977, at Kolkata as a national centre for advanced work in nuclear chemistry, nuclear physics, production of isotopes for various applications and radiation damage studies on reactor materials.

Centre for Advance Technology (CAT) It was established in 1984, at Indore to coordinate research in high technology fields like lasers, fusion and accelerators.

Nuclear Power Stations At a Glance

Location	State	Number of Reactors
I. Functional		
1. Tarapur	Maharashtra	4
2. Kaiga	Karnataka	4
3. Kalpakkam	Tamil Nadu	2
4. Kakrapar	Gujarat	2
5. Rawatbhata	Rajasthan	6
6. Narora	Uttar Pradesh	2
7. Kudankulan	Tamil Nadu	1
II. Under Construction		
1. Kudankulam	Tamil Nadu	1
2. Kalpakkam	Tamil Nadu	1
3. Rawatbhata	Rajasthan	2
4. Kakrapar Unit 344	Gujarat	2

There are now 21 operating nuclear power reactors (two boiling water reactors and nineteen PHWRs (Pressurised Heavy Water Reactors) with a total installed capacity of 5780 MW (3.5% of total installed base).

Heavy Water Production

1. Nangal (Punjab) First heavy water plant in the country
2. Baroda (Gujarat)
3. Talchar (Odisha)
4. Tuticorin (Tamil Nadu)
5. Thal (Maharashtra)
6. Hazira (Gujarat)
7. Manuguru (Andhra Pradesh)
8. Rawatbhata (Rajasthan)

India's Nuclear Test

- On 18th May, 1974, India conducted her first underground nuclear explosion at Pokhran (Rajasthan) in the Thar desert at a depth of 100 m. The code name used to convey the success of the test to the then Prime Minister, Indira Gandhi, was 'Buddha is Smiling'.

- For the second time, India conducted on 11th May, 1998 three underground nuclear explosions at the same place i.e, Pokhran in the Thar desert of Rajasthan at a depth of 100 m. The test were code named 'Operation Shakti'.

Space Programme of India

- The Indian Space Programme was launched in 1962, when the Indian National Committee for Space Research was formed. To this were added the Indian Space Research Organisation in 1969 and the Space Commission and Department of Space in 1972. The Indian Space Research Organisation (ISRO) is responsible for the planning, execution and management of space research activities and space application programmes.
- The ISRO has headquarters at Bengaluru.
- India's first satellite communication Earth station was set-up at Arvi near Pune. The first Indian Satellite Aryabhatta was launched on 19th April, 1975 from Baikonur (erstwhile USSR). The first Indian Remote Sensing Satellite was launched on 17th March, 1988.
- The first Indian Communication Satellite, APPLE was launched on 19th June, 1981 from Kourou in French Guyana (South America). It was the first Indian satellite that was placed in geostationary orbit.

ISRO Establishments

SHAR Centre, Sriharikota

- It is located on the East coast of Andhra Pradesh, SHAR is the main launch centre of ISRO. This centre also undertakes large scale production of solid rocket propellant and ground testing of solid fulled rocket stages of the Indian launch vehicles. In September 2002, the Sriharikota Space Centre was renamed as Professor Satish Dhawan Space Centre.

ISRO Telemetry, Tracking and Command Network (ISTRAC)

- It has headquarters and Spacecraft Control Centre at Bengaluru and a network of ground stations at Sriharikota, Thiruvananthapuram, Bengaluru, Lucknow, Car Nicobar and Mauritius. The ISTRAC provides Telementry, Tracking and Command (TTC) support for the launch vehicles and satellite missions of ISRO and for other space agencies.

Master Control Facility

- It is located at Hassan in Karnataka and Bhopal in Madhya Pradesh, is responsible for all post launch operations of INSAT satellites including orbital manoeuvres, station keeping and in-orbit operations on the spacecraft.

ISRO Inertial Systems Unit (IISU)

- It is located in Thiruvananthapuram, carries out development of inertial systems for both satellites and launch vehicles.

Space Applications Centre (SAC)

- It is located in Ahmedabad, is ISRO's research and development centre for conceiving, organising and building systems for practical applications of space technology. The major fields of activity cover satellite communication, remote sensing, meteorology and geodesy.

Physical Research Laboratory (PRL)

- It is located in Ahmedabad under Department of Space and is the premier national centre for research in space and allied sciences.

National Remote Sensing Agency (NRSA)

- It is located in Hyderabad under the Department of Space, has facilities for surveying, identifying, classifying and monitoring Earth resources using serial and satellite data.

Development and Educational Communication Unit (DECU)

- It is located in Ahmedabad, is involved in the conception, definition, planning and socio-economic evaluation of space application programmes. Besides carrying out research and programme production with themes of development and educational oriented communications, the unit provides training services in this area.

Vikram Sarabhai Space Centre (VSSC)

- It is located in Thiruvananthapuram, is the leading centre for launch vehicle development and it pioneers in rocket research and planning and execution of launch vehicle development projects.

ISRO Satellite Centre (ISAC)

- It is located in Bengaluru, is responsible for the design, fabrication, testing and management of satellite systems for scientific, technological and application missions.

National Atmospheric Research Laboratory

- At Gadanki near Tirupathi, is used by scientists for carrying out atmospheric research.

Laboratory for Electro-Optics Systems (LEOS)

- It is located in Bengaluru and is engaged in design, development and production of Electro-Optic sensors and camera optics for satellites and launch vehicles. The sensors include star trackers, Earth sensors, Sun sensors and processing electronics.

Liquid Propulsion Systems Centre (LPSC)

- It is located at Thiruvananthapuram and Bengaluru. The LPSC undertakes research, development and testing of liquid propulsion systems for ISRO's launch vehicle and satellite programmes. LPSC, Mahendragiri (Tamil Nadu) has been elevated as ISRO Propulsion Complex (IPRC) with effect from 1st February, 2014.

The Indian Institute of Remote Sensing (IIRS)

- It is located in Dehradun, is a premier training and education institute dealing with Remote Sensing, Geoinformation Science and GPS Technology and their Applications.

North Eastern-Space Applications Centre (NE-SAC)

- It is located at Umiam (near Shillong), Meghalaya, is a joint initiative of Department of Space (DoS) and North-Eastern Council to provide developmental support to the North-Eastern region using space science and technology. The centre has the mandate to develop high technology infrastructure support to enable North-East states to adopt space technology inputs for their development.

Regional Remote Sensing Service Centres (RRSSCs)

- Five RRSSCs have been established by the DoS at Bengaluru, Jodhpur, Kolkata and Nagpur. RRSSCs support the various remote sensing tasks specific to their regions as well as at the national level.

Indian Space Programme At a Glance

Satellite	Date	Launch Vehicle	Place	Type
Aryabhatta	19th April, 1975	Cosmos	Baikonur	Experimental
Bhaskara I	7th June, 1979	Cosmos	Baikonur	Earth Observation
Rohini	10th August, 1979	S L V-3	Sriharikota	Experimental
Rohini RS-1	18th July, 1980	S L V-3	Sriharikota	Experimental
Rohini D1	31st May, 1981	S L V-3	Sriharikota	Earth Observation
Apple	19th June, 1981	Ariane	Kourou	Communication
Bhaskara II	20th November, 1981	Cosmos	Baikonur	Earth Observation
INSAT-IA	10th April, 1982	Delta	America	Communication
SROSS I	24th March, 1987	ASLV D-1	Sriharikota	Science and Exploration
SROSS II	13th July, 1988	ASLV-D2	Sriharikota	Earth Observation
IRS-IB	29th August, 1991	Vostok	Baikonur	Earth Observation
INSAT 2A	10th July, 1992	Ariane-4	Kourou	Communication
INSAT 2B	23rd July, 1993	Ariane-4	Kourou	Communication
SROSS-C2	4th May, 1994	ASLV-D4	Sriharikota	Science and Exploration
IRS P2	15th October, 1994	PSLV-D2	Sriharikota	Earth Observation
IRS-IC	28th December, 1995	Molniya	Baikonur	Earth Observation
IRS-P3	21st March, 1996	PSLV-D3	Sriharikota	Earth Observation
OceanSat-1 or IRS P4	26th May, 1999	PSLV-C2	Sriharikota	Earth Observation
INSAT-3B	22nd March, 2000	Ariane-5	Kourou	Communication
GSAT-1	18th April, 2001	GSLV-D1	Sriharikota	Communication
INSAT-3A	10th April, 2003	Ariane-5	Kourou	Communication
GSAT-2	8th May, 2003	GSLV-D2	Sriharikota	Communication
EDUSAT	20th September, 2004	GSLV-F01	Sriharikota	Communication
CARTOSAT 1	5th May, 2005	PSLV-C6	Sriharikota	Earth Observation
HAMSAT	5th May, 2005	PSLV-C6	Sriharikota	Communication
SRE-1	10th January, 2007	PSLV-C7	Sriharikota	Experimental
AGILE	23rd April, 2007	PSLV-C8	Sriharikota	Astronomy
Tech SAR	21st January, 2008	PSLV-C10	Sriharikota	Surveillance
IMS-1	28th April, 2008	PSLV-C9	Sriharikota	Earth Observation
CHANDRA-YAAN-1	22nd October, 2008	PSLV-C11	Sriharikota	Moon Mission
OCEANSAT-2	23rd September, 2009	PSLV-C14	Sriharikota	Earth Observation
CARTOSAT-2B	12th July, 2010	PSLV-C15	Sriharikota	Earth Observation
GSAT-5P	25th December, 2010	GSLV-F06	Sriharikota	Communication
RISAT-1	26th April, 2012	PSLV-C19	Sriharikota	Radar Imaging
YOUTHSAT	20th April, 2011	PSLV-C16	Sriharikota	Experimental/Small Satellite
RESOURCESAT-2	20th April, 2011	PSLV-C16	Sriharikota	Earth Observation Satellite
GSAT-8	21st May, 2011	Ariane-5 VA-202	Kourou	Communication

Satellite	Date	Launch Vehicle	Place	Type
GSAT-12	15th July, 2011	PSLV-C17	Sriharikota	Communication
SRMSat	12th October, 2011	PSLV-C18	Sriharikota	Experimental/Small Satellite
Megha-Tropiques	12th October, 2011	PSLV-C18	Sriharikota	Earth Observation Satellite, Climate and Environment
Jugnu	12th October, 2011	PSLV-C18	Sriharikota	Student Satellite
RISAT-1	26th April, 2012	PSLV-C19	Sriharikota	Earth Observation Satellite
GSAT-10	29th September, 2012	Ariane-5 VA-209	Kourou	Communication
SARAL	25th February, 2013	PSLV-C20	Sriharikota	Earth Observation Satellite
IRNSS-1A	1st July, 2013	PSLV-C22	Sriharikota	Navigation Satellite
INSAT-3D	26th July, 2013	Ariane-5 VA-214	Kourou	Communication Disaster Management, Earth Observation Satellite
GSAT-7	30th August, 2013	Ariane-5 VA-215	Kourou	Communication
MOM	5th November, 2013	PSLV-C25	Sriharikota	Geo-Stationary Satellite
GSAT-14	5th January, 2014	GSLV-D5	Sriharikota	Communication
IRNSS-18	4th April, 2014	PSLV-24	Sriharikota	Navigation
IRNSS-IC	16th October, 2014	PSLV-C26	Sriharikota	Navigation
GSAT-16	7th December, 2014	Ariane-5 VA-221	Kourou	Communication
GSAT-15	11th November, 2015	Ariane-5 VA 227	Kourou	Communication
GSAT-18	5th October, 2016	Ariane-5 ECA	Kourou	Communication
Resourcesat-2A	7th December, 2016	PSLV-C16	Sriharikota	Remote Sensing
Cartosat-2	15th February, 2017	PSLV-C37	Sriharikota	Remote Sensing Satellite
GSAT-9	5th May, 2017	GSLV Mark-2	Sriharikota	Communication Satellite
Cartosat-2	23rd June, 2017	PSLV-C38	Sriharikota	Remote Sensing Satellite
GSAT-17	29th June, 2017	Ariane-5	Kouron	Communication Satellite
Cartosat-2	12th January, 2018	PSLV-C40	Sriharikota	Remote Sensing Satellite

History of Satellite Launch Vehicles

Rocket	Satellite	Date	Result
SLV-3	Rohini	10th August, 1979	Unsuccessful
SLV-3	Rohini	18th July, 1980	Successful
SLV-3	Rohini	31st May, 1981	Unsuccessful
SLV-3	Rohini	17th April, 1983	Successful
ASLV-D1	SROSS-1	24th March, 1987	Unsuccessful
ASLV-D2	SROSS-2	13th July, 1988	Unsuccessful
ASLV-D3	SROSS-C	20th May, 1992	Successful

Rocket	Satellite	Date	Result
PSLV-D1	IRS-P1	20th September, 1993	Unsuccessful
PSLV-D2	IRS-P2 (Ocean Sat)	15th October, 1994	Successful
PSLV-C1	IRS-1D	29th September, 1997	Successful
PSLV-C2	IRS-P4 or OceanSat-1	26th May, 1999	Successful
GSLV-D1	GSAT	18th April, 2001	Unsuccessful
GSLV-D2	GSAT-2	8th May, 2003	Successful
PSLV-C5	Resource Sat-1	17th October, 2003	Successful
GSLV-F01	EDUSAT	20th September, 2004	Successful
PSLV-C6	CARTOSAT-1 and HAMSAT	5th May, 2005	Successful
GSVL-F02	INSAT-4C	10th July, 2006	Unsuccessful
PSLV-C7	CARTOSAT-2 and SRE-1	10th January, 2007	Successful
PSLV-C8	AGILE	23rd April, 2007	Successful
PSLV-C10	Tech SAR	21st January, 2008	Successful
PSLV-C9	CARTOSAT-2A, IMS-1	28th April, 2008	Successful
PSLV-C11	CHANDRAYAAN-1	22nd October, 2008	Successful
PSLV-C12	RISAT-2	20th April, 2009	Successful
PSLV-C14	OCEANSAT-2	23rd September, 2009	Successful
GSLV-D3	GSAT-4	12th April, 2010	Unsuccessful
PSLV-C15	CARTOSAT-2B	12th July, 2010	Successful
GSLV-F06	GSAT-5P	25th December, 2010	Unsuccessful
PSLV-C16	Resource Sat-2, Youth sat and X-Sat	20th April, 2011	Successful
PSLV-C17	GSAT-12	15th July, 2011	Successful
PSLV-C18	Jugnu, Megha-Tropiques	12th October, 2011	Successful
PSLV-C19	RISAT-1	26th April, 2012	Successful
PSLV-C20	SARAL	25th February, 2013	Successful
PSLV-C22	IRNSS-1A	1st July, 2013	Successful
PSLV-C25	MOM	5th November, 2013	Successful
GSLV-D5	GSAT-14	5th January, 2014	Successful
PSLV-C24	IRNSS-1B	4th April, 2014	Successful
PSLV-C23	SPOT-7	30th June, 2014	Successful
PSLV-C26	IRNSS-1C	16th October, 2014	Successful
Ariane-5	GSAT-16	7th December, 2014	Successful
Ariane-5	GSAT-15	11th November, 2015	Successful
PSLV-31	IRNSS-IE	20th January, 2016	Successful
PSLV-32	IRNSS-IF	10th March, 2016	Successful
PSLV-33	IRNSS-IG	28th April, 2016	Successful
PSLV-34	Cartosat-2C	22nd June, 2016	Successful
PSLV-35	Seatsat	26th September, 2016	Successful
PSLV-36	Resourcesat-2A	7th December, 2016	Successful

Awards and Honours

INTERNATIONAL AWARDS

Nobel Prize

- The Nobel Prizes are given under the will of **Alfred Bernhard Nobel**, who died in 1896. He was a noted Swedish chemist and engineer, who discovered Nitroglycerine and its use in the manufacture of dynamite.
- Nobel Prizes are given each year in the six fields. The Nobel Prizes for Peace, Physics, Chemistry, Medicine and Literature were started in 1901. The Nobel Prize for Economics was started in 1968. *The prize awarding bodies are*
1. The Swedish Academy of Literature awards the prize in **Literature**.
2. The Royal Swedish Academy of Sciences awards the prize in **Physics** and **Chemistry**. The Nobel Assembly of Karolinska Chirugical (Swedan) awards the prize in **Medicine** (Physiology).
3. The Bank of Sweden awards the prize in **Economics**.
4. The Committee of the Norwegian Parliament, awards the prize for **Peace**.

- Each recipient or laureate, receives a gold medal, a diploma and a sum of money, which depends on the Nobel Foundations income that year. The Noble Prize amount for 2014 is set at SEK (Swedish Krona) 8.0 million.
- The awards are presented in Stockholm in an annual ceremony on 10th December, the anniversary of Nobel's death.
- The awards can be given to maximum three persons in the same field at the same time. The Nobel Prize was not awarded between 1940 and 1942 due to the outbreak of World War II.

Indian Nobel Laureates

Name	Field	Year
• Rabindranath Tagore	Literature (*Gitanjali*)	1913
• CV Raman	Physics (*Raman Effect*)	1930
• Har Gobind Khorana (*of Indian Descent*)	Medicine (*Genetic Code*)	1968
• Mother Teresa	Peace	1979
• Subramaniyan Chandrasekhar (*of Indian Descent*)	Physics (*Chandrasekhar's Limit*)	1983
• Amartya Sen	Economics (*Welfare Economics*)	1998
• Sir VS Naipaul (*of Indian Descent*)	Literature	2001
• Venkatraman Ramakrishnan (*of Indian Descent*)	Chemistry (*Ribosomes*)	2009
• Kailash Satyarthi	Peace (Struggle against Child Labour)	2014

Important Facts related with Nobel Prize

Unique Winners

Pierre Curie	Father
Marie Curie,	Mother
Irene Ioliot Curie	Daughter

Person Refusing Nobel Prize

Jean-Paul Sartre (*Literature*)	1964
Le Duc Tho (*Peace*)	1973

Posthumous Winners

Erik Axel Karlfeldt (*Literature*)	1931
Dag Hammarskjold (*Peace*)	1961

Award to American Presidents

Theodore Roosevelt (*Peace*)	1906
Woodrow Wilson (*Peace*)	1919
Jimmy Carter (*Peace*)	2002
Barack Obama (*Peace*)	2009

Winners of Nobel Prize More than Once

• John Bareteen	1956 (Transistor), 1972 (Superconductivity) Both in Physics
• Marie Curie	1903 (Physics), 1911 (Chemistry)
• Linus Pauling	1954 (Chemistry), 1962 (Peace)
• Frederick Sanger	1958, 1980 (Chemistry)
• International Committee of Red Cross	1917, 1944, 1963 (Peace)
• United Nations High Commissioner for Refugees	1954, 1981 (Peace)

Women Nobel Peace Prize Winners

• Bertha Von Suttner	1905	• Aung San Suu Kyi	1991
• Jane Addams	1931	• Rigoberta Menchu	1992
• Emily Greene Balch	1946	• Joddy Williams	1997
• Betty Williams	1976	• Shirin Ebadi	2003
• Mairead Coarrigan	1976	• Wangari Maathai	2004
• Mother Teresa	1979	• Ellen Johnson Sirleaf, Leymah Gbower Tawakkol Kormor	2011
• Alya Myrdal	1982	• Malala Yousafzai	2014

Nobel Peace Prize Winning Organisation

• Institute of International Law	1904
• Permanent International Peace Bureau	1910
• International Committee of the Red Cross (ICRC)	1917, 1944, 1963
• Nansen International office for Refugees	1938
• United Nations High Commissioner for Refugees	1954, 1981
• United Nations International Children's Emergency Fund (UNICEF)	1965
• International Labour Organisation (ILO)	1969
• Amnesty International	1977
• International Physicians for the Prevention of Nuclear War	1985
• United Nations Peace-keeping Forces	1988
• Pugwash Conferences on Science and World Affairs	1995
• International Campaign to Ban Landmines (ICBL)	1997
• Medicins Sans Frontiers	1999
• United Nations	2001
• International Atomic Energy Agency (IAEA)	2005
• Grameen Bank (Bangladesh)	2006
• Intergovernmental Panel on Climate Change	2007
• European Union	2012
• Organisation for the Prohibition of Chemical Weapons (OPCW)	2013
• Tunisian National Dialogue Quartet	2015
• International Campaign to Abolish Nuclear Weapon (ICAN)	2017

Oscar Awards *or* **Academy Awards**

Awarded for	Excellence in cinematic achievements
Presented by	Academy of Motion Picture Arts and Sciences
Country	United States
First awarded	16th May, 1929

The Oscar statuette is officially named 'The Academy Award of Merit'.

The Indian films nominated for Oscars are

1. Mother India (1957)
2. Salam Bombay (1988)
3. Lagan (2001)

- The Oscar award is given every year in the month of February at Hollywood Kodek Theatre.
- **Bhanu Athaiya** was the first Indian to win an Oscar Award in 1982 for costume design in film *Gandhi*.

Grammy Awards

Awarded for	Outstanding achievements in the music industry
Presented by	National Academy of Recording Arts and Sciences
Country	United States
First awarded	1959

Grammy Awards Winner Indians

Pandit Ravi Shankar (3 times)	1967, 1972, 2001
Zakir Hussain	1992 and 2009
Vikku Vinayak	1991
Vishwa Mohan Bhatt	1993
AR Rehman	2009
Ricky Kej, Neela Vaswani	2015

Golden Globe Awards

Awarded for	Excellence in film and television
Presented by	Hollywood Foreign Press Association
Country	United States
First awarded	1944

- AR Rehman is the first Indian to win Golden Globe Award.

Pulitzer Prize

Awarded for	Excellence in newspaper journalism, literary achievements and musical composition
Presented by	Columbia University
Country	United States
First awarded	1917

Indians Winning Pulitzer Prize

Gobind Behari Lal (for 'Reporting')	1937
Jhumpa Lahiri (for her book 'Interpreters of Maladies')	2000
Geeta Anand (for 'Journalism')	2003
Dr Siddhartha Mukherjee (for his book on The Emperor of all maladise; 'A Biography of Cancer')	2011
Vijay Seshadri (for 3 sections) (Poet Category)	2014

Man Booker Prize

Awarded for	Best full-length English Novel
Presented by	Man Group
Country	Commonwealth of Nations, Ireland and Zimbabwe
First awarded	1968

Indians Winning Man Booker Prize

Arundhati Roy (*Novel*-The God of Small Things)	1997
Kiran Desai (*Novel*-The Inheritance of Loss)	2006
Aravind Adiya (*Novel*-The White Tiger)	2008

Man Booker International Prize

Awarded for	Best English (or available for translation into English) fiction
Presented by	Man Group
Country	United Kingdom
First awarded	2005

- The award is worth 60000£ and an author can win only once. It is awarded for best English (or available translation into English) fiction.
- Albanian novelist Ismail Kadare was named the inaugural International Booker Prize winner in 2005. In 2013, It is given to Lydia Davis (American). In 2015, Laszlo Kraszna horkai won the Man Booker Internation Prize.

Orange Prize for Fiction

Awarded for	Best full-length novel written in English by a woman of any nationality
Presented by	Orange, A Telecom Company
Country	United Kingdom
First awarded	1996

- The winner of the prize receives $ 30000, along with a bronze culture called the 'Bessie' created by artist Grizel Niven, the sister of actor and writer David Niven.

Ramon Magsaysay Award

Awarded for	Outstanding contributions in six categories of government. Service, public service and other fields (Given to Asian Individuals)
Presented by	Ramon Magsaysay Award Foundation
Country	Philippines
First awarded	1957

Indians Winning Ramon Magsaysay Award

- *For Government Service* (GS)
  - CD Deshmukh — 1959
  - Kiran Bedi — 1994
  - TN Seshan — 1996
  - James Michael Lyngdoh — 2003
- *For Public Service* (PS)
  - Jayaprakash Narayan — 1965
  - MS Subbulakshmi — 1974
  - Manibhai Desai — 1982
  - Baba Amte — 1985
  - Lakshmi Chand Jain — 1989
  - Banoo Jehangir Coyaji — 1993
  - Mahesh Chandra Mehta — 1997
  - V Shanta — 2005
- *For Community Leadership* (CL)
  - Vinoba Bhave — 1958
  - Veghese Kurien, Dara Khurodi and Tribhuvandas Patel — 1963
  - Kamaladevi Chattopadhyay — 1966
  - MS Swaminathan — 1971
  - Ela Bhatt — 1977
  - Pramod Karan Sethi — 1981
  - Chandi Prasad Bhatt — 1982
  - Pandurang Shastri Athavale — 1996
  - Aruna Roy — 2000
  - Rajendra Singh — 2001
  - Shantha Sinha — 2003

- Dr Prakash Amte *and* Dr Mandakini Amte — 2008
- Deep Joshi — 2009
- Kujandel-Francis — 2012
- *For Peace and International Understanding* (PIU)
  - Mother Teresa — 1962
  - Jockin Arputham — 2000
  - Laxminarayan Ramdas — 2004
- *For Emergent Leadership*
  - Sandeep Pandey — 2002
  - Arvind Kejriwal — 2006
  - Nileema Mishra and Harish Hande — 2011
  - Bezwada Wilson — 2016
- *For Journalism, Literature and the Creative Communication Arts* (JLCCA)
  - Amitabh Chaudhary — 1961
  - Satyajit Ray — 1967
  - Boobli George Verghest — 1975
  - Sombhu Mitra — 1976
  - Gour Kishore Ghosh — 1981
  - Arun Shourie — 1982
  - RK Laxman — 1984
  - KV Subbanna — 1991
  - Ravi Shankar — 1992
  - Mahasweta Devi — 1997
  - P Sainath — 2007
  - Sanjiv Chaturvedi and Anshu Gupta is awarded Magsaysay Award for 2015.
  - TM Krishna — 2016

World Food Prize

The prize was created in 1986 by Nobel Peace Prize Laureate Norman Borlaug. The prize recognises contributions in all fields involved in the world food supply. First award was given to Professor MS Swaminathan (India) in 1987. In 2014 Dr Sanjaya Rajaram (Indian Origin American) won this award. Sir Fazle Hasan Abed of Bangladesh is to be honored as the 2015 World Food Prize Laureate. Dr. Akinwumi Adesina from Nigeria won the World Food Prize 2017.

The Right Livelihood Award

Awarded for	"Practical and exemplary solutions to the most urgent challenges facing the world today"
Presented by	Right Livelihood Award Foundation
Country	Sweden
First awarded	1980
Prize Money	2 Lakh Euro

The Right Livelihood Award is also referred as the 'Alternative Nobel Prize'. It was established by Jakob von Uexkull in 1980.

Indian Laureates

Laureates	Years
Self-Employed Women's Association/Ela Bhatt	1984
Lokayan/Rajni Kothari	1985
Ladakh Ecological Development Group	1986
Chipko Movement	1987
Narmada Bachao Andolan	1991
Vandana Shiva	1993
Vevekananda Girijana Kalyana Kendra	1994
People's science Movement of Kerala (Kerala Safthra Sahithya Parishad)	1996
Swami Agnivesh/Asghar Ali Engineer	2004
Ruth Manorama	2006
Krishanammal Jagannathan and Sankaralingam Jagannathan LAFI	2008
Colin Gonsalves	2017

UNESCO Peace Prize

It is presented by United Nations Educational, Scientific and Cultural Organisation (UNESCO) for extraordinary contributions for international peace.

UNESCO Human Rights Award

It is also presented by UNESCO for contributions in the field of Human Rights Awareness. It is given every alternate year created in 1978.

UN Human Rights Award

It is presented by United Nations (UN) for personal contribution for the cause of human rights. It is presented every 6th years.

BEAUTY CONTESTS

Miss Universe

- It is an annual international beauty contest that is run by the Miss Universe Organisation. The contest was founded in 1952, by California Clothing Company Pacific Mills. Its headquarters is at New York City (US).
- **Sushmita Sen** is the first Indian woman to win the Miss Universe contest in 1994.
- **Pia Alonzo Wurtzbach** won the crown of Miss Universe 2015.
- **Demi Leight Nel-Peters** from South Africa won the Miss Universe 2017 contest.

Miss World

The Miss World pageant is the oldest surviving international beauty pageant. It was created in the United Kingdom by Eric Morley In 1951. Since his death in 2000, Morley's wife, Julia Morley, co-chairs the pageant. Its headquarter is at London (UK).

Reita Faria Powell became the first Indian to win the Miss World title in 1966. Miss Stephanie Del Valle of Puerto Rico is crowned the Miss World title for 2016.

India's **Manushi Chhillar** won the Miss World 2017 contest.

Miss Earth

- Miss Earth is an annual international beauty pageant promoting environmental awareness. Miss Earth is also one of the most publicised beauty contest in the world. It was formed in 2001 and its headquarters is at Manila, Philippines. Catharina Svensson of Denmark is the first winner of Miss Earth contest (2001). Katherine Espin of Ecuador, was crowned Miss Earth 2016.
- Karen Ibasco from Philippines won the coverted title of Miss Earth 2017.

Miss India

- Miss India or Femina Miss India is a national beauty pageant in India. It is organised by Femina, a women's magazine published by Bennett, Coleman and Co Ltd.
- Its headquarters is at Mumbai and it was formed in 1963. Miss India beauty contest started on 1947.
- Pramila was the first woman to win the Miss India contest in 1947.

INDIA'S INTERNATIONAL AWARDS

Mahatma Gandhi Peace Prize

It was instituted in 1995 and awarded by Government of India to encourage and promote Gandhian values worldwide. The award carries ₹1 Crore in cash, convertible in any currency in the world, a plaque and a citation.

- First recipient (1995) *Julius Nyerere*
- Last recipient (2014) *ISRO*

Indira Gandhi Peace Prize

It was instituted in 1986 and awarded by Indira Gandhi Memorial Trust. It is awarded for peace, disarmament and development. The prize carries a cash award of 25 lakh Indian rupees and a citation.

- First recipient (1986)
  Parliamentarians for Global Action
- Manmohan Singh (2017)

Jawaharlal Nehru Award

It was instituted in 1965 and awarded by Government of India for international understanding, goodwill and friendship. The money constituent of this award is 25 Lakh Indian rupees.

- First recipient (1965) *U Thant (3rd UN Secretary-General)*
- Last recipient (2009)
- Angela Markel *(Germany's First Female Chancellor)*

National Awards

BHARAT RATNA

- Bharat Ratna is India's highest Civilian Award. It was first awarded in 1954. The actual award is designed in the shape of a Peepal leaf with *Bharat Ratna* inscribed in Devanagri script in the Sun Figure.

- The reverse side of the decoration *Satyamev Jayate* has been written in Hindi with an inscription of state emblem. The emblem, the Sun and the rim are of platinum. The inscriptions are in burnished bronze.

Note The Padma Awards were suspended between 1977 and 1980 as well as between 1992 and 1998.

Winners of Bharat Ratna

Year	Recipient	Year	Recipient
2014	Madan Mohan Malaviya*	1990	Dr Bhimrao Ramji Ambedkar *
	Atal Bihari Bajpayee	1988	Marudur Gopalan Ramachandran *
2013	Sachin Tendulkar, CNR Rao	1987	Khan Abdul Ghaffar Khan
2009	Pandit Bhimsen Joshi	1983	Acharya Vinoba Bhave *
2001	Ustad Bismillah Khan	1980	Mother Teresa-Agnes Gonxha Bojaxhiu
2001	Lata Dinanath Mangeshkar		
1999	Lokpriya Gopinath Bordoloi *	1976	Kumaraswamy Kamraj *
1999	Professor Amartya Sen	1975	Varahagiri Venkata Giri
1999	Loknayak Jayprakash Narayan *	1971	Indira Gandhi
1999	Pandit Ravi Shankar	1966	Lal Bahadur Shastri *
1998	Madurai Shanmukhavadivu Subbulakshmi	1963	Dr Zakir Hussain
		1963	Dr Pandurang Vaman Kane
1998	Chidambaram Subramaniam	1962	Dr Rajendra Prasad
1997	Dr Avul Pakir Jainulabdeen Abdul Kalam	1961	Dr Bidhan Chandra Roy
		1961	Shri Purushottam Das Tandon
1997	Aruna Asaf Ali *	1958	Dr Dhonde Keshav Karve
1997	Gulzari Lal Nanda *	1957	Pt Govind Ballabh Pant
1992	Maulana Abul Kalam Azad *	1955	Pandit Jawaharlal Nehru
1992	Satyajit Ray	1955	Dr Mokshagundam Visvesvaraya
1992	Jehangir Ratanji Dadabhai Tata	1955	Dr Bhagwan Das
1991	Rajiv Gandhi *	1954	Dr Chandrashekhar Venkata Raman
1991	Sardar Vallabhbhai Patel *	1954	Dr Sarvapalli Radhakrishnan
1991	Morarji Ranchhodji Desai	1954	Chakravarti Rajagopalachari
1990	Dr Nelson Rohihlahla Mandela		

Note * Posthumous Recipient

PADMA AWARDS

There are three Padma Awards given on Republic Day (26th January) every year.

1. Padma Vibhushan

* This is the second highest National Award.
* Instituted on 2nd January, 1954 by the Government of India.
* It is awarded to recognise exceptional and distinguished service to the nation in any field.

2. Padma Bhushan

* This is the third largest National Awards.
* Instituted on 2nd January, 1954 by the Government of India.
* It is awarded to recognise distinguished service of a high order to the nation, in any field.

3. Padma Shri

* This is the fourth highest National Award instituted on 2nd January, 1954 by Government of India.
* In 1960, Dr MG Ramachandran refused to accept the award as the wordings of the award is in Hindi.
* It recognises the contribution of Indian citizens (generally) in various spheres of activity including Arts, Education, Industry, Literature, Science, Sports, Social Service and Public life.

MILITARY AWARDS

To be given on Republic Day (26th January)

Wartime Valour Awards

(Awarded to officers or enlisted personnel from all branches of the Indian Military).

Award	Year of Institution	Awarded by	Awarded for
Paramvir Chakra	Established on 26th January, 1950 wef 15th August, 1947	Government of India	Most conspicuous bravery or some daring or pre-eminest valour or self-sacrifice.
Mahavir Chakra	Established on 26th January, 1950 wef 15th August, 1947	Government of India	Acts of gallantry in the Presence of the enemy on land, at sea or in the air.
Vir Chakra	Established on 26th January, 1950 wef 15th August, 1947	Government of India	Acts of bravery in the battle field

Note All the three awards are also given posthumously.

* Subedar Major Bana Singh of the 8th Jammu and Kashmir light infantry was the only serving personnel of the Indian defence establishment with a Param Vir Chakra till the Kargil operations.

Recipient of Param Vir Chakra

Name	Regiment	Date	Place
Major Som Nath Sharma	4th Battalion, Kumaon Regiment	3rd November, 1947	Badgam, Jammu and Kashmir
Lance Naik Karam Singh	1st Battalion, Sikh Regiment	13th October, 1948	Tithwal, Jammu and Kashmir
Second Lieutenant Rama Raghoba Rane	Bombay Sappers Corps of Engineers	8th April, 1948	Naushera, Jammu and Kashmir
Naik Jadu Nath Singh	1st Battalion, Rajput Regiment	February 1948	Naushera, Jammu and Kashmir
Company Havaldar Major Piru Singh Shekhawat	6th Battalion, Rajputana Rifles	17th July, 1948, 18th July, 1948	Tithwal, Jammu and Kashmir
Captain Gurbachan Singh Salaria	3rd Battalion, 1st Gorkha Rifles (The Malaun Regiment)	5th December, 1961	Elizabethville, Katanga, Conga
Major Dhan Singh Thapa	1st Battalion, 8th Gorkha Rifles	20th October, 1962	Ladakh, India
Subedar Joginder Singh	1st Battalion, Sikh Regiment	23rd October, 1962	Tongpen La, North-East Frontier Agency, India
Major Shaitan Singh	13th Battalion, Kumaon Regiment	18th November, 1962	Rezang La
Company Quarter Master Havaldar Abdul Hamid	4th Battalion, Grenadiers	10th September, 1965	Chima, Khem Karan Sector Pakistan
Lieutenant-Colonel Ardeshir Burzorji Tarapore	17th Poona Horse	15th October, 1965	Phillora, Sialkot Sector, Pakistan
Lance Naik Albert Ekka	14th Battalion, Brigade of the Guards	3rd December, 1971	Gangasagar, Agartala Sector
Flying Officer Nirmal Jit Singh Sekhon	No. 18 Squadron, Indian Air Force	14th December, 1971	Srinagar, Kashmir
2/Lieutenant Arun Khetarpal	17th Poona House	16th December, 1971	Barapind Jarpal, Shakargarh Sector
Major Hoshiar Singh	3rd Battalion, The Grenadiers	17th December, 1971	Basantar River, Shakargarh Sector
Naib Subedar Bana Singh	8th Battalion, Jammu and Kashmir Light Infantry	23rd May, 1987	Siachen Glacier, Jammu and Kashmir
Major Ramaswamy Parameshwaran	8th Battalion, Mahar Regiment	25th November, 1987	Sri Lanka
Captain Manoj Kumar Pandey	1st Battalion, 11th Gorkha Rifles	3th July, 1999	Khaluber/Juber Top, Batalik Sector, Kargil area, Jammu and Kashmir
Grenadier Yogendra Singh Yadav	18th Battalion, The Grenadiers	4th July, 1999	Tiger Hill, Kargil Area

Name	Regiment	Date	Place
Rifleman Sanjay Kumar	13th Battalion, Jammu and Kashmir Rifles	5th July, 1999	Area Flat Top, Kargil Area
Captain Vikram Batra	13th Battalion, Jammu and Kashmir	6th July, 1999	Point 5140, Point 4875, Kargil Area

Peace Time Gallantry Awards
Awarded Either to Military or Civilian Personnel

Award	Year of Institution	Awarded by	Awarded for
Ashoka Chakra	4th January, 1952 with effect-from 15th August, 1947	Government of India	Most conspicuous bravery or some act of daring or preeminent act of valour or self-sacrifice otherwise than in the face of the enemy.
Kirti Chakra	4th January, 1952 with effect-from 15th August, 1947	Government of India	Conspicuous gallantry otherwise than in face of the enemy.
Shaurya Chakra	4th January, 1952 with effect-from 15th August, 1947	Government of India	National bravery generally for counter insurgency operations and actions against the enemy during peace time

Note All the three awards are also given posthumously.

Other Military Awards

Category	Award
Wartime/ Peacetime Service and Gallantry	Sena Medal (Army), Nao Sena Medal (Navy), Vayusena Medal (Air Force)
Wartime Distinguished Service	Sarvottam Yudh Seva Medal, Uttam Yudh Seva Medal, Yudh Seva Medal
Peacetime Distinguished Service	Param Vishisht Seva Medal, Ati Vishisht Seva Medal, Vishisht Seva Medal

Sports Awards

Rajiv Gandhi Khel Ratna Award

- The Rajiv Gandhi Khel Ratna Award (RGKR) is India's highest honour given for achievement in sports. The words 'Khel Ratna' literally means 'Sports Gem' in Hindi. The award is named after late Rajiv Gandhi, former Prime Minister of India.
- The award was instituted in the year 1991-1992 and was awarded by the ministry of youth affairs and sports.
- Upto 2004-05, the cash component was ₹ 500000. The money has been increased from ₹ 500000 to ₹ 750000.
- First Awardees - 1991-92 Viswanathan Anand (Chess).
- 2009-10 Saina Nehwal, (Badminton), 2010-11 Gagan Narang (Shooting), 2011-12 Vijay Kumar (Shooting) 2011-12 Yogeswar Dutt (Wrestling), 2013-14 Ronjan Sodhi (Shooting).
- Four athletes namely PV Sindhu, Dipa Karmakar, Sakshi Malik and Jitu Rai were awarded Rajiv Gandhi Khel Ratna Award for 2015-16.
- In 2017, Devendra Jhajharia (Para Athlete) and Sardara Singh (Hockey) won the Rajiv Gandhi Khel Ratna Award.

Arjuna Award

- The Arjuna Awards were instituted in 1961 by the Ministry of youth affairs and sports, Government of India to recognise outstanding achievement in National Sports. The award carries a cash prize of ₹ 500000, a bronze statuette of Arjuna and a scroll.
- From the year 2001, the award is given only in disciplines falling *under the following categories*
  - Olympic Games
  - Asian Games
  - Commonwealth Games
  - World Cup
  - World Championship Disciplines and Cricket
  - Indigenous Games
  - Sports for the physically challenged

Dronacharya Award

Dronacharya Award is an award presented by the ministry of youth affairs and sports, Government of India for excellence in sports coaching. The award comprises a bronze statuette of Dronacharya a scroll of honour and a cash component of ₹ 500000. The award was instituted in 1985. Nagapuri Ramesh (Athletics), Sagar Mal Dhayal (Boxing), Raj Kumar Sharma (Cricket), Bishweshwar Nandi (Gymnastics), S Pradeep Kumar (Swimming) and Mahabir Singh (Wrestling) were awarded Dronacharya Award for 2016. In 2017, R Gandhi (Athletics), Heera Nand Kataria (Kabaddi), GSSV Prasad (Badminton), Brij Bhushan Mohanty (Boxing), PA Raphel (Hockey), Sanjay Chakrarverthy (Shooting), Roshan Lal (Wrestling).

Dhyanchand Award

Dhyanachand Award is India's highest award for lifetime achievement in sports and games, given by the Government of India. The award is named after the legendary Indian hockey player Dhyanchand. The awards was instituted in 2002. The award carries a cash prize of ₹ 500000. Satti Geetha (Athletics), Sylvanus Dung Dung (Hockey) and Rajendra Pralhad Shelke (Rowing) were awarded Dhyanchand Award for 2016.

In 2017, Bhupendra Singh (Athletics), Syed Shahid Hakim (Football), Sumrai Tete (Hockey).

Some Famous Awards by State Governments

Award	Awarded/Instituted by	Field of Honour
Mahatma Gandhi Award	Madhya Pradesh Government	To an institution working according to Gandhi philosophy and ideology
Tansen Award	Madhya Pradesh Government	Indian classical music
Kalidas Award	Madhya Pradesh Government	Classical dance and music, theatre, painting, sculpture and plastic arts
Tulsidas Award	Madhya Pradesh Government	Folk and traditional tribal art (only for male artist)
Lata Mangeskar Award	Madhya Pradesh Government	For music direction and playback singing in field of light music
Santhala Natya Award	Karnataka Government	Santhal dance (a tribal dance form)
Konark Samman	Odisha State Council of Culture	Literature, art sculpture, music, dance and socio-cultural work

Film Awards

National Film Awards

- The National Film Awards are the most prominent film award ceremony in India, established in 1954 and it is administered, along with the international film festival of India and the Indian Panorama, by the Indian Government's Directorate of Film Festivals since 1973.
- Due to the national character of the National Film Awards, it is considered to be the equivalent of the American Academy Awards.

Dada Saheb Phalke Award

- The Dada Saheb Phalke Award is India's highest award in cinema given annually by the Government of India for lifetime Contribution to Indian Cinema.
- It was instituted in 1969, the birth centenary year of Dada Saheb Phalke, considered as the Father of Indian Cinema.
- Phalke Award carries a 'Swarna Kamal', a shawl and a cash prize of ₹ 1000000.

Recipients of Dada Saheb Phalke Award

Recipients	Years
Mrs Devika Rani Roerich	1969 (First)
B N Sirkar	1970
Prithvi Raj Kapoor	1971
Pankaj Mallick	1972
Mrs Ruby Myers	1973
BN Reddy	1974
Dhiren Ganguly	1975
Mrs Kanan Devi	1976
Nitin Bose	1977
RC Boral	1978
Sohrab Modi	1979
P Jai Raj	1980
Naushad Ali	1981
L V Prasad	1982
Mrs Durga Khote	1983
Satyajit Ray	1984
V Shantaram	1985
B Nagi Reddy	1986

Recipients	Years
Raj Kapoor	1987
Ashok Kumar	1988
Lata Mangeshkar	1989
A Nageshwar Rao	1990
Bhalji Pendharkar	1991
Bhupen Hazarika	1992
Majrooh Sultanpuri	1993
Dilip Kumar	1994
Dr Raj Kumar	1995
Shivaji Ganeshan	1996
Kavi Pradeep	1997
B R Chopra	1998
Hrishikesh Mukherjee	1999
Asha Bhosle	2000
Yash Chopra	2001
Dev Anand	2002
Mrinal Sen	2003
Adoor Gopalakrishnan	2004
Shyam Benegal	2005
Tapan Sinha	2006
Manna Dey	2007
VK Murthy	2008
D Ramanaidu	2009
K Balachander	2010
Soumitra Chatterjee	2011
Pran Krishan Sikand	2012
Sampooran Singh Kalra (Gulzar)	2013
Shashi Kapoor	2014
Manoj Kumar	2015
Kasinathuni Viswanath	2016

Filmfare Awards

- The Filmfare Awards are presented annually by the Times group to honour both artistic and technical excellence of professionals in the Hindi language film industry of India. The awards were first introduced in 1954, the same year as the National Film Awards.
- They were initially referred to as the Clare Awards after the editor of the Times of India, Clare Mendonca.

Literary and Cultural Awards

Sahitya Akademi Award

It is a literary honour in India instituted in 1954, by which Sahitya Akademi, India's National Academy of Letters, annually confers on writers of outstanding works in twenty-four major Indian languages.

Jnanpith Award

- The Jnanpith Award is a literary award in India. The award was instituted in 1961. It is presented by the Bharatiya Jnanpith, a trust founded by the Sahu Jain family, the publishers of the Times of India newspaper.
- It carries a check of ₹ 7 lakh, a citation plaque and a bronze replica of Saraswati, the Indian Goddess of knowledge, music and arts. First awarded in 1965 to Sankar Kurup (Malayalam).

Recipients of the Jnanpith Award

Recipients	Years
G Shankar Kurup (Malayalam)	1965
TS Bandopadhyaya (Bengali)	1966
Uma Shankar Joshi (Gujarati)	1967
R S Firaq Gorakhpuri (Urdu)	1969
Sumitra Nandan Pant (Hindi)	1968
Vishwanath Satyanarayan (Telugu)	1970
Vishnu Dey (Bengali)	1971
Ram Dhari Singh Dinkar (Hindi)	1972
Dr D R Bendre (Kannada) and Gopinath Mohanty (Oriya)	1973
V S Khandekar (Marathi)	1974
PV Akilandam (Tamil)	1975
Mrs Asha Purna Devi (Bengali)	1976
K Shiv Ram Karanth (Kannada)	1977
H S Vatsayan 'Ageya' (Hindi)	1978
V K Bhattacharya (Assamese)	1979
S K Pottekat (Malayalam)	1980
Mrs Amrita Pritam (Punjabi)	1981
Mrs Mahadevi Verma (Hindi)	1982
M V Iyengar (Kannada)	1983
T S Pillai (Malayalam)	1984
Panna Lal Patel (Gujarati)	1985
Sachida Nand Routory (Oriya)	1986
V V Shirvadkar (Marathi)	1987
C Narayana Reddy (Telugu)	1988
Qurtul-ain-Haider (Urdu)	1989

Recipients	Years
Vinayak Krishna Gokak (Kannada)	1990
Subhash Mukhopadhyay (Bengali)	1991
Naresh Mehta (Hindi)	1992
Dr Sitakant Mahapatra (Oriya)	1993
U R Anantha Murthy (Kannada)	1994
M T Vasudevan Nair (Malayalam)	1995
Smt Mahasweta Devi (Bengali)	1996
Ali Sardar Jafri (Urdu)	1997
Girish Karnad (Kannada)	1998
Nirmal Verma (Hindi) and Gurdayal Singh (Punjabi)	1999
Dr Indira Goswami (Assamese)	2000
Rajendra Keshavlal Shah (Gujarati)	2001
D Jaya Kanthan (Tamil)	2002
Vinda Karandikar (Marathi)	2003
Rehman Rahi (Kashmiri)	2004
Kunwar Narayan (Hindi)	2005
Ravindra Kelekar (Konkani) and Satyavrat Shastri (Sanskrit)	2006
O N V Kurup (Malayalam)	2007
Akhlaq Khan Shaharyar (Urdu)	2008
Amar Kant (Hindi)	2009
Shrilal Shukla (Hindi)	2009
Chandrashekhara, Kambara (Kannada)	2010
Pratibha Ray (Odiya)	2011
Ravuri Bharadhwaja (Telugu)	2012
Kedarnath Singh (Hindi)	2013
Bhalchandra Nemade (Marathi)	2014
Raghuveer Chadhari (Gujarati)	2015
Shankha Ghosh (Bengali)	2016
Krishana Sobti (Hindi)	2017

Bhasha Samman

Instituted in 1996, Sahitya Akademi gives these special awards to writers for significant contribution to Indian languages other than the above 24 major ones and also for contribution to classical and medieval literature.

Translation Awards

Established in 1989, Sahitya Akademi annually gives these awards for outstanding translations of major works in other languages into one of the 24 major Indian languages.

Anand Coomarswamy Fellowships

Named after the Indian writer Ananda Coomarswamy, the fellowship was started in 1996. It is given to scholars from Asian countries to spend 3 to 12 months in India to pursue a literary project.

Premchand Fellowships

Named after Hindi writer Premchand, the fellowship was started in 2005. It is given to persons of eminence in the field of culture from SAARC countries.

Sangeet Natak Akademi Puraskar (Akademi Award)

Awarded by the Sangeet Natak Akademi, India's National Academy of Music, Dance and Drama. This award was constituted in 1952. It is the highest Indian recognition given to practising artists in the categories of music, dance, theatre, other traditional/ folk/ tribal/dance/music/ theatre and puppetry and contribution/scholarship in performing arts.

Lalit Kala Academy Ratna

Instituted in 1955 by the Government of India, is an honour for the fine arts given to eminent artists for their lifetime achievements in the field of visual arts. It is awarded by the Lalit Kala Academy, India's National Academy of Art. It is the highest honour in the fine arts conferred by the Government of India.

Saraswati Samman

The Saraswati Samman is an annual award for outstanding prose or poetry literacy works in any Indian language listed in Schedule VII of the Constitution of India. The Saraswati Samman was instituted in 1991 by the KK Birla foundation. The award consist of ₹ 10 lakh, a citation and a plaque.

Tansen Award

These awards are given by Government of Madhya Pradesh for the outstanding contribution in the field of music. This award was constituted in 1980 and compreses ₹ 2 lakh.

Vyas Samman

The Vyas Samman is a literary award in India, first awarded in 1991. It is awarded annually by the KK Birla Foundation and includes a cash payout of ₹ 2.5 lakh.

Iqbal Samman

These awards are given by the Literary Council of Madhya Pradesh for the outstanding contribution in the field of urdu literature. This award was constituted in 1987 and comprises ₹ 1 lakh and certificate.

Murtidevi Award

This award was constituted in 1984 and is given for extra ordinary performance in literature. It is given by Indian Jnanpith Trust.

Science Awards

Shanti Swarup Bhatnagar Award

- This prize for science and technology in awarded annually by the Council of Scientific & Industrial Research (CSIR) for notable and outstanding research, applied or fundamental, in biology, chemistry, environmental science, engineering, mathematics, medicine and physics under the age of 65 years.

- It is the highest award for science in India. It was first awarded in 1958.
- The Prize comprises a citation, a plaque and a cash award of ₹5 lakh.

DHANWANTARI AWARD

- It is given for Medical field. This award comprises a certificate, Gold Medal and ₹ 1 lakh Dhanvantari award.
- Instituted in 1971 and given for 'Excellence in Medical Services'.
- Thus, award is given by 'Dhanvantari Foundation'.

Dr BC Roy Award

- Medical Council of India instituted Dr BC Roy Award in 1976, in memory of Bharat Ratna Dr Bidhan Chandra Roy. The award is given annually in each of the following categories: statesmanship of the highest order in India, Medical man-cum- statesman, eminent medical person, eminent person in philosophy and arts.
- It is presented by the President of India in New Delhi on 1st July the National Doctor's Day.
- This award comprises a Silver Medal, certificate and ₹ 1 lakh cash.

Jamnalal Bajaj Award

It is a prestigious Indian award, for promoting Gandhian values, social work and social development. It is established in 1978 by the Jamnalal Bajaj Foundation of Bajaj Group. This award contains ₹ 5 lakh, a certificate and a trophy.

Homi Bhabha Award

- Instituted in 1990, and given for excellence in field of Atomic energy.
- This award comprises ₹ 50000 and a certificate.

Vikram Sarabhai Award

- Instituted in 1990 and given for excellence in field of Space Research.
- This award is given by 'Birla Foundation'.
- This award comprises medals, certificate and ₹ 50000.

GD Birla Award

- GD Birla award for scientific research is conferred by KK Birla Foundation. KK Birla Foundation was established in 1991, by Krishna Kumar Birla.
- This award comprises ₹ 1.45 lakh and certificate.